D0342484

HUNTER PUBLISHING, INC.
130 Campus Drive, Edison NJ 08818
(732) 225 1900, (800) 255 0343; fax (732) 417 0482

IN CANADA
Ulysses Travel Publications
4176 Saint-Denis
Montreal, Quebec H2W 2M5 Canada
(514) 843 9882, ext. 2232; fax 514 843 9448

ISBN 1-55650-900-6
Fourth Edition

Copyright © 2001 by Payot/Rivages

For complete information about the hundreds of other travel guides offered
by Hunter Publishing, visit our website at **www.hunterpublishing.com**

**Hotels and Country Inns
of Character and Charm in Italy**
Translator: Bobin Buss, Jack Monet, and Anne Norris
Front cover photograph: La Chiara di Prumiano (Tuscany)
Back cover: Hotel Villa San Michele (Campania)

All rights reserved. No part of this book may be reproduced, transmitted or
utilized in any form or by any means, electronic or mechanical, including
photocopying, recording, or by any information storage and retrieval system,
without permission in writing from the publisher. Brief extracts to be
included in reviews or articles are permitted.

Special Sales
Hunter Travel Guides can be purchased in quantity at special discounts. For
more information, contact us at the address above.

Printed in Italy by Litho Service
10 9 8 7 6 5 4 3 2 1

HOTELS AND COUNTRY INNS
of Character and Charm
IN ITALY

Hunter Publishing, Inc.
www.hunterpublishing.com

Important

In accordance with standard jurisprudence (Toulouse, 14.01.1887), the publisher of this guide cannot be held responsible for any errors or omissions that may have remained despite the best efforts of the writing and editing staff.

We also inform readers that we can in no case be held responsible for any litigation arising between the users of this guide and the owners of the houses.

HUNTER RIVAGES

HOTELS AND COUNTRY INNS
of Character and Charm
IN ITALY

Project editor
Michelle Gastaut

Conceived by
Michelle Gastaut
and Fabrice Camoin

Hunter Publishing, Inc.
www.hunterpublishing.com

WELCOME

Welcome to the world of hotels with character and charm in Italy. This edition contains 506 hotels. All have been selected for charm, quality of welcome, food, and hotelkeeping. They range from the comparatively simple to the luxurious.

When choosing among them, remember that you cannot expect as much of a room costing 90,000L as you can of one costing 180,000L or more. Please note that the prices given may change.

When you make your reservation be sure to ask for the exact prices for half board *(mezza-pensione)* or full board *(pensione)* as they can vary depending on the number in your party and the length of your stay.

STAR RATING

The government's hotel rating organization assigns stars, from one to four, based on the comfort of a hotel, with special weight given to the number of bathrooms and toilets in relation to the number of rooms. This star rating has nothing at all to do with subjective criteria such as charm or the quality of the hospitality which are among our most important criteria. Some of the hotels in this guide have no stars–and that is because the hoteliers have never asked the government to rate them.

HOW TO USE THE GUIDE

Hotels are listed by region, and within each region by district. The number of the page on which a hotel is described corresponds to the number on the flag that pinpoints the property's location on the road map and to the numbers in the table of contents and index. The phrase "major credit cards" means that Diner's, Amex, Visa, Eurocard and MasterCard are all accepted.

PLEASE LET US KNOW...

If you are impressed by a small hotel or inn not featured here, one that you think ought to be included in the guide, let us know so that we can visit it.

Please also tell us if you are disappointed by one of our choices. Write us at:

Michelle Gastaut – Editions Rivages
10, rue Fortia
13001 Marseille – FRANCE

You can also contact us on the Guides Rivages' website at:
http://www.guidesdecharme.com

Or get in touch via our US website at
http://www.hunterpublishing.com

CONTENTS LIST

Contents
Restaurants listing by region
Map of Italy
Road Maps

Basilicata - Calabria...1
Campania 4
Emilia-Romagna...45
Latium - Abruzzi 63
Liguria 96
Lombardy 111
Marches...149
Umbria 155
Piemont Valle d'Aosta 192
Puglia 216
Sardinia 227
Sicily..239
Tuscany 274
Trentino-Dolomites 419
Veneto..441

RESTAURANTS
LISTING BY REGION

Basilicata - Calabria..508

Campania 510

Emilia-Romagna..515

Latium - Abruzzi 520

Liguria 525

Lombardy 528

Marches..534

Umbria 535

Piemont Valle d'Aosta 537

Puglia/Apulia..542

Sardinia 544

Sicily..546

Tuscany 549

Trentino-Dolomites 560

Veneto..563

CONTENTS

Agriturismo, Bed and breakfasts, Villas to rent:

B A S I L I C A T A - C A L A B R I A

Altomonte (Cosenza) - Map 21
– Hotel Barbieri 1
Maratea (Potenza) - Map 21
– Locanda delle Donne Monache 2
Matera - Map 21
– Hotel Sassi 3

C A M P A N I A

Telese Terme (Benevento) - Map 20
– Grand Hotel Telese 4
Baia Domizia (Caserta) - Map 19
– Hotel della Baia 5
Napoli - Map 19
– Hotel Santa Lucia 6
– Hotel Excelsior 7
– Grand Hotel Parker's 8
– Hotel Paradiso 9
Isola di Capri (Napoli) - Map 19
– Villa Brunella 10
– Hotel Palace 11
– Hotel Luna 12
– Hotel Punta Tragara 13
– Albergo Villa Sarah 14
– Pensione Quattro Stagioni 15
Isola d'Ischia (Napoli) - Carta 19
   Sant'Angelo
   – Park Hotel Miramare 16

    – Pensione Casa Sofia 17
    – Pensione Casa Garibaldi 18
    Porto d'Ischia
    – La Villarosa 19
    Forio d'Ischia
    – La Bagattella Hotel 20
    Lacco Ameno
    – Albergo Terme San Montano 21
    Sorgeto - Panza d'Ischia
    – Hotel Residence Punta Chiarito 22
Cenito - Santa Maria di Castellabate (Salerno) - Map 20
    – Giacaranda 23
Santa Maria di Castellabate (Napoli) - Map 20
    – Palazzo Belmonte 24
Sorrento (Napoli) - Map 20
    – Grand Hotel Excelsior Vittoria 25
    – Hotel Bellevue Syrene 26
Vico Equense (Napoli) - Map 20
    – Capo La Gala Hotel 27
Amalfi (Salerno) - Map 20
    – Hotel Luna Convento 28
    – Hotel Santa Caterina 29
    – La Conchiglia 30
Conca dei Marini - Amalfi (Napoli) - Map 20
    – Hotel Belvedere 31
Castiglione di Ravello (Salerno) - Map 20
    – Hotel Villa San Michele 32
Positano (Salerno) - Map 20
    – Hotel San Pietro 33
    – Le Sirenuse 34
    – Hotel Poseidon 35
    – Hotel Palazzo Murat 36
    – Albergo Casa Albertina 37
    – La Fenice 38
    – Casa Cosenza 39
Ravello (Salerno) - Map 20
    – Hotel Palumbo - Palazzo Confalone 40
    – Palazzo Sasso 41
    – Hotel Caruso Belvedere 42
    – Villa Cimbrone 43
    – Villa Maria 44

E M I L I A - R O M A G N A

Bologna - Map 10
    – Hotel Corona d'Oro 45
    – Hotel Commercianti 46
    – Hotel Orologio 47
Ferrara - Map 10
    – Hotel Duchessa Isabella 48

  – Locanda della Duchessina 49
  – Locanda Borgonuovo 50
Modena - Map 9
  – Canalgrande Hotel 51
Castelfranco Emilia (Modena) - Map 9
  – Villa Gaidello 52
Portico di Romagna (Forlì) - Map 10
  – Hotel Al Vecchio Convento 53
Santarcangelo di Romagna (Rimini) - Map 11
  – Hotel della Porta 54
Parma - Map 9
  – Hotel Verdi 55
Busseto (Parma) - Map 9
  – I Due Foscari 56
Soragna (Parma) - Map 9
  – Locanda del Lupo 57
Brisighella (Ravenna) - Map 10
  – Il Palazzo 58
Cavina - Brisighella (Ravenna) - Map 10
  – Relais Torre Pratesi 59
Reggio nell'Emilia - Map 9
  – Hotel Posta 60
  – Albergo delle Notarie 61
Puinello (Reggio Nell'Emilia) - Map 9
  – Albergo Casa Matilde 62

L A T I U M - A B R U Z Z I

Formia (Latina) - Map 19
  – Hotel Castello Miramare 63
Gaeta (Latina) - Map 19
  – Gran Hotel Le Rocce 64
Isola di Ponza (Latina) - Map 18
  – Hotel Cernia 65
San Felice Circeo (Latina) - Map 18
  – Hotel Punta Rossa 66
Sperlonga (Latina) - Map 19
  – Parkhotel Fiorelle 67
Poggio (Rieti) - Map 14
  – Hotel Borgo Paraelios 68
Roma - Map 14
  – Hotel Lord Byron 69
  – Hotel Giulio Cesare 70
  – Hotel d'Inghilterra 71
  – Hotel Raphaël 72
  – Hotel Sole Al Pantheon 73
  – Hotel dei Mellini 74
  – Hotel Carriage 75
  – Mecenate Palace Hotel 76

– Hotel Villa Grazioli 77
– Hotel Gregoriana 78
– Hotel Locarno 79
– Teatro di Pompeo 80
– Hotel Sant'Anselmo 81
– Hotel Villa del Parco 82
– Pensione Scalinata di Spagna 83
– Pensione Parlamento 84

Grottaferratta (Roma) - Map 14
– Park Hotel Villa Grazioli 85

Tivoli (Roma) - Map 14
– Hotel Ristorante Adriano 86

Palo Laziale (Roma) - Map 14
– La Posta Vecchia 87

Vignola (Chieti) - Map 16
– Villa Vignola 88

Viterbo - Map 14
– Country Club Rinaldone 89

Bolsena (Viterbo) - Map 13
– Hotel Royal 90

Civitella d'Agliano (Viterbo) - Map 14
– L'Ombricolo 91

Farnese (Viterbo) - Map 13
– Il Voltone 92

Seripola - Orte (Viterbo) - Map 14
– La Chiocciola 93

Tuscania (Viterbo) - Map 13
– Hotel Al Gallo 94

Venafro (Isernia) - Map 19
– Dimora delPrete di Belmonte 95

L I G U R I A

Camogli (Genova) - Map 8
– Hotel Cenobio dei Dogi 96
San Fruttuoso (Genova) - Map 8
– Albergo da Giovanni 97
Portofino (Genova) - Map 8
– Albergo Splendido 98
– Splendido Mare 99
– Hotel Piccolo 100
– Hotel Nazionale 101
Sestri Levante (Genova) - Map 8
– Grand Hotel Villa Balbi 102
– Hotel Helvetia 103
– Hotel Miramare 104
Grimaldi Inferiore - Ventimiglia (Imperia) - Map 7
– Baia Beniamin 105
San Remo (Imperia) - Map 7
– Royal Hotel 106

Castelvecchio di Rocca Barbena (Savona) - *Map 7*
  – Casa Cambi 107
Finale Ligure (Savona) - *Map 8*
  – Hotel Punta Est 108
Garlenda (Savona) - *Map 7*
  – La Meridiana 109
Monterosso al Mare (La Spezia) - *Map 9*
  – Hotel Porto Roca 110

L   O   M   B   A   R   D   Y

Bergamo - *Map 3*
  – Agnello d'Oro 111
Colline di Iseo - Iseo (Brescia) - *Map 3*
  – I Due Roccoli 112
Cologne Franciacorta (Brescia) - *Map 3*
  – Cappuccini 113
Erbusco (Brescia) - *Map 3*
  – L'Albereta - Ristorante G. Marchesi 114
Lago di Garda (Brescia) - *Map 3*
  Fasano di Gardone Riviera
  – Hotel Villa del Sogno 115
  – Grand Hotel Fasano 116
  – Villa Fiordaliso 117
  Gargnano
  – Hotel Baia d'Oro 118
  – Villa Giulia 119
  Salò
  – Hotel Laurin 120
  Sirmione
  – Villa Cortine Palace Hotel 121
Lago di Como - *Map 2*
  Como
  – Albergo Terminus 122
  – Hotel Villa Flori 123
  Bellagio (Como)
  – Grand Hotel Villa Serbelloni 124
  – Hotel Florence 125
  Cernobbio (Como)
  – Grand Hotel Villa d'Este 126
  Moltrasio (Como)
  – Grand Hotel Imperiale 127
  Lenno (Como)
  – San Giorgio Hotel 128
  Menaggio (Como)
  – Grand Hotel Victoria 129
  San Mamete (Como)
  – Hotel Stella d'Italia 130
  Tremezzo (Como)
  – Grand Hotel Tremezzo 131

Varenna (Como)
– Hotel Royal Victoria 132
– Hotel Olivedo 133
San Fedele d'Intelvi (Como) - *Map 2*
– Villa Simplicitas e Solferino 134
Mantova - *Map 9*
– Albergo San Lorenzo 135
Pomponesco (Mantova) - *Map 9*
– Il Leone 136
Milano - *Map 2*
– Four Seasons Hotel 137
– Excelsior Hotel Gallia 138
– Grand Hotel Duomo 139
– Hotel Pierre Milano 140
– Hotel Diana Majestic 141
– Hotel Spadari al Duomo 142
– Hotel de la Ville 143
– Antica Locanda dei Mercanti 144
Cantello (Varese) - *Map 2*
– Albergo Madonnina 145
Maleo (Milano) - *Map 9*
– Albergo del Sole 146
Varese - *Map 2*
– Hotel Colonne 147
Lago Maggiore
  Ranco (Varese) - *Map 2*
– Il Sole di Ranco 148

M A R C H E S

Portonovo (Ancona) - *Map 11*
– Hotel Fortino Napoleonico 149
– Hotel Emilia 150
Sirolo (Ancona) - *Map 11*
– Hotel Monteconero 151
Pesaro - *Map 11*
– Hotel Vittoria 152
– Villa Serena 153
Urbino - *Map 11*
– Hotel Bonconte 154

U M B R I A

Perugia - *Map 14*
– Locanda della Posta 155
Perugia-Cenerente - *Map 14*
– Castello dell' Oscano 156
– Villa Ada 157

Castel del Piano Umbro (Perugia) - Map 14
  – Villa Aureli 158
Torgiano (Perugia) - Map 14
  – Relais Le Tre Vaselle 159
  – La Bondanzina 160
Montone (Perugia) - Map 14
  – La Locanda del Capitano 161
Assisi (Perugia) - Map 14
  – Hotel Fontebella 162
  – Hotel Umbra 163
Armenzano - Assisi (Perugia) - Map 14
  – Le Silve di Armenzano 164
Tordibetto di Assisi - Assisi (Perugia) - Map 14
  – Podere La Fornace 165
Bevagna (Perugia) - Map 14
  – L'Orto degli Angeli 166
Bovara di Trevi (Perugia) - Map 14
  – Casa Giulia 167
Canalicchio (Perugia) - Map 14
  – Relais Il Canalicchio 168
Citta di Castello (Perugia) - Maps 10 and 14
  – Hotel Tiferno 169
Colle San Paolo di Tavernelle (Perugia) - Map 13
  – Villa di Monte Solare 170
Montali - Tavernelle di Panicale - Map 13
  – Azienda Agrituristica Montali 171
Gùbbio - Monteluiano (Perugia) - Map 14
  – Villa Montegranelli Hotel 172
Lago Trasimeno (Perugia) - Map 13
  Passignano sul Trasimena
  – Poggio del Belveduto 173
  Isola Maggiore
  – Hotel da Sauro 174
Montefalco (Perugia) - Map 14
  – Hotel Villa Pambuffetti 175
Paciano (Perugia) - Map 13
  – Locanda della Rocca 176
Pissignano-Campello (Perugia) - Map 14
  – Residenza Vecchio Molino 177
Spoleto (Perugia) - Map 14
  – Hotel Gattapone 178
  – Palazzo Dragoni 179
  – Hotel San Luca 180
Spoleto - Monteluco (Perugia) - Map 14
  – Hotel Eremo delle Grazie 181
Spello (Perugia) - Map 14
  – Hotel Palazzo Bocci 182
  – Hotel La Bastiglia 183
Todi (Perugia) - Map 14
  – Hotel Fonte Cesia 184
Todi-Asproli (Perugia) - Map 14
  – Poggio d'Asproli 185
Todi-Canonica (Perugia) - Map 14
  – Tenuta di Canonica 186

Titignano-(Terni) - *Map 14*
  – Titignano 187
Amelia (Terni) - *Map 14*
  – Il Piccolo Hotel del Carléni 188
Orvieto (Terni) - *Map 13*
  – Hotel Ristorante La Badia 189
  – Villa Ciconia 190
  – Hotel Virgilio 191

PIEMONT VALLE D'AOSTA

Alba (Cuneo) - *Map 7*
  – Villa La Meridiana - Cascina Reine 192
Canelli (Asti) - *Map 7*
  – La Luna e i Falo' 193
Torino - *Map 7*
  – Villa Sassi 194
  – Hotel Victoria 195
Sauze d'Oulx (Torino) - *Map 6*
  – Il Capricorno 196
Cioccaro di Penango (Asti) - *Map 7*
  – Locanda del Sant'Uffizio 197
Verduno (Cuneo) - *Map 7*
  – Albergo del Castello 198
Lago Maggiore - *Map 2*
  Cannobio (Novara)
  – Hotel Pironi 199
  Ghiffa (Novara)
  – Hotel Ghiffa 200
  Stresa (Novara)
  – Hotel Verbano 201
Lago d'Orta - *Map 2*
  Orta San Giulio (Novara)
  – HotelVilla Crespi 202
  – Hotel San Rocco 203
San Giorgio Montferrato (Alessandria) - *Map 8*
  – Castello di San Giorgio 204
Breuil-Cervinia (Aosta) - *Map 1*
  – Hotel Hermitage 205
  – Les Neiges d'Antan 206
Champoluc (Aosta) - *Map 1*
  – Albergo Villa Anna Maria 207
Cogne (Aosta) - *Map 1*
  – Hotel Bellevue 208
Valnontey (Aosta) - *Maps 1 and 7*
  – Hotel Herbetet 209
  – Hotel Petit Dahu 210

Courmayeur-Arnouva (Aosta) - Map 1
  – Chalet Val Ferret 211
Courmayeur-Entrèves (Aosta) - Map 1
  – La Grange 212
  – Hotel La Brenva 213
Gressoney-Saint-Jean (Aosta) - Map 1
  – Hotel Gran Baita 214
Gressoney-la-Trinité (Aosta) - Map 1
  – Hotel Lo Scoiattolo 215

P U G L I A

Alberobello (Bari) - Map 22
  – Hotel dei Trulli 216
Monopoli (Bari) - Map 22
  – Il Melograno 217
Cisternino (Brindisi) - Map 22
  – Villa Cenci 218
Fasano (Brindisi) - Map 22
  – Masseria Marzalossa 219
Pezze di Greco (Brindisi) - Map 22
  – Masseria Salamina 220
Salvetrini di Fasano (Brindisi) - Map 22
  – Masseria San Domenico 221
Selva di Fasano (Brindisi) - Map 22
  – Hotel Sierra Silvana 222
Ostuni - Costa Meriata (Brindisi) - Map 22
  – Grand Hotel Masseria Santa Lucia 223
Ostuni (Brindisi) - Map 22
  – Il Frantoio 224
Lecce (Salento) - Map 22
  – Hotel Patria 225
Martina Franca (Taranto) - Map 22
  – Hotel Villa Ducale 226

S A R D I N I A

Isola di San Pietro - Carloforte (Cagliari) - Map 28
  – Hotel Hieracon 227
Isola di Sant Pietro - Tacca Rossa (Cagliari) - Map 28
  – Albergo Paola e Primo Maggio 228
Santa Margherita di Pula (Cagliari) - Map 28
  – Is Morus Relais 229
Su Gologone - Oliena (Nuoro) - Map 28
  – Hotel Su Gologone 230
Alghero (Sassari) - Map 28
  – Villa Las Tronas 231

Arzachena - Cannigione (Sassari) - Map 28
 – Hotel Li Capanni 232
Costa Dorata - Porto San Paolo (Sassari) - Map 28
 – Hotel Don Diego 233
Costa Smeralda - Porto Cervo (Sassari) - Map 28
 – Hotel Cala di Volpe 234
 – Hotel Le Ginestre 235
 – Hotel Romazzino 236
San Panteleo-Sasima (Sassari) - Map 28
 – La Sasima 237
Porto Conte (Sassari) - Map 28
 – El Faro 238

S I C I L Y

Agrigento - Map 26
 – Villa Athena 239
 – Foresteria Baglio della Luna 240
Menfi (Agrigento)- Map 26
 – Villa Ravidá 241
Canizzaro-Catania - Map 27
 – Grand Hotel Baia Verde 242
Palermo - Map 26
 – Grand Hotel Villa Igiea 243
 – Centrale Palace Hotel 244
 – Grand Hotel et des Palmes 245
 – Hotel Principe di Villafranca 246
 – Massimo Plaza Hotel 247
Gangi (Palermo) - Map 27
 – Tenuta Gangivecchio 248
Trabia (Palermo) - Map 26
 – Hotel Tonnara Trabia 249
Ragusa-Giubiliana - Map 27
 – Eremo della Giubiliana 250
Siracusa - Map 27
 – Villa Lucia 251
 – Grand Hotel di Siracusa 252
Castel di Tusa (Messina) - Map 27
 – Museo Albergo L'Atelier sul Mare 253
Pettineo (Messina) - Map 27
 – Casa Migliaca 254
Cesaro (Messina) - Map 27
 – Villa Miraglia 255
Taormina (Messina) - Map 27
 – San Domenico Palace Hotel 256
 – Hotel Villa Belvedere 257
 – Hotel Villa Ducale 258
 – Hotel Villa Paradiso 259
 – Hotel Villa Schuler 260
 – Hotel Villa Sant'Andrea (at Mazzarro) 261

Erice (Trapani) - Map 26
  – Hotel Erimo Erice 262
Scopello (Trapani)- Map 26
  – Pensione Tranchina 263
Isola di Lampedusa (Agrigento) - Map 26
  – Club Il Gattopardo 264
Isole Eolie o Lipari (Messina) - Map 27
  Isola Lipari
  – Hotel Carasco 265
  – Hotel Villa Augustus 266
  – Hotel Villa Meligunis 267
  Isola Panarea
  – Hotel Raya 268
  Isola Salina
  – Hotel Signum 269
  Isola Stromboli
  – Hotel La Sciara Residence 270
  – La Locanda del Barbablú 271
  – La Sirenetta Park Hotel 272
  Isola Vulcano
  – Les Sables Noirs 273

T U S C A N Y

Castiglion Fiorentino (Arezzo) - Map 13
  – Relais San Pietro in Polvano 274
Cortona (Arezzo) - Map 13
  – Hotel San Michele 275
Cortona - San Martino (Arezzo) - Map 13
  – Relais Il Falconiere 276
Montebenichi - Bucine (Arezzo) - Map 13
  – Castelletto di Montebenichi 277
Monte San Savino (Arezzo) - Map 13
  – Castello di Gargonza 278
San Pietro a Dame (Arezzo) - Map 13
  – Stoppiacce 279
Poggio d'Ancona (Arezzo) - Map 10
  – Il Trebbio 280
Firenze - Map 10
  – Hotel Helvetia & Bristol 281
  – Hotel Regency 282
  – Hotel Brunelleschi 283
  – Hotel J and J 284
  – Hotel Monna Lisa 285
  – Grand Hotel Minerva 286
  – Hotel Montebello Splendid 287
  – Hotel Lungarno 288
  – Hotel de la Ville 289
  – Torre di Bellosguardo 290
  – Villa Belvedere 291

   – Villa Carlotta 292
   – Hotel Hermitage 293
   – Hotel Loggiato dei Serviti 294
   – Hotel Splendor 295
   – Hotel Morandi alla Crocetta 296
   – Hotel Pensione Pendini 297
   – Pensione Annalena 298
   – Hotel Tornabuoni Beacci 299
   – Hotel David 300
   – Hotel Botticelli 301
   – Residenza Johanna I 302
   – Residenza Johanna II 303

Firenze-Candeli - Map 10
   – Villa La Massa 304

Firenze-Fiesole - Map 10
   – Villa San Michele 305
   – Pensione Bencistà 306

Firenze - Trespiano - Map 10
   – Hotel Villa Le Rondini 307

Firenze - Giogoli - Map 10
   – Fattoria Il Milione 308

Firenze - Scandici- Map 10
   – Tenuta Le Viste 309

Sesto Fiorentino (Firenze) - Map 10
   – Villa Villoresi 310

impruneta (Firenze) - Map 10
   – Castello di Cafaggio 311

Le Valli-Incisa Val d'Arno (Firenze) - Map 10
   – Residenza San Nicolo d'Olmeto 312

Mercatale (Firenze) - Map 10
   – Salvadonica 313

Montagnane (Firenze) - Map 10
   – Castello di Montegufoni 314

Montefiridolfi (Firenze) - Map 10
   – Fattoria La Loggia 315

Panzano in Chianti (Firenze) - Map 10
   – Villa Le Barone 316

Castiglioni di Rufina (Firenze) - Map 10
   – La Sosta a' Busini 317

Pomino-Rufina (Firenze) - Map 10
   – Fattoria di Petrognano 318

Reggello - Vaggio (Firenze) - Map 10
   – Villa Rigacci 319

Barberino Val d'Elsa (Firenze) - Map 13
   – La Callaiola 320

San Filippo - Barberino Val d'Elsa (Firenze) - Map 13
   – Il Paretaio 321

Scheto - Barberino Val d'Elsa - (Firenze) - Map 13
   – La Spinosa 322

Cortine - Barberino Val d'Elsa - (Firenze) - Map 13
   – Fattoria Casa Sola 323

Prumiano - Barberino Val d'Elsa - (Firenze) - Map 13
　– La Chiara di Prumiano 324
Pontessieve (Firenze) - Map 10
　– Tenuta Bossi 325
Vicchio (Firenze) - Map 10
　– Villa Campestri 326
Certaldo Alto (Firenze) - Map 13
　– Osteria del Vicario 327
Prato - Map 10
　– Villa Rucellai - Fattoria di Canneto 328
Artimino - Carmignano (Prato) - Map 10
　– Hotel Paggeria Medicea ....:.................329
　– Fattoria di Bacchereto 330
Siena - Map 13
　– Park Hotel 331
　– Hotel Certosa di Maggiano 332
　– Grand Hotel Villa Patrizia 333
　– Hotel Villa Scacciapensieri 334
　– Palazzo Ravizza 335
　– Hotel Antica Torre 336
　– Hotel Santa Caterina 337
　– Villa dei Leicci 338
Castelnuovo Berardenga (Siena) - Map 13
　– Castello di Montalto 339
San Gusmè - Castelnuovo Berardenga (Siena) - Map 13
　– Hotel Villa Arceno 340
San Felice - Castelnuovo Berardenga (Siena) - Map 13
　– Hotel Relais Borgo San Felice 341
Tornano - Lecchi (Siena) - Map 13
　– Castello di Tornano 342
San Sano - Lecchi (Siena) - Map 13
　– Residence San Sano 343
Monteriggioni (Siena) - Map 13
　– Hotel Monteriggioni 344
Pieve a Elsa - Colle di Val d'Elsa (Siena) - Map 13
　– La Piccola Pieve 345
Poggibonsi (Siena) - Map 13
　– Hotel Villa San Lucchese 346
San Gimignano (Siena) - Map 13
　– Hotel L'Antico Pozzo 347
　– Hotel La Cisterna 348
　– Hotel Bel Soggiorno 349
　– La Collegiata 350
　– Villa San Paolo 351
　– Hotel Le Renaie 352
Casaglia - San Gimignano (Siena) - Map 13
　– Villa Remignoli 353
Il Cotone - San Gimignano (Siena) - Map 13
　– Il Casale del Cotone 354
Libbiano - San Gimignano (Siena) - Map 13
　– Il Casolare di Libbiano 355
Pescille- San Gimignano (Siena) - Map 13
　– Hotel Pescille 356
　– Casanova di Pescille 357

Castellina in Chianti (Siena) - Map 13
- Palazzo Squarcialupi 358
- Hotel Salivolpi 359
- Tenuta di Ricavo (Ricavo) 360
- Hotel Villa Casalecchi 361
- Locanda Le Piazze 362
- Hotel Belvedere di San Leonino (San Leonino) 363

Gaiole in Chianti (Siena) - Map 13
- Castello di Spaltenna 364

Argenina - Gaiole in Chianti (Siena) - Map 13
- Borgo Argenina 365

La Ripresa di Vistarenni - Gaiole in Chianti (Siena) - Map 13
- L'Ultimo Molino 366

Radda in Chianti (Siena) - Map 13
- Relais Fattoria Vignale 367

Volpaia - Radda in Chianti (Siena) - Map 13
- La Locanda 368
- Podere Terreno 369

Vescine - Radda in Chianti (Siena) - Map 13
- Vescine - Il Relais del Chianti 370

La Villa - Radda in Chianti (Siena) - Map 13
- Torre Canvalle 371

Sovicille - Pretale- (Siena) - Map 13
- Hotel Borgo Pretale 372

Rosia (Siena) - Map 13
- Azienda Agricola Montestigliano 373

Montauto - Monteroni (Siena) - Map 13
- Casa Bolsinina 374

Montalcino (Siena) - Map 13
- Hotel Vechia Oliviera 375

Modanella-Serre di Rapolano (Siena) - Map 13
- Castello di Modanella 376

Lucignano d'Asso (Siena) - Map 13
- Azienda Lucignanello Bandini 377

Sinalunga (Siena) - Map 13
- Locanda dell'Amorosa 378

Montefollonico (Siena) - Map 13
- La Chiusa 379

Montepulciano (Siene) - Map 13
- La Dionora 380

Sovana - Sarteano (Siena) - Map 13
- La Sovana 381

Pienza (Siena) - Map 13
- La Saracina 382
- Relais Il Chiostro di Pienza 383

Monticchiello di Pienza (Siena) - Map 13
- L'Olmo 384

San Quirico d'Orcia - Ripa d'Orcia (Siena) - Map 13
- Castello di Ripa d'Orcia 385

Castiglione d'Orcia - Rocca d'Orcia (Siena) - Map 13
- Cantina Il Borgo 386

Cetona (Siena) - *Map 13*
 – La Frateria 387
San Casciano dei Bagni (Siena) - *Map 13*
 – Albergo Sette Querce 388
Le Vigne (Siena) - *Map 13*
 – La Palazzina 389
Lucca- *Map 9*
 – Locanda l'Elisa 390
 – La Principessa 391
Forte dei Marmi (Lucca) - *Map 9*
 – California Park Hotel 392
 – Hotel Byron 393
 – Hotel Tirreno 394
Pietrasanta (Lucca) - *Map 9*
 – Albergo Pietrasanta 395
Santa Maria del Guidice (Lucca) - *Map 9*
 – Hotel Villa Rinascimento 396
Viareggio (Lucca) - *Map 9*
 – Hotel Plaza e de Russie 397
Montecatini Val di Cecina (Pisa) - *Map 12*
 – Il Frassinello 398
Pugnano (Pisa) - *Map 9*
 – Casetta delle Selve 399
Rigoli - San Giuliano Terme (Pisa) - *Map 9*
 – Hotel Villa di Corliano 400
Volterra (Pisa) - *Map 12*
 – Albergo Villa Nencini 401
Monsummano Terme (Pistoia) - *Map 9*
 – Hotel Grotta Giusti 402
Montecatini Terme (Pistoia) - *Map 9*
 – Grand Hotel e La Pace 403
Montevettolini (Pistoia) - *Map 9*
 – Villa Lucia 404
Pontenuovo (Pistoia) - *Map 9*
 – Il Convento 405
Manciano (Grosseto) - *Map 13*
 – Le Pisanelle 406
Montieri (Grosseto) - *Map 13*
 – Rifugio Prategiano 407
Porto Ercole (Grosseto) - *Map 13*
 – Hotel Il Pellicano 408
Punta Ala (Grosseto) - *Map 12*
 – Hotel Cala del Porto 409
 – Piccolo Hotel Alleluja 410
Roccatederighi (Grosseto) - *Map 13*
 – Fattoria di Peruzzo 411
 – Auberge Azienda Pereti 412
 – Pieve di Caminino 413
Saturnia (Grosseto) - *Map 13*
 – Hotel Terme di Saturnia 414
 – Hotel Villa Clodia 415

Isola d'Elba (Livorno) - *Map 12*
  – Parkhotel Napoleone 416
  – Hotel Hermitage 417
  – Hotel da Giacomino 418

T R E N T I N O - D O L O M I T E S

Bolzano - *Map 4*
  – Parkhotel Laurin 419
Merano (Bolzano) - *Map 3*
  – Hotel Castel Labers 420
  – Hotel Castel Fragsburg 421
Merano - Marling (Bolzano) - *Map 3*
  – Hotel Oberwirt 422
Missiano - Appiano (Bolzano) - *Map 4*
  – Hotel Schloss Korb 423
Caldaro (Bolzano) - *Map 4*
  – Pensione Leuchtenburg 424
Redagno (Bolzano) - *Map 4*
  – Berghotel Zirmerhof 425
San Vigilio - Lana (Bolzano) - *Map 3*
  – Albergo Monte San Vigilio 426
Fié Allo Sciliar (Bolzano) - *Map 4*
  – Hotel Turm 427
Castelrotto-Siusi (Bolzano) - *Map 4*
  – Hotel Cavallino d'Oro 428
  – Albergo Tschötscherhof 429
Ortisei (Bolzano) - *Map 4*
  – Hotel Adler 430
Bulla - Ortisei (Bolzano) - *Map 4*
  – Pension Uhrerhof Deur 431
Bressanone (Bolzano) - *Map 4*
  – Hotel Elephant 432
Corvara in Badia (Bolzano) - *Map 4*
  – La Perla 433
San Cassiano (Bolzano) - *Map 4*
  – Hotel Armentarola 434
San Candido (Bolzano) - *Map 4*
  – Parkhotel Sole Paradiso 435
Santa Cristina (Bolzano) - *Map 4*
  – Albergo Uridl 436
Trento - *Maps 3 and 4*
  – Albergo Accademia 437
Pergine Valsugana - *Map 4*
  – Castello Pergine 438
Lago di Garda - Riva del Garda (Trento) - *Map 3*
  – Lido Palace Hotel 439
Roncegno (Trento) - *Map 4*
  – Palace Hotel 440

V E N E T O

Venezia - Map 4
- Hotel Cipriani et Palazzo Vendramin 441
- Bauer Gründwald et Grand Hotel 442
- Gritti Palace Hotel 443
- Hotel Monaco e Grand Canal 444
- Hotel Londra Palace 445
- Hotel Gabrielli Sandwirth 446
- Hotel Metropole 447
- Pensione Accademia-Villa Maravegie 448
- Hotel Flora 449
- Hotel Torino 450
- Hotel Bel Sito & Berlino 451
- Hotel La Fenice et des Artistes 452
- Hotel Do Pozzi 453
- Hotel Panada 454
- Hotel Ai due Fanali 455
- Hotel Residenza 456
- Locanda Ai Santi Apostoli 457
- Hotel Santo Stefano 458
- Pensione Seguso 459
- Pensione La Calcina 460
- Pensione Alla Salute da Cici 461
- Hotel Pausania 462
- Hotel Agli Alboretti 463
- Hotel Belle-Arti 464
- Hotel La Galleria 465
- Palazetto da Schio 466
- Palazetto S. Lio 467

Venezia-Lido - Map 4
- Hotel des Bains 468
- Albergo Quattro Fontane 469
- Hotel Villa Mabapa 470

Venezia - Torcello - Map 4
- Locanda Cipriani 471

Dolo (Venezia) - Map 4
- Villa Ducale 472

Mira Porte (Venezia) - Map 4
- Hotel Villa Margherita 473

Scorzé (Venezia) - Map 4
- Villa Soranzo Conestabile 474

Cortina d'Ampezzo (Belluno) - Map 4
- Hotel Bellevue 475
- Hotel de la Poste 476
- Hotel Ancora 477
- Hotel Pensione Menardi 478
- Franceschi Park Hotel 479

Cortina d'Ampezzo - Fraina (Belluno) - Map 4
- Baita Fraina 480

Tai di Cadore (Belluno) - Map 4
- Villa Marinotti 481

San Floriano del Collio (Gorizia) - Map 5
- Golf Hotel 482

Sappada - Map 5
  – Haus Michaela 483
Padova - Map 4
  – Albergo Leon Bianco 484
Rovigo - Map 10
  – Hotel Villa Regina Margherita 485
Asolo (Treviso) - Map 4
  – Hotel Villa Cipriani 486
  – Albergo del Sole 487
Follina (Treviso) - Map 4
  – Hotel Abbazia 488
Mogliano Veneto (Treviso) - Map 4
  – Villa Stucky 489
Portobuffolé (Treviso) - Map 5
  – Villa Giustinian 490
Solighetto (Treviso) - Map 4
  – Locanda Da Lino 491
Zerman Mogliano Veneto (Treviso) - Map 4
  – Hotel Villa Condulmer 492
Cividale del Friuli (Udine) - Map 5
  – Locanda Al Castello 493
Verona - Maps 3 and 4
  – Hotel Gabbia d'Oro 494
  – Hotel Due Torri 495
  – Albergo Aurora 496
Pedemonte (Verona) - Map 3
  – Hotel Villa del Quar 497
Gargagnago di Valpolicella (Verona) - Map 3
  – Foresteria Serègo Alighieri 498
Villabella - San Bonifacio (Verona) - Map 4
  – Relais Villabella 499
Sant'Ambrogio di Valpolicella (Verona) - Map 3
  – Coop. 8 Marzo-Ca'Verde 500
Torri del Benaco (Verona) - Map 3
  – Hotel Gardesana 501
Arcugnano (Vicenza) - Map 4
  – Hotel Villa Michelangelo 502
Barbarano Vicentino (Vicenza) - Map 4
  – Il Castello 503
Costozza di Longare (Vicenza) - Map 4
  – Azienda A & G da Schio 504
Trissino (Vicenza) - Map 4
  – Relais Ca' Masieri 505
Trieste - Map 5
  – Duchi d'Aosta 506

MAPS

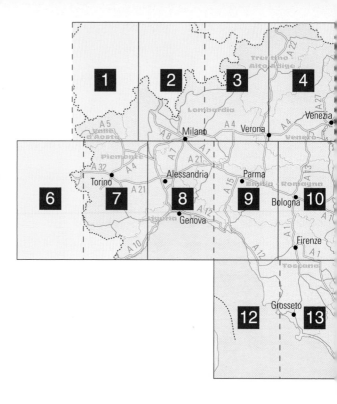

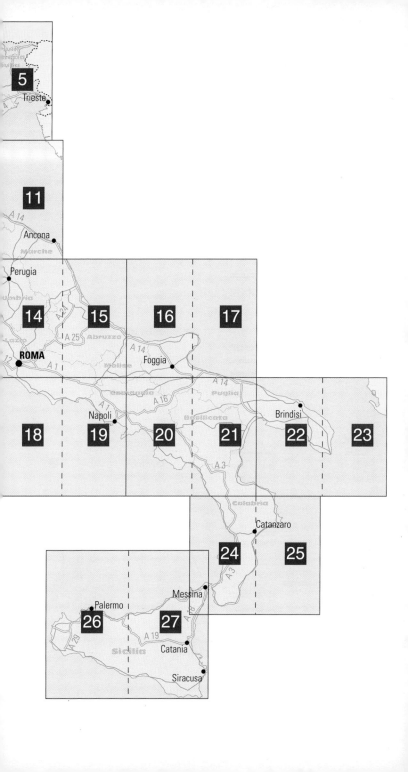

KEY TO THE MAPS

Scale : 1:1,000,000
maps 26 and 27 : scale 1:1,370,000
maps 28 : scale 1:1,250,000

MOTORWAYS

A9 - L'Océane

Under construction
projected

ROADS
Highway
Dual carriageway
Four lanes road
Major road
Secondary road

TRAFFIC
National
Regional
Local

JUNCTIONS
Complete
Limited

DISTANCES IN KILOMETRES
On motorway
On other road

BOUNDARIES
National boundary
Region area
Department area

URBAIN AREA

Town
Big city
Important city
Medium city
Little city

AIRPORTS

FORESTS

PARKS
Limit
Center

Created by

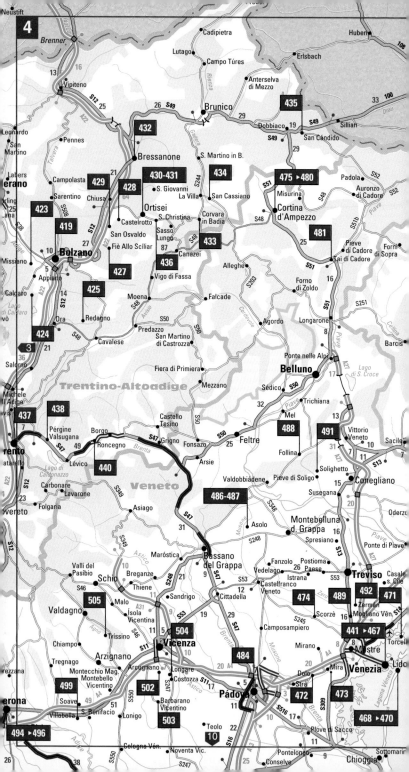

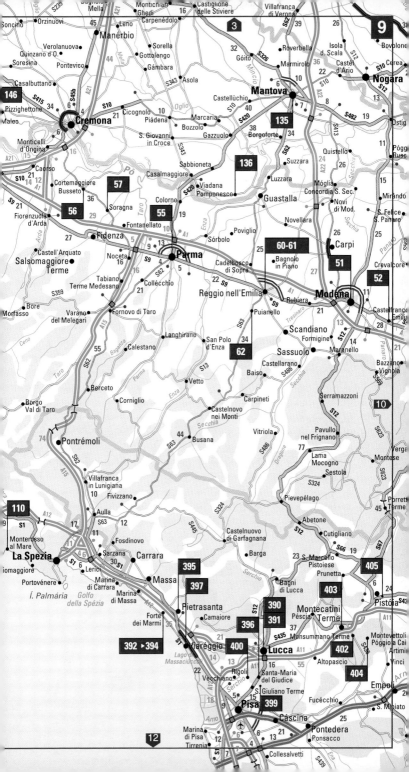

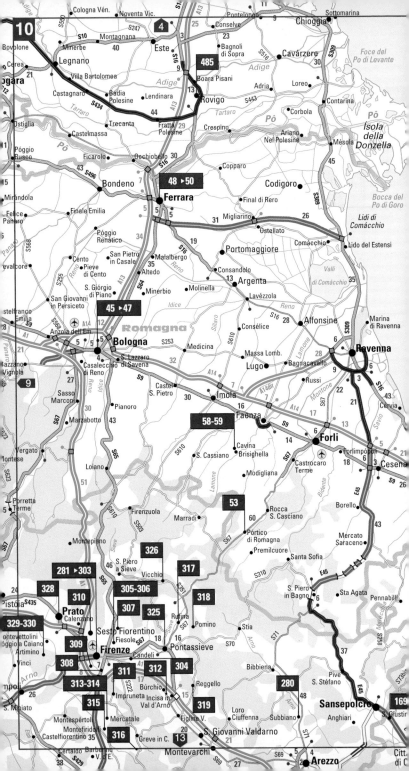

Rovinj
Bale
Vodnjan
Marcana
Pula
Premántura

M2

*Bocche del Po
della Pilla*

MAR   ADRIÁTICO

Cesenatico

54

S16

Savignano
sul Rubicone

Santarcangelo
Romágna

Rímini

11

7

S258

S72

23

Sogliano
al Rubicone

Riccione

Cattólica

Gabicce
Mare

12

152-153

16

S423

19

Pésaro

15

Montecchio

Foglia

A14

17

Fano

14

154

S3

Metauro

S16

Mercatale

Urbino

S423

Fossombrone

27

12

10

Scapezzano

149-150

9

Senigállia

S73bis

4

Foglia

Corinaldo

S360

Marzocca

16

**Falconara
Maríttima**

S16

17

4

Ancona

11

4

Portonov

S. Angelo
in Vado

Urbánia

11

Ostra

Mise

Chiaravalle

Esino

19

A14

11

8

Siról o

Acqualagna

S. Lorenzo
in Campo

14

151

Píobicco

S3

S257

Cagli

26

Montecarotto

S360

Jesi

38

S78

Musane

Osimo

S361

13

Loretó

Pérgola

Fílottrano

S362

Recanati

S571

Pietralunga

Schéggia

S360

Sassoferrato

14

10

S76

Marche

Cíngoli

S362

Tréia

Poten
Picen

Pola

Metauro

4

Maticchia

Poen

S. Mariono

Osra

Scéggia

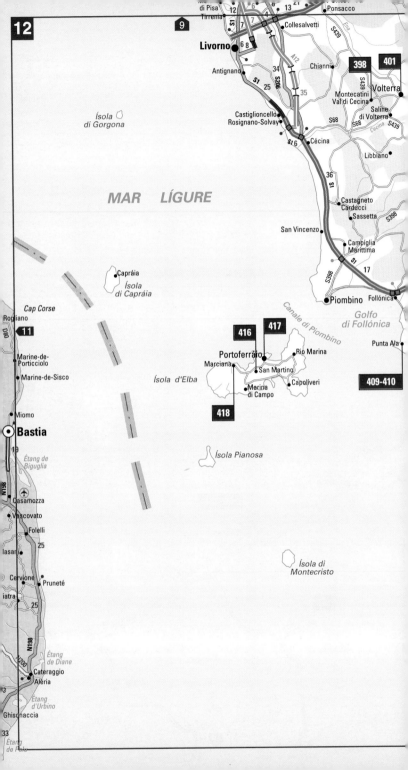

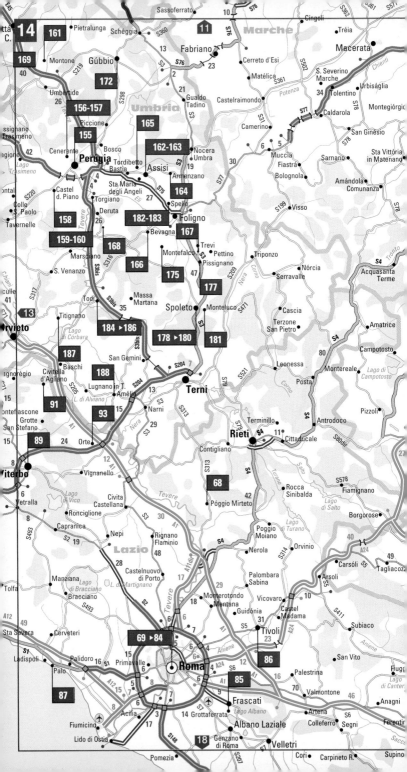

Komiza

VIS

MAR

ADRIÁTICO

15

88

Punta
Penne

Vasto

upello

San Salvo

20 S16

Térmoli

Campomarino

Montenero
di Bisáccia

Guglionesi

Palata

Castelmàuro

Trivento

67

Casacalenda

Molise

Sant'Elia
a Pianisi

S87

Casalvécchio
di Púglia

Lago
di Occhito

Pietramontecorvino

Campobasso

Riccia

Cercemaggiore

oiano

S. Bartolomeo
in Galdo

Ísole
Trémiti

I. Capráia

Í. S. Nicola

Ísola
S. Dómino

Rodi Garganico S89

Lago
di Lésina

Lago
di Varano

Carpi

Cagnano
Varano

S89

Sannicandro
Gargánico

San Marco
in Lámis

S272

S272

Apricena

Rignano
Gargánico

S89

S273

San Severo

31

Candelaro

30

Celone

S88

Cervaro

Torremaggiore

5

26

S16

A14

San Páolo
di Civitate

S160

Triolo

Castelnuovo
della Daunia

Volturara
Appula

Lucera 16

S17

29

Fóggia

6

7

A14

36

5

14

S16

Alberona

20

S160

23

S835

Orta Nova

S16

Tróia

14

20 Stornarella

9

12

25 S645

S88

S17

S25

S589

12

S90

Ururi

Chiéuti

Serracapriola

S16ter

S87

30 A14

45

16

S16

58

A14 24

9

S16

Biferno

S650

Trigno

S647

Biferno

S647

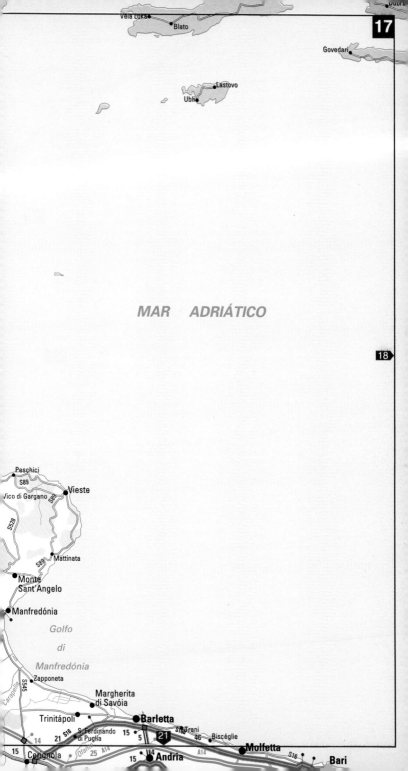

Vela Luka
Blato

Govedari

Lastovo
Ublí

MAR   ADRIÁTICO

Peschici
S89
Vico di Gargano S89 **Vieste**
S528

S89 Mattinata

Monte
Sant'Angelo

Manfredónia

Golfo

di

Manfredónia

S545
Zapponeta

Carapelle

Margherita
di Savóia

Trinitápoli **Barletta**
S. Ferdinando *S16* Trani
14 21 *S16* di Puglia 15 *S16* 46 Biscéglie
5 **21**
15 **Cerignola** *Ofanto* 25 A14 15 A14 **Andria** A14 **Molfetta** S16 **Bari**

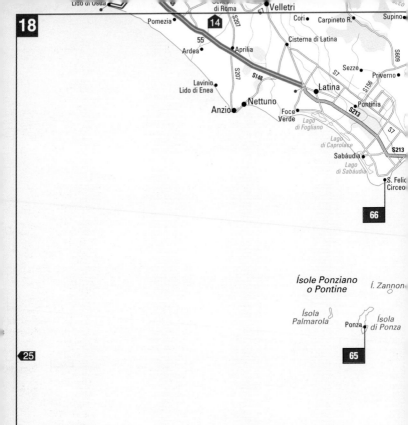

18

Lido di Ostia

di Roma
Velletri

Pomezia

14

Cori
Carpineto R.
Supino

S207

55

Cisterna di Latina

Ardea
Aprilia

S609

S207

Sezze
Priverno

S148

S7

Latina

S156

Lavinio
Lido di Enea
Nettuno

Pontinia

S213

Anzio
Foce
Verde
*Lago
di Fogliano*

*Lago
di Caprolace*

S7

S213

Sabáudia
*Lago
di Sabáudia*

S. Felic
Circeo

66

*Ísole Ponziano
o Pontine*
Í. Zannon

*Ísola
Palmarola*

Ponza
*Ísola
di Ponza*

65

◄25

MAR TIRRENO

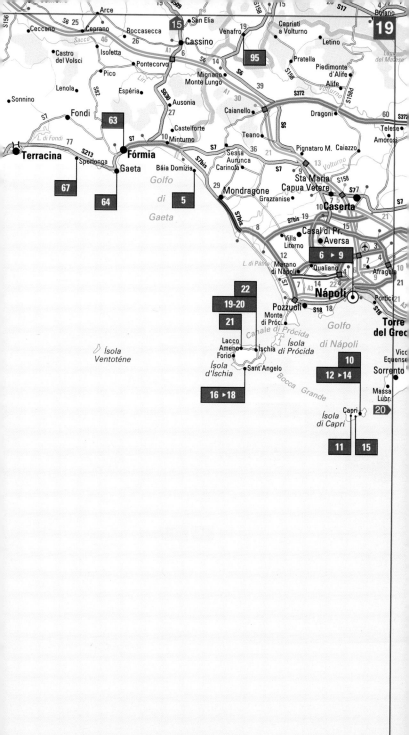

ALBANIA

Novosele

Vlore

MAR ADRIÁTICO

San Cataldo

S543

S611

Vérnole

Melendugno

22

S16

Martano

8

S16

Otranto

15

S173

Máglie

S487

5

6

Uggiano
la Chiesa

S275

Poggiardo

27

Supersano

S275

S173

Casarano

Taurisano

Tricase

S274

Ugento

Presicce

S274

Gagliano
del Capo

Marina
di Leuca

*Capo Santa Maria
di Leuca*

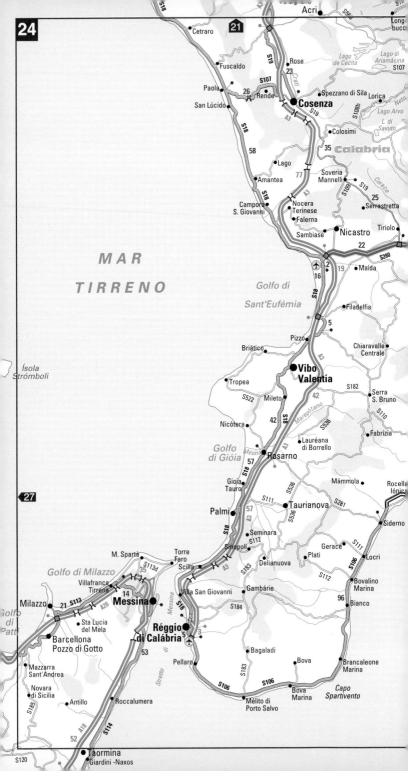

Campana

Cirò Marina

Savelli

S492

Pallagorio

S106

Vitravo

S. Giovanni
in Fiore

Lago
mpollino

S107

S107

Neto

S179

Cotronei

S106

Crotone

11

Capo Colonna

Petilia
Policastro

Tacina

Mesoraca

S109

Cutro

25

Taverna

Sersale

S106

Isola di
Capo Rizzuto

S109

S180

36

Capo Rizzuto

S1790

S106

Capo Rizzuto

Catanzaro

12

S280

S384

Catanzaro Lido

Squillace

Golfo di

Staletti

Squillace

Soverato

S106

47

Badolato

Stilo

S110

Monasterace
Marina

S106

3

M A R   I Ó N I O

Ísola di Ústica

MAR TIRRENO

Capo Gallo **243 ▸ 247**
Mondello
Partanna
Golfo
di Palermo
Capo San Vito
San Vito
lo Capo Terrasini **249** Golfo di
263 Monte- Monreale **Palermo** Bagheria Términi Imerese
Capo San Vito lepre Términi
Golfo di S113 Imerese
Castellammare Monte- Misilmeri Trabia Collesano
262 Scopello Balestate Partinico S113
Castellammare S.Giuseppe Iato Piana Cáccamo
Érice del Golfo del Albanesi Cerda
Trápani Valdérice S187 Alcamo L. di Piana
Paceco d. Albanesi Villafrati Alia Valledolmo
S115 Calatafimi Villalunga Pratameno
Salemì Camporeale Corleone Lercara Friddi Villalba
Santa Ninfa Prizzi
Marsala Partanna Montevago Palazzo Adriano
Strasatti Sta Margherita Chiusa Casteltérmini
Castelvetrano di Belice Sclàfani
241 Lago Aráncio
Mazara Menfi Burgio Canicatti
del Vallo Campobello Caltabellotta **239-240**
di Mazara Marinella
Torretta Sciacca Ribera **Agrigento**
Granítola Porto Naro
Capo Granítola Empédocle
Palma di
MAR MEDITERRÁNEO Montechiaro

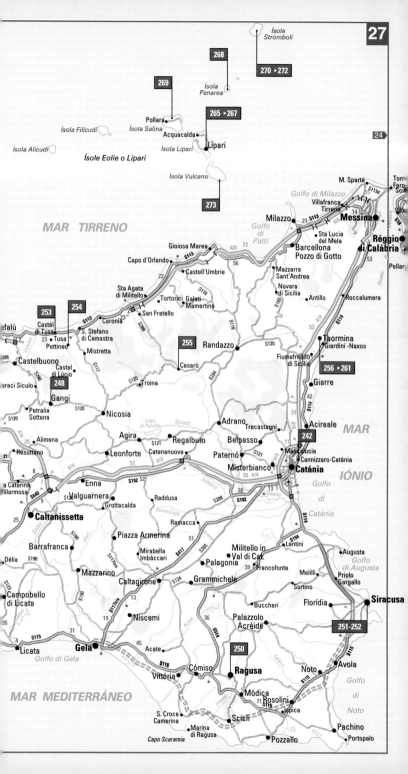

MAR TIRRENO

MAR DI SARDEGNA

MAR MEDITERRÁNEO

Ísola Maddalena

Sta Teresa Gallura
La Maddalena
12
S133b
Ísola Caprera

Palau
Baia Sardinia
Porto Cervo
Arzachena
43
San Pantaleo
234 ▸ 236

232
237
Golfo Aranci

Olbia
29 S125
Costa Dorata
Ísola Tavolara
Ísola Molara

233

S199
Monti
Padru
13

Témpio Pausánia
25
Berchidda
Padru
Brunella
13

Calangiánus
19
Oschiri
Lodè
Siniscóla

Punta Caprara

Ísola Asinara
Fornelli

Golfo dell'Asinara

Stintino

Castelsardo S200
Sedini
Nulvi
S127

Porto Tórres
14 S131
Sorso
Senneri
Chiaramonti
Lago di Coghinas
Oschiri

Sass. Argentiera S291
Sássari 8
8
Ploaghe S597
36
S199

Florinas
19
Ozieri
Buddusó

Bitti
31

Porto Conte
238
231
Alghero
Villanova Monteleone
S292
Thiesi
Mores
S128b
Benetutti
Orune
11
230

Montresta
S292
Pádria
Bonorva
34
Bono
Búrgos
Orune
Núoro

Bosa
S129b
Sindia
Macomer
Bolotana
58 S129
Orotelli
Orani
Orosei

Tresnurághes
Scano Montiferro
Cúglieri
16
Silánus
Bortigali
17
41
Sarule
Mamoiada
Orgósolo
Dorgali
80

Santu Lussúrgiu
37
S131
S388
Lago Omodeo
Fonni

Zeddiani
Bauladu
Tramatza
Busachi
Sórgono
Tonara
Aritzo
Lago Alto Flumendosa
Baunei
Lotzorai

Cábras
Simáxis
S128
Sadali
Lanusei
Bari Sardo

Oristano
Arsuni
Láconi
Tertenia

Golfo di Oristano
Marrubiu
46
Terralba
Uras
Nurallao
Lago di Mulargia
S125

Sant'Antonio de Santadi
Sardara
Pabillónis
S131 S128
Villamar
Mandas
Escalaplano
106

Gúspini S197
Strovina
Samassi
Serrenti
20
Suelli
Senorbi
S. Nicoló Gerrei
Villasalto
Villaputzu

Gonnosfanádiga
Villacidro
Fluminimaggiore
Nuraminis
Vilasor
San Andrea Frius
San Vito
Muravera

Buggérru
Serramanna
S293
Vallermosa S196
Monastir
16
S387
Burcei
Dolianova
Sinnai
S125

Domusnóvas
Siliqua
S130
Decimomannu
Sestu
13
Castiádas

Iglésias
S130
26
Sánluri
S554
5
8
Quartu Sant'Elena
Geremèas
Villasimius

228 227
Gonnesa
Cágliari

Portoscuso
Narcao
S293
Capoterra
Golfo di Cágliari
Capo Carbonara

Ísola di San Pietro
Carloforte
Calasetta
S126d
S. Giovani Suergiu
Giba
Santadi
229
Pula

Sant'Antioco
Porto Botte
Sta Anna Arresi
S195
Teulada
Sta Margherita

Ísola di Sant'Antioco
Golfo di Pálmas
Chia

Capo Sperone

HOTELS AND
COUNTRY INNS

Hotel Barbieri

87042 Altomonte (Cosenza)
Via San Nicola, 30
Tel. 0981-94 80 72 - Fax 0981-94 80 73 - Sig. Barbieri
Web: www.casabarbieri.it

Category ★★★ **Rooms** 30 with air-conditioning, telephone, shower, WC, minibar, TV. **Price** Single 80,000L, double 140,000L. **Meals** Breakfast included, served 6:30-10:00 - half board 110,000L, full board 140,000L (per pers., 3 days min.). **Restaurant** Service 12:30PM-4:00PM, 7:30PM-12:00AM - mealtime specials 65-75,000L - Specialties: Pasta fatta in casa - Funghi - Salumi tipici. **Credit cards** All major. **Pets** Dogs allowed. **Facilities** Swimming pool in casa Barbieri, tennis (5,000L), parking. **Nearby** Altomonte (with Cathedral tomb of Filippo Sangineto 14th-century and "Saint Ladislas" attributed to Simone Martini) - excursions to Monte Pollino from Castrovillari - old Calabrian villages (Stilo, Sibari and Paola as well as Altomonte). **Open** All year.

One may be surprised to find the best restaurant in Calabria in this rather out-of-the-way village. You can savor excellent regional dishes while enjoying a marvelous view of the town of Altomonte, a vista framed by a 15th-century monastery and splendid houses. Italian-style breakfast is a real delight. You can, if you like, have it by the shores of Lago del Fareto: the first bite of your day will be delicious if you have the warm ricotta cheese on lightly toasted bread, topped with home-made berry confiture, also available in the gift shop next door. Rooms are spacious, pleasant and unpretentiously decorated (some have small balconies with great views). The hotel has a family atmosphere.

How to get there (Map 21): 50km north of Cosenza via A3, Altomonte exit.

Locanda delle Donne Monache

85046 Maratea (Potenza)
Via Carlo Mazzei, 4
Tel. 0973-87 74 87 - Fax 0973-87 76 87 - Sig. Raffaele Bruno
E-mail: locdonnemonache@crosswinds.net - Web: //web.tiscalinet.it/locdonnemonache

Category ★★★★ **Rooms** 24 and 6 suites with air-conditioning, telephone, bath, satellite TV, minibar. **Price** Single 185-225,000L, double 320-360,000L, suite 520-560,000L. **Meals** Breakfast included (buffet), served 7:30-10:30 - half board and full board 200-240,000L (per pers.), +60,000L per pers. in double room. **Restaurant** Service 12:30PM-2:30PM, 8:00PM-11:00PM - à la carte - Italian and regional cooking. **Credit cards** All major. **Pets** Dogs not allowed. **Facilities** Swimming pool, private beach, parking. **Nearby** Maretea - Sanctuario Monte San Biagio - Rivello - S. Lorenzo in Padula - Monte Pollino. **Open** 1 week before Easter to end Oct.

This charming hotel between the mountains and the sea, is in Maratea, a village nestled in a cove on the Tyrrhenian coast. Once an old monastery in the center of the village, it has been completely refurbished and decorated with sobriety and elegance, except for the slightly Baroque-like lobby. The rooms, which have kept a monastic air, are very comfortable, with canopy beds and simple, tasteful furniture in the best tradition of modern Italian design. In front of the house there is a secluded garden with a nice swimming pool. The hotel's private beach is even better; a boat at your disposal can take you out to view the Gulf of Policastro. Those who prefer to go hiking and horseback riding will want to head for the back country: the Basicilata is mostly mountains and hills, with beautiful wildlife preserves.

How to get there *(Map 21): 176km southeast of Salerno via A3, Lagonegro-North Maratea exit, S585 and Maratea.*

Hotel Sassi

75100 Matera
Via San Giovanni Vecchio, 89
Tel. 0835-33 10 09 / 33 10 90 - Fax 0835-33 37 33 - Sig. Cristallo
E-mail: hotelsassi@infinito.it

Category ★★★ **Rooms** 15 with telephone, shower, WC, TV, minibar. **Price** Single 80,000L, double 150,000L, triple 180,000L, suite 210,000L. **Meals** Breakfast included, served 8:00-10:00. **Restaurant** See p. 508. **Credit cards** All major. **Pets** Dogs allowed. **Nearby** Les Sassi: Sassi road, le duome in Matera, Chiese rupestri on the Tarento road. **Open** All year.

The main points of interest in Matera are the cave dwellings and shrines of Sasso Caveoso that have just been listed by UNESCO as a World Heritage site and the rock-hewn churches of the Basilian monks nearby. This little hotel has been installed by the Cristallo family in one of these ancient dwellings. It reflects all the architecture of Sassi: a succession of vaulted rooms on different levels, small terraces offering surprising views of the nearby Duomo. Although great care has been taken to preserve the typical look and feel of the place, the owners have in no way neglected modern comforts. No two rooms are alike, in size or appearance, but all are well-decorated and comfortable. For years the Italians used to represent Dante's "Inferno" as a kind of Sassi, inhabited by the wretched of the earth (as described by Carlo Levi in "Christ Stopped at Eboli"). Today the houses tend to be occupied by architects, intellectuals and hotels of charm.

How to get there *(Map 21): 67km south of Bari.*

Grand Hotel Telese

82037 Telese Terme (Benevento)
Piazza Minieri, 1
Tel. 0824-94 05 00 - Fax 0824-94 05 04 - Sig. Michele Montagna
E-mail: termetel@tin.it

Category ★★★★ **Rooms** 110 with telephone, bath or shower, WC, TV, minibar. **Price** Single 110-130,000L, double 180-230,000L. **Meals** Breakfast included, served 7:00-9:30 - half board 110-160,000L, full board 140-190,000L. (per pers., 3 days min.). **Restaurant** Service 12:30PM-2:30PM, 7:30PM-9:30PM - à la carte - Specialties: Risotto con brocoli - Agnello. **Credit cards** Amex, Visa, Eurocard, MasterCard. **Pets** Small dogs allowed. **Facilities** Swimming pool, tennis (8,000L), sauna, parking. **Nearby** Telesia - Faicchio - Cerreto Sannita - Benevento. **Open** All year.

The Grand Hotel Telese built at the turn of the century has preserved the old-fashioned charm typical of the spas of this resort town. Ouside, its neoclassical façade is chic. Inside, you will be impressed by the grand staircase, the beautiful ground-floor rooms with painted ceilings and the second-floor–Louis XV lounge. All the guest rooms are luxurious. The restaurant is in the cellar between the billiard and chess rooms. All in all, it would be a perfect hotel, except for its proximity to a highway, which sometimes disturbs the prevailing tranquility.

How to get there *(Map 20): 65km north of Napoli via A1, Caserta-South exit, then S265 towards Maddaloni to Telese.*

Hotel della Baia

Baia Domizia - 81030 Cellole (Caserta)
Via dell' Erica
Tel. 0823-72 13 44 - Fax 0823-72 15 56
Sig.ra Sello

Category ★★★★ **Rooms** 56 with air-conditioning, telephone, bath or shower, TV, WC. **Price** Single 90-115,000L, double 140-170,000L. **Meals** Breakfast 15,000L, served 7:30-9:30 - half board 150-170,000L, full board 160-180,000L (per pers.). **Restaurant** Service 12:30PM-2:15PM, 7:30PM-9:00PM - mealtime specials 55-65,000L, also à la carte - Specialties: Tonnarelli freddi con crema di trota affumicata - Coquilles Saint-Jacques farcite di gamberi. **Credit cards** All major. **Pets** Small dogs allowed (except in the restaurant). **Facilities** Tennis (20,000L), privat beach, parking. **Nearby** Gaeta - Caserta - Napoli - Pompeii. **Open** May 12 – Sept 30.

Elsa, Imelde and Velja Sello are three charming sisters who have been running this hotel since the 1970s. After living in Venice and in Rome, they decided that this would now be their family home and have put into it all their sisterly care and attention. It is a modern Mediterranean-style building that stands with its white walls in the midst of a large green lawn planted with bamboo and many other exotic species. Both in the guest rooms and the public areas, the interior decoration is spare and meticulously done. Terra cotta and pastel colors create a fresh, summery appearance. Among other assets are the home-cooked meals and the proximity of the sea.

How to get there *(Map 19): 67km northwest of Napoli. Via A1 (Rome-Napoli), Cassino exit, towards Formia and Napoli to the stoplight of Cellole, then on the right.*

Hotel Santa Lucia

80121 Napoli
Via Partenope, 46
Tel. 081-764 06 66 - Fax 081-764 85 80 - Sig. Ferraro
E-mail: reservations@santalucia.it - Web: www.santalucia.it

Category ★★★★ **Rooms** 95 with air-conditioning, tel, bath or shower, WC, satellite TV, minibar –
Elevator. **Price** Single 349,000L, double 549,000L, suite 600-3 000,000L. **Meals** Breakfast included,
served 7:00-11:00. **Restaurant** Service Mon to Sat: 12:30PM-3:30PM and Sun: 7:30PM-11:00PM - à la
carte 75,000L - Specialties: Casarecce ai sapori mediterranei - Tagliatelle ai broccoli e frutti di mare
- Pesce fresco del golfo all'acqua pazza. **Credit cards** All major. **Pets** Dogs not allowed. **Facilities**
Garage (30,000L). **Nearby** Napoli: Archaeology museum, Capodimonte National Gallery and Museum,
Villa Floridiana, Certosa di San Martino - Estate of Napoli - Pompeii - Ercolano - Cuma - La solfatara
in Pozzuoli - Capri - Ischia - Amalfi coast - Paestum. **Open** All year.

The Bay of Naples, with Vesuvius rising out of the mist and the peninsula
of Sorrento in the background, is certainly one of the most famous
panoramas in the world. The hotel is right on the bay, near the little port of
Santa Lucia, facing the Castel dell'Ovo, and taking in this whole breathtaking
sight, like a Neapolitan painting. The neoclassic façade and Liberty-style
interior were renovated in 1999. The maze of little salons are tastefully
furnished in elegant tones of gray and blue, which beautifully set off the
magnificence of the marble, moldings and stuccos. The bedrooms have the
same classical decor, brightened with cheerful prints, comfortable amenities,
and those on the front have a view of the bay. The Santa Lucia offers its guests
the luxury of a grand hotel combined with a feeling of intimacy.

How to get there *(Map 19): Along the bay, between Castel dell'Ovo, the port
of Santa Lucia and the Palazzo Reale.*

Hotel Excelsior

80121 Napoli
Via Partenope, 48
Tel. 081-764 01 11 - Fax 081-764 97 43 - Sig. Vincenzo Pagano
E-mail: info@excelsior.it - Web: www.excelsior.it

Category ★★★★ **Rooms** 122 with air-conditioning, tel, bath or shower, WC, satellite TV, minibar, safe – Elevator. **Price** Single 450,000L, double 550,000L, suite 850-1,800,000L. **Meals** Breakfast included, served 7:00-10:30. **Restaurant** Service 1:00PM-3:30PM, 8:00PM-11:30PM - à la carte 60-90,000L - Regional cooking and pesce. **Credit cards** All major. **Pets** Dogs allowed. **Facilities** Garage (40-45,000L). **Nearby** Naples: Archaeology museum, Capodimonte National Gallery and Museum, Villa Floridiana, Certosa di San Martino - Estate of Napoli - Pompeii - Ercolano - Cuma - La solfatara in Pozzuoli - Capri - Ischia - Amalfi coast - Paestum. **Open** All year.

T he recent renovations in the center have at last made Naples an easier and more pleasant city to explore. Many of its monuments, like the Capodimonte Museum, with its treasures of Italian art, have become more accessible. The world-famous Excelsior, with its mirrors and stuccos and turn-of-the-century splendor, has all the charm of its bygone era. The salons have preserved their flamboyant style, but the bedrooms are not always as tasteful, and the bathrooms, though large, could sometimes do with a little renovation. Still, on the whole, the hotel has the quiet feel of its time. The bedrooms face the Bay and the Castel dell'Ovo. In clear weather you can see Capri and the majestic silhouette of Vesuvius. In the Terrazza restaurant with its view across the bay you can enjoy the delights of the local cuisine, with its subtle combinations of pasta and fish.

How to get there *(Map 19): Along the bay, between Castel dell'Ovo, the port of Santa Lucia and the Palazzo Reale.*

Grand Hotel Parker's

80121 Napoli
Corso Vittorio Emanuele, 135
Tel. 081-761 24 74 - Fax 081-663 527 - Sig. Luigi Richard
E-mail: ghparker@tin.it - Web: www.bcedit.it/parkershotel.htm

Category ★★★★ **Rooms** 83 with air-conditioning, tel, bath or shower, WC, satellite TV, minibar, safe – Elevator. **Price** Single 315-370,000L, double 385-450,000L, suite 900-1 800,000L. **Meals** Breakfast included, served 7:00-10:00. **Restaurant** Service 12:30PM-2:30PM, 7:30PM-10:30PM - closed Sun - à la carte 80-100,000L - Regional cooking and pesce. **Credit cards** All major. **Pets** Dogs not allowed. **Facilities** Garage. **Nearby** Naples: Archaeology museum, Capodimonte National Gallery and Museum, Villa Floridiana, Certosa di San Martino - Estate of Napoli - Pompeii - Ercolano - Cuma - La solfatara in Pozzuoli - Capri - Ischia - Amalfi coast - Paestum. **Open** All year.

For 130 years now, this hotel has been synonymous with elegance and chic. An imposing entrance hall with wood panneling, marble and club chairs gives it a rather English look, as does Bidder's Bar, a piano-bar where guests meet for cocktails in the evening. The bedrooms are classical and comfortable, and each floor is in a different style, ranging from Louis XVI to Charles X. The building is on a small hill in the center of Naples, in the residential district, and overlooks the bay. The best place to see the view is George's, the gastronomic restaurant that serves candle-lighted dinners in an atmosphere of great refinement. An additional feature at the Parker's is the availability of a fine library with a nice collection of old books.

How to get there *(Map 19): In the town center.*

Hotel Paradiso

80122 Napoli
Via Catullo, 11
Tel. 081-761 4161 - Fax 081-761 3449
Sig. Vincenzo di Donato

Category ★★★★ **Rooms** 72 with air-conditioning, tel, bath or shower, WC, satellite TV, minibar – Elevator. **Price** Single 165-190,000L, double 240-290,000L, suite 400,000L. **Meals** Breakfast included, served 7:00-10:30 - half board 160-180,000L. **Restaurant** Service 12:30PM-2:45PM, 7:15PM-10:30PM - closed Sun - mealtime specials, also à la carte 45,000L - Italian and Napolitan cuisine. **Credit cards** All major. **Pets** Dogs not allowed. **Facilities** Garage (25,000L). **Nearby** Archaeology museum, Capodimonte National Gallery and Museum, Villa Floridiana, Certosa di San Martino - Estate of Napoli - Pompeii - Ercolano - Cuma - La solfatara in Pozzuoli - Capri - Ischia - Amalfi coast - Paestum. **Open** All year.

The Hotel Paradiso is an ideal choice for anyone looking for a quiet haven away from the storms of Neapolitan life. Perched on the Posillipo hill, an airy residential quarter of Naples ten minutes from the historic center, it has a wonderful view of the Bay, Mount Vesuvius and the islands of Ischia and Capri. It is a totally modern hotel, whose main assets are calm, comfort and the view. At the panoramic restaurant you can taste the local dishes, with an emphasis on all the products of the sea.

How to get there *(Map 19): Posillipo hill.*

Villa Brunella

Isola di Capri - 80073 Capri (Napoli)
Via Tragara, 24
Tel. 081-837 01 22 - Fax 081-837 04 30 - Sig. Ruggiero
E-mail: villabrunella@capri.it - Web: www.caprionline.com/villabrunella

Category ★★★★ **Rooms** 8 and 12 suites with air-conditioning, telephone, bath, WC, satellite TV, minibar. **Price** Double 430,000L, suite 550,000L. **Meals** Breakfast included, served 8:30AM-12:00PM. **Restaurant** Service 12:30PM-3:30PM, 7:30PM-11:00PM - mealtime specials 50-60,000L, also à la carte - Specialties: Ravioli alla caprese - Frutti di mare - Linguine al cartoccio. **Credit cards** Amex, Visa, Eurocard, MasterCard. **Pets** Dogs not allowed. **Facilities** Swimming pool. **Nearby** Capri (Certosa di San Giacomo, Villa Jovis, Punta Tragara, Blue Grotto, Villa Malaparte) - Monte Solaro - Napoli - Pompeii - Herculaneum - Cuma - Pozzuoli sulphur springs - Vesuvius - Ischia - Amalfi coast. **Open** Mar 19 – Nov 6.

This hotel, near the road that leads to Villa Tiberio, has a nice family atmosphere. Its terraces, which are on several levels and are protected from the wind by berry bushes, jut excitingly out over the sea. It's a marvelous place to enjoy the relaxing lunchtime buffet. The rooms are spacious and comfortable. The ones facing the sea are nicer than those facing the courtyard. The suites have individual terraces. There is no elevator, and it is necessary to climb stairs to even get to the rooms on the ground-floor due to Capri's hilly terrain.

How to get there *(Map 19): Ferry services from Napoli (40mn-70mn), from Sorrento (35mn); in Capri, from Piazzetta towards Villa Tiberio, via Camerelle and via Tragara.*

Capri Palace Hotel & SPA

Isola di Capri
80071 Anacapri (Napoli)
Tel. 081-837 38 00 - Fax 081-837 31 91 - A. Cacace
E-mail: info@capri-palace.com - Web: www.capri-palace.com

Category ★★★★ **Rooms** 83 with air-conditioning, telephone, bath, WC, minibar, TV, (4 with private swimming pool). **Price** Single 260-400,000L, double 440-700,000L, with private swimming pool 800-1 150,000L, suite 1 150-3 000,000L. **Meals** Breakfast included, served 7:00AM-12:00PM - half board +80,000L (per pers.). **Restaurant** Service 12:00PM, 7:30PM - mealtime specials 80-100,000L, also à la carte - Specialties: Tagliolini al limone - Ravioli alla caprese - Torta di mandorla, torta di limone. **Credit cards** All major. **Pets** Dogs not allowed. **Facilities** Swimming pool. **Nearby** Anacapri (Villa San Michele, Monte Solaro) - Capri (Certosa di San Giacomo, Villa Jovis, Punta Tragara, Blue Grotto, Villa Malaparte) - Napoli - Pompeii - Herculaneum - Cuma - Pozzuoli sulphur springs - Vesuvius - Ischia - Amalfi coast. **Open** Apr – Oct.

The Palace Hotel is situated at Anacapri, the wildest part of the island, and has just undergone a complete refurbishment, right down to a change of name. The refitting has raised the standard of comfort and luxury with 22 suites. Most have a garden and four have their own private swimming pool, like the Megaron, a real apartment of 150 square metres overlooking the Bay of Naples. The rooms, too, are very comfortable, with a terrace where guests can take breakfast and enjoy the sea air as soon as they get up. The restaurant carries on the family tradition by providing tasty Mediterranean dishes, with barbecued fish and regional specialties. In the evening, candlelight dinners are served amid the palm trees, the air heavy with the scent of the sea pines. There is also a "Beauty Farm" that offers fitness sessions – nothing new, for weren't the emperors Augustus and Tiberius already praising the health-giving climate of Capri?

How to get there *(Map 19): Ferry services from Napoli (40mn-70mn), from Sorrento (35mn); in Capri, at the port, take a taxi or the private bus of the hotel.*

Hotel Luna

Isola di Capri - 80073 Capri (Napoli)
Viale Matteotti, 3
Tel. 081-837 04 33 - Fax 081-837 74 59 - Sig. Vuotto
E-mail: luna@capri.it - Web: www:capri.it/it/hotels/luna/home.htlm

Category ★★★★ **Rooms** 48 with air-conditioning, telephone, bath, WC, satelliteTV, safe, minibar – Elevator. **Price** Single 200-250,000L, double 290-600,000L. **Meals** Breakfast included, served 7:30-11:30 - half board 200-360,000L (per pers.). **Restaurant** Service 12:30PM-2:30PM, 7:30PM-9:30PM - mealtime specials 60,000L, also à la carte - Italian and Neapolitan cuisine. **Credit cards** All major. **Pets** Dogs not allowed. **Facilities** Swimming pool. **Nearby** Capri (Certosa di San Giacomo, Villa Jovis, Punta Tragara, Blue Grotto, Villa Malaparte) - Anacapri (Villa San Michele, Monte Solaro) - Napoli - Pompeii - Herculaneum - Cuma - Pozzuoli sulphur springs - Vesuvius - Ischia - Amalfi coast. **Open** Apr 1 – Oct 31.

This is a delightful hotel in an exceptional location. The rooms are large and freshly decorated in a classical style. They are a touch overdone, but very comfortable. Irresistible attractions for visitors are the terraces jutting out over the sea, the large floral garden and the pool close to the Carthusian monastery. Though only a few minutes from the center of Capri, it is a perfect place to get away from it all. One of the best situated hotels on the island.

How to get there *(Map 19): Ferry services from Napoli (40mn-70mn), from Sorrento (35mn); in Capri, from the Piazzetta towards Giardini di Augusto via Vittorio Emanuele and via F. Serena.*

Hotel Punta Tragara

Isola di Capri - 80073 Capri (Napoli)
Via Tragara, 57
Tel. 081-837 08 44 - Fax 081-837 77 90 - Sig. Ceglia
E-mail: hotel.tragara@capri.it

Category ★★★★ **Rooms** 47 with air-conditioning, telephone, bath or shower, WC, TV, minibar – Elevator. **Price** Double 500-650,000L, suite 800-1 000,000L. **Meals** Breakfast included, served 7:00-11:00. **Restaurant** Service 1:15PM-3:30PM, 8:00PM-10:30PM - mealtime specials 80,000L, also à la carte - Mediterranean cuisine. **Credit cards** All major. **Pets** Dogs not allowed. **Facilities** 2 swimming pools. **Nearby** Capri (Certosa di San Giacomo, Villa Jovis, Punta Tragara, Blue Grotto, Villa Malaparte) - Anacapri (Villa San Michele, Monte Solaro) - Napoli - Pompeii - Herculaneum - Cuma - Pozzuoli sulphur springs - Vesuvius - Ischia - Amalfi coast. **Open** Apr – Oct.

The last place you might expect to find a project designed by Le Corbusier is on Capri, but this group of ochre-colored brick houses–built into a stone cliff, hanging over the sea–bears the signature of the celebrated 20th-century architect. Today, it is a luxury hotel with more suites than rooms. The entire hotel is sumptuously decorated with antique furniture, paintings, rugs and old tapestries. Its two restaurants are very pleasant; La Bussola has a terrace for outside dining and a marvelous view. The tropical garden overflowing with giant bougainvilleas and other exotic plants, contains two beautiful salt-water pools continually heated to 94°. You can expect a luxury hotel-style welcome and service.

How to get there *(Map 19): Ferry services from Napoli (40mn-70mn), from Sorrento (35mn); in Capri, from the Piazzetta, towards the Villa Tiberio, via Camerelle and via Tragara.*

Albergo Villa Sarah

Isola di Capri - 80073 Capri (Napoli)
Via Tiberio, 3/A
Tel. 081-837 06 89/837 78 17 - Fax 081-837 72 15 - Sig. de Martino Domenico
E-mail: info@villasarah.it - reserve@villasarah.it - Web: www.villasarah.it

Category ★★★ **Rooms** 20 with, telephone, bath or shower, WC, satellite TV. **Price** Single 180-220,000L, double 280-320,000L. **Meals** Breakfast included, served 8:00-10:00. **Restaurant** See pp. 511-512. **Credit cards** All major. **Pets** Dogs not allowed. **Facilities** Solarium. **Nearby** Capri (Certosa di San Giacomo, Villa Jovis, Punta Tragara, Blue Grotto, Villa Malaparte) - Anacapri (Villa San Michele, Monte Solaro) - Napoli - Pompeii - Herculaneum - Cuma - Pozzuoli sulphur springs - Vesuvius - Ischia - Amalfi coast. **Open** Easter – Oct.

Typical of the villas built in the Capri hills, the Villa Sarah has, just beyond its garden, its own vineyard and orchard that supply all the delicious jams served at breakfast. Though it is located near the center, the quarter is a quiet one and the crowds are not too bad even in midsummer. The atmosphere is friendly and it's nice to relax in the garden or the solarium. The rooms are all equipped with the usual amenities. The beauty of Capri has made it a chic and expensive holiday spot. The Villa Sarah allows you to enjoy it in good conditions and at a reasonable price.

How to get there *(Map 19): Ferry services from Napoli (40mn-70mn), from Sorrento (35mn); in Capri, from the Piazzetta towards the Villa Tiberio, via Camerelle and via Tragara.*

Pensione Quattro Stagioni

Isola di Capri
80073 Marina Piccola (Napoli)
Tel. 081-837 00 41 - Sig.ra Salvia
E-mail: quattro.stagioni@libero.it

Category ★ **Rooms** 12 with air-conditioning, bath or shower, WC. **Price** Double 150-210,000L (but if you come with the Guide, reduction in Apr, May, Jun and Oct). **Meals** Breakfast included, served 8:00-10:00 - half board 120-150,000L (per pers.). **Restaurant** Service 8:00PM - mealtime specials - Specialties: Pasta alle zucchine - Pollo caprese. **Credit cards** Visa, Eurocard, MasterCard. **Pets** Dogs not allowed. **Nearby** Capri (Certosa di San Giacomo, Villa Jovis, Punta Tragara, Blue Grotto, Villa Malaparte) - Anacapri (Villa San Michele, Monte Solaro) - Napoli - Pompeii - Herculaneum - Cuma - Pozzuoli sulphur springs - Vesuvius - Ischia - Amalfi coast. **Open** Mar 15 – end Oct.

Italy is gradually losing its famous *Pensione* where the traveler was enveloped in family warmth and fed on the generous home cooking of la *mamma*. Capri, sophisticated though it may be, still has one. And it is located right at the Marina Piccola, the place where everyone goes to swim by day and dine by night in the little restaurants facing the sea. The Quattro Stagioni occupies one of those flower-clad houses that overlook the bay between Mount Solaro and Mount Castiglione. Today all the rooms have their own bath. As is customary in a real *pensione,* the half-board is obligatory and dinner is at 8. But this is a minor constraint when you consider the prices you pay. There is a lovely promenade that links Marina Piccola with the center of Capri, through the garden of Augustus and with a splendid view.

How to get there *(Map 19): Ferry services from Napoli (40mn-70mn), from Sorrento (35mn).*

Park Hotel Miramare

Isola d'Ischia
80070 Sant'Angelo (Napoli)
Tel. 081-999 219 - Fax 081-999 325 - Sig.ra Calise
E-mail: hotel@hotelmiramare.it - Web: www.hotelmiramare.it - www.aphrodite.it

Category ★★★★ Rooms 50 with bath or shower, telephone, WC, satellite TV, minibar, fan. **Price** Single 193,000L, double 336,000L. **Meals** Breakfast 18,000L, served 7:00-10:00 - half board 215-225,000L, 245-255,000 (per 1 pers.). **Restaurant** Service 1:00PM-2:00PM, 7:30PM-9:00PM - mealtime specials, also à la carte 75,000L - Regional cooking. **Credit cards** Diners, Visa, Eurocard, MasterCard. **Pets** Small dogs allowed. **Facilities** Thermal baths "Giardini Aphrodite". **Nearby** Ischia (Boat or car tour of the island, Castello, Mont Epomeo (788m) from Serrara-Fontana (1h), Beach of Citara in Forio, Lacco Ameno) - Lido S. Montano - Capri - Napoli - Pompeii - Herculaneum - Cuma - Pozzuoli sulphur springs - Amalfi coast to Salerno - Paestum. **Open** Apr – end Sept.

The short ferry ride to the island of Ischia is delightful. On the way, you will cross the sumptuous Gulf of Naples below the majestic silhouette of Vesuvius, and sail along the Procida peninsula. The Hotel Miramare is in Sant Angelo, one of the few unspoiled places on the island. Directly overhanging the sea, it is just a few steps from the small port and the pretty piazzetta. The hotel has a pleasant atmosphere of longstanding tradition. The rooms are comfortable and warmly decorated, some with balconies with a spectacular panoramic view. A restaurant on the terrace will entice you with classic island seafood. A few steps away, a private flower-lined path leads to the marvelous Aphrodite-Apollo Thermal Garden (at a reduction of 25 percent for guests), which has twelve pools of varying temperatures that are built into the cliff in a series of descending terraces.

How to get there *(Map 19): Boat from Napoli to Molo Beverello (1:15 by ferry); or from Napoli to Mergellina: 40mn by hydrofoil.*

Pensione Casa Sofia

Isola d'Ischia - 80070 Sant'Angelo (Napoli)
Via Sant'Angelo, 29/B
Tel. 081-999 310 - Fax 081-999 859 - Sig.ra Bremer-Barricelli
E-mail: htlsofia@pointel.it

Rooms 8 and 2 apartments with shower, WC, satellite TV. **Price** With half board 120,000L (per 1 pers.). **Meals** Breakfast included, served from 8:00. **Restaurant** Service 7:30PM - mealtime specials - Regional cooking. **Credit cards** All major. **Pets** Small dogs allowed. **Facilities** Thermal baths. **Nearby** Ischia (Boat or car tour of the island, Castello, Mont Epomeo (788m) from Serrara-Fontana (1h), Beach of Citara in Forio, Lacco Ameno) - Lido S. Montano - Capri - Napoli - Pompeii - Herculaneum - Cuma - Pozzuoli sulphur springs - Amalfi coast to Salerno - Paestum. **Open** All year.

Signora Dolly Bremer-Barricelli has made her large and beautiful house with its incomparable sea view a perfect place for anyone seeking a quiet family holiday. The rooms are all attractively decorated and from the terrace, where you have your very copious breakfast, you can look out over the entire Bay of Sant'Angelo. This ancient fishing village is only one that has kept the charm that must have once been everywhere on Ischia and is today sadly spoiled by tourism. Close by the hotel you can unwind in the thermal pools of the Garden of Aphrodite (there are 12 pools and you go from one to the other.) If your vacation takes you to Ischia, don't miss this invigorating spot. Signora Bremer-Barricelli, who is of German origin, serves dinner at 6.30 p.m. If this is too early for your taste, you may be able to negotiate for a later hour.

How to get there *(Map 19): South of Napoli via A3, Castellammare di Stabia exit, then towards S145. Ferry service from Napoli (70mn) and from Pozzuoli (40mn).*

Pensione Casa Garibaldi

Isola d'Ischia
80070 Sant'Angelo (Napoli)
Via Sant'Angelo, 52
Tel. 081-99 94 20 - Fax 081-99 94 20 - Sig. Di Iorio

Rooms 20 with shower, WC. **Price** Single 63,000L, double 110,000L, suite 130,000L. **Meals** Breakfast 8,000L, served 8:00-10:30. **Restaurant** See p. 512. **Credit cards** Not accepted. **Pets** Dogs allowed. **Facilities** Swimming pool. **Nearby** Ischia (Boat or car tour of the island, Castello, Mont Epomeo (788m) from Serrara-Fontana (1h), Beach of Citara in Forio, Lacco Ameno) - Lido San Montano - Capri - Napoli - Pompeii - Herculaneum - Cuma - Pozzuoli sulphur springs - Amalfi coast to Salerno - Paestum. **Open** Easter – Nov.

The village of Sant'Angelo, some 300 yards from the dock, is accessible only on foot, but you will find porters and parking facilities the moment you get off the boat. This unpretentious white house, surrounded by fig trees, overlooks the beach and the picturesque fishing village. The rooms are in small individual houses linked by terraced roofs. On the highest terrace is a swimming pool. Despite its sobriety of style, Casa Garibaldi is a pleasure to be in. The atmosphere is welcoming, the view superb and the rooms, simply furnished, are all equipped with showers. No dining room, but a large kitchen where guests may prepare a meal for themselves whenever they like. The transfer from Naples to Ischia and the hotel (by boat and taxi) may be reserved through the hotel at 120,000L (for two persons) or 105,000L (one person).

How to get there *(Map 19): Boat from Napoli-Molo Beverello (1:15 by ferry) and from Napoli-Mergellina (40mn by hydrofoil); tel. 081 551 32 36*

La Villarosa

Isola d'Ischia
80077 Porto d'Ischia (Napoli)
Via Giacinto Gigante, 5
Tel. 081-99 13 16 / 98 44 90 - Fax 081-99 24 25 - Sig. Pepe
E-mail: hotel@lavillarosa.it - Web: www.lavillarosa.it

Category ★★★★ **Rooms** 33 and 4 suites (20 with air-conditioning) with telephone, bath, WC, satellite TV, minibar – Elevator. **Price** Single 130-180,000L, double 220-300,000L. **Meals** Breakfast included, served 7:00-10:00 - half board 130-200,000L, full board 150-220,000L (per pers.). **Restaurant** For residents, service 1:00PM-2:00PM, 7:30PM-9:00PM - mealtime specials 40-60,000L. **Credit cards** All major. **Pets** Small dogs allowed. **Facilities** Swimming pool, thermal baths, hydrotherapy. **Nearby** Ischia (Boat or car tour of the island, Castello, Mont Epomeo (788m) from Serrara-Fontana (1h), Beach of Citara in Forio, Lacco Ameno) - Lido S. Montano - Capri - Napoli - Pompeii - Herculaneum - Cuma - Pozzuoli sulphur springs - Amalfi coast to Salerno - Paestum. **Open** Mar 22 – end Oct.

L a Villarosa is a hard place to say goodbye to. You will see this as soon as you arrive. This enchanting hotel is set in the middle of a lush tropical garden. Good taste and the best of everything prevail: simplicity, discretion and refinement are evident down to the last detail. An elegant salon opens onto a garden with a springfed swimming pool. The rooms, some with a terrace or a flowering balcony, all have the discreet charm of an old-fashioned country house. You can enjoy your meals in the rooftop restaurant or, in summer, on the marvelous wisteria-covered terrace. The hotel spa is discreetly located in the basement.

How to get there *(Map 19): Ferry services from Napoli-Molo Beverello (1:15 by ferry from Napoli-Mergellina; 40mn by hydrofoil). Tel. 081 551 32 36.*

La Bagattella Hotel

Isola d'Ischia - 80075 Forio d'Ischia (Napoli)
Spiaggia di San Francesco - Via Tommaso Cigliano
Tel. 081-98 60 72 - Fax 081-98 96 37 - Sig.ra Lauro
E-mail: labagattella@flashnet.it - Web: www.labagattella.it

Category ★★★★ **Rooms** 56 with air-conditioning, telephone, bath, WC, TV. **Price** With half board 147-167,000L, full board 177-197,000L (per pers., 3 days min.). **Meals** Breakfast included, served 7:30-10:00. **Restaurant** For residents, service 1:00PM-2:00PM, 7:00PM-8:30PM - mealtime specials 103,000L, also à la carte - Specialties: Seafood. **Credit cards** Visa, Eurocard, MasterCard. **Pets** Dogs not allowed. **Facilities** Swimming pool, hydrotherapy, parking. **Nearby** Ischia (Boat or car tour of the island, Castello, Mont Epomeo (788m) from Serrara-Fontana (1h), Beach of Citara in Forio, Lacco Ameno) - Lido S. Montano - Capri, Napoli - Pompeii, Herculaneum - Cuma - Pozzuoli sulphur springs - Amalfi coast to Salerno - Paestum. **Open** Apr – Oct.

La Bagatella looks like an oversize Moorish wedding cake dropped into a tropical garden ablaze with oleander bushes and bouganvilleas. The fresh-looking rooms are very luxurious. Some are slightly overdone but are nonetheless pleasant and some have flowering balconies. A modern wing has been added, with simple, functional rooms and efficiency apartments. The new wing and the restaurant open onto a garden with a springfed swimming pool, surrounded by hibiscus bushes and palm trees. There is also a beautiful sand beach just five minutes away on foot.

How to get there *(Map 19): Ferry services from Napoli-Molo Beverello (1:15 by ferry, 40mn by hydrofoil); 10km from Porto d'Ischia.*

Albergo Terme San Montano

Isola d'Ischia
80076 Lacco Ameno (Napoli)
Tel. 081-99 40 33 - Fax 081-98 02 42 - Sig. Farace
E-mail: sanmontano@ischiagrandialberghi.it

Category ★★★★★ **Rooms** 65 and 2 suites with air-conditioning, telephone, bath, WC, satellite TV, minibar. **Price** Single 240-310,000L, double 400-640,000L, suite +100,000L. **Meals** Breakfast included, served 7:30-10:30 - half board 240-360,000L, 300-420,000L (per pers. 8 days min. in Aug). **Restaurant** Service 1:00PM-3:00PM, 8:00PM-10:00PM - à la carte. **Credit cards** All major **Pets** Small dogs allowed only in the room. **Facilities** 2 swimming pools, tennis, private beach, water-skiing, sauna, private bus, parking. **Nearby** Ischia (Boat or car tour of the island, Castello, Mont Epomeo (788m) from Serrara-Fontana (1h), Beach of Citara in Forio, Lacco Ameno) - Lido S. Montano - Capri - Napoli - Pompeii - Herculaneum - Cuma - Pozzuoli sulphur springs - Amalfi coast to Salerno - Paestum. **Open** Apr – Oct.

This hotel enjoys one of the most beautiful locations on Ischia. It sits on the top of a hill, overlooking the countryside on one side and the sea on the other, with a great view of the Vivara and Procida Islands, and the slightly hazy outline of Vesuvius in the distance. The San Montano tends to be austerely modern in both its appearance and personality, but the great luxury and comfort of the place more than compensate. The rooms, all with superb view, are decorated in a nautical style. Some have a balcony, others a private garden. On the terraced hillside grounds are two swimming pools and a tennis court. A shuttle bus will take you to the private beach. The prices are high, but well worth it.

How to get there *(Map 19): Ferry services from Napoli-Molo Beverello (1:15 by ferry); from Napoli-Mergellina: 40mn by hydrofoil.*

Hotel Residence Punta Chiarito

Isola d'Ischia
80074 Sorgeto - Panza d'Ischia (Napoli)
Tel. 081-908 102 - Fax 081-909 277 - Sig. Impagliazzo
E-mail: puntachiarito@pointel.it - Web: www.puntachiarito.it

Rooms 8 and 7 studios with air-conditioning, tel., shower, WC, TV, minibar. **Price** Double 200-260,000L (per pers.), studio for 1 week 1,300,000-1,600,000L (2 pers.). **Meals** Breakfast included, served 8:00-10:00 - half board 120-150,000L (per pers.). **Restaurant** Service 12:40PM-2:15PM, 8:00PM-9:30PM - à la carte. **Credit cards** Visa, Eurocard, MasterCard. **Pets** Dogs not allowed. **Facilities** Swimming pool, sauna, parking. **Nearby** Ischia (Boat or car tour of the island, Castello, Mont Epomeo (788m) from Serrara-Fontana (1h), Beach of Citara in Forio, Lacco Ameno) - Lido S. Montano - Capri - Napoli - Pompeii - Ercolano - Cuma - La Solfatara in Pozzuoli - Ischia - Amalfi coast to Salerno - Paestum. **Open** All year.

If you're looking for a break from your busy round of sightseeing and want a retreat alone with the sea, try the Punta Chiarito. Perched on a rocky promontory just over the sea, it is a wonderful place to rest and catch your breath. You can swim at the hotel in two pools filled with mineral water from a nearby spring or at the beach (access by a steep stairway), where the water is warm even in winter. The bedrooms are modern and simple but comfortable and your sleep is lulled by the sound of the waves. Ask for a room facing the Sant'Angelo peninsula. In the restaurant, Caterina cooks with local produce. If you're traveling with your family, each bedroom can have a private kitchenette. In the summer, when the entire island may be in a state of effervescence, Punta Chiarito is one of the rare spots where it always feels like "low season."

How to get there *(Map 19): Ferry services from Napoli-Molo Beverello (1:15 by ferry); from Napoli-Mergellina: 40mn by hydrofoil; tel. 081 551 32 36 towards Forio, Panza and Sorgeto.*

Giacaranda

Cenito 84071 San Marco di Castellabate (Salerno)
Tel. 0974-96 61 30 - Fax 0974-96 68 00
Sig.ra Cavaliere
E-mail: giaca@costacilento.it - Web: www.giacaranda.it

Rooms 7 and 2 apartments with bath. **Price** With half board 156,000L (1 pers.), 280,000L (2 pers.), apartments 280,000L (2 pers.), 560,000L (4 pers.). **Meals** Breakfast included, served 9:00-11:30. **Restaurant** Service 1:00PM-3:00PM, 7:30PM-10:00PM - vegetarian mealtime specials - Mediterranean cuisine. **Credit cards** All major. **Pets** Small dogs allowed. **Facilities** Tennis, parking at hotel. **Nearby** Amalfi coast - Napoli - Pompeii - Paestum - Velia - Capri - Padula. **Closed** Dec 24, 25 and 30.

The back country of the Gulf of Salerno offers some extraordinary Greek temples, like Paestum (if you're staying in the area, make sure to go back and see it again at sunset) and the monumental Porta Rossa de Velia, less visited but famous for being the only example of a semicircular arch in Greek architecture. These two monuments will help to situate Giacaranda, which is halfway between them. It is a beautiful estate, where the hosts' constant preoccupation is to make their guests feel at home. The rooms and apartments are perfectly kept: fine bedding, comfortable bathrooms, antique furniture and lovely household linens make for a decor that is simple yet refined. As much care goes into the cooking, based on the classic Italian recipes, with all the flavors of the region. You will sample a variety of pastas including homemade ravioli, and for the last night's dinner, the famous local pizza. Mrs Cavaliere will give you good advice about excursions in the area. A place you'll want to come back to.

How to get there *(Map 20): 120km south of Napoli. Via A3 (Salerno/Reggio) Battipàglia exit, then SS18 (towards Agropoli) bis Santa Maria de Castellabate.*

Palazzo Belmonte

84072 Santa Maria di Castellabate (Salerno)
Tel. 0974-96 02 11 - Fax 0974-96 11 50
Sig.ra Wilkinson
Web: www.palazzobelmonte.it

Suites 20 with telephone, bath, WC, kitchenette. **Price** Suite 275-625,000L (2 pers.), 640-1 110,000L (4 pers.). **Meals** Breakfast included. **Restaurant** Service 1:00PM-2:30PM, 8:00PM-10:30PM - à la carte - Regional and Italian cuisine. **Credit cards** Visa, Eurocard, MasterCard **Pets** Dogs not allowed. **Facilities** Swimming pool, private beach, parking. **Nearby** Napoli - Pompeii - Paestum - Capri - Amalfi coast - Padula Vietri. **Open** May – Oct.

Several months a year, the prince of Belmonte opens up his palace to the outside world. This beautiful historical monument was built in the 17th century in the small fishing village and is still used by his family as a hunting lodge to receive royal visitors from Spain and Italy. The prince and his family live in one wing and there are suites for guests in another part of the palazzo. They are unpretentiously but elegantly decorated in light colors and have nice bamboo furniture. Certain guest rooms open onto a pretty courtyard full of fragrant Chilian jasmine; others overlook a garden of fragrant pine trees, magnolias, hibiscus and oleanders; and still others have a terrace on the sea with views of the island of Capri when the weather is clear. The regional specialties served in the restaurant are made with fresh produce from the palace's vegetable garden. The swimming pool and private beach at the edge of a pine forest may make you want to take it easy, but the enticements of Naples, Pompeii and the Amalfi coast are so close by!

How to get there *(Map 20): 120km south of Napoli via A3, Battipàglia exit, then towards Paestum, Agropoli and Castellabate.*

Grand Hotel Excelsior Vittoria

80067 Sorrento (Napoli)
Piazza Tasso, 34
Tel. 081-807 10 44 - Fax 081-877 12 06 - Sig. L. Fiorentino
E-mail: exvitt@exvitt.it - Web: www.exvitt.it

Category ★★★★ **Rooms** 107 with air-conditioning, telephone, bath or shower, WC, TV, safe, minibar. **Price** Single 370,000L, double 450-655,000L, suite 842-2,900,000L. **Meals** Breakfast 20-26,000L, served 7:30-9:30 - half board +66,000L (per pers. 3 days min.). **Restaurant** Service 12:30PM-2:00PM, 7:30PM-10:00PM - mealtime specials 75,000L, also à la carte - Italian and Neapolitan cuisine. **Credit cards** All major. **Pets** Dogs allowed (extra charge). **Facilities** Swimming pool, parking. **Nearby** Villa Comunale - Bay of Sorrento - Napoli - Pompeii - Paestum - Capri. **Open** All year.

Overlooking the Gulf of Naples from the top of a rocky crag, this palace-hotel is one of the most prestigious in Sorrento. The garden, with a terrace facing the open sea, is an enchanting mixture of fragrant flowers, rose bushes and vines. A highlight is the winter garden overflowing with dwarf palm trees and turquoise flowers. The interior of the palace still has its original frescoes, stucco trimming and ceilings painted in Liberty style. The salons and rooms are all spacious and comfortable and furnished with beautiful antiques. In summer, meals are served on the panoramic terrace, and on Sundays you can join in a *buffet dansant*. Many illustrious personages have stayed here, including Goethe, Wagner and Verdi. The most requested room is the one Caruso lived in at the end of his life, a stay immortalized in a renowned song often sung by Luciano Pavarotti.

How to get there *(Map 20): 48km south of Napoli via A3 to Castellammare di Stabia, then S145.*

Hotel Bellevue Syrene

80067 Sorrento (Napoli)
Piazza della Vittoria, 5
Tel. 081-878 10 24 - Fax 081-878 39 63 - Sig. Russo
E-mail: info@bellevue.it - Web: www.bellevue.it

Category ★★★★ **Rooms** 73 with telephone, bath or shower, WC, TV, minibar, safe – Elevator. **Price** Single 220-385,000L, double 330-485,000L, suite 550-600,000L. **Meals** Breakfast included (buffet), served 7:00-10:00 - half board +70,000L (per pers.). **Restaurant** Service 7:00PM-9:00PM - mealtime specials 70,000L, also à la carte - Specialties: Spaghetti con cozze - Gnocchi - Pesce. **Credit cards** All major. **Pets** Dogs allowed in the rooms only. **Facilities** Private beach, garage (30,000L). **Nearby** Bay of Sorrento - Napoli - Paestum - Capri. **Open** All year.

On the site of an ancient Roman villa where Virgil and Tiberius once lived, there now stands a handsome 18th-century building, perched just over the sea. Not all the rooms are equally interesting: The large dining room was recently redecorated, but the two small sitting rooms that follow it have frescoes and mosaics that recall its long eventful history. There is an elevator that takes guests down to a private beach. But just for fun, try the old staircase and vaulted passage which are both, along with the columns in the garden, vestiges of the Roman villa. Our favorite room is number 4, one of the few with a balcony facing the sea.

How to get there *(Map 20): 48km south of Napoli via A3 to Castellammare di Stabia, then S145.*

Capo La Gala Hotel

80069 Vico Equense (Napoli)
Via Luigi Serio, 7
Tel. 081-801 57 58 - Fax 081-879 87 47 - Sig.ra Savarese
Web: www.venere.it/campania/vico equense/capo la gala

Category ★★★★ **Rooms** 18 (9 with air-conditioning, +50,000L) with telephone, bath or shower, WC, TV, minibar. **Price** Single 190,000L, double 280,000L. **Meals** Breakfast included (buffet), served 7:30-10:30 - half board 245,000L (per 1 pers.), 195,000L (per pers. in double); full board 295,000L (per 1 pers.), 245,000L (per pers. in double). **Restaurant** Service 1:00PM-3:00PM, 8:00PM-10:00PM - mealtime specials 60,000L, also à la carte - Specialties: Seafood - Frutti di mare. **Credit cards** All major. **Pets** Small dogs allowed. **Facilities** Swimming pool, private beach, parking. **Nearby** Gulf of Salerno and Amalfi coast - Napoli - Paestum - Capri. **Open** Apr – Oct.

Designed around a series of terraces and small stairways cut into the stone hillside, the Capo La Gala blends so well into its surrounding that it seems more a part of the sea than of the land. The rooms, few in number, are all identical and could do with more air-conditioning. Each one, distinguished by the name of a wind instead of a number, has a balcony facing the sea. You will find a homey atmosphere here, and will enjoy relaxing beside the sulphur-water swimming pool. The restaurant serves mainly seafood and fresh vegetables. The service lacks enthusiasm.

How to get there *(Map 20): 39km south of Napoli via A3 to Castellammare di Stabia, then S145, towards Sorrento.*

Hotel Luna Convento

84011 Amalfi (Salerno)
Via P. Comite, 19
Tel. 089-871 002 - Fax 089-87 13 33 - Sig. Milone
E-mail: info@lunahotel.it - Web: www.lunahotel.it

Category ★★★★ **Rooms** 48 with telephone, bath or shower, WC, TV. **Price** Single 300-360,000L, double 330-390,000L, suite 500-800,000L; extra bed 90,000L. **Meals** Breakfast included, served 7:30-10:00 - half board 370-430,000L (per 1 pers.), 235-265,000L (per pers. in double); full board 420-480,000L (per 1 pers.), 285-315,000L (per pers. in double). **Restaurant** Service 12:30PM-2:30PM, 7:30PM-9:30PM - mealtime specials 80,000L, also à la carte - Specialties: Cannelloni del convento - Crespoline - Risotto pescatore - Gamberoni alla griglia. **Credit cards** All major. **Pets** Dogs not allowed. **Facilities** Swimming pool, private beach, parking. **Nearby** Amalfi (Duomo, "Cloisters of Paradise," Emerald Grotto) - Gulf of Salerno and Amalfi coast (Positano, Ravello, Salerno) - Paestum - Capri - Napoli - Pompeii - Herculaneum - Cuma - Pozzuolo sulphur springs - Ischia. **Open** All year.

Above the Saracen Tower that looks out over the Gulf, the Luna Convento, clinging to a rock facing the sea, occupies a historic building, an old Franciscan convent mainly known for its superb Byzantine cloister. This magnificent hotel has been in the same family for several generations. It underwent some transformations in the 1950s, namely, an annex that was added to provide more rooms. The amenities vary from room to room. Those in the main house, of course, benefit from the old-fashioned charm of their ancient walls. Over the years, the house has hosted famous guests – there exists, in particular a whole correspondence between Ibsen and the hotel's first owner, Signora Barbano. Although certain improvements could be wished, this is still a delightful spot.

How to get there *(Map 20): 25km west of Salerno via A3, Vietri sul Mare exit, then S163 along the coast.*

Hotel Santa Caterina

84011 Amalfi (Salerno)
Via S.S. Amalfitana, 9
Tel. 089-87 10 12 - Fax 089-87 13 51
E-mail: s.caterina@starnet.it - Web: www.starnet.it/santacaterina

Category ★★★★★ **Rooms** 68 with air-conditioning, telephone, bath, WC, TV, minibar. **Price** Single 370-500,000L, double 400-680,000L, suite 700-1 500,000L. **Meals** Breakfast 25,000L, served 7:30-10:00 - half board +95,000L, full board +180,000L. (per pers., 2 days min.). **Restaurant** Service 1:00PM-3:00PM, 8:00PM-10:00PM - mealtime specials 75,000L, also à la carte - Specialties: Linguine al limone - Limoni farciti Santa Caterina - Crespoline all'amalfitana - Penne alla saracena. **Credit cards** All major. **Pets** Dogs not allowed. **Facilities** Swimming pool, private beach, parking. **Nearby** Amalfi (Duomo, "Cloisters of Paradise," Emerald Grotto) - Gulf of Salerno and Amalfi coast (Positano, Ravello, Salerno) - Paestum - Capri - Napoli - Pompeii - Herculaneum - Cuma - Pozzuolo sulphur springs - Ischia. **Open** All year.

For three generations now, the Hotel Santa Caterina has belonged to a family which understands and enjoys the art of hospitality. The furniture, mostly antiques, has been meticulously selected, giving each room a particular flavor. The bathrooms, are very modern–some even have a whirlpool bath. An elevator will take you down to the sea or the salt-water swimming pool. Ask to stay in the "chalet," a small house tucked away among the lemon trees in the garden.

How to get there *(Map 20): 25km west of Salerno via A3, Vietri sul Mare exit, then S163 along the coast.*

La Conchiglia

84011 Amalfi (Salerno)
Piazzale dei Protontini, 9
Tel. 089-87 18 56 - Fax 089-87 18 56
Sig. Torre

Category ★★ **Rooms** 11 with bath or shower, WC. **Price** Single 100,000L, double 180,000L. **Meals** Breakfast 10,000L, served 7:30-9:30. **Restaurant** Open Jul –Aug, service 7:30PM- 9:00PM - mealtime specials 25,000L - Regional cooking and fish. **Credit cards** Not accepted. **Pets** Dogs not allowed. **Facilities** Parking. **Nearby** In Amalfi (Duomo and Paradise Cloister, Emerald Grotto) - Gulf of Salerno and Amalfi coast (Positano, Ravello, Salerno) - Paestum - Capri - Napoli - Pompeii - Herculaneum - Cuma - Pozzuolo sulphur springs - Ischia. **Open** All year

We have no hesitation once again in praising the beauty of the Amalfi Coast with the cultivated terraces on its cliffs, full of the odor of lemon groves and overlooking a coast made up of a multitude of little bays and beaches. This small hotel at the very far end of the village, set in the rocks between the sea and the mountain, has everything going for it. The house, with its blue shutters is charming, the rooms are large and plainly furnished, some with a balcony and sea view. The best of them, no. 4, has an even larger terrace and an even more extensive view. Another pleasant surprise: La Conchiglia has its own little private beach. Simple as it is, this appealing and friendly house is a good place to stay for anyone who wants to enjoy the exceptional ameneties of Amalfi without expecting the comfort of a large hotel.

How to get there *(Map 20): 25km west of Salerno on the A3, exit Vietri sul Mare, then S163 along the sea coast.*

Hotel Belvedere

84010 Conca dei Marini (Salerno)
Tel. 089-83 12 82 - Fax 089-83 14 39
Famiglia Lucibello
E-mail: belvedere@belvederehotel.it - Web: www.belvederehotel.it

Category ★★★★ **Rooms** 36 with telephone, bath, WC – Elevator. **Price** Single 135-175,000L, double 200-270,000L, suite 280-350,000L. **Meals** Breakfast 15,000L, served 7:00-10:00 - half board 165-200,000L, full board 195-230,000L. (per pers., 3 days min.). **Restaurant** Service 12:30PM-2:00PM, 7:30PM-9:30PM - mealtime specials 60,000L, also à la carte - Specialties: Crespolini - Timballo di maccheroni - Fusilli Belvedere. **Credit cards** All major. **Pets** Dogs allowed. **Facilities** Swimming pool, private beach, parking. **Nearby** Amalfi (Duomo, "Cloisters of Paradise," Emerald Grotto) - Gulf of Salerno and Amalfi coast (Positano, Ravello, Salerno) - Paestum - Capri - Napoli - Pompeii - Herculaneum - Cuma - Pozzuolo sulphur springs - Ischia. **Open** Apr – Oct.

You may be impressed by the classical façade of the Belvedere, or by the fact that it is built into a cliff over the sea, but what is truly extraordinary is its view of the entire Amalfi coast with its steep hillsides and beautiful lemon tree orchards. The rooms are modern and very comfortable, with either a balcony or terrace overlooking the sea. An interior elevator will take you down to the pool on the rocks and to the walkway to the sea. The Belvedere is a singularly professional hotel, the cuisine excellent, and the service impeccable yet friendly. And the welcome afforded by the Lucibello family adds that atmosphere of warm, unimposing hospitality, that makes a true hotel of character and charm.

How to get there *(Map 20): 65km southeast of Napoli via A3, Castellammare di Stabia exit, then N336, towards Amalfi. From Salerno (1-4 pers.): 110,000L, from Napoli Airport: 160,000L.*

Hotel Villa San Michele

84011 Castiglione di Ravello (Salerno)
SS. 163 Costiera Amalfitana
Tel. 089-87 22 37 - Fax 089-87 22 37 - Nicola Dipino
E-mail: smichele@starnet.it - Web: www.amalfi.it/smichele

Rooms 12 with air-conditioning, telephone, shower, WC, TV, minibar. **Price** Double 180-230,000L.
Meals Breakfast included, served 8:00-10:00 - half board +40,000L, full board + 75,000L (per pers.,
2 days min.). **Restaurant** Service 12:30PM-2:00PM, 7:30PM-9:45PM - mealtime specials - Specialties:
Fish. **Credit cards** All major. **Pets** Dogs not allowed. **Facilities** Private rocks, parking. **Nearby** In
Amalfi: Duomo and Paradise Cloister - Sorrento - Gulf of Salerno and Amalfi coast (Positano, Ravello,
Salerno) - Paestum - Capri - Napoli - Pompeii - Herculaneum - Cuma - Pozzuolo sulphur springs.
Closed Feb 7 – 12.

As soon as you arrive, the delightful owner who meets you in reception tells
you that you are coming into paradise… And he is right. The hotel is
reached through a delightful trellised garden with vines and bougainvillea, and
the scent of lemon trees. The pretty white house with its blue shutters is
practically on the sea front, so the rooms, all at the front of the building, enjoy
sea views, while most have a blacony or even a terrace. The design is simple
but the majolica tiled flooring and the natural décor easily make up for more
sophisticated decoration. Nicola himself plays a large part in the easygoing
and convivial atmosphere in his hotel, creating a relaxed and friendly holiday
mood. If you want to swim, you have only to go down a few steps to reach the
rocks, which have been supplied with deck chairs and ladder so that you can
enjoy an unforgettable swim in complete comfort. Finally, the prices are such
as to put paradise well within reach.

How to get there *(Map 20): 27km west of Salerno by A3, exit Vietri sul Mare,*
then SS163 along the sea front.

Hotel San Pietro

84017 Positano (Salerno)
Tel. 089-87 54 55 - Fax 089-81 14 49
Sig. Attanasio
E-mail: info@ilsanpietro.it - Web: ilsanpietro.it

Category ★★★★★ **Rooms** 60 with air-conditioning, telephone, bath, WC, minibar, satellite TV.
Price Single 680-780,000L, double 700-800,000L, triple 800,000L. **Meals** Breakfast included, served
7:00-11:30. **Restaurant** Service 1:00PM-3:00PM, 8:00PM-9:30PM - à la carte - Italian and Napolitan
cuisine. **Credit cards** All major. **Pets** Dogs not allowed. **Facilities** Swimming pool, private beach,
tennis, windsurfing, parking. **Nearby** Sorrento - Gulf of Salerno and Amalfi coast (Positano, Amalfi,
Ravello, Salerno) - Paestum - Capri - Napoli - Pompeii - Cuma - Pozzuolo sulphur springs - Ischia.
Open Apr – Oct.

From the sea, the San Pietro looks like a cascade of greenery flowing from
terrace to terrace down the slope of Mount Lattari. It is a model of
architecture integrated with its environment, covered with bougainvillea and
Virginia creeper so thick they nearly invade the rooms. From inside, the view
is stupendous. Each room is more sumptuous than the next, and the bathrooms
are like something out of a Hollywood fantasy. Each room has a sea view and
a ceramic tile balcony. An elevator shaft has been carved out of the rock wall
for a height of 88 meters, to take the guests down to a private beach at the foot
of the cliff. There is a snack bar down below and a tennis court in another cove
nearby. The hotel restaurant serves excellent Italian food and the welcome is
exceptional. For safety reasons, the hotel does not accept children under 12.

How to get there *(Map 20): 57km south of Napoli via A3, Castellammare di
Stabia exit, towards Sorrento, Positano.*

Le Sirenuse

84010 Positano (Salerno)
Via C. Colombo, 30
Tel. 089-87 50 66 - Fax 089-81 17 98 - Sig. Sersale
E-mail: info@sirenuse.it - Web: www.sirenuse.it

Category ★★★★★ **Rooms** 60 with air-conditioning, telephone, bath or shower, WC, TV, minibar.
Price Single 418-1 056,000L, double 462-1 100,000L, suite 825-1 402,500L. **Meals** Breakfast
included, served 7:00-11:00 - half board +100,000L (per pers., 3 days min.). **Restaurant** Service
1:00PM-2:30PM, 8:00PM-10:00PM - à la carte - Specialties: Pasta - Seafood. **Credit cards** All major.
Pets Dogs not allowed from Apr to Oct. **Facilities** Heated swimming pool, fitness, sauna, parking
(35,000L). **Nearby** Gulf of Salerno and Amalfi coast - Positano - Grotta di Smeraldo - Ravello -
Salerno - Paestum - Capri - Napoli - Pompeii - Ercolano - Cuma - Pozzuolo sulphur springs - Ischia.
Open All year.

B ehind the red-ochre façade of Le Sirenuse you'll find one of the best hotels
on the Amalfi coast. This former 18th-century palace looks out over the
bay of Positano. It has been modified and expanded over the years, and today
the hotel appears to be an odd but charming series of angles, often extended by
terraces (in fact, for reasons of security, children of under eight years old are
not accepted in the hotel from April to October). The rooms are extremely
comfortable and decorated with lovely Venetian and Neapolitan furniture.
Certain rooms in the oldest part still have their original ceramic tile floors. You
can have lunch and dinner at tables set around the pool. The new chef offers
innovative cuisine based on traditional Neapolitan recipes. The staff is friendly
and efficient.

How to get there *(Map 20): 57km south of Napoli via A3, Castellammare di
Stabia exit, then S145 and S163 to Positano.*

Hotel Poseidon

84017 Positano (Salerno)
Via Pasitea, 148
Tel. 089-81 11 11 - Fax 089-87 58 33 - Famiglia Aonzo
E-mail: poseidon@starnet.it - Web: www.starnet.it/poseidon

Category ★★★★ **Rooms** 45 and 3 suites with air-conditioning, telephone, bath, WC, TV, minibar – Elevator. **Price** Double 320-470,000L, junior suite 450-610,000L, suite 580-780,000L, extra bed 150,000L. **Meals** Breakfast included, served 7:00-11:00 - half board +70,000L (per pers.). **Restaurant** Service 1:00PM-2:30PM, 8:00PM-10:00PM - à la carte. **Credit cards** All major. **Pets** Dogs allowed. **Facilities** Swimming pool, health center, parking (40,000L). **Nearby** Sorrento - Gulf of Salerno and Amalfi coast (Positano, Amalfi, Ravello, Salerno) - Paestum - Capri - Napoli - Pompeii - Cuma - Pozzuolo sulphur springs - Ischia. **Open** Apr 18 – Jan 8.

As the Aonzo family likes to recall, the initial idea, back in the 1950s, was to build a nice little place to spend the holidays... Today it is a friendly hotel which, despite its stars, has kept a certain simplicity and conviviality that make guests feel right at home. The attentive hospitality adds to this feeling. Like the rest of the village, the house is built right onto the hill overlooking the bay, an exceptional location which means a wonderful view from the bedrooms, each with an individual terrace. The rooms are spacious and elegant, with all the comfort you expect from a 4-star hotel. The salons have the same refined sobriety. The panoramic terrace has been organized like a large living space – during the summer the restaurant is set up under the bougainvillea and a bit farther on is the swimming pool and the solarium. The hotel has recently opened a fitness center where you can treat yourself to a real cure, provided you can resist the attractions of Positano night life.

How to get there *(Map 20): 57km south of Napoli via A3, Castellammare di Stabia exit, towards Sorrento, Positano.*

Hotel Palazzo Murat

84017 Positano (Salerno)
Via dei Mulini, 23
Tel. 089-875 177 - Fax 089-811 419 - Famiglia Attanasio
E-mail: http@starnet.it - Web: www.starnet.it/murat/welcome.html

Category ★★★★ **Rooms** 30 with air-conditioning, telephone, bath, WC, satellite TV, minibar. **Price** Single 250-300,000L, double 320-600,000L. **Meals** Breakfast included (buffet), served 8:00-11:00. **Restaurant** Solo la Sera - à la carte **Credit cards** All major. **Pets** Dogs not allowed. **Nearby** Sorrento - Gulf of Salerno and Amalfi coast (Positano, Amalfi, Ravello, Salerno) - Paestum - Capri - Napoli - Pompeii - Herculaneum - Cuma - Pozzuolo (sulphur springs) - Ischia. **Open** All year.

Built as the summer home of Joachim Murat, Marshal of France and King of Naples, the *palazzo* was converted into a hotel several years ago. It is in Baroque style and has preserved the greater part of its original features, including an enchanting patio where chamber music concerts are sometimes held. The nicest rooms are those in the old part of the building (they are also the most expensive), in particular rooms 1 to 5, which have a balcony facing the Bay of Positano. However, most of those in the newer part of the house also have a balcony with a view of the sea. A few of the rooms have air-conditioning. There is no access directly to the hotel by car, but you can park in the Piazza dei Mulini, some 50 meters away.

How to get there *(Map 20): 57km south of Napoli via A3, Castellammare di Stabia exit, towards Sorrento, Positano. In the old town.*

Albergo Casa Albertina

84017 Positano (Salerno)
Via Tavolozza, 3
Tel. 089-87 51 43 - Fax 089-81 15 40 - Sig. L. Cinque
E-mail: info@casalbertina.it - Web: www.casalbertina.it

Rooms 21 with air-conditioning, telephone, bath and shower, WC, minibar – Elevator. **Price** Half board in single 170-260,000L, in double 160-190,000L, in suite 190-290,000L (per pers.). **Meals** Breakfast included, served 7:30AM-12:00PM. **Restaurant** Service 8:00PM-9:30PM - à la carte - Specialties: Risotto alla pescatora - Penne all'impazzata - Zuppa di pesce - Pesce alla griglia. **Credit cards** All major. **Pets** Dogs allowed. **Facilities** Parking (30-35,000L). **Nearby** Sorrento - Gulf of Salerno and Amalfi coast (Positano, Amalfi, Ravello, Salerno) - Paestum - Capri - Napoli - Pompeii - Herculaneum - Cuma - Pozzuolo sulphur springs - Ischia. **Open** All year.

Take a few steps up a steep little street and you will discover the simple but charming Albergo Casa Albertina. This old village house is run by the son of a fisherman, a former employee of the nearby Sirenuse. Apart from the marvelous 18th-century wooden doors, most of the hotel has a rakish 60's-style decor. However, the dishes, chairs and knick-knacks crafted by local artisans give the place an atmosphere typical of the region. Most of the rooms have a sea-view balcony–it's the perfect place to have breakfast. The service is particularly warm and friendly. You cannot reach the hotel by car, but porter service is available.

How to get there *(Map 20): 57km south of Napoli via A3, Castellammare di Stabia exit, then S145 to Meta and S163 to Positano.*

La Fenice

84017 Positano (Salerno)
Via G. Marconi, 4
Tel. 089-87 55 13 - Fax 089-81 13 09
Famiglia Mandara

Rooms 14 with bath or shower, 13 with WC. **Price** Double 200,000L, suite 400,000L. **Meals** Breakfast included, served 8.00-10.00. **Restaurant** See pp. 513-514. **Credit cards** Not accepted. **Pets** Dogs not allowed. **Facilities** Swimming pool, private beach, garage (20,000L). **Nearby** Sorrento - Gulf of Salerno and Amalfi coast (Positano, Amalfi, Ravello, Salerno) - Paestum - Capri - Napoli - Pompeii - Herculaneum - Cuma - Solfatara at Pozzuloli - Ischia. **Open** All year.

Clinging to the side of the cliff, the villa is on several levels between shady terraces and lush vegetation. The main asset of La Fenice is undoubtedly its position. Fans of Positano who are looking chiefly for the delights of the view will not flinch at the simple furniture and plain bathrooms, particularly with prices to match. If you can, book one of the rooms overlooking the sea which are often reserved in advance from one year to the next. Those in the other rooms can enjoy the superb panorama by taking breakfast under the trellis on the vine-covered terrace, surrounded by flowers and fig trees. Nor should you neglect the fact that the hotel has access to a tiny creek which has the enormous advantage of giving you a little "private" beach where you can enjoy unforgettable swims morning or evening when the bay and its waters are still calm.

How to get there *(Map 20): 57km south of Napoli by A3, exit Castellammare di Stabia, towards Sorrento, Positano; in the old town.*

Casa Cosenza

84017 Positano (Salerno)
Via Trara Genoino, 18
Tel. and Fax 089-875 06 - Sig.ra Maria Rosaria Vitaglione-Cosenza
E-mail: casacosenza@divinacostiera.it

Rooms 9 with shower, WC. **Price** Single for double use 120-160,000L, double with balcony 200,000L, double with terrace 220-240,000L, triple 300,000L, suite with 2 rooms and terrace 380,000L. **Meals** Breakfast 17,500L, served 8:00-9:30. **Restaurant** See pp. 513-514. **Credit cards** Not accepted. **Pets** Dogs not allowed. **Nearby** Sorrento - Gulf of Salerno and Amalfi coast (Positano, Amalfi, Ravello, Salerno) - Paestum - Capri - Napoli - Pompeii - Cuma - La Solfatara at Pozzuoli - Ischia. **Open** All year.

Casa Cosenza is one of those many little houses painted in various pastel shades which cling to the rocks in Positano, overlooking the beach and the blue waters of the Mediterranean. You reach it along one of the various small streets and stairways that wind their way between the houses of the village. Like any good boarding house you will find all the charm of simplicity and conviviality, without too much interference from your fellow-guests. All the rooms look out on the sea and are pleasantly decorated with a few pieces of antique furniture. However we recommend the one which still has its dome, which dates like the rest of the house from the 17th Century. Some rooms share a terrace, others have a private balcony. Here again breakfast with a view through the trellis is a moment to savor.

How to get there (Map 20): *57km south of Napoli on the A3, exit Castellammare di Stabia, towards Sorrento and Positano; in the old town.*

Hotel Palumbo - Palazzo Confalone

84010 Ravello (Salerno)
Via San Giovanni del Toro, 16
Tel. 089-85 72 44 - Fax 089-85 81 33 - Sig. Vuilleumier
E-mail: palumbo@amalfinet.it - Web: www.hotel-palumbo.it

Category ★★★★★ **Rooms** 21 with air-conditioning, telephone, bath or shower, WC, TV, safe, minibar.
Price Half board in the palazzo 440-510,000L, suite 625-775,000L, in the annex 310-340,000L. **Meals**
Breakfast included, served 7:30-10:30. **Restaurant** Service 12:30PM-2:30PM, 8:00PM-10:00PM - mealtime
specials 105,000L, also à la carte - Specialties: Crespelle Palumbo - Ravioli alla menta - Filetto al
Confalone. **Credit cards** All major. **Pets** Small dogs allowed. **Facilities** Garage (30,000L). **Nearby**
Ravello (Villa Rufolo and Villa Cimbrone) - Gulf of Salerno and Amalfi coast (Positano, Amalfi, Ravello,
Salerno) - Paestum - Capri - Napoli - Pompeii - Cuma - Pozzuolo sulphur springs - Ischia. **Open** All year.

When Pasquale Palumbo came here from Switzerland in the 19th century, he opened a hotel in the Episcopal Palace, which quickly became the aristocratic rendez-vous of the whole Amalfi coast. When he opened his hotel in the Palazzo Confalone, his fame grew greater yet. This superb 18th-century mansion in Arab-Norman style has majolica-tiled floors, a patio with arcades of pointed arches and five labyrinthine stories opening on the sea. The interior decoration is beautiful, with antique furniture and paintings, including a large canvas from the school of Caravaggio in an alcove of the main salon. Each room has a particular character, as witnessed in the names they bear: Suite Blu, Torre or Romantica. There are simpler and less expensive rooms in the annex. Situated between mountains and sea, there is a wonderful view from every side. The garden is as romantic as can be, with rosebushes, arbors and trellises. The grandeur of the site adds to the luxury of the place, especially the endless view of the sea broken only by the white cliffs of the Cilento coast and the ruins of Paestum.

How to get there (Map 20): 65km southeast of Napoli.

Palazzo Sasso

84010 Ravello (Salerno)
Via San Giovanni del Toro, 28
Tel. 089-81 81 81 - Fax 089-85 89 00 - Attilis Marro
E-mail: info@palazzosasso.com - Web: www.palazzosasso.com

Category ★★★★ **Rooms** 43 with air-conditioning, telephone, bath or shower, satellite TV, minibar, safe – Elevator. **Price** Double 550-850,000L, junior suite 1 000-1 200,000L, senior suite 1 000-1 400,000L. **Meals** Breakfast included, served 7:00-11:00. **Restaurant** Service 12:00PM-3:00PM, 7:00PM-11:00PM - mealtime specials 95,000L, also à la carte - Italian cuisine. **Credit cards** All major. **Pets** Small dogs allowed. **Facilities** Solarium with 2 jacuzzi, parking. **Nearby** Ravello (Villa Rufolo and Villa Cimbrone) - Gulf of Salerno and Amalfi coast (Positano, Amalfi, Ravello, Salerno) - Paestum - Capri - Napoli - Pompeii - Ischia. **Closed** Nov 1 – Feb 28.

This palace has belonged to the same family for seven hundred years. Altered over the centuries and turned into a hotel in the Fifties, it has just been renovated as a luxurious palace by the American firm Virgin Hotels. Now its ochre colored walls, its terraces covered in flowers overlooking the sea, and its vaulted loggias and colonnades rise once more magnificently above the Bay. The interior décor is luxurious, with its marble-covered floors, stylish antique furniture (tending towards the rococo) and contemporary paintings by Ferdinando Ambrosiano. In the rooms, the more modern furniture is both functional and refined. Service and comfort are naturally those of a great hotel. Yet the whole lacks the depth and the soul that transform a palace into a historic location. However, what the American Gore Vidal called "the loveliest panorama in the world", is still to be found right in front of the hotel.

How to get there *(Map 20): 65km southeast of Napoli by A3, exit Vietri sul Mare, then towards Costiera amalfitana and Ravello.*

Hotel Caruso Belvedere

84010 Ravello (Salerno)
Piazza San Giovanni del Toro, 2
Tel. 089-85 71 11 - Fax 089-85 73 72
Sig. Caruso

Category ★★★★ **Rooms** 24 with telephone, bath or shower, WC. **Price** With half board 330-460,000L, full board 410-540,000L (per 2 pers.). **Meals** Breakfast included, served 7:30-10:00. **Restaurant** Service 12:30PM-2:30PM, 7:30PM-9:00PM - closed 15 days in Feb - mealtime specials 60,000L, also à la carte - Specialties: Crespolini al formaggio - Scaloppina alla Caruso - Soufflé di limone e cioccolata. **Credit cards** All major. **Pets** Dogs allowed (with extra charge). **Nearby** Ravello (Villa Rufolo and Villa Cimbrone) - Gulf of Salerno and Amalfi coast (Positano, Amalfi, Ravello, Salerno) - Paestum - Capri - Napoli - Pompeii - Cuma - Pozzuolo sulphur springs - Ischia. **Open** All year.

The Caruso is tucked away in a quiet garden spot at the end of the little road that links it with the church of San Giovanni del Tore. You enter through a gate flanked by two ancient stone lions and framed by columns and pilasters, then go up one flight to reach the reception. The *palazzo* has well-preserved frescoes and tiled floors in geometric patterns. The walls of the large sitting room are thickly hung with an extensive collection of 19th-century paintings representing landscapes and interiors, and the room is brightened by a number of gaily-colored armchairs. The bedrooms are spacious and most of them offer an extraordinary panorama. The owner is attentive to the needs of his guests, both in the comfort of the surroundings and the quality of the cooking, which he himself supervises. Even though you have to take half-board, the prices here are quite reasonable. So come to Ravello and treat yourself to the unforgettable spectacle of the Gulf of Salerno from your window.

How to get there *(Map 20): 65km southeast of Napoli via A3, Salerno exit, towards Vietri sul Mare and Ravello.*

Villa Cimbrone

84010 Ravello (Salerno)
Via Santa Chiara, 26
Tel. 089-85 74 59 - Fax 089-85 77 77 - Famiglia Vuilleumier
E-mail: info@villacimbrone.it - Web: www.villacimbrone.it

Category ★★★★ **Rooms** 19 with telephone with bath or shower, WC, minibar. **Price** Single 280-300,000L, double and suite 380-650,000L. **Meals** Breakfast included, served 7:30-10:30. **Restaurant** See p. 512. **Credit cards** Amex, Visa, Eurocard, MasterCard. **Pets** Dogs not allowed. **Nearby** Ravello (Villa Rufolo and Villa Cimbrone) - Gulf of Salerno and Amalfi coast (Positano, Amalfi, Ravello, Salerno) - Paestum - Capri - Napoli - Pompeii - Cuma - Pozzuolo sulphur springs - Ischia. **Open** Easter – Dec.

The wonderful gardens of the Villa Cimbrone are, along with those of the Villa Rufolo, one of the recommended sights for tourists visiting Ravello. From its belvedere and its antique-style terraces lined with statues you can admire the view and the spot where, according to legend, God once argued with the devil. But this is a nice place to stay as well as to look at. Periodic renovations have made sure that this historic hotel (Greta Garbo stayed here for some time with Leopold Stokowski) maintains a level of comfort in keeping with the grandeur of the site. Many of the rooms are quite comfortable; all of them have a fine view. Inside there are frescoes, chimneys, majolica tiles and above all a beautiful cloister that adds a touch of magic to the place.

How to get there *(Map 20): 65km southeast of Napoli via A3, Salerno exit, towards Vietri sul Mare and Ravello.*

Villa Maria

84010 Ravello (Salerno)
Via Santa Chiara, 2
Tel. 089-85 72 55 - Fax 089-85 70 71 - Sig. Ginepro
E-mail: villamaria@amalfinet.com - Web: www.villamaria.it

Category ★★★★ **Rooms** 23 with telephone, 6 with bath and 17 with shower, WC, satellite TV, minibar. **Price** Double 300-380,000L, suite 400-680,000L. **Meals** Breakfast included, served 8:00-10:00 - half board 190-230,000L, full board 220-275,000L (per pers.). **Restaurant** Service 12:30PM-2:30PM, 7:30PM-9:30PM - mealtime specials 70,000L, also à la carte - Specialties: Crespolini soffitini - Scialatielle ai frutti di mare - Spigole in crosta - Profiterolle al limone. **Credit cards** All major. **Pets** Dogs not allowed. **Facilities** Swimming pool and parking in Hotel Giordano. **Nearby** Ravello (Villa Rufolo and Villa Cimbrone) - Gulf of Salerno and Amalfi coast (Positano, Amalfi, Ravello, Salerno) - Paestum - Capri - Napoli - Pompeii - Cuma - La Solfatara at Pozzuoli - Ischia. **Closed** Dec 24 – 25.

The owner had two hotels in Ravello, but we definitely prefer the Villa Maria. The exquisite 19th-century atmosphere of the house evokes those travellers of the period who would stop over in Ravello, like Richard Wagner who found the inspiration for the second act of Parsifal in the gardens of the Villa Rufolo, just nearby. The salons of the hotel have deeply upholstered settees, flowered prints, oriental carpets and furniture overloaded with china and curios. The rooms are more soberly decorated, some with a private terrace, have an unforgettable view over the Bay and the mountains, on the sides of which are vineyards and orchards of lemon trees. The restaurant is undoubtedly a place to remember. The owner takes great care with the quality of the produce and the cooking, while inventive, respects the traditions of the region. The maître d'hôtel will offer you a white wine from Ravello which will set your palate dancing.

How to get there *(Map 20): 65km southeast of Napoli by A3, exit Vietri sul Marte, then towards Costiera amalfitana and Ravello.*

Hotel Corona D'Oro 1890

40126 Bologna
Via Oberdan, 12
Tel. 051-23 64 56 - Fax 051-26 26 79 - Sig. Mauro Orsi
E-mail: hotcoro@tin.it - Web: www.cnc.it/bologna

Category ★★★★ **Rooms** 35 with air-conditioning, telephone, fax connexion, shower, WC, satellite TV, minibar, safe – Elevator, wheelchair access. **Price** Single 265-370,000L, double 380-525,000L (–10% reduction for readers of the Guide, except during trade fair periods). **Meals** Breakfast included, served 7:30-11:00. **Restaurant** See pp. 515-516. **Credit cards** All major. **Pets** Dogs allowed. **Nearby** Bologna (Piazza Maggiore and Piazza del Nettuno, churches of S. Petronio, S. Domenico, S. Francesco, National Picture Gallery) - Madonna di San Lucca - San Michele in Bosco - "Giro sulle colline" (car tour around Bologna) - Road of the castles (Bazzano, Monteveglio, S. Maria) – Golf Course (18-hole) in Chiesa Nova di Monte San Pietro and golf course (18-hole) in Bologna. **Closed** Jul 25 – Aug 20.

The blend of styles in this small, four-star hotel right in the historical center of Bologna gives it a pleasant, informal atmosphere. Although the building dates from the 8th century, it has been modified several times; You can now admire a Madonna and Child from the 15th century as well as the Liberty-style stucco decoration circa 1900. The hotel continues to improve on what has been its reputation up to now: comfort, service, and quiet.

How to get there *(Map 10): Via A14, Bologna-Arcoveggio exit. On the "Tangenziale," number 7 exit towards center and piazza Maggiore.*

Hotel Commercianti

40124 Bologna
Via de' Pignattari, 11
Tel. 051-23 30 52 - Fax 051-22 47 33 - Sig.ra Serena Orsi
E-mail: hotcom@tin.it - Web: www.cnc.it/bologna

Category ★★★ **Rooms** 34 with air-conditioning, telephone, shower, WC, satellite TV, safe, minibar – Elevator, wheelchair access. **Price** Single 235-370,000L, double 335-525,000L, suite 510-770,000L (-10% reduction for readers of the Guide, except during trade fair periods). **Meals** Breakfast included, served 7:00AM-12:00PM. **Restaurant** See pp. 515-516. **Credit cards** All major. **Pets** Small dogs allowed. **Facilities** Bikes, Parking (40,000L). **Nearby** Bologna (Piazza Maggiore and Piazza del Nettuno, churches of S. Petronio, S. Domenico, S. Francesco, National Picture Gallery) - Madonna di San Lucca - San Michele in Bosco - "Giro sulle colline" (car tour around Bologna) - Road of the castles (Bazzano, Monteveglio, S. Maria) – Golf Course (18-hole) in Chiesa Nova di Monte San Pietro and golf course (18-hole) in Bologna. **Open** All year.

The most convenient feature of this hotel is its location: right next to the San Petronio cathedral in a special traffic-free zone (which, however, hotel guests can enter with car to use the hotel garage). The Commercianti has just been completely refurbished. A modern décor has been replaced by a more traditional style closer to the atmosphere of the former palazzo, with pastel colors in the reception rooms, and fine papers in the guest rooms ; there are frescos on the walls of Room 319. Rooms 310, 312, 316 and 325 have terraces with views of the nearby church, while the rooms built in the old tower have a remarkable view of the stained-glass windows and roof of the cathedral. The other rooms look out on the Piazza Maggiore.

How to get there *(Map 10): Via A14, Bologna-Arcoveggio exit. On the "Tangenziale," number 7 exit towards center and piazza Maggiore.*

Hotel Orologio

40123 Bologna
Via IV Novembre, 10
Tel. 051-231 253 - Fax 051-260 552 - Sig.ra Cristina Orsi
E-mail: hotoro@tin.it - Web: www.cnc.it/bologna

Category ★★★ **Rooms** 35 with air-conditioning, telephone, bath or shower, WC, satellite TV, safe, minibar, fax connection – Elevator. **Price** Single 235-370,000L, double 335-525,000L, suite 510-770,000L (-10% reduction for readers of the Guide, except during trade fair periods). **Meals** Breakfast included, served 7:00-11:30. **Restaurant** See pp. 515-516. **Credit cards** All major. **Pets** Dogs allowed. **Facilities** Bikes, Parking (40,000L). **Nearby** Bologna (Piazza Maggiore and Piazza del Nettuno, churches of S. Petronio, S. Domenico, S. Francesco, National Picture Gallery) - Madonna di San Lucca - San Michele in Bosco - "Giro sulle colline" (car tour around Bologna) - Road of the castles (Bazzano, Monteveglio, S. Maria) – Golf Course (18-hole) in Chiesa Nova di Monte San Pietro. **Open** All year.

This small well-located hotel is next to the Piazza Maggiore in Bologna, one of the most visited towns in Italy, where it can be especially difficult to find a place to stay in professional exhibit season. This town is also a great place for tourism and gastronomy. The Hotel Orlogio offers comfortable rooms, most of which have a nice view on the oldest vestiges of the town. The planned restoration of the rooms has been delayed but is due to start in 2000. It should give them the charm which they still lack. However, the professionalism of the Orsi family, which runs some of the finest establishments in town, is evident in the quality of the service.

How to get there *(Map 10): Via A14, Bologna-Arcoveggio exit. On the "Tangenziale," number 7 exit towards center and piazza Maggiore.*

Hotel Duchessa Isabella

44100 Ferrara
Via Palestro, 70
Tel. 0532-20 21 21 - Fax 0532-20 26 38 - Sig.ra Evelina Bonzagni
E-mail: isabelld@tin.it

Category ★★★★★ **Rooms** 21 and 7 suite with air-conditioning, telephone, bath, WC, satellite TV, minibar. **Price** Double 450-570,000L, suite 770-1 600,000L. **Meals** Breakfast served 7:00-10:00 - half board 330-380,000L (per pers.). **Restaurant** Service 12:00PM-2:30PM, 7:30PM-9:30PM - closed Sun evening and Mon - mealtime specials 100-150,000L, also à la carte - Regional cooking. **Credit cards** All major. **Pets** Dogs allowed. **Nearby** Parking. **Nearby** In Ferrara: Duomo, Palazzo Ludovico il Moro, Castello Estense, Palazzo dei Diamanti - Events: Palio in May, concerts at the Abbey of Pomposa in Jul and Aug - Comacchio - Abbey of San Bartolo - Cento and Pieve di Cento. **Closed** Aug.

An exceptional luxury hotel in a 15th-century palazzo in the very heart of Ferrara. For a long time, the city was ruled by the d'Este family and Isabella, the daughter of Ercole I, was famous throughout Europe in the 15th Century for the brilliance and refinement of her entertainments. The palace still has many of its former splendors, including the ceilings with their painted panels in the magnificent salons. Most of the rooms and suites open on a garden full of birds; they are luxuriously decorated, though in a rather ordinary style, with many frills, furbelows, lace and pastel colors suggesting the very romantic décor of "young girls rooms"... Having said that, the service is impeccable, the restaurant delicious and the welcome exceptionally gracious. At present, the best Grand Hotel in Ferrara.

How to get there *(Map 10): 47km northeast of Bologna by A13, exit Ferrara-North.*

Locanda della Duchessina

44100 Ferrara
Vicolo Voltino, 11
Tel. 0532-20 69 81 - Fax 0532-20 26 38 - Sig.ra Evelina Bonzagni
E-mail: isabelld@tin.it

Category ★★★ **Rooms** 5 with air-conditioning, tel, bath or shower, WC, satellite TV, minibar, safe. **Price** Single 140,000L, double 180-220,000L, suite 270,000L. **Meals** Breakfast served 7:00-10:00. **Restaurant** In Hotel Duchessa Isabella: L. 60 000. Or see pp. 516-517. **Credit cards** All major. **Pets** Dogs allowed. **Nearby** Ferrara (Duomo, Palace of Ludivic the Moor, Castello Estense, Diamond Palace, spectacle of the traditional Palio in May) - Abbey of S. Bartolo - Cento and Pieve di Cento. **Closed** Aug.

Ferrara is well worth a visit, with its Renaissance houses and art treasures, the heritage of its long and splendid past. The Locanda della Duchessina is a small and much less expensive annex to the luxurious Duchessa Isabella. It is a little building with a garden and a few pleasant, functional rooms, though their style (like that of the Duchessa, for that matter) is a bit too "cute" for our taste. Nevertheless, it has a good location near the center of town and makes a nice stopover in a city that still lacks a "hotel of charm." Guests can take their meals at the Duchessa Isabella, which offers excellent cooking. An added plus is that guests who present this guide will get an 8% reduction on the price of a room.

How to get there *(Map 10): 47km northeast of Bologna via A13, Ferrara-North exit.*

Locanda Borgonuovo

44100 Ferrara
Via Cairoli, 29
Tel. 0532-21 11 00 - Fax 0532-24 80 00 - Sig.ra Adèle Orlandini
Web: www.4net.com/business/borgonuovo

Rooms 4 with air-conditioning, tel, shower, WC, TV, safe, minibar. **Price** Single 100,000L, double 140-200,000L; extra bed 50,000L. **Meals** Breakfast included, served 7:30-10:00. **Restaurant** See pp. 516-517. **Credit cards** Amex, Visa, Eurocard, MasterCard. **Pets** Dogs allowed. **Facilities** Bikes. **Nearby** Ferrara (Duomo, Palace of Ludivic the Moor, Castello Estense, Diamond Palace, spectacle of the traditional Palio in May) - Abbey of S. Bartolo - Cento and Pieve di Cento. **Open** All year.

In the heart of this old city that was once the home of the Dukes of Este, the Borgonuovo offers all the intimacy of a little guest house. Built within the walls of a 15th-century monastery, it is a nice stopping place in a city that really lacks hotels of charm and where all the accommodations tend to be on the expensive side, particularly for someone traveling alone. The four rooms in the house are fairly small. Pleasantly decorated, they with all the necessary amenities and even, in one case, a kitchenette (5,000 L. extra per person/per day) for guests who plan a longer stay. In fine weather, the copious breakfast is served on the patio of the locanda. Or you can breakfast in the living room you share with the owners, who are both friendly and helpful. They have bicycles for rent to tour the historic center, which is now (like elsewhere in Italy) completely off-limits to cars. A good address to keep in mind to visit a city that deserves to be better known.

How to get there *(Map 10): 47km northeast of Bologna via A13, Ferrara-North exit; in the old city.*

Canalgrande Hotel

41100 Modena
Corso Canalgrande, 6
Tel. 059-21 71 60 - Fax 059-22 16 74
E-mail: info@canalgrandehotel.it - Web: www.canalgrandehotel.it

Category ★★★★ **Rooms** 79 with air-conditioning, telephone, bath or shower, WC, TV, minibar – Elevator. **Price** Single 210,000L, double 305,000L, suite 445,000L. **Meals** Breakfast included, served 7:00-10:30. **Restaurant** Service 12:30PM-1:45PM, 7:30PM-9:45PM - closed Wed - mealtime specials 50-70,000L, also à la carte - Specialties: Paste modenesi - Verdure ai ferri - Dolci casalinghi. **Credit cards** All major. **Pets** Dogs allowed. **Facilities** Garage (15,000L). **Nearby** Modena (Duomo, Estense Gallery and Library) - Roman churches of San Cesario sul Panano and of Pieve Trebbio near Monteorsello - Abbey of Nonantola – Golf course (18- and 19-hole) in Colombaro di Formigine. **Open** All year.

The Canalgrande is located right in the center of town, and has a large garden with a charming fountain surrounded by enormous several-hundred-year-old trees. Formerly a patrician villa, it is today a hotel with Neoclassical architecture. The foyer and the series of salons around the entry are handsomely done in stucco. Contemporary armchairs and beautiful old paintings give the place a cozy atmosphere. The guest rooms and bathrooms are comfortable. Be sure to check out La Secchia Rapita, the restaurant in the cellar, with its beautiful vaulted brick ceiling.

How to get there *(Map 9): 39km northwest of Bologna via A1, Modena-South exit, then S9 (via Emilia-East) to Corso Canalgrande and to the left (near by the church).*

Villa Gaidello

41013 Castelfranco Emilia (Modena)
Via Gaidello, 22
Tel. 059-92 68 06 - Fax 059-92 66 20 - Sig.ra Bini
E-mail: gaidello@tin.it - Web: members.aol.com/gaidello

Apartments 9 and 2 rooms with bath or shower, WC, TV, minibar. **Price** With half-board 100-150,000L (per pers.). **Meals** Breakfast included, served 8:00-10:00. **Restaurant** By reservation. Service 1:00PM, 8:00PM - mealtime specials 75,000L - Regional cooking. **Credit cards** All major. **Pets** Dogs not allowed. **Facilities** Lake in the park, parking. **Nearby** Church in Castelfranco - Modena - Roman churchs of San Cesario sul Panano and of Pieve Trebbio near by Monteorsello - Abbey of Nonantola - Bologna - Modena. **Closed** Aug, Sun evening, Mon.

If you plan to stay a while in Bologna or Modena and if you like country living, perhaps you will decide to stay at Signora Bini's lovely farmhouse, several miles away from these two large towns. She has only three apartments, each sleeping from 2 to 5 persons. Somewhere between an inn and a guest house, the appeal of this place lies in the arts of hospitality and a cuisine based largely on homemade products. You must book in advance, whether for lodging or for meals. Whether in the villa or its extension, the lodgings are justly appreciated for their country charm and Signora Bini's cooking for the quality and freshness of the products: her pasta is made the day it is used, fruits and vegetables come from her garden and the wine is grown in the estate vineyards. An appealing spot.

How to get there *(Map 9): 13km southeast of Modena - 26km northwest of Bologna via S9 (the hotel is in the country, 1km from the city).*

Hotel Al Vecchio Convento

47010 Portico di Romagna (Forlì)
Via Roma, 7
Tel. 0543-96 70 53 - 96 70 14 - Fax 0543-96 71 57 - Sig.ra Raggi
E-mail: info@vecchioconvento.it - Web: www.vecchioconvento.it

Category ★★★ **Rooms** 15 with telephone, bath, WC, TV. **Price** Single 100,000L, double 130,000L. **Meals** Breakfast 17,000L, served at any time - half board 130,000L, full board 150,000L (per pers. 3 days min.). **Restaurant** Service 12:30PM-2:00PM, 7:30PM-10:00PM - closed Wed except in summer - mealtime specials 35-55,000L, also à la carte - Specialties: Funghi tartufi - Cacciagione - Pasta fatta in casa. **Credit cards** All major. **Pets** Dogs not allowed in restaurant. **Facilities** Parking. **Nearby** Church of Polenta - Biblioteca Malatestiana in Cesena - Abbey of Madona del Monte near Cesena - Ravenna. **Open** All year.

This former convent now converted into a hotel adjoins the palace of Beatrice Portinari – the famous "Beatrice" who so inspired Dante. Here all the skills of local artists and craftsmen were put to use to restore the antique furniture – wooden or iron beds, period chests and chairs – and the original architecture of the building. In the cooking as well, tradition is respected: Many dishes are based on vegetables, rice or pasta and you can end the meal with a glass of laurino, the local liqueur. Breakfast is now served in a new dining room near the garden and the jams and preserves on the breakfast table are also homemade. Hospitality is another tradition and you won't be disappointed here, either. An address that's worth a detour to sample the charm of old Italy.

How to get there *(Map 10): 97km southeast of Bologna via A14, Forli exit - S67 (towards Firenze).*

Hotel della Porta

47822 Santarcangelo di Romagna (Rimini)
Via Andrea Costa, 85
Tel. 0541-62 21 52 - Fax 0541-62 21 68

Category ★★★ **Rooms** 22 and 2 suites with air-conditioning, telephone, bath, WC, TV, minibar –
Elevator, wheelchair access. **Price** Single 100-120,000L, double 140-170,000L, suite 240,000L.
Meals Breakfast included, served 7:00-10:30. **Restaurant** See p. 519. **Credit cards** All major.
Pets Dogs allowed. **Facilities** Sauna (15,000L), parking. **Nearby** Santarcangelo (museum, Rocco
Malatestiana, San Michele) - Verruchio - Longiano - Rimini - San Marino – Amalia Golf Course (9-
hole). **Open** All year.

The Hotel Della Porta is in Santarcangelo, several miles from Rimini, in Montefeltro, between Romagna and the Marches. This region was the cradle of the famous Malatesta family, and is dotted with splendid Renaissance monuments, along with traces of the forbidden romance of Francesca and Paolo, which Dante immortalized in his "Divine Comedy." It consists of two houses in the old village. The spacious salon-reception area serves as a tourist information office. It is illuminated by a sizeable skylight, and decorated in contemporary style. The guest rooms are large and very comfortable and have a more traditional decor. A nice touch is that each one has a work or living area. Our favorite rooms are in the adjoining house, with its antique furniture and ornate frescoes of flowers on the ceiling. There is no restaurant, but the hotel will help make arrangements with the best ones in the village.

How to get there *(Map 11): 15km west of Rimini; via A14 Rimini-North exit, then towards Santarcangelo.*

Hotel Verdi

43100 Parma
Viale Pasini, 18
Tel. 0521-29 35 39 - Fax 0521-29 35 59 - Sig.ra Dondi
E-mail: hotelverdi@libero.it

Category ★★★★ **Rooms** 20 with air-conditioning, telephone, bath and shower, WC, satellite TV, minibar, safe – Elevator. **Price** Single 175-220,000L, double 255-290,000L, suite 285-330,000L. **Meals** Breakfast 18,000L, served 7:00AM-12:00PM - half board +35,000L (per pers., 3 days min.). **Restaurant** "Santa Croce", service 12:00PM-2:00PM, 8:00PM-10:00PM - closed Sat lunch and Sun - mealtime specials, also à la carte 60-70,000L - Specialties: Culatello - Tortelli - Brasato - Duchessa di Parma. **Credit cards** All major. **Pets** Dogs allowed by reservation. **Facilities** Parking, garage. **Nearby** Parma (Duomo, Baptistery, Abbey of St. John, National Gallery, Farnese Theater, Arturo Toscanini's Birthplace) - House of Verdi in Roncole - Verdi Theater in Busseto - Villa Verdi in Sant'Agata - Mantova - Sabbioneta. **Open** All year.

Surprisingly little known, the city of Parma shines like a little Mannerist jewel set into northern Italy with its palaces and churches that so many illustrious painters (Coregio and Parmigiano, among others) adorned with their works. The city is also known for its cooking and boasts more fine restaurants than it does hotels of charm. The Hotel Verdi is one of the rare ones. Near the gardens of the Ducal Palace, it started out as a Liberty-style villa. Now restored, it is a pleasant, charming place to stay for anyone who wants to explore Parma. Just a few steps from the hotel, you mustn't miss the famous restaurant Santa Croce where you can taste the specialties: culatello and the homemade tortelli and lasagna. The rooms overlooking the street have now been soundproofed.

How to get there *(Map 9): 100km southeast of Milano - 96km northwest of Bologna via A1.*

I Due Foscari

43011 Busseto (Parma)
Piazza Carlo Rossi, 15
Tel. 0524-93 00 39 - Fax 0524-91 625
Sig. Marco Bergonzi - Sig. Roberto Morsia

Category ★★★ **Rooms** 20 with air-conditioning, telephone, bath or shower, WC, satellite TV, minibar, safe. **Price** 110,000L, double 150,000L **Meals** Breakfast included 15,000L, served 7:30-10:00 - half board 135-170,000L (per pers., 3 days min.). **Restaurant** Service 12:00PM-2:00PM, 8:00PM-10:00PM - mealtime specials, also à la carte - Regional cooking. **Credit cards** All major. **Pets Varie** Dogs not allowed. **Facilities** Parking. **Nearby** Teatro Verdi a Busseto - Verdi's house in Roncole - Villa Verdi at Sant'Agata di Villanova by appointment: tel 0532-83 00 00 - Villa Verdi at Sant'Agata - Parma - Castles at Torrechiara - Fontanello - Soragna - Certosa di Parma (under restoration) - Mantova - Sabbioneta. **Open** All year.

B ussetto is a charming little agricultural town set in the Emilian countryside which still shows traces of its past as the capital of the little State of Pallavicino (until 1588) and as a home of bel canto with its pretty Verdi theatre. From that point of view, I Due Foscari, which is housed in a noble building behind the town square and named after one of the great composer's operas, is the ideal stopping-place – and all the more so since the owner has a name which will not be unknown to music lovers. The hotel has been entirely renovated and its furnishings, in Venetian-Arab style, were inspired by the libretto of the opera. The rooms and bathrooms are very comfortable; don't hesitate to accept those in the front, because the street is pedestrianized for the summer months. The hotel inevitably honors the culinary traditions of the region and its restaurant, under the guidance of Enrico Piazzi, justifies its reputation, in particular during the celebration of the Verdi Sapori from September 10 to 12, which highlights regional products and Verdi's music.

How to get there *(Map 9): 40km northwest of Parma by A1, exit Firenze-Salsomaggiore Terme, then S359 to Soragna.*

Locanda del Lupo

43019 Soragna (Parma)
Via Garibaldi, 64
Tel. 0524-59 71 00 - Fax 0524-59 70 66 - Sig. E. Dioni
E-mail: info@locandadellupo.com - Web: www.locandadellupo.com

Category ★★★★ **Rooms** 46 with air-conditioning, telephone, bath or shower, WC, satellite TV.
Price Single 140,000L, double 230,000L, suite 300,000L. **Meals** Breakfast included, served 7:30-
10:30 - half board 140-160,000L (per pers.). **Restaurant** Service 12:00PM-2:00PM, 7:30PM-10:00PM -
mealtime specials 55,000L, also à la carte - Specialties: Salami tipici - Formaggi di Parma - Tortelli
di ricotta. **Credit cards** All major. **Pets** Dogs allowed except in restaurant. **Facilities** Parking. **Nearby**
Parma - Verdi pilgrimage tour: Arturo Toscanini's birthplace in Parma - House of Verdi in Roncole -
Verdi Theater in Busseto - Villa Verdi in Sant'Agata — La Rocca golf course (9-hole) in Sala Barganza.
Closed Aug 10 – 20.

For years, Locanda del Lupo was famous locally for its fine cuisine, and
appreciated as well by Parisian gastronomic critics, which now offers
rooms. The rooms and salons are simply decorated but refined and
comfortable. The main attraction, however, remains the restaurant where early
recipes from the archives of Prince Meli Lupi, a former resident, are brilliantly
prepared and served. The wine cellar is well stocked. You may count on a
warm welcome here.

How to get there *(Map 9): 33km northwest of Parma via A1, Fidenza exit.*

Il Palazzo ♟

48013 Brisighella (Ravenna)
Via Baccagnano, 110
Tel. and Fax 0546-803 38 - Sig. Matarese
E-mail: ematarese@racine.ra.it

Rooms 6 and 1 apartment (4-5 pers.) with shower. **Price** Double 100-120,000L, apart. 700-800,000L (per 1 week). **Meals** Breakfast included, served 8:30-10:00. **Restaurant** Service 12:30PM-8:00PM - mealtime specials 25,000L - Organic cooking. **Credit cards** All major. **Pets** Dogs not allowed. **Facilities** Parking. **Nearby** In Brisighella: La Rocca, sanctuary of Monticino, Termes, Pieve del Tho (S.Giovanni in Ottovano), Park Carnè (walks), Park della Vena del Gesso (la Tanaccia) - Modigliona - Faenza (museum) - Ravenna - Rimini – Riolo Terme golf course (18-hole). **Open** All year.

Brisighella, a medieval village in the foothills of the Appenines, is also a health spa with thermal springs. The Adriatic beaches are close by and an excursion to Rimini is a must: One should make sure to see the Temple Malatestino for the grandiose architecture of Leon Battista Alberti and for the lovely fresco by Piero della Francesca. Ravenna, with its celebrated mosaics, is also nearby. If you plan to visit this region, this simple inn is a nice place to stay. Its architect/owner has designed the rooms in a style that is modern and rustic at the same time, with a charm of their own. Their windows look out over the vineyards and orchards all around. In May, impressive numbers of fireflies will accompany your evening strolls. If you eat on the premises, you will be pleased to know that the bread and all the specialties are made by the mistress of the house, with organically-grown products.

How to get there *(Map 10): 12km from Faenza. On the A14, Faenza exit, towards Brisighella-Firenze. In Brisighella, towards Terme/Modigliona. Il Palazzo is the third house on the left after the Hôtel Terme.*

Relais Torre Pratesi

Cavina 48013 Brisighella (Ravenna)
Via Cavina, 11
Tel. 0546-845 45 - Fax 0546-845 58 - Sig. and Sig.ra Raccagni
E-mail: torrep@tin.it - Web: web.tin.it/torrepratesi

Category ★★★★ **Rooms** 3 and 5 suites with air-conditioning, telephone, bath or shower, WC, TV, minibar, safe. **Price** Double 250,000L, suite 300,000L. **Meals** Breakfast included, served to 2:00PM - half board 150-175,000L (per pers.). **Restaurant** Service 8:00PM-10:00PM - closed Tues - mealtime specials, also à la carte 70,000L - Regional cooking. **Credit cards** All major. **Pets** Dogs allowed. **Facilities** Swimmin pool, palestra. **Nearby** Faenza - Brisighella - Church of San Pietro at Sylvis - Ravenna – Golf Club la Torre, Manneggio Villa Corte, thermal baths "Riolo Terme". **Open** All year.

This massive hotel towers deep in the lush Romagnian countryside, which is famous for its wine, oil and truffles. It was built in 1510, and a farm was added in the 19th century. Renovated with careful attention to artistic detail, the rooms have the spacious dimensions of days gone by. The elegant simplicity of the furniture highlights the materials, stone and wood. The modern conveniences do not at all detract from the beautiful restoration work. Home-style cuisine allows you to savor products fresh from your hosts' farm. This place is magical–it's a great way to experience the beautiful, well-preserved Lamona valley, which extends all the way to Florence.

How to get there *(Map 10): 28km south of Faenza, via A14, Faenza exit, then S302 (Brisighella-Firenze) to Fognano, then towards Valletta during 4km.*

Hotel Posta

42100 Reggio nell'Emilia
Piazza Del Monte, 2
Tel. 0522-43 29 44 - Fax 0522-45 26 02 - Sig.ra Caroline Salomon
E-mail: info@hotelposta.re.it - Web: www.hotelposta.re.it

Category ★★★★ **Rooms** 43 with air-conditioning, telephone, bath or shower, WC, TV, minibar – Elevator. **Price** Single 240,000L, double 310,000L, suite 360,000L, apartment 450,000L. **Meals** Breakfast included, served 7:00-10:30. **Restaurant** See p. 519. **Credit cards** All major. **Pets** Dogs not allowed. **Facilities** Parking (20,000L). **Nearby** Church of San Faustino at Rubiera - Church of Novallara - Château of Scandiano - Parma – Matilde di Canossa Golf Course (18-hole) in Reggio. **Open** All year.

This former palace is in an ideal location in the heart of the historic town center, on Cesare Battisti Square. The austere medieval façade conceals the rococo interior which is embellished with old stucco ornaments from the walls of a famous local bakery frequented by the notables of the town. The rooms are highly original and offer all the comforts you would expect from a four-star hotel.

How to get there *(Map 9): 27km southeast of Parma via A1, Reggio Nell'Emilia exit.*

Albergo delle Notarie

42100 Reggio nell'Emilia
Via Palazzolo, 5
Tel. 0522-45 35 00 - Fax 0522-45 37 37
Dr. Stefano Zanichelli

Category ★★★★ **Rooms** 34 with air-conditioning, telephone, bath or shower, WC, satellite TV, minibar – Elevator. **Price** Single 240-280,000L, double 320-360,000L, suite (3-4 pers.) 360-460,000L. **Meals** Breakfast included, served 7:00-10:00. **Restaurant** Service 12:30PM-2:30PM, 7:30PM-10:30PM - closed Sat evening, (Jun - Sept closed Sat and Sun) - mealtime specials 55,000L, also à la carte - Regional cooking. **Credit cards** All major. **Pets** Dogs allowed. **Facilities** Parking (30,000L). **Pets** Dogs not allowed. **Nearby** Church of San Faustino at Rubiera - Novallara churches - Château of Scandiano - Canossa - Parma – Golf course (18-hole). **Closed** Aug.

The town of Reggio nell'Emilia may not have the splendor if its more famous neighbors, Parma and Modena, but it is still an interesting and pleasant stop. The two basilicas of San Prospero and della Ghiara, near the hotel, bear witness to the artistic treasures of its past. The Albergo delle Notarie is located in the old quarter and shares the town's discreet yet colorful elegance. The recent renovation opted for simplicity and comfort: a spare, refined look determined by the size of the rooms and choice of furniture, whether modern or period. A major asset is an excellent gastronomic restaurant where you can sample the pasta, ham, sausages and the specialities that make the province of Emilia a famous culinary center.

How to get there *(Map 9): 27km southwest of Parma via A1, Reggio nell'Emilia exit.*

Albergo Casa Matilde

42030 Puianello (Reggio Emilia)
Via A. Negri, 11
Tel. 0522-88 90 06 - Fax 0522-88 90 06
Famiglia Bertolini

Category ★★★★ **Rooms** 5 and 2 suites (with air-conditioning) with telephone, bath, WC, minibar, TV. **Price** Double 330,000L, suite 450,000L. **Meals** Breakfast included, served from 7:30. **Restaurant** Only for residents - mealtime specials. **Credit cards** Amex, Visa, Eurocard, Mastercard. **Pets** Dogs not allowed. **Facilities** Swimming pool. **Nearby** Parma - Verdi pilgrimage tour: Arturo Toscanini's Birthplace in Parma, House of Verdi in Roncole, Verdi Theater in Busseto, Villa Verdi in Sant'Agata – Matilde di Canossa golf course (9-hole) in Reggio. **Open** All year.

If you would like to get away from it all in a country setting, where fine dining is time-honored tradition, Casa Matilde is a destination to consider. This friendly inn, in the shady hills of the Parmesan Appenines, is in the middle of a small park full of flowers. The spacious rooms are individually decorated. The large beautiful salons have been carefully laid out to ensure that you have all of the comforts of home. The surroundings are perfect for long romantic walks. Your hostess will be happy to answer any questions you might have. She knows all about this queen-valkyrie named Matilda and the mysteries of the region.

How to get there *(Map 9): 35km southwest of Parma; 10km of Reggio Emilia. Via A1, Reggio Emilia exit, then towards Puianello-Quattro Castella.*

Hotel Castello Miramare

04023 Formia (Latina)
Via Pagnano
Tel. 0771-70 01 38 - Fax 0771-70 01 39 - Sig.ra Celletti
E-mail: info@hotelcastellomiramare.it - Web: www.hotelcastellomiramare.it

Category ★★★★ **Rooms** 10 with air-conditioning, telephone, bath or shower, WC, TV, safe, minibar.
Price Single 130-160,000L, double 170-200,000L. **Meals** Breakfast 18,000L, served 7:30AM-12:00PM
- half board 160-190,000L, full board 180-210,000L. (per pers., 3 days min.). **Restaurant** Service
12:30PM-3:00PM, 7:30PM-9:30PM - mealtime specials 65,000L, also à la carte - Specialties: Tonnarelli
all'aragosta e funghi - Cocktail di astice alla catalana. **Credit cards** All major. **Pets** Dogs allowed.
Facilities Parking. **Nearby** Cicero's Tomb - Church of San Pietro in Minturno - Abbey of Montecassino
- Island of Ponza. **Open** All year.

The Castello Miramare is a good stopping place on the way to the south of
Italy. The town of Formia is of no particular interest except for Latin
scholars who may want to visit Cicero's tomb, 2 kilometers away along the
Appian way. The castle itself has several rooms with modern comfort and old-
style decor, handsome gardens and numerous public rooms. These facilities
are often used for receptions, but the staff members are very nice and they will
go out of their way to make sure that these events do not in any way
inconvenience individual clients.

How to get there *(Map 19): 76km southeast of Latina via A2, Cassino exit,
then S630 towards Formia and SS7.*

Grand Hotel Le Rocce

04024 Gaeta (Latina)
Via Flacca,km 23,300
Tel. 0771-74 09 85 - 0771-74 16 33 - Sig. Viola
E-mail: lerocce@lerocce.com - Web: www.lerocce.com

Category ★★★ **Rooms** 48 and 6 suites with telephone, bath or shower, WC, TV, minibar (air-conditioning in suites). **Price** Single 140-280,000L, double 160-370,000L, suite 340-470,000L. **Meals** Breakfast included, served 8:00-10:00 - half board 130-280,000L (per pers., 3 days. min.). **Restaurant** Service 1:00PM-2:30PM, 8:00PM-9:30PM - à la carte 55-60,000L. **Credit cards** All major. **Pets** Dogs not allowed. **Facilities** Private beach, parking. **Nearby** Gulf of Gaeta. **Open** Mar – Oct.

This is an ideal spot for those who dream of a holiday close to the sea. Nestled in a little bay of the Gulf of Gaeta, the hotel has lush Mediterranean gardens on terraces that descend to a solarium just over the private beach. The interior architecture echoes the style of the region, favoring generous dimensions and repeated arcades, with a majolica-tiled floor. Whatever their category, all the rooms have a balcony or terrace facing the sea. Most are spacious, all are comfortable and those called superiore boast air-conditioning as well. Salons and dining room, inside and out, have been arranged so as to provide the best view of the gardens and the sea. A good place to stop on a trip south, or as a base for visiting Rome or Naples. Gaeta is on the autostrada, just about halfway between these two principal cities of the south of Italy.

How to get there *(Map 19): 140km south of Roma, 95km north of Napoli. 7km west of Gaetaon the S213 road.*

Hotel Cernia

Isola di Ponza - Chiaia di Luna 04027 Ponza (Latina)
Via Panoramica
Tel. 0771-804 12/80 99 51 - Fax 0771-80 99 55 - Sig. Paolo Greca
E-mail: pagreca@tin.it - Web: www.emmeti.it/cernia

Rooms 60 with air-conditioning, telephone, bath or shower, WC, TV, minibar – Elevator. **Price** Single 180-260,000L, double 280-450,000L. **Meals** Breakfast included, served 8:30-10:30. **Restaurant** Service 1:00PM-2:30PM, 8:00PM-9:30PM - mealtime specials 60-70,000L, also à la carte - Italian, regional cooking and seafood. **Credit cards** All major. **Pets** Dogs allowed. **Facilities** Swimming pool, tennis, private bus. **Nearby** Beach of Chaia di Luna - Pesca subacquea. **Open** Apr 1 – Oct 15.

Buried in a dense and fragrant garden, the Cernia is just a five minute walk from the beautiful Chiaia di Luna beach, and near the port where you will find the most famous restaurant on the island, Gennarino a Mare, with landing stages for the 10m or 25m boats that can be hired through the hotel of the same name. The hotel is vast and the rooms numerous. Certain rooms-201, 202, 203 and 204–have a large terrace and a rewarding view of the sea. The straw window-shades, wicker furniture, rocking chairs and white couches create a friendly vacation atmosphere in the salon enfilade. The beach isn't far away, but a swim in the large hotel swimming pool set in the shade can also be nice on a hot summer day.

How to get there *(Map 18): Ferry services from Rome, Napoli, Anzio, San Felice Circeo, Terracina, Formia (1:30/2:00) - cars are permitted in summer if you stay 15 days minimum on the island.*

Hotel Punta Rossa

04017 San Felice Circeo (Latina)
Via delle Batterie, 37
Tel. 0773-54 80 85 - Fax 0773-54 80 75 - Sig. and Sig.ra Battaglia
E-mail: punta_rossa@iol.it - Web: www.venere.it.lazio, san felice circeo

Category ★★★★ **Rooms** 36 and 4 suites and 20 mini-apartments with air-conditioning, telephone, bath, WC, TV, video, minibar. **Price** Double 260-330,000L, suite 460-530,000L. **Meals** Breakfast included, served 8:00-11:00 - half board in high season 280-380,000L (per pers.). **Restaurant** Service 1:00PM-2:30PM, 8:00PM-10:30PM - mealtime specials 65,000L - Specialties: Tonnarelli seafood - Frutti di mare. **Credit cards** All major. **Pets** Dogs allowed. **Facilities** Swimming pool, sauna (+20,000L), private beach, health center. **Nearby** Terracina - Abbey of Fossanova - Temple of Jupiter Anxur - National park of Circeo. **Open** All year.

The seven-and-a-half acres of the Hotel Punta Rossa lie within a protected site on the San Felice Circeo peninsula, a truly unique location. The architecture is slightly dated, but the hotel is otherwise fully up-to-date. It looks like a miniature village set into the contours of a hill abounding with lush vegetation. The rooms are vast in size, simply decorated, and very comfortable. They all face the sea, and most of them have landscaped terraces. Several mini-apartments, suitable for four to six people are tucked away in the garden; there can be rented by the week. The hotel has a health-and-beauty center, a nice salt-water swimming pool, a private beach, and a small port at the end of a path that winds through the rocks and plantings. The restaurant is excellent.

How to get there *(Map 18): 106km southeast of Rome via A1, exit N148, towards Latina then Terracina.*

Parkhotel Fiorelle

04029 Sperlonga (Latina)
Via Fiorelle, 12
Tel. 0771-548 092 / 549 246 - Fax 0771-548 092
Sig. Cosmo Di Mille

Category ★★★ **Rooms** 33 with telephone, bath or shower, WC, safe. **Price** Single 135,000L, double 155,000L. **Meals** Breakfast 10,000L, served 8:00-9:30 - half board 95-135,000L, full board 105-145,000L (per pers.). **Restaurant** Only for residents - Service 1:00PM-2:00PM, 7:30PM-10:00PM - closed Fri - mealtime specials 40,000L, also à la carte - Regional cooking and seafood. **Credit cards** Visa, MasterCard. **Pets** Dogs allowed. **Facilities** Swimming pool, private beach, parking. **Nearby** In Sperlonga: National Archeological Museum and Tiberius, Grotto - Terracina (Duomo and Piazza del Municipio) - Abbey of Fossanova. **Open** Easter – Oct 1.

The regulars who come to the Fiorelle to unwind year after year tend to keep their distance from newcomers. This works out very well within the overall peaceful ambiance which the owners carefully cultivate for all their guests. No one from outside the hotel is admitted to the bar, the pool, or the private beach. The garden, an important part of the pleasant experience of the hotel, is well kept and has flowers blooming year-round. Meals are prepared with fresh vegetables from the garden, and menus are submitted to the guests the day before for selection.

How to get there *(Map 19): 57km southeast of Latina via S148 to Terracina, then S213 to Sperlonga.*

Hotel Borgo Paraelios

Valle Collicchia
02040 Poggio Mirteto Scalo (Rieti)
Tel. 0765-26 267 - Fax 0765-26 268 - Sig. Salabe
E-mail: borgo@fabaris.it

Category ★★★★★ **Rooms** 13 and 2 suites with air-conditioning, telephone, bath or shower, WC, TV. **Price** single 350,000L, double 450,000L, junior suite 550,000L. **Meals** Breakfast included, served 8:30-10:30 - half board 670,000L. (per 2 pers.). **Restaurant** Service 1:00PM-3:00PM, 8:00PM-10:30PM - mealtime specials 110-130,000L, also à la carte - Italian cuisine. **Credit cards** All major **Pets** Dogs allowed (with extra charge). **Facilities** 2 swimming pools (1 indoor), tennis, sauna, parking, private bus to the station or airport, parking. **Nearby** Roma – Colle dei Tetti golf course (9-hole). **Open** All year.

The Borgo Paraelios is amazing: there are few rooms but many salons of all sizes. It is, above all, a haven of elegance in the Roman countryside. The sumptuous decor of this splendid house compares favorably with the luxury level typically found in palaces. There are very beautiful furnishings and paintings in every room, including the garden-level rooms. Try your best billiard shots under the stony gaze of Roman emperors carved in marble. This place is quiet, luxurious, exquisite.

How to get there *(Map 14): 40km north of Rome via A1, Fiano Romano exit - until S4 to Passo Corese, S313, Poggio Mirteto, towards Cantalupo Terni to km17,6.*

Hotel Lord Byron

00197 Roma
Via G. de Notaris, 5
Tel. 06-322 04 04 - Fax 06-322 04 05 - Sig. Ottaviani
E-mail: info@lordbyronhotel.com - Web: www.lordbyronhotel.com

Category ★★★★★ **Rooms** 37 with air-conditioning, telephone, bath, WC, TV, safe, minibar –
Elevator. **Price** Double 440-695,000L, suite 950-1 650,000L. **Meals** Breakfast (buffet) included,
served 7:00-10:30. **Restaurant** Service 12:30PM-3:00PM, 8:00PM-10:30PM - closed Sun except for
residents - à la carte - Seasonal cooking. **Credit cards** All major. **Pets** Small dogs allowed by
reservation with extra charge. **Facilities** Parking (40-50,000L). **Nearby** Castelli Romani: Aldobrandini
villa and gardens at Frascati, Tusculum, Abbey of Grottaferrata, Piazza della Repubblica (Bernini) at
Ariccia - Tivoli (bus from station): Villa d'Este and Villa Adriana (6km before arriving at Tivoli) -
Palestrina - Anagni – Acquasanta golf course, (18-hole); Golf ad Olgiata, Rome, (9- and 18-
hole). **Open** All year.

The Lord Byron is located in the heart of the Parioli district–the most
fashinable in Rome–facing the Villa Borghese gardens. Amadeo Ottaviani,
the owner, has given it a high-style look. Thick luxurious carpeting, capacious
white armchairs bearing the initials of the hotel, lacquered white ceilings,
sumptuous bouquets and many other details reflect his taste for perfection. The
Relais du Jardin restaurant is popular with Romans, who come for the fine
dining and the lovely decor. Spend some time at the bar; your companion
might turn out to be a countess.

How to get there *(Map 14): Near the Galleria Nazionale d'Arte Moderna -
and the Villa Borghese gardens.*

Hotel Giulio Cesare

00192 Roma
Via degli Scipioni, 287
Tel. 06-321 07 51 - Fax 06-321 17 36 - Sig. Pandolfi
E-mail: giulioce@uni.net - Web: www.travel.giulioce/giulioce.html

Category ★★★★ **Rooms** 90 with air-conditioning, telephone, bath, WC, satellite TV, minibar – Elevator. **Price** Single 440,000L, double 540,000L. **Meals** Breakfast included (buffet), served 7:00-10:30. **Restaurant** See pp. 520-523. **Credit cards** All major. **Pets** Dogs not allowed. **Facilities** Parking. **Nearby** Castelli Romani: Aldobrandini villa and gardens at Frascati, Tusculum, Abbey of Grottaferrata, Piazza della Repubblica (Bernini) at Ariccia - Tivoli (bus from station): Villa d'Este and Villa Adriana (6km before arriving at Tivoli) - Palestrina - Anagni – Acquasanta golf course, (18-hole); Golf ad Olgiata, Rome (9- and 18-hole). **Open** All year.

An atmosphere of elegance pervades this large hotel, the former residence of Countess Solari. Antique furniture, rugs, and tapestries give the rooms a feeling of well-being and comfort. Breakfast is served in the garden as soon as the weather permits. You may want to spend some time there, as it is one of the most charming parts of this lovely hotel.

How to get there *(Map 14): Near the Piazza del Popolo.*

Hotel d'Inghilterra

00187 Roma
Via Bocca di Leone, 14
Tel. 06-699 811 - Fax 06-679 86 01 - Sig. Sarlo
E-mail: reservation_hir@charminghotels.it - Web: www.charminghotels.it/inghilterra

Category ★★★★ **Rooms** 86 and 12 suites with air-conditioning, telephone, bath, WC, TV, minibar – Elevator. **Price** Single 370-620,000L, double 490-730,000L, suite 780-1 235,000L. **Meals** Breakfast 40,000L, served 7:30-10:30. **Restaurant** Service 12:30PM-3:00PM, 7:30PM-10:30PM - mealtime specials 70-100,000L, also à la carte - New italian cuisine. **Credit cards** All major. **Pets** Dogs not allowed. **Nearby** Castelli Romani: Aldobrandini villa and gardens at Frascati, Tusculum, Abbey of Grottaferrata, Piazza della Repubblica (Bernini) at Ariccia - Tivoli (bus from station): Villa d'Este and Villa Adriana (6km before arriving at Tivoli) - Palestrina - Anagni – Acquasanta golf course, (18-hole); Golf ad Olgiata, Rome (9- and 18-hole). **Open** All year.

Anatole France, Franz Liszt, and Felix Mendelssohn have all stayed at the Hotel d'Inghilterra, a first-class grand hotel and a favorite among celebrities all over the world. It is on a pedestrian cul-de-sac near the Piazza di Spagna, and has recently been carefully restored. The lobby is superb, done in black and white marble, with stucco columns decorated with white palm trees. The salon is decorated with both antique and contemporary furniture, oriental rugs, and marvelous Neapolitan gouache paintings. The rooms are all excellent, but if you want to have the rare pleasure of breakfast overlooking the rooftops of Rome, ask for ones with a terrace on the top floor. Room service is available for light meals. The service is impeccable.

How to get there (Map 14): Near the Piazza di Spagna.

Hotel Raphaël

00186 Roma
Largo Febo, 2
Tel. 06-68 28 31 - Fax 06-68 78 993 - Sig. Vannoni
E-mail: info@raphaelhotel.com - Web: www.raphaelhotel.com

Category ★★★★ **Rooms** 69 with air-conditioning, telephone, bath, WC, TV (7 with terrace) – Elevator. **Price** Single 435-480,000L, double 650-695,000L, deluxe 825-865,000L, suite 990-1 100,000L. **Meals** Breakfast (buffet) 25-37,000L, served 7:00-10:30. **Restaurant** "Relais Picasso", service 12:30PM-2:30PM, 7:30PM-10:30PM - closed Sun - à la carte - Or see pp. 520-523. **Credit cards** All major. **Pets** Dogs allowed. **Facilities** Sauna, Fitness center. **Nearby** Castelli Romani: Aldobrandini villa and gardens at Frascati, Tusculum, Abbey of Grottaferrata, Piazza della Repubblica (Bernini) at Ariccia - Tivoli (bus from station): Villa d'Este and Villa Adriana (6km before arriving at Tivoli) – Palestrina - Anagni – Acquasanta golf course, (18-hole); Golf ad Olgiata, Rome (9- and 18-hole). **Open** All year.

The Raphaël is one of the best-known hotels in Rome, frequently playing host to international events and world-famous people. It is ideally located, just near the Piazza Navona. Its rooms are all comfortable but some of the bathrooms have not yet been renovated, as some clients have learned to their regret. However, the rooms of "luxury" category have been redone, with furniture of exceptional quality and wonderful decoration by a Venetian artist. Lunch and dinner can be taken at the Relais Picasoon, and snacks are available at any time. In summer, dinners are held for hotel guests (by reservation only) on the marvelous panoramic terrace.

How to get there *(Map 14): Near the Piazza Navona.*

Hotel Sole Al Pantheon

00186 Roma
Piazza della Rotonda, 63
Tel. 06-678 04 41 - Fax 06-699 406 89
E-mail: hotsole@flashnet.it - Web: www.hotelsolealpantheon.com

Category ★★★★ **Rooms** 26 with air-conditioning, telephone, bath or shower, WC, TV, minibar –
Elevator. **Price** Single 400,000L, double 600,000L, suite 650-700,000L. **Meals** Breakfast included,
served 7:00-11:00. **Restaurant** See pp. 520-523. **Credit cards** All major. **Pets** Dogs not allowed.
Facilities Parking (+35-45,000L). **Nearby** Castelli Romani: Aldobrandini villa and gardens at
Frascati, Tusculum, Abbey of Grottaferrata, Piazza della Repubblica (Bernini) at Ariccia - Tivoli (bus
from station): Villa d'Este and Villa Adriana (6km before arriving at Tivoli) - Palestrina - Anagni –
Acquasanta golf course, (18-hole); Golf ad Olgiata, Rome (9- and 18-hole). **Open** All year.

This hotel, picturesquely located on the Piazza della Rotonda facing the
Pantheon, has recently been completely renovated, with special care taken
to preserving its old world charm. There are only twenty-six rooms, all very
comfortable (request a quiet back room). Each one bears the name of a
celebrity who stayed there, among them Jean-Paul Sartre, who was a regular.
The bathrooms are particularly well-equipped. A whirlpool bath can be a real
delight after a day out and about in Rome. In addition to the list of restaurants
we recommend at the end of this guidebook, try the little trattorias on the
square, where on summer evenings you can dine very pleasantly just across
from the Pantheon, Imperial Rome's best-preserved monument.

How to get there *(Map 14): In front of the Pantheon.*

Hotel dei Mellini

00193 Roma
Via Muzzio Clementi, 81
Tel. 06-324 771 - Fax 06-324 77 801 - Sig. Daniel N. Barr
E-mail: info@hotelmellini.com - Web: www.hotelmellini.com

Rooms 80 with air-conditioning, telephone, bath or shower, satellite TV, minibar, safe, fax, PC connexion – Wheelchair access, elevator, no smoking floor. **Price** Single 430,000L, double 530,000L, suite 800-1 320,000L. **Meals** Breakfast included (buffet), served 6:30-10:30. **No restaurant** But snacks via room service (see our selection of restaurants, pp. 520-523). **Credit cards** All major. **Pets** Dogs not allowed. **Facilities** Roof garden, Garage (35,000L). **Nearby** Castelli Romani: Aldobrandini villa and gardens at Frascati, Tusculum, Abbey of Grottaferrata, Piazza della Repubblica (Bernini) at Ariccia - Tivoli (bus from station): Villa d'Este and Villa Adriana (6km before arriving at Tivoli) - Palestrina - Anagni – Acquasanta golf course, (18-hole); Golf ad Olgiata, Rome (9- and 18-hole). **Open** All year.

The hotel is situated in the district near Castel Sant'Angelo, that is to say near to St Peter's Basilica and, on the right bank of the Tiber, the Piazza del Popolo. It has recently been completely restructured and redecorated in a 19th-century building; the restoration suggests a fine, luxurious modern apartment rather than a hotel, with lots of furniture, objets d'art and paintings giving a very distinctive, personal atmosphere. The décor conjures up in a stylized way that of the Thirties and Forties, with a selection of very warm colors and materials. The same elegant comfort is to be found in the rooms and bathrooms. The American Bar is a pleasant place for a drink on returning to the hotel at the end of the day. The service is very prompt, attentive and courteous. A good hotel.

How to get there *(Map 14): Near Castel Sant'Angelo.*

Hotel Carriage

00187 Roma
Via delle Carrozze, 36
Tel. 06-699 01 24 - Fax 06-678 82 79
Sig. Jean Piero Cau

Category ★★★ **Rooms** 24 with air-conditioning, telephone, bath, WC, TV, minibar – Elevator. **Price** Single 320,000L, double 430,000L, triple 540,000L, suite 620,000L. **Meals** Breakfast included, served 7:00-11:00. **Restaurant** See pp. 520-523. **Credit cards** All major. **Pets** Dogs not allowed. **Nearby** Castelli Romani: Aldobrandini villa and gardens at Frascati, Tusculum, Abbey of Grottaferrata, Piazza della Repubblica (Bernini) at Ariccia - Tivoli (bus from station): Villa d'Este and Villa Adriana (6km before arriving at Tivoli) - Palestrina - Anagni – Acquasanta golf course, (18-hole); Golf ad Olgiata, Rome, (9- and 18-hole). **Open** All year.

The Carriage is a small hotel in the heart of a quarter where many of the capital's luxury boutiques are located, near the Piazza di Spagna. The entry, the salon, and the ground-floor breakfast room all have an elegant 18th-century decor. The rooms are comfortable, and air-conditioned, which means you won't hear street noise. If you make your reservation in time, ask for Rooms 501 or 601, which are on a terrace with a beautiful view of the rooftops of the Eternal City. Even if you don't get these rooms, you can still have breakfast on the terrace. The suites accommodate up to four people.

How to get there *(Map 14): Near the Piazza di Spagna.*

Mecenate Palace Hotel

00185 Roma
Via Carlo Alberto, 3
Tel. 06-44 70 20 24 - Fax 06-44 61 354 - Sig.ra Capuzzo
E-mail: info@mecenatepalace.com - Web: www.mecenatepalace.com

Category ★★★★ **Rooms** 62 with air-conditioning (5 no smoking), telephone, bath, WC, satellite TV, minibar, safe – Elevator. **Price** Single 500,000L, double 680,000L, triple 820,000L, suite 1 200,000L. **Meals** Breakfast included, served 7:00-10:00. **Restaurant** See pp. 520-523. **Credit cards** All major. **Pets** Small dogs allowed. **Facilities** Garage (45,000L). **Nearby** Castelli Romani: Aldobrandini villa and gardens at Frascati, Tusculum, Abbey of Grottaferrata, Piazza della Repubblica (Bernini) at Ariccia - Tivoli (bus from station): Villa d'Este and Villa Adriana (6km before arriving at Tivoli) - Palestrina - Anagni – Acquasanta golf course, (18-hole); Golf ad Olgiata, Rome, (9- and 18-hole). **Open** All year.

Situated near the Termini railroad station and facing the church of Santa Maria Maggiore, the Mecenate has just emerged as a luxury hotel after a long renovation. The owner's aim was to give the hotel the atmosphere of a private apartment. This is particularly true for the three suites, each of which is named after a Roman poet: Horace, Virgil and Propertius. One touch, for example, is the kettle in your room, where you can make a cup of tea and relax in your room before going out to dinner; another is the jacuzzi in the suites. The decoration is elegant and meticulous and the marble bathrooms are spacious. Half the rooms have a view of the church. The hotel restaurant, the Terrazza dei Papi, is only open for functions, but still serves as a dining room for breakfast. A nice spot to know, lacking until now in this neighborhood.

How to get there *(Map 14): Near the rail station (stazione Termini). La via Carlo Alberto is on the piazza Santa Maria Maggiore.*

Hotel Villa Grazioli

00199 Roma
Via Salaria, 241
Tel. 06-841 65 87 - Fax 06-841 33 85
Sig. Gianpaolo Italo

Category ★★★ **Rooms** 30 with air-conditioning, telephone, bath or shower, WC, satellite TV, minibar – Elevator. **Price** Single 250,000L, double 315,000L. **Meals** Breakfast included, served 7:00-10:30. **Restaurant** See pp. 520-523. **Credit cards** All major. **Pets** Small dogs allowed. **Facilities** Parking. **Nearby** Castelli Romani: Aldobrandini villa and gardens at Frascati, Tusculum, Abbey of Grottaferrata, Piazza della Repubblica (Bernini) at Ariccia - Tivoli (bus from station): Villa d'Este and Villa Adriana (6km before arriving at Tivoli) - Palestrina - Anagni – Acquasanta golf course, (18-hole); Golf ad Olgiata, Rome, (9- and 18-hole). **Open** All year.

The building that houses the Villa Grazioli was constructed very recently on the ancient Via Salaria, in the Parioloi green zone, near the parks of the Villa Borghese and the Villa Ada (note that the Borghese Museum has reopened after a complete restoration lasting several years). This district, though very central, is relatively calm, making it pleasant to return here after a full day of visits and shopping. The thirty rooms are not very large but well and comfortably equipped, decorated with ostentation and supplied with fine marble bathrooms. The reception, the adjoining little salon and the breakfast room are equally elegant. A free, private garage is also an advantage not to be overlooked.

How to get there *(Map 14): Near Villa Borghese.*

Hotel Gregoriana

00187 Roma
Via Gregoriana, 18
Tel. 06-679 42 69 - Fax 06-678 42 58
Sig. Panier-Bagat

Category ★★★ **Rooms** 19 with air-conditioning, telephone, bath or shower, WC, TV, minibar – Elevator. **Price** Single 230,000L, double 380,000L. **Meals** Breakfast included, served 7:00-11:00. **Restaurant** See pp. 520-523. **Credit cards** Not accepted **Pets** Dogs allowed (with extra charge). **Nearby** Castelli Romani: Aldobrandini villa and gardens at Frascati, Tusculum, Abbey of Grottaferrata, Piazza della Repubblica (Bernini) at Ariccia - Tivoli (bus from station): Villa d'Este and Villa Adriana (6km before arriving at Tivoli) - Palestrina - Anagni – Acquasanta golf course, (18-hole); Golf ad Olgiata, Rome, (9- and 18-hole). **Open** All year.

The Via Gregoriana is in an ideal spot: just above the Spanish Steps, near the church of Trinita dei Monti. Fortunately, though, the street is a quiet one, which adds to the intimate atmosphere of the hotel. We don't much care for the decor, which is a mixture of Art Deco and Liberty with a touch of exotica, but it is quiet and comfortable, and some of the rooms have a nice view over the rooftops of Rome. What does make this hotel stand out is the warmth with which you are welcomed as soon as you arrive and the attentiveness of the staff throughout your stay. You are instantly made to feel like a privileged guest, which explains the loyalty of the clientele and hence, the need to reserve your rooms well in advance.

How to get there *(Map 14): From Piazza di Spagna ascend the Spanish Steps.*

Hotel Locarno

00186 Roma
Via della Penna, 22
Tel. 06-36 10 841 - Fax 06-32 15 249 - Sig.ra Celli
E-mail: info@hotellocarno.com - Web: www.vhotellocarno.com

Category ★★★ **Rooms** 60 and 6 apartments with air-conditioning, telephone, bath or shower, WC, satellite TV, safe, minibar — Elevator, 2 rooms for disabled persons. **Price** Single 240-290,000L, double 360-450,000L, suite 600,000L, apartment (3-4 pers.) for 1 day per pers. 260,000L. **Meals** Breakfast included, served 7:00-11:00. **Restaurant** See pp. 520-523. **Credit cards** All major. **Pets** Dogs not allowed. **Facilities** Bikes. **Nearby** Castelli Romani: Aldobrandini villa and gardens at Frascati, Tusculum, Abbey of Grottaferrata, Piazza della Repubblica (Bernini) at Ariccia - Tivoli (bus from station): Villa d'Este and Villa Adriana (6km before arriving at Tivoli) - Palestrina - Anagni — Acquasanta golf course, (18-hole); Golf ad Olgiata, Rome, (9- and 18-hole). **Open** All year.

Right in the center of Rome, just a few steps from the Piazza del Popolo, the Hotel Locarno offers attractive rooms, all renovated and furnished in an antique style, with bathrooms decorated with pretty, handmade tiles. In a small palazzo just across the street there are several apartments for rent by the week, complete with hotel services. In the summer, breakfast is served under large white sun umbrellas on the ground floor patio-terrace. This also doubles as a bar open until midnight. In the winter, you can sit before a roaring fire in the large living room fireplace. There is also a terrace with a bar that affords a wonderful view of Rome. The welcome is always charming, the prices reasonable and the location excellent. All in all, a pleasant place to stay.

How to get there *(Map 14): Next to the Piazza del Popolo.*

Teatro di Pompeo

00186 Roma
Largo del Pallaro, 8
Tel. 06-872 812 - Fax 06-880 55 31
Sig. Mignoni

Category ★★★ **Rooms** 12 with air-conditioning, telephone, bath or shower, WC, TV, safe, minibar – Elevator. **Price** Single 270,000L, double 350,000L. **Meals** Breakfast included, served 7:00-10:00. **Restaurant** See pp. 520-523. **Credit cards** All major. **Pets** Dogs allowed. **Nearby** Castelli Romani: Aldobrandini villa and gardens at Frascati, Tusculum, Abbey of Grottaferrata, Piazza della Repubblica (Bernini) at Ariccia - Tivoli (bus from station): Villa d'Este and Villa Adriana (6km before arriving at Tivoli) - Palestrina - Anagni – Acquasanta golf course, (18-hole); Golf ad Olgiata, Rome, (9- and 18-hole). **Open** All year.

If you are looking for a quiet but centrally located hotel for your Roman vacation, this is the place. Located right in the heart of Rome, with its back to the Campo dei Fiori and close to the Piazza Navona, the hotel is on a quiet little square. All of the rooms, under the roof, have sloping ceilings, and half of them open onto the square. Though the decor is simple, the size of the hotel makes it a warm friendly place, with the charm of an old-fashioned pensione (plus modern conveniences). The adjoining restaurant "Costanza" is independent of the hotel and serves fine cuisine. The arched ruins of the old theatre of Pompeii, inaugurated in the year 55 B.C. provide the decor. The service is discreet but efficient.

How to get there *(Map 14): Near Piazza Campo dei Fiori and the church of S. Andrea della Valle.*

Hotel Sant' Anselmo

00153 Roma
Piazza Sant' Anselmo, 2
Tel. 06-574 35 47 - Reservation: 06-574 52 32/31 - Fax 06-578 36 04/574 11 12
Sig.ra R. Piroli - Web: www.aventinohotels.com

Category ★★★ **Rooms** 45 with telephone, bath or shower, WC, TV. **Price** Single 210,000L, double
320,000L. **Meals** Breakfast included, served 7:00-10:30. **Restaurant** See pp. 520-523. **Credit cards**
All major. **Pets** Dogs not allowed. **Facilities** Parking. **Nearby** Castelli Romani: Aldobrandini villa and
gardens at Frascati, Tusculum, Abbey of Grottaferrata, Piazza della Repubblica (Bernini) at Ariccia -
Tivoli (bus from station): Villa d'Este and Villa Adriana (6km before arriving at Tivoli) - Palestrina -
Anagni – Acquasanta golf course, (18-hole); Golf ad Olgiata, Rome, (9- and 18-hole). **Open** All year.

Already prized in antiquity for its quiet (the Romans built their thermal
baths here) Aventino Hill is a haven of tranquility from the summer heat
of Rome even today. There are three old patrician houses there, submerged in
verdant shaded alleyways, which are hotels. The S. Anselmo and the Villa
S. Pio are right next door to each other, and the Aventino is nearby. There is
one reservation number for all three hotels; ask for the first or second one. The
rooms are small and could benefit from a little more attention, but they are
comfortable and not without charm. The upper rooms overlooking the whole
south side of the town are the nicest ones. Breakfast is simple, but served in a
cool interior garden. This is one of the rare places in Rome with quiet,
elegance, and reasonable prices.

How to get there *(Map 14): Near Termal of Cracalla.*

Hotel Villa del Parco

00161 Roma
Via Nomentana, 110
Tel. 06-442 377 73 - Fax 06-442 375 72 - Famiglia Bernardini
E-mail: villaparco@mclink.it - Web: www.venere.it/roma/villaparco

Category ★★★ **Rooms** 31 with air-conditioning, telephone, bath or shower, WC, TV, minibar –
Elevator, 2 rooms with wheelchair access. **Price** Single 190 (weekend)-225,000L, double 250
(weekend)-290,000L, triple 295 (weekend)-325,000L. **Meals** Breakfast included, served 7:00-10:30.
Restaurant See pp. 520-523. **Credit cards** All major. **Pets** Dogs allowed. **Facilities** Parking
(15,000L). **Nearby** Castelli Romani: Aldobrandini villa and gardens at Frascati, Tusculum, Abbey of
Grottaferrata, Piazza della Repubblica (Bernini) at Ariccia - Tivoli (bus from station): Villa d'Este and
Villa Adriana (6km before arriving at Tivoli) - Palestrina - Anagni – Acquasanta golf course, (18-hole):
Golf ad Olgiata, Rome, (9- and 18-hole). **Open** All year.

This beautiful turn-of-the-century house, with its gracefully fading pink
façade, is located in a quiet residential quarter, a twenty-minute walk from
the Via Veneto, just outside of the historic district. The shady trees in the little
garden and the park nearby keep it cool in the summertime. You will like the
series of small salons (several in the basement remind one of similar rooms
you might find in London), the small bar tucked into an alcove, and the tables
under the trees where you can have tea and light snacks. This will quickly
become your Rome home-away-from-home. Redecoration has been somewhat
in the English style. The rooms each have an individual character. The most
attractive are 5, 7, 12, and 22.

***How to get there** (Map 14): North of Rome, next to the Porta Bologna.*

Pensione Scalinata di Spagna

00187 Roma
Piazza Trinita dei Monti, 17
Tel. 06-69 94 08 96 - Fax 06-69 94 05 98 - Sig. Bellia
E-mail: info@hotelscalinata.com - Web: www.hotelscalinata.com

Category ★★★ **Rooms** 16 with air-conditioning, telephone, bath or shower, WC, TV, safe, minibar.
Price Single 450,000L, double 550,000L, triple 650,000L, suite (4-5 pers.) 1 100,000L. **Meals**
Breakfast included, served 7:30-11:00. **Restaurant** See pp. 520-523. **Credit cards** All major.
Pets Dogs allowed. **Nearby** Castelli Romani: Aldobrandini villa and gardens at Frascati, Tusculum,
Abbey of Grottaferrata, Piazza della Repubblica (Bernini) at Ariccia - Tivoli (bus from station): Villa
d'Este and Villa Adriana (6km before arriving at Tivoli) - Palestrina - Anagni – Acquasanta golf
course, (18-hole); Golf ad Olgiata, Rome, (9- and 18-hole). **Open** All year.

Near the chic shopping streets of the city and famous Spanish steps, this
intimate and elegant little hotel has a location every bit as good as its
luxurious neighbor, the Hassler Medici. The rooms which have just been
completely refurbished are comfortable, with air-conditioning (indispensable
in summer) and tasteful decoration. A terrace affords a fine view over the
rooftops of Rome, many of which have their own little terraces. You will find
a courteous welcome and attentive service. In short, for a pleasant stay in the
Eternal City, this is one of the best addresses to be found.

How to get there (Map 14): Up the stairs of the Piazza di Spagna.

Hotel Pensione Parlamento

00187 Roma
Via delle Convertite, 5
Tel. 06-679 20 82/699 41 697 - Fax 06-699 21 000
Plinio Chini - Daniela Ciarri Chini - E-mail: hotelparlamento@galactica.it

Rooms 23 (17 with air-conditioning) with telephone, bath or shower, WC, satellite TV, safe – Elevator.
Price Single 160-170,000L, double 190-220,000L. **Meals** Breakfast included, served 7:30-10:00.
restaurant See pp. 520-523. **Credit cards** Amex, Visa, Eurocard, MasterCard. **Pets** Small dogs
allowed. **Nearby** Castelli Romani: Aldobrandini villa and gardens at Frascati, Tusculum, Abbey of
Grottaferrata, Piazza della Repubblica (Bernini) at Ariccia - Tivoli (bus from station): Villa d'Este and
Villa Adriana (6km before arriving at Tivoli) - Palestrina - Anagni – Acquasanta golf course, (18-hole);
Golf ad Olgiata, Rome, (9- and 18-hole). **Open** All year.

Situated in the district of Piazza di Spagna, this former guest house which
owes its name to the proximity of the parliament building, has charm
despite the fact that its fixtures and fittings tend towards the practical and the
functional. Occupying the third and fourth floors of an apartment block, it
enjoys those roof terraces that we all dream about. In the fine weather, if you
want the good fortune to get the room with terrace, reserve number 108; but
don't worry too much if it is already taken, because number 110 is also very
pleasant, spacious and light. Moreover, there are still another 21 where you can
enjoy a very agreeable stay, with another terrace where you can go and have a
drink. The management is exemplary and the whole is personalized by some
interesting prints and a few pieces of antique furniture. For Rome (and for this
district) the prices are reasonable.

How to get there *(Map 14): Near Piazza di Spagna.*

Park Hotel Villa Grazioli

00046 Grottaferrata (Roma)
Tel. 06-94 54 001 - Fax 06-94 13 506 - Sig. Rolf Rampf
E-mail: info@villagrazioli.com - Web: www.villagrazioli.com

Rooms 58 with air-conditioning, bath, satellite TV, minibar, safe – Elevator, wheelchair access. **Price** Single 330-370,000L, double 390-430,000L, suite 700-800,000L. **Meals** Breakfast included, served 7:00-10:00 - half board +70,000L, full board +120,000L (per pers.). **Restaurant** Service 12:30PM-2:30PM, 8:00PM-10:30PM - mealtime specials 75,000L (local wine included). **Credit cards** All major. **Pets** Dogs allowed. **Facilities** Shuttle to Roma and Fiumicino; parking. **Nearby** Castelli Romani: Aldobrandini villa and gardens at Frascati, Tusculum, Abbey of Grottaferrata, Piazza della Repubblica (Bernini) at Ariccia - Tivoli (bus from station): Villa d'Este and Villa Adriana (6km before arriving at Tivoli) - Palestrina - Anagni – Acquasanta golf course, (18-hole); Golf ad Olgiata, Rome, (9- and 18-hole). **Open** All year.

The Castelli Romani refers to the collection of villages perched on the Alban Hills which overlook the vineyards of the Roman campagna to the southeast of Rome. People have always come to these hills, a mere ten kilometers from the capital, to seek cool and calm in summer, as the Pope's annual summer retreat to Castelgandolfo reminds us. The historic Villa Grazioli dates from the 16th Century and was also built for this purpose. Following a superb restoration of the house and garden, it has now become a hotel, offering its residents a lesson in art history with (in particular) some especially magnificent frescoes in the Stanza di Eliseo and still more in the Galleria del Pannini. The rooms are situated on the upper floor. They are comfortable and quite luxurious, almost all having a view across the campagna which is enhanced in the evening by an exceptional golden light.

How to get there (Map 14): 10km southeast of Roma by Via Tuscolana towards Frascati; on the raccordo anulare take the Napoli exit to exit 21-22 for Frascati. At Frascati, follow the signs (the hotel is between Frascati and Grottaferrata).

Hotel Ristorante Adriano

Villa Adriana 00010 Tivoli (Roma)
Via di Villa Adriana, 194
Tel. 0774-38 22 35 / 53 5028 - Fax 0774-53 51 22
Famiglia Cinelli

Rooms 7 and 3 suites with air-conditioning, telephone, bath or shower, WC, TV, minibar. **Price** Double 180-220,000L, suites 270,000L. **Meals** Breakfast included, served 8:30-10:00. **Restaurant** Service 12:30PM and 8:00PM - à la carte 70-80,000L. **Credit cards** All major. **Pets** Dogs not allowed. **Facilities** Tennis, parking. **Nearby** Tivoli: duomo, Villa Adriana, Villa d'Este, Villa Gregoriana - Roma. **Open** All year.

Hadrian's Villa, always a tourist highlight, then immortalized by Marguerite Yourcenar's excellent book, has become a must for all visitors to Rome. If you are among these visitors, why not spend a night (or more) at the Adriano, just next to Hadrian's Villa and then take the opportunity also to visit the Villa d'Este and the Villa Gregoriana, both at Tivoli, only six kilometers away. You will never regret either the visit or the hotel: the lovely gardens with their bubbling fountains and waterfalls that inspired Fragonard, Hubert Robert, Corot and even Maurice Ravel, and the hotel-restaurant, both comfortable and gastronomic. It is a beautiful fuschia-colored building standing on a broad lawn shaded by palms and cypress trees. The room are upstairs. Luxurious rather than charming, they are very comfortable and some even have a view of the ancient walls of the famous neighbor. The restaurant is decorated with great elegance, and the white walls beautifully set off the 19th-century furniture and the fine china and crystal on the tables. Excellent cuisine prepared by Gabriella, in charge of the kitchen, and Patrizia, who does the sweets and pastries. Umberto offers a kind and thoughtful welcome. A fine place for a Roman holiday.

How to get there (Map 14): 36km from Rome, 6km before Tivoli.

La Posta Vecchia

Ladispoli 00055 Palo Laziale (Roma)
Tel. 06-994-95 01 - Fax 06-994 95 07
Sig. Harry Charles Mills Sció
E-mail: info@postavecchia.com - Web: www.lapostavecchia.com

Rooms 10 and 8 suites with air-conditioning, telephone, bath, satellite TV, safe - Elevator. **Price** Standard 775,000L, superieur 990,000L, junior suite 1 600,000L, senior suite 2 200,000L, master suite 2 400,000L. **Meals** Breakfast included, served 8:00-10:00. **Credit cards** All major. **Pets** Dogs not allowed. **Restaurant** Service 1:00PM-3:00PM, 8:00PM-10:00PM - mealtime specials 150,000L - Specialties: Fish. **Facilities** Covered swimming pool, parking. **Nearby** Tivoli: duomo, Villa Adriana, Villa d'Este, Villa Gregoriana - Roma. **Open** Mar – Nov.

Some thirty kilometers from Rome, overlooking the Mediterranean, Prince Odelscalchi's former palazzo (15th Century), became a post stage then the property of John-Paul Getty – and it still inspires dreams. After it had been purchased by a Swiss company, it was handed over to a decorator who was instructed to preserve Mr Getty's sumptuous, historical fixtures and fittings, not least a a little museum that he created with the illustrious Frederico Zero in the course of excavations in the cellars of the palazzo to uncover the Roman remains. Nowadays the rooms and bathrooms are marvellously refined and the suites are true apartments, like the Castello, where the drawing-room walls are decorated with a delightful collection of small pictures of great Roman houses. In the restaurant, the chef, Pino Redaelli, will ensure moments to remember, especially when the food is being served on the terrace above the sea.

How to get there *(Map 14): 37km northwest of Rome by SS1 towards Aurelia then Ladispoli.*

Villa Vignola

Vignola 66054 Vasto (Chieti)
Corso Vannucci, 97
Tel. 0873-31 00 50 - Fax 0873-31 00 60
Sig. Mazzetti

Category ★★★★ **Rooms** 5 with air-conditioning, telephone, bath and shower, WC, TV, minibar.
Price Single 160,000L, double 280,000L. **Meals** Breakfast included, served 7:30-10:30. **Restaurant**
Service 12:30PM-2:30PM, 7:30PM-10:30PM - mealtime specials 75,000L, also à la carte - Specialties:
Seafood. **Credit cards** All major. **Pets** Dogs allowed (with extra charge). **Facilities** Parking. **Nearby**
Vasto (3km). **Open** All year.

The Villa Vignola is a very intimate place, scaled for a limited clientele, as there are only five rooms and about ten tables. You can see the sea from the rooms and the terraces through a multitude of trees growing close to the beach. The place has the air of a private vacation house on the beach. The cozy salon, the small number of rooms, and their intimate, elegant decor certainly have a lot to do with this effect. This is a great place to come for a rest.

How to get there *(Map 16): 74km south of Pescara via A14, Vasto exit, then towards Porto di Vasto (6km north of Vasto).*

Country Club Rinaldone

01100 Viterbo
Strada Rinaldone, 9
Tel. 0761-35 21 37 - Fax 0761-35 31 16 - M. Lamani
E-mail: rinaldone@hesnet.net - Web: www.touring.it/rinaldone

Rooms 20 with telephone, bath or shower, TV, minibar. **Price** Single 95-110,000L, double 130-160,000L, suite +10,000L. **Meals** Breakfast 10,000L, served 8:30-10:00 - half board: 105-120,000L (per pers., 2 days min.). **Restaurant** Service 12:30PM-2:30PM, 8:00PM-10:00PM - mealtime specials, also à la carte 30-35,000L - Italian cuisine. **Credit cards** Visa, Eurocard, MasterCard. **Pets** Dogs allowed. **Facilities** Swimming pool, mountain bike, tennis, garage and parking. **Nearby** Viterbo and the Etruscan country - Santa Maria della Quercia - Bagnaia: Villa Lantea - Ferentium: Etruscan ruins - Bomarzo "The Saced Wood" (7:00PM to 8:00PM) - Lake of Bolsena - Lago di Vico - Caprarola: Farnese Palace. **Closed** Jan and Feb.

The Sabine women famously carried off by the Romans came from the region of Viterbo and it may be from that time that dates the proverb naming the town as one of beautiful women and beautiful fountains... The Second World War spared the historic center inside the ramparts. The inn is in the country, north of the town, on a 180 ha estate. The atmosphere is that of a country club with comfortably rustic fittings. The rooms also have a rural décor with brick walls preserved in places and regional furniture. Etruscan remains have been discovered in the restaurant, situated in the oldest of the buildings, and this offers an added attraction for diners. The Rinaldone, 80km from Rome, is a good overnight stopping place or even a pleasant place for a longer stay from which one can visit the medieval town and the amazing monster park of Bomarzo, a symbolic wonderland inhabited by strange sculptures.

How to get there *(Map 14): 3km north of Viterbo. The hotel is on SS Cassia, at kilometer sign 86.*

Hotel Royal

01023 Bolsena (Viterbo)
Piazzale D. Alghieri, 8/10
Tel. 761-79 70 48/49 - Fax 0761-79 60 00
Sig. Paolo Equitani
E-mail: info@atihotels.it - Web: www.atihotels.it

Rooms 37 with air-conditioning, telephone, shower, satellite TV, minibar, safe – Elevator, wheelchair access. **Price** Single 115-175,000L, double 165-255,000L, suite 205-315,000L. **Meals** Breakfast (buffet) 18,000L, served 7:30-10:00. **Restaurant** See p. 524. **Credit cards** Visa, Eurocard, MasterCard. **Pets** Dogs not allowed. **Facilities** Swimming pool, parking. **Nearby** Orvieto - Lago di Bolsena and Etruscan country: Chiusi, Pitigliano, Sorano and Sovana - Isola Bisentina (palazzo Farnese and church by antonio Sangallo the younger) - Chapels on Monte Tabor (frescoes) - Montefiascone - Viterbo. **Open** All year.

Bolsena, on the northeast shore of the lake that bears its name, is the heart of ancient Etruria. Though archeological exploration has not so far discovered the site of the great Etruscan sanctuary to the goddess Voltumna, the surroundings are rich in grottoes and other remains. Another nearby Italian cultural treasure is the private island of Bisentina, former summer residence of the Popes. The hotel, situated by the dark waters of the lake, is the oldest in the town, and this no doubt is what gives it the atmosphere of a cozy Grand Hotel which really knows its business. Luxury and elegance rule in the public rooms where marble and columns form a fine backdrop to damask sofa and Venetian chandeliers. The bedrooms are more traditional, with hotel furniture that is elegant and functional, but rather ordinary. The prices, given the standard of service and décor, are reasonable, allowing one to discover painlessly the pleasures of this little visited Italian lake.

How to get there *(Map 13): 31km north of Viterbo.*

L'Ombricolo

01020 Civitella d'Agliano (Viterbo)
Tel. 0761-91 47 35 - Fax 0761-91 47 35
Dawne Alstrom-Viotti

Rooms 5 with telephone, bath or shower, safe. **Price** Single 120-180,000l, double 180-240,000L. **Meals** Breakfast included (buffet). **Evening meals** On request - mealtime specials 80,000L, lunch at swimming pool 30,000L. **Credit cards** Visa, Eurocard, MasterCard. **Pets** Dogs not allowed. **Facilities** Swimming pool, parking. **Nearby** Nearby Orvieto - Lago di Bolsena and Etruscan country: Chiusi, Pitigliano, Sorano and Sovana - Farnese - Isola Bisentina Tarquinia Tuscania - Viterbo - Roma (70km). **Closed** May.

The Teverina valley contains a few villages and some of the most interesting Etruscan sites, which is why we suggest you consider staying in this region, crossed by the Florence-Rome autostrada. L'Ombricolo is, moreover, a house of rare charm, equal to that of its owner, an Englishwoman who came to Rome to work in the cinema and who one day decided to settle down in this village less than a hundred kilometers from the capital. The ground floor of the house, surrounded by a loggia, has single storey above it, topped with a pinnacle turret, and the whole lies in a delightful garden of climbing plants and flowering shrubs. Very fine recovered materials have been added to the original broad outliens, so the kitchen-dining room, which still has its wood oven, houses a large table made out of the beams of old mangers, and the chimney place in the salon is made up of four lengths of monumental stone. The standard of comfort in the rooms and bathrooms is perfect, characterized by refined simplicity. The atmosphere is that of a welcoming country house that has been transformed into a guest house and will soon become a house of friends.

How to get there (Map 14): 31km south of Orvieto. On the A1, exit Attigliano, towards Civitella. Take the road on the left before reaching the village.

Il Voltone

Voltone 01010 Farnese (Viterbo)
Tel. 0761-42 25 40 - Fax 0761-42 25 40
Sig.ras Parenti
E-mail: info@voltone.it - Web: www.voltone.it

Rooms 30 with telephone, bath, WC. **Price** Single 130-150,000L, double 200-240,000L, suite 240-260,000L. **Meals** Breakfast included, served 8:00-10:00 - half board 150-180,000L (per pers.). **Restaurant** Service 1:00PM and 8:00PM - mealtime specials 45-70,000L - Regional cooking. **Credit cards** Visa, Eurocard, MasterCard. **Pets** Dogs allowed by reservation. **Facilities** Swimming pool, parking. **Nearby** Viterbo - Tarquinia - Ortebello - Cerveteri - Véio - Isola Bisantina - Lago di Bolsena – "Le Querce" golf course in Viterbo, (18-hole). **Open** Apr 5 – Nov 8.

Between Latin Rome and Florentine Tuscany, why not stop and see this lovely region of the Etruscans? Il Voltone is a rare find - all alone in the middle of a large agricultural estate in a tiny 17th-century village that has been wonderfully renovated and transformed, this hotel gives you the feeling that you are a guest in a private home. The yellow, ochre and pale pink colors outside and the antique furniture and carpets inside reinforce this gentle, homey atmosphere. The bedrooms are comfortable and each is personalized. You can go horseback riding or mountain-biking on the estate and there is also a lovely swimming pool with a view over the entire valley. The area was the home of the powerful Farnese family and boasts a wealth of historic points of interest. Your hosts will advise you on things to see and itineraries to choose. This place makes a wonderful retreat.

How to get there *(Map 13): 45km north of Viterbo, via A1 (Roma-Firenze), Orte exit then Viterbo, Capodimento, Valentano, Voltone. On the A1 (Firenze-Roma), Orvieto exit.*

La Chiocciola

Seripola 01028 Orte
Tel. 0761-40 27 34 - Fax 0761-49 02 54
Roberto and Maria-Cristina de Fonseca Pimentel
E-mail: info@lachiocciola.net - Web: www.lachiocciola.net

Rooms 8 with air-conditioning, bath or shower, TV (by request). **Price** Single 115-125,000L, double 170-180,000L, apart. (2-4 pers.) 1 000,000L/week. **Meals** Breakfast included, served 8:30-10:30 - half board 110,000L (per pers.). **Restaurant** By reservation, service 7:30PM-9:00PM - closed Mon to Thurs - mealtime specials 50,000L - Regional cooking. **Credit cards** Visa, Eurocard, MasterCard. **Pets** Dogs not allowed. **Facilities** Swimming pool, mountain bike, parking. **Nearby** Nearby Viterbo and Etruscan country - Bomarzo "Sacred Wood" - Rome - Todi. **Closed** Mid Jan – mid Feb.

Halfway between Rome and Orvieto, this could be a good base for excursions to discover the Etruscan remains, the cities of Umbria or the Italian capital (the motorway junction is nearby), while at the same time enjoying the charm and comfort of a house in the countryside. A few kilometers from Orte – a fortified town which has to be seen – a young couple has painstakingly restored this former fattoria, to give it the highest standards of comfort. The whole house has a pleasant smell of polish and the rooms, with their old-fashioned furniture and comfortable bathrooms, are very well kept; La Chiocciola is the largest and most beautiful. Every care has been taken with the well-being of the guests: the dining room opens on the garden, a large airconditioned salon with a billiard table occupies on the the annexes and the swimming pool offers another chance to cool down in summer (which can be very hot in these parts). Set in some twenty hectares of vines and fruit trees, it enjoys tranquillity even though the trains pass quite nearby. A very good place to stay.

How to get there *(Map 14): 10km northeast of Orte. On A1 or SSE45, exit Orte. Take the first exit to Orte, then after 3km the Amelia exit on the right and 300m further on the road on the left for Penna in Teverina.*

Hotel Al Gallo

01017 Tuscània (Viterbo)
Via del Gallo, 22
Tel. 0761-44 33 88 - Fax 0761-44 36 28 - Sig. José Pettiti
E-mail: gallotus@tin.it - Web: www.algallo.it

Category ★★★ Rooms 10 with air-conditioning, telephone, bath or shower, WC, TV – Elevator. **Price** Single 104-158,000L, double 140-224,000L. **Meals** Breakfast included, served 7:00-10:00 - half board 128-178,000L, full board 178-228,000L (per pers, in double room, 3 days min.). **Restaurant** Service 12:00PM-2:00PM, 7:00PM-10:00PM - mealtime specials 50-80,000L, also à la carte - Specialties: Ventaglio di proscuitto d'oca al pepe nero con carfiofi e peperoni arrostiti - Ravioli di petto di anatra e tartufo nero all'olio di canino - Involtini di manzo alla brace con basilico ed alloro - Stogliatina di ricotta e miele. **Credit cards** All major. **Pets** Dogs not allowed. **Facilities** Tennis, parking. **Nearby** Viterbo - Tarquinia - Ortebello - Cerveteri - Véio - Isola Bizantina - Lago di Bolsena – "Le Querce" golf course in Viterbo, (18-hole). **Open** All year.

On the border between Tuscany and Latium, the little town of Tuscània is one of those mysterious Etruscan cities, with tumuli and galleries of tombs scattered through the surrounding countryside. In addition, there are vestiges of the Middle Ages: the basilicas of San Pietro and Santa Maria Maggiore are jewels of early Christian and Romanesque architecure. The bedrooms are nicely decorated (except for the apple green carpeting) with blond wood furniture and flowered wallpaper. Choose rooms 7, 8 or 9 which overlook the lower part of town or number 6, which has a balcony. A few small rooms for one can be let out as doubles. Al Gallo is known for its restaurant, where the menu varies each month with the season and the market. But if you prefer to eat à la carte, even guests on half-board can pick from the full menu.

How to get there (Map 13): *20km of Viterbo, via A1, Orte exit. A12, exit Civitavecchia.*

Dimora del Prete di Belmonte

86079 Venafro (Isernia)
Via Cristo, 49
Tel. 0865-900 159 - Fax 0865-900 159 - Luigi and Dorothy del Prete
E-mail: dorvolpe@tin.it - Web: dimoradelprete.it

Rooms 4 with bath, WC. **Price** Double 150,000L. **Meals** Breakfast included, served 8:00-10:00. **Restaurant** Only for residents - mealtime specials 40,000L. **Credit cards** Diners, Visa, Eurocard, MasterCard. **Pets** Dogs allowed. **Nearby** Venafro: archeological museum, Roman theatre and amphitheatre, romanesque cathedral, palazzo Caracciolo, Chiesa dell'Annunziata, castello Pandone - Isernia - Capua - Caserta - Abbazia de Montecassina - Grotte di Pasena - Naples (1 hour). **Open** All year.

An ideal stopover for anyone travelling towards the South on the Roma-Napoli autostrada. Here, less than twenty kilometers after leaving Cassino, you will find yourself in the smallest and least known of the regions of Italy, the Molise, in a village which, despite its insignificant appearance, still has many traces of the old Roman town of Venafrum, as well as a palace restored in the 19th Century in neo-classical style. The descendants of the family who now own the Dimora, left Naples a few years ago to make this their main home and their natural sense of hospitality encouraged them to open four rooms to guests adventurous enough to wander a little off the beaten track. You will be welcomed as a friend. The villa houses archeological treasures, most of them in the museum which contains the grandfather's collection; and don't miss the family furniture and pictures. The bedrooms are less luxurious than the public areas, done up simply and in good taste with brand new bathrooms. Breakfast is served beneath the frescoes in the dining room, but you can also enjoy the shade of the hundred-year old palm trees in the garden.

How to get there *(Map 19): 140km southeast of Rome by A1, exit S. Vittore, towards Venafro, Isernia.*

Hotel Cenobio dei Dogi

16032 Camogli (Genova)
Via Nicolo Cuneo, 34
Tel. 0185-72 41 - Fax 0185-77 27 96 - Sig. Siri
E-mail: cenobio@canobio.it - Web: www.cenobio.it

Category ★★★★ **Rooms** 107 with air-conditioning, telephone, bath or shower, WC, TV, minibar – Elevator. **Price** Single 180-240,000L, double 260-510,000L, suite 400-700,000L; extra bed 50-70,000L. **Meals** Breakfast included, served 7:30-10:15 - half board +65,000L, full board +130,000L (per pers., 3 days min.). **Restaurant** Service 12:45PM-2:15PM, 8:00PM-9:30PM - à la carte - Specialties: Seafood. **Credit cards** Amex, Visa, Eurocard, MasterCard. **Pets** Dogs allowed. (+15,000 L). **Facilities** Swimming pool, solarium, tennis (+25,000L), private beach, parking. **Nearby** Ruta and Portofino Vetta (Monte di Portofino) - Punta Chiappa and the Abbey of S. Fruttuoso by foot or boat - Portofino - Rapallo and the Riviera di Levante – Rapallo golf course (18-hole). **Open** All year.

This large and beautiful villa stands at one end of the Gulf, in the pretty little seaside resort of Camogli, the twin city of Portofino. For a long time it was the property of an eminent family that gave the city of Genoa a number of its Doges. When it was bought in the 1950s and transformed into a hotel, it quite naturally kept the memory of the Doges in its name. Today it is one of the luxury hotels of the Ligurian Riviera. All the rooms and the en-suite bathrooms have been refurbished, giving the hotel a level of decoration and comfort befitting its four stars. The rooms overlooking the sea enjoy an undeniable advantage. The facilities are, of course, in keeping with the status of the hotel: a beautifully planted garden, a swimming pool and a private beach right at the foot of the building guarantees absolute tranquility even at the height of the season.

How to get there *(Map 8): 26km east of Genova via A12, Recco exit, then S333 to Recco, Camogli, along the coast.*

Albergo da Giovanni

15032 San Fruttuoso - Camogli (Genova)
Casale Portale, 23
Tel. 0185-77 00 47
Famiglia Bozzo

Rooms 7 with shower (indoor). **Price** Rooms with half board and full board (per pers.) 150,000L, 190,000L. **Restaurant** Service 1:00PM-2:30PM, 8:00PM-9:15PM - mealtime specials, also à la carte - Specialties: Seafood. **Credit cards** Visa, Eurocard, MasterCard. **Pets** Dogs not allowed. **Nearby** Abbey of S. Fruttuoso - Camogli - Portofino. **Open** Jun – Sept (open weekends Oct – May).

The Albergo da Giovanni is in San Fruttuoso, a magical, forgotten-by-time town dating from Roman antiquity, which most people stop off and visit during boat trips from Camogli and Portofino. The city is set on a small inlet surrounded by woods that border the sea, and has a cathedral, an abbey, a bell-tower and the Andréa Doria tower. Previously regarded as a day-trip destination, San Fruttuoso now welcomes adventurous overnighters, thanks to this beach house. The comfort is basic and the service nonexistent, but the restaurant is great and serves dishes made with fish fresh from the sea. The most magical part is being able to stay behind in this wonderfully evocative place and wave goodbye as the last boat of the day sails away.

How to get there *(Map 8): 26km east of Genova via A12, Recco exit, then S333 to Recco then Camogli along the coast. Ferry services from Camogli to San Fruttuoso. (Information: 39-185-77 10 66).*

Albergo Splendido

16034 Portofino (Genova)
Salita Baratta, 16
Tel. 0185-26 78 01 - Fax 0185-26 78 06 - Sig. Saccani
E-mail: reservations@spendido.net

Category ★★★★ **Rooms** 69 with air-conditioning, telephone, bath, WC, TV, minibar – Elevator. **Price** With half board 780-860,000L (single), 1 540-1 920,000L (2 pers. in double room), 2 350-3 280,000L (2 pers. in suite), with full board +125,000L; extra bed 140,000L. **Meals** Breakfast included, served 7:30-10:30. **Restaurant** Service 1:00PM-2:30PM, 8:00PM-9:45PM - à la carte - Italian and regional cooking. **Credit cards** All major. **Pets** Dogs allowed (except in restaurant and in the swimming pool). **Facilities** Swimming pool, tennis (+40,000L), sauna, health center, parking (+38,000L). **Nearby** Fortezza di San Giorgio in Portofino - Abbey of S. Fruttuoso by foot or boat - Rapallo and the Riviera di Levante – Golf course of Rapallo (18-hole). **Closed** Nov 12 – Mar 30.

The Splendido, nestled amid woods on the heights over Portofino, is part of the landscape of the famous port. It is a real jewel of a place, admirably preserved. If possible, you should avoid coming in July and August, or if you do, at least avoid arriving toward the end of the day — the access from Santa Margherita is really quite difficult. Nevertheless, what a reward when you walk through the leafy gardens, with the scent of flowers in bloom, and catch sight of the port, with the sailboats crisscrossing the bay. It is as romantic as it is luxurious. The lounges are cool and comfortable, and the lovely terrace is used as a dining room in summer. The garden is filled with walks and paths leading to the village or the beach, and there are many quiet places to sit and enjoy the view. Our favorite rooms are those with a balcony in the trees. The rates are quite steep, but it's truly like paradise.

How to get there *(Map 8): 36km east of Genova via A12, Rapallo exit, S227 along the coast to Portofino.*

Splendido Mare

16034 Portofino (Genova)
Via Roma, 2
Tel. 0185-267 802 - Fax 0185-267 807 - Sig. Saccani
E-mail: reservations@spendido.net

Rooms 16 and 8 suites with air-conditioning, telephone, bath, WC, TV, minibar – Elevator. **Price** With half board: single 700,000L, 2 pers. in double 1 210-1 400,000L (2 pers. in double), 1 920-2 970,000L (2 pers. in suite); extra bed 140,000L. Full board: +125,000L. **Meals** Breakfast (buffet) included, served 7:00-11:00. **Bar** "Chuflay Bar", service 12:00PM-4:00PM and 7:30PM-11:00PM - mealtime specials 130,000L, also à la carte. **Credit cards** All major. **Pets** Dogs allowed (except in restaurant and in the swimming pool). **Facilities** Swimming pool and tennis (35,000L), sauna (40,000L), health center, parking (38,000L). **Nearby** Corniche road from Portofino to Rapallo (8km, not recommended in summer) - walk to lighthouse and fortezza di San Giogio in Portofino – Golf course at Rapallo, (18-hole) Chuflay. **Open** All year.

The Splendido has opened a luxurious annex a stone's throw from the jetties of the little port that shelters the finest boats on the Ligurian coast. At the very beginning of the century, Silvio Gazzolo decided to transform his fisherman's house into a little hotel, to give him something to do in his retirement… The Hotel Nazionale and the more recent Splendido Mare occupy what remains of the property which has recently been acquired by Orient Express Hotels. This means that the rooms are marvellously placed to enjoy the life of one of the smartest ports of call in Italy, the best rooms being the ones with terraces. Comfort and service are what one would expect from the famous mother house, which allows guests to share the use of its gardens and swimming pool. If you wish to see and be seen, you absolutely must stop in the Chuflay Bar, which from breakfast to supper time serves the beautiful people who come off the yachts.

How to get there *(Map 8): On the port.*

Hotel Piccolo

16034 Portofino (Genova)
Via Duca degli Abruzzi, 31
Tel. 0185-269 015 - Fax 0185-269 621 - Sig. Tirabuschi
E-mail: dopiccol@tin.it - Web: www.domina.it

Category ★★★★ **Rooms** 22 with tel, bath, WC, TV, minibar – Elevator. **Price** Single 150-240,000L, double 220-360,000L, suite 360-440,000L. **Meals** Breakfast included, served 7:30-10:00 - half board 240,000L, full board 280,000L (per pers.). **Restaurant** Service 12:30PM-2:00PM, 7:30PM-9:00PM - mealtime specials, also à la carte 40,000L. **Credit cards** All major. **Pets** Dogs allowed. **Facilities** Parking and garage (10,000L). **Nearby** Road from Portofino to Rapallo (8km, not counsel in summer) - Walk to lighthouse and fortezza di San Giogio in Portofino - Abbey of S. Fruttuoso di Camogli by foot or boat – Golf course of Rapallo (18-hole). **Closed** Nov – end Dec.

The Hotel Piccolo stands just at the last curve, from which you catch your first glimpse of Portofino (anyway, unless you have a resident's pass, you have to wait at the exit of Santa Margherita until a parking place becomes free in the Portofino parking lot). The hotel has been nicely renovated, with a good utilization of all available space, as the house really is piccolo. There is a small but inviting reception area, a few meters from where you park your car. The rooms, (reminiscent of a ship's cabin) are cozy and pleasant to live in, each with a living room corner and a shower room equipped with all you need. Some rooms have terraces and those on the higher floors have a view of the sea. For swimming, you just have to cross the road to reach the little cove (complete with beach chairs) with its own private access, a great plus in this town where access to the beach is not always easy. There is a welcoming atmosphere as well.

How to get there (Map 8): *30km east of Genova via A12, Rapallo exit, then S227 along the coast to Portofino.*

Hotel Nazionale

16038 Portofino (Genova)
Via Roma, 8
Tel. 0185-26 95 75 - Fax 0185-26 91 38
E-mail: reservation@nazionaleportofino.com - Web: www.nazionaleportofino.com

Category ★★★★ **Rooms** 12 with air-conditioning, telephone, bath or shower, WC, TV, minibar.
Price Double 400,000L, suite 500-600,000L. **Meals** Breakfast included, served 7:30AM-12:00PM.
Restaurant See pp. 526-527. **Credit cards** Visa, Eurocard, MasterCard. **Pets** Dogs allowed. **Nearby**
Road from Portofino to Rapallo (8km, not counsel in summer) - Walk to lighthouse and fortezza di San
Giogio in Portofino - Abbey of S. Fruttuoso di Camogli by foot or boat, Rapallo and the Riviera di
Levante – Rapallo golf course (18-hole). **Open** Mar 15 – Nov 30.

You can find the Hotel Nazionale by going down to the port. If you really
want to feel a part of every event that takes place in the life of Portofino,
this hotel occupies one of those fisherman's houses in pink, yellow, orange or
ochre tints that lend their traditional charm to this village. Though the entrance
is in Via Roma, some of the rooms look directly across the square and a few
over the port. But be forewarned — the show goes on by night as well as by
day. The hotel was renovated a few years ago with a view to comfort but the
décor lacks personality. But it must be said that the rooms are comfortable and
this offers the best quality for its price in Portofino. The hospitality may not be
outstanding, but hotels are few and rooms are hard to find around here.

How to get there *(Map 8): 36km east of Genova via A12, Rapallo exit, S227
along the coast to Portofino. (Parking is 300 meters from the hotel).*

Grand Hotel Villa Balbi

16039 Sestri Levante (Genova)
Viale Rimembranza, 1
Tel. 0185-42 941 - Fax 0185-48 24 59 - Sig. Rossignotti
E-mail: villabalbi@pn.itnet.it

Category ★★★★ **Rooms** 99 with air-conditioning, telephone, bath, WC, TV, minibar – Elevator. **Price** Single 120-210,000L, double 280-380,000L, suite 350-480,000L. **Meals** Breakfast included, served 7:30-10:00 - half board 190-250,000L, full board 220-280,000L (per pers. 3 days min.). **Restaurant** Service 12:30PM-2:00PM, 7:30PM-9:00PM - mealtime specials 65-75,000L, also à la carte - Italian and regional cooking. **Credit cards** All major. **Pets** Dogs not allowed. **Facilities** Heated swimming pool and private beach (40,000L), parking (+15,000L). **Nearby** Church of San Nicolo - Sestri Levante (Baia del Silenzio, coast road from Sestri Levante to Monterosso al Mare) - Cinque Terre by boat or by train – Rapallo golf course (18-hole). **Closed** Oct 15 – Dec 27.

The Villa Balbi is one of those historic houses built for princes, then later, for want of a king, converted into luxury summer residences. The decor has changed in the course of centuries and the clientele as well, judging from the number of Mercedes parked all over the grounds, but the salons that look out on the *passagiata* of palm trees and the pines in the garden still have their air of mystery. There is some antique furniture in the large guest rooms and the service is what you would expect from a luxury hotel. Although it is right in the center of town, only the street separates you from the private beach, where you will have your cabin, sun umbrella and beach chair. Children seem to prefer the swimming pool. An ideal hotel place if you can afford it.

How to get there *(Map 8): 50km east of Genova via A12, Sestri Levante exit.*

Hotel Helvetia

16039 Sestri Levante (Genova)
Via Cappuccini, 43
Tel. 0185-41 175 - Fax 0185-45 72 16 - Sig. Pernigotti
E-mail: helvetia@rainbownet.it - Web: www.rainbownet.it/helvetia

Category ★★★ **Rooms** 24 with air-conditioning, telephone, bath or shower, WC, satellite TV, minibar, safe – Elevator. **Price** Single 190,000L, double 260,000L, suite 290,000L. **Meals** Breakfast included (buffet), served 7:30-10:30. **Restaurant** See p. 527. **Credit cards** Visa, Eurocard, MasterCard. **Pets** Dogs not allowed. **Facilities** Private beach, bikes, parking (+20,000L). **Nearby** Church of San Nicolo - Sestri Levante (Baia del Silenzio, coast road from Sestri Levante to Monterosso al Mare) - Cinque Terre by boat or by train – Rapallo golf course (18-hole). **Open** Mar – Oct.

In this pretty little beach resort of the Ligurian Riviera, the Helvetia is our favorite hotel. Sheltered in the little Bay of Silence, it has been lovingly looked after for many years by the Pernigotti family. All the rooms were recently re-done: bright and luminous, with well-equipped bathrooms, they face either the sea or the garden. It would be a pity not to have the sea view, but the salons and the terrace are also a good vantage point from which to see it. The morning is a wonderful time to enjoy the panorama, as you help yourself from the delicious and copious buffet breakfast, served until 10 o'clock. The beach is right at your feet, to go swimming whenever you feel like. The kind, attentive hospitality of Signor Pernigotti makes this the sort of place you want to come back to.

How to get there *(Map 8): 50km east of Genova via A12, Sestri Levante exit. Pedestrian way but you can used for deposit your luggages.*

Hotel Miramare

16039 Sestri Levante (Genova)
Via Cappellini, 9
Tel. 0185-48 08 55 - Fax 0185-41 055 - Sig. Carmagnini
E-mail: hrm.rainbownet.it@miramare - Web: www.miramaresestrilevante.com

Category ★★★★ **Rooms** 43 with air-conditioning, telephone, bath or shower, WC, satellite TV, minibar – Elevator. **Price** Single 240,000L, double 350,000L, suite 500,000L. **Meals** Breakfast 20,000L, served 7:30-10:00 - half board 185-250,000L (1 pers.), 155-230,000L (per pers., 3 days min), full board +40,000L. **Restaurant** Service 12:30PM-2:00PM, 7:30PM-10:30PM - mealtime specials 60-70,000L, also à la carte - Specialties: Risotto all'aragosta - Filetto di pesce in crosta alle erbe - Torte artigianali del giorno. **Credit cards** Diners, Visa, Eurocard, MasterCard. **Pets** Dogs not allowed. **Facilities** Private beach, parking by reservation (20,000L). **Nearby** Hotel dei Castelli's park - Church of San Nicolo - Rizzi museum - Sestri Levante (Baia del Silenzio, coast road from Sestri Levante to Monterosso al Mare) - Cinque Terre – Rapallo golf course (18-hole). **Closed** Dec and Jan.

The Miramar has been converted into a luxury hotel, and this is obvious as soon as you walk in. The lobby is busy and inviting. All the common areas are on the ground floor: salons and restaurants, but also shops and meeting rooms. Everything is bright and neat. The rooms have modern style decor. Most are set up as small apartments and they can be combined to accommodate up to six persons. The nicest are those with a sea view. There is a large terrace and a garden just facing the beach of the Bay of Silence. In short, a very comfortable hotel - although the renovation was essential, it is true that it has lost a little of its former charm.

How to get there *(Map 8): 50km east of Genova via A12, Sestri Levante exit. Pedestrian street but you can go with your car to deposit luggage.*

Baia Beniamin

18036 Grimaldi Inferiore - Ventimiglia (Imperia)
Corso Europa, 63
Tel. 0184-380 02/380 27 - Fax 0184-380 02/380 27
Sig. Brunelli

Rooms 5 with tel, bath or shower, WC, TV. **Price** Double 400,000L. **Meals** Breakfast (at any time).
Restaurant Service 12:30PM-2:00PM, 8:00PM-9:30PM - closed Mon - mealtime specials lunch 70,000L
(except national holidays), 120,000L; also à la carte - Specialties: Agnolotti di nasello - Taglioni ai
crostacei e fiori di zucchine - Branzino con funghi porcini - Medaglioni di pescatrice di timp - Piccata
di branzino con petali di melone al'acto balsamico. **Credit cards** All major. **Pets** Dogs not allowed.
Facilities Parking. **Nearby** Menton - Villa Hambury's garden - Monaco - San Remo — San Remo golf
course (18-hole). **Closed** Nov.

The Baia Beniamin stands amid oleanders, geraniums, eucalyptus and palm
trees on a rocky outcrop descending to a little beach, just a few hundred
yards from the port of Menton. Frederic Cartier has taken over in the kitchen
from Carlo Brunelli and has a good track record: his "business lunch" will give
you an idea of his talent. There are five rooms over the restaurant and a stay in
one of them makes a nice gourmet holiday. They are comfortable and elegant
and open onto a large covered terrace. Our favorite is number 5, with its double
exposure. The house is at the water's edge and has its own beach chairs on the
little beach. A good stopping place for fine dining while you discover Menton,
the last pearl of the French Riviera on the Ligurian coast.

How to get there *(Map 7): 3km from Menton, 8km from Vintimille on the
inferior cornice.*

Royal Hotel

18038 Sanremo (Imperia)
Corso Imperatrice, 80
Tel. 0184-53 91 - Fax 0184-661 445 - Famiglia Bertolini
E-mail: royal@royalhotelsanremo.com - Web: www.royalhotelsanremo.com

Category ★★★★★ L **Rooms** 140 with air-conditioning, telephone, bath, WC, satellite TV, minibar, safe – Elevator, wheelchair access. **Price** Single 200-380,000L, double 345-600,000L, suite 600-1 050,000L. **Meals** Breakfast included, served 7:30-10:15 (2:30PM in the room) - half board 245-395,000L, full board 290-450,000L (per pers. 3 days min.). **Restaurant** Service 12:30PM-2:30PM, 7:30PM-9:30PM - mealtime specials 98,000L, also à la carte. **Credit cards** All major. **Pets** Small dogs allowed (+25,000L). **Facilities** Heated seawater pool, tennis (30,000L), fitness, minigolf, parking (+20,000L), garage (35,000L). **Nearby** San Remo: Casino and market, Bussana Vecchia, Taggia (Church of San Domenico) - Ceriana and Baiardo villages – San Remo golf course (18-hole). **Open** 20 Dec – 7 Oct.

The picturesque historic center of town is at Pigna, on the heights. It was only in the 19th century, when Sanremo (which takes its name from Saint Romolo) became a famed beach resort that it began to spread down towards the sea The Royal Hotel, along with the luxurious Liberty-style Municipal Casino, bear witness to this luxury life of that era on the Riviera di Ponente. The comfort is perfect, while preserving all that gave it its charm. The hotel still has luxuriously fitted rooms, as well as vast salons and smaller rooms opening on the subtropical park full of lush vegetation. As soon as the weather is warm enough, one can have lunch in the swimming-pool snack bar and in summer one can dine in the outdoor restaurant with piano-bar. The service and hospitality are in high style.

How to get there *(Map 7): 56km east of Nice (France) via A10, San Remo exit.*

Casa Cambi

17024 Castelvecchio di Rocca Barbena (Savona)
Via Roma, 42
Tel. 0182-780 09 - Fax 0182-780 09
Anna Bozano

Rooms 5 with telephone, bath or shower. **Price** Simple 100,000L, double 140-160,000L. **Meals** Breakfast included, served 8.00-10.00 - half board 110-140,000L (per pers.). **No restaurant** But light meals on request. **Credit cards** Not accepted. **Pets** Dogs allowed. **Nearby** Albenga - Alasio - Finale ligure - Isola di Gallinara - Garessio – Garlenda golf course (18-hole). **Closed** Nov 15 – Dec 15, Jan 15 – Mar 15.

On the recommendation of a Swiss reader, we ventured into the hinterland of Liguria. Castelvecchio is a typical small town of this region, its pink and grey houses clinging to the rocks and dominated by the castello. The narrow medieval streets are cooled by the sea breeze blowing in from the coast. Casa Cambi, situated just oppoosite the castle, is an old family house, now restored. There are few rooms, but each is different from the rest, with its own character, enjoying space and the view. Two of them can communicate through a shared drawing room. Others open on a wide terrace looking out across the village and the mountains. All have very comfortable bathrooms and are elegantly furnished by the owner, a Florentine and an antiques expert. Breakfast is served in a pretty ground-floor room or in summer in the garden. Lovingly restored, the village is peaceful, within easy reach of fine walks by the sea or in the mountains.

How to get there *(Map 7): 17km northeast of Albenga. On the A10, exit Albenga.*

Hotel Punta Est

17024 Finale Ligure (Savona)
Via Aurelia, 1
Tel. 019-60 06 11 - Fax 019-60 06 11 - Sig. Podesta
Web: www.puntaest.com

Category ★★★★ **Rooms** 40 with telephone, bath or shower, WC (30 with TV, 30 with minibar) – Elevator. **Price** Single 160-250,000L, double 300-400,000L, suite 400-800,000L. **Meals** Breakfast 25,000L, served 8:00-10:00 - half board 180-300,000L, full board 220-350,000L (per pers.). **Restaurant** Service 1:00PM-2:00PM, 8:00PM-9:00PM - mealtime specials 60-120,000L, also à la carte - Specialties: Branzino al sale - Pennette al profumo di mare - Terrina di basilico e olive. **Credit cards** Amex, Visa, Eurocard, MasterCard. **Pets** Dogs not allowed. **Facilities** Swimming pool, private beach, parking. **Nearby** Abbey of Finale Pia - Prehistoric caves near by Toirano - Noli – Golf Garlenda Course (18-hole). **Open** May – Sept.

The Hotel Punta Est is perched on a little promontory overhanging the beach. It consists of two buildings–an 18th-century villa and a modern addition–set in the middle of a trellised garden with large pine trees, palms, bougainvillea and hibiscus. The rooms are comfortably furnished and all have a view of the sea. The private swimming pool and reserved spaces on the beach across from the hotel allow you to escape the summer crowds. The large, panoramic terrace with piano bar is a nice place to spend an evening.

How to get there *(Map 8): 30km south of Savona via A10, Finale Ligure exit.*

La Meridiana

17033 Garlenda (Savona)
Via ai Castelli, 11
Tel. 0182-58 02 71 - Fax 0182-58 01 50
Sig. and Sig.ra Segre

Category ★★★★ **Rooms** 32 (suite with air-conditiong), with telephone, bath, WC, satellite TV, safe, minibar – Elevator; wheelchair access. **Price** Double 350-480,000L, apart. 550-1 200,000L. **Meals** Breakfast 30,000L - half board 300-700,000L (per pers. 3 days min.). **Restaurant** In summer, lunch at the swimming pool (by reservation). Service 8:00PM-10:00PM - mealtime specials 90,000L, also à la carte - Regional cooking. **Credit cards** All major. **Pets** Small dogs allowed in some rooms (+25,000L). **Facilities** Covered swimming pool (Jun – Sept), bike, sauna (20,000L), moutain bikes, golf, parking. **Nearby** Roman remains, baptistry and beaches at Albenga – Garlenda golf course (18-hole). **Open** Mar 15 – Dec.

The road to the Meridiana is not always pleasant, but once you have arrived, you will have no regrets. The atmosphere is one of a large country house, opening on the countryside, with beautiful grounds and a swimming pool. You will find the same airy comfort in the rooms. The hotel restaurant, Il Rosmario, is one of the better ones in the area. Mr. Segre, the dynamic owner, sees to it that only the best local products are used in the fine cuisine. A plus for many is the golf course right next door. This is a great place for a get away; ask about the special weekend package and golf rates.

How to get there *(Map 7): 100km east to Nice (France) via A10, Albenga exit, then S453 towards Garlenda.*

Hotel Porto Roca

19016 Monterosso Al Mare (La Spezia)
Via Corone, 1
Tel. 0187-81 75 02 - Fax 0187-81 76 92
Sig.ra Guerina Arpe

Rooms 43 with air-conditioning, telephone, shower, WC, TV, minibar. **Price** Single 280,000L, double 290-450,000L. **Meals** Breakfast included, served 7:30-10:00 - half board 220-255,000L, full board 240-300,000L (per pers. 3 days min.). **Restaurant** Service 12:30PM-1:30PM, 7:30PM-9:00PM - mealtime specials 60-70,000L, also à la carte - Specialties: Sfogliatelle Porto Roca - Straccetti "paradiso" - Branzino al sale, crostate di frutta fresca. **Credit cards** Amex, Visa, Eurocard, MasterCard. **Pets** Dogs allowed (+15-20,000L). **Facilities** Private beach in summer, parking in the village. **Nearby** The Riviera di Levante - Cinque Terre by boat or by rail - Riomaggiore - Manarola - Corniglia - Vernazza and Monterosso al Mare – Marigola golf course (9-hole) in Lerici. **Open** Apr 20 – Nov.

Monterosso rivals the charms of the neighboring villages of "Cinqueterra." The access road was built very recently and you still have to leave your car in the village parking lot. In the summer, it is guarded night and day, and if you inform the hotel of your arrival, they can arrange to have you picked up. The 43-room Porto Roca, the only hotel of this category to be found in these villages, towers over the Bay of Porticciolo and the beach of Monterosso. The interior furnishings are pleasantly kitsch, a mixture of different styles from the medieval to the 18th century. For sunbathing, you have a choice between the beach at the foot of the hotel and the terrace that overlooks the cliffs.

How to get there *(Map 9): 32km northwest of La Spezia via S370, along the coast*

Agnello d'Oro

24129 Bergamo Alta
Via Gombito, 22
Tel. 035-24 98 83 - Fax 035-23 56 12
Sig. Capozzi

Category ★★★ **Rooms** 20 with tel, bath or shower, WC, satellite TV – Elevator. **Price** Single 90,000L, double 155,000L. **Meals** Breakfast 10-000L, served 7:30-10:00. **Restaurant** Service 12:30PM-2:30PM, 7:30PM-10:00PM - closed Mon and Sun evening - mealtime specials 55-65,000L, also à la carte - Regional cooking. **Credit cards** All major. **Pets** Dogs allowed. **Nearby** In Bergamo: Piazza Vecchia, S. Maria Maggiore, Church of Colleoni, Galeria Carrara, International Piano Festival - Abbey of Pontida - Treviglio and Church of Rivolto d'Adda – La Rossera golf course (9-hole) in Chiuduno. **Open** All year.

This small inn stands on a tiny piazza in the upper town of Bergamo. It is first of all a typical restaurant with solid wooden chairs and tables, red checkered tablecloths and shiny brass decorations on the walls. The specialties are the tasty dishes of Lombardy and if you order the risotto al profumo del bosco, you can have your souvenir plate to take with you. The rooms have been renovated and are simple but comfortable enough for a stopover in this town, whose artistic and historic heritage make it one of the most interesting in Lombardy. If no one is there to greet you on arrival, don't hesitate to ring the bell - the owner is undoubtedly busy in his kitchen.

How to get there *(Map 3): 47km northeast of Milano. Airport di Oria al Serio, 4km.*

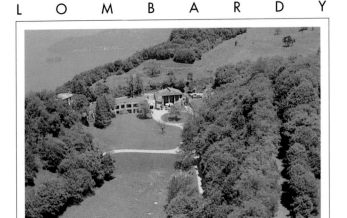

I Due Roccoli

25049 Iseo (Brescia)
Via Silvio Bonomelli, 54
Tel. 030-982 29 77 - Fax 030-982 29 80 - Sig. Agoni
E-mail: relais@idueroccoli.com - Web: www.idueroccoli.com

Category ★★★★ **Rooms** 13 with telephone, bath or shower, WC, TV, safe, minibar **Price** Single 170,000L, double 220-240,000L, suite 280,000L. **Meals** Breakfast 16,000L, served 7:30-10:00. **Restaurant** Service 12:00PM-2:00PM, 7:30PM-10:00PM - mealtime specials 45-65,000L, also à la carte - Specialties: Fagotino di ricotta - Code di gamberi - Pesce. **Credit cards** All major. **Pets** Small dogs allowed. **Nearby** Lake Iseo - Bergamo - Val Camonica - Church of S. Pietro in Provaglio d'Iseo - Brescia - Bergamo – Franciacorta golf course (18-hole). **Open** Mar 16 – Oct 31.

Thanks to its mild climate, Lake Iseo has become a tourist haven, bordered by little lakefront resorts. The Mediterranean vegetation and forests that seem to plunge straight into the water give the place an almost Alpine look, although the altitude is only 185 meters. The architecture of the resort houses is not always very attractive. To find buildings of character, it's best to go a bit further from the lake shores. I Due Roccoli is on the heights overlooking the lake. It consists of the old villa and a new building with guest rooms that are comfortable and decorated in a pleasant country style. If you have the choice, take a room facing the water. In short, this is a good spot, slightly off the beaten track but not too far away from the tourist highlights of Lombardy.

How to get there *(Map 3): 25km north of Brescia (via A4 Milano/Venezia, Rovato exit), towards Lago Iseo, then Polaveno (4km of Iseo).*

Cappuccini

25033 Cologne Franciacorta (Brescia)
Via Cappuccini, 54
Tel. 030-715 72 54 - Fax 030-715 72 57 - M. Massimo Pelizzari
E-mail: cappucini@numerica.it - Web: freeyellow.com/members3/cappuccini

Category ★★★ **Rooms** 7 with air-conditioning, telephone, bath, WC, satellite TV, minibar. **Price** Single 200,000L, double 300,000L, suite 350,000L. **Meals** Breakfast 25,000L served 9:30-11:00. **Restaurant** Service 12:30PM-2:30PM, 7:30PM-10:00PM - closed Wed - mealtime specials 60-85,000L, also à la carte - Specialties: Manzo all' olio - Stracotto con polenta - Seafood. **Credit cards** Diners, Visa, Eurocard, MasterCard. **Pets** Dogs not allowed. **Nearby** Lake Iseo, San Pietro Chirch in Lamosa in Provaglio d'Iseo, Bergamo, Brescia, Sirmione – Franciacorta golf course (18-hole). **Closed** Jan 1 – 20, Aug 1 – 20, and Wed.

Austere elegance and refinement, these are the qualities of this former monastery respectfully converted into a hospitable holiday spot. This lovely region on the border of Lombardy and Venetia, with its landscape of rolling hills and vineyards, is still little known by the masses of tourists. A serene landscape with plain stone houses whose only adornment is often their large canvas sunshades. The building still has the long corridors and vaulted passages of its monastic past. They lead to bedrooms that are very comfortable, yet even here the decor is minimal in style. The largest, which open onto the countryside, have a mezzanine and a small living room with a fireplace. A series of small dining rooms make it possible for guests to dine without being inconvenienced by the dinners or receptions that are sometimes held on the convent grounds. The cuisine, based largely on regional recipes and local products, will give you a taste of yet another aspect of the dolce vita in Franciacorta.

How to get there (*Map 3*): *27km west of Brescia, towards Bergamo.*

L'Albereta Ristorante G. Marchesi

Erbusco (Brescia)
Via Vittorio Emanuele, 11
Tel. 030-776 05 50 - Fax 030-776 05 73 - Mme Moretti de Rosa
E-mail: albereta@terramoretti.it

Category ★★★★ **Rooms** 41 with air-conditining, telephone, bath, WC, TV, minibar. **Price** Single from 235,000L, double from 3620,000L, suite from 790,000L. **Meals** Breakfast 35-45,000L, served 7:30-10:30 - half board 240,000L, full board 260,000L (per pers.,3 days min.). **Restaurant** "Gualtiero Marchesi", service 12:30PM-2:00PM, 7:30PM-10:00PM - closed Sun evening, Mon - mealtime specials 200-240,000L, also à la carte - Italian "nouvelle cuisine". **Credit cards** All major. **Pets** Dogs allowed. **Facilities** Swimming pool, tennis, sauna, parking, garage. **Nearby** Lake Iseo - Bergamo - Brescia - Lake Garda - Lake Como – Franciacorta golf course (9- and 18-hole). **Open** All year.

The Albereta is reputed to be the finest country inn in Lombardy, both for the cooking of Gualtieri Marchesi, who offers his own interpretations of traditional specialties, and for the winecellar, made up essentially of Italian and French wines. A stay here will also give you the chance to discover the region, with the softly rounded hills of Bellavista that form a backdrop for the verdant vineyards of Franciacorta. The dining room, under a large portico, faces the pleasant grounds that surround this fine 18th-century villa and its outbuildings. The rooms have comfort and refinement, the meals are delicious and as other distractions there are a library, a billiard room, plus a swimming pool and tennis court for sunny days. All the ingredients for an ideal weekend.

How to get there *(Map 3): 80km of Milano; 20km west of Brescia, via A4 (Milano/Venezia) Rovato.*

Hotel Villa del Sogno

Lago di Garda
25083 Fasano di Gardone Riviera (Brescia)
Via Zanardelli, 107
Tel. 0365-29 01 81 - Fax 0365-29 02 30 - Famiglia Calderan
E-mail: villadelsogno@gardalake.it - Web: www.gardalake.it/villadelsogno

Category ★★★★★ **Rooms** 31 with air-conditioning, telephone, bath, WC, TV, minibar – Elevator. **Price** Single 200-320,000L, double 350-550,000L, suite 650-850,000L. **Meals** Breakfast included, served 7:30-10:00 - half board +55,000L, full board +95,000L (per pers.,3 days min.). **Restaurant** Service 12:30PM-2:30PM, 7:30PM-9:30PM - mealtime specials 90,000L, also à la carte - Specialties: Coregone alla gardesana - Spaghetti alla trota. **Credit cards** All major. **Pets** Dogs not allowed. **Facilities** Swimming pool, tennis, sauna, parking **Nearby** Botanical garden of Gardone di Sotto - The Vittoriale (D'Annunzio estate) - Belvedere San Michele - Verona – Soiano golf course (27-hole). **Open** Apr – Oct 20.

A symphony of pale yellow and ochre tones lights the façade of this romantic turn-of-the-century villa, with a terrace like something out of a dream. On a slight rise, towering over Lake Garda amid the lush vegetation of its wonderful garden, this is an elegant hotel, decorated with antique furniture and paintings of various epochs, and with here and there a touch or a detail that is odd or unexpected, but which in no way spoils the ensemble. The rooms are perfect — spacious, some in Liberty style, others Venetian. One room has a small loggia, and others, below the main terrace, have their own private terraces. Not all of them have a direct view of the lake, so guests must make their requirements clear when booking. There is a very pleasant bar. A nice swimming pool and tennis court have been built in the grounds.

How to get there *(Map 3): 130km east of Milano - 36km northeast of Brescia via S45bis the left bank (Fasano, 2km).*

Grand Hotel Fasano

Lago di Garda
25083 Fasano di Gardone Riviera (Brescia)
Corso Zanardelli, 190
Tel. 0365-290 220 - Fax 0365-290 221 - Sig.ra Mayr
E-mail: reservation@grand-hotel-fasano.it - Web: www.grand-hotel.fasano.it

Category ★★★★ **Rooms** 87 (30 with air-conditioning) with telephone, bath or shower, WC – Elevator, wheelchair access. **Price** Double 180-480,000L. **Meals** Breakfast included, served 7:30-10:30 - half board +50,000L (per pers.). **Restaurant** Service 12:30PM-2:00PM, 7:30PM-9:30PM - mealtime specials 75,000L, also à la carte - Italian cuisine. **Credit cards** Not accepted. **Pets** Dogs allowed (+25,000L). **Facilities** Heated swimming pool and private beach, tennis (25,000L), parking (10,000L), garage (25,000L). **Nearby** Lake Garda - Villa Martinengo in Barbarno - botanical garden of Gardone di Sotto - The Vittoriale (D'Annunzio estate) - Belvedere San Michele - Verona – Soiano golf course (9- and 18-hole). **Open** Easter – Nov.

The Grand Hotel Fasano used to be a hunting lodge belonging to the imperial family of Austria, which perhaps explains, apart from the origins of the owner, the number of German tourists who come here. The hotel is comfortable, if a little over-decorated. The rooms are all pleasant, but ask for one in the older part. The garden, right on the lake, consists of beautiful plantings of palm trees, flowers, and greenery.

How to get there *(Map 3): 130km east of Milano - 36km northeast of Brescia via S45bis, on the left bank (Fasano Gardone, 1km).*

Villa Fiordaliso

Lago di Garda
25083 Gardone Riviera (Brescia)
Corso Zanardelli, 132
Tel. 0365-20 158 - Fax 0365-29 00 11 - Sig. Tosetti

Category ★★★★ **Rooms** 6 and 1 suite with air-conditioning, telephone, bath, WC, TV, minibar.
Price Double 350-700,000L, suite 950,000L. **Meals** Breakfast included, served 8:00-10:00.
Restaurant Service 12:30PM-2:00PM, 7:30PM-10:00PM - closed Mon and Tues lunch - mealtime
specials 150,000L, also à la carte - Season cooking. **Credit cards** All major. **Pets** Dogs not allowed.
Facilities Private embarcadère, parking. **Nearby** Villa Martinengo in Barbarno - botanical garden of
Gardone di Sotto - The Vittoriale (D'Annunzio estate) - Belvedere San Michele - Verona – Bogliaco golf
course (9-hole). **Closed** Nov 20 – Feb 10.

The 4-story Villa Fiordaliso stands on the shores of Lake Garda, the front
facing the lake, but the rear of the building is directly on the road. The
architecture could be termed eclectic, happily mingling Renaissance loggias and
neoclassical Venetian-style windows. In 1985, restoration work was begun, its
aim to preserve the original charm of this building that was once the home of
Gabriele D'Annunzio (before he moved a little further away) and later, from 1943
to 1945, became the residence of Mussolini's mistress, Clara Petacci. The rooms
are all wonderful. Iris and Mimosa are small, but overlook the lake, Gardenia and
Magnolia have a view of the lake but windows overlooking the raod, while little
Camelia, and the Orchidea and Claretta suites, described as "historical", have a
terrace which looks over the lake while the Rose room has a sumptuous bathroom
all done in Carrara marble. The restaurant is known for its gastronomic quality
and it is well worth stopping for a meal there even if you don't stay at the hotel.

How to get there *(Map 3): 130km east of Milano. On the left bank of the lake
(1km from Gardone Riviera).*

Hotel Baia d'Oro

Lago di Garda
25084 Gargnano (Brescia)
Via Gamberera, 13
Tel. 0365-71 171 - Fax 0365-72 568 - Sig. Terzi

Category ★★★ **Rooms** 12 with air-conditioning, telephone, bath, WC, TV, minibar. **Price** Double 160-240,000L. **Meals** Breakfast included, served 8:00-10:00. **Restaurant** Service 7:30PM-8:30PM - à la carte - Specialties: Pasta fatta in casa - Pesce del lago e di mare. **Credit cards** Not accepted. **Pets** Dogs allowed. **Facilities** Garage (15,000L). **Nearby** Villa Feltrinelli - Lake Idro - Church of Madonna di Monte Castello - Pieve di Tremosine - Verona – Bogliaco golf course (9-hole). **Open** Apr – Oct.

The colored façade of the Baia d'Oro, formerly a smallish house belonging to a fisherman, makes it easy to spot on the edge of Lake Garda. A private wharf keeps a *motoscaffo* at the disposal of the guests. On the picturesque lakeside terrace, you can enjoy lunch or dinner based on some of the best cuisine of the region–the hotel even recommends guests choose the half-board option so as not to miss out on the local treats. The rooms are comfortable and most have a small balcony, where you can have a pleasant breakfast while taking in the superb view. On the dining room walls are complimentary letters with famous signatures, notably one from Winston Churchill.

How to get there *(Map 3): 46km northwest of Brescia via S45bis, on the left bank.*

Villa Giulia

Lago di Garda
25084 Gargnano (Brescia)
Tel. 0365-71 022/71 289 - Fax 0365-72 774 - Famiglia Bombardelli
E-mail: info@villagiulia.it - Web: www.villagiulia.it

Category ★★★ **Rooms** 24 with air-conditioning, telephone, shower, WC, satellite TV, minibar, safe.
Price Single 180,000L, double 305-360,000L, suite 395-410,000L. **Meals** Breakfast (buffet)
included, served 7:30-11:00. **Restaurant** Service 12:30PM-3:00PM, 6:30PM-8:30PM - à la carte -
Regional cooking. **Credit cards** Visa, Amex, Diners, MasterCard. **Pets** Dogs not allowed. **Facilities**
Swimming pool, sauna, private beach, parking. **Nearby** Villa Feltrinelli - Lake Idro - Church of
Madonna di Monte Castello - Pieve di Tremosine - Verona – Bogliaco golf course (9-hole). **Open** 1 week
before Easter – Oct 10.

Success is often a question of passion and perseverance, two qualities which
helped Rina Bombardelli turn the family *pensione* into a hotel of
considerable charm. This Gothic-style villa, right on Lake Garda, has a great
view of the lake and the Baldo mountains, which appear green or snowy white
according to the season. The atmosphere is very cozy. The salon-bar is divided
into distinctly different areas by wing and club chairs. The dining room,
similarly divided, is lit by two beautiful Murano crystal chandeliers. In
summer, the restaurant is set up on the veranda. The well-furnished rooms
have a view of either the garden or the lake. Off to one side there is a
swimming pool and a solarium on the lawn.

How to get there *(Map 3): 46km northwest of Brescia via S45bis, on the left
bank.*

Hotel Laurin

Lago di Garda
25087 Salò (Brescia)
Viale Landi, 9
Tel. 0365-220 22 - Fax 0365-223 82 - Sig. Rossi
E-mail: laurinbs@tin.it - Web: www.laurinsalo.com

Rooms 36 (18 with air-conditioning) with telephone, bath or shower, WC, TV, minibar. **Price** Single 300,000L, double 600,000L. **Meals** Breakfast included, served 8:00-10:00 - half board 250-350,000L (per pers., 3 days min.). **Restaurant** Service 12:30PM-2:30PM, 8:00PM-9:30PM - à la carte 120,000L - Specialties: Fish. **Credit cards** All major. **Pets** Small dogs allowed. **Facilities** Swimming pool, parking. **Nearby** Villa Martinengo in Barbarano - Garden of Gardone di Sotto - Vittoriale degli Italiani - Belvedere San Michele - Verona – Bogliaco golf course (9-hole). **Open** Feb – Nov.

A popular vacation spot in the last century, Lake Garda has kept beautiful vestiges of this era. Salo, one of the rare villages to have kept the luster of the old days, is also etched painfully into the history of Italy, having been the last bastion of Mussolini's supporters. The Hotel Laurin is an admirably preserved Liberty-style villa, one of the precious jewels of the area. The salons are decorated with frescoes of voluptuous romantic subjects. The rooms have parquet floors and delicate furniture adding to the elegant harmonious atmosphere. While some of them overlook the road at the back of the hotel, most have delightfully romantic views over the lake. The staff will welcome you warmly. Be sure to take a walk along the banks up to the village and visit the very unusual "Vittoriale," the palace-museum of the poet Gabriele d'Annunzio.

How to get there *(Map 3): 130km east of Milano - 35km northeast of Brescia via S45 on the left bank (1km from Gardone Riviera).*

Villa Cortine Palace Hotel

Lago di Garda
25019 Sirmione (Brescia)
Via Grotte, 12
Tel. 030-99 05 890 - Fax 030-91 63 90 - Sig. Cappelletto
E-mail: info@hotelvillacortine.com - Web: www.hotelvillacortine.com

Category ★★★★★ **Rooms** 54 with telephone, bath, WC, TV — Elevator. **Price** Double 550-700,000L, deluxe 780-1 000,000L, junior suite 800-1 100,000L, suite 900-1 200,000L. **Meals** Breakfast included, served 7:30-10:30 - half board 730-1 180,000L (per pers. in double), 980-1 380,000L (per pers. in suite), obligatory in hight season. **Restaurant** Service 12:30PM-2:15PM, 7:30PM-9:15PM - mealtime specials 100-130,000L, also à la carte - Italian and international cuisine. **Credit cards** All major. **Pets** Dogs allowed (+60,000L). **Facilities** Swimming pool, tennis, private beach, parking. **Nearby** Rocca Scaligera - Grotte di Catullo Peschiera del Garda - Desenzano - Brescia - Verona — Soiano golf course (9- and 18-hole). **Open** Apr 5 – Oct 21.

This lovely house in neo-classical style was built by Count von Koseritz, who was later killed in World War II. Later, a rich industrialist from Milan renovated the property and converted it into a luxury hotel. The interior is adorned with fluted columns and Corinthian capitals, with marble, gilded wood and frescoes. A second building, recently added in order to increase the capacity, has unfortunately spoiled the ensemble. The luxuriousness is all a bit too strident, but the quality of amenities and service is up to the highest expectations. Besides, the site is marvelous: The lovely grounds with ornamental fountains and balconies over the lake confirm what Catullus said so many centuries ago — that Sirmione was the jewel of the entire peninsula.

How to get there *(Map 3): 127km east of Milano - 40km east of Brescia via A4, Sirmione exit - San Martino di Battaglia.*

Albergo Terminus

Lago di Como
22100 Como - Lungo Lario Trieste, 14
Tel. 031-329 111 - Fax 031-302 550 - Dr Passera
E-mail: larioterminus@galactica.it

Category ★★★★ **Rooms** 38 with air-conditioning, telephone, bath or shower, WC, satellite TV, minibar, safe – Elevator. **Price** Single 195-240,000L, double 240-356,000L, suite 500-680,000L. **Meals** Breakfast 27,000L (buffet), served 7:15-10:30. **Restaurant** "Bar delle Terme", service 12:30PM-3:00PM, 7:30PM-10:30PM - closed Tues - à la carte - Italian cuisine. **Credit cards** All major. **Pets** Dogs allowed. **Facilities** Sauna, parking and garage at hotel (30,000L). **Nearby** Menaggio - Villa Carlotta in Tremezzo - Garden of the Villa Serbelloni and Villa Melzi – Villa d'Este golf course (18-hole) in Montorfano. **Open** All year.

All along the Como waterfront the imposing villas stand shoulder to shoulder, but you can't miss the little French-style garden with its lawns and pebbled paths just in front of the Albergo Terminus. The hotel has kept intact its Liberty-style stuccos and woodwork and floral decorations as well as the fantasy of its interior architecture, with a central great hall surrounded by salons and a veranda dining room extending onto a pleasant terrace in summer. All the bedrooms are comfortable, but the prettiest are those facing the lake. One worthy of special mention is La Torretta, a suite with a terrace and a panoramic view of Como.

How to get there (Map 2): 48km from Milano; on the harbor.

Hotel Villa Flori

Lago di Como
22100 Como - Via Cernobbio, 12
Tel. 031-573 105 - Fax 031-570 379 - Famiglia Passera
E-mail: lariovillaflori@galactica.it - Web: hotelvillaflori.com

Rooms 44 with air-conditioning, telephone, bath or shower, WC, TV, minibar – Elevator. **Price** Single 195-283,000L, double 240-356,000L, suite 400-570,000L. **Meals** Breakfast (buffet) 27,000L, served 7:15-11:00. **Restaurant** Service 12:30PM-2:30PM, 7:30PM-9:00PM - closed Mon and Sat noon - mealtime specials 65-90,000L, also à la carte - Italian cuisine. **Credit cards** All major. **Pets** Dogs allowed (except in restaurant). **Facilities** Parking and garage (25,000L). **Nearby** Menaggio - Villa Carlotta in Tremezzo - Bellagio - Garden of the Villa Serbelloni and Villa Melzi – Villa d'Este golf course (18-hole) in Montorfano. **Open** Mar – Dec 2.

The Villa Flori was originally intended as a wedding present from the Marchese Raimondi to his daughter Giuseppina, who was to marry Garibaldi. But the wedding never took place as the general discovered that the girl's past was not above reproach, and for a long time the house remained uninhabited. Today it is one of Lake Como's very pleasant hotels. The entrance hall gives not a clue to what you will find inside. The salons and dining room are richly appointed in pleasing pastel tones. All the bedrooms face the lake and some have a large living room and balcony. The silky fabrics, thick carpets and large modern bathrooms make them very comfortable to live in. With Milan so close by, the hotel is often used for seminars and receptions, but all is done to see that these events do not inconvenience the guests.

How to get there (Map 2): 48km from Milano; 2km from Como. Cernobbio road.

Grand Hotel Villa Serbelloni

Lago di Como - 22021 Bellagio (Como)
Tel. 031-95 02 16 - Fax 031-95 15 29
Sig. Spinelli
E-mail: inforequest@villaserbelloni.it - Web: www.villasebelloni.it

Category ★★★★★ **Rooms** 85 with air-conditioning, telephone, bath, WC, TV, minibar – Elevator. **Price** Single 365-440,000L, double 515-790,000L, suite 990-1 250 000L. **Meals** Breakfast included, served 7:30-10:30 - half board +95,000L, full board +180,000L (per pers., 3 days min.). **Restaurant** Service 12:30PM-2:30PM, 8:00PM-10:00PM - mealtime specials 110,000L, also à la carte - Specialties: Pasta della casa - Pesce del lago. **Credit cards** All major. **Pets** Dogs allowed. **Facilities** Heated swimming pool, tennis (20,000L), sauna, fitness and beauty, squash, private garage (25,000L), parking. **Nearby** Milan - Lake Como (Villa Melzi, Erba to Bellagio by the Vallassina) - Bellagio to Como - Villa Trotti - Grotta verde in Lezzeno - Careno - Villa Pliniana in Riva di Faggetto – Grandola golf course (18-hole). **Open** Apr – end Oct.

The Serbelloni is one of those historic villas built in the 19th century all along this lovely section of the lake to provide the aristocratic families of Lombardy with all the grandeur they could possibly desire. Others were the Villa d'Este at Cernobbio, the Villa Carlotta at Tremezzo, the Villa Olmo in Como or the Villa Ricordi in Cadenabbia where Verdi wrote part of "La Traviata." The Serbelloni, with its impressive Liberty-style façade stands overlooking the lakefront in its magnificent English-style garden, planted with an incredible variety of trees. Stuccos and columns add a further note of luxury to the public rooms. As for the bedrooms, most of them have retained their original size, painted ceilings and furniture. It is clearly best to reserve those overlooking the lake in order to enjoy the magnificent view. The Serbelloni is a wonderful place in which to enjoy gracious living, Italian style, in a baroque setting that delighted Flaubert and Liszt.

How to get there *(Map 2): 31km north of Como.*

Hotel Florence

Lago di Como
22021 Bellagio (Como)
Piazza Mazzimi
Tel. 031-950 342 - Fax 031-951 722 - Sig. and Sig.ra Ketzlar

Category ★★★ **Rooms** 32 with telephone, bath or shower, WC, satellite TV, safe, hairdryer, minibar. **Price** Single 190-210,000L, double 280-350,000L, suite 400-450,000L. **Meals** Breakfast included, served 7:30-10:15 - half board 155-160,000L (per pers.). **Restaurant** Service 12:30PM-2:30PM, 7:30PM-10:00PM - à la carte - Specialties: Stracci di pasta agli spinaci e pecorino - Cappellacci - Barbabiet - Pesce persico con salsa di porri e tortino di mais. **Credit cards** Visa, Eurocard, MasterCard. **Pets** Dogs allowed (except in restaurant). **Nearby** Villa Serbelloni - Villa Melzi - Erba to Bellagio by the Vallassina - Bellagio to Como - Villa Trotti - Grotta verde in Lezzeno - Careno - Villa Pliniana in Riva di Faggetto – Grandola golf course (18-hole). **Open** Apr – Oct.

Under the arcades that line Bellagio's port, just near the entrance to the Hotel Serbelloni, one notices a small hotel with a terrace where refreshments are served to tourists waiting for the ferry. This is the Hotel Firenze. It also has a cocktail lounge where jazz concerts are given on Sunday. The dining room and bedrooms are on the upper floors. They are all nicely appointed with antique furniture and fine fabrics. All have a view of the lively port and the lake. The dining room with its fireplace has a convivial atmosphere, but in the summer meals are also served on the terrace facing the lake. The owners will give you a warm welcome. The Firenze is less luxurious than its neighbor but far less expensive as well. It is a hotel of charm and quality, well worth discovering.

How to get there (Map 2): 31km north of Como via S583; on the right bank.

Grand Hotel Villa d'Este

Lago di Como - 22012 Cernobbio (Como) - Via Regina, 40
Tel. 031-348 1 - Fax 031-348 844
Sig. Ceccherelli
E-mail: info@villadeste.it - Web: www.villadeste.it

Category ★★★★★ **Rooms** 164 with telephone, bath, WC, satellite TV, safe, minibar — Elevator.
Price Single 590-697L, double 920-1 045,000L. **Meals** Breakfast (buffet) included. **Restaurant** Service
12:00PM-2:30PM, 7:30PM-10:00PM - à la carte - International cooking. **Credit cards** All major. **Pets** Dogs
allowed. **Facilities** 2 swimming pools, sauna, tennis, beauty center, squash, garage, parking. **Nearby**
Villa Arconati in Punta di Balbianello - Villa Carlotta in Tremezzo - Mennagio - Lugano - boat for
Bellagio in Tremezzo — Villa d'Este golf course (18-hole) in Montorfano. **Open** Mar 1 — Nov 18.

The Villa d'Este has always been a favorite of celebrities - those whose
names grace the pages of the popular magazines. Built in the 16th century,
it was even then favored by the aristocracy and now that the horse-drawn
coaches are gone, the Rolls and Mercedes have taken their place in the little
village streets of Cernobbio. The interior still bears traces of these illustrious
visitors: The Napoleon room has its original silk hangings and a statue
attributed to Canova attests to the stay by the famous sculptor. Each room is
unique, a personalized decor of silk draperies and antique furniture. But the
gardens are even more unforgettable: ruins and columns, rockwork and basins
are set amid a vegetation of rare species. To entertain its demanding clientele,
the hotel provides such a variety of sports facilities that it is possible to do just
about everything without leaving the grounds — a large swimming pool built
out over the lake, all the water sports available, and a health center. After an
excellent dinner (with dancing, if you wish) you can always end the evening
in the private night club. The staff is uniformly excellent.

How to get there *(Map 2): 5km north of Como.*

Grand Hotel Imperiale

Lago di Como
22010 Moltrasio (Como)
Via Durini
Tel. 031-346 111 - Fax 031-346 120 - E-mail: grandimp@tin.it

Category ★★★★ **Rooms** 92 with air-conditioning, tel, bath, WC, satellite TV, minibar, safe –
Elevator. **Price** Single 218-288,000L, double 260-420,000L, suite 480-590,000L. **Meals** Breakfast
included - half board 165-432,000L, full board 195-463,000L (per pers. 3 days min.). **Restaurant**
Service 12:00PM-2:30PM, 7:30PM-10:00PM - à la carte - Italian cuisine. **Credit cards** All major. **Pets**
Dogs allowed. **Facilities** Heated swimming pool, tennis, squash, garage (18,000L). **Nearby** Ossuccio
and gardens of the Villa Arconati in Punta di Balbia - Menaggio - Villa Carlotta in Tremezzo - boat for
Bellagio - gardens of the Villa Serballoni and Villa Melzi – Golf Villa d'Este (18-hole) in Montorfano.
Open Mar 1 – Oct 31.

If the Villa d'Este is an impossible dream, drive on for a few more kilometers
till you reach Moltrasio. There a beautiful villa that has been completely
transformed stands between its park and the lakefront. At the rear of the old
house they have built a new addition linked to the rest by a large and very
modern atrium which serves as the reception area. Metallic corridors lead to
the modern rooms of the new wing. Although these are perfectly adequate, we
recommend you book one of the ten rooms in the Villa Stucchi facing the
garden, and if you can afford it, La Romantica, opening onto the lake. There
are two restaurants, one overlooking the swimming pool and a man-made
private beach on the lake. The prices are not too steep, but you should know
that the hotel has several conference rooms, and a seminar might possibly
disturb your stay.

How to get there *(Map 2): 7km north of Como.*

San Giorgio Hotel

Lago di Como
Tremezzo 22016 Lenno (Como) - Via Regina, 81
Tel. 0344-40 415 - Fax 0344-41 591
Sig.ra Cappelletti

Category ★★★ **Rooms** 26 with telephone, bath or shower, WC. **Price** Double 230-250,000L. **Meals** Breakfast included, served 8:00-11:00. **Restaurant** Only for residents; service 12:30PM-1:30PM, 7:30PM-8:30PM - mealtime specials. **Credit cards** All major. **Pets** Dogs not allowed. **Facilities** Tennis (25,000L), parking. **Nearby** Mennagio - Villa Carlotta in Tremezzo - boat for Bellagio in Tremezzo – Golf course (18-hole) in Grandola e Uniti. **Open** Apr – mid Oct.

The San Giorgio is a gracious hotel, run as a family affair. It's located in the heart of the Bay of Tremezzina–the dreamiest part of Lake Como. The main building, next to the small old house, was built by the current owner's grandfather. The dining room and the grand salon, which still have the family furniture, 19th-century chairs and couches and a mahogany roll-top desk, open onto a garden-level porch. The rooms are all large and have functional bathrooms, balconies and a view of the bay and the mountains. The grounds, formerly an olive grove, dip gently downward to the lake. They bloom with wisteria and magnolia flowers in the spring, and in the fall are full of the fragrance of exotic plants. The hotel is only a few miles from the wharves of Tremezzo, Cadenabbia and Menaggio–perfect for sailing buffs eager to explore the Italian lakes.

How to get there *(Map 2): 27km north of Como via S340, on the left bank.*

Grand Hotel Victoria

Lago di Como
22017 Menaggio (Como)
Tel. 0344-32 003 - Fax 0344-32 992 - Sig. Proserpio - Sig. Palano
E-mail: hotelvictoria@palacehotel.it - Web: www.palacehotel.it

Category ★★★★ **Rooms** 53 with air-conditioning, telephone, bath or shower, WC, satellite TV – Elevator. **Price** Single 155-185,000L, double 240-280,000L, suite 390,000L. **Meals** Breakfast 25,000L (buffet), served 7:30-11:00 - half board +55,000L (per pers.). **Restaurant** Service 12:30PM- 2:00PM, 7:30PM-10:00PM - mealtime specials 60,000L, also à la carte - Italian cuisine. **Credit cards** All major. **Pets** Dogs allowed. **Facilities** Swimming pool, parking. **Nearby** Villa Carlotta in Tremezzo - Mennagio - Lugano – Golf course (18-hole) in Grandola e Uniti. **Open** All year.

Set on magnificent grounds with enormous trees facing Lake Como, the Grand Hotel Victoria is a late 1880s-style palace. The vast salons have parquet floors, stucco ceilings and a quiet and harmonious atmosphere. As soon as the weather allows, meals are served on the terrace facing the lake under a big striped tent. The most recently refurnished rooms gained in comfort what they may have lost of their former personality.

How to get there *(Map 2): 35km north of Como via S340, on the left bank.*

Hotel Stella d'Italia

Lago di Lugano San Mamete 22010 Valsolda (Como)
Piazza Roma, 1
Tel. 0344-68 139 - Fax 0344-68 729 - Sig. Ortelli
E-mail: info@stelladitalia.com - Web: www.stelladitalia.com

Category ★★★ **Rooms** 34 (15 with air-conditioning) with telephone, bath or shower, WC, satellite TV, safe – Elevator. **Price** Single 125-175,000L, double 215-295,000L. **Meals** Breakfast included, served 7:30-10:00 - half board 130-155,000L (per pers., 3 days min.). **Restaurant** Service 12:30PM-2:00PM, 7:30PM-9:00PM - mealtime specials 35,000L, also à la carte -Specialties: Seafood - Pasta. **Credit cards** All major. **Pets** Small dogs allowed. **Facilities** Private beach, garage (16,000L). **Nearby** Lake Lugano - Villa Favorita - Lugano-Mennagio - Villa Carlotta in Tremezzo. **Open** Apr 1 – Oct 15.

On the shores of Lake Lugano, San Mamete is a pretty little village, home to the Stella d'Italia, which has been run by the Ortelli family for three generations. Many readers have written to us about the beautiful interiors adorned with Madame Ortelli's interesting collection of paintings, artistic lighting and comfortable furniture. The rooms are continually being improved and the most agreeable ones, in the front, have large door-windows facing on the lake. The lakeside garden is marvelous and here you can dine pleasantly under a large trellis smothered with Virginia creeper and roses. There is a small beach where you can sunbathe and go for a swim in the lake. The panorama and surroundings are superb, the prices moderate and the service friendly.

How to get there *(Map 2): 42km north of Como via A9, Lugano-South exit, then towards Gandria-Saint Moritz.*

Grand Hotel Tremezzo

Lago di Como 22019 Tremezzo (Como)
Via Regina, 8
Tel. 0344-42 491 - Fax 0344-40 201 - Famiglia De Santis and Sig. De Bolfo
E-mail: info@grandhoteltremezzo.com - Web: www.grandhoteltremezzo.com

Rooms 100 with telephone, bath or shower, satellite TV, minibar, safe **Price** Standard 388-446,000L, superior 465-535,000L, deluxe 558-641,000L, suite 852-969,000L; extra bed +97,000L. **Meals** Breakfast (buffet) included, served 7:00-10:00 - half-board +51-66,000L. **Restaurant** Open from 12:30PM-2:00PM, 7:30PM-10:00PM - mealtime specials 95,000L, also à la carte. **Credit cards** accepted. **Pets** Small dogs allowed except in restaurant. **Facilities** Sauna, fitness, beauty Center, tennis, swimming pools, solariums, parking, garage (30,000L). **Nearby** Villa Carlotta - Bellagio Villa Melzi - Lake Como. **Open** Mar 4 – Nov 13.

A typical turn-of-the-century palace, the Grand Hotel Temezzo still welcomes an international clientele which comes here to enjoy the climate – pleasant in any season – and to savor the elegant and well-organizaed surroundings of a hotel where the service is courteous and discreet but always available. The hotel has been restored, bringing the décor of a great classic up-to-date. The sixty or so windows in the façade allow many rooms to have views over the lake. All of them have also benefitted from modernization to an impeccable standard of comfort. Salons and dining rooms have retained their space, columns, moulded ceilgns and collections of sculptures or Pompeian engravings. At noon, one can take lunch by the swimming pool; and dinner in summer by candlelight on the terrace overlooking the lake is a wonderful moment. The park, lushly supplied with trees and bushes, has been designed to provide small corners for escape or relaxation. In the evening, l'Escale and its piano-bar reinforce the feeling of a Grand Hotel of the old days.

How to get there (Map 2): 30km from Como.

Hotel Royal Victoria

Lago di Como
23829 Varenna (Lecco)
Piazza San Giorgio, 5
Tel. 0341-81 51 11 - Fax 0341-83 07 22 - Sig. Sorrentino
E-mail: hotelroyalvictoria@promo.it - Web: www.royalvictoria.com

Categorie ★★★★ **Rooms** 43 with telephone, bath, WC, satellite TV, minibar, safe. **Price** Single 110-190,000L, double 160-240,000L, +60,000L with view over the lake; extra bed +100,000L. **Meals** Breakfast 30,000L, served from 7:00-10:00 - half-board 120-160,000L, full board 160-200,000L (per pers. in double room). **Restaurant** Service 12:30PM-2:00PM, 7:30PM-9:30PM - mealtime specials 60,000L, also à la carte. **Credit cards** All major. **Pets** Dogs not allowed. **Facilities** Garage (30,000L). **Nearby** In Varenna: gardens of the Villa Mornico (Apr to Oct) - In Lecco: Villa Manzoni - Tremezo Villa Carlotta - Bellagio Villa Melzi - Lake Como. **Open** all year

The east bank of the legendary (and Stendhalian) Lake Como enjoys less sunshine than the west bank. This may be what discourages certain tourists; but so much the better to take advantage of this exceptional spot. The hotel owes its name to the occasion in 1838 when the Queen of England stayed here and is on the edge of the road that runs around the banks of the lake, but far enough back for one to enjoy the calm of the little square surrounded by old plane trees. On the other side, it looks directly out across the lake. The reception rooms on the ground floor still suggest a certain old-fashioned, nostalgic splendour. The bedrooms are comfortable, but simpler – and it is essential to choose one with the magnificent lake view that is the chief delight of this hotel. The Royal Victoria's other assets are the romantic garden and the good restaurant which, in summer, overlook the waters of the lake.

How to get there *(Map 2): 50km from Como.*

Hotel Olivedo ★★

Lago di Como
23829 Varenna (Lecco)
Piazza Martiri de la Liberta', 4
Tel. 0341-83 01 15 - Fax 0341-83 01 15 - Sig.ra Laura Colombo
E-mail: olivedo@tin.it - Web www.olivedo.it

Category ★★ **Rooms** 15 (6 with bath or shower). **Price** Double 110-120,000L (without bath), 140-180,000L (with bath). **Meals** Breakfast included, served 8:30-10:30 - half board 100-108,000L (without bath.) and full board 115-130,000L (with bath.) per pers. **Restaurant** Service 12:30PM-2:00PM, 7:30PM-9:00PM - mealtime specials 40,000L - Specialties: Pesce di lago - Antipasti i dolci fatti in casa. **Credit cards** Visa, Eurocard, MasterCard. **Pets** Dogs allowed. **Facilities** Parking. **Nearby** Varenna: Villa Monastero Mornico gardens, (Apr – Oct) - Lecco (villa Manzoni) - Lake Como. **Open** Dec 15 – Oct 10.

The nicest way to get to Varenna is to put the car on the ferry and cross the lake from Menaggio or Bellagio - you get a wonderful view of the pretty multicolored houses that descend right down to the water's edge. The hotel is just there, facing the dock. On its shaded terrace stand several tourists, waiting for the boat. The house is a noble yellow building with green shutters, where all is simple but arranged with utmost care. This is clear from the first look at the dining room (with its pretty tablecloths and candles just waiting for the evening meal) or the charming little village bistro. The rooms are extremely well-kept and Laura points out with pride that she still has laundry staff who know how to use starch. However, the rooms are not equally comfortable: not all of them have a private bathroom and some of the furniture has seen better days. To be sure that you won't be disappointed, ask to reserve a room facing the lake. This is a friendly and unpretentious place, in a village a bit off the main tourist paths, which is perhaps something of an advantage.

How to get there (Map 2): 50km from Como.

Villa Simplicitas e Solferino

22028 San Fedele d'Intelvi (Como)
Tel. 031-83 11 32
Sig.ra Ulla Wagner

Category ★★ **Rooms** 10 with shower, WC. **Price** With half board 115,000L (per pers.). **Restaurant** Service 12:30PM-2:30PM, 8:30PM-10:00PM - mealtime specials 40-55,000L - Italian and regional cooking. **Credit cards** All major. **Pets** Dogs allowed (fee). **Facilities** Parking. **Nearby** Cernobbio - Church of Sala Comacina - Val d'Intelvi - Lanzo d'Intelvi - Lugano **Open** Apr – Oct.

Let us say at the outset, this is a real inn of charm and one of our favorite places of all. First the site: You leave the shores of the lake, which can get a bit too touristy, and head for the mountainous countryside, into a landscape of large chestnut trees, larches and ferns. The villa is built on a rise surrounded by verdant meadowland. The cat and the dogs of the house will be the first to greet you and bid you welcome. The interior is delightfully simple, with worn floorboards, faded curtains and yellowed old engravings, but the rooms are as cozy as can be (with comfortable bathrooms) and the cooking, Trentino style, is excellent. A perfect spot if you're seeking inspiration, or a lovers' retreat, or just a wonderful house for a family vacation.

How to get there *(Map 2): 30km north of Como via S340, on the left bank to Argegno, then left towards San Fedele Intelvi.*

Albergo San Lorenzo

46100 Mantova
Piazza Concordia, 14
Tel. 0376-22 05 00 - Fax 0376-32 71 94 - Sig. Tosi
E-mail: hotel@hotelsanlorenzo.it - Web: www.hotelsanlorenzo.it

Category ★★★★ **Rooms** 21 and 9 junior suite with air-conditioning, telephone, bath or shower, WC, satellite TV, minibar, safe – Elevator. **Price** Single 300,000L, double 360,000L, suite 420,000L. **Meals** Breakfast (buffet) included, served 7:00-10:00. **Restaurant** See p. 532. **Credit cards** All major. **Pets** Dogs not allowed. **Facilities** Rooms service (24h), garage (35-50,000L). **Nearby** Mantova: Piazza Sordelo, Duomo, Palazzo Ducale, Piazza delle Erbe, S. Andrea - Santuario delle Grazie (6km) site of the national meeting of Madonnari (mid Aug) - Trips down the Mincio and the Pô (Mar – Oct, starting in front of Castello di San Giorgio), on the Andes 2000 for Venice, return in pullman for the Abbey of San Benedetto Pô and Mincio Park - Sabbioneta: Park of Palazzo del Giardino, Olympic Theater and Ducale Palace, Church of Villa Pasquali (2km) and Viadana (11km) - Verona. **Open** All year.

The Albergo San Lorenzo is the ideally place for visiting the wealthy town of Mantua (Mantova). It is in the middle of a pedestrian area close to the Duomo and the Palazzo Ducale. Decorated with antique furniture and a rococo decor, it is spacious and comfortable. Breakfast is served on a pretty rooftop terrace. The hotel does have three conference rooms but the absence of a restaurant means that it remains a very restful place despite these additional residences. Mantua offers the considerable advantage of being off the beaten tourist track, even though it is undeniably beautiful. One should note, too, that the villages along the river after la Foce dell'Oglio (the place where the Oglio and the Po meet) have very lovely settings.

How to get there *(Map 9): 62km northeast of Parma via S343. 45km southwest of Verona.*

Il Leone

46030 Pomponesco (Mantova)
Piazza IV Martiri, 2
Tel. 0375-86 077 - Fax 0375-86 770
Famiglia Mori

Category ★★★ **Rooms** 8 with air-conditioning in the double room, telephone, shower, WC, TV, minibar. **Price** Single 110,000L, double 160,000L. **Meals** Breakfast included, served 8:00-10:00 - half board 135-145,000L, full board 155-165,000L (per pers., 3 days min.). **Restaurant** Service 12:00PM-2:00PM, 8:00PM-10:00PM - closed Sun evening, Mon - à la carte - Specialties: Salumeria - Ravioli al zucca - Tartufi - Risotto - Zabaione e semi-freddo. **Credit cards** All major. **Pets** Small dogs allowed. Facilities Swimming pool. **Nearby** Church in Viadana - Church in Villa Pasquali - Sabbioneta - Mantova - Parma. **Open** Jan 27 – Dec 26.

Behind the austere façade of this house in the village of Pomponesco–formerly the fiefdom of the celebrated Gonzagua family–you will find a swimming pool and a lovely patio. The salons are impressive: they have superb furniture and high ceilings, and one is decorated with magnificent frescoes. The rooms are large and comfortable. Ask for one by the pool. Breakfasts are copious, the cuisine is perfect and the risotto unforgettable. The wine cellar is well stocked with Italian and international wines.

How to get there (Map 9): *32km northwest of Parma via S62 to Viadana, then on the right towards Pomponesco.*

Four Seasons Hotel

20121 Milano
Via Gesù, 8
Tel. 02-77 088 - Fax 02-77 08 5000 - Sig. V. Finizzola
Web: www.fourseasons.com

Category ★★★★★ **Rooms** 77 and 41 suites with air-conditioning, telephone, bath, WC, satellite TV, videorecorder, safe, minibar – Elevator. **Price** Single 830-980,000L, double 960-1 120,000L, suite 1 240-6 750,000L. **Meals** Breakfast 50,000L, served 7:00-11:30. **Restaurants** "La Veranda", service 11:30AM-11:00PM - mealtime specials 80,000L, also à la carte. "Il teatro", service 7:30PM-11:00PM - mealtime specials 110,000L - Italian cuisine. **Credit cards** All major. **Pets** Dogs allowed except in restaurant. **Facilities** Fitness club, garage (75,000L). **Nearby** Milano Duomo - Brera-Museum - Opening Dec 7 of the lyric season at the Scala - Piccolo teatro di Milano - Abbey of Chiaravalle - Villa Reale in Monza - Abbey of Viboldone - Lake Como - Piazza Ducale in Vigevano - Certosa di Pavia – golf course (9- and 18-hole) at Parco di Monza. **Open** All year.

A superb oasis in a lively triangle of culture and fashion, the Four Seasons is in a former Franciscan monastery built in the 15th century, preserving the original cloister, colonnade and some frescoes. Discreetly luxurious, the hotel features more or less spacious rooms, characterized by sober elegance and accented with Fortuny fabrics in faded colors, sycamore wood furniture and marble baths. Everything is comfortable and very quiet. The Superiors overlook the Via Gesù, the Deluxes and the Suites overlook the cloister. Room service is available around the clock, so if you prefer to have dinner in your room after your evening at La Scala, all you need do is ring. Otherwise, you can enjoy fine savory cuisine at one of two restaurants before having one last drink at the Foyer, the hotel bar. Dream on…

How to get there *(Map 2): In the center of the town.*

Excelsior Hotel Gallia

20124 Milano
Piazza Duca d'Aosta, 9
Tel. 02-67 851 - Fax 02-66 713 239 - Sig. Pietro di Panizza
E-mail: sales@excelsiorgallia.com - Web: www.excelsiorgallia.it

Category ★★★★★ **Rooms** 237 with air-conditioning, telephone, bath, WC, satellite TV, minibar.
Price Single from 600,000L, double from 800,000L, suite 1 000-2 000,000L. **Meals** Breakfast 38-
55,000L, served 7:00-10:30. **Restaurant** Service 12:30PM-2:30PM, 19.30PM-22.30PM - mealtime
specials 90,000L, also à la carte. **Credit cards** All major. **Pets** Dogs not allowed. **Facilities** Fitness
club, garage (60,000L). **Nearby** Milano Duomo - Brera-Museum - Opening Dec 7 of the lyric season
at the Scala - Piccolo teatro di Milano - Abbey of Chiaravalle - Villa Reale in Monza - Abbey of
Viboldone - Lake Como - Piazza Ducale in Vigevano - Certosa di Pavia — Golf course (9- and 18-hole)
at Parco di Monza. **Open** All year.

Just across from the train station, the Excelsior Gallia is one of the great
institutions of Milan. It was built in the 30s and its interior announces
comfort and luxury. The elegant, comfortable rooms have 30s, 50s, and
contemporary decor. You will find excellent cuisine (one of the best restaurant
in Milan) and perfect service here. Night owls can sip a nightcap while
listening to the piano music in *The Baboon*. This classic grand hotel is a great
find.

How to get there *(Map 2): In front of the station.*

Grand Hotel Duomo

20121 Milano
Via San Raffaele, 1
Tel. 02-88 33 - Fax 02-864 620 27/864-50 54 - Sig. Marabini
E-mail: info@grandhotelduomo.com - booking@grandhotelduomo.com
Web: www.grandhotelduomo.com

Category ★★★★★ **Rooms** 160 with air-conditioning, tel, bath, WC, satellite TV, minibar, safe – Elevator. **Price** Single 440-550,000L, double 620-715,000L, triple 700-850,000L, suite 850-1 800,000L. **Meals** Breakfast included, served 7:00-11:00. **Restaurant** Service 12:30PM-2:30PM, 7:30PM-11:00PM - mealtime specials 75-100,000L, also à la carte. **Credit cards** All major. **Pets** Dogs allowed. **Facilities** Garage (75,000L). **Nearby** Milan: Duomo, Brera museum, Piccolo teatro di milano - Abbey of Chiaravalle - Villa Reale in Monza - Abbey of Chiaravalle - Villa Reale in Monza - Abbey of Viboldone - Lake of Como - Piazza Ducale in Vigevano - Certosa di Pavia – Golf course (9- and 18-hole) at Parco di Monza. **Open** All year.

The Duomo is Milan's traditional luxury hotel. Its location just opposite the cathedral has contributed to its reputation. The common areas (lobby and great hall) are still in the modern style of the 1950s, but this look does have a certain allure. The bedrooms, however, have been redone to suit today's taste. They are spacious and elegant and offer good comfort and excellent service. As for the suites, each one is a real duplex with a view of the cathedral. In winter breakfast and meals are served in the large dining room whose windows are under the arcades along the piazza, but in fine weather they are served on the panoramic terrace, just a few yards from the lacy stonework of the towers and spires of the Duomo.

How to get there (Map 2): Piazza del Duomo.

Hotel Pierre Milano

20123 Milano
Via de Amicis, 32
Tel. 02-720 005 81 - Fax 02-805 2157
E-mail: photel@punto.it - Web: www.hotelpierre.it

Category ★★★★★ **Rooms** 49 with tel, bath, WC, TV, minibar. **Price** Single 250-350,000L, double 460-550,000L, suite 690-000L. **Meals** Breakfast included, served 7:00-10:30. **Restaurant** "Petit Pierre", service 12:30PM-2:30PM, 7:30PM-10:30PM - mealtime specials 50-70,000L, also à la carte - Italian and regional cooking. **Credit cards** All major. **Pets** Dogs allowed by reservation. **Facilities** Parking at hotel. **Nearby** Milan: Duomo, Brera museum, Piccolo teatro di milano - Abbey of Chiaravalle - Villa Reale in Monza - Abbey of Chiaravalle - Villa Reale in Monza - Abbey of Viboldone - Lake of Como - Piazza Ducale in Vigevano - Certosa di Pavia – Golf course (9- and 18-hole) at Parco di Monza. **Closed** Aug.

Near the Ticinese quarter, just behind the Via Lanzone and the Via del Torchio, famous for the antique and fine crafts shops, a stay at the Pierre Milano is a good way to get to appreciate this city, which is the heart of modern Italy. A visit to the Brera is a must, if only for the Christ of Mantegna, but you shouldn't miss seeing the boutiques and galleries that show the latest creations of Italian design. The Pierre is a perfect illustration of the spirit of Milan, which blends tradition with great modernity and technological sophistication. For example, the bedrooms are the height of functional and contemporary style, yet on the beds you will find wonderful old linen sheets. The service is perfect. The elegant atmosphere of the piano bar makes it a favorite meeting place for guests, who often stop here for cocktails before dinner and sometimes drop in for a nightcap as well.

How to get there *(Map 2): Ticinese quarter.*

Hotel Diana Majestic

20129 Milano
Viale Piave, 42
Tel. 02-20 581 - Fax 02-2058 2058

Category ★★★★ **Rooms** 94 with air-conditioning, telephone, bath, WC, satellite TV, minibar – Elevator. **Price** Single 650-730,000L, double 700-780,000L. **Meals** Breakfast 45-60,000L. **Restaurant** "La Véranda", open only in summer excepting weekend. Service 1:00PM-2:30PM, 7:30PM-11:00PM - Or see pp. 528-532. **Credit cards** All major. **Pets** Small dogs allowed. **Facilities** Parking. **Nearby** Milano Duomo, Brera-Museum - Opening Dec 7 of the lyric season at the Scala, Piccolo teatro di Milano - Abbey of Chiaravalle - Villa Reale in Monza - Abbey of Viboldone - Lake Como - Piazza Ducale in Vigevano - Certosa di Pavia – Golf course (9- and 18-hole) at Parco di Monza. **Open** All year.

W ell-situated at the end of the Corso Venezia, this hotel of the Ciga-Sheraton group has now recovered all its authenticity, after a restoration carried out with great respect. The Art Deco architecture and features have been preserved: On the ground floor, the little reception room leads to the circular grand salon, a lounge with wicker furniture opening onto a garden. This garden is the last trace of the countryside that once began at the Porta Venezia. The statue of Diana the Huntress that still stands here recalls the inauguration on this site of the Diana Baths, the first public swimming pool for women in Italy. In April, when the wisteria is in bloom, it forms an enormous flowering arbor, under which the restaurant is installed. The bedrooms have been entirely refurbished, with improved comfort and modern technology. An address of charm in Milan.

How to get there (Map 2): *Near the Corso Venezia.*

Hotel Spadari al Duomo

20123 Milano
Via Spadari, 11
Tel. 02-720 023 71 - Fax 02-861 184
E-mail: reservation@spadarihotel.com - guest@spadarihotel.com
Web: www.spadarihotel.com

Category ★★★★ **Rooms** 38 and 1 suite with air-conditioning, tel, bath, WC, satellite TV, minibar, safe – Elevator. **Price** Single 368-428,000L, double 398-498,000L, suite 650,000L. **Meals** Breakfast included. **Restaurant** See pp. 528-532. **Credit cards** All major. **Pets** Dogs not allowed. **Facilities** Parking. **Nearby** Milano: Brera museum, Piccolo teatro - Abbey of Chiaravalle - Villa Reale in Monza - Abbey of Chiaravalle - Villa Reale in Monza - Abbey of Viboldone - Lake Como - Piazza Ducale in Vigevano - Certosa di Pavia – Golf course (9- and 18-hole) at Parco di Monza. **Open** All year.

With the Duomo as a landmark, the ease with which you can find the Hotel Spadari will reassure all those who feel nervous about finding their way around Milan. All visitors interested in food will appreciate the proximity of Speck's, the well-known gourmet boutique of Milan. Aside from the usual assets of a four-star hotel, the Spadari gets its personality from that of its owners, fervent collectors of contemporary art. The total space of the hotel has been redesigned with a view to showing off the works of young Milanese artists, whose murals, paintings and sculptures adorn the reception rooms. There is some offbeat furniture by Ugo La Pietra in postmodern style. The bedrooms retain a classic look even with the abstract paintings that add a modern but never aggressive touch. The bathrooms are thoroughly modern as well. One of the top-floor suites has a view on the spires of the Duomo. A fine address for all who like or are curious about modern art.

How to get there *(Map 2): Near the Duomo.*

Hotel de la Ville

20121 Milano
Via Hoepli, 6
Tel. 02-86 76 51 - Fax 02-86 66 09 - Sig. Giuliano Nardiotti
E-mail: delaville@tin.it - Web: www.delavillemilano.it

Category ★★★★ **Rooms** 109 with telephone, bath, WC, satellite TV, minibar, safe – Elevator. **Price** Single 410-500,000L, double 530-580,000L, suite 750-1 200,000L. **Meals** Breakfast included. **Restaurant** See pp. 528-532. **Credit cards** All major. **Pets** Small dogs allowed. **Facilities** Parking. **Nearby** Milano Duomo, Brera-Museum - Opening Dec 7 of the lyric season at the Scala, Piccolo teatro di Milano - Abbey of Chiaravalle - Villa Reale in Monza - Abbey of Viboldone - Lake of Como - Piazza Ducale in Vigevano - Certosa di Pavia – Golf course (9- and 18-hole) at Parco di Monza. **Open** All year.

The elegant Hotel de la Ville is ideal for active vacationers, as it is close to stores, the Duomo and La Scala. The walls and chairs of the salons and the smoking room are monochromatic shades of pink and blue. The very comfortable rooms are carefully decorated with beautiful fabrics on the walls, matching the bedspreads and curtains. The most spacious suites also enjoy the privilege of a view of the spires of the Duomo. Those who are exhausted by sightseeing and shopping can dine pleasantly on the spot in the hotel restaurant.

How to get there *(Map 2): Between piazza S. Babila and piazza della Scala.*

Antica Locanda dei Mercanti

20123 Milano
Via San Tomaso, 6
Tel. 02-805 40 80 - Fax 02-805 40 90 - Sig.ra Paola Ora - Sig. Bruce
E-mail: locanda@locanda.it - Web: www.locanda.it

Rooms 14 (4with air-conditiong and terrace) with telephone, shower, WC, (TV on request). **Price** 210,000L, 450,000L with terrace. **Meals** Breakfast 15,000L, served 7:30-11:00. **Restaurant** See pp. 528-532. **Credit cards** Visa, Eurocard, MasterCard. **Pets** Dogs not allowed. **Nearby** Milan: Duomo, Teatro alla Scala, Pinacoteca di Brera, Piccolo Teatro di Milano - Abbey of Chiaravalle - Villa Reale in Monza - Lake of Como - Certosa di Pavia — Golf course (9- and 18-hole) at Parco di Monza. **Open** All year.

In Milan, charming often means pricey. This little hotel proves that one can find an attractive hotel in Italy without paying a ruinous price. Located in the quarter of La Scala, the hotel occupies the second floor of an old building. Be careful - the Locanda has no street sign, just a name-plate along with others on the list of bells at the front door. The suggested rooms are all nicely decorated. The shower rooms are small but adequate. The building is extremely quiet. Breakfast is served in the rooms because there is only a tiny reception area, no sitting room, and service is kept to a minimum. But we wouldn't dream of complaining - we're delighted to find a charming hotel at a decent price (at least in the ten rooms without terrace or air-conditioning, which makes the other four much more expensive). Though smoking is not absolutely forbidden in the rooms, it will be appreciated if you keep it to a minimum or refrain altogether. Give advance notice if you intend to arrive after 5 pm.

How to get there *(Map 2): In the Scala neighborhood. Parking nearby, see with the hotel.*

Albergo Madonnina

21050 Cantello (Varese)
Largo Lanfranco da Ligurno, 1
Tel. 0332-417 731 - Fax 0 332-418 403 - Famiglia Limido
E-mail: elmado@working.it - Web: www.madonnina.it

Rooms 14 and 3 suites with telephone, bath, WC, satellite TV. **Price** Single 118,000L, double 167,000L, suite 250-350-500,000L. **Meals** Breakfast 16,000L, half board 176,000L (per pers.). **Restaurant** Service 12:30PM-2:00PM, 7:30PM-9:30PM - closed Mon - mealtime specials 55-75,000L - Regional cooking. **Credit cards** All major. **Pets** Dogs allowed. **Facilities** Parking. **Nearby** Lake Como - Lake majeur - Lake Varèse - Monte Campo dei Fiori (view) - Castiglione Olona - Castelseprio (S. Maria Foris portas). **Open** All year.

Cantello is a little country village between Lake Como and Lake Maggiore, a few kilometers from Varese, near the Italian-Swiss border at Staggio-Gaggiolo. The Madonnina owes its reputation mainly to its restaurant, specially known for its spring menus featuring fresh asparagus. Each season meals are built around a theme, based on local produce. This former coaching inn, covered and surrounded by lush vegetation, also has fourteen rooms and two suites. The decoration is simple and elegant, which nicely sets off the architecture of the place. The amenities are very good, particularly the bathrooms. A very useful address for its cuisine and refinement in a region rich in tourist attractions, and a good stopping place on the road to southern Italy.

How to get there (Map 2): 9km from Varese. From the Saint-Gothard pass, motorway exit Stabio-Gaggiolo. Cantello is then 2km away. Malpensa airport: 27km.

Albergo del Sole

20076 Maleo
Via Trabattoni, 22
Tel. 0377-58 142 - Fax 0377-45 80 58
Francesca and Mario Colombani

Category ★★★★ **Rooms** 8 with air-conditioning, telephone, bath or shower, WC, TV, minibar **Price** Single 160,000L, double 260,000L, apartment (4 pers.) 360,000L. **Meals** Breakfast included. **Restaurant** Service 12:15PM-2:15PM, 8:15PM-9:45PM - closed Sun and Mon - mealtime specials 60-90,000L, also à la carte - Specialties: Spaghetti con pomodori - Olive e capperi - Fegato di vitello all'uva - Seafood. **Credit cards** All major. **Pets** Dogs allowed. **Facilities** Parking. **Nearby** Cremona - Piacenza - Certosa di Pavia. **Closed** Jan, Aug, Sun evening and Mon.

Situated at the point where the plain of the river Adda meets that of the Po, some 60km south of Milan, Maleo has has long been a celebrated stopping place, and visitors would stop at the Sole to enjoy the inn's excellent Lombard cooking. The they had to find somewhere to stay… To please customers who wished to prolong the pleasure, a few rooms were opened, reviving the traditions of this former coaching stop. The rooms are simple, elegant and very comfortable. Nowadys it is Franco Colombani's children who carry on his work in the kitchen. This is a great place to stop off for a fine meal or to spend a pleasant weekend if you are visiting the Pavia or Crémona monasteries.

How to get there *(Map 9): 60km south of Milano via A1 Casalfusterlengo exit, towards Codogno, then Maleo at 5km.*

Hotel Colonne

Sacro Monte 21100 Varese
Via Fincarà, 37
Tel. 0332-224 633 - Fax 0332-821 593

Category ★★★★ **Rooms** 10 with telephone, bath, WC, satellite TV, minibar – Elevator, wheelchair access. **Price** Single 180,000L, double 250,000L. **Meals** Breakfast included, served 6:30-11:30. **Restaurant** Service 12:30PM-2:30PM, 7:45PM-10:00PM - closed Tues - mealtime specials, also à la carte. **Credit cards** All major. **Pets** Small dogs allowed. **Nearby** Santa Maria del Monte Sanctuary - Monte Campo dei Fiori (panorama) - Lake Varese - Lake Lugano - Castiglione Olona: casa Castiglioni, la Chiesa di villa – Golf course di Luvinate (18-hole). **Closed** Jan.

The Hotel Colonne in on Sacro Monte which, along with Monte Campo dei Fiori, tower over Varese and its lake. The access is by car, of course, but don't miss a walk around the 14 identical chapels built in the 17th century and decorated with frescoes and sculptures by Lombard artists. As for the hotel itself, it is a lovely place combining all the qualities of a hotel of charm: "an elegant and refined decor in an attractive setting, comfortable and well-kept rooms, a good view, an excellent restaurant, a warm welcome, a thoughtful staff... The weak points? Just one: the hotel and the restaurant are closed on Tuesday." This was an opinion we received from a couple of our readers, and it was exactly what we found when we went to check out the Colonne at their excellent suggestion.

How to get there *(Map 2): 56km northwest of Milano. In Varese, leave town via the viale Aguggiari to Sacro Monte.*

Il Sole di Ranco

Lago Maggiore - 21020 Ranco (Varese)
Piazza Venezia, 5
Tel. 0331-97 65 07 - Fax 0331-97 66 20 - Famiglia Brovelli
E-mail: ivanett@tin.it

Category ★★★★ **Apart.** 4 and 10 suites with air-conditioning, telephone, bath or shower, WC, TV, safe, minibar. **Price** Double 350,000L, suite 500-700,000L. **Meals** Breakfast not included, served 7:30-11:00 - half board 300-470,000L (per pers., 3 days min.). **Restaurant** Service 12:30PM-2:00PM, 7:45PM-9:30PM - closed Tues - mealtime specials 95-135,000L, also à la carte - Regional cooking. **Credit cards** All major. **Pets** Dogs not allowed. **Facilities** Parking. **Nearby** Santa Caterina del Sasso (sanctuary) - Arcumeggia - Stresa - Borromean islands - Villa Bozzolo - Villa Taranto - Casalzuigno - Rocca di Angera. **Closed** Jan 1 – Feb 14.

For three generations, Il Sole has been famous for its fine restaurant. Eight duplex suites have been added, each with a balcony or terrace on Lake Maggiore. The year 2000 will mark the two hundred and fiftieth anniversary of the firm. Ettore Machetti's décor is a good example of Italian design, which is not incompatible with outstanding comfort and a warm appearance which results from skilful harmonization of fabric shades and colors. Carlo and David Brovelli's cooking is outstanding, but guests will also enjoy the preserves and other Itala specialties, which you can buy at the Bottega del Sole gift shop. All this without mentioning Andrea's friendly welcome, plus beautiful grounds, a delightful terrace and excellent service at Il Sole.

How to get there *(Map 2): 67km northwest of Milano via A8, Sesto Calende exit; then S33 and S629 towards Laveno, on the right bank; 30km from the airport Mimano-Malpensa.*

Hotel Fortino Napoleonico

60020 Portonovo (Ancona)
Via Poggio
Tel. 071-80 14 50 - Fax 071-80 14 54
Sig. Roscioni

Category ★★★★ **Rooms** 30 with air-conditioning, telephone, bath or shower, WC, TV, minibar. **Price** Single 200-250,000L, double 270-350,000L, junior suite 300-400,000L, suite 360-450,000L; extra bed 70,000L. **Meals** Breakfast included, served about 7:30-10:30 - half board 180-240,000L, full board 220-280,000L (per pers., 3 days min.). **Restaurant** Service 1:00PM-2:30PM, 8:00PM-10:00PM - mealtime specials 80,000L, also à la carte - Specialties: Seafood. **Credit cards** All major. **Pets** Dogs allowed. **Facilities** Swimming pool, tennis (20,000L), gym, private beach, parking. **Nearby** Portonovo (Abbey of Santa Maria di Portonovo) - Fermo (Duomo and diocesano museum) – Conero golf course (27-hole) in Sirolo. **Open** All year.

The "Fort Napoleon," erected on Bay of Portonovo in 1808, is now an extraordinary hotel. The road that winds around this former military edifice has been transformed into flowering terraces with laurel and other fragrant plants and the old arms room has metamorphosed into multiple salons and dining rooms filled with Empire-style furniture. Carefully selected antique furniture and contemporary materials coexist in perfect harmony in the guest rooms. The seafood-based cuisine is innovative and excellent.

How to get there *(Map 11): 10km south of Ancona via A14, Ancona-South exit, towards Camerano.*

Hotel Emilia

60020 Portonovo (Ancona)
Poggio di Portonovo, 149
Tel. 071-80 11 45 - Fax 071-80 13 30 - Sig. Fiorini
E-mail: info@hotelemilia.com - Web: www.hotelemilia.com

Category ★★★★ **Rooms** 26 and 3 suites with air-conditioning, telephone, bath or shower, WC, TV, minibar – Wheelchair access. **Price** Single 200-250,000L, double 300-400,000L, suite 400-600,000L. **Meals** Breakfast included, served at any time - half board 250-300,000L (per pers., 3 days min.). **Restaurant** Service 12:45PM-2:00PM, 8:00PM-10:00PM - mealtime specials 80,000L, also à la carte - Specialties: Seafood - Pasta fatta in casa e verdure. **Credit cards** All major. **Pets** Dogs not allowed. **Facilities** Swimming pool, tennis, parking. **Nearby** Portonovo (Abbey of Santa Maria di Portonovo) - Ancona - Fermo (Duomo and diocesano museum) – Conero golf course (27-hole) in Sirolo. **Open** All year.

The Hotel Emilia is in the heart of the Conero park, halfway up a hill, between he bay of Portonovo and mount Conero, overlooking the beaches from its natural terrace among the broom, beech trees and the arbutus. A beautiful green lawn extends from the foot of the hotel to the cliff overhanging the ocean. The twittering of the swallows living on the rooftops will wake you in the morning. The pleasant rooms look out over the sea. This family estate, named after a woman who actively campaigned for the preservation of the region, has an atmosphere of deep tranquility. Today, father and son, continuing the family tradition, manage the hotel and restaurant. A wonderful place to know.

How to get there *(Map 11): 10km south of Ancona via A14, Ancona-South exit, towards Camerano.*

Hotel Monteconero

60020 Sirolo (Ancona)
Via Monteconero, 26
Tel. 071-93 30 592 - Fax 071-93 30 365
E-mail: monteconero.hotel@fastnet.it - Web: www.fastnet.it/monteconerohotel

Category ★★★ **Rooms** 41 and 9 suites (einige with air-conditioning) with bath or shower, WC – Elevator. **Price** Double 180-230,000L. **Meals** Breakfast included, served 8:00-9:45 - half board 135-170,000L (per pers., 2 days min.). **Restaurant** Service 1:00PM-3:00PM, 8:00PM-10:00PM - à la carte. Specialties: Seafood. **Credit cards** All major. **Pets** Small dogs allowed except in restaurant. **Facilities** Swimming pool, tennis (15,000L), parking. **Nearby** Abbey of San Pietro - Abbey of Santa Maria di Portonovo - Ancona – Conero golf course (27-hole) in Sirolo. **Open** Mar 15 – Nov 15.

At the summit of the regional park bearing the same name, this 12th century Carmaldosian abbey overlooks the sea and the village of Sirolo. Around the abbey the owners have built a comfortable, modern hotel with a panoramic restaurant. The simple rooms are well equipped and face the sea. The rooms over the restaurant have a private terrace. Since the beaches of Sirolo are only two-and-a-half miles away, the Monte Conero is filled with Italian tourists in the summer and at such times, seems like a typical tourist resort. Summer, therefore, is not the best season to visit this beautiful place. There is a large, inviting pool on the grounds, as well as a golf course two-and-a-half miles away.

How to get there *(Map 11): 26km southeast of Ancona via the coast to Fonte d'Olio, towards Sirolo, then towards Badia di San Pietro to Monte Conero.*

Hotel Vittoria

61100 Pesaro
Piazzale della Libertà, 2
Tel. 0721-34 343 - Fax 0721-65 204 - Alex Marcucci Pinoli
E-mail: vittoria.viphotels.it - Web: www.viphotels.it

Category ★★★★ **Rooms** 27 with air-conditioning, bath, WC, TV – Elevator. **Price** Single 220-260,000L, double 300-360,000L, apartment 500-600,000L. **Meals** Breakfast 30,000L (buffet), served 7:30-10:30. **Restaurant** Service 1:00PM-3:00PM, 8:00PM-10:00PM - mealtime specials 70-90,000L, also à la carte - Specialties: Seafood. **Credit cards** All major. **Pets** Dogs not allowed. **Facilities** Swimming pool, sauna, garage. **Nearby** Pesaro: Piazza del popolo (Palazzo Ducale), house of Rossini, Civici museum, Rossini Opera Festival in Aug - Villa Caprile - Villa Imperiale - Gradara - Urbino. **Open** All year.

Meeting place for the stars of the Rossini Opera Festival in August, the Hotel Vittoria is on the sea and is one of the best hotels in town. The salon still has its original 1900 stucco finish; it opens onto a restaurant on a large Scandinavian-style porch. In summer, the large windows are opened and you can dine outside with a view of the sea. The rooms are simple, elegant and provide every comfort; the same is true for the bathrooms. The owners have several similar estates in the area, so if you like variety you can enjoy a meal in one these.

How to get there *(Map 11): Between Bologna and Rome via A14.*

Hotel Villa Serena

61100 Pesaro
Via San Nicola, 6/3
Tel. 0721-55 211 - Fax 0721-55 927 - Sig. Pinto
Web: www.villa—serena.it

Category ★★★ **Rooms** 8 and 1 suite with bath or shower, WC. **Price** Double 190-270,000L, suite 260-350,000L. **Meals** Breakfast 18,000L, served 8:00-11:30; half board 140-190,000L, full board 190-240,000L (per pers. 3 day min.). **Restaurant** Service 1:30PM-3:00PM, 8:30PM-10:00PM - mealtime specials 75-120,000L, also à la carte - Specialties: Salmone marinato con rucola - Filetto di branzino - Carre di vitello in crosta. **Credit cards** All major. **Pets** Small dogs allowed. **Facilities** Swimming pool, parking. **Nearby** In Pesaro: piazza del Popolo (Palazzo Ducale), house of Rossini, Civici museum, Rossini Opera Festival in Aug - Villa Caprile - Villa Imperiale - Colle San Bartolo o Accio - Gradara - Urbino. **Closed** Jan 2 – 20.

If you are coming to Pesaro for the Rossini festival, or for another event, and if you prefer not to stay in the city itself, nor on the rather crowded Adriatic coast, then your only choice is to head for the surrounding hills. Four kilometers from the sea and three from the town center, the summer residence of the Counts of Pinto de Franca (in a landmark building) has been a hotel since the 1960s. Built in 1600, decorated with 17th-century frescoes and ancient paintings and filled with the furniture of the Pinto family (which still runs the place) this hotel is an ideal spot for anyone who seeks peace and quiet. The swimming pool, surrounded by orange and lemon trees, overlooks the peaceful Umbrian plain. Don't be put off by a certain austerity - the rooms and bathrooms are done with great sobriety. The central part of the house, with its three bedrooms and a living room, can be used as an independent apartment with its own private entrance.

How to get there *(Map 11): Between Bologna and Roma via A14.*

Hotel Bonconte

61029 Urbino
Via della Mura, 28
Tel. 0722-2463 - Fax 0722-4782 - Sig. A.F. Marcucci Pinoli
E-mail: bonconte.viphotels.it - Web: www.viphotels.it

Category ★★★★ **Rooms** 23 with air-conditioning, telephone, bath or shower, WC, satellite TV, minibar. **Price** Single 120-140,000L, double 190-260,000L, suite 300-400,000L. **Meals** Breakfast 25,000L, served 7:30-10:30. **Restaurant** Service 8:00PM-10:30PM - closed Tues - mealtime specials 28,000L - Specialties: Antipasti vegetali - Passatelli in brodo - Ravioli agli asparagi - Agnello - Filetto G. Cesare. **Credit card** All major. **Pets** Dogs allowed (8-10,000L). **Facilities** Parking. **Nearby** Urbino (Palazzo Ducal, Galleria delle Marche, San Giovanni Battista) - Urbania - Sant'Angelo in Vado - Castles and villages of Montefeltro: Sassocoruaro, Macereta, Feltria - Pesado ("Victoria Club" beach). **Open** All year.

The Hotel Boconte is in the historic town of Urbino. This old duchy seems unchanged since the days of splendor of its prince of light, Federico de Montefeltro. He wanted it to be a model for a new society where the refinement of manners would reflect the elegance of thought and taste, as described by Castiglione in *The Perfect Courtisan (Il Cortegiano)*. The hotel is on the outskirts of this pink village, close to the Ducal Palace. It has a splendid view of the magical hills of Umbria which illuminate the backgrounds of the paintings of Piero della Francesca. This will make you forget the small sized but comfortable rooms.

How to get there *(Map 11): 36km southwest of Pesaro via A14, Pesado-Urbino exit, then S423*

Locanda della Posta

06100 Perugia
Corso Vanucci, 97
Tel. 075-57 28 925 - Fax 075-57 32 562
Sig. Bernardini

Category ★★★★ **Rooms** 40 with air-conditioning, telephone, bath or shower, WC, TV, minibar –
Elevator. **Price** Single 160-190,000L, double 210-300,000L, suite 320-360,000L. **Meals** Breakfast
included, served 7:30-10:30. **Restaurant** See p. 535. **Credit cards** All major. **Pets** Dogs allowed.
Nearby Perugia: Corso Vanucci, Duomo, Palazzo dei Priori, Fontana Maggiore, National Gallery,
oratorio S. Bernardino, via Bagliona - Events: festival of La Desolata, Good Friday, antiques market
on last weekend of the month - Torgiano - Assisi - Bettona - Ipogeo etrusco dei Volumni in Ponte San
Giovanni (N 75) - Spello - Spoleto – Ellera golf course (18-hole) in Perugia. **Open** All year.

The Locanda della Posta is an old palace which has been entirely restored.
On the Corso Vanucci, one of the most beautiful and famous
avenues–which can get pretty noisy–you will have a chance to feel the pulse
of the town and enjoy the Peruginian pace of life. The rooms are extremely
comfortable. The decor is subtle, elegant and very pleasant. The salons still
have their original frescoes. The service is friendly. Be sure to spend some time
visiting this historic city, on whose walls you can actually see traces of the
Etruscan, Roman and Renaissance periods.

How to get there (Map 14): In the old city.

Castello dell'Oscano

Cenerente 06134 (Perugia)
Tel. 075-58 43 71 - Fax 075-69 06 66
Sig. Bussolati
E-mail: info@oscano.com - Web: www.oscano.com

Category ★★★★ **Rooms** 10 with telephone, shower, WC, satellite TV, minibar – Elevator, 1 room for disabled persons. **Price** Single 300,000L, double 320,000L, suite 420-460,000L; extra bed 110,000L. **Meals** Breakfast included, served 8:00-11:00. **Restaurant** Only for residents, service 8:30PM - mealtime specials 60,000L. **Credit cards** All major. **Pets** Dogs allowed. **Facilities** Swimming pool, parking. **Nearby** Perugia - Torgiano - Church of Madonna del Miracoli at Castel Rigone - Etruscan hypogeum of the Volumni at Ponte San Giovanni (N 75) - Spello - Spoleto – Ellera golf course (18-hole) in Perugia. **Open** All year.

Just a few kilometers from beautiful Perugia, the ancient towers and crenellated walls of the Castello dell'Oscano rise up amid a forest of cedars, sequoias and cypresses. It is a historic castle that has preserved its interesting library and large wood-paneled salons. The rooms in the Castello are all spacious, comfortable and luxurious suites. They all, too, have a fine view over the grounds, but we were especially taken with the one that looks over the loggia and by La Torre which will have you hurrying back to bed just to enjoy the view over the large private terrace on the roof. In order to preserve the intimate character of this privileged spot, the restaurant only serves residents. A marvellous base from which to discover Perugia and the Umbrian countryside, at prices still below those usually charged by hotels in this class.

How to get there *(Map 14): 8km of Perugia, towards Firenze, Madonna alta exit; stade Renato Curi; railway bridge; south Marco; Cenerente.*

Villa Ada

06134 Cenerente (Perugia)
Tel. 075-58 43 71 - Fax 075-69 06 66
Sig. Ravano
E-mail: info@oscano.com - Web: www.oscano.com

Rooms 12 with air-conditioning, telephone, shower, WC, TV, minibar. **Price** Single 180,000L, double 240,000L; extra bed 60,000L. **Meals** Breakfats in the château included, served 7:00-11:00. **Restaurant** In Castello "Turandot", only for residents - Service 8:30PM - mealtime specials 60,000L. **Credit cards** All major. **Pets** Dogs allowed. **Facilities** Swimming pool, parking. **Nearby** Perugia - Torgiano - Assisi Bettona - Church of the Madonna dei miracoli at Castel Rigone - Etruscan hypogeum (underground burial chamber) of the Volumni at Ponte San Giovanni (N 75) - Spello - Spoleto – Golf courses at Ellera, (18-hole), and Antognolla **Open** All year.

On the same estate (of some 250 hectares) as the Castello Oscano, you can also stay at the Villa Ada. This is an aristocratic house built in the 19th Century. Here the décor is less imposing, but no less elegant. The rooms are less luxurious , but equally comfortable, and guests can also take their meals at the restaurant of the château, the Turandot. This proves to be an excellent way to enjoy the very beautiful setting without paying so much for it. Finally, if you want to stay a long time, you might choose to go a few kilometers away to La Macina and rent an apartment, minimally furnished, but with a swimming pool, and the opportunity to buy wine, cheese and honey on the spot. Prices vary according to the number of bedrooms in the house; enquiries to reception/reservation.

How to get there *(Map 14): 8km from Perugia. On the SS Florence-Rome, exit Madonna alta, continue on the right as far as the stadium, then the railway bridge, Santa Lucia, San Marco and Generente (10km).*

Villa Aureli 🌳

06071 Castel del Piano Umbro (Perugia)
Via Cirenei, 70
Tel. 075-51 59 186 - Fax 075-514 94 08 - Dott. L. di Serego Alighieri

Apartments 2 (4-6 pers.) with kitchen, sitting room, lounge, 2 rooms, telephone, bath, TV. **Price** For 1 week 1 650,000L in low season, 2 200,000L (Jun – Sept). **Credit cards** Not accepted. **Pets** Dogs not allowed. **Facilities** Swimming pool, parking. **Nearby** Perugia - Assisi - Spello - Collegio del Cambio (Perugin fresco) - Montefalco – Ellera golf course (18-hole) in Perugia. **Open** All year.

Our arrival at the Villa Aureli was like something out of a Visconti film, a scene full of charm that seemed to belong to another time. The old Count di Serego Alighieri was walking in the magnificent garden surrounded by a flock of grandchildren who had come, as they do every summer, from the four corners of Europe to see their grandfather and touch their roots. One of the grandchildren showed us around the villa. It was a marvel. The building dates from the 16th century, but the facilities inside are in the finest tradition of the 18th, the time when the Alighieris acquired the villa. The present descendant and owner has worked hard to find old documents that would enable him to preserve or recreate the decor of the past: decorative rock work, Chinese ornaments, Persian prints, painted furniture and the baroque Italian gardens, making the whole place a sort of museum of the art of living of that bygone age... The villa is large and has two handsome apartments, comfortable and elegant, and marked with the same historic grace. The larger and finer of the two is on the second floor. It goes without saying that if you want to stay at the Aureli, you will have to contact the Count early enough to settle all the details well in advance. A stay at the Villa Aureli is quite an experience.

How to get there (*Map 14*): *10km of Perugia, Madonna Alta exit, statale 220 towards Città della Pieve.*

Relais Le Tre Vaselle

06089 Torgiano (Perugia)
Via G. Garibaldi, 48
Tel. 075-98 80 447 - Fax 075-98 80 214 - G. Margheritini
E-mail: 3vaselle@3vaselle.it - Web: www.3vaselle.it

Category ★★★★★ **Rooms** 48 and 12 suites with telephone, bath or shower, WC, minibar. **Price** Single 240-260,000L, double 340-380,000L, suite 440,000L. **Meals** Breakfast included, served 7:30-10:00 - half board +80,000L, full board +160,000L (per pers. 3 days min.). **Restaurant** Service 12:30PM-2:30PM, 8:00PM-10:30PM - mealtime specials 65-75,000L, also à la carte - Italian and regional cooking. **Credit cards** All major. **Pets** Dogs not allowed. **Facilities** 2 Swimming pool, health fitness club, parking. **Nearby** In Torgiano: wine museum (home to the famous Lungarotti winery) - Perugia - Assisi - Bettona – Ellera golf course (18-hole) in Perugia. **Open** All year.

Perugia is only 8 kilometers away, so if you like the country, with tradition, refinement and good cuisine, then stay at the Tre Vaselle. The hotel has a handsome stone façade and below it a superb terrace where breakfast and meals are served in good weather. When the weather is not so fine, the living and dining rooms have fireplaces and a nice log fire creates a homey, intimate atmosphere. The rooms are sober and elegant, the service discreet and courteous. Add to all this the interest of the site: The beautiful fortified village of Torgiano is known for its Lungarotti wines, and you will find a wine museum with a nice collection. Other places too will allow you to sample local produce, like the Osteria del Museo where you can taste or buy olive oil, fine wines and honey from the Azienda Lungarotti. Those with a real interest in wine production can visit the estate itself, to see the vines and storerooms.

***How to get there** (Map 14): 16km from Perugia via SS3 towards Todi.*

La Bondanzina

06089 Torgiano (Perugia)
Tel. 075-98 80 447 - Fax 075-98 80 214
G. Margheritini

Category ★★★★★ Rooms 4 and 1 suite with air-conditioning, tel, shower and 1 bath, WC, minibar. **Price** Single 200,000L, double 340,000L, suite 440,000L. **Meals** Breakfast included, served 7:00-10:30 - half board +80,000L (per pers. 3 day min.). **Restaurant** In the Tre Vaselle hotel. **Credit cards** All major. **Pets** Dogs not allowed. **Facilities** Swimming pool and health center in the Tre Vaselle hotel, Sauna (30,000L). **Nearby** In Torgiano: Cellar, Wine museum - Perugia - Bettona - Assisi – Ellera golf course (18-hole) in Perugia. **Open** All year.

Still in Torgiano, La Bondanzina, named after its former owners, is a village house dating from the 19th century. With the same management, the same quality of service and the same refinement as the Tre Vaselle, except that there are only a few rooms, each one meticulously arranged. There are two small singles, two doubles and a suite. Some fine pieces of antique furniture and amazing panoramic murals create a very poetic setting. Meals are served in the main house, just a few yards away, but if you like, breakfast can be brought to you in your room. This is a little hotel of great charm.

How to get there *(Map 14): 16km from Perugia via SS3bis towards Todi.*

La Locanda del Capitano

06014 Montone (Perugia)
Via Roma, 7
Tel. and Fax 075-93 06 521 - 075-93 06 455 - G. Polito
E-mail: locanda_del_capitano@hotmail.com
Web: www.umbriatravel.com/locandadelcapitano/locandadelcapitano.htm

Rooms 8 with telephone, shower and 1 with bath, TV, minibar. **Price** Double (for 1 pers.) 100-130,000L, double 140-180,000L. **Meals** Breakfast included, served 8:00-10:00 - half board 100-120,000L (per pers., 3 days min.). **Restaurant** Service 12:30PM-2:00PM, 7:30PM-9:30PM - mealtime specials, also à la carte - Regional cooking. **Credit cards** All major. **Pets** Small dogs allowed. **Nearby** Perugia - Bettona - Assisi - Gubbio - Trasimène Lake – Ellera golf course (18-hole) in Perugia. Antognolla **Closed** Feb.

Montone is a charming little medieval town typical of those around Perugia, set in the midst of the countrywide where it dominates a valley. The Locanda del Capitano is a typcial village inn, which you will find round a bend in a narrow street, and owes its name to the famous condottiere Braccio Fontebraccio who lived here: there is a reminder of his presence on the fresco at the entrance. The stairs leading to the bedrooms are decorated with wooden frames carved with images of gorgons. All the rooms themselves are simple and charming, fitted out with old regional furniture. The largest (nos. 7 and 8), on the second floor, have a terrace which overlooks the tiled roofs and the church tower. Everything is very well kept. The dining room, on the ground floor, is spacious, but as soon as the fine weather arrives, food is served on the terrace overlooking the street. Your welcome will be warm and the village, which is not a tourist attraction, gives an idea of country life in this region.

How to get there (Map 14): 35km north of Perugia by E45, Montone exit.

Hotel Fontebella

06082 Assisi (Perugia)
Via Fontebella, 25
Tel. 075-81 28 83/81 64 56 - Fax 075-81 29 41 - G. and E. Angeletti
E-mail: fontebel@krenet.it - Web: www.fontebella.com

Rooms 46 with air-conditioning, telephone, bath, satellite TV, minibar, safe – Elevator. **Price** Single 140-190,000L, double 190-380,000L, suite 450,000L. **Meals** Breakfast included, served 7:00-10:00 - half board 180,000L (per pers.). **Restaurant** "Il Frantoio", service 12:00PM-2:30PM, 7:00PM-9:30PM - mealtime specials 40-80,000L, also à la carte - Specialties: Tartufi - Funghi - Porcini - Strangozzi. **Credit cards** All major. **Pets** Dogs allowed. **Facilities** Parking. **Nearby** Assisi (Basilica S. Francesco, Santa Chiara, Duomo, Ermitage Eremo delle Carceri, Basilica San Damiano, Basilica Santa Maria degli Angeli) - Church of Santa Maria di Rivortolo - Perugia - Abbey of San Benetto - Spello – Ellera golf course (18-hole) in Perugia. **Open** All year.

In the heart of the historical town center, the recently established Hotel Fontebella occupies a 17th-century palazzo. In the front, an austere and noble façade looks out on the street, while at the back, in contrast, a terrace covered in greenery overhangs the valley. The building has been restored in a way that respects its old stones while offering guests the best modern comforts. Hence the décor is classical and expensive looking, both in the public rooms and in the bedrooms where carpets, pictures and furniture are modish or antique. In the breakfast room one can admire the forms of a typically Umbrian vaulted ceiling. The dining room of the restaurant, Il Frantoio, is more impersonal, but its cooking (which earns a Michelin rosette) and the view from its windows easily make up for that. Another undoubted asset is the car park situated right opposite the hotel in this pedestrian town.

How to get there *(Map 14): 25km east of Perugia; in the historic center.*

Hotel Umbra

06081 Assisi (Perugia)
Via degli Archi, 6
Tel. 075-81 22 40 - Fax 075-81 36 53 - Sig. Laudenzi
E-mail: humbra@mail.caribusiness.it - Web: www.caribusiness.it/carifo/az/hotelumbra

Category ★★★ **Rooms** 25 (20 with air-conditioning), with telephone, bath or shower, WC, TV, minibar. **Price** Single 110-130,000L, double 160-200,000L. **Meals** Breakfast included, served 8:00-10:00. **Restaurant** Service 12:30PM-2:00PM, 8:00PM-9:15PM - closed Sun - à la carte - Specialties: Delizia di cappelletti - Crespelle all' Umbra - Friccò - Piccione alla ghiotta - Zabaione al cioccolato. **Credit cards** All major. **Pets** Dogs not allowed. **Nearby** Assisi (Basilica S. Francesco, Santa Chiara, Duomo, Ermitage Eremo delle Carceri, Basilica Santa Maria degli Angeli) - Church of Santa Maria di Rivortolo - Perugia - Abbey of San Benetto - Spello – Ellera golf course (18-hole) in Perugia. **Closed** Jan 16 – Mar 14.

A centrally-located and yet quiet hotel in the middle of historic Assisi, with the front on the pedestrian zone of the city and the back overlooking the lower town and the valley. All the rooms are pleasant, installed like real little apartments with living area and balcony, but we would recommend the ones with the view of the valley. In summer, the restaurant serves on the terrace, under a flowered trellis. If you have succumbed to the beauty of the lovely basilica of Saint Francis, now you can discover the delights of Umbrian cooking, with local wines and specialities.

How to get there *(Map 14): 25km east of Perugia via S75, then S147 to Assisi; in the old city.*

Le Silve di Armenzano

Armenzano 06081 Assisi (Perugia)
Tel. 075-801 90 00 - Fax 075-801 90 05
Sig.ra Taddia

Category ★★★★ **Rooms** 15 with telephone, bath or shower, WC, TV, minibar. **Price** Single 150,000L, double 300,000L. **Meals** Breakfast included, served 8:00-10:00 - half board 200,000L. **Restaurant** Mealtime specials 50-65,000L, also à la carte - Regional cooking and produce from the estate. **Credit cards** All major. **Pets** Dogs not allowed. **Facilities** Swimming pool, tennis, sauna, mini golf, parking. **Nearby** In Assisi: Ermitage Eremo delle Carceri, Basilica Convento San Damiano, Basilica Santa Maria degli Angeli - Church of Santa Maria di Rivortoto - Abbey of San Benedetto - Spello - Spoleto — Ellera golf course (18-hole) in Perugia. **Closed** Nov 20 — Mar 1.

The quiet and solitude of the mountains await you at the Armenzano. Only seven-and-a-half miles from Assisi, this restored medieval hamlet has been transformed into a hotel. Set in a wild and grandiose landscape, the Silve has retained its rustic charm, while offering comfortable, tastefully furnished rooms, a swimming pool and tennis court. The Silve also has facilities for horseback riding and mountain motorbiking. The owners of this private estate try to outdo the professionals. A glance through the guest book will reveal all the nice things guests have written about the service and the cuisine enjoyed during their visits.

How to get there *(Map 14): 32km east of Perugia to Assisi via S75 - when you leave Assisi, turn on the right towards Armenzano (12km).*

Podere La Fornace

Tordibetto d'Assisi 06081 Assisi (Perugia)
Via Ombrosa, 3
Tel. 075-801 95 37 - Fax 075-801 96 30
E-mail: info@lafornace.com - Web: www.lafornace.com

Apartment 4 with telephone, satellite TV. **Price** Apartment (min. 2 nights): 140-200,000L/day/pers. apartment 2-3 pers. - 200-315,000L/days/pers. apartment 4-6 pers. **Meals** No breakfast. **No restaurant** But products of the estate for sale (see our selection of restaurants, p. 535). **Credit cards** Visa, Eurocard, MasterCard. **Pets** Small dogs allowed. **Facilities** Swimming pool, bikes, parking. **Nearby** In Assisi: Ermitage Eremo delle Carceri, Basilica Convento San Damiano, Basilica Santa Maria degli Angeli - Church of Santa Maria di Rivortoto - Abbey of San Benedetto - Spello - Spoleto – Ellera golf course (18-hole) in Perugia. **Closed** Feb.

At the foot of Assisi, before going up into the historic town, a little road goes off to the left owards the village of Tordibetto which is only two kilometers away. On this plain a large family estate has been equipped to take in tourists. The three large stone houses have been entirely reconstructed to provide apartments to a very high standard of comfort. The rustic decor, too, has been very carefully arranged: attractive regional furniture and beams in the ceiling. The apartments are of different sizes, very well done up with the usual basic domestic appliances supplied, as well as dishwasher, safe and bed linen. The shady garden has a little stream running through it and overlooks a field of sunflowers, which are splendid when in flower. A little further away is the swimming pool. The old stables have been transformed into a room where the guests can meet. Bicycles are at their disposal, allowing the more courageous of them to climb up to Assisi, which is entirely pedestrianized.

How to get there *(Map 14): 32km east of Perugia as far as Assisi by SS75. Before going up into Assisi, take the road on the left for Tordibetto.*

L'Orto degli Angeli

06031 Bevagna (Perugia)
Via Dante Alghieri, 1
Tel. 0742-36 01 30 - Fax 0742-36 17 56 - T. and F. Antonini Mongalli
E-mail: ortoangeli@ortoangeli.it - Web: www.ortoangeli.it

Rooms 9 with air-conditioning, telephone, bath or shower, WC, satellite TV, minibar. **Price** Double 250-300,000L, suite 400,000L. **Meals** Breakfast included, served 8.00-10.30. **Restaurant** Service 12:30PM-1:30PM only Sat and Sun except in summer. 8:00PM-9:30PM - closed Thus - mealtime specials, also à la carte 50-70,000L. **Credit cards** All major. **Pets** Dogs not allowed. **Nearby** Bevagna: Piazza S. Silvestro: Palazzo dei Consoli, Romanesque churches of S. Silvestro and S. Michele, Pinacoteca F. Torti - Il Mercato delle Gaite fine giugno - Foligno - Montefalco - Abbazia di Sassovino - Spello - Assisi - Perugia - Trevi - Spoleto. **Open** All year.

In Bevagna you are at the heart of historic Umbria and its remains. The town itself is essentially medieval, as one can see from the buildings around the attractive Piazza San Silvestro and the very interesting folklore festival at the end of June when the inhabitants harmonize with the town's monuments and its history. Built on the remains of a Roman temple and theatre, the Orto degli Angeli is also an important archeological site. A delightful hanging garden, where breakfast is served in fine weather, separates the Palazzo Alberti (14th – 17th Century) from the fine patrician home (1710), which since 1788 has belonged to the Nieri Mongalli family whose descendants welcome you here today. A monumental staircase leads up to the drawing room, which is notable for its frescoed ceiling and its fine fireplace. The bedrooms are elegant, fitted out with fine linen and supplied with excellent bathrooms. Tradition is also respected in the preparation of specialties which are served with simplicity and refinement. A warm welcome.

How to get there *(Map 14): 32km south of Perugia.*

Casa Giulia

06039 Bovara di Trevi (Perugia)
Via S.S.Flaminia,km 140,100
Tel. 0742-78 257 - Fax 0742-38 16 32 - Sig.ra Alessandrini-Petrucci
E-mail: info@casagiulia.com - Web: www.casagiulia.com

Rooms 4 and 1 suite (4 pers.) with bath or shower, WC and 2 apartments. (2-4 pers.) – 1 room for disabled persons. **Price** Single 110,000L, double 170-190,000L, 345,000L (4 pers.), apart. 200,000L (3-4 pers./day.). **Meals** Breakfast included in the room, served 8:30-9:30. Evening meals. **Credit cards** Not accepted. **Pets** Dogs not allowed. **Facilities** Swimming pool, parking. **Nearby** Assisi - Perugia - Abbey of Sassovino - Montefalco - Spello - Tempietto del Clitunno - Fonti del Clitunno - Spoleto. **Open** All year.

The home of grandmother Giulia, who inherited it from her grandparents, is now a lovely guest house for visitors who want to tour Umbria. Off the main road that serves the large towns of the region, it offers travelers a quiet retreat. The old red-brick house that contains most of the rooms, now has an annex in which there are two small apartments. The rooms in the main house have kept the family furniture and those on the third floor still have traces of 17th century frescoes showing landscapes of the region. The garden is pleasantly shaded by large pines. Its finest site is occupied by the swimming pool, which has a wonderful view of the wheat fields and the village bell tower. For those who feel like lazing here all day, a snack bar is available. The countryside has a gay and smiling look, and if you're wondering what are all those large jars bordering the farms, let us inform you that the olive trees of the Trevi Hills have the largest yield of olive oil in all of Italy.

How to get there *(Map 14): On the S75 Perugia-Spoleto, after Trevi and Campello.*

Relais Il Canalicchio

06050 Canalicchio di Collazzone (Perugia)
Via della Piazza, 13
Tel. 075-87 07 325 - Fax 075-87 07 296 - Sig. Orfeo Vassallo
E-mail: relais@ntt.it - Web: www.wel.it/rcanalicchio.html

Rooms 35 with air-conditioning, telephone, bath or shower, WC, satellite TV, minibar. **Price** Single 200-240,000L, double 250-360,000L, suite 350-400,000L. **Meals** Breakfast included, served 8:00-10:30 - half board +60,000L (per pers. 2 day min.). **Restaurant** Service 12:00PM-2:30PM, 8:00PM-10:30PM - mealtime specials 60,000L, also à la carte - Regional cooking. **Credit cards** Allo major. **Pets** Dogs not allowed. **Facilities** Swimming pool, sauna, mountain bikes, billiard, tennis, gymnase room, enclosed parking. **Nearby** Perugia - Assisi - Todi. **Open** All year.

The little fortified village of Canalicchio, not far from Assisi, has been in existence at least as far back as the 9th century. With its ancient keep and chapel within the old stone walls, it stands surrounded by woods in the middle of 50 hectares of farmland. The hotel reflects this noble rural heritage: sturdy walls of Umbrian stone, floors of terra cotta tile. The rooms bear "aristocratic" names like Contessa di Oxford or Duca di Buckingham and have the cozy charm and comfort of an English manor: wrought iron bedsteads, flower-patterned wallpaper with matching striped cotton fabrics, small armchairs in the parlor and a small writing table near the window, to enjoy the view over the green hills that are every bit as lovely as those of Tuscany. The restaurant, in one of the narrow village lanes, features local specialties and produce of the azienda. This is a pleasant, restful place to spend a holiday, for you can indulge in all the pleasures of country living - riding, fishing, hunting or just strolling through the countryside.

How to get there *(Map 14): 50km south of Perugia. A1 Ripabianca exit - Foligno, towards "Relais il Canalicchio".*

Hotel Tiferno

06012 Città di Castello (Perugia)
Piazza R. Sanzio, 13
Tel. 075-85 50 331 - Fax 075-85 21 196 - Sig. Luigi Neri
E-mail: hoteltiferno@lineanet.net - Web: www.hoteltiferno.it

Rooms 38 with air-conditioning, telephone, bath or shower, hairdryer, WC, satellite TV, minibar – Elevator. **Price** Single 98-140,000L, double 180-220,000L, suite 280,000L. **Meals** Breakfast included, served 7:30-10:00 - half board 130-165,000L, full board 155-190,000L (per pers. 3 day min.). **Restaurant** Service 12:30PM-2:30PM, 7:30PM-10:00PM - closed Mon - mealtime specials 35-50,000L - Regional cooking. **Credit cards** All major. **Pets** Dogs not allowed. **Facilities** Garage (30,000L). **Nearby** In Città di Castello: Duomo, Pinacoteca - Perugia - Assisi - Lake Trasimeno - Evens: Antiques fair on the third Sun in the month, local market on Thurs and Sat, festival of classical music and jazz in Jul and Aug. **Open** All year.

Città di Castello is a typical small Umbrian Renaissance town, one of its main claims to fame being that the young Raphael was among its citizens. Don't miss his double-faced painting, the "Creation of Eve" on one side and a "Trinity and the Saints" on the other, in the fascinating little Pinacoteca that has the second largest collection (after Perugia) of Umbrian paintings. Tiferno was the Roman name of the town, and the hotel has preserved the original architecture of this former convent, with its ribbed vaults and large chimneys, but has also acquired a small collection of paintings by Alberto Burri, whose work is also to be seen in the museum dedicated to him. The modern rooms are functional and very comfortable. This sober and elegant establishment is a good stopping point for a tour of Umbria. There is a good restaurant at the hotel, but if you wish to dine in town we recommend Amici miei, which should not be missed.

How to get there (Maps 10 and 14): 50km south of Perugia.

Villa di Monte Solare

Colle San Paolo - Tavernelle di Panicale
06136 Fontignano (Perugia) - Via Montali, 7
Tel. 075-83 23 76/835 58 18 - Fax 075-83 554 62
Sig. and Sig.ra Iannarone Strunk
E-mail: info@villamontesolare.it - Web: www.villamontesolare.it

Rooms 13 and 7 suites with shower, WC. **Price** Double 240-310,000L, suite 280-360,000L. **Meals** Breakfast included, served 8:00-10:30 - half board 160-195,000L in double room, 180-230,000L in suite (per pers.). **Restaurant** Service 1:00PM, 8:00PM - mealtime specials. **Credit cards** All major. **Pets** Small dogs allowed in the annex. **Facilities** Swimming pools, tennis, riding, parking, wine taost, Classic music concert. **Nearby** Perugia - Assisi - Bettona - Church of Madonna dei Miracoli in Castel Rigone near by Passignano - Lake Trasimeno – Ellera golf course (18-hole) in Perugia. **Open** All year.

The road is long to Monte Solare and unpaved, but driveable, and so pretty with its Umbrian landscapes planted with vineyards and olive orchards, devoted since antiquity to the sun-god Apollo. The fine house when you reach it is a patrician residence of the 18th century which has preserved all its style: original cotto floor, period furniture, and breakfast room frescoes. The rooms each with private bath have a lot of charm. The suites in the nearby 17th-century farmhouse are very comfortable. The Italian-style garden has been replanted and a swimming pool is being built. The one-hundred-and-thirty-eight acre (56 ha) farm produces olive oil, wine, and produce that are used in the food that you will be served, alongside a splendid list of Umbrian wines. A good place to stay in the region.

How to get there *(Map 13): 25km southwest of Perugia, via SS220 towards Città delle Pieve; before Tavernelle, take the road on the right for Colle San Paolo to Monte Solare.*

Azienda Agrituristica Montali

Montali 06068 Tavernelle di Panicale (Perugia)
Via Montali, 23
Tél. 075-835 06 80 - Fax 075-835 01 44 - M. Alberto Musacchio
E-mail: montali@edisons.it - Web: www.edisons.it/montali

Rooms 10 with telephone, shower, WC. **Price** With half board obligatory: 120-130,000L (per pers.).
Meals Breakfast included, served 8:30-10:00. **Restaurant** Service 1:30PM and 8:30PM - mealtime
specials 25,000L (snacks in the swimming pool/35,000L) - Specialties: Ravioli alla sudtirolese -
Parmigiana alle zucchine - Charlot dell'abate. **Credit cards** Visa, Eurocard, MasterCard. **Pets** Dogs
not allowed. **Facilities** Swimming pool, parking. **Nearby** Perugia - Assisi - Bettona - Church of
Madonna dei Miracoli at Castel Rigone near Passignano - Lake Trasimeno - Todi - Orvieto - Cortona
– Santa Sabina golf course (18-hole). **Open** All year.

Along, dusty road with splendid paroramas over Lake Trasimene leads to
the hamlet where you find this farm and a few houses which have been
arranged to take guests. A green meadow, shaded by olive trees makes a large
garden for all these various dry-stone buildings, hung with vines and
bougainvilleas. Everything has been fitted out by the charming and talented
Brazilian owner: she has had regional furniture reproduced in teak, put
flowered prints in the bedrooms and decorated the walls of the house with
abstract paintings. Only vegetarian cooking is served in the restaurant, but the
menus are in fact very varied, including creative reinterpretations of local
specialties. Set in the midst of the Umbrian countryside, the place exudes calm
and serenity. Ideal for anyone seeking solitude.

How to get there *(Map 13): 25km southwest of Perugia, take SS220 towards
Città delle Pieve, and before Tavernelle, take the road to the right for Colle
San Paolo. At Colle San Paolo, turn right for Montali.*

Villa Montegranelli Hotel

Monteluiano
06024 Gùbbio (Perugia)
Tel. 075-92 20 185 - Fax 075-92 73 372 - Sig. Mongelli
E-mail: montegra@tin.it

Category ★★★ **Rooms** 21 with telephone, bath or shower, WC, TV, minibar – Elevator, wheelchair access. **Price** Single 160,000L, double 200,000L, suite 280,000L. **Meals** Breakfast 10,000L, served 7:30-10:30 - half board 165,000L, full board 220,000L (per pers.). **Restaurant** Service 12:30PM-2:30PM, 7:00PM-10:30PM - mealtime specials 60-70,000L, also à la carte - Specialties: Caciotta fusa al coccio con tartufo - Filetto con salsa ghiotta di fegatelli - Tozzetti al vino santo - Crespella di gelato alla vanilla con salsa calda di frutti di bosco. **Credit cards** All major. **Pets** Dogs allowed. **Facilities** Garage and parking. **Nearby** In Gùbbio: S. Francesco, Piazza della Signoria, Palazzo dei Consoli (museum), Duomo, Palazzo Ducale, Via dei Consoli - Festival of the Candles ("Ceri") every May 15 - Perugia - Assisi. **Open** All year.

A long path lined with cypress trees leads slowly up the slope to this large stone house that was, in the 18th century, the summer residence of an Italian aristocrat. From the garden, the view extends from the little village of Gobbio in the foreground all the way to the edge of the Appenines. The restoration has preserved most of the original features. The bedrooms are on the third floor, in what used to be the lofts. They are done in an attractive country style and are quite comfortable. The floor below is occupied by the suites — larger and more elegant, but less appealing. The restaurant is attractive for all its simplicity, with a vaulted ceiling and the decorative pattern of its stone walls. The menu consists of delicious local specialties that vary with the season and the market. There is a gourmet-style menu as well as country dishes, with fish as a highlight on Thursday and Friday. A good wine list is a final asset of this pleasant country stopover.

How to get there *(Map 14): 35km northwest of Perugia, 4km of Gùbbio.*

Poggio del Belvedere

06065 Passignano sul Trasimena (Perugia)
Via San Donato, 65
Tel. 075-84 53 22 - Fax 075-84 51 97
Dr. Lorenzo Rondini

Apartments 13 (4 with telephone), shower, WC, TV. **Price** Apartments/week 750,000L (2 pers.), 1 100,000L (2 pers. + 2 pers.), 1 430,000L (4 pers. + 2 pers.). **Restaurant** Service 12:30PM-2:30PM, 8:00PM-10:30PM - mealtime specials, aslo à la carte - Regional cooking. **Credit cards** Not accepted. **Pets** Dogs allowed. **Facilities** Swimming pool - Western and English riding schools, horse riding, Parking. **Nearby** Lake Trasimène - Isola Maggiore - Perugia - Assisi - Città del Castello - Spello. **Open** All year.

On the shores of Lake Trasimene, in an ambiance that has something of a Fifties resort, you may be enchanted by the gentle countryside, unless you are here solely for the riding. From Poggio del Belveduto, the view over the lake and the surrounding hills is splendid, but if you want to enjoy your stay here you must not be upset by a slightly unpolished, sporting atmosphere, and a welcome that will be rough and ready, though well-meaning. The truth is that the manager, a delightful veterinary surgeon, is more accustomed to looking after his horses than worrying about the detailed upkeep of the rooms. The estate has two riding schools with forty well-bred horses. As for Hermann, the manager of the restaurant, he is inclined to turn into a crooner after a certain time in the evening. So if you do not want to take part, except from afar, in the nocturnal revels, choose the new, simply furnished apartments on the top of the hill.

How to get there *(Map 13): 25km west of Perugia. On the A1 (Firenze-Roma), take the exit for Passignano (from Firenze) or Torricella (from Roma).*

Hotel da Sauro

Lago Trasimeno
06060 Isola Maggiore (Perugia)
Tel. 075-82 61 68 - Fax 075-82 51 30
Sig. Sauro

Category ★★★ **Rooms** 10 with telephone, bath or shower, WC, TV. **Price** Double 110,000L, apart. (2-4 pers.) 130-170,000L. **Meals** Breakfast included, served 7:00-10:00 - half board 75,000L, full board 90,000L (per pers., 3 day min.). **Restaurant** Service 12:00PM-2:00PM, 7:00PM-8:30PM - mealtime specials 20-30,000L, also à la carte - Regional cooking and seafood. **Credit cards** Diners, Visa, Eurocard, MasterCard. **Pets** Dogs allowed. **Nearby** In Isola Maggiore: Church of Salvatore - Perugia - Spello - Assisi - Città del Castello. **Closed** Nov 8 – 30 and Jan 10 – Feb 28.

If you have decided to visit Umbria, why not take the time to go all the way and explore the little islands of Lake Trasimeno. As yet undiscovered by mass tourism, they are frequented largely by the locals, which is part of their charm. The Sauro is a simple village inn, comfortable enough for a stopover of a few days. The food is good, with lots of fish, naturally, but also a variety of pasta and antipasto, like everywhere in Italy. Informality is the key word both for atmosphere and service.

How to get there *(Map 13): 20km west of Perugia. Ferry services from Passignano and Tuoro (Navaccia) to Isola Maggiore (15mn).*

Hotel Villa Pambuffetti

06036 Montefalco (Perugia)
Via della Vittoria, 20
Tel. 0742-379 417 - Fax 0742-379 245 - Sig.ra Angelucci
E-mail: villablanca@interbusiness.it - Web: www.umbria.org

Category ★★★★ Rooms 15 with air-conditioning, telephone, bath or shower, WC, safe, minibar. **Price** Single 180,000L, double 285,000L, suite 370,000L. **Meals** Breakfast included - half board 208-275,000L. **Restaurant** Service 8:00PM-9:00PM - closed Mon - mealtime specials 75,000L - Regional cooking. **Credit cards** All major. **Pets** Dogs not allowed. **Facilities** Swimming pool, parking. **Nearby** In Montefalco: Pinacoteca di San Francesco, Church of S. Agostino, Palazzo Comunale (view) - Bevagna - Assisi - Perugia - Bettona - Spello - Spoleto - Todi - Orvieto. **Open** All year.

The Villa Pambuffetti, a former country house now maintained as a combination private residence and guest house, has always belonged to the same family. It is in the middle of beautiful grounds which overlook the valley. The house has been reorganized to create spacious rooms each meticulously decorated with antique furniture, and all different. The most amazing one is is located in the little tower and has six windows from which create a panoramic view of the entire valley. The restaurant serves regional specialties and has an excellent wine list, including the notable Sagranito, a specialty of Montefalco. This is an elegant address in the D'Annunzio's fabled "town of silence."

How to get there (Map 14): *41km southeast of Perugia to Foligno, then to Montefalco.*

Locanda della Rocca

06060 Paciano
Viale Roma, 4
Tel. 075-83 02 36 - Fax 075-83 01 55 - Sig. and Sig.ra Buitoni
E-mail: l.buitoni@tin.it

Rooms 9 and 1 suite (4 pers.) with bath or shower, WC, TV, minibar. **Price** Double 180-200,000L, suite 420-450,000L. **Meals** Breakfast included (buffet), served 8:30-10:30 - half board 135,000L (per pers. in double room). **Restaurant** Service 7:30PM-9:00PM - closed Tues - mealtime specials-carte 40-70,0000L. **Credit cards** All major. **Pets** Small dogs allowed (except in restaurant). **Facilities** Swimming pool, parking. **Nearby** "Museo Aperto" for Castiglione del Lago - Città della Pieve - Paciano - Panicale - Lago Trasimeno. **Closed** Jan 15 – Feb 15.

Paciano is a peaceful medieval village, lovingly looked after by its residents, if we can judge by the excellent state of preservation of the fortifying walls, with seven towers and three gates, that surround the old streets and homes with flower-laden balconies. Part of the locanda is in the torrione, built in the 17th century to defend the Rastella Gate. On a level with the terrace is a beautiful vaulted dining room with arches cut into the wall that are used as a wine cellar. Here you will enjoy the fine cuisine of Luigi Buitoni, who also organises groups for cookery classes; these must be reserved. A mezzanine sitting room is very comfortable, with soft sofas and lots of green plants. The bedrooms are upstairs. Apart from the suite, which is in the torrione and has a balcony, the other rooms are rather small but the amenities are adequate. Most look out over the amphitheater of greenery that stretches out in front of the hotel. Paciano and the other villages around Lake Trasimeno have grouped together to offer a short tour to introduce visitors to their artistic heritage. Caterina provides a warm welcome to the hotel.

How to get there *(Map 13): On highway A1, Valdichiana exit (Firenze) or Chiusi/Chiancano Terme (Roma), towards Lago Trasimeno.*

Residenza Vecchio Molino

06042 Pissignano - Campello sul Clitunno (Perugia)
Via del Tempio, 34
Tel. 0743-52 11 22 - Fax 0743-27 50 97 - Sig. Eredi Rapanelli
E-mail: vecchiomolino@perugiaonline.com
Web: www.perugiaonline.com/vecchiomolino

Category ★★★★ **Rooms** 13 with air-conditioning, telephone, bath, WC, minibar. **Price** Single 142,000L, double 200,000L, suite 240,000L. **Meals** Breakfast included, served 7:30-11:30. **Restaurant** In Spoleto and Campello sul Clitunno, see p. 536. **Credit cards** All major. **Pets** Dogs not allowed. **Facilities** Parking. **Nearby** Fonti del Clitunno - Tempietto del Clitunno - Ponte delle Torri - Church of S. Pietro - Basilica of S. Salvatore - Church of S. Ponziano - Monteluco and Convento of S. Francesco - Trevi - Spoleto - Spello - Orvieto — Santa Sabina (9-hole) and Antognolla golf course. **Open** Apr — end Oct.

The small Christian temple just above the Vecchio Molino is a reminder of the cultural and artistic past of the cheery Clitunno Valley. This 15th-century mill is now a very pleasant hotel. Inside you can see the original equipment, and watch the river flow by. The decor is very simple, almost entirely white, which enhances the antique lines of the building. The rooms are large and superbly decorated. Each one is different, and some have a salon. On every floor are spots to read and relax. Only a few miles from Spoleto, this is one of the favorite hotels of the culture-seeking clientele which attends the Festival of Two Worlds run by Gian Carlo Menotti.

How to get there (Map 14): 50km southeast of Perugia via SS75 to Foligno, then S3.

Hotel Gattapone

06049 Spoleto (Perugia)
Via del Ponte, 6
Tel. 0743-223 447 - Fax 0743-223 448 - Sig. Pier Giulio Hanke
E-mail: gattapone@mail.caribusiness.it - Web: www.caribusiness.it/gattapone

Category ★★★★ **Rooms** 16 with air-conditioning, telephone, bath or shower, WC, TV, minibar. **Price** Single 230,000L, double 300,000L, suite 420,000L. **Meals** Breakfast included, served 7:30-10:30. **Restaurant** See p. 536. **Credit cards** All major. **Pets** Dogs allowed. **Nearby** In Spoleto: Ponte delle Torrri, Duomo, Arch of Druso, church, San Pietro, Festival of Two Worlds from mid Jun to mid Jul - Monteluco and the Convento di San Francesco - Fonti del Clitunno - Tempietto del Clitunno - Trevi - Spello – Santa Sabina (9-hole) and Antognolla golf course. **Open** All year.

Just outside the village of Spoleto, the Hotel Gattapone is the secret address of music fans who attend the celebrated festival. Built into a cliff overlooking the entire Tessino Valley, facing the Roman aqueduct beloved by Lucrecia Borgia, the duchess of Spoleto, the Gattapone is perfectly integrated into the landscape. Its interior decor is a model of comfort and harmony. The rooms are superb, modern, and have in common a panoramic view on the countryside, which gives them an atmosphere of quiet serenity. Professor Hanke, the owner, has a real sense of hospitality, and makes sure his guests feel at home.

How to get there *(Map 14): 65km southeast of Perugia via SS3, towards Terni to Acquasparta, then S418 to Spoleto.*

Palazzo Dragoni

06049 Spoleto (Perugia)
Via del Duomo, 13
Tel. 0743-22 22 20 - Fax 0743-22 22 25
E-mail: rodiota@tin.it

Rooms 15 with air-conditioning, telephone, bath or shower, WC, TV, minibar – Elevator. **Price** Single and double 230,000L, suite 280,000L. **Meals** Breakfast included, served 7:30-10:30. **Restaurant** See p. 536. **Credit card** Visa, Eurocard, MasterCard. **Pets** Small dogs allowed. **Nearby** In Spoleto: Ponte delle Torrri, Duomo, Arch of Drusus, Church of San Pietro, Festival of Two Worlds from mid Jun to mid Jul - Monteluco and the Convento di San Francesco - Fonti del Clitunno - Tempietto del Clitunno - Trevi - Spello – Santa Sabina (9-hole) and Antognolla golf course. **Open** All year (by reservation).

This 15th-century *residenza d'epoca* just near the Duomo of Spoleto was once the palace of the Dragoni family. Upstairs in the bedrooms and salons you will admire the beautiful ceilings and an interior architecture that has been scrupulously preserved. The rooms are well-decorated with chairs, sofas, elegantly skirted tables and a number of nice antique pieces. The bedrooms are large and some have a real salon. There are two dining rooms: one, with arched windows that face the medieval part of town, is used as a breakfast room. The other, more intimate, with old stone walls and vaulted ceilings, is used only for private dinners. And you can rest assured that you'll be safe and snug — three green-headed dragons have been keeping watch over this house for centuries.

How to get there *(Map 14): 65km southeast of Perugia via SS3bis, towards Terni to Acquasparta, then S418 to Spoleto.*

Hotel San Luca

06049 Spoleto (Perugia)
Via Interna delle Mura, 21
Tel. 0743-22 33 99 - Fax 0743-22 38 00 - Sig.ra Zuccari
E-mail: sanluca@hotelsanluca.com - Web: www.hotelsanluca.com

Rooms 35 with air-conditioning, telephone, bath or shower, WC, satellite TV, safe, minibar – Elevator, rooms and access for disabled persons. **Price** Single 150-420,000L, double 200-420,000L, suite 400-520,000L; extra bed 80,000L. **Meals** Breakfats included, served 7:30-10:00. **Restaurant** See p. 536. **Credit cards** All major. **Pets** Small dogs allowed. **Facilities** Garage (25,000L). **Nearby** In Spoleto: Ponte delle Torrri, Duomo, Arch of Drusus, Church of San Ponziano, Festival of Two Worlds from mid Jun to mid Jul - Monteluco and the Convento di San Francesco - Fonti del Clitunno - Tempietto del Clitunno - Trevi – Santa Sabina (9-hole) and Antognolla golf course. **Open** All year.

The hotel occupies what was once a former tannery. Though the architects have respected the external structure of the 19th-century buildings, the interior has been entirely remodelled. All the rooms now communicate with the interior courtyard and the garden by a series of corridors, passageways and iron stairways creating a surprising labyrinth. The rooms open on the garden lawn, the courtyard or the old town with its surrounding orchards. They are decorated with refined taste, spacious (some can accommodate three people) and have comfortable bathrooms, some with jacuzzi. The public rooms, always full of flowers, provide a pleasant space with comfortable sofas and well-designed furniture. You will notice the collection of prints and drawings around the walls as well as the old soup tureens in two large glass cases. A spring with legendary therapeutic properties still runs on the premises of the hotel, so don't forget to drink a glass.

How to get there *(Map 14): 65km southeast of Perugia.*

Hotel Eremo delle Grazie

Monteluco
04960 Spoleto (Perugia)
Tel. 0743-49 624 - Fax 0743-49 650
Professore Lalli

Rooms 11 with telephone, bath or shower, WC. **Price** Single 300,000L, double 350,000L, suite 450-500,000L. **Meals** Breakfast included. **Restaurant** Only by reservation - closed Mon. **Credit cards** Diners, Visa, Eurocard, MasterCard. **Pets** Small dogs allowed. **Facilities** Swimming pool. **Nearby** In Spoleto: Ponte delle Torrri, Duomo, Arch of Drusus, Church of San Ponziano, Festival of Two Worlds from mid Jun to mid Jul - Monteluco and the Convento di San Francesco - Fonti del Clitunno - Tempietto del Clitunno - Trevi – Santa Sabina (9-hole) and Antognolla golf course. **Open** All year.

The Eremo was a *residenza d'epoca* before it was a hotel, as the owner Pio Lalli insists on pointing out. One might add it was a *residenza historica*, built to be the mother house of the Monteluco Order, which explains why the surrounding woods became a place of refuge for many anchorites. It had its share of illustrious visitors in those days, including no less than Michelangelo and Pope Pius VI. It is also like a residenza museo, so filled is it with interesting souvenirs, like the library of Cardinal Cybo (who once lived here), available to anyone who likes old books. The bedrooms, once the cells, have kept their monastic atmosphere but improved their amenities. The salons are more convivial, with antique furniture and a terrace that offers an impressive view of Spoleto and the surrounding forest.

How to get there *(Map 14): 65km southeast of Perugia via SS3bis, towards Terni to Acquasparta, then S418 to Spoleto - 8km southeast of Spoleto.*

Hotel Palazzo Bocci

06038 Spello (Perugia)
via Cavour, 17
Tel. 0742-30 10 21 - Fax 0742-30 14 64 - Sig. Buono
E-mail: bocci@bcsnet.it - Web: www.emmeti.it/pbocci.it.html

Category ★★★★ **Rooms** 23 with air-conditioning, telephone, bath or shower, WC, satellite TV, safe, minibar – Elevator. **Price** Single 130-150,000L, double 220-260,000L, suite 320-460,000L. **Meals** Breakfast included, served 7:30-10:00 - half board +50,000L, full board +100,000L. **Restaurant** "Il Molino", service 12:30pm-3:00PM, 7:30PM-10:00PM - closed Tues - mealtime specials 40-60,000L, also à la carte - Specialities: Pinturicchio - Tagliatelle alla molinara - Oca alla fratina - Funghi porcini - Tartufo. **Credit cards** All major. **Pets** Dogs not allowed. **Nearby** In Spello: Church of Santa Maria Maggiore (cappella Baglioni), Palazzo Comunale, Ponte Venere, Belvedere, Church of Tonda (2km) - Assisi - Perugia - Trevi - Bevagna - Montefalco - Spoleto - Fonti del Clitunno - Tempietto del Clitunno. **Open** All year.

Frescoes, stuccos and panoramic murals, wooden beams and stone vaults, the Palazzo Bocci offers its guests all the surroundings and atmosphere of a real little palace. The furniture is more classical and less elaborate than the decor. The rooms are large and equipped with the amenities one expects nowadays in a recently-done quality hotel (the suites have bathrooms with jacuzzis). In the summer, breakfast is served on the terrace overlooking the twisting lanes and rooftops of the old city. Just across the street is the restaurant Il Molino: known for both its cuisine and its winecellar, it brings an added plus to this hotel.

How to get there *(Map 14): 31km southeast of Perugia.*

Hotel La Bastiglia

06038 Spello (Perugia)
Piazza Vallegloria, 7
Tel. 0742-65 12 77 - Fax 0742-30 11 59 - Sig. L. Fancelli
E-mail: fancelli@labastiglia.com - Web: www.labastiglia.com

Category ★★★ **Rooms** 31 and 2 junior suites with air-conditioning, telephone, bath or shower, WC, TV, minibar. **Price** Double 120-250,000L, suite 500-700,000L. **Meals** Breakfast included, served 8:00-10:00 - half board +50,000L (per pers. 3 days min.). **Restaurant** Service 1:00PM-2:30PM, 8:00PM-10:00PM - closed Wed, Thurs noon, Jan and 1 week in Jul - mealtime specials 70,000L, also à la carte - Umbrian cuisine. **Credit cards** All major. **Pets** Dogs not allowed. **Facilities** Parking. **Nearby** In Spello: Church of Santa Maria Maggiore (cappella Baglioni), Palazzo Comunale, Ponte Venere, Belvedere, Church of Tonda (2km) - Assisi - Perugia - Trevi - Bevagna - Montefalco - Spoleto - Fonti del Clitunno - Tempietto del Clitunno. **Closed** Jan and 1 week in Jul.

This charming little hotel is in the historical center of Spello, an ancient Roman town on the slopes of Mount Subasio. Formerly an old mill, it still has certain elements of its original architecture, such as the arches in the reception rooms. There is a superb terrace off of the salon with a lovely view of the olive trees and the valley. The dining room has a very convivial atmosphere and the cuisine features old Umbrian specialties prepared with carefully selected regional products. The rooms are light and comfortable, with somewhat old-fashioned bathrooms. Ask for the ones on the upper floors on the terrace side, which have a view of the countryside. (The suites have a private garden and a separate entry.) Work is underway to increase the capacity of the hotel by eleven rooms and to build a swimming pool. Watch this space.

How to get there *(Map 14): 31km southeast of Perugia.*

Hotel Fonte Cesia

06059 Todi (Perugia)
Via Lorenzo Leonj, 3
Tel. 075-894 37 37 - Fax 075-894 46 77 - Sig. Felice
E-mail: f.cesia@full-service.it - Web: www.fontecesia.it

Category ★★★★ **Rooms** 32 and 5 suites with air-conditioning, telephone, bath or shower, WC, satellite TV, minibar. **Price** Single 200,000L, double 280,000L, suite 360,000L. **Meals** Breakfast included, served 8:00-10:00 - half board 190-230,000L, full board 220-260,000L (per pers, 3 days min.). **Restaurant** Service 1:00PM-2:30PM, 8:00PM-9:30PM - mealtime specials, à la carte - Italian and umbrian cuisine. **Credit cards** All major. **Pets** Dogs allowed on request. **Facilities** Parking. **Nearby** In Todi: Church of Santa Maria della Consolazione (1km) - Orvieto - Perugia - Assisi - Spoleto - Gubbio – Ellera golf course (9-hole) in Perugia. **Open** All year.

The Hotel Fonte Cesia has recently opened its doors in a setting charged with history, the ancient Etruscan town of Todi, home of Jacopone da Todi, poet and author of the famous "Stabat Maler". You can still find traces of the flourishing medieval period in its small winding streets. The hotel is in a beautiful 17th century palace, a harmonious blend of tradition, elegance, and modern comfort. The well-preserved architecture is the most beautiful decorative element, notably its superb vaulted ceilings in small bricks. It is an intimate, tasteful decorated hotel with comfortable well-furnished rooms, some of which have a trompe-l'œil decor. The Umbrian delicacies served in the restaurant will convince you, if you still need convincing, that this is a great place for fine living.

How to get there *(Map 14): 45km south of Perugia, via SS3bis, Todi exit.*

Poggio d'Asproli

06059 Todi (Perugia)
Frazione Asproli N.7
Tel. 075-885 33 85 - Fax 075-885 33 85
Sig.ra Maria Claudia Pagliari

Rooms 7 and 2 suite with telephone, shower, WC. **Price** Double 200,000L, suite 290-360,000L (2 and 4 pers.). **Meals** Breakfast included, served 8:00-10:00. **Restaurant** Service ab 8:30PM - mealtime specials 40,000L, also à la carte. **Credit cards** All major. **Pets** Dogs not allowed. **Facilities** Swimming pool, parking. **Nearby** Todi: Church of S. Maria della Consolazione (1km) towards Orvieto - Orvieto - Perugia - Spoleto - Assisi - Gùbbio —Ellera golf course (18-hole) in Perugia. **Open** All year.

You can't miss the entrance to this estate - it is marked by a sculpture made by the master of the house. Several other of his works stand in the garden. The building is a beautiful old farmhouse and its architecture is suitably rustic, but inside the decor is of the most refined. There are of course some bare stone walls and archways and exposed beams in the ceiling, but the choice of fabrics, hangings and antique objects gives the whole place an elegant feel. The rooms are laid out with variations in level, creating many nooks and corners where it's nice to read or write postcards or have a quiet drink. As soon as the weather permits, meals and breakfasts are served on the terrace with its impressive view. The rooms are all attractive, the suites even more so. The swimming pool is on a par with the rest. This is not just an inn or a guest house, but in the words of the brochure, a residenza de campagna. The owner also lets some apartments for two or three people about eight kilometers away in a house with a swimming pool, which we were unable to visit.

How to get there (Map 14): In Todi take the road towards Orvieto and turn left towards Izzalini.

Tenuta di Canonica

Canonica 06059 Todi (Perugia)
Tel. 075-894 75 45 - Fax 075-894 75 81
Sig. Daniele Fano
E-mail: tenutadicanonica@tin.it - Web: www.tenutadicanonica.com

Rooms 11 with telephone, bath or shower, WC. **Price** Double 180-200,000L. **Meals** Breakfast included, served 8:30-10:30 - half board 135,000L (per pers., 2 nights min.). **Diner** Service 8:30PM – mealtime specials 35,000L - Specialties: Risotti al tartufo e provolone affumicato - Lasagne maialino all'umbra - Melanzane alla parmigiana. **Credit cards** Not accepted. **Pets** Dogs not allowed. **Facilities** Swimming pool, mountain bikes, parking. **Nearby** Todi: Church of S. Maria della Consolazione (1km) towards Orvieto - Orvieto - Perugia - Spoleto - Assisi - Gùbbio –Santa Sabina golf course (9-hole) in Perugia. **Closed** Jan and Feb.

On the hills opposite Todi, a young couple has skillfully restored a medival tower, then linked it to an old building beside it. The whole creates a delightful maze of rooms for the visitor to discover. On the ground floor, there are several public rooms, including the drawing room in the tower which occupies a very attractive space. All the rooms are different and all are utterly charming: waxed colored plaster on the walls, family furniture or pieces found in antique shops, and attractive, brand new bathrooms. Everywhere, the view is magnificent: a glimpse of the Lake of Corbara, or a panorama of Todi. The lovely countryside is all around and children will be in heaven in the meadows on the estate. An informal and very friendly holiday atmosphere.

How to get there *(Map 14): 35km south of Perugia, exit Todi, towards Oriveto by N448 for 5km, then Prodo, Titgnano to the sign for Cordigliano; the road for Tenuta is just at this fork in the road.*

Titignano

06039 Titignano (Perugia)
Tel. 0763-30 80 00/30 80 22 - Fax 0763-30 80 02
Famiglia Corsini
E-mail: fattoria@orvienet.it

Rooms 6 in the Castel and 5 mini-apartment in the annexes, with shower, WC. **Price** 70,000L (per pers.). **Meals** Breakfast included, served 8:30-10:30 - half board 170,000L, full board 120,000L (per pers.). **Evening meals** By reservation. **Credit cards** Not accepted. **Pets** Dogs allowed. **Facilities** Swimming pool, mountain bike, tasting of wines, parking. **Nearby** Todi - Della Piana cave - La Roccacia - Lake Corbara - Orvieto - Lake Bolsena and Etruscan country. **Open** All year.

Going to Titignano is liking traveling backwards in time. The estate, which still covers 2000 hectares, has lived through the centuries in an unchanged environment. Its buildings, still intact, form by themselves a veritable little village. Don't be surprised that you have to cross woods and fields once you have left the road - Titignano is in a way the end of the world. The main house facing the small piazza is the most comfortable place to stay and the one that has best preserved the charm of the interior architecture (the furniture has not been so fortunate). The very pleasant living room is extended by a loggia arranged for rest and recreation, and the dining room has a magnificent fireplace. The mini-apartments are in buildings that face both the piazza and the valley, but some are a little dark. Down below, overlooking the meadows and hills that border the little Lake Cobara, the swimming pool will provide some magical moments as you look out over one of the loveliest landscapes of the Umbrian countryside.

How to get there *(Map 14): On the highway A1 (Roma-Firenze), Orvieto exit, towards Prodo on the N79bis, then turn right towards Titignano. At 35km south of Perugia, take the Todi exit twoards Orvieto by the N448 for 5km, then towards Prodo.*

Il Piccolo Hotel del Carléni

05022 Amelia (Terni)
Via Pellegrino Carleni, 21
Tel. 0744-98 39 25 - Fax 0744-97 81 43 - Sig. Ralli - Sig. F. de Boiscuille
E-mail: carleni@tin.it - Web: www.giubileoitalia.com/carleni

Rooms 4 and 3 suites with air-conditiong, telephone, bath, WC, satellite TV, safe, minibar - Wheelchair access. **Price** Single 140-180,000L, double 150-170,000L, suite 180-210,000L. **Meals** Breakfast included, served 8:30-10:30. **Restaurant** Service 12:00PM-2:30PM, 7:00PM-10:00PM - closed Mon and Thus (except national holidays) for non resident - mealtime specials 50,000L, vegetarian 30,000L, kid 20,000L, also à la carte. **Credit cards** All major. **Pets** Dogs not allowed. **Nearby** Amelia (Roman remains, duomo) - villages in the Monti Amerino - Narni Perugia - Orvieto - Roma. **Closed** Aug 27 – Sept 4.

Between Orvieto and Rome, the A 1 runs beside the Monti Amerino which lie between the Tiber and the Nera. This is a region of wooded hills with pretty medieval villages perched upon them and the oldest town in Umbria; this is Amelia, on the frontier with Latium. While the surroundings have deteriorated somewhat, the tortuous little streets goiing up towards the Duomo and the belfrey reveal the medieval remains of the town, including the Palazzo Carléni, which has been renovated as a delightful little hotel. The interior is very welcoming, its attractive regional furniture harmonizing with the elegantly rustic style of the house. The rooms are just as carefully designed, both in their décor and in the immaculate comfort of the bathrooms. In summer breakfast is served under wide parasols in the garden smelling of roses and jasmin. As for the vegetable garden, it allows you to savor in advance the freshness of the tomatoes and rocket salad served in the restaurant. If you are staying longer, ask for the no. 1 suite, where the terrace has views over the roofs of Amelia.

How to get there *(Map 14): 30km south of Orvieto via A1, exit Orte. SS Terni-Perugia for 9km before turning off for Amelia.*

Hotel Ristorante La Badia

La Badia 05019 Orvieto (Terni)
Tel. 0763-30 19 59 / 30 18 76 - Fax 0763-30 53 96
Sig.ra Fiumi
E-mail: labadia.hotel@tiscalinet.it - Web: www.paginegialle.it/la badia-01

Category ★★★★ **Rooms** 24 and 7 suites with air-conditiong, telephone, bath or shower, WC, TV, minibar. **Price** Single 215-235,000L, double 285-325,000L, suite 440-550,000L. **Meals** Breakfast 20,000L, served 7:30-10:00 - half board required in high season 236-368,000L (per pers.). **Restaurant** Service 12:30PM-2:30PM, 7:30PM-9:30PM - closed Wed - mealtime specials 70,000L, also à la carte - Specialties: Panicetti - Coccinillo - Scaloppe Badia. **Credit cards** Amex, Visa, Eurocard, MasterCard. **Pets** Dogs not allowed. **Facilities** Swimming pool (Jun to Oct), 2 tennis courts, parking. **Nearby** In Orvieto: Duomo, Palazzo del Popolo - Bolsena (Church of Santa Cristina) - Lake Bolsena - Etruscan country from San Lorenzo Nuovo to Chiusi (Grotta di Castro, Pitigliano, Sorano, Sovana, Chiusi) - Todi – Golf course (9-hole) in Tarquinia and golf course (18-hole) in Sutri. **Closed** Jan and Feb.

This former monastery is a wonderful stopping place in a lovely countryside. From its perch on a rock, it looks down over the town of Orvieto and the Umbrian landscape. It is a very comfortable hotel with well-appointed rooms and suites, a good restaurant, swimming pool and tennis court, all the ingredients for a perfect country inn only 5 kilometers from the historic center. And a warm, friendly welcome in addition.

How to get there (*Map 13*): *86km south of Perugia via SS3bis to Todi exit, then S448 suivre les indications pour la plazza Duopo - In La Badia, 5km south of Orvieto.*

Villa Ciconia

Ciconia 05019 Orvieto Scalo (Terni)
Via dei Tigli, 69
Tel. 0763-30 55 82 - Fax 0763-30 20 77 - Sig. Falcone
E-mail: villaciconia@libero.it

Category ★★★★ **Rooms** 12 with air-conditioning, telephone, bath or shower, WC, satellite TV, hairdryer, minibar. **Price** Double 200-250,000L. **Meals** Breakfast 18,000L, served 7:30-10:30 - half board +50,000L, full board +85,000L (per pers.). **Restaurant** Service 1:00PM-3:00PM, 8:00PM-10:00PM - closed Mon - mealtime specials 45-55,000L. **Credit cards** All major. **Pets** Dogs not allowed. **Facilities** Parking. **Nearby** Orvieto: Duomo, Palazzo del Popolo - Bolsena - Lake Bolsena - Etruscan country from San Lorenzo Nuovo to Chiusi - Todi — Golf course (9-hole) in Viterbo. **Closed** 15 days in Feb.

Orvieto has more than one claim to fame. The first is certainly its wine. When Signorelli painted the Duomo, he asked for part of his remuneration to be paid in wine. The wines, both red and white, are excellent and there is also a regional production of *vin santo*. Stop in at the wine bar at no. 2, Piazza del Duomo, and you'll be able to taste some of the fine vintages. The other famous attraction of Orvieto is, of course, its Duomo. The Villa Ciconia is only a few kilometers away, but it's already the country, at the confluence of two streams that cross the property. It is a superb 15th-century gray stone building attributed to a student of Michelangelo. It is said he also painted the landscapes and allegorical scenes in what is today a restaurant. The rooms are large and comfortable; facing the park, they are decorated with antique furniture and traditional materials. Despite the small number of rooms, the fact that there are three restaurants shows that the Ciconia is used for meetings and receptions. You should find out what events are scheduled when making your reservation.

How to get there *(Map 13): 86km south of Perugia via SS3bis to Todi exit, then S448 towards Orvieto; Orvieto Scalo, drive under the motorway towards Todi-Perugia and left towards Arezzo via SS71 to 35km.*

Hotel Virgilio

05019 Orvieto (Terni)
Piazza Duomo, 5-6
Tel. 0763-34 18 82 - Fax 0763-34 37 97
Sig. Vladimiro Belcapo

Rooms 15 with telephone, bath, TV. **Price** Single 120,000L, double 165,000L. **Meals** Breakfast 10,000L, served 8:00-11:00. **Restaurant** See p. 536. **Credit cards** All major. **Pets** Dogs not allowed. **Nearby** Orvieto: Duomo, Palazzo del Popolo - Bolsena - Lake Bolsena - Etruscan country from San Lorenzo Nuovo to Chiusi - Todi – Golf course (9-hole) in Tarquinia and in Sutri (18-hole). **Open** All year.

Simple though it is, the Hotel Virgilio has long been the only hotel with some personality in the historic center of Orvieto. The ground-floor rooms, that is the salon, the bar and the breakfast room, have typically Seventies furniture in plastic and stainless steel tubing, which will please the more "trendy" guests. In more conventional taste is the series of ink drawings of nudes hanging on the walls. The rooms are simply furnished but rather pretty with their flowered frieze matching the bed covers. But the Hotel Virgilio's greatest asset is its situation on the Piazza del Duomo, giving its guests a superb view over the cathedral, a masterpiece of Italian Gothic. To console those whose rooms are at the back – though even these look over gardens – the benches in front of the house are strictly reserved for guests.

How to get there *(Map 13): 86km south of Perugia.*

Villa La Meridiana - Cascina Reine

12051 Alba (Cuneo)
Altavilla, 9
Tel. 0173-44 01 12 - Fax 0173-44 01 12 - G. Pionzo - A. Giacosa
E-mail: cascinareine@libero.it

Rooms 5 and 3 apartments with kitchen, bath or shower, WC, TV (telephone on request). **Price** Double 120-130,000L, apartment 140,000L (2 pers. +20,000L extra bed.). **Meals** Breakfast included, served 8:00-10:00. **Restaurant** See p. 538. **Credit cards** Not accepted. **Pets** Dogs allowed. **Facilities** Swimming pool, Training center, billard, parking. **Nearby** Alba: Wine fair in Apr, white truffles fair in Oct, panoramic road (Langhe towards Ceva), Barbaresco and vermouth and spumante road d'Asti towards Canelli - Asti: cathedral, S. Secondo, Pallio de Asti in Sept, Sanctuary of Crea, Abbey of Vezollano – "Le Chocciole" golf course (18-hole). **Open** All year.

If you give yourself half a chance, you will be enthralled by the vine-clad hills of Piedmont that produce the famous Asti Spumante and such highly appreciated wines as Barolo and Barbaresco. Asti and Alba are charming medieval villages where life flows slowly on in the rhythm of the seasons and the work in the fields, punctuated by the traditional celebrations. Built on the heights of the town, La Meridiana is in art nouveau style, with a modern wing recently added to provide more rooms. Some pieces of family furniture add a note of charm and the bathrooms are completely modern and comfortable. The garden is inviting, well-placed for viewing the landscape of vineyards and poplars, with the towers of the historic old town in the distance. The kitchen, where breakfast is prepared daily, can occasionally be put at your disposal, if you feel like dining in one evening. However, one should really make it a point to discover the cuisine of Piedmont, so different from what we usually think of as Italian cooking.

How to get there *(Map 7): 62km from Torino.*

La Luna e i Falo'

14053 Canelli (Asti)
Regione Aie, 37
Tel. 0141-83 16 43 - Fax 0141-83 16 43
Sig. Carnero

Rooms 5 with bath or shower, WC, TV. **Price** Double 180,000L. **Meals** Breakfast included, served until 10:00 - half board 280,000L (2 pers., 1 day min.). **Restaurant** (by reservation). Service 7:30PM - mealtime specials 65,000L and 75,000L (wine incl.) - Specialties: Monferrina - Lungana. **Credit cards** Not accepted. **Pets** Dogs allowed. **Facilities** Parking. **Nearby** Canelli: historical feast day in Jun "l'ossedio", wine fair and white truffles fair (autumn), Alba - Asti: cathedral, S.Secondo, Pallio de Asti in Sept, Monferatto, Sanctuary of Crea, Abbey of Vezollano. **Open** All year (on request).

Owner Franco Carnero is a fervent admirer of Cesare Pavese. That is why he named his house after the writer's best-known masterpiece, "La Luna e i Falo" (The Moon and the Fires). This is Pavese country: the hills of Piedmont where every June, under a full moon, peasants light the fires that announce the start of the harvest. It is a magnificent and moving sight that you will witness from the large terrace overlooking the vineyards. The interior is inviting, though a little surprising, with its profusion of imposing furniture and its large and varied painting collection. The bedrooms have the same cozy and comfortable feel. The cooking lives up to the reputation the Carnero family had already acquired in Turin before they decided to settle here at Canelli. The region boasts a wealth of historic, cultural and gastronomic treasures that promise a wonderful vacation.

How to get there *(Map 7): 26km from Asti. In Canelli, take the road towards "Castello Gancia".*

Villa Sassi

10132 Torino Sassi
Strada Traforo del Pino, 47
Tel. 011-89 80 556 - Fax 011-89 80 095 - Sig.ra Aonzo
E-mail: info@villasassi.com - Web: www.villasassi.com

Category ★★★★ **Rooms** 16 with air-conditioning, telephone, bath, WC – Elevator. **Price** Single 330,000L, double 420,000L. **Meals** Breakfast included, served 7:00-10:30. **Restaurant** Service 12:30PM-2:30PM, 8:00PM-10:30PM - closed Sun - 110,000L à la carte - Local and Italian dishes. **Credit cards** All major. **Pets** Dogs not allowed. **Facilities** Parking. **Nearby** In Torino: Palazzo Madama, Museo Egizio (Egyptian Museum) and Galleria Sabauda (16th- and 17th-century Dutch and Flemish paintings), Mole Antonelliana, Sanctuario della Consolata, Galleria d'Arte Moderna - Basilica de Superga - Villa Reale in Stupinigi - Cathedral in Chieri - Church of Sant'Antonio di Ranverso - Abbey of Sacra di San Michele – I Roveri golf course in La Mandria. **Closed** Aug.

This 17th-century villa, which stood in open country when it was first built, is now practically in the center of Turin, though it still benefits from the tranquility of the large grounds that surround it. Of the interior features, it has preserved the wooden staircase and a fine fresco on one wall. Each room has a personalized decoration and excellent amenities. The modern design of the restaurant with its large glazed walls makes it seem part of the garden and gives fine views over the grounds. The farm adjoining the property guarantees the availability of fresh produce and contributes to the quality of the Piedmontese cuisine, a little different and very tasty.

How to get there *(Map 7): Torino-West exit; towards Pino Torinese or Chieri.*

Hotel Victoria

10123 Torino
Via Nino Costa, 4
Tel. 011-56 11 909 - Fax 011-56 11 806
Sig. Vallinotto

Category ★★★ **Rooms** 100 with air-conditioning, telephone, bath or shower, WC, TV, minibar – Elevator. **Price** Single 180-220,000L, double 260-290,000L, suite 335,000L. **Meals** Breakfast included (buffet), served 7:30-11:00. **Restaurant** See p. 537. **Credit cards** All major. **Pets** Dogs not allowed. **Nearby** In Torino: Palazzo Madama, Museo Egizio (Egyptian Museum) and Galleria Sabauda (16th- and 17th-century Dutch and Flemish paintings), Mole Antonelliana, Sanctuario della Consolata, Galleria d'Arte Moderna - Basilica de Superga - Villa Reale in Stupinigi - Cathedral in Chieri - Church of Sant'Antonio di Ranverso - Abbey of Sacra di San Michele – I Roveri golf course in La Mandria. **Open** All year.

The Hotel Victoria, hidden in the middle of this secret town, is a place to experience. This recently built, modern building is in the heart of the shopping district, near the Piazza San Carlo, the Duomo, and the train station. The decor is an innovative blend of function, fantasy and humor. The rooms are all very pretty; you will have trouble choosing between the Egyptian room, the more romantic ones with their Art Nouveau prints, or the ones with a New Orleans motif. They are all very quiet, overlooking either a pedestrian street or the chamber of commerce garden. The breakfast room has all the charm of a winter garden, and the very cozy salon offers a peaceful view of a patio full of green plants. This three-star hotel offers four-star comfort. You will like the Victoria for the quiet, the nice decor, and the reasonable prices.

How to get there *(Map 7): Near Piazza San Carlo and train station.*

Il Capricorno

10050 La Sauze d'Oulx (Torino)
Le Clotes
Tel. 0122-850 273 - Fax 0122-850 055
Sig. and Sig.ra Sacchi

Category ★★★★ **Rooms** 7 with telephone, bath, WC, TV. **Price** Single 220,000L, double 300,000L. **Meals** Breakfast included, served 8:00-10:30 - half board 250,000L (per pers., 3 days min.). **Restaurant** Service 12:30PM-2:30PM, 7:30PM-9:00PM - à la carte - Specialties: Antipasti di Mariarosa - Scottata rucola e Parmigiano - Tacchino su zucchini - Gnocchi alla menta - Ravioli alla crema di zucchini - Portofoglio alla Capricorno - Maltagliati al ragù di verdure. **Credit cards** Visa, Eurocard, MasterCard. **Pets** Dogs not allowed. **Facilities** Parking in summer. **Nearby** Skiing (from the hotel), Bardonecchia - Sestriere - Briançon (France) –golf course (18-hole) in Sestriere. **Open** Dec – Apr 25, Jun 15 – Sept 15.

Sauze d'Oulx is a ski resort town located at an altitude of 4875 feet (1500 meters), near the Franco-Italian border at Clavière Montgenèvre. Il Capricorno is even higher, deep in the mountains, at 5850 feet (1800 meters). This pretty chalet has only seven rooms, all with small but very functional bathrooms. The small number of boarders allows Mariarosa, the owner, to pamper her guests. Her cuisine is absolutely delicious. Il Capricorno, in a location well adapted for both hikers and skiers, is as pleasant in summer as it is in winter, as it is only a few miles from Bardonecchia and Sestrière, and 18 miles (30km) from Briançon. Reservations are a must.

How to get there *(Map 6): 40km north of Briançon via the Col de Montgenève to Oulx, then towards Saure-d'Oulx. 81km west of Torino via A70.*

Locanda del Sant' Uffizio

14030 Cioccaro di Penango (Asti)
Tel. 0141-91 62 92 - Fax 0141-91 60 68
Sig. Beppe

Category ★★★★ **Rooms** 35 and 5 in annex, with telephone, bath or shower, WC, TV, minibar – Wheelchair access. **Price** With half board 260-320,000L (per pers. in double room), 360,000L (single room). **Meals** Breakfast included, served 7:30-10:30. **Restaurant** Service 12:30PM-1:30PM, 7:30PM-9:00PM - mealtime specials 100,000L, also à la carte - Specialties: Funghi tartufi - Gnocchi de fonduta - Cinghiale di bosco - Lasagne con verdurini del orto - Anatra stufata al miele e rhum. **Credit cards** Diners, Visa, Eurocard, MasterCard. **Pets** Small dogs allowed in rooms. **Facilities** Swimming pool, tennis, parking. **Nearby** Asti - Abbey of Vezzolano in Albrugnano - Sanctuario of Crea in Monferrato hills – Golf course (18-hole) in Margara. **Closed** Jan 6 – 16, Aug 9 – 20.

The Locanda del Sant' Uffizio is a former 15th-century convent nestled in the Monferrato hills, surrounded by vineyards. The small chapel, the marvelous and comfortable rooms, the absolute quiet, the beauty of the surrounding countryside and the red brick buildings make this, in our opinion, one of the most charming hotels in this book. Breakfast is served is a beautifully furnished room, and when the weather is warm, next to the swimming pool. The restaurant features exceptional regional cuisine accompanied by delicious wines including one produced right here. Meals are very generous. This place is not to be missed.

How to get there *(Map 7): 64km east of Torino - 21km north of Asti via S457 towards Moncalvo (3km before Moncalvo).*

Albergo del Castello

12060 Verduno (Cuneo)
Via Umberto I, 9
Tel. 0172-47 01 25 - Fax 0172-47 02 98 - Sig.ra Elisa Burlotto
E-mail: real.cast@tin.it - Web: www.castellodiverduno.com

Category ★★ **Rooms** 13 with shower, WC (12 with tel.). **Price** Double 180-250,000L, suite 330,000L.
Meals Breakfast included, served 8:00-11:00 - half board +70,000L (1 pers. 3 days min.).
Restaurant Service from 8:00PM - mealtime specials 85,000L - Specialties: Giura (stracotto di vacca)
- Carne di verduno, risotti albarolo - Anatra con insalata - Panna cotta - Torta nocciole. **Credit cards**
All major. **Pets** Dogs not allowed. **Facilities** Parking at hotel. **Nearby** Torino - Asti - Bra - Alba - Abbey
of Vezzolano. **Open** Feb – end Nov.

This little castle, built according to a design by the 18th-century architect Juvarra, belonged after 1837 to the Savoia family, the royal family of Italy. Located in a region known for its fine wines, barolo and barbera, the hotel still cultivates the vines on the estate and boasts an excellent wine cellar. The interior has undergone a discreet renovation, keeping the original appearance of the castle: frescoes, impressive antique furniture and some of the royal family paintings. The rooms in the main building have a monastic austerity. Those in the outbuilding, the Rose Room and the Blue Room, are more luxurious and decorated with beautiful frescoes. From the wonderful garden you can contemplate all the charms of the Piedmontese countryside. The art-loving Elisa has founded a cultural association called Arte nel Castello which regularly holds exhibits on her premises and which will organize cookery lessons on request.

How to get there *(Map 7): 50km south of Torino; on A21 Asti-East exit; on A6 Marene exit.*

Hotel Pironi

Lago Maggiore
28822 Cannobio (Verbania)
Via Marconi, 35
Tel. 0323-70 624/70 871 - Fax 0323-72 184 - Famiglia Albertella
E-mail: hotel.pironi@carnnobio.net

Category ★★★ **Rooms** 12 with telephone, bath or shower, WC, hairdryer, safe, minibar – Elevator.
Price Single 130-150,000L, double 190-240,000L. **Meals** Breakfast included (buffet). **Restaurant**
See p. 539. **Credit cards** Amex, Visa, Eurocard, MasterCard. **Pets** Dogs not allowed. **Nearby**
Sanctuario della Pietà - Lake Maggiore: Stresa, Borromean islands, Verbania, Villa Taranto, Ascona -
Locarno (Switzerland). **Open** Mid Mar – Oct.

In the old town of Cannobio, the Pironi rises like a ship's prow over the little *piazza*, at the intersection of two streets that descend toward the lake. Solidly built over an elegant portico, the hotel is made up of two adjoining palaces, which have been very ably renovated and restored in such a way as to enhance the capacity of the hotel while preserving the architectural heritage. The bedrooms are not luxurious but very comfortable. Our favorite room is number 12, which gives onto a lovely Renaissance loggia. The salon, which doubles as a breakfast room, is like a little jewel box, its walls entirely covered with frescoes from the *cinquecento*. Situated close to the Swiss border, it is a good point from which to explore the two wild and beautiful valleys of Cannobina and Vissezo.

How to get there *(Map 2): 117km northwest of Milano via A8 (Milan/Torino), Verbiania exit, towards Locarno.*

Hotel Ghiffa

Lago Maggiore
28823 Ghiffa (Verbiana)
Corso Belvedere, 88
Tel. 0323-59 285- Fax 0323-59 585 - Sig. Valerio Cattaneo
E-mail: info@hotelghiffa.com - Web: www.hotelghiffa.com

Category ★★★ **Rooms** 39 (35 with air-conditioning) with telephone, bath or shower, WC, satellite TV – Elevator. **Price** Single 195,000L, double 275,000L; +20,000L with balcon, +40,000L with terrasse. **Meals** Breakfast included, served 7:15-9:45 - half board +30,000L (per pers., 3 days min.). **Restaurant** Service 12:15PM-2:00PM, 7:15PM-9:00PM - mealtime specials 50,000L - Specialties: Filetti di pesce persico alle erbe - Bianco di rambo al finocchio selvatino - Cannelloni alla nizarda - Torta Daverina. **Credit cards** All major. **Pets** Dogs allowed on request. **Facilities** Swimming pool, garage (18,000L), parking. **Nearby** Stresa - Borromean islands - Locarno - Ascona – Pian golf course di Sole. **Closed** Jan 1 – Mar 25, Oct 20 – Dec 21.

On the lush banks of Lake Maggiore, its luxuriant vegetation tamed by artistic landscape gardening, Ghiffa is a quiet and romantic resort town. The hotel, directly on the lakefront, has preserved in its salons something of its aristocratic past. The bedrooms have a rather cold, modern look, but those with views over the lake and the mountains amply make up for the slight shortcoming. A swimming pool and a small private beach are attractive during the summer season. The restaurant offers the same fine panorama. A refreshing place to stop before a visit to the Borromean Islands, though the service, the cooking and the management suffer from the excess of customers in summer.

How to get there (*Map 2*): *102km northwest of Milano via A8, Gravellona Toce exit, towards Verbania/Lago Maggiore, Locarno.*

Hotel Verbano

Lago Maggiore
Isole Borromee 28838 Stresa (Novara) - Isola dei Pescatori
Tel. 0323-30 408/32 534 - Fax 0323-33 129 - Sig. Zacchera
E-mail: hotelverbano@tin.it - Web: www.hotelverbano.it

Category ★★★ **Rooms** 12 with telephone, bath or shower, WC. **Price** Double 250,000L. **Meals** Breakfast included - half board 180,000L, full board 230,000L (per pers.). **Restaurant** Service 12:00PM-2:30PM, 7:00PM-9:30PM - mealtime specials 45-75,000L, also à la carte - Specialties: Antipasti - Pesce del lago. **Credit cards** All major. **Pets** Dogs allowed. **Facilities** Boat. **Nearby** Isola Bella (Palazzo Borromeo and his gardens) - Isola Madre (botanical garden) – Isole Borromee golf course (18-hole) in Stresa. **Closed** Jan and Feb.

An excursion to the Borromean Islands is one of the highlights of Lake Maggiore. If you want a tour, you can catch the boat at the port of Stresa. But these wonderful little islands, with their charming villas whose lush gardens extend right up to the dock, are really worth a stay. Isola dei Pescatori is one of the smallest and the Hotel Verbano is quite small itself. Toscanini used to like to come here and work. Charming though not luxurious, the bedrooms, with their creaking wood floors, are decorated with old-fashioned family furniture and most have a splendid view of the lake. In case all this is not romantic enough, dinner in the evening is served by candlelight.

How to get there *(Map 2): Northwest of Milano via A8 and A26, towards Lake Maggiore; in Stresa or in Pallanza, ferry services for the Borromean Islands, stop at Isola dei Pescatori. Ferry service for the coast from 6:30PM or bus-boat and taxi-boat.*

Hotel Villa Crespi

Lago d'Orta
28016 Orta San Giulio (Novara)
Via Generale Fava, 8
Tel. 0322-91 19 02 - Fax 0322-91 19 19 - Famiglia Primatesta

Category ★★★★ **Rooms** 14 and 8 suites with air-conditioning, telephone, bath, WC, TV, minibar – Elevator. **Price** Single 200-310,000L, double 320-420,000L, suite 420-700,000L. **Meals** Breakfast included, served 7:00-10:30 - half board 90,000L (per pers.). **Restaurant** Service 12:00PM-2:30PM, 7:30PM-10:00PM - mealtime specials 90-140,000L - Specialties: Fantasia di astice e caviale con agrumi e zenzero - Petto di quaglia glassato - San Pietro croccante con julienne di verdure alla soja e sesamo - Anatro glassata a miele d'acacia e cedro. **Credit cards** All major. **Pets** Small dogs allowed. **Facilities** Sauna, parking. **Nearby** Orta San Giulio - Sacro Monte (view) - Island of San Giulio - Fondation Calderana in Vacciago – Golf course in Gignese. **Open** All year (only by reservation).

The hotel has just changed hands, though no great difference can be observed for the time being. On the banks of the very romantic Lake Orta you will notice an unusual Moorish minaret, a luxurious homage to the Orient built by a cotton industrialist, Benigno Crespi. The villa (1880) stands in the middle of marvelous grounds shaded by pine trees. The salons and rooms are a successful blend of a somewhat heavy orientalism with more classical furniture. The rooms have a Romantic decor with imposing canopy beds and lovely velvet fabrics. The spacious marble bathrooms feature ultramodern facilities including "matrimonial" jacuzzis. This is a professionally run, family hotel. This is a nice place in an ideal location for wandering down the narrow cobblestone streets of the peninsula.

How to get there *(Map 2): 20km west of Stresa and of Lago Maggiore.*

Hotel San Rocco

Lago d'Orta - 28016 Orta San Giulio (Novara)
Via Gippini, 11
Tel. 0322-91 19 77 - Fax 0322-91 19 64 - Sig. Barone
E-mail: sanrocco@giacomini.com - Web: www.hotelsanrocco.it

Category ★★★★ Rooms 74 with telephone, bath, WC, TV, minibar – Elevator. **Price** Single 180-270,000L, double 260-390,000L, suite 400-460,000L. **Meals** Breakfast included, served 7:00-10:00. **Restaurant** Service 12:30PM-2:00PM, 8:00PM - mealtime specials 75,000L - Specialties: Filetti di salmerino con farcia di coregone - Risotti - Medaglioni di vitello agli agrumi - Zabaglione frappè all'aceto balsamico. **Credit cards** All major. **Pets** Dogs not allowed. **Facilities** Sauna (26,000L), health center, parking, garage (15,000L). **Nearby** Orta San Giulio - Sacro Monte (view) - Island of San Giulio - Fondation Calderana in Vacciago – Golf course in Gignese. **Open** All year.

The Hotel San Rocco is right on the lake across from the Romanesque landscape of the island of San Giulio. Built on the foundations of a 17th century monastery, the hotel has kept its original architectural structure, enclosed shell-like on the lake and on its cloister. Inside you will find all of the efficiency of a modern hotel. The rooms all have a beautiful view and are simply decorated but very comfortable. When the weather gets warm, you can have breakfast in the garden on the lake and relax in the pool. The hotel also provides a private boat to explore all of the nooks and crannies of the island with. The restaurant features delicate variations on traditional recipes.

***How to get there** (Map 2): 20km west of Stresa and Lago Maggiore.*

Castello di San Giorgio

15020 San Giorgio Monferrato (Alessandria)
Via Cavalli d'Olivola, 3
Tel. 0142-80 62 03 - Fax 0142-80 65 05
Sig. Cavaliere

Category ★★★★ **Rooms** 10 and 1 suite with telephone, bath, WC, TV, minibar. **Price** Single 170-190,000L, double 240-260,000L, suite 340,000L. **Meals** Breakfast 25,000L (buffet), served 8:00-10:00 - half board 240,000L (per pers.). **Restaurant** Service 12:00PM-2:30PM, 7:30PM-9:30PM - closed Mon - mealtime specials 95,000L, also à la carte - Specialties: Agnolotti alla monferrina - Seafood - Tartufi. **Credit cards** All major. **Pets** Dogs allowed. **Facilities** Parking. **Nearby** Marengo (Villa Marengo) - Asti - Abbey of Vezzolano in Albugnano. **Closed** Jan 3 – 10.

This hotel and remarkable restaurant are located in the outbuildings (the farmhouse and stables) of Monferrat Castle, an enormous dark brick edifice built in the 14th century for Gonzague de Mantoue. On magnificent grounds inside its original walls, the buildings have been superbly renovated and partly decorated with furniture and old paintings from the castle. The luxurious rooms have been tastefully done, and have a very pretty view of the vast, quiet plain dotted with hills. Management and chef have changed in the restaurant, but the staff are still the same. One can only hope that, since they were trained in a good school, the cooking will be as delicious as before. And since the setting and service go hand-in-hand, we suggest you give it a try.

How to get there *(Map 8): 26km northwest of Alessandria via A26, Casale-South exit, 6km towards Alessandria - Asti, road on the right towards San Giorgio Monferrato.*

Hotel Hermitage

11021 Breuil-Cervinia (Aosta)
Tel. 0166-94 89 98 - Fax 0166-94 90 32
E-mail: info@hotelhermitage.com - Web: www.hotelhermitage.com

Category ★★★★ **Rooms** 28, 7 suites and 1 apartment with telephone, bath or shower, WC, satellite TV, safe, minibar – Elevator. **Price** Double 300-400,000L (classical), suite 400-600,000L (junior suite), 500-1 000,000L (junior with camine). **Meals** Breakfast included (buffet), served 7:30-10:30 - half board 220-380,000L (classical), 400,000L in suite. **Restaurant** Service 1:00PM-2:00PM, 8:00PM-10:00PM - mealtime specials 70-90,000L, also à la carte - Italian and local cooking. **Credit cards** All major. **Pets** Dogs not allowed. **Facilities** Covered swimming pool, sauna, health center, parking and garage (+30,000L). **Nearby** Ski - cable car to Plateau Rosà (view) – Cervino golf course (9-hole). **Closed** May, Jun, Oct and Nov.

A stay at the Hermitage combines the joys of skiing with all the well-being of a luxury hotel. You gan get your fill of thrills on the slopes of the Matterhorn at 3,000 meters or have the pleasure of skiing all the way to Zermatt on the Swiss side. Back at the hotel, you'll find excellent amenities, spacious rooms done with an Alpine flavor, both elegant and cozy, or some new attic rooms, very romantic with their sloping ceilings. In the evening, pleasant après-ski activities round the swimming pool or at the health and fitness club. And to end the day, a dinner at the hotel restaurant, known for its old family recipes, lives up to its very fine reputation. Everything here is homemade, including the Viennese pastries and the jams on the breakfast table. During certain off-season periods of December, January and April, the Hermitage offers five-day packages at affordable prices that make it possible to enjoy all the advantages of a hotel of charm in one of the finest skiing areas in Europe. Two small things to note: gentlemen, please wear a jacket for dinner; and children are welcome from ten years up.

How to get there *(Map 1): 50km northeast of Aosta via A5 Aosta-West exit, then RR47.*

Les Neiges d'Antan

11021 Breuil-Cervinia (Aosta)
Frazione Cret Perrères
Tel. 0166-94 87 75 - Fax 0166-94 88 52 - Sig. and Sig.ra Bich
E-mail: ludo@netvallee.it - Web: www.lesneigesdantan.com

Category ★★★ **Rooms** 28 with telephone, bath or shower, WC, safe, TV. **Price** Single 120,000L, double 220,000L, suite (4 pers.) 380,000L. **Meals** Breakfast included, served 7:30-10:00 - half board 95,000L, full board 170,000L. **Restaurant** Service 12:30PM-2:00PM, 7:30PM-9:30PM - mealtime specials 50,000L, also à la carte - Italian and local cooking. **Credit cards** Visa, Eurocard, MasterCard. **Pets** Dogs allowed except in restaurant. **Facilities** Private shuttle to the pister, parking. **Nearby** Skiing - cable car to Plateau Rosà (view) – Cervino golf course (9-hole). **Closed** Sept 17 – Dec 5, May 3 – Jun 29.

Isolated high up in the mountains, facing the Matterhorn, the Neiges d'Antan is a charming hotel, the reflection of the soul and the passion of an entire family. The decor is simple but warm and personal. The bar has paneled walls covered with a collection of photos. You can find books, magazines and newspapers to read in the large, modern salon and music room. This is a place of simple luxury, reflected in the excellent cuisine carefully supervised by Sig.ra Bich, who also makes the jellies you will be served at breakfast, in the wine list selected by Sig. Bich and his son, the wine-waiter, and in the old, lace doily upon which you will place your wine glass. The rooms all have the same good taste and great comfort. This is a quality hotel, run by quality people.

How to get there *(Map 1): 49km northeast of Aosta via A5, Saint-Vincent exit - Chatillon, then S406 - 4km before Cervinia.*

Albergo Villa Anna Maria

11020 Champoluc (Aosta)
5, rue Croues
Tel. 0125-30 71 28 - Fax 0125-30 79 84 - Sig. Origone and Sig. Origone
E-mail: hotelannamaria@tiscalinet.it - Web: www.hotelvillaannamaria.com

Category ★★★ **Rooms** 20 with telephone, TV (14 with bath or shower, WC). **Price** With half board 125,000L, full board 140,000L. (per pers., 3 days min.). **Meals** Breakfast included, served 8:15-11:00. **Restaurant** Service 12:45PM-2:00PM, 7:45PM-9:00PM - closed Sept 16 – Dec 1, Apr 20 – Jun 20 - mealtime specials 30-40,000L, also à la carte - Specialty: Fonduta with melted Fontina. **Credit cards** Visa, Eurocard, MasterCard. **Pets** Small dogs allowed. **Nearby** Skiing - Hamlets in the Valle d'Ayas: Antagnod, Perrias, Saint-Jacques - Castles of Verrès and Issogne - Church of Antagnod. **Open** All year.

This incontestably charming chalet is one of our favorite properties. Hidden behind spruce trees, covered with flowers in the summer and buried in snow in the winter, the Villa Anna Maria is perfect for people seeking for quiet. The dining room has a rustic, natural atmosphere with its gleaming copper pots and lovely polished wood walls. The cuisine is simple and sophisticated. The rooms have low ceilings and are a little dark, as mountain refuges often are. The hosts extend a warm and genuine welcome.

How to get there *(Map 1): 63km east of Aosta via A5, Verrès exit, then SR45 (Valley of Ayas) to Champoluc.*

Hotel Bellevue

11012 Cogne (Aosta)
Via Gran Paradiso, 22
Tel. 0165-74 825 - Fax 0165-74 91 92 - Sigg. Jeantet and Roullet
E-mail: info@hotelbellevue.it - Web: www.hotelbellevue.it

Category ★★★★ **Rooms** 32, 3 chalets with telephone, bath or shower, WC, TV, minibar, safe – Elevator. **Price** Single 190-240,000L, double 280-540,000L. **Meals** Breakfast included, served 8:00-10:00 - half board 170-300,000L (per pers., 3 days min.). **Restaurants** Service 12:30PM-1:30PM, 7:30PM-9:00PM - mealtime specials 50-80,000L, also à la carte - Regional cooking. **Credit cards** All major. **Pets** Dogs not allowed. **Facilities** Swimming pool (indoor), whirlpool, turkish bath, sauna, mountain bikes, cooking lesson, wine toast, garage and parking. **Nearby** Alpine Garden of Valnontey - Gran Paradiso National Park - Waterfall of Lillaz. **Closed** Oct 1 – Dec 22.

The Hotel Bellevue is located in the heart of the Gran Paradiso National Park, very near the center of Cogne, yet isolated in a field which goes on as far as the eye can see. The service is warm and the white wood and pastel decor is simple. The personnel, dressed in traditional costume, add to the charm of the place. The cuisine is exquisite and made with fine regional products; the bread, pastries, and jellies are homemade, and the hotel has its own private supplier of cheeses. The hotel owns three restaurants, two of which are at the hotel: one is for boarders, and the other small one is a place where you can dine à la carte. The third, *La Brasserie du Bon Bec,* is in the center of the village, and serves mountain specialties. The rooms, which all have a superb view, are very elegantly decorated. The hotel now has modern entertainment facilities and offers music and movie evenings.

How to get there *(Map 1): 27km south of Aosta by the Mont-Blanc motorway (reopening Fall 2000), then exit Aosta-West and RR47.*

Hotel Herbetet

Valnontey 11012 Cogne (Aosta)
Tel. 0165-74 372 - Fax 0165-74 180
Sig. Carlo Cavagnet
E-mail: ccavagnet@hotmail.com

Category ★★ **Rooms** 22 with bath or shower, WC. **Price** Single 40-50,000L, double 80-130,000L. **Meals** Breakfast 8,000L, served 7:30-9:30 - half board 65-100,000L, full board 75-120,000L (per pers.). **Restaurant** Service 12:30PM-1:00PM, 7:30PM-8:00PM - closed Thurs in low season - mealtime specials 26,000L. (all incl.), also à la carte - Specialties: Fondue alla valdotena - Sosa. **Credit cards** All major. **Pets** Dogs allowed. **Facilities** Parking at hotel. **Nearby** Alpine Garden of Paradidia - Gran Paradiso National Park. **Open** May 15 – Sept 25.

For those who love the mountains, Cogne is a strategic spot. At an altitude of 1,535 meters, you find yourself at the foot of the high mountains. Hiking in summer, cross-country skiing in winter, here you feel really close to nature. The greatest asset of the Hotel Herbetet is its view. Bedrooms, balconies and terraces face the majestic panorama of Gran Paradiso National Park. It is a little away from the village and from your room you may even catch a glimpse of the mountain goats that live protected in the park. Inside the hotel, everything is very rustic, simple and comfortable. This is a good stop for anyone who feels like spending a few days in quiet communion with the mountains.

How to get there *(Maps 1 and 7): 27km south of Aosta. By the Turin-Milan motorway, Aosta-West exit then R47.*

Hotel Petit Dahu

11012 Valnontey (Aosta)
Tel. 0165-74 146 - Fax 0165-74 146
Sig. and Sig.ra Cesare - Ivana Charruaz
E-mail: hpdahu@aostanet.com

Category ★★ **Rooms** 8 with telephone, shower, WC, (3 rooms with TV). **Price** 85-135,000L in half board (per pers., 3 days min.). **Meals** Breakfast included, served 8:00-10:00. **Restaurant** Service 7:30PM - mealtime specials 42,000L - Specialties: Carbonade - Fondutte - Raclette. **Credit cards** Visa, Eurocard, MasterCard. **Pets** Dogs not allowed. **Facilities** Parking at hotel. **Nearby** Alpine Garden of Valnontey - Gran Paradiso National Park. **Closed** May.

If you're not in the mood for the luxury of Cogne, you can lose yourself in this tiny hamlet of the Gran Paradiso National Park, as rustic as can be and consisting today only of hotels. In the heart of the village, two small houses linked by a little footbridge make up the Petit Dahu. A miniature hotel, with little rooms, a little garden and a little restaurant, it is for all its small size a place of warmth, well-kept and friendly. The owner can serve as guide if you want to hike through the valley or explore the park for marmots, deer and mountain goats, which have become quite tame in their protected environment. Excursions are proposed to Vittorio Sella, Roccia Viba or Becca di Gay, and when you return you can delight in the home cooking of Ivana, with local specialties like fondue and raclette. Once a week they organize (for a set price) a dinner by candlelight. This is a simple and convivial place.

How to get there *(Maps 1 and 7): 27km south of Aosta via S26 to Sarre, then S47.*

Chalet Val Ferret

Arnouva 11013 Courmayeur (Aosta)
Tel. 0165-84 49 59 - Fax 0165-84 49 59 - Marcella and Stefano Biondi
E-mail: chalet@netvallee.it

Category ★★ **Rooms** 7 with telephone, bath or shower, WC – Wheelchair access. **Price** Double 120-140,000. **Meals** Breakfast included, served 8:00-10:30 - half board and full board 100-110,000L, 110-130,000L (per pers.). **Restaurant** Service 12:30PM-2:00PM, 7:30PM-9:30PM - mealtime specials 35-50,000L, also à la carte - Regional cooking. **Credit cards** Visa, Eurocard, MasterCard. **Pets** Dogs allowed. **Facilities** Parking. **Nearby** Skiing - Waterfalls and Lac du Ruitor near Thuile - Col du Géant and Aiguille du Midi by Cablecar - Cablecar at Chécrouit - Val Veny and Val Ferret - Chamonix – Plainpincieux golf course (9-hole), golf course in Chamonix (18-hole). **Closed** Sept 15 – Jun 15.

With the Mont-Blanc tunnel, the Valle d'Aosta is the quickest way to reach northern Italy via France. On emerging from the tunnel, one reaches the little village of Entrèves, the starting point of two valleys which share the celebrated Mont Blanc massif with the valley of Chamonix: to the southwest, the Val Veny and to the northeast the Val Ferret. Together these offer everything that could be wanted by walkers and climbers in summer, or skiers in winter (since the famous resort of Courmayeur is only a few kilometers away). At the bottom of this valley of larch trees with its lush vegetation, on the banks of the River Ferret, you find this chalet, the last stop before the high summits. The owners have managed to make the best possible use of this former sheepfold and to adapt traditional décor in very good taste to modern standards of comfort. You will be greeted with warmth and friendliness. The team is young and energetic and the cooking of high quality. All the rooms overlook the mountain stream and the moutain itself. Ideal for anyone who loves silence, as well as for sports enthusiasts and simple holidaymakers.

How to get there *(Map 1): 20km from Chamonix through the Mont-Blanc tunnel (reopening 2002) - Entrèves, then Val Ferrat road.*

La Grange

Entrèves 11013 Courmayeur (Aosta)
Strada La Brenva
Tel. 0165-86 97 33 - Fax 0165-86 97 44
Sig.ra Berthod

Category ★★★ **Rooms** 23 with telephone, bath, WC, TV, radio, minibar. **Price** Single 100-200,000L, double 150-250,000L, suite (4 pers.) 300-450,000L. **Meals** Breakfast included, served 8:00-10:30. **Restaurant** See. p. 540. **Credit cards** All major. **Pets** Dogs allowed (5,000L). **Facilities** Sauna (15,000L), parking. **Nearby** Skiing - Ruitor Lake - cable car to Col du Géant and Aiguille du Midi - Val Veny and Val Ferret - Chamonix (in France) – Golf course (18-hole) in Chamonix, golf course (9-hole) in Plainpincieux. **Open** Dec – end Apr, Jul – end Sept.

Despite its charm and its success, this small hotel has remained a little-known find. Hidden in what was once the depths of Val d'Aosta, at the foot of the Brenva glacier and Mont Blanc, it is today close to the tunnel that links Courmayeur to Chamonix (tourists coming from France should inform themselves about the reopening of the Mont-Blanc tunnel). Fortunately, the village of Entreves has remained an unspoiled mountain village. The interior of what was once an old barn has been beautifully restored and is warm and welcoming: antique furniture, old objects and engravings adorn the sitting room and the lovely breakfast room. (Breakfast, by the way, is absolutely delicious.) The rooms are comfortable, cozy and intimate. There is a possibility of a half-board arrangement with a restaurant 50 meters from the hotel (30,000L a meal).

How to get there *(Map 1): 42km west of Aosta via S26, Courmayeur, towards the Mont-Blanc tunnel.*

Hotel La Brenva

Entrèves 11013 Courmayeur (Aosta)
Tel. 0165-869 780 - Fax 0165-869 726
Sig. Egidio Biondi
E-mail: labrenva@tin.it - Web: www.labrenva.com

Category ★★★ **Rooms** 14 with telephone, shower, WC, TV. **Price** Double 120-220,000L, suite 180-280,000L (4 pers.). **Meals** Breakfast included, served 8:00-10:00. **Restaurant** Service 7:30PM-9:30PM - closed Mon - mealtime specials 50-70,000L, also à la carte - Regional cooking. **Credit cards** All major. **Pets** Dogs allowed. **Facilities** Parking at hotel. **Nearby** Skiing - Waterfalls and Lac du Ruitor near Thuile - cable car to "Col du Géant" and "Aiguille du midi" - cable car to Chécrouit - Val Veny and Val Ferret - Chamonix – Golf course (9-hole) in Plainpincieux, golf course (18-hole) in Chamonix. **Closed** May.

Located just at the base of the towering Mont Blanc, Entrèves combines the assets of a skiing resort with those of a little Alpine village. The inn has all the cozy atmosphere of a mountain chalet: thick stone walls, fireplaces, exposed beams. The rooms are paneled in wood and their balconies look out on the stunning Alpine peaks. It is rustic yet comfortable and in the evening it is an ideal retreat to rest and replenish your strength. The owner, an excellent cook, will introduce you to the local specialties, imaginatively prepared. Gourmets take note.

How to get there *(Map 1): 42km west of Aosta via S26, Courmayeur, the Mont-Blanc tunnel road, Entrèves.*

Hotel Gran Baita

11025 Gressoney-Saint-Jean (Aosta)
Strada Castello Savoia, 26
Tel. 0125-35 64 41 - Fax 0125-35 64 41 - Sig. Francesco Mattai del Moro
E-mail: granbaita@netsurf.it - Web: www.hotelgranbaita.it

Category ★★★ **Rooms** 12 with telephone, bath, hairdryer, satellite TV – Elevator, wheelchair access. **Price** Double 140-180,000L. **Meals** Breakfast (buffet) 12,000L, served 8:00-10:00 - half board and full board 95-160,000L, 106-165,000 (per pers.). **Restaurant** Service 12:30PM-1:00PM, 7:30PM-8:30PM - mealtime specials, also à la carte - Italian and regional cooking. **Credit cards** Visa, Eurocard, MasterCard. **Pets** Dogs not allowed. **Facilities** Turkish bath, sauna, fitness, UVA (12,000L), parking. **Nearby** Skiing (1km from chair lift) - Excursion and climbs on Monte Rosa – Golf Gressoney Monte Rosa (green fee not charged to residents). **Closed** Mid Apr – end Jun, mid Sept – beg Dec.

At the bottom of the valley of La Lys, the two villages of Gressoney can offer moutain sports at every level and in all seasons, including trips to Monte Rosa for the more experienced. The Gran-Baita occupies a typical local chalet, the interior of which has been converted into a comfortable hotel with a desire to preserve the Val d'Aosta atmosphere. Hence the lavish use of wood - old wood for the framework, the beams and some fittings, but more modern for the furniture in regional style. The result is warm, providing a convivial space both in the reading room, with its rich library of documents about the area, in the dining room, where you can sample the local cuisine or in the bar, open at all hours. The rooms have a high standard of comfort in a modernized moutain-style décor. Most have a balcony. Finally, there are some useful extras, such as a minibus which will take you to the start of skiing pistes, or on trips. And after a hard day, you can soothe your aching limbs in the sauna or the Turkish bath...

How to get there *(Map 1): 100km east of Aosta by A5, exit Pont-Saint-Martin, then S505.*

Hotel Lo Scoiattolo

11020 Gressoney-la-Trinité (Aosta)
Tel. 0125-366 313 - Fax. 0125-366 220
Sig.ra Bethaz
E-mail: hotelloscoiattolo@tiscalinet.it

Category ★★★ **Rooms** 14 with telephone, bath or shower, WC, TV. **Price** With half board 70-140,000L (per pers.). **Meals** Breakfast 15,000L, served 8:00-10:00. **Restaurant** For residents; service 1:00PM and 7:30PM - mealtime specials - Local cooking. **Credit cards** Visa, Eurocard, MasterCard. **Pets** Dogs not allowed. **Facilities** Garage. **Nearby** Skiing - Mont Rosa. **Open** Dec – Apr, Jun 25 – Sept.

Gressoney-la Trinité is the last in a string of villages in the Val d'Aoste at the foot of Mount Rose. Frequented mainly by Italian families and couples, this village has a very different atmosphere from the other more urbane resorts in the area, and the hotels here cater to the needs of their clientele. The nicest one is this small hotel run by Silvana and her two daughters. The rooms are large and well furnished. Every room is paneled in light wood, giving them a real mountain feel. Sig.ra Bethaz can sometimes be a little gruff, but she does see to it that everything in the hotel and the kitchen runs smoothly. This is a good hotel for an economical vacation.

How to get there *(Map 1): 100km east of Aosta via A5, Pont-Saint-Martin exit, then S505.*

Hotel dei Trulli

70011 Alberobello (Bari)
Via Cadore, 28
Tel. 080-432 35 55 - Fax 080-432 35 60 - Sig. Farace - Sig. Cottino
E-mail: hoteldeitrulli@inmedia.it

Category ★★★★★ **Rooms** 19 with air-conditioning, telephone, bath or shower, WC, TV, minibar.
Price (with half board), single 170-200,000L, double 140-170,000L (per pers. 3 days min.).
Restaurant Service 12:30PM-2:30PM, 7:30PM-10:30PM - mealtime specials 60,000L. Specialties:
Orecchiette alla barese - Purè di fave con cicoria - Agnello Alberobellese. **Credit cards** All major. **Pets**
Dogs allowed. **Facilities** Swimming pool, parking. **Nearby** Alberobello (Trulli district) - Castel del
Monte - Locorotondo - Martina Franca - Taranto (Museo Nazionale: Greek and Roman artifacts
collection) - Castellana Grotte. **Open** All year.

Alberobello is the world capital of *trulli*, cute little houses which, at first
glance, might remind you of the ones the dwarves live in at Disneyland,
but they are, in fact, authentic old houses, typical of the region. The hotel
is entirely made up of recently built trulli, which imitate the local style; each one
is freshly whitewashed and has an arbor, one or two rooms, and a small living
room with a fireplace. They are all charming, comfortable, and air-
conditioned. The restaurant is in the main building. The hotel swimming pool
is not very attractive, but you will really appreciate it on hot summer days.

How to get there *(Map 22): 55km southeast of Bari via S100 to Casamàssima,
then S172 to Putignano and Alberobello.*

Il Melograno

70043 Monopoli (Bari)
Contrada Torricella, 345
Tel. 080-690 90 30 - Fax 080-74 79 08 – Sig. Guerra
E-mail: melograno@melograno.com - Web: www.melograno.com

Category ★★★★★ **Rooms** 37 with air-conditioning, telephone, bath or shower, WC, satellite TV, minibar. **Price** Single 230-340,000L, double 460-720,000L, suite 720-1 260,000L. **Meals** Breakfast included, served 7:30-11:00 - half board 320-430,000L, full board 360-470,000L. (per pers., 3 days min.). **Restaurant** Service 12:30PM-2:30PM, 8:00PM-10:30PM - mealtime specials 80,000L - Specialties: Salmone affumicato in casa - Agnello al forno. **Credit cards** All major. **Pets** Dogs allowed by request. **Facilities** Swimming pool, tennis, parking. **Nearby** Ruins of Egnazia - Polignano a Mare - Alberobello (Trulli district) - Castel del Monte - Locorotondo - Martina Franca - Taranto (Museo Nazionale: Greek and Roman artifacts collection) - Castellana Grotte. **Closed** Jan 7 – Apr 4.

Here, in the hot region of Apulia, is an oasis of coolness, greenery and taste. Il Melograno was originally a sharecropper's fortified farmhouse from the 16th century. It is surrounded by a maze of white buildings which blend in with bouganvilleas, and olive, lemon, and pomegranate trees. Formerly a vacation house, it has been transformed into a hotel but has kept its characteristic personal touch. The rooms are very elegant, with their antique furniture and paintings, beautiful fabrics and traditional *cotto* (ceramic tile) floors. The salons seem lost in the orange grove seen through a picture window. The dining room-veranda, where you'll dine under a white canopy next to an ancient olive tree, is on the other side of the garden. The hosts are very nice. Note that sometimes there are seminars which can disturb guests.

How to get there *(Map 22): 50km south of Bari, 3km from Monopoli towards Alberobello.*

Villa Cenci

72014 Cisternino (Brindisi)
Via per Ceglie Messapica
Tel. 080-444 82 08 - Fax 080-444 33 29
Sig.ra Bianco

Category ★★★ **Rooms** 25 with telephone, bath or shower, WC. **Price** Double 130-170,000L.
Meals Breakfast 10,000L, served 8:30-10:30. **Restaurant** Service 8:00PM-10:00PM - mealtime
specials 30,000L - Italian and regional cooking. **Credit cards** Visa, Eurocard, MasterCard. **Pets** Dogs
allowed. **Facilities** Swimming pool, parking. **Nearby** Alberobello (Trulli district) - Castellana Grotte -
Locorotondo - Martina Franca - Tàranto (Museo Nazionale: Greek and Roman artifacts collection) –
Golf course (18-hole) in Riva dei Tessali. **Open** End Mar – end Sept.

Far from the hordes of tourists in this very busy region, this agricultural
estate will host you for a very modest price. The beautiful white house,
isolated among the grapevines, offers its guests tranquility, which you will feel
as you walk along the paths lined with white laurels. It is surrounded by *trulli*,
conic constructions typical of Apulia; those here have cool rooms with simple,
tasteful decor. In the villa itself there are other more classical rooms, as well
as several functional small apartments. The hotel is frequented by numerous
Italian and English regulars. From the swimming pool you can have a nice
view of the countryside. The fruit and vegetables served at meals are fresh
from the garden, and the wine is "home made."

How to get there *(Map 22): 74km southeast of Bari via SS16, coast to the
Ostuni-Pezze-di-Greco-Cisternino exit. At Cisternino, take the strada
provinciale towards Ceglie Messapico.*

Masseria Marzalossa

72015 Fasano (Brindisi)
C.da Pezze Vicine, 65
Tel. 080-44 13 780 - Fax 080-44 13 780 - Sig. Mario Guarini
E-mail: masseriamarzalossa@puglianet.it - Web: www.marzalossa.puglianet.it

Rooms 6 and 1 suite with bath, WC, TV on request, fridge. **Price** Double 140-150,000L (per pers.), junior suite 150-170,000L, suite 180-200,000L. **Meals** Breakfast included, served 8:30-10:00 - half board 160-180,000L in double room, 180-230,000L in suite (per pers., 3 day min.). **Restaurant** Service 8:00PM-9:30PM - mealtime specials 60,000L. **Credit cards** Visa, Eurocard, MasterCard. **Pets** Dogs not allowed. **Facilities** Swimming pool, bicycles, parking. **Nearby** Ruins of Egnazia - Alberobello - Locorotondo - Martina Franca - Tàranto - Castellana Grotto. **Open** Apr – end Sept.

An exceptional site, lost in the middle of an olive grove, not far from Ostuni and Fasano with its strange local architecture typical of Puglia. A fortified 17th-century farmhouse, it has been subtly and tastefully restored. The house is built around several patios: one planted with orange trees, one with lemon trees, and one with a swimming pool entirely surrounded by columns. The dimensions are modest and the atmosphere intimate. The masseria has only a few apartments, elegant and well-decorated with period furniture. Once owned by an ecclesiastical family, it still has traces of that past, which lend a somewhat mysterious air. You will also enjoy the wonderful local cooking based on the produce of the estate: an outstanding olive oil and delicious home-made jams for breakfast. The isolation of the place is part of its charm and you may wish to stay put and savor it. But you can easily explore the region - for a modest price, the owners can put a boat at your disposal, or another means of transport, if you wish.

How to get there *(Map 22): 60km southwest of Bari via SS379, Bari-North exit. Towards Brindisi, Fasano exit, 2km towards SS16, Ostoni exit.*

Masseria Salamina

72010 Pezze di Greco (Brindisi)
Tel. 080-489 73 07 - Fax 080-489 85 82
G.V. de Miccolis Angelini
E-mail: salamina@mailbox.media.it - Web: www.joynet.it/salamina

Rooms 7 and 8 apartments (2-4 pers.) with bath, WC. **Price** Double 140-180,000L, apartment 805-1 350,000L (weekly). **Meals** Breakfast included, served 8:00-10:00 - half board 100-120,000L (per pers.). **Restaurant** Service from 8:00PM - closed Tues in winter - mealtime specials 35-50,000L - Regional cooking. **Credit cards** All major. **Pets** Digs allowed. **Facilities** Parking. **Nearby** Medieval town of Ostuni (the white town) - Egnatia - Martina Franca (Baroque town) - Alberbello (trulli) - Castellana grotte. **Open** All year.

B etween Fasano and Ostuni the landscape alternates between olive groves bathed in the sea mists of the Adriatic and the chalk plateau of the Murge, with its gottoes and caves, ending in the dazzling città bianca. This is the site in which in the 17th Century this fortress was constructed; with its elegant gilded tower, it dominates the valley. The estate of seven hectares surrounding this fortified masseria is still cultivated, but also offers rooms or apartments on the property. The contrast between the impressive building and the austerity of the internal fittings may be disconcerting. In fact, only the spaces survive, most of the furniture of the rooms being made up essentially of beds and small cane or rattan pieces and chairs in willow. The decoration is minimal, with white walls and flowered bedspreads in pastel colors. Some rooms have a view of the coast which can be seen between the olive trees. As with many agriturismi, you can enjoy the fresh products of the estate in the restaurant.

How to get there *(Map 22): 18km from Ostuni, 5km from Fasano.*

Masseria San Domenico

72010 Savelletri di Fasano (Brindisi)
Tel. 080-482 79 90 - Fax 080-955 79 78
Sig. Luigi Anfosso
E-mail: masseriasandomenico@puglianet.it - Web: www.masseriasandomenico.com

Rooms 31 and 1 suite with air-conditioning, telephone, bath or shower, WC, haidryer, safe, satellite TV, minibar. **Price** Single 1580-240,000L, double 320-580,000L, suite on request. **Meals** Breakfast 15,000L, served 7:30-10:30 - half board +60,000L, full board +100,000L (per pers., 3 day min.). **Restaurant** Service 12:30PM-2:00PM, 7:30PM-10:00PM - closed Tues - mealtime specials 80-120,000L - Local cooking. **Credit cards** All Major. **Pets** Dogs not allowed. **Facilities** Swimming pool, bicycles, golf, sauna (25,000L), parking. **Nearby** Ruins of Egnazia, Alberobelloa (Trulli district) - Locorotondo - Martina Franca - Taranto (Museo Nazionale: Greek artifacts collection) - Castellana Grotte – Golf course (18-hole) in Riva dei Tessali, Castellaneta-Taranto. **Closed** Jan 6 – Feb 10.

This is one of the finest examples of a fortified farmhouse in the entire Puglia region. Between the 15th and 17th centuries the landowners built these masserie a torre with surrounding walls, moats and sentry posts as protection against the pirates who used to attack this coast. The San Domenico has been wonderfully restored and furnished and the result is splendid, notably the vast room that serves as living- dining- and billiard-room all in one. Bedrooms and apartments are tasteful and comfortable. There are good recreational facilities available on the spot. As for the surroundings, various excursions are possible: The beach is 800 meters away, there are walks in the Murgia hills and cultural sightseeing in the historic hinterland.

How to get there (Map 22): 60km southeast of Bari via the superstrada 379, Fasano- Savelettri exit.

Hotel Sierra Silvana

72010 Selva di Fasano (Brindisi)
Via Don Bartolo Boggia
Tel. 080-433 13 22 - Fax 080-433 12 07
E-mail: htlsierra@mail.media.it - Web: www.sierrasilvana.com

Rooms 120 with air-conditioning, telephone, bath, WC, satellite TV – Elevator, wheelchair access. **Price** Double 150-232,000L. **Meals** Breakfast included, served 7:00-10:00 - half board 88-160,000L, full board 102-170,000L (per pers.). **Restaurant** Service 12:30PM-2:00PM, 7:30PM-9:00PM - mealtime specials 40,000L, also à la carte - Italian and regional cooking. **Credit cards** All major. **Pets** Dogs allowed. **Facilities** Swimming pool, parking. **Nearby** Ruins of Egnazia near by Monopoli - Alberobello (Trulli district) - Locorotondo - Martina Franca - Tàranto (Museo Nazionale: Greek and Roman artifacts collection) - Castellana Grotte – Golf course (18-hole) in Riva dei Tessali. **Open** All year.

The Hotel Sierra Silvana is built around an imposing old *trulli* (a conical structure common to the Apulia region). In many primitive societies, social status was reflected in the size of the dwelling. Someone important must have lived in this one, because it is enormous, with enough space for four rooms. There is a great demand for these simple and elegantly decorated rooms. The other rooms are in more modern buildings, and are quiet and comfortable; all have a balcony on the garden. The hotel is well equipped for receptions, but the staff ensures that guests are not disturbed. Located 30 miles (50km) from Brindisi, this hotel is an interesting stopover on your way to Greece.

How to get there (Map 22): 60km southeast of Bari.

Grand Hotel Masseria Santa Lucia

Ostuni Marina 72017 Ostuni (Brindisi)
Tel. 0831-3561 - Fax 0831-30 40 90
Sig. Bartolo d'Amico
E-mail: info@masseriasantalucia.it - Web: www.masseriasantalucia.it

Category ★★★★ **Rooms** 88 and 4 suites with air-conditioning, telelephone, bath or shower, WC, satellite TV, minibar, safe. **Price** Single 190-290,000L, double 230-340,000L, triple 270-390,000L. **Meals** Breakfast included, served 7:30-9:30 - half board 150-235,000L, full board 175-250,000L (per pers., 3 day min.). **Restaurant** Service 12:30PM-2:30PM, 7:30PM-10:00PM - mealtime specials 60,000L, also à la carte - Regional cooking and fish. **Credit cards** All major. **Pets** Dogs not allowed. **Facilities** Swimming pool, tennis (20,000L), archery, parking. **Nearby** Ostuni - Carovigno - Martina Franca - Alberobello and Castellana cellars - Ceglie Messapico. **Open** All year.

Ostuni is undoubtedly one of the wonders of Puglia. The town, perched high on its hilltop, has preserved a vague hint of Iberia, a leftover from its period of Spanish domination. Down below, some 500 meters from the sea, the very modern Masseria Santa Lucia has tried to recover this ancient charm. Built like a small hacienda, the hotel has within its walls a swimming pool and a little Gallo-Roman theater, in which shows and concerts are held in summer. The decor is resolutely "modern design" and can be quite attractive, unless you are completely allergic to that rather bare, cold style. Each bedroom has a little terrace, protected by a hedge. Ask for a room overlooking the swimming pool and a view of the sea. Ambitious building projects are still going on, which will eventually extend the complex as far as the seafront. For the moment, the place feels rather like a building site, and the beach, which could be sumptuous, is not always as clean as one might expect.

How to get there (Map 22): 25km from Brindisi; 7km from Ostuni.

Il Frantoio

72017 Ostuni (Brindisi)
SS 16, km 874
Tel. 0831-33 02 76 - Fax 0831-33 02 76 - Famiglia Balestrazzi
E-mail: armaredo@trecolline.it - Web: www.trecolline.it

Rooms 8 with bath or shower. **Price** Single 110-125,000L, double 220-250,000L. **Meals** Breakfast included, served 8.30-11.00 - half board 160-180,000L (per pers., 3 days min.). **Restaurant** Service 13.00, 20.30 - closed Sun - mealtime specials 75,000L (wine incl.), child's mealtime specials 45,000L - Specialties: Vermicelli agli odori dell'orto - Zuppa di cavetelli e ceci - Agnello con patate in coccio - Salsiccia di maiale in intingolo. **Credit cards** Not accepted. **Pets** Dogs allowed (+20,000L). **Facilities** Mountain bike, private beach (5km), parking. **Nearby** Medieval town of Ostuni - Carovigno - Ceglie Massapico. **Open** Apr – Oct.

A whole family from Bari has come to live in this former masseria (some parts of which are more than four hundred years old) a few kilometers from the white town of Ostuni. This is a rare spot, where the eye is lost in distant prospects of the sea and olive groves. There is one garden after another in the seventy hectares of the estate: a pleasure garden of roses and papyrus, a bio garden, a formal garden of aromatic herbs, an orchard of lemon and orange trees, and an olive grove, prdoucing a famous olive oil. You will find all these products available to try during your stay. Breakfast is a delight: focacce which you can accompany with zabaglione alla marsala or with yoghurt, fresh ricotta with bitter orange marmalade... In the restaurant, which is also open to non-residents, there is a feast of house specialties: orechiette, ravioli, panzerotti with quince... After these delights, we must mention the rooms. Each has its own personality and all are comfortable. There is a lot of atmosphere throughout the house where the half-closed shutters still let the sea breezes through in summer.

How to get there (Map 22): 40km from Brindisi.

Hotel Patria

73100 Lecce (Salento)
Piazzetta Riccardi
Tel. 0832-24 51 11 - Fax 0832-24 50 02
Sig. Antonio Mauro

Category ★★★★★ **Rooms** 67 with air-conditioning, telephone, bath or shower, WC, satellite TV, minibar, safe – Elevator. **Price** Single 250-260,000L, double 350-380,000L, junior suite 400-450,000L. **Meals** Breakfast included, served 7:00-10:30 - half board +50,000L (per pers.). **Restaurant** "Atenze", service 12:30PM-3:00PM, 7:30PM-11:00PM - mealtime specials 50,000L, also à la carte - Salentine cuisine. **Credit cards** All major. **Pets** Dogs not allowed. **Facilities** Garage (20,000L). **Nearby** Lecce: Piazza del Duomo, Santa Croce, Santi Nicolo and Cataldo, provincial museum, old town - Salentine peninsula (the heel of Italy) - beach at San Cataldo - Abbey of Santa Maria di Cerrate. **Open** All year.

Lecce is a major town on the European baroque tour and we are delighted by the reopening of this hotel which allows one to stay in comfort. It is also an aristocratic and university town which in the 17th Century faced its medieval buildings with this soft, golden-colored local stone (which is tufa) and then decorated it with a whole repertory of animal and floral designs of the time. The hotel is in a little 18th-century palazzo in the center of town, though only the internal spaces remain: the vaults in the hall and the restaurant and the frameworks of some doors or windows. The interior tends towards a comfortable version of art déco, with the emphasis on yellow woods and fine leathers in the reception rooms, while the bedrooms have heavy hangings, thick carpets and "modern-style" reproductions of frescoes. The comfort is evident in the superb marble bathrooms. When you reserve, try to get one of the sixteen rooms overlooking Santa Croce, probably the most representative monument of the wildy exuberent Lecce baroque.

How to get there (Map 22): *In the town center.*

Hotel Villa Ducale

74015 Martina Franca (Taranto)
Piazzetta Sant'Antonio
Tel. 080-480 50 55 - Fax 080-480 58 85
Sig. A. Sforza

Category ★★★★ **Rooms** 24 with air-conditiong, telephone, bath, WC, minibar. **Price** Single 100,000L, double 150,000L, suite 160,000L. **Meals** Breakfast included, served 7:30-11:30. **Restaurant** Service 12:30PM-2:30PM, 8:00PM-10:00PM - mealtime specials 40,000L, also à la carte - Italian and regional cooking. **Credit cards** All major. **Pets** Dogs allowed. **Nearby** In Martina Franca: Piazza Roma (Palazzo Ducale), Ruins of Egnazia near by Monopoli, Alberobello (Trulli district), Castel del Monte - Locorotondo - Martina Franca - Taranto (Museo Nazionale: Greck and Roman artifacts collection) - Castellana Grotte. **Open** All year.

L ike all of the hotels in town, the Villa Ducale has gone the modern road. The building itself is unappealing but well located, close to the old town and next to a large public garden and a 16th-century convent. Once inside, however, you will forget all about the façade; the decor is very avant-garde, and the lobby, the bar and the rooms all have a designer look. The hotel is pretty incongruous but very comfortable. Ask for the corner rooms (105, 205, 305) which have two windows and are very light, though sometimes a little noisy despite the double-panes. Be sure to visit the splendid Ducal palace. The entire town has interesting architecture, though it is off the beaten tourist track and you will need to stay here awhile to appreciate it.

How to get there *(Map 22): 74km southeast of Bari via S100, Locorotondo and Martina Franca.*

Hotel Hieracon

Isola di San Pietro
09014 Carloforte (Cagliari)
Corso Cavour, 62
Tel. 0781-85 40 28 - Fax 0781-85 48 93 - Sig. Ferrando

Category ★★★ **Rooms** 17 and 7 suites with air-conditioning, telephone, shower, WC, TV, minibar. **Price** Single 80,000L, double 140,000L, triple 160,000L. **Meals** Breakfast 6,000L, served 8:30-10:30 - half board 110,000L, full board 150,000L. (per pers., 3 days min.). **Restaurant** Service 12:30PM-2:00PM, 7:30PM-9:30PM - mealtime specials 30,000L - Italian and regional cooking. **Credit cards** All major. **Pets** Small dogs allowed. **Nearby** Beach (2km) - boat rentals - walking in the island. **Open** All year.

The Hotel Hieracon is located in San Pietro, a pretty little island with a rocky coastline dotted with inlets and beaches. This lovely Art Nouveau-style building is right on the port. The interior is a blend of light tile work and pastel colors. We recommend the rooms on the second floor, which have nice turn-of-the-century furniture. The ones on the other floors are darker and less comfortable. Behind the hotel there is a large terraced garden set in the shade of a tall palm tree. Four small ground floor apartments open onto the garden. The restaurant is superb with its black flagstones and its curving mezzanine which looks like the bridge of an old pre-war ocean liner. The cuisine is good and features typical island dishes. Dr. Ferrando will make you feel at home.

How to get there *(Map 28): 77km west of Cagliarii via SS130 to Portoscuro; ferry service from Porto Vesme (40mn).*

Albergo Paola e Primo Maggio

Isola di San Pietro
Tacca Rossa
09014 Carloforte (Cagliari)
Tel. 0781-85 00 98 - Fax 0781-85 01 04 - Sig. Ferraro
E-mail: hotelpaola@tiscalinet.it

Category ★★ **Rooms** 24 with shower, WC. **Price** Double 60-120,000L. **Meals** Breakfast 5,5-10,000L, served 8:00-11:00 - half board 65-100,000L, full board 70-120,000L. (per pers.). **Restaurant** Service 1:00PM-2:30PM, 7:00PM-11:00PM - à la carte - Specialties: Seafood. **Credit cards** Amex, Visa, Eurocard, MasterCard, Diners. **Pets** Dogs allowed. **Nearby** Beach (2km) - boat rentals - walking in the island. **Open** Apr 16 – end Oct.

The Pensione Paola, about a mile and a half from Carloforte, faces the sea and offers rooms–at very reasonable prices–which all enjoy the beautiful maritime view. In the main house, a restaurant with a large shady terrace serves fine, solid cuisine featuring many dishes typical of the island. Rooms 7, 8, and 9 are our favorites, as they are more modern and comfortable than the others. Downstairs, there are six garden-level rooms which are just as nice as the other three in a bungalow nearby.

How to get there *(Map 28): 77km west of Cagliari via SS130 to Portoscuro; ferry services from Porto Vesme (40mn) - 3km north of Carloforte.*

Is Morus Relais

09010 Santa Margherita di Pula (Cagliari)
Tel. 070-92 11 71 - Fax 070-92 15 96
Sig.ra Maffei
E-mail: ismorusrelais@tin.it

Category ★★★★ **Rooms** 85 with air-conditioning, telephone, bath or shower, WC, TV, minibar.
Price With half board 170-430,000L (per pers.). **Meals** Breakfast included, served 7:30-10:00.
Restaurant Service 1:00PM-2:30PM, 8:00PM-9:30PM - mealtime specials 70,000L - Italian and regional
cooking, seafood. **Credit cards** All major. **Pets** Small dogs allowed. **Facilities** Swimming pool, tennis,
miniature golf, private beach, parking. **Nearby** Nora (ancient city: ruins of temples, amphitheater,
Roman theater, mosaic pavement) – Is Molas golf course (18-hole) at S. Margherita di Pula.
Open Apr – end Oct.

Just like the Costa Smeralda, the coast south of Cagliari has been
experiencing a boom in beach construction. The Is Morus is in Santa
Margherita di Pula, right next to the golf course. It is a luxury hotel with a
marvelous location, in the middle of a pine forest and on the superb turquoise-
blue sea. Some of the rooms are in villas set in the cool shade of pine trees,
something very rare in this part of Sardinia. The other rooms are in the main
house, a low building with white walls, which looks like a large Spanish villa.
The well-equipped beach is very pleasant, with a snack bar where one can take
a light midday meal.

How to get there *(Map 28): 37km southwest of Cagliari via the coast (S195)*
to Santa Margherita (6.5km from Pula).

Hotel Su Gologone

Sorgente Su Gologone
08025 Oliena (Nuoro)
Tel. 0784-28 75 12 - Fax 0784-28 76 68 - Famiglia Palimodde
E-mail: gologone@tin.it - Web: www.sugologone.it

Category ★★★★ **Rooms** 65 with air-conditioning, telephone, bath, WC, TV, minibar, safe. **Price** Single 180-270,000L, double 250-310,000L, suite +100,000L. **Meals** Breakfast included, served 8:00-9:30 - half board 200-265,000L (1 pers.), 160-205,000L; full board 200-255,000L (per pers., in double). **Restaurant** Service 12:30PM-3:00PM, 8:00PM-10:00PM - mealtime specials 70-80,000L, also à la carte - Sardinian cuisine and seafood. **Credit cards** All major. **Pets** Dogs allowed. **Facilities** Swimming pool, tennis, riding, miniature golf, Bikes, trekking, trips in Land Rover, parking. **Nearby** Sorgente su Gologone - Chapel of San Lussurgiu at Oliena. **Open** Apr – Oct and Dec.

The main attraction of Sardinia is its coast, but the beautiful inland part really deserves more than a quick detour. The Su Gologone has it all, located about 12 miles from the coast between Dorgali and Oliean, at the foot of superb rocky mountains, the Supramonten. The restaurant, open since 1961, made a name for itself before the hotel and its excellent regional cuisine still attracts many gourmets. The architecture of the hotel, inspired by the houses in Oliena, is a great achievement. The interior has been decorated with uncommon taste, with old exposed beams complementing the beautiful antique furniture and the paintings by Biasi, a talented Sardinian painter. The rooms are all different and very pleasant. The spring-fed swimming pool is splendid. The hotel organizes numerous excursions by Land Rover in the surrounding area. The staff is very friendly.

How to get there *(Map 28): 20km southeast of Nuoro to Oliena, then towards Dorgali. Follow signs.*

Villa Las Tronas

07041 Alghero (Sassari)
Lungomare Valencia, 1
Tel. 079-98 18 18 - Fax 079-98 10 44

Category ★★★★ **Rooms** 28 and 1 suite with air-conditioning, telephone, bath or shower, WC, TV, safe, minibar – Elevator. **Price** Single 273-313,000L, double 327-520,000L, suite 640-787,000L. **Meals** Breakfast included, served 7:30-10:30 - half board 209-305,000L, full board 249-345,000L. **Restaurant** Service 1:00PM-2:30PM, 8:00PM-9:30PM - mealtime specials 88-99,000L, also à la carte - Sardinian cuisine and seafood. **Credit cards** All major. **Pets** Dogs not allowed. **Facilities** Swimming pool (sea water), private cliff, gym, bikes, fishing, parking. **Nearby** Cathedral in Alghero - Church and Cloister of San Francesco - Nuraghe de Palmavera - Porto Conte - Grotte of Neptune - Necropolis of Anghelu Ruiu - Bosa road - Antiquarium (Porto Torres) - Sanna museum in Sassari - Church of Santissima Trinità di Saccargia (15km of Sassari). **Open** All year.

The Villa Las Tronas, surrounded by very well kept garden, is on a small peninsula overlooking the Gulf of Alghero. Once a vacation spot for Italian kings during their visits to Sardinia, this unusual Moorish-style building is today a hotel with a Baroque atmosphere created by vast rooms with painted ceilings and gleaming chandeliers, and numerous salons of different colors. The spacious, high-ceilinged rooms all overlook the sea; spacious and comfortable, they are all different, with antique furniture. The suite and Rooms 110, 112, 114, 116, 118, and 216 are the nicest ones, with a very large common terrace from which you can take in the superb panoramic view. You can enjoy the same view in the lovely dining room. There is a pretty swimming pool, with access to the sea. The style and presence of the personnel contribute to the elegant atmosphere of this hotel.

How to get there (Map 28): *35km southwest of Sassari via S291 to Alghero.*

Hotel Li Capanni

Cannigione
07020 Arzachena (Sassari)
Tel. 0789-86 041 - Fax 0789-86 200
Sig. Pagni

Category ★★★ **Rooms** 23 and 2 suites with shower, WC. **Price** With half board 160-260,000L (per pers.). **Meals** Breakfast included. **Restaurant** For residents, service 1:00PM-2:00PM, 8:30PM-9:00PM - mealtime specials 30-35,000L - Sardinian and Italian cuisine. **Credit cards** Not accepted. **Pets** Dogs not allowed. **Facilities** Private beach, parking. **Nearby** Tombe di Giganti (giants' tombs) and ancient city of Li Muri - San Pantaleo – Pevero golf course (18-hole) in Porto Cervo. **Open** May 1 – end Sept.

G o a few kilometers from the village, and suddenly, as if by magic, you will find yourself far from the throngs of the Costa Smeralda (where the environment is nonetheless protected and campgrounds restricted). The Hotel Li Capanni aspires to be more of a club than a hotel, to highlight its uniqueness and preserve its tranquility. It is on a very lovely site facing the archipelago of the Maddalena Islands, overlooking the sea. The small ochre houses are scattered here and there on ten-acre grounds which slope gently down to the sea and a very pretty, private beach. The rooms are simply decorated and comfortable. The dining room and salons are grouped in the main building. The dining room overlooks the bay and is very inviting with its small blue wood tables and chairs. A cozy salon looks just like the living room of a private home. For security reasons, the hotel does not accept children under 14.

How to get there *(Map 28): 32km north of Olbia via S125 towards Arzachena, then along the sea twoards Palau as far as Cannigione; the hotel is 3.5km after Cannigione.*

Hotel Don Diego

Costa Dorata
07020 Porto San Paolo (Sassari)
Tel. 0789-40 006 - Fax 0789-40 026
Web: www.hoteldondiego.com

Category ★★★★ **Rooms** 50 and 6 suites with air-conditioning, telephone, bath or shower, WC, TV.
Price Double 300-500,000L. **Meals** Breakfast 30,000L, served 8:00-10:00 - half board 200-450,000L
(per pers.). **Restaurant** Service 12:30PM-2:00PM, 8:00PM-9:30PM - mealtime specials 80-90,000L, also
à la carte - Sardinian cuisine and seafood. **Credit cards** All major. **Pets** Dogs not allowed. **Facilities**
Swimming pool (sea water), tennis, beach, parking. **Nearby** Church of San Simplicio in Olbia -
Tavolara Island – Golf course in Punta Aldia. **Closed** Oct – Apr.

Located south of Olbia, the Hotel Don Diego is a series of small villas
facing the sea, scattered among beautiful bouganvilles and pine trees.
Each one has a separate entry and six to eight rooms, and there's a pleasant
coolness inside. The reception area, bar, restaurant, and salons are located in
the closest house to the water. You will also find a sea-water swimming pool
and a sand beach here. Just across from the hotel is Tavolara Island, an
impressive rocky spur jutting into the clear blue water. The Don Diego is a
great place for a family vacation.

How to get there *(Map 28): 16km southeast of Olbia via S125 until just after
Porto San Paolo, then turn left towards the Costa Dorata coast.*

Hotel Cala di Volpe

Porto Cervo
07020 Cala di Volpe (Sassari)
Tel. 0789-97 6111 - Fax 0789-97 6617 - Sig. Koren
E-mail: res059caladivolpe@luxurycollection.com
Web: www.luxurycollection.com/caladivolpe

Category ★★★★★ L **Rooms** 125 with air-conditioning, telephone, bath, WC, TV, safe, minibar. **Price** With half board 405-1 240,000L, full board 455-1 290,000L. **Restaurant** Service 12:30PM-2:30PM, 8:00PM-10:30PM - Italian cuisine and seafood. **Pets** Dogs not allowed. **Facilities** Swimming pool, sauna, tennis, Fitness Centre, putting-green, private beach, wather skiing, private port, parking. **Nearby** Costa Smeralda - Tombe di Giganti (giants' tombs) and ancient city of Li Muri - San Pantaleo – Pevero golf course (18-hole) in Porto Cervo. **Closed** Nov 1 – Mar 28.

This beautiful wild region of rolling hills and valleys was luxuriously fitted out by a few millionaires and reborn as the Costa Smeralda. The buildings are a sort of cocktail of Mediterranean architectural styles–Spanish, Moorish, and Provençal. The most famous hotel in the region, the Cala di Volpe faces an enchanting bay, and was designed by a French architect, Jacques Couelle. He used a medieval village as a model, inspired by its towers and terraces, arcades and wooden bridges.The rooms are furnished with antiques and the products of local craftsmen. Naturally, the standard of comfort is impeccable. You can have meals in either the traditional restaurant or the barbecue. There is a magnificent salt-water swimming pool in the grounds, or a shuttle boat service can take you to the hotel's private beach. This is an exctirely exceptional hotel.

How to get there *(Map 28): 25km north of Olbia via S125, then towards Porto Cervo to Abbiadori and take a right towards Capriccioli to Cala di Volpe.*

Hotel Le Ginestre

07020 Porto Cervo (Sassari)
Tel. 0789-92 030 - Fax 0789-94 087
Sig. Costa
E-mail: info@leginestrehotel.com - Web: leginestrehotel.com

Category ★★★★ **Rooms** 78 with air-conditioning, telephone, bath or shower, WC, TV, minibar. **Price** With half board 195-390,000L, full board +50,000L (per pers.); single +50-200,000L. **Meals** Breakfast included, served 8:00-10:30. **Restaurant** Service 1:00PM-2:30PM, 8:00PM-10:00PM - mealtime specials, also à la carte - Specialties: Seafood. **Credit cards** All major. **Pets** Dogs not allowed. **Facilities** Swimming pool, tennis (35,000L), private beach, parking. **Nearby** Costa Smeralda - Tombe di Giganti (giants' tombs) and ancient city of Li Muri - San Pantaleo – Pevero golf course (18-hole) in Porto Cervo. **Open** May – Sept 30 or Oct 15.

There are luxury hotels on the Costa Smeralda which are more affordable than the Ginestre, but not all of them have its charm. The rooms are in a series of small villas at the edge of a pine forest, slightly overhanging the Gulf of Pevero. It looks like a small hamlet, with its tangle of little streets on grounds with fragrant bushes and trees with brightly colored flowers typical of the Mediterranean region. As is common in this area, the Neo-Realist architecture recalls Tuscan villages with their faded ochre façades. The rooms have pretty furniture, and most of them have balconies. A little off to one side, under a large thatched sunscreen, there is a pleasant restaurant. Because of the number of rooms, the hotel loses in intimacy what it gains in atmosphere.

How to get there *(Map 28): 30km north of Olbia via S125, towards Porto Cervo.*

Hotel Romazzino

Porto Cervo
07020 Romazzino (Sassari)
Tel. 0789-97 7111 - Fax 0789-96 258 - 0789-96 292
Web: www.luxurycollection.com/romazzino

Category ★★★★★ **Rooms** 93 with air-conditioning, telephone, bath, WC, TV, minibar. **Price** With half board and full board (2 pers., 3 days min.) 1 210-2 233,000L. **Meals** Breakfast included, served 7:30-11:00. **Restaurant** Service 1:00PM-2:30PM, 8:00PM-10:00PM - mealtime specials - Italian and international cuisine. **Credit cards** All major. **Pets** Dogs not allowed. **Facilities** Swimming pool, tennis, private beach, putting green, wather skiing, parking. **Nearby** Costa Smeralda - Arcipelago di la Maddalena - Tombe di Giganti (giants' tombs) and ancient city of Li Muri - San Pantaleo - Pevero golf course (18-hole) in Porto Cervo. **Open** Apr 20 – Oct 15.

Next door to "Medieval village," the Romazzino, with its white walls, vaulted windows, and pink tiles, looks like an Andelusian–if not Mexican–village. It looks magical when you see it from the road as you arrive, its superb silhouette rising in front of the sea. The Romazzino is a quiet hotel–a great place for resting and enjoying the sea. The fine sand beach is superb. A delicious barbecue awaits you at lunchtime. The interior is all curves, and gives the impression of sumptuous caverns or imaginary palaces. The bar is unique with a floor inlayed with juniper trunks. All the rooms are perfect and have private terraces. This dreamy place is all about the pleasures of the sea.

How to get there *(Map 28): 25km north of Olbia via S125, then towards Porto Cervo to Abbiadoni, then turn right towards Capriccioli to Cala di Volpe - Romazzino is after Capriccioli.*

La Sasima

La Sasimedda
07020 San Pantaleo (Sassari)
Tel. 0789-98 755
Sandro and Carla Contis

Rooms 5 with shower. **Price** On request. **Meals** Breakfast included, served 8:30-11:00. **Evening meals** Only for residents, service 8:00PM-10:30PM - mealtime specials - Regional cooking. **Credit cards** Not accepted. **Pets** Dogs not allowed. **Facilities** Parking. **Nearby** Costa Smeralda - Arcipelago della Maddelena - Tombs of giants at Capichera and Li Muri necropolis - Pevero golf course (18-hole), 15mn. **Open** All year.

Inland, some twenty kilometers from the most sophisticated and expensive area of the Costa Smeralda, lies a bucolic spot in the Sardinian heartland. This region to the south of Obia is so poor and dry that it had the name of Inferno and long remained uninhabited before the arrival of the peasants and shepherds who built these stazzi, stone houses on one level. La Sasima is housed in one of these former stazzi which has been very well restored and transformed into a fine locale for agriturismo by Sandro and Carla Contis. Here, the emphasis is on the raw authenticity of stones, beams, fences, furniture and everyday objects. Yet comfort has not been overlooked. The cooking is based on simple dishes using basic products - you will discover the real taste of bread, of home-made cheese, of gallurese soup and other traditional foods that the poverty of the soil has always led people to share. A good place to learn a little about Sardinian culture.

How to get there (*Map 28*): *25km north of Olbia as far as San Pantaleo and La Sasimedda.*

El Faro

Porto Conte
07041 Alghero (Sassari)
Tel. 079-94 20 10 - Fax 079-94 20 30
Sig. Sarno

Category ★★★★ **Rooms** 92 with air-conditioning, telephone, bath or shower, WC, TV, minibar.
Price Double (per. pers.) 110-240,000L. **Meals** Breakfast included, served 7:30-10:00 - half board
140-287,000L (per pers., 3 days min.). **Restaurant** Service 1:00PM-2:00PM, 8:00PM-10:00PM -
mealtime specials 70,000L, also à la carte - Specialties: Lobsters - Seafood. **Credit cards** All major.
Pets Dogs allowed except in restaurant and on the beach. **Facilities** Swimming pool, tennis, sauna
(25,000L), parking. **Nearby** Cathedral in Alghero - Grotto of Neptune - heights of Capo Caccia -
Nuraghe Palmavera. **Open** Apr – Oct.

This hotel is superbly located on a small peninsula next to an old lighthouse,
facing Cap Caccia with it famous Neptune caverns. The view encompasses
all of the splendid Gulf with its banks almost totally unspoiled by construction.
This large, ninety-two room hotel is a special place, thanks to the quality of the
service and the simple, well-planned Mediterranean decor. All the rooms have
a balcony and a view of the sea, with white walls brightened by engravings of
nautical themes, wooden furniture, and pretty bathrooms. Down below,
between several terraces, there is a superb semi-covered swimming pool
overlooking the waves, and a little further beyond, a beach among the rocks.
This is a luxury hotel which is still affordable.

How to get there *(Map 28): 41km southwest of Sassari via S291 to Alghero
and S127 bis to Porto Conte.*

Villa Athena

92100 Agrigento
Via dei Templi
Tel. 0922-59 62 88 - Fax 0922-40 21 80
Sig. Montalbano

Category ★★★★ **Rooms** 40 with air-conditioning, telephone, bath or shower, WC, TV. **Price** Single 240,000L, double 350,000L. **Meals** Breakfast included, served 7:30-10:00 - half board +40,000L (per 2 pers., 3 days min.). **Restaurant** Service 12:30PM-2:30PM, 7:30PM-10:00PM - mealtime specials 45,000L, also à la carte - Specialties: Involtini di pesce spado - Cavatelli Villa Athena - Pesce fresco. **Credit cards** All major. **Pets** Dogs not allowed. **Facilities** Swimming pool, parking. **Nearby** In Agrigento: Valley of the Temples, birthhouse of Luigi Pirandello - Naro - Palma di Montechiano. **Open** All year.

There are many Easter festivities in the region of Agrigento, the festa degli Archi at San Biagio Platini, 60km east, being particularly remarkable (the arks are displayed for one month) - Be sure to stop off at Agrigento and visit the Valley of the Temples, an epicenter of archaeology if ever there was one. Once you are there, you will see that there is only one hotel which has any charm: the Villa Athena. The major asset of this former princely villa, dating from the 18th century, is its outstanding position, across from the Concord Temple; of which the best view is from Room 205. The rooms and bathrooms are standard, functional and comfortable. A large salon opens onto the terrace and the temple. The swimming pool is very pleasant.

How to get there *(Map 26): 2km south of Agrigento towards "Valle dei Templi."*

Foresteria Baglio della Luna

92100 Agrigento
Contrada Maddalusa - Valle de' Templi
Tel. 0922-51 10 61 - Fax 0922-59 88 02
Sig. Altieri

Categoty ★★★★ **Rooms** 24 with air-conditioning, telephone, bath or shower, WC, TV, minibar. **Price** Single 285,000L, double 400-480,000L, suite 580-880,000L. **Meals** Breakfast included served 7:30-10:30 - half board +65,000L, full board +95,000L (per pers., 2 day min.). **Restaurant** Service 1:00PM-2:30PM, 7:30PM-10:00PM - mealtime specials 65-70,000L, also à la carte - Regional cooking and pesce. **Credit cards** All major. **Pets** Small dogs allowed in room. **Facilities** Parking. **Nearby** In Agrigento: Valley of the Temples, birthhouse of Luigi Pirandello - Naro - Palma di Montechiaro. **Open** All year.

There are many Easter festivities in the region of Agrigento, the festa degli Archi at San Biagio Platini, 60km east, being particularly remarkable (the arks are displayed for one month) If you want to visit the Valley of the Temples without being encircled by the rather wild urban development of Agrigento, the Foresteria can offer a nice retreat. Outside of town and in the heart of an archeological site, this 13th-century tower was transformed into a country house in the 18th century. Today it is a hotel, but with its thick stone surrounding walls, it looks like an old walled inn. The atmosphere of the hotel is commonplace and the "antiques" with which is it furnished are sometimes of questionable antiquity, but the comfort is there (even though not up to the standard expected of its four stars), complete with air-conditioning, a delightful element after sightseeing in these arid valleys. From the hotel, you can see the temples on the surrounding hills, even more poetic when viewed at sunset. The restaurant does a version of Sicilian cooking, with views over the temples and the sea.

How to get there *(Map 26): 2km south of Agrigento (south coast); toward "Valle dei Templi" and SS115, towards Trapani.*

Villa Ravidà

92013 Menfi (Agrigente)
Via Roma, 173
Tel. 0925-71 109 - Fax 0925-71 180 - Sig. Nicolo Ravidà
E-mail: ravidasrl@tiscalinet.it

Rooms 7 (4 with air-conditioning) with shower. **Price** Single 190,000L., double 200-240,000L. **Meals** Breakfast included, served 8:00-10:00. **Evening meals** (By reservation 24 hours before) service 9:00PM - mealtime specials 45-50,000L - Seasonal specialties with product of the estate. **Credit cards** Not accepted. **Pets** Dogs not allowed. **Nearby** Burgio - Salemi - Segesta - Isola di Mozia - Marsala - Trapani - Erice - Monreale - Palermo. **Closed** Jan and Feb, Aug 5 – 20.

The ochre façade of this 18th-century Sicilian palazzo is magnificent. Surmounted by a pediment supported on four Doric columns, it stands majestic in a paved courtyard shaded by palms. The surprise is all the greater since the banality of the architecture in the rest of the village might make you want to go straight home and gives no hint of such a discovery. The interior lives up to the façade with its vast entrance hall, its salons opening on the sea which can be seen in the distance, and the dining room with its grand scale and frescoes across the walls and ceilings. Three rooms have a view over the Mediterranean, but the finest is the one that occupies the former chapel with its frescoes, small balcony and sea view. For generations (since 1700, in fact) the owners have been producing a well-known olive oil and, rather than letting rooms, they receive guests in their home, giving you the opportunity to live in a Sicilian palazzo. The surroundings, rich in archeological sites and fine beaches, mean that one may profitably consider spending a few days here.

How to get there (Map 26): 78km west of Agrigento by S115, 105km from Palermo airport.

Grand Hotel Baia Verde

95020 Cannizzaro-Catània
Via Castello, 6
Tel. 095-49 15 22 - Fax 095-49 44 64 - Sig. Claudio Robba

Category ★★★★ **Rooms** 127 with air-conditioning, telephone, bath or shower, WC, satellite TV, minibar. **Price** Single 220-260,000L, double 320-360,000L. **Meals** Breakfast included, served 7:00-10:00. **Restaurant** Service 1:00PM-2:30PM, 8:00PM-10:00PM - mealtime specials 55,000L, also à la carte - Specialties: Cernia all'acqua di mare - Fish. **Credit cards** All major. **Pets** Dogs not allowed. **Facilities** Swimming pool, tennis (20,000L), parking. **Nearby** In Catania: Duomo, Ursino castle (Municipal Museum), Museo Bellini, via dei rociferi (Barqoue palace), Church of S. Nicolovia Etna and piazza dell'Università - Etna - Taormina - Siracusa. **Open** All year.

Catania is situated at the foot of Mount Etna and its fate has always been tied to the goodwill of the volcano. As a result it was completely reconstructed in the 18th Century by the architect G B Vacarinio who gave the center of town its decidedly baroque appearance. The large modern Hotel Baia Verde is a few kilometers from the town center and the port, beside the water with its black rocks of volcanic lava, typical of all Sicilian coasts close to volcanoes. The rooms are comfortable and functional, the most expensive being the ones overlooking the sea. The public areas are spacious and make good use of the panoramic views. One should note, however, that the size and arrangement of the hotel make it an ideal place for conventions and congresses. Even so, with its situation and the warm welcome you will find here, this is a pleasant stopping place for those who have landed in Catania and are about to start a Sicilian tour. It goes without saying that it is preferable to have a room with a view and a balcony.

How to get there *(Map 27): On the east coast between Taormina and Siracusa. 12km from the airport, 4km from the center of town.*

Grand Hotel Villa Igiea

90142 Palermo
Via Belmonte, 43
Tel. 091-54 37 44 - Fax 091-54 76 54
Sig. Maurizio Viviani

Category ★★★★★ **Rooms** 114 with air-conditioning, telephone, bath, WC, minibar — Elevator, wheelchair access. **Price** Single 210-285,000L, double 280-450,000L, suite 720-920,000L. **Meals** Breakfast included, served 7:00-10:00 - half board +70,000L (per pers.). **Restaurant** Service 12:30PM-2:30PM, 7:30PM-10:30PM - mealtime specials 80,000L, also à la carte - Specialties: Pennette alla lido - Spada al forno. **Credit cards** All major. **Pets** Dogs allowed in rooms. **Facilities** Swimming pool, tennis, parking. **Nearby** In Palermo: Church of Martorana, Church of Del Gesu, Palazzo dei Normanni (Norman Royal Palace), Church of San Giovanni degli Eremiti, S. Francesco d'Assisi, Oratorio S. Lorenzo, Regional Archeological Museum, Palazzo Abatellis (Annunciation by Antonello da Messina) - Mondello - Villa Palagonia in Bagheria - Solonte - Piana degli Albanesi - Cefalù. **Open** All year.

A superb example of Art Nouveau-style, the Villa Igiea is certainly the most beautiful hotel in the west of Sicily, and its location allows it to escape from the hustle and bustle of Palermo. It's hard to find fault with this grand hotel which has kept its period furniture and decor while guaranteeing its guests almost flawless service and comfort. The bar, the winter dining room, the veranda and the rooms are so pleasant that the most sophisticated Palermians come here every night. The swimming pool and the terraced gardens overlook the bay where you can go for a swim. In summary it is impossible to pass the Villa Igiea by when you are in Palermo.

How to get there *(Map 26): Towards district of Acquasanta, by via dei Cantieri Navali.*

Centrale Palace Hotel

90134 Palermo
Corso Vittorio Emanuele, 327
Tel. 091-33 66 66 - Fax 091-33 48 81 - Sig. Schifano
E-Mail: cphotel@tin.it - Web: www.bestwestern.it/centralepalace_pa

Category ★★★ **Rooms** 63 with air-conditioning, telephone, shower (6 with bath), WC, minibar – 2 rooms for disabled persons. **Price** Single 265,000L, double 380,000L; extra bed 123,000L. **Meals** Breakfast included, served 7.00-11.00 - half board +65,000F. **Restaurant** Small restaurant at hotel; or see p. 546. **Credit cards** All major. **Pets** Dogs not allowed. **Nearby** In Palermo: Church of Martorana, Church of Del Gesu, Palazzo dei Normanni (Norman Royal Palace), Church of San Giovanni degli Eremiti, S. Francesco d'Assisi, Oratorio S. Lorenzo, Regional Archeological Museum, Palazzo Abatellis (Annunciation by Antonello da Messina) - Mondello - Villa Palagonia in Bagheria - Solonte - Piana degli Albanesi - Cefalù. **Open** All year.

Here is just the type of "little hotel" that we needed in Palermo. Located right in the historic center of town, a recent renovation has enabled this hotel to recover its former splendor. The rooms combine modern amenities, like the very welcome air-conditioning, with traditional charm. In the summer the dining room is set up on the terrace, with a marvelous view over the rooftops of the city. An excellent place to stay to explore the mysteries of Palermo.

How to get there *(Map 26): The Corso Vittorio Emanuele begins at the piazza Independenza.*

Grand Hotel et des Palmes

90142 Palermo
Via Roma, 398
Tel. 091-58 39 33 - Fax 091-33 15 45
E-mail: des-palmes@thi.it - Web: www.thi.it

Category ★★★★ **Rooms** 183 and 4 suites with air-conditioning, telephone, bath, WC, minibar – Elevator. **Price** Single 230-290,000L, double 340,000L, suite +200,000L. **Meals** Breakfast included served 7:00-10:00. **Restaurant** Service 12:30PM-3:00PM, 7:30PM-11:00PM - mealtime specials 70,000L, also à la carte. **Credit cards** All major. **Pets** Dogs allowed. **Nearby** In Palermo: Church of Martorana, Church of Del Gesù, Cappella palatina (Palatine Chapel), Church of San Giovanni degli Eremiti, S. Francesco d'Assisi, Oratorio S. Lorenzo, Archaeological museum, Palazzo Abatellis (Annunciation by Antonello da Messina), Duomo and Cathedral of Monreale - Mondello and Mont Pellegrino - Cefalù - Villa Palagonia in Bagheria - Solonte - Piana degli Albanesi. **Open** All year.

This grand old hotel, located in the heart of Palermo, seat of so many legends and so many rumors, has the tired charm of its bygone age. A palace first converted into a hotel in 1874, it would be hard to list all the celebrities who sojourned here: from Wagner, who came here to finish "Parsifal," to Auguste Renoir, from De Maupassant to Lucky Luciano. The salons still have the luster of their former prestige. The hall was decorated by Ernesto Basile, the great artist of Italian Art Nouveau. The other salon has a great fireplace, an ornate inlaid ceiling, frescoes, gilding and stained-glass windows. The amenities are rather more modest in the bedrooms, some of which could do with a serious renovation. The hotel restaurant, La Palmetta, serves local cuisine in a sumptuous setting. Don't hesitate to treat yourself to a taste of this Sicilian legend, for a price that's really quite reasonable.

How to get there (Map 26): Town center.

Hotel Principe di Villafranca

90141 Palermo
Via G. Turrisi Colonna, 4
Tel. 091-61 18 523 - Fax 091-58 87 05 - Sig.ra Licia Guccione
E-mail: info@principedivillafranca.it - Web: www.principedivillafranca.it

Category ★★★★ **Rooms** 40 with air-conditioning, telephone, bath or shower, WC, satellite TV, minibar, safe. **Price** Single 210-230,000L, double 300-330,000L, junior suite 420-460,000L. **Meals** Breakfast included, served 7:00-10:00. **Restaurant** Service 1:00PM-3:00PM, 8:00PM-10:30PM - mealtime specials 40,000L, also à la carte - Regional cooking. **Credit cards** All major. **Pets** Dogs not allowed. **Facilities** Fitness, garage. **Nearby** In Palermo: Church of la Martorana, Chiusa del Gesù, Paraltine chapel in the Normal palazzo, S. Giovanni degli Eremiti, S. Francesco d'Assisi, oratorio S. Lorenzo, archeological museum, palazzo Abatellis (Annunciation by A. de Messina), botanical garden - Events: feast of Saint Rosalie (Jul 11 – 15), flea market near the cathedral - Duomo and cloister of Monreale - Mondello and Monte Pellegrino - Cefalù - Vailla Palagonia in Bagheria - Solunto - Piana degli Albanesi. **Open** All year.

This hotel, close to the luxury shops in the center of town and also to the Teatro Massimo, has only recently opened. While the building, dating from the 1970s, is without interest, the interior has been tastefully arranged and the designers have made judicious use of old pictures and furniture. The dining room is elegant, while deep sofas in the drawing room invite the guests to explore the library and browse through the books on Sicily. This same discreet luxury is to be found in the spacious bedrooms. The soundproofing is perfect and the bathrooms very well equipped. The whole lacks a certain patina, but this is still one of the best hotels in Palermo.

How to get there *(Map 26): Near the Teatro Massimo.*

Massimo Plaza Hotel

90133 Palermo
Via Maqueda, 437
Tel. 091-32 56 57 - Fax 091-32 57 11 - Sig. Farruggio
E-mail: booking@massimoplazahotel.com - Web: www.massimoplazahotel.com

Category ★★★ **Rooms** 11 with air-conditioning, telephone, shower, WC, satellite TV, radio, minibar, safe. **Price** Single 180,000L, double 240,000L, triple 300,000L, junior suite 270,000L. **Meals** Breakfast included, served 7:00-10:30 - half board and fulml board +35,000L, +70,000L (per pers., 3 days min.). **Restaurant** See p. 546. **Credit cards** All major. **Pets** Dogs not allowed. **Facilities** Audioguide, private beach, garage (15,000L). **Nearby** In Palermo: Church of la Martorana, Chiusa del gesù, Paraltine chapel in the Normal palazzo, S. Giovanni degli Eremiti, S. Francesco d'Assisi, oratorio S. Lorenzo, archeological museum, palazzo Abatellis (Annunciation by A. de Messina), botanical garden - Events: feast of Saint Rosalie (Jul 11– 15), flea market near the cathedral - Duomo and cloister of Monreale - Mondello and Monte Pellegrino - Cefalù - Vailla Palagonia in Bagheria - Solunto - Piana degli Albanesi. **Open** All year.

A little hotel has just opened opposite one of the most famous lyric theatres in the world, the Teatro Massimo; photographs remind us of some famous productions. This is a precious find in a city where up to now quality was only to be found in the large, late-19th-century hotels. Occupying the first floor of a palazzo, in the delightfully busy Via Maqueda, the Plaza is run more like a guest house than a hotel. The public areas have been decorated with art nouveau motifs by some fine local artists. The rooms are comfortable and functional. Most overlook the imposing theatre building, put up at the end of the last century by Ernesto Basile. Breakfast is served in your room and accompanied by the daily newspaper. The service is attentive.

How to get there (Map 26): Near the Teatro Massimo.

Tenuta Gangivecchio

Gangivecchio 90024 Gangi (Palermo)
Tel. 0921-64 48 04 - Fax 0921-68 91 91
Sig. Paolo Tornabene

Rooms 8 and 1 suite with telephone, shower, WC. **Price** With half board 200,000L, with full board 240,000L (per pers., 3 days min.). **Meals** Breakfast included, served 8:15-10:00. **Restaurant** Service 1:30PM and 8:30PM - closed Mon - mealtime specials 30,000L. **Credit cards** Diners, Visa, Eurocard, MasterCard. **Pets** Dogs not allowed. **Facilities** Pont-swimming pool, parking. **Nearby** Excursions into the massif of Madonie: Castelbuono, Gangi (vecchio), Petralia, Sottana, Collesano - Cefalù. **Closed** Jul 15 – 31.

If you have an urge to leave the coast and the coastal roads for a countryside that is more austere and wild, you will find old Sicilian villages where traditions die hard, and where you meet mainly men and old people, the latter sitting on their front porches in the evening. Gengi is one of those villages in the Madonie massif where the highest peaks in Sicily lie, and might form a stopover if one wishes on the autostrada travelling from Catania to Palermo, with a pause in Cefalu. While the historic center is well preserved, unregulated building rather disfigures the outskirts beyond the walls. Go at once towards the imposing monastery of Gangivecchio, now owned by a patrician family. The ladies of the house have installed some rooms in an annex with a decent standard of comfort, but not too much concern for décor. However the terraces all have a fine view over the mountains, the lovely old stones of the cloister and the age-old trees in the park. Take advantage too of the welcome offered by this Sicilian family and enjoy an authentic local meal with no less than five dishes, not forgetting the delicious cannoli.

How to get there (Map 27): A19 Catania-Palermo, exit Tremonzelli, then S120 to Gengi.

Hotel Tonnara Trabia

90019 Trabia (Palermo)
Largo Tonnara S.s. 113
Tel. 091-814 79 76 - Fax 091-812 48 10 - Sig. Salvo Di Maio
E-mail: info@tonnara.com - Web: www.tonnara.com

Category ★★★ **Rooms** 111 with air-conditioning, shower, WC, satellite TV, minibar – 2 elevators, wheelchair access. **Price** Single 90-150,000L, double 130-250,000L, suite 190-300,000. **Meals** Breakfast included, served 7:30-10:00. **Restaurant** Service 12:30PM-2:00PM, 7:30PM-10:00PM - mealtime specials 45,000L, also à la carte. **Credit cards** Amex, Visa, Eurocard, MasterCard. **Pets** Dogs allowed. **Facilities** Parking. **Nearby** Bagheria (villa Palagonia) - Solunto - Termini Imerese - Cefalù. **Open** All year.

One of the chief economic activities of the north coast of Sicily is tuna fishing which in May is the occasion for the collective fishing known as la mattanza, the most famous of which - and the most interesting for tourists - is the one that takes place off Trapani. In Trabia, this hotel occupies a former tuna fishmarket, a tonnara, which lies alongside the road without revealing that two floors lower down, the back of the hotel opens directly on a lawn that runs down to the waters of the Gulf of Termini. This, as it happens, is the façade that most clearly reveals the industrial character of the building. The whole has an appearance of authenticity, the architects having used traditional materials such as stone and tufa, while conserving the forms and frameworks of the original. The rooms are comfortable, all identically decorated in blue or green. Demand to be given one that overlooks the bay. Situated between Palermo and Cefalù, Trabia is an excellent base in summer to visit the historical and tourist sites while enjoying the beaches or the hotel's two swimming pools, one of which is covered, thus prolonging the season.

How to get there (Map 26): 35km from Palermo, 25km from Cefalù.

Eremo della Giubiliana

Giubiliana 97100 Ragusa
Tel. and Fax 0932-669 119 - Fax 0932-623 891
Sig.ra Nifossi

Category ★★★★★ **Rooms** 9 and 2 suites with telephone, bath, satellite TV, safe. **Price** Double 298,000L, suite 770,000L. **Meals** Breakfast included, served 7:30-10:00 - half board and full board 194,000L, 239,000L (per pers.). **Restaurant** Service 12:30PM-2:00PM, 7:30PM-10:00PM - closed mon - mealtime specials 50-90,000L, also à la carte. **Credit cards** All major. **Pets** Dogs not allowed. **Facilities** Prvated beach (shuttle service). **Nearby** Ragusa - Marina di Ragusa and ruins of Camarina - Noto - Siracusa. **Open** All year.

In a protected natural region, in the midst of oak woods, white dry stone walls still protect this hermitage which its last owner has opened to guests. The transformation was keen to preserve the original plan and the old stones, but not only these. Indeed, the spirit of retreat - which was by turns that of the hermit and of the warrior - is still predominant today, in a different manner of course, guests finding a haven here from which to discover another Sicily. Sobriety, rigor and refinement are the luxury of this house. The rooms occupy the former monks' cells, and are fitted out with discreet but exemplary comfort. The fittings consist in old regional furniture and family hierlooms. The cooking is to match: biological products from the garden, homemade bread and fresh pasta, traditional recipes of the island and a cellar well-supplied with Sicilian wines will help you to discover new flavors of Mediterranean cuisine. Don't be surprised when you hear that the hotel has its own private aerodrome. The son, a skilled pilot whose business is known on all the tourist circuits of the area, offers day trips to the islands of Malta, Lampedusa and Pantelleria, as well as trips flying over Etna and the surrounding baroque cities.

How to get there *(Map 27): 80km southwest of Siracuse. At 9km from Ragusa Iba, towards Marina di Ragusa.*

Villa Lucia

96100 Siracusa
Traversa Mondello, 1 - Contrada Isola
Tel. and fax 0931-721 007 - Fax 0931-72 15 87
Sig.ra Maria Luisa Palermo

Rooms 7 with air-conditioning, telephone, bath or shower, WC, minibar, TV; 5 in the annex and 7 small apartments. **Price** Single 195,000L, double 290,000L, annex: single 105,000L, double 150,000L; apartment (2-5 pers.) 60,000 (per pers., 2 nights min.). **Meals** Breakfast included (for the rooms), served 8:00-9:30. **Restaurant** See p. 547. **Credit cards** Visa, Eurocard, MasterCard. **Pets** Small dogs allowed in room (with extra charge). **Facilities** Swimming pool, parking. **Nearby** In Siracusa: Archeological Museum, Ortygia island, Catacombs, Castle of Euryale, Fountain of Arethusa. **Open** All year.

The Villa Lucia is a valuable address to know, for this is not a classic hotel, but a family country home outside the center of town whose owner, Marquisa Maria Luisa Palermo, has been gradually adapting it to receive guests. A path lined with pine trees leads up to the villa whose faded rosy-tinted façade gives the visitor a first taste of the charm of the place. A few rooms are in the villa, the rest in its annexes. Nothing is ostentatious, but you will find antique furniture assembled over generations, family portraits and travel souvenirs. There is a very pleasant park with lush Mediterranean vegetation. Maria Luisa can also provide information on where to find all that is most authentic in Sicily. A charming place with a charming hostess.

How to get there *(Map 27): 6km from Siracusa. At the highway, exit Catania/Siracusa, then take SS115. When you leave the town, take the bridge on the river Ciane, first road on the left, go around the port, Contrada Isola.*

Grand Hotel di Siracusa

96100 Siracusa
Via Mazzini, 12
Tel. 0931-46 46 00 - Fax 0931-46 46 11
Sig. Calandruccio

Apartments 38 and 20 with bath, WC, TV satellite, minibar – Elevator, wheelchair access and rooms for disabled persons. **Price** Single 260,000L, double 380,000L, suite 480-580,000L. **Meals** Breakfast included, served 7:30-10:00. **Restaurant** Service 12:00PM-2:30PM, 8:00PM-10:30PM - à la carte - Italian and Sicilian cuisine. **Credit cards** All major. **Pets** Dogs not allowed. **Facilities** Shuttle service for private beach. **Nearby** in Siracusa: Archaeological museum and Origia island, ruins of Neapolis, catacombs - Castel of Euryale. **Open** All year.

After four long years of costly restoration, Syracuse at last has a hotel worthy of the city. The goal the architects set was to create new spaces, like the panoramic terrace-restaurant, to refurbish the entire ground floor as reception rooms, and to keep intact as many of the original features as possible. During the renovation work, the builders uncovered vestiges of Spanish fortifications from the 16th century, which are now on display in the hotel's small museum. In the two grand salons they found antique Sicilian furniture or had new pieces made by artists like Carlo Moretti, who did the Murano chandelier that hangs in the Minerva Room. The Athena Room, with its stuccos and frescoes, is in a rotunda illuminated at night and looking out over the port. A large semi-circular staircase with columns leads upstairs to the bedrooms, with luxurious comfort and a view of the sea. Every bit as stunning is the interior garden, with a panoramic elevator amid palm trees and fragrant shrubs.

How to get there (Map 27): On Oetigia island.

Museo Albergo L'Atelier sul Mare

98070 Castel di Tusa (Messina)
Via Cesare Battisti, 4
Tel. 0921-33 42 95 - Fax 0921-33 42 83 - Sig. Antonio Presti
E-mail: ateliersulmare@nebro.net - Web: www.ateliersulmare.com

Rooms 40 with telephone, bath or shower, WC – Elevator. **Price** Single 80-105,000L, double 120-160,000L, "chambre d'artiste" 200,000L. **Meals** Breakfast included, served 7:30-9:30 - half board 95-140,000L, full board 100-165,000L (per pers., 3 days min.). **Restaurant** Service 1:00PM-3:00PM, 8:30PM-10:30PM - mealtime specials 30-40,000L, also à la carte - Specialties: Seafood. **Credit cards** Amex, Visa, Eurocard, MasterCard. **Pets** Dogs allowed (with extra charge). **Facilities** Privat beach, parking. **Nearby** Halaesa - S. Stefano di Camastra (Terracotta potteries) - Cefalù. **Open** Apr – Nov.

The road from Messina to Palermo follows the coast of the Tyrrhenian Sea with its many resorts, including Castel di Tusa. Museo Albergo is a Mediterranean-style building right on the water, set on several levels. But what is really interesting is the concept which the hotel and especially the rooms are based on: art as an integral part of daily life. Each room is an "event" designed by a contemporary artist. By staying here, you will inhabit a unique work of art. In the lobby and the salon, you will find a series of paintings and sculptures. You may like to note that the French Ministry of Culture has chosen the Atelier sul Mare to put up its artists on their visits to Italy. The art may not be to everyone's taste, but this hotel does fulfill all the criteria of a good hotel: It has comfort, good service, and a fine restaurant where you will enjoy the hotel's fine fish dishes.

How to get there *(Map 27): 90km east of Palerme; via A20 to Cefalù then along the coast towards Messina.*

Casa Migliaca

Migliaca 98070 Pettineo (Messina)
Tel. 0921-33 67 22 - Fax 0921-39 11 07
Maria Teresa Allegra
E-mail: casa.migliaca@sicilyonline.it - Web: www.casamigliaca.com

Rooms 8 with bath. **Price** 80,000L (per pers.). **Meals** Breakfast included - half board 105,000L (per pers.). **Credit cards** Amex, Visa, Eurocard, MasterCard. **Pets** Dogs not allowed. **Facilities** Parking. **Nearby** Cefalù - Mistretta - Castel of Lucio - Craft pottery at S. Stefano di Camastra - Nicosia. **Open** All year.

A visit to Cefalù is a must, for its setting, its Norman cathedral and its mosaics. Casa Migliaca may be the ideal stopping place if you would rather stay inland. As you leave Pettineo, take the road towards Castel di Lucio for 500 m until you see the old mill, looking out over fields of olive trees. The surrounding garden is charming, with trees among the roses, the geraniums and the ivy that climbs up the walls of the building. Inside, the materials, the flooring and the original forms have been respected to create an authentic atmosphere, with the old millstone serving as a dining table. The bedrooms have been done up with the same attention to detail and now all have a private bathroom. In summer, dinner will be served to you in the pergola, accompanied by the scents from the citrus fruits in the garden. The prices are reasonable and the welcome friendly.

How to get there *(Map 27): 47km north of Cefalù. Follow the coast as far as Castel di Tusa, and after Halesa, turn right towards Pettineo.*

Villa Miraglia

Portella Miraglia 98033 Cesaro' (Messina)
SS 289
Tel. 095-77 32 133
Sig. Calogero Pedala

Rooms 5 with shower. **Price** Single 50,000L, double 105,000L. **Meals** Breakfast 9,000L, served 8:30-9:30 - half board and full board 90,000L, 120,000L (per pers.). **Restaurant** Service 12:00PM-1:30PM, 7:30PM-9:00PM - mealtime specials 35,000L. **Credit cards** Not accepted. **Pets** Dogs not allowed. **Facilities** Parking. **Nearby** Craft pottery at S. Stefano di Camastra - Nicosia - Troina. **Open** All year.

Leaving the coast, you take the mountain road into the Regional Park of Nebrodi. The Villa Miraglia is a very friendly and welcoming guest house, somewhere between an inn and a hostel. A house int eh forest in stone and wood, with five small rooms on the first floor, some of which open on a balcony. The comfort is minimal but the establishment well kept, with a warm interior and walls covered in ceramics and typical local craft objects. In winter, meals are served in the dining room on the ground floor with a view of the forest, but as soon as the fine weather comes, large tables are set up outside, the wine comes in jugs and there is a great barbecue. After lunch the families separate to have a siesta in the grass or a little stroll. The owner will give you all the information you need and any available leaflets on long-distance walking, bathing in lakes and waterfalls, cycling and so on... A week-end, a stopover or a longer stay will also give you the chance to meet Sicilian families.

How to get there (Map 27): 70km north of Cefalù. Follow the coast as far as Acquedolci, then S289 towards Cesaro as far as Portella.

San Domenico Palace Hotel

98039 Taormina (Messina)
Piazza San Domenico, 5
Tel. 0942-23 701 - Fax 0942-62 55 06 - F. Cozzo
E-mail: san-domenico@thi.it - Web: www.thi.it

Category ★★★★★ **Rooms** 111 with telephone, bath, WC, satellite TV, minibar – Elevator. **Price** Single 405-470,000L, double 670-800,000L. **Meals** Breakfast included, served 7:00AM-12:00PM - half board 505-570,000L (in single), 870-1 000,000L (in double). **Restaurant** Service 12:30PM-2:30PM, 7:30PM-10:00PM - mealtime specials 100,000L, also à la carte - Sicialian and Italian cuisine. **Credit cards** All major. **Pets** Dogs not allowed. **Facilities** Heated swimming pool, fitness center. **Nearby** In Taormina: Castello San Pancrazio, gorges of Alcantara, Castelmola (panorama from Cafe S. Giorgio) - Forza d'Agro - Alcantara - Capo Schiso - Naxos – Il Picciolo Golf course (18-hole). **Open** All year.

The San Domenico Palace, formerly a monastery built in 1430, is no doubt the most beautiful hotel in Sicily. It is frequented by a rich international clientele and some top-notch tour operators. To get to the marvelous garden, meticulously kept and flowering year-round, you walk through a cloister and numerous, long hallways decorated with 17th- and 18th-century paintings, which lead to luxurious rooms resembling monk's cells from the outside. You will spend dreamlike days next to the swimming pool, from which you can enjoy the view of the Greek theater, the sea, and Mount Etna. A dinner by candlelight on the terrace will prove that the San Domenico also has the finest restaurant in Taormina.

How to get there *(Map 27): 52km south of Messina via A18 Taormina-North exit; near the belvedere of the via Roma.*

Hotel Villa Belvedere

98039 Taormina (Messina)
Via Bagnoli Croci, 79
Tel. 0942-237 91 - Fax 0942-62 58 30 - Sig. Pécaut
E-mail: info@villabelvedere.it - Web: www.villabelvedere.it

Category ★★★ **Rooms** 51 (32 with air-condiditiong), telephone, bath or shower, WC, TV on request. **Price** Single 110-190,000L, double 180-290,000L. **Meals** Breakfast included, served 7:00AM-12:00PM - snacks from Apr to Oct, service 11:30PM-6:00PM. **Restaurant** See pp. 546-547. **Credit cards** Visa, Eurocard, MasterCard. **Pets** Dogs allowed. **Facilities** Swimming pool, parking (6,000L). **Nearby** In Taormina: Greek Theater, Castello San Pancrazio, Castelmola (panorama from Cafe S. Giorgio) - Forza d'Agro - Alcantara - Capo Schiso - Mazzaro beach - Messina – Il Picciolo Golf Course (18-hole). **Open** Mar 10 – Nov 25.

The discreet Hotel Belvedere stands very close to the enchanting public garden of Taormina. Unlike most of the hotels of Taotmina which suffer from frenetic delusions of grandeur, the Belvedere has remained simple, comfortable and charming. It is remarkably managed by its French director, and who runs it according to three rules which have made is so popular among its clientele of artists and regulars: cleanliness, comfort, and silence. Five new very pretty rooms have been opened, with large balconies with a view of the sea. You couldn't ask for more, but the view on the Bay of Taormina and a beautiful swimming pool under the giant palm trees give it additional allure which, fortunately, you won't see in the final bill.

How to get there *(Map 27): 52km south of Messina via A18, Taormina exit - the hotel is next to the "belvedere dei giardini pubblici".*

Hotel Villa Ducale

96039 Taormina (Messina)
Via Leonardo da Vinci, 60
Tel. 0942-28 153 - Fax 0942-28 710 - Sig. and Sig.ra Quartucci
E-mail: villaducale@tao.it - Web: www.hotelvilladucale.it

Category ★★★ **Rooms** 14 with air-conditioning, telephone, bath or shower, WC, satellite TV, safe, minibar. **Price** Single 200-250,000L, double 270-400,000L, junior suite 380-440,000L, suite 550-750,000L. **Meals** Breakfast included, served 8:00-11:00. **Restaurant** See pp. 546-547. **Credit cards** All major. **Pets** Small dogs allowed. **Facilities** Parking. **Nearby** In Taormina: Greek Theater, Castello San Pancrazio, Castelmola (panorama from Cafe S. Giorgio) - Forza d'Agro - Alcantara - Capo Schiso - Naxos - Mazzaro beach - Messina – Il Picciolo Golf Course (18-hole). **Closed** Dec 1 – Feb 21.

The patrician Villa Ducale is a very comfortable and elegant hotel, built by the great grandfather of the current owners at the beginning of the century. The rooms, carefully decorated and furnished with antiques, are all different, but all have an incredible view of the sea, Etna and the valley. The ones on the third floor have a pleasant terrace with a table and lounge chairs. A very interesting library provides reading material on Sicily and its history; you can also play chess there. Don't miss the delicious breakfasts–served on the terrace–of Viennese pastries, jelly and honey from Etna, fresh fruit juice and other local products. The staff is very friendly.

How to get there *(Map 27): 52km south of Messina via A18, Taormina-North exit.*

Hotel Villa Paradiso

98039 Taormina (Messina)
Via Roma, 2
Tel. 0942-239 21 22 - Fax 0942-625 800
Sig. Salvatore Martorana

Category ★★★★ **Rooms** 25 and 13 suites with air-conditioning, telephone, bath or shower, WC, satellite TV – Elevator. **Price** Single 140-170,000L, double 180-270,000L, suite 280-320,000L. **Meals** Breakfast included served 7:30-10:00. **Restaurant** Service 1:00PM-2:00PM, 8:00PM-9:15PM - mealtime specials 35-45,000L, also à la carte - Sicilian cuisine and pesce. **Credit cards** All major. **Pets** Small dogs allowed. **Nearby** In Taormina: Greek Theater, Castello San Pancrazio, Castelmola (panorama cafe S.Giorgio) - Forza d'Argo - Alcantara - Capo Schiso - Naxos - Mazzaro beach - Etna – Il Picciolo golf course (18-hole). **Open** All year.

Set between the sea and the majestic Mount Etna, Taormina is like a sampler of Sicily, all in one stunning package. The Villa Paradiso is the creation of an English adventuress of the last century who fell in love with an Italian doctor and with what was then just a little village. She built the house as a hunting lodge and it still bears the mark of its history - a blend of Sicily with far-off Albion and an air of intimacy as in a family guest house. The bedrooms have elegant painted wood furniture, the larger suites look out on the sea. The salons are a series of connecting rooms, some with a covered gallery facing the winter garden, others facing the sea. A well-appointed terrace and a winter garden offer grandiose panoramas of the bay. As soon as weather permits, a private bus will take you to Letojanni, where the hotel owns Paradise Beach, a private club on the beach with swimming pool and a restaurant (from June to the end of October).

How to get there (Map 27): 52km south of Messina via A18, Taormina exit.

Hotel Villa Schuler

98039 Taormina
Piazzetta Bastione/Via Roma
Tel. 0942-23 481 - Fax 0942-23 522 - Sig. Gerardo Schuler
E-mail: schuler@tao.it - Web: www.villaschuler.com

Rooms 21 and 5 junior suites (some with air-conditioning) with telephone, bath or shower, WC, satellite TV, radio, safe. **Price** Single 120,000L, double 180-204,000L, junior suite 230,000L. **Meals** Breakfast included, served 7:00-10:00. **Restaurant** See pp. 546-547. **Credit cards** All major. **Pets** Dogs not allowed. **Facilities** Bicycle, Shuttle to beach and car park (6,000L/per pers.), garage (18,000L). **Nearby** In Taormina: Greek theatre, Castello on Monte Tauro, Castelmola (terrace, belvedere opf Café S. Giorgio) - Forza d'Agro - Gorges of the Alcantara - Capo Schiso - Naxos - Mazzaro beach - Etna – Il Picciolo Golf Club (18-hole). **Open** Mar 10 – Nov 15.

Taormina lies some two hundred meters above sea level, overhanging the sea, already providing a very beautiful natural setting. The main attraction of this villa is its situation: it is both in the historic center of twon, near the public gardens and the Corso Umberto, and in a garden that allows you from its terrace to overlook the sea and to have a view of Etna through the palm trees. The surrounding grounds are bursting with wild, exotic vegetation and colorful mixed borders. The interior is comfortable and most of the rooms, though simply furnished and not very large, have sea views. Those on the top floor enjoy a veritable roof terrace with chaises longues. The prices are kind, the welcome friendly. A good family hotel.

How to get there *(Map 27): 52km south of Messina by A18, exit Taormina.*

Hotel Villa Sant'Andrea

98030 Mazzaro - Taormina (Messina)
Via Nazionale, 137
Tel. 0942-23 125 - Fax 0942-24 838
E-mail: santandrea@framon-hotels.com - Web: www.framon-hotels.com

Category ★★★★ **Rooms** 67 with air-conditioning, tel., bath or shower, WC, TV. **Price** Single 215-395,000L, double 310-550,000L, junior suite +120,000L. **Meals** Breakfast included, served 7:30-10:00 - half board and full board 260-440,000L (1 pers.), 200-320,000L (per pers. in double), 235-355,000L (per pers.). **Restaurant** Service 1:00PM-2:30PM, 8:00PM-10:30PM - mealtime specials 55,000L, also à la carte - Specialties: Tagliolini con scampi e pesto alla Sant'Andrea - Spigoletta creazione "Olivero" - Parfait alle mandorle. **Credit cards** All major. **Pets** Small dogs allowed. **Facilities** Privat beach, parking (27,000L). **Nearby** In Taormina: Greek Theater, Castello on the Monte Tauro, Castelmola (terrace, panorama from Cafe S. Giorgio) - Forza d'Agro - Gorges of the Alcantara - Capo Schiso - Naxos - Mazzaro beach - Trip to the Etna — Il Picciolo Golf Club (18-hole). **Open** All year.

At the Villa Sant'Andrea it is possible to enjoy the advantages of Taormina without suffering from the drawbacks. At the water's edge and away from the narrow village lanes crowded with tourists, it is only 5 minutes from town by cable car. This charming place has managed (unlike its neighbors in Mazzaro) to avoid becoming just another address for group tours. The hotel dates from the 1950s. Most of its rooms face the sea and it is very quiet. Restaurants, private beach and terrace bar are arranged with discretion and good taste. From August 8 to 21, the hotel reserves the right to accept only guests staying for a minimum of one week.

How to get there (Map 27): 52km south of Messina via A18, Taormina-North exit - The hotel is 5,5km north of Taormina, along the coast.

Hotel Elimo Erice

91016 Erice (Trapani)
Via Vittore Emanuele, 75
Tel. 0923-86 93 77 / 86 94 86 - Fax 0923-86 92 52 - Sig. Tilotta
E-mail: elimoh@comeg.it

Rooms 21 with telephone, bath or shower, WC, TV – Elevator. **Price** Single 170,000L, double 330,000L. **Meals** Breakfast included, served 7:30-10:00 - half board 140,000L, full board 180,000L (per pers., 3 days min.). **Restaurant** Service 12:30PM-2:30PM, 7:30PM-8:00PM - mealtime specials 30-60,000L, also à la carte - Sicilian cuisine. **Credit cards** All major. **Pets** Dogs allowed. **Facilities** Parking. **Nearby** Trapani - Egadi islands and island of Pantelleria. **Open** All year.

At the western end of Sicily, Erice, which rises straight up from a rock, seems to keep watch over a peaceful and silent world. The historical center is a labyrinth of narrow little streets, Renaissance palaces and churches from the Middle Ages, all of which seem to fit together like pieces of a jigsaw puzzle. Life goes on behind these façades, in the inner courtyards which are characteristic of the houses in Erice. The hotel Elimo is in one of these old houses. Carefully restored and comfortably furnished, the hotel's decor, inspired by the colors and materials of ancient motifs, is nevertheless a bit common. This is, however, a very pleasant place to stay in this beautiful town of Erice, with its remarkable architectural heritage. Be sure to go for a walk along the fortified walls surrounding the town from which you will have stunning views of the coast. From the Castello di Venere, you can see Trapani and the islands, and on a clear day, Tunisia. Don't be surprised if you hear people speaking foreign languages–the town is the headquarters for the International Center of Scientific Culture "Ettore Majorana."

How to get there (Map 26): 13km north of Trapani.

S I C I L Y

Pensione Tranchina

91014 Scopello (Trapani)
Via A. Diaz, 7
Tel. 0924-54 10 99 - Fax 0924-54 10 99
Sig. Salvatore Tranchina

Category ★ **rooms** 10 with shower, WC. **Price** With half board 85-105,000L (per pers.). **Meals** Breakfast included, served 8:00-10:00. **Restaurant** Service 8:00PM - mealtime specials 30-35,000L - Regional cooking. **Credit cards** All major. **Pets** Dogs not allowed. **Nearby** Riserva naturale dallo Zingaro - Tonnara in disuso - Segesta - Erice - Trapani - Mozia - Palermo. **open** All year.

Scopello is a good stopping place on your journey towards the unmissable sites of the northeast coast, because it will show you a delightful little village off the tourist track. Built around its traditional square and fountain, this particular village prides itself on housing the hunting lodge of King Ferdinand de Bourbon, to be found among the gelaterie and their terraces. The Pensione Tranchina is like the village itself, simple and quiet. The rooms are more or less spacious, the bathrooms are not large, the furniture is unpretentious, yet one feels good here. Some rooms have sea views. It should be said that the owner and his wife go to immense trouble to please their guests. The obligatory half-board will ensure that you taste Sicilian pasta, vegetables from the garden, home-made jams and the fish of the day. One thing: please do not miss the walk down through the fields towards the magnificent tonnara at Scopello, situated between the rocks and overlooking the Gulf of Castellamare. Also quite near is the very lovely coast of the Zingaro nature reserve.

How to get there *(Map 26): 30km east of Trapani. On the A29. Exit towards Castellamare del Golfo, then coastal road towards Scopello.*

Club Il Gattopardo

Isola di Lampedusa (Agrigento)
Tel. 0922-97 00 51 - Fax 011-817 83 87
Reservation: 011-817 83 85

Rooms 12 and 2 suites with bath, WC. **Price** With full board 1 800-2 850,000L (per pers. for 1 week with car and boat rental included). **Restaurant** Service 1:00PM and 8:30PM - mealtime specials, also à la carte - Sicilian cuisine and seafood. **Credit card** Not accepted. **Pets** Dogs not allowed. **Nearby** Lampedusa island - Linosa island. **Open** Jun – mid Oct.

Lampedusa, the largest of the Pelagien Islands, which are scattered between the coasts of Sicily and Tunisia, was inhabited in the Bronze Age, then deserted from antiquity until 1843. Roberto and his French wife Annette opened this hotel-club because Roberto, who loves scuba diving, wanted to become better acquainted with this still unspoiled island. Here, the word "club" takes on an intimate connotation, as Il Gattopardo is a guest house with only a few rooms. In the purest architectural tradition of the island, the ochre stone and white domes blend perfectly with the coast and the sea nearby. The rooms are decorated in a Mediterranean style and are very comfortable. Everything is organized to take full advantage of the sea: You will have two boats (fishing and motor) at your disposal, as well as six dromedaries, which will allow you to explore the island. In the evening, you can enjoy the chef's cuisine, and in the morning, the delicious breakfasts prepared by Annette. From May to September, sea turtles come to Lampedusa to lay their eggs on the beaches at night. The best time to visit is in September and October, when the water is warm and the sky full of birds migrating towards Africa. Children under 18 are not accepted at this hotel.

How to get there *(Map 26): From Palermo by plane (30mn). Lampedusa Airport, tel. 922-97 02 99.*

Hotel Carasco

Isole Eolie o Lipari
98055 Lipari (Messina)
Porto delle Genti
Tel. 090-981 16 05 - Fax 090-981 18 28 - Sig. Marco del Bono
E-mail: carasco@tin.it - Web: www.carasco.com

Category ★★★ **Rooms** 89 with telephone, bath or shower, WC. **Price** With half board 85-170,000L, full board 100-185,000L (per pers.). **Meals** Breakfast included, served 7:30-9:30. **Restaurant** Service 12:30PM-2:30PM, 8:00PM-10:00PM - à la carte - Sicilian and Italian cuisine. **Credit cards** All major. **Pets** Dogs not allowed. **Facilities** Swimming pool, piano-bar, parking. **Nearby** Aeolian museum in Lipari - Canneto - Acquacalda - Puntazze (view) - Ovattropani - Piano Conte - Quattrocchi - Lipari island. **Open** Apr – Oct.

Lipari is the biggest and most visited island of the archipelago.The Hotel Carasco, run by an Anglo-Italian couple who are the descendants of the first owners, offers all the comfort of a grand hotel. The rooms are very large and most of them have a terrace with a view of the sea. The swimming pool (you can have lunch at the poolside in Summer) and the beach right at the foot of the hotel allow full enjoyment of the sea and the sun. The prices are reasonable and if you visit between April and July, or in October, you will benefit from special rates. Everything, in fact, makes this one of the best little addresses on the Aeolian Islands.

How to get there (Map 27): *Hydrofoil service from Messina all year; from Napoli, Reggio, Cefalù and Palermo Jun – Sept; car ferry service from Messina, Napoli and Milazzo (50mn-2hrs).*

Hotel Villa Augustus

Isole Eolie o Lipari - 98055 Lipari (Messina)
Vico Ausonia, 16
Tel. 090-981 12 32 - Fax 090-981 22 33 - Sig. D'Albora
E-mail: villaaugustus@tin.it - Web: www.emmeti.it/hvillaaugustus

Category ★★★ **Rooms** 35 with air-conditiong, telephone, bath or shower, WC, modem outlet, satellite TV. **Price** Single 80-160,000L, double 100-260,000L, suite 350,000L. **Meals** Breakfast 10-20,000L, served 7:00-11:30 - half board 100-180,000L (per pers.). **Restaurant** See p. 548. **Credit cards** Amex, Visa, Eurocard, MasterCard. **Pets** Dogs allowed. **Facilities** Parking. **Nearby** Aeolian museum in Lipari - Canneto - Acquacalda - Puntazze (view) - Ovattropani - Piano Conte - Quattrocchi. **Open** Mar – Oct.

Concealed close to the archeological museum, this is in an old family villa transformed into a hotel in the 1950s and now one of the most pleasant hotels in Lipari. We like this hotel for its simplicity, its garden, and its relatively spacious and comfortable rooms. Each one has a balcony or a terrace and a view of either the sea or the Lipari castle. It is more of a boarding house than a luxury hotel, but is nonetheless one of the more pleasant hotels in town. Although there is no hotel restaurant, there are several fine restaurants in the area where you can have lunch or dinner.

How to get there *(Map 27): Hydrofoil service from Messina all year; from Napoli, Reggio, Cefalù and Palermo Jun – Sept; car ferry service from Messina, Napoli and Milazzo (50mn-2hrs); the hotel is 100m from the port where the boats arrive.*

Hotel Villa Meligunis

Isole Eolie o Lipari - 98055 Lipari (Messina)
Via Marte, 7
Tel. 090-98 12 426 - Fax 090-98 80 149 - Sig. Guisina D'Ambra
E-mail: villameligunis@netnet.it - Web: www.netnet.it/villameligunis

Category ★★★★ **Rooms** 32 with air-conditioning, telephone, bath, WC, satellite TV, minibar –
Elevator. **Price** Single 150-350,000L, double 200-500,000L, suite +120,000L. **Meals** Breakfast
included - half board 200-400,000L (1 pers.), 300-600,000L (2 pers.); full board 250-450,000L
(1 pers.), 400-700,000L (2 pers.). **Restaurant** "Le Terrasse", service 12:30PM-1:30PM, 8:00PM-10:00PM
- mealtime specials 50-100,000L, also à la carte - Regional cooking and fish. **Credit cards** All major.
Pets Dogs not allowed. **Nearby** Aeolian museum in Lipari - Canneto - Acquacalda - Puntazze (view)
- Ovattropani - Piano Conte - Quattrocchi. **Open** All year.

The Aeolian Islands are one of the few remaining Mediterranean paradises
which are still relatively unspoiled. The director of the Villa Meligunis has
opened this hotel in hopes of attracting people from northern Europe in winter.
The name Meligunis is meaningful and appropriate: It is the ancient Greek
name for Lipari and means "gentleness". You will find this in the climate, the
wine and the color of the sea. The hotel is in an old house, to which more
modern Mediterranean-style buildings have been added. There is a large
terrace overlooking the sea. The rooms, which have every comfort, are
spacious and simply decorated. The restaurant serves local cuisine and features
mainly fish dishes.

How to get there *(Map 27): Hydrofoil service from Messina, Milazzo, all year;
from Napoli, Reggio, Cefalù and Palermo Jun – Sept; car ferry service from
Messina, Napoli and Milazzo (50mn-2hrs).*

Hotel Raya

Isole Eolie o Lipari
Via San Pietro 98050 Isola Panarea (Messina)
Tel. 090-98 30 29 - Fax 090-98 31 03
Sig.ra Beltrami and Sig. Tilche
E-mail: htlraya@netnet.it - Web: www.netnet.it/hotel/raya/index

Category ★★ **Rooms** 36 with telephone, shower, WC, minibar. **Price** Per pers. with half board 250-370,000L, double 300-460,000L. **Meals** Breakfast included, served 8:00AM-12:00PM. **Restaurant** Service 8:30PM-12:00AM - mealtime specials 70,000L - Specialties: Fish and seafood. **Credit cards** All major. **Pets** Dogs allowed, boat rentals, shops of the Raya, beach (20 mm). **Nearby** Bronze Age village at Capo Milazzese - Basiluzzo - Scuba Diving Center. **Open** Apr 10 – Oct 15.

It is surprising on this little Sicilian island to find a very trendy hotel–considered a local institution. It was built twenty years ago and consists of a series of pink and white bungalows which extend from the hillside (no elevator) down to the sea. Its Mediterranean architecture is ideal for its clean and modern interior decorated with beautiful, primitive art objects from Polynesia, Africa and the Orient. The lounges and all rooms, which are very sparse, overlook the sea. Each one has a terrace with a view of the Aeolian archipelago and Stromboli. A few more basic rooms are to be found in an annex in the village, more accessible and only a few minutes from Raya. The restaurant and the open-air bar (where breakfast is also served) look towards the sea. In the evening the scarlet fumazroles of Stromboli provide a magnificent spectacle. The guests are mostly regulars and the hotel staff is hip. Young children are not allowed and anyone looking for a traditional hotel will not be comfortable here.

How to get there (Map 27): Hydrofoil service from Milazzo and Napoli. No cars allowed on the island.

Hotel Signum

Isole Eolie o Lipari - Isola Salina 98050
Malfa (Messina), via Scalo, 15
Tel. 090-98 44 222 - Fax 090-98 44 102
Sig.ra Clara Rametta

Category ★★ **Rooms** 23 with telephone, bath or shower, WC. **Price** Single 135-200,000L, double 85-150,000L (per pers.), double superior +25,000L. **Meals** Breakfast included, served 8:00-10:00 - half board +45,000L (per pers.). **Restaurant** Service 8:30PM-10:00PM - closed Nov – Feb - mealtime specials 25-50,000L, also à la carte - Regional cooking and pesce. **Credit cards** All major. **Pets** Dogs allowed on request. **Nearby** Santa Marina (ecomuseum) - vineyard of malvoisie - Malfa - Valley of Valdichies - Monte Fossa - the volcano. **Open** All year.

We fell in love with this hotel as soon as we arrived by a narrow village lane that winds its way among the vines, oleanders and barbary fig trees. The Hotel Signum is built in the traditional style of the Aeolian Islands. From the broad terrace, the true heart of the house, there is a magical view of the Bay of Malfa, with Stromboli in the distance. The bedrooms are laid out around the terrace and each one has something special, like the rooms of an old family home. Some have terraces, others overlook the garden with their pergola of vines. The place owes its charm to its owners as well, Clara, always kind and helpful, and her husband, Michele, who is in charge of the cooking - refined dishes based on the local produce and the catch of the day. Clara can help you organize excursions to the other islands or boat trips to the cove of Pollara (where the film "Il Postino" was shot) or scooter rides around the local vineyards. This is the sort of place you can't leave without a twinge of sadness

How to get there *(Map 27): Hydrofoil service from Milazzo. No cars allowed on the island.*

Hotel La Sciara Residence

Isole Eolie o Lipari - 98050 Isola Stromboli (Messina)
Tel. 090-98 60 05/98 61 21 - Fax 090-98 62 84
Famiglia d'Eufemia
E-mail: info@lasciara.it - Web: www.lasciara.it

Category ★★★ **Rooms** 62 with telephone, bath or shower, WC. **Price** With half board 120-220,000L, (per pers., 7 day min. in high season). **Meals** Breakfast included, served 7:30-10:00. **Restaurant** Service 1:00PM-2:30PM, 8:00PM-9:30PM - mealtime specials 50-75,000L, also à la carte - Regional cooking and seafood. **Credit cards** All major. **Pets** Small dogs allowed. **Facilities** Swimming pool, tennis, private beach. **Nearby** The volcano - Sciara del Fuoco - Strombolicchio - Ginostra. **Open** May 20 – Oct 10.

Stromboli is a place to see, even if it's just for the Hotel La Sciara. The garden is splendid and filled with flowers–mostly fuchsia, pink and orange bougainvillea–which testify to the exceptional quality of the fertile volcanic soil. The rooms are spacious, comfortable and filled with antique furniture and objects of diverse origin, selected by the owner. In addition to the hotel, there are five old restored houses you can stay in, each with several rooms, one or two bathrooms, and a kitchenette. They overlook the sea and offer some hotel services.

How to get there (*Map 27*): *Hydrofoil service from Milazzo and Napoli. No cars allowed on the island.*

La Locanda del Barbablù

Isole Eolie o Lipari - 98050 Isola Stomboli (Messina)
Via Vittorio Emanuele, 17-19
Tel. 090-98 61 18 - Fax 090-98 63 23 - Sig. Andrea Fabbricino

Rooms 6 with telephone, shower, WC. **Price** Double 180-320,000L. **Meals** Breakfast included, served 7:30-11:00. **Restaurant** Service 8:00PM-10:00PM - mealtime specials 85,000L, also à la carte - Regional cooking. **Credit cards** Amex, Visa, Eurocard, MasterCard. **Pets** Dogs not allowed. **Nearby** The volcano - Sciara del Fuoco - Strombolicchio - Ginostra. **Closed** Nov and Feb.

Up to now, Barbablú has been the unmissable restaurant for connoisseurs of Stromboli. Now the owners have added on a few rooms so that their guests can experience even more intensely the peculiar relationship that one can achieve here with nature, with sea and fire side-by-side, under the auspices of a master of ceremonies that one can never forget - Stromboli. When you arrive, an Ape taxi will take you to the locanda which has retained all the simplicity and intimacy of the fisherman's house that it used to be. The rooms often still have their original floors and are fitted out with old furniture and small, but well-equipped shower rooms. All have a balcony with an uninterrupted view over the volcano and the sea. Add to this sense of well-being the gastronomic pleasure supplied by talented cooks interpreting the great classics of Sicilian cuisine. In the evening, do not forget to go up to the Observatory to admire the breath-taking spectacle of the volcano which produces an eruption like a firework display every ten minutes.

How to get there *(Map 27): Hydrofoil from Milazzo or Napoli - No cars allowed on the island.*

La Sirenetta Park Hotel

Isole Eolie o Lipari - 98050 Isola Stromboli (Messina)
Via Marina, 33
Tel. 090-98 60 25 - Fax 090-98 61 24 - Sig. Vito Russow
E-mail: lasirenetta@netnet.it - Web: www.netnet.it/hotel/lasirenetta

Category ★★★ **Rooms** 55 with air-conditiong, telephone bath or shower, WC, satellite TV, minibar.
Price Single 135-190,000L, double 240-410,000L, suite 290-490,000L. **Meals** Breakfast included
served 7:30-10:00 - half board 140-225,000L (per pers.) and full board 180-270,000L (per pers.).
Restaurant Service 1:00PM-2:30PM, 8:00PM-9:30PM - mealtime specials 45-70,000L, also à la carte -
Sicilian cuisine and pesce. **Credit cards** All major. **Pets** Small dogs allowed. **Facilities** Swimming
pool, tennis. **Nearby** The Volcano - Sciara del Fuoco - Strombolicchio - Ginostra. **Open** Mar - end Oct.

For many people, the name Stromboli evokes the film of Roberto Rosselini
and the famous love affair with Ingrid Bergman that began right here.
Domenico, the owner of the hotel, still remembers how he met Rosselini when
he came scouting for locations. Desperate at the thought that there was no
place on the island for the crew to stay, he rented the director his own house
and worked as an aide on the production. With the money he earned he built a
hotel facing the black waters of the sea and called it La Sirenetta after the
sirens in the tale of Ulysses. It's a hotel, in a nice location facing the beach,
and a favourite stopping-place for volcanologists. Choose a room with a
terrace or balcony that faces the Strombolicchio. The hotel is also noted for its
bar, the Tartana Club, where you can spend the evening. If you want to go up
to the crater (an unforgettable sight) the trip takes 3 hours and you must hire a
guide. The best time to do it is late afternoon, to see the sunset.

How to get there *(Map 27): Hydrofoil service from Milazzo and Napoli. No
cars allowed on the island.*

Les Sables Noirs

Isole Eolie o Lipari
98050 Isola Vulcano (Messina)
Porto Ponente
Tel. 090-98 50 - Fax 090-98 52 454 - M. Coppola
E-mail: lesablesnoirs@framon-hotels.com - Web: www.framon-hotels.com

Category ★★★★ **Rooms** 48 with air-conditioning, telephone, bath or shower, TV, minibar, WC. **Price** 155-250,000L (per pers.). **Meals** Breakfast included, served 7:00-10:00 - half board 180-275,000L, full board 210-305,000L (per pers., special rates for 10 or 14 days). **Restaurant** Service 1:00PM-2:30PM, 8:00PM-10:30PM - mealtime specials 65,000L, also à la carte - Mediterranean cuisine and seafood. **Credit cards** All major. **Pets** Small dogs allowed (+20,000L). **Facilities** Swimming pool, tennis, bike, private beach, parking. **Nearby** Access to the volcano's crater. **Open** End Apr – Oct 10.

The white houses of Porto Ponente are spread out along the black sand beaches at the foot of the Piana volcano. One of them is the Hotel La Scaria Residence. It has been recently renovated, and is now a comfortable luxury hotel with four-star service. You will find both heaven and hell on this Aeolian island dedicated to the Roman god-Vulcan and the farthest south in the Lipari archipelago. Hell is near the large 500-meter crater continually belching up ash, steam, smoke and gas. Heaven is the verdant surroundings of the volcano and the coast, with its mysterious hidden grottos, inlets, beaches and transparent turquoise water. The biggest tourist attraction is, however, the large crater, which puts on a show unique to the archipelago, the coasts of Sicily and Etna.

How to get there *(Map 27): Hydrofoil services from Milazzo and Napoli. Cars subject to restrictions.*

Relais San Pietro in Polvano

Loc. Polvano, 3 - 52043 Castiglion Fiorentino (Arezzo)
Tel. 0575-65 01 00 - Fax 0575- 65 02 55 - Sig. Luigi Protti
E-mail: polvano@technet.it - Web: www.cotona.net/polvano

Category ★★★ **Rooms** 5 and 2 suites with telephone, bath. **Price** Single 240,000L, double 300,000L, junior suite 400,000L, senior suite 350-480,000L. **Meals** Breakfast included, served 8:00-10:00. **Restaurant** By reservation, service 7:30PM-8:00PM. **Credit cards** All major except Diners. **Pets** Dogs not allowed. **Facilities** Swimming pool, parking. **Nearby** Cortona - Arezzo - Val di Chiana: Abbey of Farneta, Lucignano, Sinalunga - Lake of Trasimeno - Perugia **Closed** Nov 6 - Mar 15.

This is a wonderful place for anyone looking for calm, refinement and good taste (in the gastronomic sense of the term). After leaving the village of Castiglion Fiorentino, one plunges a little deeper into the oak woods and the olive groves until one reaches the hamlet of Polvano where you will find this large mansion. It enjoys a unique situation, with the Valley and Plain of the Chio at your feet. The house has been renovated with exquisite good taste. The original forms, vaults, arcades in pink brickwork and the tiled floors have been preserved and fitted out with comfortable, modern furniture which harmonizes elegantly with the old architecture. Each room has the name of a flower and these decorate a hat which is at your disposal. Here again elegant décor is allied to the highest standard of comfort. The suites are still more spacious with a drawing-room corner. The plentiful breakfast, home made and served on the terrace, is worth visiting just for itself, but everything here encourages you to stay: the region, the delicious dinner, the welcome offered by Luigi Protti and his wife and rates which are less expesnive than they may seem.

How to get there *(Map 13): 25km south of Arezzo by S71 as far as Castiglion Fiorentino than Polvano.*

Hotel San Michele

52044 Cortona (Arezzo)
Via Guelfa, 15
Tel. 0575-60 43 48 - Fax 0575-63 01 47 - Dr. Alunno
E-mail: sanmichele@ats.it - Web: www.cortona.net/sanmichele

Category ★★★★ **Rooms** 40 with air-conditioning, telephone, bath or shower, WC, TV, minibar – Elevator. **Price** Single 160,000L, double 250,000L, triple 270-280,000L (triple), 300,000L (for 4 pers.). **Meals** Breakfast included, served 7:30-9:30. **Restaurant** See p. 556. **Credit cards** All major. **Pets** Dogs not allowed. **Facilities** Garage (20,000L). **Nearby** Cortona (Church of Madonna del Calcinaio, Museo dell' Accademia Etrusca) - Arezzo - Val di Chiana (Abbey of Farneta, Lucignano, Sinalunga) - Lake of Trasimeno - Perugia. **Open** Mar – Dec.

The fortified town of Cortona has, from time immemorial, stood watch over the valley, a bit away from the main roads down in the plain that link Arezzo to Perugia, Tuscany to Umbria. The town still has its fortress look today. You enter through gates in the medieval walls and walk around steep, narrow lanes, often ending in stairways. There are still traces of the Etruscan epoch, and a fine collection can be seen at the Museo dell'Accademia Etrusca. The Renaissance has also left its mark, notably with the Madonna del Calcinaio church. The Albergo San Michele itself is situated in a former Renaissance palace. Simply and intelligently restored, it offers rooms with pleasant decoration and good amenities. The most charming are the attic rooms with their sloping ceilings. The largest ones have a mezzanine. The welcome is friendly but the standard is not up to the level of the four stars that the establishment boasts – though this is not a drawback as far as we are concerned, seeing that the hotel is pleasant to stay in and reasonably priced.

How to get there (Map 13): 28km south of Arezzo via SS71.

Hotel Il Falconiere

San Martino a Bolena 52044 Cortona (Arezzo)
Tel. 0575-61 26 79 - Fax 0575-61 29 27
Silvia and Riccardo Baracchi
E-mail: ilfalcon@ilfalconiere.com - Web: www.ilfalconiere.com

Category ★★★★ **Rooms** 19 with air-conditioning, telephone, bath (some with jacuzzi), WC, TV, minibar, safe – Elevator, room for disabled persons. **Price** Standard 430,000L, superior 530,000L, junior suite 670,000L, suite 900,000L; extra bed 100,000L. **Meals** Breakfast included, served 7:00-10:30 - half board +90,000L **Restaurant** Service 1:00PM-2:00PM, 8:00PM-10:00PM - also à la carte - Specialties: Fmosaico di fegatini con pane casareccio e cipollata al vinsanto - Pici con pomodoro fresco e olio dell'aromario - Agnello al rosmarino cun purea d'aglio dolce e germogli di spinaci - Terrina di pere al moscato con salsa vaniglia e gelato al latte di mandorle. **Credit cards** All major. **Pets** Dogs not allowed. **Facilities** Swimming pools, parking. **Nearby** Church of Madonna del Calcinaio - Museo dell' Accademia Etrusca - Arezzo - Val di Chiana (Abbey of Farneta, Lucignano, Sinalunga) - Lake of Trasimeno - Perugia. **Open** All year.

This magnificent 17th century villa stands on a hill covered with olive trees and vineyards, facing Cortona. This family house, transformed into a hotel, has kept all of the charm and polished luxury of the old days. The spacious, quiet rooms have beautiful classical furniture. Comfort and refinement pervade the hotel, creating a feeling of real well-being. We suggest, apart from the three garden-level suites (with pool-jacuzzis), the pretty little attic room from which you can see the majestic contours of the Etruscan town. And should you be inspired by "The Annunciation" by Fra' Angelico in the Diocese museum, there is a private chapel painted with frescoes at your disposal in the hotel garden.

How to get there (Map 13): 3km north of Cortona.

Castelletto di Montebenichi

52020 Montebenichi-Bucine (Arezzo)
Tel. 055-99 10 110 - Fax 055-99 10 113 - Marco Gasparini
E-mail: monteben@val.it - Web: www.val.it/hotel/castelletto

Category ★★★★ **Rooms** 5 and 4 suites with bath, WC, satellite TV, minibar, safe - No smoking.
Price Double 400-480,000L. **Meals** Breakfast included, served 8:00-11:00. **Restaurant** See p. 557.
Credit cards All major. **Pets** Dogs not allowed. **Facilities** Swimming pool, sauna, parking. **Nearby**
Siena - Il Chianti - Firenze - Arezzo - Convent of San Francesco d'Assisi at Verna and La Penna
(1.283m) **Closed** Nov – Mar.

One of the most refined hotels in Italy is situated in the tiny medieval
village of Montebenichi, between Arezzo and Siena, hidden among the
vineyards and olive groves of Chianti. The castelletto, situated on the flowery
little town square is itself an historical monument dating from the 12th
Century, its rich past still visible in its 13th-century frescoes. But this
castelletto conceals many other precious surprises, in its very fine collections
of objets d'art and old furniture, as well as the manuscripts in the library, a
collection of Greek and Etruscan vases and many paintings, ranging from the
Italian primitives to the present time. The rooms, too, have preserved all their
charm and their secrets, including the littlest under the roof, with its lovely
view and its walls decorated with erotic drawings attributed to Bonnard, or one
very spacious suite which is situated on two floors. The owners have tried to
preserve the intimacy of a private house, so the drawing rooms are open to you
for you relax at your leisure or pour yourself a drink. Given the above, you
must forgive the owners if they do not accept either children or smokers.

How to get there *(Map 13): 30km east of Siena (towards Colonna di Grillo,
then Bucine); before reaching Ambra, take the road on the left for
Montebenichi.*

Castello di Gargonza

Gargonza
52048 Monte San Savino (Arezzo)
Tel. 0575-84 70 21 - Fax 0575-84 70 54 - Sig. Fucini
E-mail: gargonza@teta.it - Web: www.gargonza.it

Category ★ **Rooms** and apartments 25 with telephone, bath or shower, WC. **Price** Single 180-320,000L, apartment 1 050-2 940,000L (for 1 week). **Meals** Breakfast included, served 8:00-10:00 - half board 140-210,000L, (per pers., 3 nights min.). **Restaurant** "La Torre di Gargonza", service 12:30PM-2:30PM, 7:30PM-9:30PM - closed Tues - mealtime specials 45-55,000L - Tuscan cuisine. **Credit cards** All major. **Pets** Dogs not allowed. **Facilities** Swimming pool. **Nearby** Monte San Savino (Loggia dei Mercanti, church and Palazzo of Monte San Savino) - Convent of San Fracesco in La Verna and La Penna (1,283m) - Arezzo. **Closed** Jan 9 – Feb 3.

If you are traveling with family or friends and if you want to choose a base from which to explore the region, the Castello di Gargonza may be just what you're looking for. In a completely restored and rehabilitated little village you can rent a furnished apartment in a very pretty site. When you arrive you will be given a map and the keys to your house and left to manage on your own. The interior is functional, not especially attractive, but with all the necessary amenities, and some of the units have a fireplace. There are some rooms to rent, as well, with hotel service. There is also a restaurant, the Torre di Gargonza, and a swimming pool. The whole place has the family atmosphere of an apartment hotel.

How to get there *(Map 13): 29km southwest of Arezzo via S73 to Monte San Savino, then right towards Gargonza.*

Stoppiacce ♠

52044 San Pietro a Dame (Arezzo)
Tel. 0575-69 00 58 - Fax 0575-69 00 58
Scarlett and Colin Campbell
E-mail: stoppiacce@technet.it - Web: www.stoppiacce.com

Rooms 3 and 1 apartment with bath, WC. **Price** Double 220,000L (2 nights min.), apartment 1 200,000-2 200,000L (1 week). **Meals** Breakfast included, served until 10:00. **Restaurant** By reservation, service 12:30PM, 8:00PM - mealtime specials 45,000L (lunch), 85,000L wine incl. **Credit cards** Not accepted. **Pets** Dogs not allowed. **Facilities** Swimming pool, parking. **Nearby** Cortona: Church of Madonna del Calcinaio, Museo dell' Accademia etrusca - Arezzo - Val di Chiana: Abbey of Farneta - Lucignano - Sinalunga - Lake of Trasimeno - Perugia. **Closed** Nov – Apr.

A stunning road from Cortona takes you through a wild and sun-drenched part of Tuscany, a landscape of green rolling hills reminiscent of nearby Umbria. It leads at last to an "end of the world" spot, but a very British one, indeed. For the three rooms in the superb setting of an old, meticulously-restored farmhouse are provided by an English couple. Both indoors and out, the setting is as trim as an English cottage: The garden beautifully kept, the rosebushes perfectly clipped, a chintz living room, old portraits, sumptuous bathrooms. In the dining room the table is set with great refinement, china and silver sparkle, awaiting the arrival of the guests, who are free to suggest their own menu. A wonderful choice for a complete rest and change of scene, suitable for anyone who wants to either laze about or explore this border region.

How to get there *(Map 13): 17km from Cortona towards Citta del Castello. In Portole, phone if you have a problem for location of the hotel.*

Il Trebbio

52010 Poggio d'Ancona (Arezzo)
Tel. 0575-487 252 - Fax 0575-487 252
Sig. Bellucci

Rooms 4 with bath or shower, TV. **Price** Double 120,000L; extra bed +35,000L. **Meals** Breakfast included, served before 10:00. **Restaurant** By reservation, service 8:00PM - mealtime specials 35,000L (wine not incl.). **Credit cards** Not accepted. **Pets** Dogs allowed. **Facilities** Parking. **Nearby** Bibbiena - La Verna - Monastery of Camaldoli - Cortona - Arezzo - Val di Chiana: Abbey of Farneta, Lucignano, Sinalunga, Sansepolcro - Anghiari - Caprese Michelangelo. **Closed** Dec 21 – 28.

Il Trebbio considers itself first and foremost a farm - not in the "agricultural" sense of the term, but rather with regard to nature, authenticity and respect for the environment and tradition. The various stone buildings thast make it up, situated in the center of the Casentino, or high valley of the Arno, overlook a beautiful landscape of woods and meadows, vines and olive trees. The business is efficently managed by a young couple, who are fit and love the region, so they will be your best guides when it comes to visits or walks in the area. The interior is nothing like a farm, more like a pleasant country house with its beamed ceilings, rustic furniture and large fireplace surrounded by appealing sofas. The whole is simple and stylish, and the uninterrupted views are always very attractive. A swimming pool is planned as an additional attraction for summer, but that is not where the interest lies in the homeland of Vasari, Michelangelo and Piero della Francesca.

How to get there *(Map 10): 25km north of Arezzo on SS71. 4km pas Subbiano, turn right for Poggio d'Ancona. On leaving the village, take the dirt road on the right. The inn (700m on your left) is not signposted.*

Hotel Helvetia & Bristol

50123 Firenze
Via dei Pescioni, 2
Tel. 055-28 78 14 - Fax 055-28 83 53 - Sig. Panelli
E-mail: hbf@charminghotels.it - Web: www.charminghotels.it/helvetia

Category ★★★★★ **Rooms** 52 with air-conditioning, telephone, bath or shower, WC, satellite TV, safe – Elevator. **Price** Single 407-495,000L, double 539-759,000L, suite 913-1 980,000L. **Meals** Breakfast 44,000L, served 7:00-10:30. **Restaurant** Service 12:30PM-2:30PM, 7:30PM-10:30PM - mealtime specials 80-120,000L - Mediterranean cuisine and old Tuscan recipes. **Credit cards** All major. **Pets** Dogs not allowed. **Facilites** Parking. **Nearby** Events in Firenze: Scoppio del Carro on Easter morning, Festa del Grillo Ascension Day, musical May, antiques biennale in odd years - Fiesole - Charterhouse of Galluzzo - Florentine villas and gardens (tel. Palazzo Pitti: 055 23 88 615) - Abbey of Vallombrosa –Dell'Ugolino golf course (18-hole) in Grassina. **Open** All year.

The Helvetia & Bristol is incontestably one of the best hotels of this category in Firenze: everything here is perfect and tasteful. This large, beautiful residence, once the meeting place of the Tuscan intellegentsia, has now regained its former prestige. The main salon sets the tone, a blend of British-style comfort and Italian luxury. Pretty old Indian calico fabrics add color to the small, very elegant dining room. The bar on the veranda has the charm of a winter garden. The exquisite rooms have beautiful fabric-covered walls, comfortable beds and marble bathrooms with whirlpools. The personnel is like the hotel–high class but irresistibly friendly and Italian.

How to get there *(Map 10): Next to Piazza della Repubblica, via Strozzi, via dei Pescioni.*

Hotel Regency

50121 Firenze
Piazza Massimo d'Azeglio, 3
Tel. 055-24 52 47 - Fax 055-234 67 35 - Sig.ra M. Landi
E-mail: info@regency-hotel.com - Web: www.regency-hotel.com

Category ★★★★★ **Rooms** 35 with air-conditiong, telephone, bath, WC, satellite TV, safe, minibar – Elevator. **Price** Single 380-445,000L, double 440-695,000L. **Meals** Breakfast included. **Restaurant** Service 12:30PM-2:30PM, 7:30PM-10:30PM - à la carte - Tuscan and Italian cuisine. **Credit cards** All major. **Pets** Dogs allowed (with extra charge). **Facilities** Garage. **Nearby** Events in Firenze: Scoppio del Carro on Easter morning, Festa del Grillo Ascension Day, musical May, antiques biennale in odd years - Fiesole - Charterhouse of Galluzzo - Florentine villas and gardens (tel. Palazzo Pitti: 055 23 88 615) - Abbey of Vallombrosa – Dell'Ugolino golf course (18-hole) in Grassina. **Open** All year.

Modern comfort and old fashioned hospitality is the motto of the owner of the Hotel Regency, Amedo Ottaviani. On the Piazza d'Azeglio, the Regency is a villa which used to belong to Florentine nobles. The almost English comfort of the rooms and the salons characterizes this place, as does the excellent cuisine served in a paneled dining room and the large glass wall opening onto the gardens. You will find great elegance here, down to the last details. One practical note: It is easy to park on the square and the streets nearby.

How to get there *(Map 10): Next to Santa Croce by the via Borgo Pinti.*

Hotel Brunelleschi

50122 Firenze
Piazza S. Elisabetta, 3
Tel. 055-27 370 - Fax 055-21 96 53 - Sig. Litta
E-mail: info@hotelbrunelleschi.it

Category ★★★★ **Rooms** 96 with air-conditioning, telephone, bath or shower, WC, TV, minibar – Elevator. **Price** Single 410,000L, double 560,000L, suite 850,000L. **Meals** Breakfast included, served 7:00-10:00 - half board +75,000L, full board +120,000L. **Restaurant** Service 12:00PM-2:00PM, 7:30PM-10:00PM - closed Sun - mealtime specials, also à la carte - Florentine and international cuisine. **Credit cards** All major. **Pets** Dogs allowed. **Facilities** Parking (55,000L). **Nearby** Events in Firenze: Scoppio del Carro on Easter morning, Festa del Grillo Ascension Day, musical May, antiques biennale in odd years - Fiesole - Certosa di Galluzzo - Villas and gardens around Firenze (tel. Palazzo Pitti: 055 23 88 615) - Abbey of Vallombrosa – Dell'Ugolino golf course (18-hole) in Grassina. **Open** All year.

The hotel was designed by Italo Gamberini, a renowned Italian architect, and set up in a 5th-century Byzantine tower and several adjoining houses, in the Duomo quarter. The decor is modern with some Art Nouveau details. There is a lot of ceruse wood, which goes nicely with the bricks in the tower and throughout the hotel. The quiet rooms all overlook pedestrian streets. The prettiest ones are on the fourth floor and have a view of the Duomo and the tower. The hotel terrace is the perfect place to watch spectacular sunsets over Firenze. This hotel, with a famous restaurant, feels like a grand hotel.

How to get there *(Map 10): Near the Duomo.*

Hotel J and J

50121 Firenze
Via di Mezzo, 20
Tel. 055-263 121 - Fax 055-24 02 82 - Famiglia Cavagnari
E-mail: jandj@dada.it - Web: www.jandjhotel.com

Category ★★★★ **Rooms** 20 with air-conditioning, telephone, bath or shower, WC, satellite TV, minibar. **Price** Double 490-550,000L, suite 700-800,000L. **Meals** Breakfast included, served 7:30-10:00. **Restaurant** See pp. 549-553. **Credit cards** All major. **Pets** Dogs not allowed. **Facilities** Public parking (50,000L). **Nearby** Events in Firenze: Scoppio del Carro on Easter morning, Festa del Grillo Ascension Day, musical May, antiques biennale in odd years - Fiesole - Certosa di Galluzzo - Villas and gardens around Firenze (tel. Palazzo Pitti: 055 23 88 615) - Abbey of Vallombrosa – Dell'Ugolino golf course (18-hole) in Grassina. **Open** All year.

Nicely located in the old quarter of Santa Croce, very close to the Duomo and the center of town, this hotel is in a 16th-century palace. Vestiges of that era, such as the cloister, the vaulted ceilings, and the frescos, have been preserved and restored. The rooms have simple, contemporary decor. Some are very large, and all have a living-room area. There can be surprises, such as the bathtub in Suite No 9, but the decoration is so well done that these flights of fancy do not at all detract from the atmosphere. The hotel has no elevator and the stairs to the upper floors are steep.

How to get there *(Map 10): Near Santa Croce by the via Borgo Pinti.*

Hotel Monna Lisa

50121 Firenze
Via Borgo Pinti, 27
Tel. 055-247 97 51 - Fax 055-247 97 55 - Sig. Agostino Cona
E-mail: monnalis@ats.it - Web: wwww.monnalisa.it

Category ★★★★ **Rooms** 30 with air-conditioning, telephone, bath, WC, satellite TV, safe, minibar.
Price Single 200-350,000L, double 350-550,000L. **Meals** Breakfast included (buffet), served 7:30-
10:00. **Restaurant** See pp. 549-553. **Credit cards** All major. **Pets** Dogs allowed. **Facilities** Parking
(20,000L). **Nearby** Events in Firenze: Scoppio del Carro on Easter morning, Festa del Grillo Ascension
Day, musical May, antiques biennale in odd years - Fiesole - Certosa di Galluzzo - Villas and gardens
around Firenze (tel. Palazzo Pitti: 055 23 88 615) - Abbey of Vallombrosa – Dell'Ugolino golf course
(18-hole) in Grassina. **Open** All year.

The atmosphere at the Monna Lisa is so warm and intimate that it feels more
like some luxury pensione than like a four-star hotel. First of all, its little
garden creates a wonderful change of scene, making you forget that you're
right in the center of Florence. Secondly, the place is run by a family of artists,
who seem to have real taste in antiques and decoration. Each room has its share
of nice antique pieces and engravings (with, of course, many interpretations of
the painting that gives the place its name). The reception room and breakfast
room overlooking the garden are as well-appointed as the rest. The entire place
is elegant and distinguished. We recommend you ask for a room in the main
house, preferably facing the garden. Those overlooking the street are, however,
well soundproofed. As for the rooms in the annex, they are very comfortable
but more impersonal. The Monna Lisa is undeniably the hotel in the centre of
Florence that most deserves the label: "hotel of character and charm".

How to get there (*Map 10*): *Near the Duomo and Santa Croce by the via Borgo
Pinti.*

Grand Hotel Minerva

50123 Firenze
Piazza Santa Maria Novella, 16
Tel. 055-27 230 - Reservations: 055-27 23 182 - Fax 055-26 82 81Sig.
Alessandro Augier
E-mail: info@grandhotelminerva.com - Web: www.grandhotelminerva.com

Category ★★★★ **Rooms** 102 with air-conditioning, telephone, bath or shower, WC, TV, minibar, safe –
Elevator. **Price** Single 310-360,000L, double 400-800,000L, suite 900-1 250,000L, apart. 750-900,000L.
Meals Breakfast included, served 7:00-10:30 - half board +60,000L (per pers.). **Restaurant** Service
12:00PM-2:00PM, 7:30PM-11:00PM - mealtime specials - also à la carte - Florentine cuisine. **Credit cards**
All major. **Pets** Dogs not allowed. **Facilities** Swimming pool, garage (45,000L). **Nearby** Events in Firenze:
Scoppio del Carro on Easter morning, Festa del Grillo Ascension Day, musical May, antiques biennale in
odd years - Fiesole - Certosa di Galluzzo - Villas and gardens around Firenze (tel. Palazzo Pitti: 055 23
88 615) - Abbey of Vallombosa – Dell'Ugolino golf course (18-hole) in Grassina. **Open** All year.

On the Piazza Santa Maria Novella you are right in the heart of Florence.
Between the famous church of polychrome marble that gave its name to
the piazza and the loggia San Paolo, adorned with medallions by Della Robbia,
the Minerva has since the 19th century occupied a building that once belonged
to a brotherhood of the nearby convent. It has recently undergone major
transformations. The architects have opted for modernity, with quality
materials, furniture often designed specially for the hotel and amenities for the
most demanding clientele. The bedrooms are soft and cozy; the largest have a
mezzanine and can sleep several people. Many have a view of the church
façade or its cloister. The salon and the bar are pleasant places to relax, but the
best surprise is the swimming pool on the rooftop, with the Duomo in the
background. Enquire about prices: the management is not very cooperative
about communicating future rates.

How to get there *(Map 10): In the town center.*

Hotel Montebello Splendid

50123 Firenze
Via Montebello, 60
Tel. 055-239 80 51 - Fax 055-21 18 67 - Sig. Lupi
E-mail: hms@tin.it - Web: www.milanflorencehotel.it

Category ★★★★ **Rooms** 54 with air-conditioning, telephone, bath or shower, WC, TV, safe, minibar; elevator. **Price** Single 300-390,000L, double 385-550,000L, triple 405-560,000L, suite 650-900,000L. **Meals** Breakfast (buffet) 35,000L, served 7:00-11:00 - half board +60,000L, full board +115,000L (per pers., 3 days min.). **Restaurant** Service 1:00PM-3:00PM, 7:30PM-11:00PM - closed Sun - mealtime specials 60-100,000L, also à la carte - Florentine and international cuisine. **Credit cards** All major. **Pets** Dogs allowed. **Facilities** Parking (100 m). **Nearby** Events in Firenze: Scoppio del Carro on Easter morning, Festa del Grillo Ascension Day, musical May, antiques biennale in odd years - Fiesole - Certosa di Galluzzo - Villas and gardens around Firenze (tel. Palazzo Pitti: 055 23 88 615) - Abbey of Vallombrosa – Dell'Ugolino golf course (18-hole) in Grassina. **Open** All year.

This elegant hotel with refined, slightly Parisian decor is in an old 14th-century villa in the heart of Firenze. The reception area, salons and bar are imbued with a sophisticated atmosphere, with their marble mosaic columns and floors, stucco ceilings, large 1900-style couches and profusion of green plants. All the rooms are extremely comfortable and have marble bathrooms. The ones overlooking the garden are quieter. Breakfasts and meals are served in a nice garden-level greenhouse.

How to get there *(Map 10): In the village center Porta al Prato, near the teatro comunale.*

Hotel Lungarno

50125 Firenze
Borgo Sant' Jacopo, 14
Tel. 055-27 26 1 - Fax 055-26 84 37

Category ★★★★ **Rooms** 54 and 6 apartments with air-conditionig, telephone, bath or shower, WC, satellite TV, minibar, safe – Elevator. **Price** Double 530-580,000L, 800-920,000L. **Meals** Breakfast included, served 7:00-11:00. **Restaurant** See p. 549-553. **Credit cards** All major. **Pets** Dogs not allowed. **Nearby** Events in Firenze: Scoppio del Carro on Easter morning, Festa del Grillo Ascension Day, musical May, antiques biennale in odd years - Fiesole - Certosa di Galluzzo - Villas and gardens around Firenze (tel. palazzo Pitti: 055 23 88 615) - Abbey of Vallombrosa – Dell'Ugolino golf course (18-hole) in Grassina. **Open** All year.

The view of the Arno from the Ponte Vecchio is one of the loveliest sights in Florence, especially at dusk when rowboats skim the waters of the river, glowing red in the setting sun. This, along with the houses on the famous bridge, is the view you will have from the salon of the Lungarno or from some of the bedrooms. Recent renovations have increased the luxury of the hotel but have still kept an elegant and contemporary atmosphere, with interesting modern paintings on the walls. Calm and comfort are its other great assets. Of course, you must book well in advance if you want to get a room facing the river. The hospitality is pleasant and professional.

How to get there *(Map 10): Beside Ponte Vecchio, near Palazzo Pitti.*

Hotel de la Ville

50123 Firenze
Piazza Antinori, 1
Tel. 055-238 18 05 - Fax 055-238 18 09
E-mail: delaville@firenze.net - Web: www.hoteldelaville.it/indexok.htm

Category ★★★★ **Rooms** 75 with air-conditioning, telephone, bath or shower, WC, satellite TV, web, minibar, safe – Elevator. **Price** Single 395-495,000L, double 520-650,000L, suite 820-965,000L. **Meals** Breakfast (buffet) 35,000L, served 7:00-10:30. **Restaurant** See pp. 549-553. **Credit cards** All major. **Pets** Small dogs allowed on request. **Facilities** Garage (45,000L). **Nearby** Events in Firenze: Scoppio del Carro on Easter morning, Festa del Grillo Ascension Day, musical May, antiques biennale in odd years - Fiesole - Charterhouse of Galluzzo - Florentine villas and gardens (tel. palazzo Pitti: 055 23 88 615) - Abbey of Vallombrosa – Dell'Ugolino golf course (18-hole) in Grassina. **Open** All year.

Piazza Antinori is at the western end of the Via Tornabuoni which has been the most aristocratic streets in Florence since the 15th century, lined with palazzi and luxury shops. The square itself owes its name to the Palazzo Antinori, which has a very good wine bar on its ground floor and adjoins the town hall. In short, the site is one of the very best. The hotel has just completed the first stage in a wide-ranging restoration which has so far affected all its rooms. The style is classical, expensive and very comfortable, the higher double rooms being very spacious with a sitting room corner and a bathroom. The suites are veritable little appartments, in duplex, with a drawing room and a bedroom which are reached via a staircase decorated with stained glass and old-fashioned frescoes. Those at the front of the building enjoy the best views, overlooking the church of San Gaetano. The reception area still needs restoring, but all the ingredients of a very good hotel are in place, including standards of service.

How to get there (Map 10): In the center of town.

Torre di Bellosguardo

50124 Firenze
Via Roti Michelozzi, 2
Tel. 055-229 81 45 - Fax 055-22 90 08 - Sig. Franchetti
E-mail: torredibellosguardo@dada.it

Category ★★★★ **Rooms** 10 and 6 suites with telephone, bath, shower, WC – Elevator. **Price** Single 290-360,000L, double 480,000L, suite 580-680,000L. **Meals** Breakfast 35-45,000L, served 7:30-10:00. **Restaurant** Lunch by the swimming pool in summer (or see pp. 549-553). **Credit cards** All major. **Pets** Dogs allowed. **Facilities** Swimming pool, parking. **Nearby** Events in Firenze: Scoppio del Carro on Easter morning, Festa del Grillo Ascension Day, musical May, antiques biennale in odd years - Fiesole - Charterhouse of Galluzzo - Florentine villas and gardens (tel. palazzo Pitti: 055 23 88 615) - Abbey of Vallombrosa – Dell'Ugolino golf course (18-hole) in Grassina. **Open** All year.

Torre di Bellosguardo is on a hill just outside the center of Firenze and has an exceptional view of the city. It is an extraordinarily quiet place with a majestic palace, a 14th-century tower, a lovely harmonious garden and a beautiful swimming pool down below. Today it is an elegant and comfortable hotel, with sixteen unusually large rooms, many salons and a spectacular sun room. Each room is unique and has period furniture, extraordinary woodwork, and frescoes. In the tower, there is a suite on two floors with a marvelous view. All rooms are superb and now have better bathrooms, raising the standard of comfort to the level of the beauty of the setting. Friendly welcome. A undeniably charming spot.

How to get there *(Map 10): Towards Forte Belvedere, Porta Romana.*

Villa Belvedere

50124 Firenze
Via Benedetto Castelli, 3
Tel. 055-222 501 - Fax 055-223 163 - Sig. and Sig.ra Ceschi-Perotto
E-mail: hotelvillabelvedere@tiscalinet.it - Web: www.villabelvedere.com

Category ★★★★ **Rooms** 26 with air-conditioning, telephone, bath or shower, WC, satellite TV, safe, minibar – Elevator. **Price** Single 220-240,000L, double 300-360,000L. **Meals** Breakfast included, served 7:15-10:00. **Restaurant** Snacks service for lunch and dinner (or see pp. 549-553). **Credit cards** All major. **Pets** Dogs not allowed. **Facilities** Swimming pool, tennis, parking. **Nearby** Events in Firenze: Scoppio del Carro on Easter morning, Festa del Grillo Ascension Day, musical May, antiques biennale in odd years - Fiesole - Charterhouse of Galluzzo - Florentine villas and gardens (tel. palazzo Pitti: 055 23 88 615) - Abbey of Vallombrosa –Dell'Ugolino golf course (18-hole) in Grassina. **Open** Mar – end Nov.

The Villa Belvedere is in the heights of Firenze, surrounded by a large quiet garden with a swimming pool and a tennis court. You will appreciate this place if you are traveling with children. The modern veranda, which has been added to the house, detracts a bit from its charm. The rooms have been entirely renovated and are all spacious and comfortable. Most have a superb view of Firenze, the countryside or the Certosa. The ones in the front have large terraces and the nicest are on the top floor. There's no restaurant, but if you are too tired to go out, snacks are available. The Ceschi family extends the warmest of welcomes.

How to get there *(Map 10): Towards Forte Belvedere - Porta Romana. Bus (300m) for the town center.*

Villa Carlotta

50125 Firenze
Via Michele di Lando, 3
Tel. 055-233 61 34 - Fax 055-233 61 47 - Sig. Gheri
E-mail: villa.carlotta@italyhotel.com - Web: www.venere.it/firenze/villacarlotta

Category ★★★★ **Rooms** 32 with air-conditioning, telephone, bath or shower, satellite TV, minibar – Elevator. **Price** Single 180-310,000L, double 280-460,000L. **Meals** Breakfast included, served 7:15-10:15 - half board 220-350,000L (per pers.). **Restaurant** Service 12:30PM-2:30PM, 7:30PM-9:30PM - closed Sun - à la carte - Tuscan and Italian cuisine. **Credit cards** All major. **Pets** Dogs allowed. **Facilities** Parking. **Nearby** Events in Firenze: Scoppio del Carro on Easter morning, Festa del Grillo Ascension Day, musical May, antiques biennale in odd years - Fiesole - Charterhouse of Galluzzo - Florentine villas and gardens (tel. palazzo Pitti: 055 23 88 615) - Abbey of Vallombrosa –Dell'Ugolino golf course (18-hole) in Grassina. **Open** All year.

Close to the Palazzo Pitti and the Boboli Gardens, the Villa Carlotta is an old patrician villa which has retained its nice proportions and harmony, which means that not far from the historic city center you can enjoy peace and calm, and relax after sightseeing in a large garden. The hotel is comfortable and well-equipped, service is efficient and friendly. The change in furniture has made the decor fresher and more modern. Depsite these improvements, prices remain moderate when one considers the quality of the amenities on offer.

How to get there *(Map 10): Towards Forte Belvedere - Porta Romana.*

Hotel Hermitage

50122 Firenze
Piazza del Pesce - Vicolo Marzio, 1 (Ponte Vecchio)
Tel. 055-28 72 16 - Fax 055-21 22 08 - Sig. Scarcelli
E-mail: florence@hermitagehotel.com - Web: www.hermitagehotel.com

Category ★★★ **Rooms** 29 with air-conditioning, telephone, bath (jacuzzi), WC, satellite TV –
Elevator. **Price** Single 350,000L, double 410,000L. **Meals** Breakfast included, served 7:30-9:30.
Restaurant See pp. 549-553. **Credit cards** Visa, Eurocard, MasterCard. **Pets** Small dogs allowed.
Nearby Events in Firenze: Scoppio del Carro on Easter morning, Festa del Grillo Ascension Day,
musical May, antiques biennale in odd years - Fiesole - Charterhouse of Galluzzo - Florentine villas
and gardens (tel. palazzo Pitti: 055 23 88 615) - Abbey of Vallombrosa – Dell'Ugolino golf course (18-
hole) in Grassina. **Open** All year.

This small hotel takes up the entire building next to the Ponte Vecchio. The
rooms have been redecorated; they are comfortable; each one done in a
slightly different antiquated style and all have double-pane windows, which
makes them pretty soundproof. The quietest rooms are those on the courtyard,
especially Rooms 13 and 14; but now that the area has become a pedestrian
zone, you may sleep just as well on the streetside. What made us choose this
hotel was its good prices and its terrace with an unforgettable view of the
Ponte Vecchio and the Pitti Palace on one side and the dome of the Duomo and
the rooftops of the Signoria on the other. If you are traveling alone, reserve the
terrace-level room. It is hard to park, but the hotel can direct you to the nearest
garage.

How to get there (Map 10): Next to Ponte Vecchio.

Hotel Loggiato dei Serviti

50122 Firenze
Piazza della SS. Annunziata, 3
Tel. 055-28 95 92 - Fax 055-28 95 95 - Sig. Budini Gattai
E-mail: loggiato.dei.serviti.@italyhotel.com

Category ★★★ **Rooms** 25 and 4 apartments with air-conditioning, telephone, bath or shower, WC, TV, minibar – Elevator. **Price** Single 250,000L, double 370,000L, suite 390-750,000L. **Meals** Breakfast included, served 7:15-10:00. **Restaurant** See pp. 549-553. **Credit cards** All major. **Pets** Dogs allowed (with extra charge). **Nearby** Events in Firenze: Scoppio del Carro on Easter morning, Festa del Grillo Ascension Day, musical May, antiques biennale in odd years - Fiesole - Charterhouse of Galluzzo - Florentine villas and gardens (tel. palazzo Pitti: 055 23 88 615) - Abbey of Vallombrosa –Dell'Ugolino golf course (18-hole) in Grassina. **Open** All year.

One of our favorites in Firenze, this hotel is on the Piazza della SS. Annunziata, just across from the Hospital of the Innocents. Like the hospital, it was designed by Brunelleschi, a brilliant architect of the Tuscan Rennaissance. The hotel decor is simple and elegant, respectful of the archictectural proportions of the period. The rooms are spare and charming; some open onto the square and have views of the equestrian statue of Ferdinand I of Médicis and the portico by Brunelleschi, embellished with medallions by Della Robbia. The other rooms open onto the Accademia garden and are quieter. The ones on the top floor have a nice view of the Duomo. The square has been surprisingly protected from the hustle and bustle of tourists; no café terraces or souvenir shops disturb the peace and quiet at nightfall–only the sound of swallows playing under the portico arches can be heard.

How to get there *(Map 10): From the piazza del Duomo via the Via dei Servi.*

Hotel Splendor

50129 Firenze
Via San Gallo, 30
Tel. 055-48 34 27 - Fax 055-46 12 76 - Sig. and Sig.ra Masoero
E-mail: info@hotelsplendor.it - Web: www.hotelsplendor.it

Category ★★★ **Rooms** 31 with air-conditioning, telephone, bath, WC, satellite TV, safe, minibar. **Price** Single 200,000L, double 300,000L, triple 380,000L. **Meals** Breakfast included, served 7:30-10:00. **Restaurant** See pp. 549-553. **Credit cards** All major. **Pets** Dogs not allowed. **Nearby** Events in Firenze: Scoppio del Carro on Easter morning, Festa del Grillo Ascension Day, musical May, antiques biennale in odd years - Fiesole - Charterhouse of Galluzzo - Florentine villas and gardens (tel. palazzo Pitti: 055 23 88 615) - Abbey of Vallombrosa — Dell'Ugolino golf course (18-hole) in Grassina. **Closed** Mar — Apr.

The 19th-century building that houses the Hotel Splendor is ideally located just a few steps from the San Marco convent, famous for its frescoes by Fra Angelico. The friendly welcome makes you feel right at home in the softly-lighted and elegantly-furnished salons with their oak floors, cozy armchairs, antique Persian rugs and lovely bouquets of flowers. The breakfast room is particularly attractive with its mural paintings and large French windows opening on a flower-decked terrace where you can take your breakfast if you so desire. You can use the place as a reading room as well, and if you want to brush up on the history of Florence, the owner will offer you an interesting little volume of stories published by the hotel. The rooms are soundproofed and decorated in the same good taste. The ones most in demand are those which face San Marco. A noteworthy nearby place for dinner is the Trattoria Tito.

How to get there *(Map 10): Near the piazza San Marco.*

Hotel Morandi alla Crocetta

50121 Firenze
Via Laura, 50
Tel. 055-234 47 47 - Fax 055-248 09 54 - Sig.ra Doyle Antuono
E-mail: welcome@hotelmorandi.it - Web: www.hotelmorandi.it

Category ★★★ **Rooms** 10 with air-conditioning, telephone, shower, WC, TV, minibar. **Price** Single 180,000L, double 290,000L, triple 380,000L. **Meals** Breakfast 20,000L, served 8:00AM-12:00PM. **Restaurant** See pp. 549-553. **Credit cards** All major. **Pets** Small dogs allowed. **Facilities** Garage (30,000L). **Nearby** Events in Firenze: Scoppio del Carro on Easter morning, Festa del Grillo Ascension Day, musical May, antiques biennale in odd years - Fiesole - Charterhouse of Galluzzo - Florentine villas and gardens (tel. palazzo Pitti: 055 23 88 615) - Abbey of Vallombrosa — Dell'Ugolino golf course (18-hole) in Grassina. **Open** All year.

The little Hotel Morandi Alla Crocetta is run by the delightful Kathleen Doyle Antuono who came to Florence for the first time many years ago when she was only 12. The pensione occupies part of a monastery built during the Renaissance on a small street near the Piazza della SS. Annunziata. The interior is as comfortable as in British homes, and the rooms all have bathrooms and air-conditioning. The decor is very tasteful; each room has antique furniture and beautiful collector's items (but with time the whole will need a thorough redecoration). Two of them have a beautiful flower-covered terrace on a countryard. The atmosphere of the hotel is quiet and serene.

How to get there (Map 10): Near Piazza della SS. Annunziata.

Hotel Pensione Pendini

50123 Firenze
Via Strozzi, 2
Tel. 055-21 11 70 - Fax 055-28 18 07 - Sigg. Abolaffio
E-mail: pendini@dada.it - Web: www.tiac.net/users/pendini

Category ★★★ **Rooms** 42 with air-conditioning, telephone, bath or shower, WC, satellite TV – Elevator. **Price** Single 140-180,000L, double 190-260,000L. **Meals** Breakfast included, served 7:30-10:00. **Restaurant** See pp. 549-553. **Credit cards** All major. **Pets** Small dogs allowed. **Nearby** Events in Firenze: Scoppio del Carro on Easter morning, Festa del Grillo Ascension Day, musical May, antiques biennale in odd years - Fiesole - Charterhouse of Galluzzo - Florentine villas and gardens (tel. palazzo Pitti: 055 23 88 615) - Abbey of Vallombrosa – Dell'Ugolino golf course (18-hole) in Grassina. **Open** All year.

When you cross the large Piazza della Repubblica or stop and have a drink on the terrace of the Gilli or the Giubbe Rosse, you won't be able to keep from noticing the building with the immense sign, which since 1879 has advertised the pensione within. The entrance is on a side street and an elevator will take you to the right floor. You will have an immediate impression of comfort as you walk in, and you won't be disappointed. All the rooms are large, mainly done up in a simple, flowered style, with small but functional bathrooms. For the sake of peace and quiet it is better not to sleep in those that overlook the Piazza della Repubblica which is outside the pedestrian area. Having said that, the double glazing is very efficient. A precious find in view of its position, the excellent welcome, the very decent level of comfort and the very reasonable prices.

How to get there *(Map 10): In the town center, near Piazza della Repubblica, entrance via Strozzi.*

Pensione Annalena

50127 Firenze
Via Romana, 34
Tel. 055-22 24 02/22 24 39 - Fax 055-22 24 03 - Sig. Salvestrini
E-mail: info@hotelannalena.it - Web: www.annalena.it

Category ★★★ **Rooms** 20 with telephone, bath or shower, WC, satellite TV, safe. **Price** Single 160-200,000, double 230-280,000L. **Meals** Breakfast included, served 8:00-10:00. **Restaurant** See pp. 549-553. **Credit cards** All major. **Pets** Dogs allowed. **Facilities** Parking (20,000L). **Nearby** Events in Firenze: Scoppio del Carro on Easter morning, Festa del Grillo Ascension Day, musical May, antiques biennale in odd years - Fiesole - Charterhouse of Galluzzo - Florentine villas and gardens (tel. palazzo Pitti: 055 23 88 615) - Abbey of Vallombrosa – Dell'Ugolino golf course (18-hole) in Grassina. **Open** All year (except May).

Located a few steps from the Pitti Palace and the Boboli Gardens, the former 15th-century palace was the home of the Orlandini and Medici families before becoming the property of the beautiful Annalena who, after a tragic love story, withdrew from the world and left her palace to the Dominicans. The place is steeped in history. The former reception hall has been turned into a large entrance area where vestiges of the old frescoes are still visible, as well as several salons and a breakfast room. The rooms furnished in traditional style are not very spacious and the bathrooms are even smaller. Our favorites are those that face the gallery with a view of the old gardens, now a tree nursery (Numbers 19, 20 and 21) and those giving onto the terrace.

How to get there *(Map 10): Near the Palazzo Pitti. You can take the via Romana at Piazzale di Porta Romana.*

Hotel Tornabuoni Beacci

50123 Firenze
Via Tornabuoni, 3
Tel. 055-21 26 45 / 26 83 77 - Fax 055-28 35 94 - Famiglia Bechi
E-mail: beacci:tornabuoni@italyhotel.com
Web: www.italyhotel.com/firenze/beacci_tornabuoni

Category ★★★ **Rooms** 29 with air-conditioning, telephone, bath or shower, WC, satellite TV, minibar – Elevator. **Price** Single 220-260,000L, double 320-400,000L, suite 500-700,000L. **Meals** Breakfast included, served 7:00-10:30. **Restaurant** Service 12:30PM-2:30PM, 7:30PM-9:30PM - mealtime specials, also à la carte (50,000L) - Italian cuisine. **Credit cards** All major. **Pets** Small dogs allowed (5,000L). **Facilities** Garage. **Nearby** Events in Firenze: Scoppio del Carro on Easter morning, Festa del Grillo Ascension Day, musical May, antiques biennale in odd years - Fiesole - Charterhouse of Galluzzo - Florentine villas and gardens (tel. palazzo Pitti: 055 23 88 615) - Abbey of Vallombrosa – Dell'Ugolino golf course (18-hole) in Grassina. **Open** All year.

This hotel, on the upper floors of a 14th-century palace, shares one of the elegant streets of Firenze with famous fashion designers and jewelers. It is one of Firenze's oldest hotels; Bismarck, himself, once stayed here. Today, many Americans like come to enjoy the excellent cuisine, the comfortable rooms with their painted furniture, the suites which can house several guests, the pretty terrace on the roof and the atmosphere of a charming family pensione. Note that special rates can be arranged for parties of ten or more. The welcome is very friendly. You can park the car in a garage close by and have access to it whenever you want.

How to get there *(Map 10): In the town center. Via lungarno Guicciardini, Ponte S. Trinita and via Tornabuoni.*

Hotel David

50129 Firenze
Viale Michelangelo, 1
Tel. 055-681 16 95 - Fax 055-680 602 - Sig. Cecioni
E-mail: david@italyhotel.com - Web: www.davidhotel.com

Category ★★★ **Rooms** 26 with air-conditioning, soundproofing, telephone, bath or shower, WC, TV, minibar. **Price** Double 270,000L. **Meals** Breakfast included, served 7:30-10:30. **Restaurant** See pp. 549-553. **Credit cards** All major. **Pets** Dogs allowed. **Facilities** Parking. **Nearby** Events in Firenze: Scoppio del Carro on Easter morning, Festa del Grillo Ascension Day, musical May, antiques biennale in odd years - Fiesole - Charterhouse of Galluzzo - Florentine villas and gardens (tel. palazzo Pitti: 055 23 88 615) - Abbey of Vallombrosa – Dell'Ugolino golf course (18-hole) in Grassina. **Open** All year.

Charm and comfort in this little villa that was enlarged when the Hotel David was created. The owner, Giovanni Cecioni, has recreated the ambiance of a private house by giving each bedroom a personalized decor. Antique furniture, either belonging to the family or acquired from local dealers, contribute to the intimate feel. The same is true for the living room, which is arranged in different areas for reading, writing or playing cards. The light from a large picture window and the foliage in the little garden add to the charm. And you don't have to search for a restaurant for dinner - the hotel has arrangements with several neighborhood trattorie.

How to get there *(Map 10): Near Arno (lungarno).*

Hotel Botticelli

50123 Firenze
Via Taddea, 8
Tel. 055-29 09 05 - Fax 055-29 43 22 - Fabrizio Gheri
E-mail: botticelli@fi.flashnet.it - Web: www.panoramahotelsitaly.com

Category ★★★ **Rooms** 34 with air-conditioning, telephone, bath or shower, WC, satellite TV, minibar, safe – Elevator. **Price** Single 230,000L, double 370,000L, triple +30%. **Meals** Breakfast included, served 7:15-10:00. **Restaurant** See pp. 549-553. **Credit cards** All major. **Pets** Small dogs allowed. **Facilities** Parking. **Nearby** Events in Firenze: Scoppio del Carro on Easter morning, Festa del Grillo Ascension Day, musical May, antiques biennale in odd years - Fiesole - Charterhouse of Galluzzo - Florentine villas and gardens (tel. palazzo Pitti: 055 23 88 615) - Abbey of Vallombrosa – Dell'Ugolino golf course (18-hole) in Grassina. **Open** All year.

The Hotel Botticelli is in the heart of the historic center of the city, near the very lively market of San Lorenzo. It is a 16th-century palazzo with arched windows which has been enlarged by the addition of a section built in the 19th Century. The vaulted ceilings of the reception area and the breakfast room on the ground floor still have their frescoes of cherubs on a flowered background. The little alleyway that once ran between the two buildings has since been covered over and made into a pleasant sitting room. Equally charming is the maze of corridors on the upper floors, which reveals the complex rearrangements that have taken place in these old palazzi. The bedrooms are spacious, more simple than the rest but elegantly decorated. The best place to stay is on the upper floors on a level with the roofs of Florence and the dome of the Duomo, a view that can also be admired from the large, divinely proportioned Renaissance loggia which is now a small terrace for aperitifs.

How to get there *(Map 10): Near Plaza San Lorenzo.*

Residenza Johanna I

50129 Firenze
Via Bonifacio Lupi, 14
Tel. 055-48 18 96 - Fax 055-48 27 21 - Sig.ra Gulmanelli and Sig.ra Arrighi
E-mail: lupi@johanna.it

Rooms 9 with shower or bath and WC, TV –ELevator. **Price** Single 80,000L, double 130,000L. **Meals** No breakfast. **Restaurant** See p. 549-553. **Credit cards** Not accepted. **Pets** Dogs not allowed. **Facilities** Garage (22,000L). **Nearby** Events in Firenze: Scoppio del Carro on Easter morning, Festa del Grillo Ascension Day, musical May, antiques biennale in odd years - Fiesole - Charterhouse of Galluzzo - Florentine villas and gardens (tel. palazzo Pitti: 055 23 88 615) - Abbey of Vallombrosa – Dell'Ugolino golf course (18-hole) in Grassina. **Open** All year.

In the heart of Florence, two young women had the unusual idea to transform one floor of a large building into a residential hotel. Built around two long corridors, it is like a real apartment, with a number of small bedrooms, nearly all with a private bath. There is no bar or television or breakfast room (though there is a kettle to prepare your morning tea or coffee), but it has an intimacy that no hotel can provide, and a gentle, tasteful decor that adds to the quiet comfort. You have your own keys, which makes you feel quite at home. And for Florence, the prices are exceptionally low. So why not try living like a Florentine for a few days?

How to get there *(Map 10): In town center, 10 minutes from Duomo.*

Residenza Johanna II

50129 Firenze
Via delle Cinque Giornate, 12
Tel. and Fax 055-47 33 77 – Sig.ra Gulmanelli
E-mail: cinquegiornate@johanna.it

Rooms 6 (3 with air-conditiong and double-glaging) with telephone (on request), bath or shower, WC, satellite TV. **Price** Double 140,0000L, triple 170,000L. **Meals** Breakfast included. **Restaurant.** See pp. 549-553. **Credit cards** Not accepted. **Pets** Dogs not allowed. **Facilities** Parking. **Nearby** Events in Firenze: Scoppio del Carro on Easter morning, Festa del Grillo Ascension Day, musical May, antiques biennale in odd years - Fiesole - Charterhouse of Galluzzo - Florentine villas and gardens (tel. palazzo Pitti: 055 23 88 615) - Abbey of Vallombrosa – Dell'Ugolino golf course (18-hole) in Grassina. **Open** All year.

The owners of the Residenza Johanna have built on their success by adding a twin. Finding such comfortable, well-kept and well-decorated rooms (most of them are quite spacious as well) with such attention to decor and furnishings - and at such prices - is something of a feat in Italy (and we can't help wondering why this is?). Perhaps the trick is that the service is left up to the clients: For example, if you like, they will give you a portable phone (but only to phone within Italy), you prepare your own breakfast in your room (each room has a kettle with tea, coffee, camomile and biscuits) and you have your own key so you are free to come and go at any hour. Three rooms overlook the street, air-conditioning and double-glazing have provided an effective solution to the problem of noise, so they are as pleasant as the ones on the second floor (not air-conditioned), which overlook the garden. The latter is also used for parking, but in Florence, who can complain? On the ground floor, there is a pleasant salon-library where you can consult a fine collection of art books on Florence and Italy.

How to get there *(Map 10): 15 minutes from the duomo.*

Villa La Massa

Candeli 50012 Firenze
Via della Massa, 24
Tel. 055-62 611 - Fax 055-633 102 - Sig. Ottazzi
E-mail: villamassa@galactica.it - Web: www.villamassa.com

Category ★★★★★ **Rooms** 38 with air-conditioning, telephone, bath, WC, satellite TV, minibar, safe – Elevator. **Price** Single 387-620,000L, double 590-830,000L, suite 970-1 452,000L. **Meals** Breakfast (buffet) included, served 7:30-10:30 - half board +105,000L (per pers.). **Restaurant** Service 12:30PM-2:30PM, 7:30PM-10:00PM - mealtime specials 90-140,000L, also à la carte - Regional cooking. **Credit cards** All major. **Pets** Small dogs allowed in bedrooms. **Facilities** Swimming pool, parking. **Nearby** Events in Firenze: Scoppio del Carro on Easter morning, Festa del Grillo Ascension Day, musical May, antiques biennale in odd years - Fiesole - Charterhouse of Galluzzo - Florentine villas and gardens (tel. palazzo Pitti: 055 23 88 615) - Abbey of Vallombrosa – Dell'Ugolino golf course (18-hole) in Grassina. **Closed** Dec - Feb.

David Bowie was so attracted by the idea of staying eight kilometers outside Florence in the villa that once belonged to the Medici on the banks of the Arno that he rented the whole house to celebrate his wedding. Bought by the Villa d'Este group, the hotel has recoved all its former glory. The great hall with its arcades surmounted by loggias is magnificent. The rooms have all been restored in a style of discreet luxury with old furniture and flowered prints which are well suited to the view over the countryside. The Verrochio restaurant is also housed in a fine room where a group of pilasters supports the arcades and vaults of the ceiling. In winter, one can enjoy its refined cuisine by the warmth of a log fire, while in summer meals are served under the loggia on the banks of the river. The garden is full of flowers, the swimming pool ideal for the Tuscan heat and the kilometers between here and the historic town center are not a problem, because a shuttle bus goes to and from the Ponte Vecchio every hours between 9:00AM and 7:00PM.

How to get there *(Map 10): Towards Pontassieve, Candeli.*

Villa San Michele

Fiesole 50014 Firenze
Via Doccia, 4
Tel. 055-567 8200 - Fax 055-567 8250 - Sig. Saccani
E-mail: reservations@villasanmichele.net

Category ★★★★★ **Rooms** 41 with air-conditioning, telephone, bath, WC, satellite TV, safe, minibar. **Price** With half board: Single 740,000L, double 1 430-1 810,000L, suite 2 360-3 000,000L. **Meals** Breakfast included (buffet), served 7:00-10:30 - full board +110,000L. **Restaurant** Service 1:00PM-2:45PM, 8:00PM-9:45PM - mealtime specials 130-160,000L, also à la carte - Tuscan and Italian cuisine. **Credit cards** All major. **Pets** Small dogs allowed (except in restaurant and in swimming pool). **Facilities** Heated swimming pool, parking. **Nearby** Events in Firenze: Scoppio del Carro on Easter morning, Festa del Grillo Ascension Day, musical May, antiques biennale in odd years - Fiesole - Charterhouse of Galluzzo - Florentine villas and gardens (tel. palazzo Pitti: 055 23 88 615) - Abbey of Vallombrosa – Dell'Ugolino golf course (18-hole) in Grassina. **Closed** Dec – mid Mar.

The Villa San Michele is a monument of the international hotel trade. A luxury hotel, to be sure, but with, in addition, the magic that comes from sheer beauty: the beauty of the site, for one, and then the beauty of the architecture. The former monastery that houses the San Michele is said to have been designed by Michelangelo himself. The villa with its gardens and terraces that take on a rosy glow as the sun sets over the Duomo and the rooftops of Florence is an unforgettable spectacle, as unforgettable as the elegance of the rooms, the meals and the service.

How to get there *(Map 10): 8km north of Firenze. Bus for Firenze 200 meters from the hotel.*

Pensione Bencistà

Fiesole 50014 Firenze
Via Benedetto da Maiano, 4
Tel. and Fax 055-59 163 - Sig. Simone Simoni
E-mail: bencista@vol.it

Category ★★★ **Rooms** 44 with telephone, bath or shower, WC. **Price** With half board 140-160,000L, full board 160-180,000L. **Meals** Breakfast included, served 7:30-10:00. **Restaurant** Service 1:00PM-2:00PM, 7:30PM-8:30PM - mealtime specials - Traditional Tuscan cuisine. **Credit cards** Not accepted. **Pets** Dogs allowed (except in restaurant). **Facilities** Parking. **Nearby** Events in Firenze: Scoppio del Carro on Easter morning, Festa del Grillo Ascension Day, musical May, antiques biennale in odd years - Fiesole - Charterhouse of Galluzzo - Florentine villas and gardens (tel. palazzo Pitti: 055 23 88 615) - Abbey of Vallombrosa — Dell'Ugolino golf course (18-hole) in Grassina. **Open** Feb 15 – Nov 15.

On the hills of Fiesole, this family pensione is a charming establishment for those who love Tuscany. It has been simply and carefully decorated with antique furniture and travel souvenirs. The library, filled with books in English, is the perfect place to spend some quiet moments. The terrace is in a natural setting, and the garden is full of flowers and trees of diverse species. The rooms, which are made more comfortable year after year, are delightful. The home-style cuisine adds to the relaxed family atmosphere.

How to get there *(Map 10): 8km north of Firenze. Bus no. 7 for Firenze 200 meters from the hotel, every 20mn.*

Hotel Villa Le Rondini

50139 Firenze - Trespiano
Via Bolognese Vecchia, 224
Tel. 055-40 00 81 - Fax 055-26 82 12 - Sig.ra Reali
E-mail: mailbox@villalerondini.it - Web: www.villalerondini.it

Category ★★★ **Rooms** 43 with air-conditioning, telephone, bath or shower, WC, satellite TV, minibar. **Price** Single 150-270,000L, double 180-330,000L, suite 250-420,000L. **Meals** Breakfast included, served 7:30-10:00 - half board +60,000L (per pers.). **Restaurant** Service 12:30PM-2:00PM, 7:30PM-9:00PM - mealtime specials 50-80,000L, also à la carte - Italian and international cuisine with farm produce. **Credit cards** All major. **Pets** Dogs allowed (10,000L). **Facilities** Swimming pool, tennis (20,000L), sauna, parking. **Nearby** Events in Firenze: Scoppio del Carro on Easter morning, Festa del Grillo Ascension Day, musical May, antiques biennale in odd years - Fiesole - Charterhouse of Galluzzo - Florentine villas and gardens (tel. palazzo Pitti: 055 23 88 615) - Abbey of Vallombrosa – Dell'Ugolino golf course (18-hole) in Grassina. **Open** All year.

Y ou reach the magnificent Rondini estate by driving through a vast olive grove. The hotel property spreads over 20 hectares and the guest rooms are divided into three villas. The ones in the original old house have the charm of their age and have been renovated to include modern comforts. Those in the two annexes, situated near the entrance to the estate, are less appealing but every bit as comfortable. It's a nice place, all in all, especially in summer, when the countryside is so beautiful. And there's no problem getting into Florence — the bus stop is just in front of the villa's gate.

How to get there *(Map 10): 7km north of Firenze, towards Fortessa da Bano until the Piazza della Libertà, via Bolognese. Bus no. 25 in front of the hotel entrance, every 20mn.*

Fattoria Il Milione 🍷

50100 Firenze - Giogoli
Via di Giogoli, 14
Tel. 055-20 48 713 - Fax 055-20 48 046 - Sig.ra Jessica Guscelli

Apartments 6 with Kitchen, bath. **Price** Apart 150,000L (2 pers.), 300,000L (4 pers.). **Evening meals** By reservation. Mealtime specials 50,000L (all incl.) - Regional cooking. **Credit cards** No accepted. **Pets** Dogs allowed on request. **Facilities** Swimming pool, parking. **Nearby** Events in Firenze: Scoppio del Carro on Easter morning, Festa del Grillo Ascension Day, musical May, antiques biennale in odd years - Fiesole - Charterhouse of Galluzzo - Florentine villas and gardens (tel. palazzo Pitti: 055 23 88 615) - Abbey of Vallombrosa – Dell'Ugolino golf course (18-hole) in Grassina. **Open** All year.

Il Milione di Brandimarte is a model of the art of living, and it would be a pity just to drop your luggage there and go off exploring the surroundings. Here the guests can truly share the emotions and the harmony of this unique land, "daughter of nature and of man." Life flows to the rhythm of the seasons and the work on the farm - plowing, seeding, harvesting, crop-picking. The countryside is always a visual delight - silver in the gray light of winter, splashed with bright color before the olive picking, when orange nets are spread out beneath the trees, red-hued as the sun sets over Florence. Like Brandimarte (the famous Florentine goldsmith) and Jessica and their seven children, we should also celebrate nature around their large table, where excellent *table d'hôte* meals are served. And if you're curious about the name of the place, the story is this: to open this farm, Brandimarte asked his friends for *un milione* in exchange for one of his works. "Craftwork and farmwork are genetically linked by a common root," says the man who is both artist and farmer.

How to get there *(Map 10): A1, Florenz-Certosa exit, towards Florenz, then right towards Scandicci.*

Tenuta Le Viste

Mosciano 50018 Scandicci
Via del Leone, 11
Tel. 055-76 85 43 - Fax 055-76 85 31 - Sig.ra Alexandra Ern
E-mail: birgiter@tin.it - Web: www.tenuta-leviste.it

Rooms 4 with air-conditioning, telephone, bath, WC, satellite TV, minibar, safe. **Price** Double 350-390,000L, family room 590,000L. **Meals** Breakfast included, served 8:30-10:30. **Restaurant** See pp. 549-553. **Credit cards** All major. **Pets** Dogs not allowed. **Facilities** Swimming pool, parking. **Nearby** Events in Firenze: Scoppio del Carro on Easter morning, Festa del Grillo Ascension Day, musical May, antiques biennale in odd years - Fiesole - Charterhouse of Galluzzo - Florentine villas and gardens (tel. palazzo Pitti: 055 23 88 615) - Abbey of Vallombrosa – Dell'Ugolino golf course (18-hole) in Grassina. **Closed** Dec 10 – Jan 10.

Situated eight kilometers outside Florence, the Tenuta Le Viste has been totally restored so that it can conveniently share the house with guests. You will not be wondering for long after your arrival why it is called "Le Viste": the great lawn in front of the house puts the countryside and the vity of Florence at your feet. There are only four rooms. The ones we prefer are those on the first floor around the little library, two of which can commuicate with each other. The largest and finest room is a duplex with a marble bathroom and a jacuzzi. The room overlooking the terrace on the ground floor is best for a guest travelling alone. The décor, combining ancient and modern, is very meticulous, even fussy. The dining room, in which breakfast is served when the weather is not good enough for the use of the terrace, is a fine room with beams, fireplace and furniture of the 17th Century. A very elegant little drawing room is also at your disposal. Not truly in the countryside, not really in town, but in the tranquillity of a garden with a view.

How to get there *(Map 10): 8km from Firenze. On A1, exit Firenze-Signa.*

Villa Villoresi

50019 Sesto Fiorentino (Firenze)
Via Ciampi, 2 - Colonnata
Tel. 055-44 32 12 - Fax 055-44 20 63 - Sig.ra Villoresi de Loche
E-mail: cvillor@tin.it - Web: www.ila-chateau.com/villores/

Category ★★★★ **Rooms** 28 with telephone, bath, WC, satellite TV – Wheelchair access. **Price** Single 180-260,000L, double 280-380,000L, double luxe 480,000L. **Meals** Breakfast 20,000L, served 7:00-10:30 - half board 225-295,000L (per pers., 3 days min.). **Restaurant** Service 12:00PM-2:30PM, 8:00PM-10:00PM - closed Mon (except for residents) - mealtime specials 50-55,000L, also à la carte - Specialties: Penne al coccio - Fagiano alla foglia di vite. **Credit cards** All major. **Pets** Dogs allowed. **Facilities** Swimming pool, parking. **Nearby** Sesto: Duomo and S. Maria dei Carceri, Castello dell'Imperatore in Prato, Firenze – Dell'Ugolino golf course (18-hole) in Grassina. **Open** All year.

The countryside around Florence has begun to suffer from urban sprawl and this Renaissance house, which used to be a country residence, now finds itself encircled by constructions of lesser interest. The house remains appealing, however, with its fresco-painted ceilings, panoramic or allegoric murals and portraits of the ancestors on the walls. A long loggia (the longest in Tuscany) extends the length of the second floor and overlooks the garden and the swimming pool (with snack bar). The dining room looks out on the cortile. Some of the bedrooms are of truly palatial dimensions and arriving via the gallery is a most impressive sight. Signora Villoresi will be very helpful with advice on the cultural aspects of your tour. The amenities are adequate. The great asset here is authenticity.

How to get there (Map 10): 10km northwest of Firenze, towards Prato-Calenzano. If you have a fax, ask for a plan.

Castello di Cafaggio

50023 Impruneta (Firenze)
Via del Ferrone, 58
Tel. 055-201 20 85 - Fax 055-231 46 33 - Sig. Enrico Bencii
E-mail: info@cafaggio.com - Web: www.cafaggio.com

Apartments 4 (2-6 pers.) with kitchen, shower, 1-2 bedrooms, TV. **Price** Apart. for 1 week 950-
1 550,000L. **Credit cards** Visa, Eurocard, MasterCard, Amex. **Pets** Dogs not allowed. **Facilities**
Cooking lessons, parking. **Nearby** Firenze - Charterhouse of Galluzzo - Greve in Chianti - Siena –
Dell'Ugolino golf course (18-hole) in Grassina. **Open** All year.

Impruneta is a wine-growing town on the Via del Chianti famous for two
important events: the wine harvest festival and the horse market which takes
place around the Feast of Saint Luke between October 15 and 18 (the event is
described in a series of engravings by Jacques Callot and the Venetian painter
Tiepolo came here to draw from life). This is also a center of the garden pottery
which has made the region famous. The Castello is very poorly signposted in
the village, no doubt because it can be seen on its hill, rising out of a grove of
olive trees, overlooking the valley of the Greve. The château goes back to the
trecento and has always exploited the traditional agricultural resources of the
area - as it still does, with a special mention for its olive oil. The apartments
are in the main part of the farm around a large terrace and decorated simply, in
country style. According to size, they have a real kichen or a kitchenette, a
bedroom and a living room with a folding bed; only the Ulivo has two rooms
upstairs (note that prices are according to the number of beds). The owners live
in the farm and you will only be able to use the fine Art Nouveau dining room
when tastings are held and the music rooms, in which Puccini worked, when
concerts are given in the château.

How to get there *(Map 10): 14km from Florence. On A1, exit Firenze-Certosa.*

Residenza San Niccolo d'Olmeto

Le Valli 50066 Incisa Valdarno (Firenze)
Tel. 055-23 45 005 - Fax 055-24 02 82
Sig.ra Valenti Cavagnari
E-mail: jandj@dada.it - Web: www.jandjhotel.com

Apartments 6 with kitchen, shower, WC, 2 with TV. **Price** 1 week 950,000L (2 pers.); extra bed 200,000L. **Credit cards** All major. **Pets** Dogs not allowed. **Facilites** Swimming pool, parking. **Nearby** Firenze - Le Valdarno between Firenze and Arezzo. **Open** Apr – Oct.

Only 18 kilometers from Florence, after crossing a landscape that lacks the gentle charm of the best Tuscan countryside, not far from the autostrada, you will be all the more surprised to come upon the orchards and olive groves that surround the former convent of San Niccolo. Beautifully restored and very well-kept by the Cavagnari family (who earlier won distinction with the Hotel J & J in Florence), the renovation is both rustic and elegant. The apartments are in the building near the cloister and the Romanesque chapel. They are all quite comfortable with a well-equipped kitchen area, functional shower rooms and meticulous decoration: floors of terra cotta tile and modern furnishings that set off a number of well-chosen antiques. Our preference goes to those that are not near the old orange grove. When the lemon and mandarin trees are in bloom their scent is all-pervasive, further adding to the serene atmosphere of the estate.

How to get there *(Map 10): 18km from Firenze via A1 Incisa Valdarno exit, then SS69 to Burchio, then Le Valli.*

Salvadonica

Val di Pesa - 50024 Mercatale (Firenze)
Via Grevigiana, 82
Tel. 055-821 80 39 - Fax 055-821 80 43 - Sig. Baccetti
E-mail: info@salvadonica.it - Web: www.salvadonica.com

Rooms 5 and 10 apartments with telephone, bath, WC, TV – Wheelchair access. **Price** Single 160,000L, double 190-220,000L, apartments (by request). **Meals** Breakfast included, served 8:00-10:00. **Restaurant** Snacks avalaible, or in San Casciano and in Val di pesa, see p. 554. **Credit cards** All major. **Pets** Dogs not allowed. **Facilities** Swimming pool with whirlpool, tennis, parking. **Nearby** Firenze - Certosa di Galluzzo - Impruneta - Siena – Dell'Ugolino golf course (18-hole) in Grassina. **Open** Apr – Nov 16.

Two Tuscan farmhouses, dating from the 14th century, have been made into this luxurious hotel in the Tuscan countryside. Its restoration is an example of one of the more successful in the region because the rustic feeling of the original buildings has been maintained in the renovation. They used old materials and decorated the place with beautiful polished farm furniture, but also added modern conveniences. The hotel consists mostly of small apartments, which you are advised to rent by the week. The housework is done for you every day. You can have breakfast around a communal table at the hotel and dine pleasantly in San Casciano and the surrounding area in the evening. You can buy wine and olive oil produced on the farm.

How to get there *(Map 10): 20km from Firenze via A1, Firenze-Certosa exit, then highway towards Siena, San Casciano exit; in San Casciano, go left towards Mercatale.*

Castello di Montegufoni

50020 Montagnana (Firenze)
Via Montegufoni, 20
Tel. 0571-67 11 31 - Fax 0571-67 15 14 - Sig. Posarelli
E-mail: mgufoni@sienanet.it

Apartments 25 fully equipped, public phone. **Price** For 2 pers., 1 000,000L (week), for 4 pers. 1 400,000L (week), for 6 pers. 1 600,000L (week). **Meals** Breakfast (fresh bread) by request. **Restaurant** By request in "La Tavena," Mon, Wed, Fri. **Credit cards** Not accepted. **Pets** Dogs not allowed. **Facilities** 2 swimming pools, parking. **Nearby** Firenze - Certosa di Galluzzo - Impruneta (Church of Santa Maria dell'Impruneta) - Siena – Dell'Ugolino golf course (18-hole) in Grassina. **Open** Mar 26 – Nov.

While you're in Florence, live like a Florentine — or better still, like a Florentine noble, in a castle of your own, the Castello di Montegufoni, some 15 kilometers from Florence. It is complete with lush gardens, towering cypresses and terra cotta jars overflowing with flowers, and the façades in those wonderful muted colors that are unique to Florence. The well-appointed, sometimes even sumptuous, apartments can sleep up to six people. As for the service, it is so well-organized that you can be completely independent and at the same time have fresh bread delivered every morning for your breakfast. It is also possible to have dinner in, if you wish. To make sure no one will feel crowded, there are two swimming pools. This is the sort of place that will please parents and their children as well.

How to get there *(Map 10): 15km west of Firenze, via highway towards Livorno-Pisa, Ginestra exit; in Ginestra, follow the signs to Montespertoli. In Ginestra take dir. Montespertoli, turn right, go 4km to Baccaiano, then turn left, the castello is 1km on left.*

Fattoria La Loggia

50020 Montefiridolfi - San Casciano (Firenze)
Via Collina, 40
Tel. 055-82 44 288 - Fax 055-82 44 283 - Sig. Baruffaldi
E-mail: fatlaloggia@ftbcc.it - Web: www.fatlaloggia.it

Rooms 3 double and 11 apartments (for 2-6 pers.) with kitchen, rooms, living room, bath, WC. **Price** 180-250,000L (per 2 pers.), apart. 250-300,000L (per day per 2 pers.). **Restaurant** Wine tasting on request and snacks. Service 8:00PM-11:00PM - mealtime specials 45-55,000L - Tuscan cuisine with products from the farm. **Pets** Dogs allowed. **Facilities** Swimming pool, mountain bikes, riding. **Nearby** Firenze - Le Chianti - Certosa di Galluzzo - Impruneta (Church of Santa Maria dell'Impruneta) - Siena - Volterra - Pisa - San Gimignano — Dell'Ugolino golf course (18-hole) in Grassina. **Open** All year.

Y ou may have to pinch yourself to make sure you're not dreaming when you cross the Tuscan countryside to one of these beautiful farmhouses perched on top of a hill among a few cypress trees with a view of the little furrowed valleys. The Fattoria is not a hotel, but a functioning agricultural estate with a carefully restored Renaissance hamlet of small private houses, which have been decorated with Tuscan-style refinement. Here, you can move at your own pace, as you would in your own country house. La Loggia also houses a contemporary art museum and a European cultural center which caters to the many artists who come to work on the farm.

How to get there *(Map 10): 21km south of Firenze via A1, Firenze-Certosa exit; then via SS Firenze-Siena, Bargino exit.*

Villa Le Barone

50020 Panzano in Chianti (Firenze)
Via S. Leolino, 19
Tel. 055-85 26 21 - Fax 055-85 22 77 - Sig.ra Buonamici
E-mail: villalebarone@libero.it - Web: www.villalebarone.it

Category ★★★ **Rooms** 27 with telephone, bath or shower, WC. **Price** With half board 195-250,000L (per pers.). **Meals** Breakfast included, served 8:00-10:00. **Restaurant** Service 1:00PM-2:00PM, 7:30PM-9:00PM - mealtime specials 65,000L, à la carte - Tuscan cuisine. **Credit cards** All major. **Pets** Dogs not allowed. **Facilities** Swimming pool, tennis. **Nearby** Greve valley via S222 (vineyards of Chianti Classico from Greve to Gaiole) - Firenze - Siena – Dell'Ugolino golf course (18-hole) in Grassina. **Open** Apr – Oct.

The Villa Le Barone has always belonged to famous owners, once the Della Robbia family, today the *duchesa* Visconti. The outside of the house has kept its original appearance while the inside has been remodeled into an inviting and intimate home. Nothing here reminds you that you're in a hotel; the living room with its reading nook and chimney-corner, the cheery bedrooms with their antique beds and brightly-colored spreads, all have a very homey feel. The swimming pool is wonderfully landscaped, its lawns well-shaded against the hot sun of a Florentine summer. And from the tennis court, the view extends far into the countryside, with olive groves and vineyards of *Chianti Classico.*

How to get there *(Map 10): 33km south of Firenze via S222 to Panzano in Chianti via Greve in Chianti.*

La Sosta a' Busini

Castiglioni di Busini 50060 Rufina (Firenze)
Scoperto, 28
Tel. 055-839 78 09 - Fax 055-839 70 04
M-Rosaria and Marcello Nicolodi

Rooms 9 (1 with bath) and 5 apartments (2-7 pers.) with kitchen, bath or shower, WC. **Price** Rooms 170,000L (whitout bath)/180,000 (with bath), Apart./week 850-1,400,000L. **Meals** Breakfast in bedrooms, served 7:30-10:00 - half board 110,000L (per pers.). **Evening meals** Service 8:00PM. **Credit cards** Visa, Eurocard, MasterCard. **Pets** Dogs not allowed. **Facilities** Small swimming pool, tennis, parking. **Nearby** Valley of Mugello: Monastory of Santa Maria di Rosano, Vicchio, San Piero a Sieve, Scarperia, Convent of Bosco ai Frati, convent of Monte Senario a Bivigliano - Firenze **Open** All year.

This is large family estate that still cultivates its land and has opened some rooms in its fine Medici villa, while transforming some outbuildings into apartments. The whole has remained in its original state, which gives a general impression of neglect, while at the same time confering on it a sort of romantic and decadent charm. The region is splendid and the winding road bordered with cypress trees is the very image of postcard Tuscany. The villa itself overlooks an Italian garden planted with box trees among which are statues in the antique style. The interior of the house combines old family furniture and collections with more recent acquisitions, creating an informal and convivial atmosphere. In summer and winter one may meet pleasantly in the main living room around the fireplace or on its terrace opening on the garden. In the main, the rooms to have not been touched, which explains why most of them have to use a bathroom on the landing. On the other hand, you can light a fire in the fireplace of some of them.

How to get there *(Map 10): 30km east of Flroence. N67 towards Forli as far as Pontassieve, Rufina, then towards Borselli-Pomino for 3km.*

Fattoria di Petrognano

Petrognano
Pomino 50060 Rufina (Firenze)
Tel. 055-831 88 67 - Reservations: 055-26 087 68 - Fax 055-26 453 07
Sig.ra Galeotti-Ottieri
E-mail: petrognano@stayinitaly.com

Rooms 7 and 5 apartments (2-8 pers.) with telephone, bath or shower, WC. **Price** Double 130,000L, apart. 650,000-1 500,000L (1 week). **Meals** Breakfast included, served 8:30-10:00. **Restaurant** Service 1:00PM-2:00PM, 8:00PM-9:00PM - mealtime specials 25,000L - Farm produce. **Credit cards** All major. **Pets** Dogs allowed. **Facilities** Swimming pool, tennis, parking. **Nearby** Valley of Mugello: Monastery of Santa Maria di Rosano, Vicchio, San Piero a Sieve, Scarperia, Convent of Bosco ai Frati, convent of Monte Senario in Bivigliano – Scarperia and Poppi golf course (9-hole). **Open** May – Oct.

This handsome estate once belonged to the bishops of Fiesole who were responsible for the famous vineyard as far back as the Renaissance. The main building, which once housed the convent, has kept its noble proportions, antique floors and monumental fireplace. Several farmhouses that belong to the Fattoria have been restored, including the Locanda Patricino, whose rooms are simply furnished, decorated with a few old family portraits, but they have a breathtaking view over the surrounding hills. The one up in the attic has the finest panorama of all. For long family stays the apartments are best. Meals are served in the rustic dining room where it is a pleasure to sit around the large family table and partake of the specialties of the house (including beef raised on the estate) and drink an excellent Pomino, drawn from the vat. A pleasant way to sample the hospitality of an old Tuscan family.

How to get there *(Map 10): 30km from Firenze. Take the N67 road via Forlì to Pontassieve, Rufina and Castiglioni-Pomino.*

Villa Rigacci

50066 Vaggio - Reggello (Firenze)
Via Manzoni, 76
Tel. 055-865 67 18 / 865 65 62 - Fax 055-865 65 37 - Famiglia Pierazzi
E-mail: hotel@villarigacci.it - Web: www.villarigacci.it

Category ★★★★ **Rooms** 25 with air-conditioning, telephone, bath or shower, WC, TV, minibar.
Price Single 170,000L, double 260-310,000L, suite 350,000L; extra bed +45,000L. **Meals** Breakfast
included, served 7:30-10:30 - half board 160-200,000L and full board 190-230,000L. **Restaurant**
Service 12:00PM-2:00PM, 8:00PM-9:30PM - mealtime specials 50,000L, also à la carte - French and
Italian cuisine. **Credit cards** All major. **Pets** Dogs allowed. **Facilities** Swimming pool, parking. **Nearby**
Abbey of Vallombrosa - Church of Montemignaio - Castello Pretorio in Poppi - Firenze - Siena. **Open**
All year.

This old farmhouse, covered with vines and surrounded by woods, has a
personality of its own. Built in the 15th century, it is now run by the
Pierazzi family. Inside, a fireplace, a richly stocked library and family
furniture which recalls Signora Pierazzi's Provencal origins make for the sort
of convivial atmosphere one yearns to find on vacation. Each of the bedrooms
is different, but all are furnished in bright cheery colors and equipped with all
the amenities. In summer you may choose to spend a whole day between
garden and swimming pool instead of going sightseeing, and in the evening
you can dine at the Vieux Pressoir or in summer on its terrace, where in
addition to the usual Italian dishes, they serve Tuscan specialties.

How to get there *(Map 10): 30km southeast of Firenze via A1, Incisa exit,
number 24, towards Matassino and Vaggio.*

La Callaiola ♀

50021 Barberino Val d'Elsa (Firenze)
Strada di Magliano, 3
Tel. and Fax 055-80 76 598
Sig.ra J. Münchenbach

Rooms 2 (4 pers.) with bath, WC. **Price** 70,000L (per pers.). **Meals** Breakfast included. **Restaurant** In Colle Val d'Elsa, see p. 555. **Credit cards** Not accepted. **Pets** Dogs not allowed. **Facilities** Parking. **Nearby** Siena - Monteriggioni - Colle di Val d'Elsa - Firenze - San Gimignano - Certaldo - Castellina in Chianti - Volterra. **Open** All year (by reservation).

L a Callaiola is a working farm run by a friendly German woman who produces organically grown products. She and her Italian husband have restored this sturdy 18th-century building, keeping intact its rustic country air. A garden lawn surrounds the house with its flower-decked façades. All around are olive trees and fields of sunflowers. The Callaiola is run like a real guest house, that is, you live in the house along with the family and share in its daily life. The house is very pleasant, perfumed by bouquets of flowers and aromatic plants set out by Jocelyne, and by the scent of hay from outside. The bedrooms are soberly but charmingly furnished, with a theatrical touch that makes them look even nicer. You reach the bedrooms through the family living room. The atmosphere is informal and living together never feels awkward.

How to get there *(Map 13): 33km south of Firenze via A1, Firenze-Certosa exit; towards Siena, Tavarnelle exit.*

Il Paretaio 🌲

San Filippo 50021 Barberino Val d'Elsa (Firenze)
Strada delle Ginestre, 12
Tel. 055-80 59 218 - Fax 055-80 59 231 - Handy: 0338-737 96 26
Sig.ra de Marchi
E-mail: ilparetaio@tin.it - Web: www.ilparetaio.it

Rooms 8 with shower, WC. **Price** Double 120-160,000L; apart. (2-4 pers.) 700-1 400,000L.
Meals Breakfast included - half board 80-120,000L (per pers.). **Evening meals** Service 8:00PM -
mealtime specials - Traditional cuisine. **Credit cards** Not accepted. **Pets** Dogs allowed. **Facilities**
Riding (35,000L), swimming pool, parking. **Nearby** Siena - Monteriggioni - Colle di Val d'Elsa -
Firenze - San Gimignano - Certaldo - Castellina in Chianti - Volterra. **Open** All year.

What a wonderful place the Paretaio is for people who like to ride horses!
This beautiful estate, in the heart of the Tuscan countryside, is
surrounded by four hundred and ninety-five acres of woods, vineyards and
olive trees. The young owners have a passion for horses and are excellent
riders, skilled in dressage, offer a series of package rates ranging from a
weekend to a week, including classes to improve riding skills for children and
adults, courses on breaking in and training horses, and rides in the country. The
house and its decor are rustic and the rooms are large and nicely arranged. The
atmosphere is very warm, especially when guests gather together in the
evening around the big table for a good meal, and a great chianti. This hotel is
especially aimed at riders because you have to know and love horses to
understand the philosophy of the Paretaio. But if you simply enjoy conviviality
and the outdoors you will also like it here.

How to get there *(Map 13): 33km south of Firenze via A1, Firenze-Certosa
exit; towards Siena, Tavarnelle exit; go past Barberino Val d'Elsa, after 2km
take road on the right towerd San Filippo.*

La Spinosa 🌳

Scheto 50021 Barberino Val d'Elsa (Firenze)
Via le Masse, 8
Tel. 055-807 54 13 - Fax 055-806 62 14
E-mail: info@laspinosa.it - Web: www.laspinosa.it

Rooms 5 and 4 suite with bath. **Price** Double 240-280,000L. **Meals** Breakfast included, served 8:00-10:30 - half board 170-190,000L (per pers., 3 days min.) **Restaurant** Only for residents. Service snacks-bar 12:30PM-1:30PM, dinner 8:00PM - mealtime specials - Regional cooking. **Credit cards** Visa, Eurocard, Mastercard. **Pets** Dogs allowed. (+20,000L). **Facilities** Swimming pool, archery, parking. **Nearby** Siena - Monteriggioni - Colle Val d'Elsa - Firenze - San Gimignano - Certaldo - Castellina in Chianti - Volterra. **Closed** Jan and Feb.

From Barberino, take a dirt road which travels across country for two kilometers then ends in a cul de sac at La Spinosa. This is a beautiful old azienda agricola which manages its affairs in a very professional way. For the past fifteen years, its products have conformed with the biological agricultural programmes of the EEC and its wine, honey, oil, jam and flowers are sold directly through the wineshop Il Canto di Baccio in the center of Barberino. It agritourist activities are managed with the same efficency. The rooms are spacious and well-kept, with old furniture and very comfortable bathrooms. The same applies to the public areas: reading room, music room and a dining room with individual tables where you can taste the products of the house. The garden is well laid out with play areas and swimming pool. An ideal spot for the family.

How to get there *(Map 13): 33km south of Florence by SS2 (Quattro Corsie) towards Siena, exit Tavarnelle. In the village, follow the signs.*

Fattoria Casa Sola

Cortine 50021 Barberino Val d'Elsa (Firenze)
Tel. 055-807 50 28 - Fax 055-805 91 94
Sig. Gambaro
E-mail: casasola@chianticlassico.com

Apartments 6 (2-8 pers.) with 2-4 rooms, kitchen, sitting room, bath, WC. **Price** 65-70,000L (per pers. for 1 day). **Restaurant** In Colle Val d'Elsa, see p. 555. **Credit cards** Visa, Eurocard, MasterCard. **Pets** Dogs not allowed. **Facilities** Swimming pool, parking. **Nearby** Siena - Monteriggioni - Colle di Val d'Elsa - Firenze - San Gimignano - Certaldo - Castellina in Chianti - Volterra. **Open** All year.

The owners' home perched on a hilltop is impressive and of fine proportions. The garden has been left to grow wild but the swimming pool amid the olive trees is pleasant and the bench under the nut trees is an invitation to reverie. The apartments are higher up, 500 meters from the main villa, near a cypress grove, in the old rose-covered houses that were once lived in by the peasants on the estate. They are simple and luxurious at the same time, well-appointed, sometimes in duplexes, with comfortable bathrooms, functional kitchens that makes you want to try your hand cooking the local produce (which includes Chianti Classico, olive oil and vin santo: visits and tastings once a week), antique furniture, soft couches and refined decoration. The Capanno apartment is a real love nest. Halfway between Florence and Siena, near the superstrada, it's a wonderful place to enjoy the Tuscan countryside.

How to get there *(Map 13): 30km south of Firenze. On the SS2 (Firenze/ Siena), take the San Donato in Poggio exit. Drive through the village of Sandonato, take the right-hand road (towards Castellina in Chianti) and after onekm turn towards Cortine, following the Casa Sola sign.*

La Chiara di Prumiano 🌳

Prumiano 50021 Barberino Val d'Elsa (Firenze)
Tel. 055-807 57 27 - Fax 055-807 56 78
Sig.ra Gaia Mezzadri
E-mail: prumiano@tin.it

Rooms 11 (7 with bath) and 2 apartments (3 bedrooms). **Price** Single 100,000L, double 130,000L.
Meals Half board and full board 90-120,000L, 115-145,000L (per pers.). **Evening meals** Mealtime
specials 25-35,000L - Vegetarian cooking. **Credit cards** Visa, Eurocard, MasterCard. **Pets** Dogs
allowed. **Facilities** Swimming poolriding, parking. **Nearby** Siena - Monteriggioni - Colle Val d'Elsa -
Firenze - San Gimignano - Certaldo - Castellina in Chianti - Volterra. **Closed** Jan – Feb.

Whether you arrive from Barberino or from San Donato you will have to travel through the woods on a little dirt road to reach La Chiara. It is worth taking the trouble: vines and olive trees, with a noble country house of the 17th Century. The estate produces wine and has specialized in organic agriculture. But receiving guests is also one of its activities. There are eleven rooms in the main house. On the first level are the dining room and kitchen where the ladies of the house officiate and offer you vegetarian cooking using only home produce. Since the owner comes from Emilia and Olivia is of multi-regional origin, the menu is always varied and appetizing. The rooms are on the first floor, large, sober (with the exception of that of la principessa) and rustic; prefer those with a private bathroom. In the garden, la Casa delle fate (the fairy house) can be rented as a whole. Here, isolated, immersed in nature, you will discover the colors of the seasons: the blues of wisteria, lilac and rosemary in spring, the silver-green of olives trees in summer and the brilliant colors of fall. Serenity cannot be far away.

How to get there *(Map 13): 30km south of Firenze, exit San Donato. Go through San Donato, turn right (towards Castellina) and at 1km take the road for Cortine, the follow the sign for Casa Sola.*

Tenuta Bossi

50065 Pontassieve (Firenze)
Via dello Stracchino, 32
Tel. 055-831 78 30 - Fax 055-836 40 08
Sig.ra Gondi

Apartments 7 (2-12 pers.) with 1-6 rooms, kitchen, sitting room, bath, WC; 3 with fireplace. **Price** 5500-2 200,000L (1 week). **Restaurant** In Firenze, see pp. 549-553. **Credit cards** Not accepted. **Pets** Dogs allowed. **Facilities** Parking. **Nearby** Firenze - Valley of Mugello - Siena – Dell'Ugolino golf course (18-hole). **Open** All year.

This vast estate just on the outskirts of Florence, which produces a fine white wine in addition to the famous Chianti Rufina, has been in the hands of the Gondi family since 1592. The palace, chapel and several farmhouses share 320 hectares of woods, vineyards and olive groves. The guest apartments have been installed in fully-renovated farmhouses. The furniture is comfortable, in country style. Each unit has a friendly living room (some with fireplace) and a small private terrace. The surrounding vegetation is lush and the gardens, though rustic, are overflowing with roses and charm. The son and daughter of the Marchese are there to help the guests: The daughter provides a delightful welcome and the son, who is in charge of the vineyard, can advise you on your choice of some good bottles of wine. Besides the wines, the Tenuta also produce a quality olive oil and a vin santo, a sweet wine to be tasted with croccanti, a specialty of the region.

How to get there (Map 10): 18km east of Firenze.

Villa Campestri

50039 Vicchio di Mugello (Firenze)
Via di Campestri, 19
Tel. 055-84 90 107 - Fax 055-84 90 108 - Sig. Pasquali
Web: www.villacampestri.it

Category ★★★ **Rooms** 15 and 6 suites with telephone, bath or shower, WC, satellite TV, minibar. **Price** Double 220-350,000L, suite 380-480,000L. **Meals** Breakfast included, served 8:00-10:00 - half board +60,000L (per pers., 3 nights min.). **Restaurant** Service 7:30PM-9:30PM - mealtime specials 70,000L. **Credit cards** Amex, Visa, Eurocard, MasterCard. **Pets** Dogs not allowed. **Facilities** Swimming pool, riding, parking. **Nearby** Firenze - Vespignano - Borgo S. Lorenzo - S. Piero a Sieve - Scarperia - convent of Bosco ai Frati - Novoli - Castello del Trebbio - Pratolino - Convent of Monte Senario in Bivigliano - Sesto Fiorentino and the strada panoràmica (panoramic road) dei Colli Alti (13km to the N15 towards Firenze). **Closed** Nov 15 – Mar 15.

The north of Florence was the place of predilection for villas belonging to the Medici family. The Villa Campestri was one of these until it was bought by Paolo Pasquali, who also cultivates the 160-hectare estate. This lovely house overlooking the Mugello Valley has been renovated with a true respect for its past. In the villa and one of the remodeled outbuildings there are rooms as well as a number of suites suitable for families. The decoration is meticulous, the furniture consists of Florentine antiques and the bathrooms are all that one could wish. The cuisine, made with the produce of the *fattoria*, will let you appreciate the flavors of Tuscany. You can go horseriding in the country and you will never forget the Florentine light once you have seen it from the Villa Campestri.

How to get there *(Map 10): 35km northeast of Firenze. Via A1, towards Bologna, Barberino exit di Mugello, towards Borgo San Lorenzo and Vicchio. 3km from Vicchio.*

Osteria del Vicario

50052 Certaldo Alto (Firenze)
Via Rivellino, 3
Tel. and Fax 0571-66 82 28 / 0571-66 86 76 - Sig. Claudio Borchi
E-mail: info@osteriadelvicario.it

Rooms 15 with shower, WC, satellite TV. **Price** Single 80,000L, double 130,000L. **Meals** Breakfast 8-18,000L, served 8:00-10:30 - half board 110,000L (per pers., 3 days min.). **Restaurant** Service 12:30PM-2:30PM, 7:30PM-10:00PM - closed Wed - mealtime specials 40-60,000L. **Credit cards** All major. **Pets** Dogs not allowed. **Nearby** Collegiata d'Empoli - Vinci and Anchiano (Leonardo de Vinci's birth house) - Certaldo Boccace's house - Church of Santi Michele e Iacopo (Boccace's tomb) - Palazzo Pretorio and chapel (frescoes) - Castelfiorentino: church of S. Verdiana Chapel of Visitation (B. Gozzoli's fresco) - San Gimignano - Montelupo Fiorentino - Church of S. Giovanni - Abbey of Badia di San Salvatore a Settimo. **Closed** Jan.

The historic center is in the upper city. Here in the narrow lanes of this charming red-brick village, Boccacio, the celebrated author of "The Decameron," lived and died. The Osteria del Vicario occupies a former monastery just next to the Palazzo Pretorio. Now it is a lovely village inn that pays particular attention to its restaurant. The location is wonderful, whether you are in the cloister, under the trellis or on the terrace overlooking the wheat fields and sunflowers of Val d'Elsa. The regional cooking is carefully prepared and the owner offers a good selection of Tuscan wines. The rooms, charming, though not very big, are spread over three buildings: the five in the same building as the restaurant have telephones and a ceiling ventilator. El Vicario is a good place to use as a base to explore the little churches of Val d'Elsa and Val d'Arno, which often contain some little-known wonders of their own.

How to get there *(Map 13): 40km south of Firenze.*

Villa Rucellai - Fattoria di Canneto

59100 Prato
Via di Canneto, 16
Tel. 0574-46 03 92 - Fax 0574-46 03 92 - Famiglia Piqué-Rucellai
E-mail: canneto@scotty.masternet.it - Web: www.itwg.com/itw11448.asp

Rooms 12 with bath or shower, WC. **Price** Double 140-160,000 L. **Meals** Breakfast included, served at 8:00. **Restaurant** See p. 553. **Credit cards** Not accepted. **Pets** Dogs not allowed. **Facilities** Swimming pool, parking. **Nearby** Prato: Duomo (Filippo Lippi frescoes), Palazzo Pretorio, Castello dell'Imperatore - Villa of Médici in Poggio a Caiano - Firenze. **Open** All year.

You are sure to fall in love with this wonderful Tuscan Renaissance villa, which has been in the Rucellai family of Florence since the middle of the 18th century. Your first welcome to the place is on the terrace of the Italian garden, where you will be offered a glass of wine produced on the property. Today the villa, partly turned into a hotel, is a favorite of international artists and entertainers passing through Prato for the theater or the museum of contemporary art. The villa is beautiful and full of charm — its salons and gardens evoke the grandeur of celebrations past. The rooms are attractive, with new and modern bathrooms, and the lack of service is made up for by the kindness of the hosts. There is no restaurant, but you can partake of a family-style breakfast in the morning. One drawback is that the railroad is quite nearby, which could disturb your sleep in the summer.

How to get there *(Map 10): 15km west of Firenze, 45km east of Lucca. Via A11, Prato-East exit. Via A1, Prato/Calenzano exit. Then towards Prato and train station, go via Machiavelli, go left via Lambruschini; then on right "Villa S. Leonardo" and "Trattoria la Fontana," follow the railway, keeping it on your left, for 1.5km.*

Hotel Paggeria Medicea

59015 Artimino - Carmignano (Firenze)
Viale Papa Giovanni XXIII, 3
Tel. 055-875 141 - Fax 055-875 14 70 - Sig. Gualtieri
E-mail: hotel@artimino.com - Web: www.artimino.com

Category ★★★★ **Rooms** 37 with air-conditioning and 37 apartments with telephone, bath, WC, satellite TV, minibar – Wheelchair access. **Price** Single 130-200,000L, double 220-280,000L. **Meals** Breakfast included, served 7:30-10:30 - half board +50,000L (per pers., 3 days min.). **Restaurant** Service 12:30PM-2:00PM, 7:30PM-10:00PM - closed Wed and Fri at noon - mealtime specials, also à la carte. **Credit cards** All major. **Pets** Dogs allowed. **Facilities** Swimming pool, 2 tennis, gymnasium, mountain bike, parking. **Nearby** Artimino (church and Etruscan ancient city of Pian di Rosello, Villa dell'Artimino) - Etruscan Tomb of Montefortini in Comeana - Médici Villa Gardens' in Poggio a Caiano - Prato - Pistoia- Firenze – Dell'Ugolino golf course (18-hole) in Grassina. **Open** All year.

If you stay at the Paggeria Medicea, your neighbor will be the lovely "La Ferdinanda," built as a hunting lodge by the Duke Ferdinand de Medici. This undoubtedly explains the sumptuous sobriety of the "fortress-villa," flanked by bastions on the four corners, and whose only adornment is the fanciful double-curved staircase that leads to the loggia. But living in this part of the villa is only a dream, though it's a mere 30 yards away — the guest quarters are in the wing that used to house the servants. Never fear, this wing has been completely transformed into a luxury hotel that offers well-appointed rooms and suites, a restaurant where you will appreciate the products of the estate, and service that is high-style, gracious and attentive.

How to get there *(Map 10): 24km north of Firenze via A1, Firenze-Signa exit; via A11, Prato exit.*

T U S C A N Y

Fattoria di Bacchereto

59015 Bacchereto - Carmignano (Prato)
Tel. 055-871 71 91 - Fax 055-055-871 71 91
Famiglia Bencini Tesi

Apartments 4 with kitchen, bath, 2, 3 or 7 bedrooms. **Price** For 1 week (poss. for 1 night) 850,000L (2 bedrooms), 1 150,000L (3 bedrooms), 2 200,000L (6 bedrooms). **Credit cards** Not accepted. **Pets** Dogs allowed. **Facilities** Swimming pool. **Nearby** Artimino - Etruscan Tomb of Montefortini in Comeana - Médici Villa Gardens' in Poggio a Caiano - Prato - Pistoia - Firenze — Pavoniere golf course (18-hole) in Prato **Open** All year.

Halfway between Florence (25km) and Pistoia, on the hills of Montalbano which produce fine wines and olive oils, a stay at the Fattoria di Bacchereto can become a total immersion in traditional life, since the fattoria is able to organize "courses" on Tuscan culture and crafts. The guest house offers four apartments of different sizes which have preserved the simple, but charming atmosphere of a country house, in some cases with huge rooms that the owners did not want to divide, so they have several beds (La Floralia). Whether they are attached or not to the main building (Orchio and Ruota) or in outbuildings, all of them have a separate entrance. The estate which was once part of a Medici hunting reservation is surrounded by a wood that offers pleasant walks. But the pretty main house also has a fine garden, with oleanders and lemon trees, cooled by a basin in the shade of some palms and a swimming pool somewhat lower down. There is no restaurant in the house but the family owns an inn, La Cantina di Toia, from which you can order Tuscan specialties to be delivered.

How to get there *(Map 10): By A11, exit Prato-East or west, towards Seano.*

Park Hotel Siena

53100 Siena
Via di Marciano, 18
Tel. 0577-44 803 - Fax 0577-490 20 - Sig. Cadirni
E-mail: info@parkhotelsiena.it - Web: www.parkhotelsiena.it

Category ★★★★ **Rooms** 65 and 5 suites with air-conditioning, telephone, bath, WC, satellite TV, safe, minibar – Elevator. **Price** Single 330-418,000L, double 440-726,000L, suite 880-990-1 430,000L; extra bed 154,000L. **Meals** Breakfast 44,000L, served 7:30-10:30. **Restaurant** Service 12:30PM-2:45PM, 7:30PM-10:00PM - à la carte 90,000L - Seasonal Tuscan cuisine. **Credit cards** All major. **Pets** Small dogs allowed. **Facilities** Swimming pool, tennis, golf practice, parking. **Nearby** Siena - Abbey of Sant'Antimo - Abbey of Monte Oliveto Maggiore and the crestroad from Asciano to Siena - Convento dell'Osservanza - Torri abbey in Rosia - Abbey of San Galgano. **Open** All year.

Built on a mountain pass, the old castle of Marciano has an exceptional view of Siena and the Tuscan countryside. This massive and imposing structure built by Peruzzi is now the Park Hotel, a large hotel which belongs to the little Italian group Charming Hotels, and has no lack of that quality. The salons, superbly furnished in Haute Epoque style, open onto a pretty inner courtyard, a replica of the famous Piazza del Campo. The restaurant is on the Italian-style garden, as are the loggia reserved for banquets. The rooms are comfortable–our favorites are on the second floor. This hotel is very good.

How to get there *(Map 13): 68km south of Firenze; take the Siena-North exit; then via Fiorentina to Perticcio and right, via di Marciano (5km northwest of the center of the town).*

Hotel Certosa di Maggiano

53100 Siena
Strada di Certosa, 82
Tel. 0577-28 81 80 - Fax 0577-28 81 89 - Sig.ra Grossi
E-mail: info@certosadimaggiano.it - Web: www.certosadimaggiano.it

Category ★★★★ **Rooms** 6 and 12 suites with air-conditioning, telephone, bath, WC, TV, safe, minibar. **Price** Single 600-700,000L, double 700-900,000L, suite 1 100-1 600,000L. **Meals** Breakfast included, served 7:15-11:00 - half board +150,000L, full board +240,000L. **Restaurant** Service 1:00PM-2:30PM, 8:00PM-10:00PM - mealtime specials 90-140,000L, also à la carte. **Credit cards** All major. **Pets** Dogs not allowed (+50,000L). **Facilities** Heated swimming pool, tennis, parking. **Nearby** In Siena: Palio in Jul and Aug, Duomo, Abbey of Sant'Antimo - Abbey of Monte Oliveto Maggiore and the crestroad from Asciano to Siena - Convento dell'Osservanza - Torri abbey in Rosia - Abbey of San Galgano. **Open** All Year.

What could be prettier than a Carthusian monastery with its vaulted ceilings, Gothic arches, columns and capitals and the serenity of its cloister. The Certosa di Maggiano, in the hills of Siena, dates from 1316 and after a painstaking renovation, it has emerged from its ruins as a luxury hotel. In this stupendous setting there are both rooms and suites, but the suites are on the whole more attractive. The common areas of the hotel are all very beautiful. The dining room in particular has a wonderful china cabinet, painted to resemble marble, in tints to match the pottery collection it holds. The floor is done in *pietra serena*, with wicker chairs and color-coordinated tablecloths, giving an atmosphere of country elegance. The salon is more imposing, with its portraits of emperors. The swimming pool is surrounded by a lovely paving of chevron-patterned terra cotta tiles and vases of flowers, and from here you look out on a verdant landscape of 6 hectares of vineyard and the Sienese hills in the background.

How to get there *(Map 13): 68km south of Firenze, Siena-South exit, Porta Romana, on the right via Certosa.*

Grand Hotel Villa Patrizia

53100 Siena
Via Fiorentina, 58
Tel. 0577-50 431 - Fax 0577-50 442 - Sig. Brogi
E-mail: info@villapatrizia.it - Web: www.villapatrizia.it

Category ★★★★ **Rooms** 33 with air-conditioning, telephone, bath, WC, TV, minibar – Elevator.
Price Single 290,000L, double 440,000L. **Meals** Breakfast included, served 7:00-10:00 - half board
+60,000L, full board +75,000L. **Restaurant** Service 12:30PM-2:00PM, 7:30PM-9:30PM - closed Nov –
Mar - mealtime specials 60,000L, also à la carte - Specialties: Ribollita - Pici alla senese.
Credit cards All major. **Pets** Dogs allowed. **Facilities** Swimming pool, tennis, parking. **Nearby** Siena:
Palio, Jul 2 and Aug 16 - Abbey of Sant'Antimo - Abbey of Monte Oliveto Maggiore and the crestroad
from Asciano to Siena - Convento dell'Osservanza - Torri abbey in Rosia - Abbey of San Galgano. **Open**
All year.

The Villa Patrizia is located outside the town walls of Siena. Most of its original architectural features have been preserved, but the interior is remodeled in a style that is modern, sober and elegant. Beneath the beamed ceilings, the walls are sparely decorated, in light colors. The living room features large leather armchairs and the dining room has white tablecloths and caned chairs. An intriguing arrangement of staircases leads to the upper stories, where the bedrooms have the same spare luxury. Some of the bathrooms are a bit small but all are perfectly well-equipped. The garden is well-tended, with flowers and trees, swimming pool and tennis court. Along with the other qualities of a good hotel, the service is attentive and courteous.

How to get there *(Map 13): 68km south of Firenze, Siena-North exit; then via Fiorentina to the intersection between viale Cavon and via Achille Sclavo; 5km northwest of the city center.*

Hotel Villa Scacciapensieri

53100 Siena
Via di Scacciapensieri, 10
Tel. 0577-41 441 - Fax 0577-27 08 54 - Famiglia Nardi
E-mail: villasca@tin.it

Category ★★★★ **Rooms** 31 with air-conditioning, telephone, bath, WC, satellite TV, minibar – Elevator. **Price** Single 200-230,000L, double 300-420,000L, suite 450-530,000L. **Meals** Breakfast included, served 7:30-10:00 - half board 265-280,000L (per pers. 3 days min.). **Restaurant** Service 12:30PM-2:00PM, 7:30PM-9:00PM - closed Wed - mealtime specials 50-70,000L, also à la carte - Tuscan cuisine - Pici alla senese. **Credit cards** All major. **Pets** Dogs allowed. **Facilities** Swimming pool, tennis, bus to Siena, parking. **Nearby** Siena: Palio, Jul 2 and Aug 12 - Abbey of Sant'Antimo - Abbey of Monte Oliveto Maggiore and the crestroad from Asciano to Siena - Convento dell'Osservanza - Torri abbey in Rosia - Abbey of San Galgano. **Open** Mar 15 – Jan 3.

A few kilometers from Siena, this old inn has been lovingly run by the same family for many years. The long ochre façade of the building is surrounded by an Italian garden with box hedges and masses of flowers. The old-fashioned charm of the comfortable rooms combines with the charm of the old traditional hospitality. A fine old house that seems to come from another time — an idea echoed in the name of the restaurant, Altri Tempi, a name that seems to sum up the atmosphere of the Villa Scacciapensieri.

How to get there *(Map 13): 68km south of Firenze-Siena, Siena-North exit; stazione ferroviara (rail station) 3km north of the city center.*

Palazzo Ravizza

53100 Siena
Pian dei Mantellini, 34
Tel. 0577-28 04 62 - Fax 0577-22 15 97
Sig. Grottanelli

Rooms 30 and 5 suites with air-conditioning, telephone, bath, WC, satellite TV – Elevator. **Price** Single 120-200,000L, double 180-240,000L, suite 450-500,000L. **Meals** Breakfast included, served 7:30-10:00 - half board 230,000L (1 pers.), 135-165,000L (per pers., in double, 3 days min.), 170-205,000L (per pers. in suite). **Restaurant** Service 12:00PM-1:30PM, 7:30PM-9:30PM - mealtime specials 50-60,000L, also à la carte. **Credit cards** All major. **Pets** Dogs allowed. **Facilities** Parking. **Nearby** The Palio, Jul 2 and Aug 16 - Abbey of Sant'Antimo - Abbey of Monte Oliveto Maggiore, returning via the peaks of Asciano-Siena - Covnento dell'Osservanza - Abbey of Torri at Rosia - Abbey of San Galgano **Open** All year.

It is a pleasure to come back to the Palazzo Ravizza after an exemplary restoration that has given it back the comfort and freshness that it had lost over the years, while still preserving the charm of an elegant Italian pensione. The building is superb and has not been altered. The entrance, with its lovely floor - in a black-and-white chessboard pattern - is a succession of vaulted rooms, the groins elegantly decorated with banches of pine or olive. Various little sitting-room corners have been created with comfrotable sofas. The rooms are now all beautiful, spacious and elegantly restrained: the floor is in red tiles or old parquet, there are flowered or damasked fabrics and 19th-century furniture in dark wood. The suites occupy the largest rooms in the palazzo, usually with frescoed ceilings. We suggest you reserve the rooms that overlook the countryside and the garden. The latter is a real source of joy, whether at breakfast, with an aperitif at sundown or for dinner outdoors in summer. Here there is more than luxury, there is loads of charm.

***How to get there** (Map 13): Exit porta S. Marco or Porta Tufi.*

Hotel Antica Torre

53100 Siena
Via di Fiera Vecchia, 7
Tel. and Fax 0577-22 22 55
Sig.ra Landolfo

Category ★★★ **Rooms** 8 with telephone, shower, WC (2 with TV). **Price** Single 160,000L, double 200,000L. **Meals** Breakfast 12,000L, served 8:00-10:30. **Restaurant** See p. 553. **Credit cards** All major. **Pets** Dogs not allowed. **Nearby** Siena: Palio, Jul 2 and Aug 16 - Abbey of Sant'Antimo - Abbey of Monte Oliveto Maggiore - Convento dell'Osservanza - Abbey of Torri in Rosia - Abbey of San Galgano. **Open** All year.

Just outside of Siena you will find one of the best hotels in Tuscany. This charming, affordable hotel in the center of town is so small and so discreet that we really had to dig it up. And what a find! It is a typical 16th century *casa torre*, on one of the quietest streets in Siena. A small central stairway (with beautiful 19th century portraits) leads to two rooms on every floor. They have travertine floors, wrought iron beds, antique furniture, engravings, and small, but well-equipped, bathrooms with showers. A former pottery store in the basement, serves as the breakfast room.

How to get there *(Map 13): SS Firneze-Siena, Siena-South exit; then towards town center (Porta Romana).*

Hotel Santa Caterina

53100 Siena
Via Enea Silvio Piccolomini, 7
Tel. 0577-22 11 05 - Fax 0577-27 10 87 - Sig.ra Minuti Stasi
E-mail: hsc@sienanet.it - Web: www.sienanet.it/hsc/

Category ★★★ **Rooms** 22 with air-conditioning, telephone, bath, WC, hairdryer, satellite TV, minibar. **Price** (Low season: Nov 3 – Dec 22); single 130-185,000L, double 185-250,000L, triple 250-330,000L, for 4 pers. 250-400,000L. **Meals** Breakfast included, served 8:00-10:00 (self-service). **Restaurant** See p. 553. **Credit cards** All major. **Pets** Dogs allowed. **Facilities** Parking (20,000L). **Nearby** Siena: Palio, Jul 2 and Aug 16 - Abbey of Sant'Antimo - Abbey of Monte Oliveto Maggiore and the crestroad from Asciano to Siena - Convento dell'Osservanza - Abbey of Torri in Rosia - Abbey of San Galgano. **Open** All year.

The Hotel Santa Caterina is in a former private home in the center of Siena, a few yards from the Porta Romana. The façade is plain and the street corner location is not wonderful, but the double pane windows make the rooms fairly soundproof. All of the rooms are comfortably furnished and have modern bathrooms. Ask for a room off the marvelous flower garden, which overlooks the valley and the red rooftops of Siena. This view is the most charming aspect of this hotel.

How to get there *(Map 13): SS Firenze-Siena, Siena-South exit; then towards town center to Porta Romana via E.S. Piccolomini.*

Villa dei Lecci

53100 Siena
Strada di Larniano, 21/1
Tel. and fax 0577-22 11 26
From Jan 6 to Mar 15: Tel. 0577-30 52 43 - Fax 0577-92 96 47
E-mail: info@villadeilecci.com - Web: www.villadeilecci.com

Rooms 3 (some with air-conditioning), with telephone, bath, WC, satellite TV. **Price** Double 380,000L (3 days min.). **Meals** Breakfast included, served 8:30-11:00. **Evening meals** Mealtime specials 70,000L. **Credit cards** Not accepted. **Pets** Dogs allowed. **Facilities** Gymnasium, garage. **Nearby** Siena: the Palio, Jul 2 and Aug 16 - Abbey of Sant'Antimo - Abbey of Monte Oliveto Maggiore, returning via the peaks of Asciano-Siena - Covnento dell'Osservanza - Abbey of Torri at Rosia - Abbey of San Galgano **Closed** Jan 6 - Mar 15.

The Villa dei Leicci has the name of the variety of oak tree that leads to this superb property only a few kilometers from Siena. This 17th-century villa has long been in the same family and is now occupied by the two sisters who have decided to settle here permanently and to open some rooms to guests. For this reason, the house is full of family souvenirs, for example the little chapel that is here because of one ancestor who was Pope; it still has its frescoes furniture and liturgical objects. The same applies to the house, which is more like a fine bourgeois family residence than a country house: mirrors of gilded wood, Chinese vases and walnut furniture oranment the sitting rooms and the dining room. The bedrooms are large, especially those on the second floor, as well as comfortable and very intimate. You will also find that the service is excellent: you can have your laundry done and they will be happy to prepare you a delicious dinner. On the first floor, a veranda decorated with 18th-century allegorical frescoes gives access to the garden, with its old roses, scents of rosemary and kitchen garden.

How to get there *(Map 13): Exit Siena-East, towards Arezzo-Grosetto, Due Ponti and signed to Larniano. Ask for a plan to be sent to you.*

Castello di Montalto

Montalto 53019 Castelnuovo Berardenga (Siena)
Tel. 0577-35 56 75 - Fax 0577-35 56 82
Sig.ra Diana Coda-Nunziante
E-mail: info@montalto.it - Web: www.montalto.it

Apartments 7 (2-6 pers.) with 1-3 rooms, kitchen, sitting room, bath, WC (4 apart. with telephone, 1 apart with TV). **Price** For 1 week 3 600-4 500,000L (in the Castle), 900-2 650,000L (in village), 1 000-2 000,000L (in farm, 2km). **Restaurant** See p. 554. **Credit cards** Visa, Eurocard, MasterCard. **Pets** Dogs allowed in the farm. **Facilities** Swimming pool, tennis, bikes, parking. **Nearby** Castello delle quattro torri near Due Ponti - Castello di Brolio and vineyards of Chianti (Meleto) - Gaiole - Badia a Coltibu ono - Radda and Castellina in Chianti. **Closed** Nov 5 – Dec 29, Jan 7 – Mar 15.

The Castello di Montalto is in itself a small fortified village with a well-preserved tower and crenellated façades of genuine beauty and nobility. It is owned by an Italian Count and run by his American wife. The outbuildings of the estate have been transformed into comfortable apartments and the atmosphere is distinguished. You may also be able to live in the castello itself, where the largest apartment is situated, with access to the tower's rooftop terrace. It is possible, too, to rent an independent farmhouse, more rustic, 2 kilometers from the castle, but provided with phone and garage for anyone who might otherwise feel too far away. The decoration varies from house to house but is always nice even when quite simple. Most of them have a fireplace and a garden where you can have lunch outdoors. An added pleasure is going to the farm to buy oil, honey, eggs and fresh vegetables. The welcome is warm and discreet. Nature lovers will be right in their element.

How to get there *(Map 13): 17km southeast of Siena via SS Siena-Perugia towards Arezzo. At the junction for Arezzo, take the road towards Bucine/Ambra; then after 3km the road on the left towards Montalto (3km).*

Relais Villa d'Arceno

53010 San Gusmè - Castelnuovo Berardenga (Siena)
Tel. 0577-35 92 92 - Fax 0577-35 92 76
Sig. Mancini

Category ★★★★ **Rooms** 16 with air-conditiong, telephone, bath, WC, TV, minibar – Elevator. **Price** Single 330,000L, double 550,000L, suite 720-800,000L. **Meals** Breakfast included, served 7:30-10:30. **Restaurant** Service 1:00PM-2:30PM, 8:00PM-9:30PM - mealtime specials about 90,000L, also à la carte - Tuscan cuisine. **Credit cards** All major. **Pets** Dogs not allowed. **Facilities** Swimming pool, moutain bike, tennis, parking. **Nearby** Siena - Arezzo - Monte San Savino - Abbey of Monte Oliveto, crest road from Asciano to Siena. **Open** Mar – Oct.

Castelnuovo Berardenga is only a few kilometers from Siena and it is a pleasure to discover the landscapes and light charactersitic of the Sienese school of painting. One drives to the little hamlet of San Gusme at the exit from the vilalge. A large arch with the word "Arceno" written on it marks the entrance to the estate. At the end of a road planted with trees, vines and olives, you come to the villa. This beautiful 17th-century country house is on a 24,700-acre estate; it is an old hunting lodge which belonged to a rich Italian family until recently when it was transformed into a very nice hotel. The 19 farms on the estate were also carefully restored. The hotel is decorated with beautiful fabrics. The rooms are spacious, furnished with antiques and with a very high standard of comfort. The setting is magnificent and the staff very welcoming.

How to get there *(Map 13): 25km east of Siena via A1; Valdichiana or Monte San Savino exit towards Monte San Savino, to Castelnuovo Berardenga, San Gusmé.*

Hotel Relais Borgo San Felice

San Felice
53019 Castelnuovo Berardenga (Siena)
Tel. 0577-35 92 60 - Fax 0577-35 90 89
Sig. Righi

Category ★★★★ **Rooms** 50 and 12 with air-conditioning, suites with telephone, bath, WC, TV, minibar. **Price** Single 355,000L, double 520,000L, suite 890,000L. **Meals** Breakfast included, served 7:30-10:30 - half board 390-575,000L, full board 495-680,000L (per pers.). **Restaurant** Service 12:30PM-2:00PM, 7:30PM-9:30PM - mealtime specials 80-150,000L - Tuscan and Italian cuisine. **Credit cards** All major. **Pets** Dogs not allowed. **Facilities** Swimming pool, tennis, parking. **Nearby** Castello delle quattro torri near by de Due Ponti - Castello di Brolio and Chianti vineyard via Meleto - Gaiole - Badia Coltibuono - Radda and Castellina in Chianti. **Open** Mar – Oct.

A little square in front of a postcard chapel, small cobblestone streets lined with houses covered with flowers, cute gardens, stone stairways, beautiful Virginia creeper-covered façades–you will find all this and more in Borgo San Felice, a Medieval Tuscan village. It feels like a village which has continued its agricultural activity of producing wine and olive oil. The houses are very tastefully decorated, with nice open spaces, shades of ochre and pretty furniture. A beautiful swimming pool, very professional service and an excellent restaurant make Borgo San Felice a hotel which we heartily recommend.

How to get there *(Map 13): 17km east of Siena; in Siena, SS Siena-Perugia towards Arezzo, then 7km to Montaperti.*

Castello di Tornano

Tornano 53013 Gaiole in Chianti (Siena)
Tel. 0577-74 60 67 - 055-80 918 - Fax 0577-74 60 94
Sigg.ra Selvolini

Apartments 10 (2-6 pers.) with rooms, kitchen, shower, WC. **Price** For 1 week (1 room) 750-
1 200,000L, (2 rooms) 1 150-2 300,000L, Torre (2 rooms) 1 950-3 700,000L. **Meals** Breakfast
10,000L. **Restaurant** Service 12:00PM-7:00PM - closed Mon - mealtime specials 30,000L - Property
produce. **Credit cards** Amex, Visa, Eurocard, MasterCard. **Pets** Small dogs allowed (on request).
Facilities Swimming pool, tennis (10,000L), parking. **Nearby** Monteriggioni - Firenze - Siena - San
Gimignano - Arezzo. **Open** May - Oct.

Castello di Tornano is a 12th century castle today officially designated as a
landmark. Beautifully set on a hilltop covered with vineyards and oak
trees, it towers over the surroundings. The farm is now run by two charming
sisters, who have also fitted out the tower as a very comfortable apartment,
with monumental rooms lit by narrow windows, and an apartment served by a
spiral staircase going up three levels to a panoramic terrace. Rooms of more
modest proportions are situated in other farm buildings. Around the castle
extends a large lawn filled with flowers and bordered by cypresses with a
swimming pool set cleverly into the former moat. At a restaurant some 500
meters away you can taste the products of the estate.

*How to get there (Map 13): 19km northeast of Siena. On Highway A1,
Valdarno exit, then SS408 towards Siena. From Siena take the road towards
Gaiole in Chianti to Lecchi. In Lecchi towards Tornano-Ristorante
Guarnelotto.*

Residence San Sano

San Sano 53010 Lecchi in Chianti (Siena)
Tel. 0577-74 61 30 - Fax 0577-74 61 56
Sig. and Sig.ra Matarazzo
E-mail: hotelsansano@chiantinet.it

Category ★★★★ **Rooms** 14 with air-conditiong, telephone, shower, WC, minibar. **Price** Double 190-250,000L. **Meals** Breakfast included, served 8:00-10:00. **Restaurant** Service 7:30PM - closed Sun - mealtime specials 40,000L - Tuscan cuisine. **Credit cards** All major. **Pets** Dogs allowed by request. **Facilities** Swimming pool, parking. **Nearby** Monteriggioni - Abbadia Isola - Colle di Val d'Elsa (colle Alta) - Firenze - Siena - San Gimignano - Arezzo. **Open** Mar 15 – Nov 3.

Foreigners who fall in love with a country, a region or a house are sometimes those who best know how to respect and preserve the soul of the place. That is the case of the Italian/German couple who settled in Tuscany and who welcome you today to this old stone farmhouse that combines the charm and warm hospitality of a guest house with the independence and service of a hotel. The rooms are each done with a particular theme; each is appealing and very comfortable. The cooking emphasizes regional specialties. Only 20 kilometers from Siena, you can enjoy the lovely countryside as you visit Tuscany.

How to get there *(Map 13): 20km north of Siena via S408; then left towards Lecchi, then San Sano.*

Hotel Monteriggioni

53035 Monteriggioni (Siena)
Tel. 0577-30 50 09 - Fax 0577-30 50 11
Sig.ra Gozzi

Category ★★★★ **Rooms** 12 with air-conditioning, telephone, bath, WC, TV, minibar – Elevator. **Price** Single 200,000L, double 380,000L. **Meals** Breakfast included, served 8:00-10:00. **Restaurant** See p. 554. **Credit cards** All major. **Pets** Dogs not allowed. **Facilities** Swimming pool. **Nearby** Siena - Abbadia Isola - Colle Val d'Elsa - Basilica dell' Osservanza and chartreuse de Pontignano - San Gimignano - Volterra **Closed** Jan 16 – Feb 14.

The towers of Monteriggioni rise like a mirage on the highway connecting Firenze and Siena. The beauty of the decapitated walls and towers, especially at sunset, will make you want get off the highway for a closer look. This small village is made up of what originally were old military buildings dating back to the time when Montérriggioni was still a Sienian garrison (the 8th century). The hotel, in the village, is discreet and luxurious. The rooms are all different and are very comfortable. We prefer the ones on the garden where breakfast is served in summer. Just across the street is one of the best restaurants in the region, Il Pozzo, which more than makes up for the lack of a restaurant in the hotel.

***How to get there** (Map 13): 12km north of Siena, on 4 Corsie, Colle di Val d'Elsa-Monteriggioni exit.*

La Piccola Pieve

Pieve a Elsa, 92 50034 Colle di Val d'Elsa (Siena)
Tel. 0577-92 97 45
Sig.ra Silvana Ravanelli
E-mail: fields@tin.it - Web: www.enet.it/wrk/colle

Rooms 4 with air-conditioning, bath or shower, TV (1 with telephone). **Price** Double 170,000L (3 days min.). **Meals** Breakfast included, served 8:00-9:30. **Restaurant** See p. 555. **Credit cards** Not accepted. **Pets** Dogs not allowed. **Facilities** Parking. **Nearby** Firenze - Siena - San Gimignano - Volterra - Monterrigioni Chianti Route. **Open** Mar – Oct.

Near to both San Gimignano and Siena, this charming bed and breakfast could be a pleasant country option for your stay in Tuscany. Colle Val d'Esta has preserved in the upper town a fine historic center with ramparts, Renaissance palaces, a baroque cathedral and the casa-torre of the famous architect and sculptor Arnolfo di Cambio. Whether in the lower or upper part of the town you will find some very fine restaurants, among them the highly recommended Arnolfo. The Piccola Pieve is situated in the plain. It is a lovely house in rough stone, wonderfully restored and decorated by its charming owner. The salon is really attractive and very convivial: well-chosen old furniture, books, personal souvenirs, comfortable sofa and a fireplace, for days when the weather is chilly. The bedrooms are very well-kept, with modern and very functional bathrooms. Two rooms can be put together to make a real family suite. The other two, which are very spacious, share a reading room and music room. Breakfast is plentiful, and the welcome warm.

How to get there *(Map 13): 27km northeast of Siena by S2, exit Monteriggioni.*

Hotel Villa San Lucchese

50036 Poggibonsi (Siena)
Via S. Lucchese, 5
Tel. 0577-93 42 31 - Fax 0577-93 47 29 - Sig. Ninci
E-mail: villasanlucchese@etr.it - Web: www.etr.it.hotel_villa_san_lucchese

Category ★★★★ **Rooms** 36 with air-conditioning, telephone, bath or shower, WC, TV, minibar – Elevator. **Price** Single 100-180,000L, double 200-320,000L, suite 250-350,000L. **Meals** Breakfast included, served 7:30-10:00 - half board +40,000L, full board +80,000L (per pers.). **Restaurant** Service 12:30PM-2:00PM, 7:30PM-10:00PM - closed Tues - mealtime specials 60,000L, à la carte - Tuscan cuisine. **Credit cards** All major. **Pets** Dogs not allowed. **Facilities** Swimming pool, tennis, parking. **Nearby** Firenze - Sienna - Colle Val d'Elsa - San Gimignano - Volterra - Monterrigioni Chianti Route. **Open** All year.

The hotel is ideally located in Poggibonsi, at the crossroads of the main cities of Tuscany, Florence and Siena. It is next to the San Lucchese monastery, overlooking the town and all of its commotion. This 15th century noble villa, has vast, light rooms and a pleasant classical decor. On the ground floor the restaurant opens onto a very large terrace, which looks out over the Val d'Elsa plain. In the garden, next to a grove of superb centenarian trees, there is a large pool. The hotel is well equipped for receptions.

How to get there *(Map 13): 19km north of Siena. Superstrada "4 Corsie," Poggibonsa exit. A1, Firenze Certosa exit.*

Hotel L'Antico Pozzo

53037 San Gimignano (Siena)
Via San Matteo, 87
Tel. 0577-94 20 14 - Fax 0577-94 21 17 - Sig. Marro and Sig. Caponi
E-mail: info@anticopozzo.com - Web: www.anticopozzo.com

Rooms 18 with air-conditioning, telephone, bath or shower, hairdryer, satellite TV, safe, minibar, internet point of access – Elevator. **Price** Single 160,000L, double 220-270,000L. **Meals** Breakfast (buffet) included. **Restaurant** See p. 556. **Credit cards** All major. **Pets** Dogs not allowed. **Nearby** San Gimignano (Church of sant'Agostino), piazza del Duomo, piazza della Cisterna - Etruscan ancient city of Pieve di Cellole - Convent of S. Vivaldo - Certaldo - Pinacoteca and Visitation chapel (frescoes of Benozzo Gozzoli) in Castelfiorentino - Firenze - Siena - Volterra – Castelfalfi golf course (18-hole). **Open** All year.

Two talented young people with impeccable taste have restored this very beautiful 15th-century residence in the heart of San Gimignano. The house still has its original architecture and frescos. There is an old well inside the house, which is why the hotel has this name. Their taste is found in the decor, which is perfect, with pretty, antique furniture and beautiful fabrics creating an atmosphere of elegance and refinement. Some rooms overlook the little patio, others the street, but when the tourists leave in the evening, this, together with air-conditioning and soon new doors and windows, will provide perfect soundproofing. If you ask for the fresco room, beware, it is unfortunately on the fire escape (but security comes first). The salon and breakfast room are very pleasant. The hotel is the jewel of San Gimignano.

How to get there *(Map 13): 38km northeast of Siena, in town center. Parking: Porta San Matteo (100m).*

Hotel La Cisterna

53037 San Gimignano (Siena)
Piazza della Cisterna, 24
Tel. 0577-94 03 28 - Fax 0577-94 20 80 - Sig. Salvestrini
E-mail: lacisterna@iol.it

Category ★★★ **Rooms** 47 and 2 suites with telephone, bath or shower, WC, satellite TV, safe. **Price** Single 125,000L, double 165-205,000L, suite 235,000L. **Meals** Breakfast included, served 7:30-10:00 - half board 130-165,000L, full board 165-200,000L (per pers.). **Restaurant** Service 12:30PM-2:30PM, 7:30PM-9:30PM - closed Tues and Wed at noon - mealtime specials 55-75,000L - Specialties: Intercosta scaloppata al chianti - Specialita' ai funghi e ai tartufi - Pasta fatta in casa - Dolci freschiescechi. **Credit cards** All major. **Pets** Dogs not allowed. **Facilities** Parking (20,000L). **Nearby** San Gimignano (church of Sant'Agostino, piazza della Cisterna, piazza della Duomo) - Etruscan ancient city of Pieve di Cellole - Monastery of S. Vivaldo - Certaldo - Pinacoteca and Visitation chapel (frescoes of Benozzo Gozzoli) in Castelfiorentino - Firenze - Siena - Volterra – Castelfalfi golf course (18-hole). **Closed** Jan 11 – Mar 3.

Situated on the main *piazza* in the very heart of San Gimignano, La Cisterna (named after the well which is, along with the famous towers, one of the attractions of San Gimignano) is a beautiful old hotel. Once a palace, it still has many vestiges of the past, like the stunning salon whose architecture is an attraction in itself. Well-chosen Florentine furniture of great refinement creates an atmosphere of elegance and comfort throughout the hotel. Worth special mention is La Terrasse, the restaurant known not only for its cuisine but also for its panoramic view over all the valley. In short, a quality hotel in this miniature city that seems to contain more than its share of the best addresses in Tuscany.

How to get there *(Map 13): 38km northeast of Siena, in town center. Parking: Porta San Matteo (200m).*

Hotel Bel Soggiorno

53037 San Gimignano (Siena)
Via San Giovanni, 91
Tel. 0577-94 03 75/94 31 49 - Fax 0577-90 75 21 - Sig. Gigli
E-mail: belsoggiorno@pescille.it - Web: www.hotelbelsoggiorno.it

Category ★★★ **Rooms** 21 with air-conditioning, telephone, bath, WC, TV (12 with minibar) –
Elevator. **Price** Double 150-250,000L, suite 280,000L. **Meals** Breakfast 15,000L, served 8:00-10:00.
Restaurant With air-conditioning. Service 12:00PM-2:30PM, 7:30PM-9:30PM - closed Jan 10 – Feb 28 -
mealtime specials about 55-80,000L, à la carte - Traditional cuisine. **Credit cards** All major. **Pets**
Dogs not allowed. **Facilities** Parking and garage (20,000L). **Nearby** San Gimignano (church of
Sant'Agostino, piazza della Cisterna, piazza della Duomo) - Etruscan ancient city of Pieve di Cellole
- Monastery of S. Vivaldo - Certaldo - Pinacoteca and Visitation chapel (frescoes of Benozzo Gozzoli)
in Castelfiorentino - Firenze - Siena - Volterra – Castelfalfi golf course (18-hole). **Closed** Jan 10 –
Feb 23.

This very beautiful 13th-century house, in the center of San Gimignano, has
belonged to the family that also runs Le Pescille, for five generations. A
warm welcome awaits you here. The rooms are unevenly charming: some are
on the street and others have a magnificent balcony overlooking the
countryside (Rooms 1, 2, and 6). The two suites (11 and 21) are the most
beautiful; they have small terraces overlooking the valley. The restaurant also
has an extraordinary view, and you can enjoy excellent traditional cuisine,
which has been the cause of Bel Soggiorno's good reputation for several
generations.

How to get there *(Map 13): 38km northeast of Siena, in town center.*

La Collegiata

Strada Nr. 27 - 53037 San Gimignano (Siena)
Tel. 0577-94 32 01 - Fax 0577-94 05 66
Sig. S. Perko

Rooms 22 with air-conditioning, telephone, bath or shower, satellite TV, minibar, safe – Elevator. **Price** Double 650-800,000L, suite 850-2 000,000L. **Meals** Breakfast included, served 7:30-10:30. **Restaurant** Service 12:30PM-2:00PM, 7:30PM-10:00PM - mealtime specials, also à la carte - Regional cooking. **Credit cards** All major. **Pets** Small dogs allowed. **Facilities** Swimming pool, parking. **Nearby** San Gimignano (church of Sant'Agostino, piazza della Cisterna, piazza della Duomo) - Etruscan ancient city of Pieve di Cellole - Monastery of S. Vivaldo - Certaldo - Pinacoteca and Visitation chapel (frescoes of Benozzo Gozzoli) in Castelfiorentino - Firenze - Siena - Volterra –Castelfalfi golf course (18-hole). **Closed** Jan.

This former Franciscan convent, built in 1587 at the request of the inhabitants of San Gimignano, is a beautiful composition of red brick and *pietra serena*, standing against a backdrop of tall cypress trees. Around the buildings are an Italian-style garden and a large swimming pool amid green lawns, which invite the visitor to enjoy the delights of the surrounding countryside. The view from the property stretches as far as the famous towers. Inside, carefully chosen fabrics and furnishings give great elegance to the hall and the salons, situated near the cloister. The restaurant has been installed in what was once the chapel, which lends it an air of nearly religious reverence. Meals are based on local specialties that change with the season and the inspiration of the market. In the tower is a suite with a view 180° around, but this is not our favorite room because of the enormous jacuzzi that takes up a good part of it. The other rooms are large, comfortable and attractive, and far less ostentatious, and the service is uniformly good.

How to get there *(Map 13): 38km northeast of Siena; 2km of San Gimignano towards Certaldo.*

Villa San Paolo

53037 San Gimignano (Siena)
Strada Provinciale per Certaldo
Tel. 0577-95 51 00 - Fax 0577-95 51 13 - Sig. Squarcia
E-mail: sanpaolo@iol.it - Web: www.sangimignano.com/sanpaolo

Category ★★★★ Rooms 18 with air-conditioning, telephone, bath, WC, satellite TV, minibar –
Elevator, wheelchair access. **Price** Double 250-400,000L. **Meals** Breakfast included, served 7:30-
10:30. **Restaurant** "Leonetto" in Hotel Le Renaie - mealtime specials, also à la carte. **Credit cards**
All major. **Pets** Dogs not allowed. **Facilities** Swimming pool, tennis, ping-pong, fitness room, parking.
Nearby San Gimignano (Church of sant'Agostino), piazza del Duomo, piazza della Cisterna, Palazzo
del Popolo - Etruscan ancient city of Pieve di Cellole - Monastery of S. Vivaldo - Certaldo - Pinacoteca
and Visitation chapel (frescoes of Benozzo Gozzoli) in Castelfiorentino - Firenze - Siena - Volterra –
Castelfalfi golf course (18-hole). **Closed** Jan 10 – Feb 10.

This small hotel in a beautiful villa is in the San Gimignano countryside on large grounds full of pine and olive trees. The owners also have a hotel next door, Le Renaie. There are only a few rooms; all are air-conditioned and extremely comfortable. The "winter-garden" decor is cheery and warm. There is a superb pool with snack service and an unforgettable view of the countryside around San Gimignano. There is no restaurant, but you can always go the "Leonetto" next door. In the local area, there are historical sites to visit and numerous trails for hiking or horseback riding (there is a club a few miles away).

How to get there *(Map 13): 38km northeast of Siena; 5km north of San Gimignano towards Certaldo.*

Hotel Le Renaie

53037 San Gimignano - Pancole (Siena)
Tel. 0577-95 50 44 - Fax 0577-95 51 26
Sig. Sabatini
E-mail: lerenaie@iol.it - Web: www.sangimignano.com

Category ★★★ **Rooms** 25 with telephone, bath, WC, satellite TV, minibar, safe. **Price** Single 120,000L, double 160-200,000L. **Meals** Breakfast 17,000L, served 8:00-10:00 - half board 140-160,000L (per pers., 3 days min.). **Restaurant** Service 12:30PM-2:30PM, 7:30PM-10:00PM - closed Tues - mealtime specials 30-60,000L, also à la carte - Specialties: Coniglio alla vernaccia - Piatti al tartufi - Piatti agli asparagi e ai funghi. **Credit cards** All major. **Pets** Dogs allowed. **Facilities** Swimming pool (May – Sept), tennis, parking. **Nearby** San Gimignano (Church of sant'Agostino), piazza del Duomo, piazza della Cisterna, Palazzo del Popolo - Etruscan ancient city of Pieve di Cellole - Monastery of S. Vivaldo - Certaldo - Pinacoteca and Visitation chapel (frescoes of Benozzo Gozzoli) in Castelfiorentino - Firenze - Siena - Volterra – Castelfalfi golf course (18-hole). **Closed** Nov 5 – Dec 5.

L e Renaie is in the countryside near San Gimignano. Recently constructed, it respects the traditional Tuscan materials and colors. Tiles, bricks, terra cotta and wood form a harmonious blend of textures and colors: pale pink and off-white colors predominate. The contemporary salon, with its large fireplace and a pretty little bar open onto a gallery surrounded by plants and flowers, particularly pleasant for having breakfast or a drink. The rooms are all comfortable and pleasant, but try to get the ones with a terrace overlooking the countryside.

How to get there *(Map 13): 38km northeast of Siena; 6km northwest of San Gimignano to Pieve di Cellole, then Pancole.*

Villa Remignoli

Casaglia Nr. 25 - 53037 San Gimignano (Siena)
Tel. and Fax 0577-95 00 48
Renato and Maria Faresi

Rooms 6 with shower. **Price** Double 180-200,000L. **Meals** Breakfast included, served 8:30-10:30.
Evening meals By reservation - Mealtime specials 15,000L (lunch), 35,000L (dinner). **Credit cards**
Not accepted. **Pets** Dogs not allowed. **Facilities** Swimming pool, tennis (15,000L), parking. **Nerby** San
Gimignano (Church of sant'Agostino), piazza del Duomo, piazza della Cisterna - Pinacoteca and
Visitation chapel (frescoes of Benozzo Gozzoli) in Castelfiorentino - Firenze - Siena - Volterra –
Castelfalfi golf course (18-hole). **Open** Mar – end Oct.

Surrounded by vineyards on one of the hills oppsoite San Gimignano, the
Villa Remignoli is reached, for the last part of the road, by a dirt track. The
owners, who cultivate the vines on the estate are always delighted to share a
moment of their lives with travelling guests. The ground floor of the house has
retained its original stonework while the first floor, where the bedrooms are,
has been entirely (and simply) renovated. The rooms are of moderate size, very
well kept up and carefully supplied with regional furniture, pretty flowered bed
covers and embroidered cloths. The bathrooms are comfortable but not very
large; one room has a bathroom in the corridor. Breakfast, a copious family
affair, is taken in the old kitchen where you can also find the good local ham.
The swimming pool is on a hillside from which you have a fine view of the
famous towers of San Gimignano. Light meals can be served on request. In the
evening, you can also arrange to dine on the panoramic terrace in the garden.
Tennis, horseriding, tourism... a full holiday programme.

How to get there *(Map 13): 7km from San Gimignano. By SS222 exit
Poggibonsi. At Poggibonsi, after the Superal supermarket, head for Ulignano,
then after 1km follow the signs towards Casaglia and Remignoli.*

353

Il Casale del Cotone

Il Cotone
53037 San Gimignano (Siena)
Tel. and Fax 0577-94 32 36
E-mail: info@casaledelcotone.com - Web: www.casaledelcotone.com

Rooms 4 and 3 apartments with shower, WC, satellite TV and minibar; 3 rooms in the annex. **Price** Single 120,000L, double 170-180,000L, triple 230,000L, apart. 160-210,000L (2-3 pers.). **Meals** Breakfast included in rooms - 10,000L in apart. served 8:00-10:30 - half board 210-260,000L. **Restaurant** See p. 556. **Credit cards** Amex, Visa, Eurocard, MasterCard. **Pets** Dogs allowed. **Facilities** Swimming pool, mountain bikes, parking at hotel. **Nearby** In San Gimignano: Etruscan ancient city of Pieve di Cellole, Convent of S.Vivaldo - Certaldo - Pinacotecaand visitation chapel (frescoes of Benozzo.Gozzoli) in Castelfiorentino - Firenze - Siena - Volterra — Castelfalfi golf course (18-hole). **Open** All year.

Beautiful little San Gimignano, situated between Siena, Florence and Pisa, is an excellent base from which to tour the region, and it abounds in nice hotels. But that's no reason to exclude another one, which is both nice and reasonably-priced. It is an 18th-century farmhouse surrounded by 30 hectares of vineyards and olive trees. The owners recently set up several rooms sleeping two or three persons and two mini-apartments, with their own separate entrance, suitable for families. Country-style decor, with some antique furniture. Brand new and very comfortable shower rooms. Breakfast is served in the hunting room or the garden, depending on the season. The owners take great pains to give guests a good welcome - there is bar service at all times and they will even prepare a light meal at your request. But San Gimignano is only 2 kilometers away and the evening is really the best time to discover this historic city.

How to get there *(Map 13): 2km from San Gimignano, towards Certaldo.*

Il Casolare di Libbiano

Libbiano 53037 San Gimignano (Siena)
Tel. and Fax 0577-94 60 02
Sig. Bucciarelli and Sig.ra Mateos
E-mail: cas.libbiano@cybermarket.it

Rooms 5 with shower, WC and 1 suite with bath, WC, lounge, terrace. **Price** Double 240,000L, suite 320,000L. **Meals** Breakfast included, served 8:30-10:00 - half board 295,000L (in double room), 370,000L in suite. **Restaurant** Service 8:00PM - Traditional Tuscan cuisine. **Credit cards** Visa, Eurocard, MasterCard. **Pets** Dogs not allowed. **Facilities** Swimming pool, mountain bikes, parking. **Nearby** San Gimignano (Sommer of San Gimignano), etruscan ancient city of Pieve di Cellole, Monastery of S. Vivaldo - Certaldo - Pinacoteca and Visitation chapel (frescoes of Benozzo Gozzoli) in Castelfiorentino - Firenze - Siena - Volterra – Castelfalfi golf course (18-hole). **Open** Mar – Oct.

L eaving San Gimignano on the road to Certaldo, you drive into the countryside of Val d'Elsa until you catch sight of a small hill on which stands the church of Cellole. A few kilometers farther on you come to Libbiano and the Casolare. A dynamic couple have completely transformed this old farmhouse into a warm and inviting holiday home that is comfortable and authentic. The hospitality is particularly attentive and your hosts are eager to tell you about their region and let you share in its varied riches — be it the cuisine, the wine or the culture. Be sure you go and see the beautiful abbeys of Sant'Antimo and San Galgano, which you can visit in complete tranquility as they are still a bit off the main tourist paths.

How to get there *(Map 13): 8km from San Gimignano, towards Gambassi, left to Libbiano.*

Hotel Pescille

Pescille 53037 San Gimignano (Siena)
Tel. 0577-94 01 86 - Fax 0577-94 31 65
Fratelli Gigli
E-mail: pescille@iol.it - Web: www.pescille.it

Category ★★★ **Rooms** 50 with telephone, bath, WC; 12 with air-conditiong, satellite TV, minibar. **Price** Double 180-230,000L, suite 260-310,000L. **Meals** Breakfast included, served 8:00-9:30. **Restaurant** See p. 556. **Credit cards** All major. **Pets** Dogs not allowed. **Facilities** Swimming pool, tennis (10,000L), parking. **Nearby** In San Gimignano, piazza della Cisterna, carnaval, San Gimignano, Etruscan ancient city of Pieve di Cellole, Convent of S.Vivaldo - Certaldo - Pinacoteca and visitation chapel (frescoes of Benozzo Gozzoli) in Castelfiorentino - Firenze - Siena - Volterra–Castelfalfi golf course (18-hole). **Closed** Nov – Mar.

The towers of San Gimignano are among the great tourist attractions of Tuscany. The Hotel Pescille, a sturdy and rustic old farmhouse converted into a hotel some years ago, is located outside of town. It was recently renovated and has all the facilities that a hotel in the city lacks: garden, tennis, swimming pool. The spot is pleasant and restful. You can relax after a hard day's sightseeing in the maze of little gardens around the hotel. The bedrooms have all the necessary amenities, in a sober decor that blends old and contemporary. All in all, a nice country inn.

How to get there *(Map 13): 38km northeast of Siena; 6km from San Gimignano towards Castel San Gimignano-Volterra after 3.5km.*

Casanova di Pescille

Pescille 53037 San Gimignano (Siena)
Tel. and Fax 0577-94 19 02
Roberto and Monica Fanciullini
E-mail: pescille@casanovadipescille.com - Web: www.casanovadipescille.com

Rooms 8 with air-conditiong, telephone and 1 apartment. (2 pers. with kitchen) with shower, satellite TV. **Price** Single 120-140,000L, double 130-150,000L, apartment 170-180,000L (2 pers.). **Meals** Breakfast included. **Restaurant** See p. 556. **Credit cards** Visa, Eurocard, MasterCard, Amex. **Pets** Dogs allowed. **Facilities** Mountain bike, archery, swimming pool, parking. **Nearby** San Gimignano: collegiata, piazza del Duomo, piazza della Cisterna, Annual carnival, Convent of S.Vivaldo - Certaldo - Pinacoteca - Visitation chapel (frescoes by B. Gozzoli) in Castelfiorentino - Firenze - Siena - Volterra – Castelfalfi golf course, (18-hole). **Open** All year.

For young people or others of limited means, or if you plan on a long stay, here is an address that will give you a base two kilometers from San Gimignano for far less money than you would pay in town. The owners of this estate, which produces the local white wine, Vernaccia, and also a good olive oil, have set up several rooms to receive guests. The house is simple but has a pleasant, well-kept garden, adorned with enormous pots of hydrangeas. Though the ground floor decor is really not to our taste, the bedrooms are nicely, if simply, decorated. They are not very large, but quite comfortable. The individual little house with its kitchenette gives a guest greater independence. One strong point: the breathtaking view from the bedrooms of the 13 towers of San Gimignano, and even better, the view from the pleasant terrace, which is open to all who want to taste the wine of the estate.

How to get there *(Map 13): 38km northeast of Siena; 5km north of San Gimignano, on the road to Volterra 2km on the left.*

Palazzo Squarcialupi

53011 Castellina in Chianti (Siena)
Via Ferruccio, 26
Tel. 0577-74 11 86 - Fax 0577-74 03 86 - Sig.ra Targioni
E-mail: squarcialupi@itzlyexpo.com - Web: www.italyexpo.com/squarcialupi

Category ★★★ **Rooms** 15 and 2 suites with air-conditioning, bath or shower, WC, satellite TV, minibar – Elevator. **Price** Double 180-290,000L. **Meals** Breakfast (buffet) included, served 8:00-10:00. **Restaurant** See p. 557. **Credit cards** Visa, Eurocard, MasterCard. **Pets** Small dogs allowed. **Facilities** Parking. **Nearby** Castellina: Wine fair (May) - Firenze - Vineyards of Chianti Classico (S 222) - Castello di Meleto - Castello di Brolio (Cappella S. Jacopo and Palazzo Padronale) - Siena - San Gimignano - Volterra. **Open** End Mar – end Oct.

In the main street of the medieval village of Castellina, the imposing Renaissance palace of Squarcialupi has just undergone a complete restoration of its upper floors and now houses a charming hotel. Part of the ground floor is occupied by the cantina enoteca. Castellina still produces Chianti, whose different vintages can be sampled in the pleasant and inviting bar. The rooms have been appointed in a sober and elegant manner. Beams and woodwork, panoramic murals and antique furniture mingle with modern paintings and pretty flower arrangements. The bedrooms, all brand new, are very comfortable. From the hotel terrace and from some of the rooms, one can admire the beauty of the Tuscan skyline, the colors and light of this lovely countryside whose praises have been sung for so many centuries. The Squarcialupi has all the charm of its roots.

How to get there *(Map 13): 21km north of Siena via S222.*

Hotel Salivolpi

53011 Castellina in Chianti (Siena)
Via Fiorentina, 13
Tel. 0577-74 04 84 - Fax 0577-74 09 98
E-mail: info@hotelsalivolpi. com - Web: www.hotelsalivolpi.com

Category ★★★ **Rooms** 19 with telephone, bath or shower, WC (9 with satellite TV). **Price** Double 170,000L; extra bed 69,500L. **Meals** Breakfast included (buffet), served 8:00-10:00. **Restaurant** See p. 557. **Credit card** Amex. **Pets** Dogs not allowed. **Facilities** Swimming pool, parking. **Nearby** Firenze - Vineyards Chianti Classico (S 222) from Impruneta to Siena - Castello di Meleto - Castello di Brolio (Cappella S. Jacopo and Palazzo padronale) - Siena - San Gimignano - Volterra. **Open** All year.

The Hotel Salivolpi consists of two old houses and a more modern annex, reconverted some years ago into an inn. Although it is on the small road from Castellina to San Donato, it is nevertheless quiet and peaceful. From the garden or the terrace, there is a lovely view of the vineyards that produce the famous Gallo Nero wine. In the old part, the rooms are delightful, with sloping ceilings and antique regional furniture. The new part, once lacking in charm, has been much improved by new amenities and decorations. Good facilities, a friendly welcome, a swimming pool (a godsend in the summer) and very advantageous prices make the Hotel Salivolpi an excellent base from which to explore the Chianti region.

How to get there *(Map 13): 21km north of Siena via S222, exit northwest of the town.*

Hotel Tenuta di Ricavo

Ricavo 53011 Castellina in Chianti (Siena)
Tel. 0577-74 02 21 - Fax 0577-74 10 14
Famiglia Lobrano
E-mail: ricavo@ricavo.com - Web: www.ricavo.com

Category ★★★★ **Rooms** 23 with air-conditiong, telephone, bath, WC, satellite TV, minibar, safe.
Price Double 300-380,000L, 335-438,000L, suite with terrace 450-600,000L. **Meals** Breakfast
included, served 7:30-10:00. **Restaurant** "La Pecora Nera", by reservation. Service 1:00PM-2:30PM,
7:00PM-10:00PM - closed Tues - à la carte 65-100,000L - Tuscan cuisine and very good Tuscan wines.
Credit cards Visa, Eurocard, MasterCard. **Pets** Dogs not allowed. **Facilities** Swimming pools (May –
Sept), ping-pong, palestre, parking (18,000L). **Nearby** Firenze - Vineyards Chianti Classico (S222)
from Impruneta to Siena - Castello di Meleto - Castello di Brolio (Cappella S. Jacopo and Palazzo
padronale) - Siena - San Gimignano - Volterra. **Closed** End Nov – Feb/Mar.

The Tenuta di Ricavo is one of the nicest restorations carried out in all of
Chianti. On this estate they have recreated a sort of village where the
farmhouses and barns now hold living rooms, a dining room and delightful
bedrooms. The windows of the bungalows are hung with pots of geraniums.
Everything has been done to enhance the surroundings so that guests can get
full enjoyment from their stay. The cooking is delicious, the swimming pool is
heated according to season. Note that the hotel offers special rates for stays
longer than four days. With all of Tuscany at your doorstep, the scent of the
pine forest and the chirping of the cicadas in summer will make you realize
why this region has been an inspiration to so many.

How to get there *(Map 13): 25km north of Siena, San Donato in Poggio exit,
then towards Castellina in Chianti, before 8km, take small road to the left and
1km.*

Hotel Villa Casalecchi

53011 Castellina in Chianti (Siena)
Tel. 0577-74 02 40 - Fax 0577-74 11 11
Sig.ra Lecchini-Giovannoni
E-mail: info@villacasalecchi.it - Web: www.villacasalecchi.it

Category ★★★★ **Rooms** 19 with air-conditioning, telephone, bath, WC, minibar, safe. **Price** Double 320-420,000L. **Meals** Breakfast included, served 8:00-10:30. **Restaurant** Service 12:30PM-2:30PM, 7:30PM-9:30PM - mealtime specials 75-95,000L - Tuscan cuisine. **Credit cards** All major. **Pets** Dogs allowed. **Facilities** Swimming pool, tennis, parking. **Nearby** Firenze - Vineyards Chianti Classico (S222) from Impruneta to Siena - Castello di Meleto - Castello di Brolio (Cappella S. Jacopo and Palazzo padronale) - Siena - San Gimignano - Volterra. **Closed** Mar – Nov.

This is the heart of that noble Tuscan vintage, Chianti Classico. The Villa Casalecchi is one of those places that offer real old-fashioned hospitality in the middle of beautiful rural surroundings. The atmosphere is serene, perhaps in part because of the very small number of rooms. There is a feeling of well-being, good food and, for those gentle country evenings, a large and wonderfully fragrant garden. This is a fine hotel that has kept its good reputation for many years.

How to get there *(Map 13): 21km north of Siena via S222, exit northwest of the town.*

Locanda Le Piazze

53011 Castellina in Chianti (Siena)
Tel. 0577-74 31 90 - Fax 0577-74 31 91 - Maureen Bonini
E-mail: lepiazze@chiantinet.it - Web: www.chiantinet.it/lepiazze

Rooms 20 with telephone, bath or shower, WC, TV on request - 1 for disabled persons. **Price** Standard double 360-380,000L, superior double 400-420,000L; extra bed +90,000L. **Meals** Breakfast (buffet) included, served 8:00-10:00 - half board 230-270,000L (per pers.). **Restaurant** By reservation for residents only - mealtime specials 60,000L. **Credit cards** All major. **Pets** Dogs allowed. **Facilities** Swimming pool, parking. **Nearby** Firenze - Vineyards Chianti Classico (S222) from Impruneta to Siena - Castello di Meleto - Castello di Brolio (Cappella S. Jacopo and Palazzo padronale) - Siena - San Gimignano - Volterra. **Open** Apr – mid Nov.

The site of the Locanda Le Piazze is quite simply astonishing, yet just what one would imagine when thinking about Tuscany and Chianti country. You leave Castellina to take a dirt road that weaves its way for five kilometers through fields of vineyards. Gradually, the stone building emerges against the horizon. Its apparent austerity from the outside makes all the more pleasant the delicious complexity of its interiors that descend gently towards the garden by half-levels. The ground floor extends into a veranda where breakfast and the menu of the day are served, then into a terrace leading to a lawn with beds of broom and oleanders which slopes gently down tyo the swimming poll - a real boon on hot summer days. Ten comfortable rooms are situated in the main house, the most charming of which has its bed in a little tower from which one can enjoy the view over the countryside. The other bedrooms are in the more modern annexes, some with a terrace level with the garden. All in all, they are spacious, independent and ideal for longer stays.

How to get there *(Map 13): On the SS Siena-Firenze, exit Poggibonsi (not Poggibonsi-North), and on reaching the bridge follow the route Alexclub, Villarosa, Belvedere; after 2km head for Le Piazze. Do not follow the direction of Castellina.*

Hotel Belvedere di San Leonino

San Leonino 53011 Castellina in Chianti (Siena)
Tel. 0577-74 08 87 - Fax 0577-74 09 24
Sig.ra Orlandi
E-mail: info@hotelsanleonino.com - Web: www.hotelsanleonino.com

Category ★★★ **Rooms** 28 with telephone, bath or shower, WC. **Price** Double 185-200,000L.
Meals Breakfast included, served 8:00-10:00. **Restaurant** Service 7:30PM - mealtime specials 32-
45,000L, also à la carte - Specialties: Bruschette toscane - Farfallette confiori di zucca - Lombo di
miale al forno con fonduta di gorgonzola pecorino e funghi - Semi freddo di ricotta e frutti di bosco.
Credit cards Amex, Visa, Eurocard, MasterCard. **Pets** Dogs not allowed. **Facilities** Swimming pool,
parking. **Nearby** Firenze - Vineyards Chianti Classico (S222) from Impruneta to Siena - Castello di
Meleto - Castello di Brolio (Cappella S. Jacopo and Palazzo padronale) - Siena. **Open** Feb – Nov.

The countryside between Florence and Siena is an ideal place to stay: the
Chianti region is superb, it is easy to reach because the two cities are
linked by a motorway and an express route and prices outside them are more
moderate. Hotel San Leonino, a few kilometers from Castellina, is a
welcoming inn, situated in very lovely country, with rooms divided between
several buildings; they are spacious and impeccably clean. The salon and the
dining room on the ground floor are newer. In summer, dinner is served in the
garden, while at noon you can take a light lunch on the terrace. The swimming
pool at the end of the garden has a panoramic view of the valley. Staying here
is a good way to get to know Tuscany, away from the hordes of tourists who
periodically overrun Firenze and Siena.

How to get there *(Map 13): 10km north of Siena via S2, Badesse exit; 8km*
south of Castellina by S222, at Quercegrossa go left towards San Leonino. On
the A1 (Firenze-Roma), exit Firenze Certosa.

Castello di Spaltenna

53013 Gaiole in Chianti (Siena)
Tel. 0577-74 94 83 - Fax 0577-74 92 69
E-mail: info@spaltenna.it - Web: www.spaltenna.it

Category ★★★★ **Rooms** 30 with air-conditiong, telephone, bath, WC, TV, minibar. **Price** Single 300,000L, double 380-480,000L, suite 580-690,000L. **Meals** Breakfast included **Restaurant** Service 1:00PM-2:30PM, 8:00PM-10:00PM - also à la carte - Specialties: Ribollita, insalata di funghi porcini con rucola e tartufi - Ravioli di zucchine al profumo di tartufo - Mdaglioni d'agnello al mosto cotto - Tortino di cioccolato caldo. **Credit cards** All major. **Pets** Dogs not allowed. **Facilities** 2 swimming pools (1 heated and covered), tennis, billard, sauna, parking. **Nearby** Firenze - Vineyards Chianti Classico (S222) from Impruneta to Siena - Castello di Meleto - Castello di Brolio (Cappella S. Jacopo and Palazzo padronale) - Siena. **Open** Mar 20 – Nov 20.

This former monastery, built between the 10th and 13th centuries, is now under new management. The renovation and conversion to a hotel have successfully preserved all its ancient majesty. Since one of the foremost assets of the place is its marvelous location, it was decided to have as many of the rooms as possible benefit from the panoramic view of the woods and vineyards of Chianti. The impressive interior architecture, always turned outward on the natural surroundings, has also been well-preserved. Calm, comfort and gastronomy are the key words here — all guarantees of an enjoyable stay at the Castello di Spaltenna.

How to get there (Map 13): 28km northeast of Siena via S408.

Borgo Argenina 🌳

Argenina 53013 Gaiole in Chianti (Siena)
Tel. and Fax 0577-74 71 17 - Sig.ra Elena Nappa
Web: www.borgoargenina.it

Rooms 5 and 2 apartments (6 with air-conditioning), with telephone, bath, WC, minibar. **Price** (2 nights min.). Single 150-180,000L, double 220,000L, suite 200-250,000L, apart. 280,000L (per 2 pers.). **Meals** Breakfast included; in bedrooms 15,000L, served 9:00-10:30. **Restaurant** See p. 555. **Credit cards** Not accepted. **Pets** Dogs not allowed. **Facilities** Parking. **Nearby** Firenze - vineyards Chianti Classico (S222) from Impruneta to Siena. **Open** All year.

In the heart of Chianti country, among the vineyards of Barone Ricasoli, the delightful Elena Nappi has devoted all her energy and love to restoring the old abandoned hamlet of Argenina. The site, like the old stones, is superb and one admires her initiative. This is the image of Tuscany as one imagines it, with its hills covered with vineyards and its rows of cypress trees rising skywards and the solitary castle of Brolio in the distance. Local craftsmen and recovered materials, used for a scrupulous restoration, have given life back to this little village, which is occupied all year round by its owners who have created a few rooms for those wish to rediscover the refinement of simplicity and tradition. The bedrooms are very comfortable, decorated with old rustic furniture and examples of Elena's needlework. The sitting room has a series of vaults and arcades, to make an elegant and convivial space. The kitchen displays the attractive disorder of preserving jars, garlic and bunches of tomatoes drying under the ceiling. The welcome is very attentive and friendly. All this beautiful nature, still enjoying the serenity it has known for centuries, is a mere fifteen kilometers from Siena.

How to get there *(Map 13): 15km northeast of Siena by SS408 towards Gaiole. Take the right towards Marcellino Monti.*

L'Ultimo Mulino

La Ripresa di Vistarenni 53013 Gaiole in Chianti (Siena)
Tel. 0577-73 85 20 - Fax 0577-73 86 59
Andrea Mencarelli
E-mail: hotelmulino@chiantinet.it - Web: www.chiantinet.it/hotelmulino

Category ★★★★ **Rooms** 12 and 1 suite with air-conditioning, telephone, bath, WC, satellite TV, minibar, safe – Rooms for disabled persons. **Price** Single 280,000L, double 350-400,000L, suite 530,000L. **Meals** Breakfast included, served 8:00-11:00. **Restaurant** Only for residents. **Credit cards** All major. **Pets** Dogs allowed. **Facilities** Swimming pool, parking. **Nearby** Siena - Vineyards Chianti Classico (S222) from Impruneta to Siena - Impruneta (grape harvets festival, Fair of Saint Luke with is an important horse market, center of porcelain manufacture) - Firenze. **Closed** Jan 7 – Mar.

In this region, with its shortage of rivers, many mills were built from the 12th Century onwards to make use of the smallest water course. L'Ultimo Mulino, dating from the 15th Century and one of the largest, therefore had an important economic role in the region. Now restored, its fine and noble structure make a charming setting for this elegrant country hotel. The main sitting room has no less than 13 arches and you can still see the wheel at twenty meters depth. The interior is soberly decorated, but there is more sophisticated comfort in the bathrooms, some of which have jacuzzi. The bedrooms too are very pleasant with a private terrace-patio. The wooden surroundings are magnificent and guarantee the most complete tranquillity. The hotel now has a restaurant service for residents, but this should not prevent you from also discovering the nearby village osterie which continue to serve healthy food and a good Chianti.

How to get there (Map 13): 35km northeast of Siena, 6km from Gaiole in Chianti.

Relais Fattoria Vignale

53017 Radda in Chianti (Siena)
Via Pianigiani, 9
Tel. 0577-73 83 00 - Fax 0577-73 85 92 - Sig.ra Kummer
E-mail: vignale@chiantinet.it

Category ★★★★ **Rooms** 34 and 3 suites with air-conditioning, telephone, bath, WC, TV, minibar –
Elevator. **Price** Single 220,000L, double 280-380,000L, suite with terrace 500-600,000L. **Meals**
Breakfast included (buffet), served 7:30-10:30. **Restaurant** Service 1:00PM-2:30PM, 7:30PM-9:00PM -
mealtime specials 70-100,000L, also à la carte - Seasonal and Tuscan cuisine. **Credit cards** All
major. **Pets** Dogs not allowed. **Facilities** Swimming pool, parking. **Nearby** Siena - Vineyards Chianti
Classico (S222) from Impruneta to Siena - Impruneta (grape harvets festival, Fair of Saint Luke with
is an important horse market, center of porcelain manufacture) - Firenze. **Closed** Dec 8 – Jan 6.

Formerly the home of wealthy landowners, it was bought and entirely
renovated in 1983. The decoration is discreet and consistent, perfectly in
tune with the surroundings, and one feels the constant fidelity to the past: the
vaulted cellar that serves as a breakfast room, the wall paintings in the library,
the austerity with which all the bedrooms have been furnished. Aside from the
traditional restaurant, there is also the Taverna, which is open from 5 p.m. to
midnight. Anyone interested in wine should make it a point to stop here. The
estate produces an excellent wine and offers its clients an *onoteca* as well as a
fine collection of books on wine for connoisseurs.

How to get there *(Map 13): 30km north of Siena via S222 to Castellina in
Chianti, then S429.*

La Locanda

Montanino - 53017 Radda in Chianti (Siena)
Tel. and fax 0577-73 88 33/32 - G. and M. Bevilacqua
E-mail: info@lalocanda.it - Web: www.lalocanda.it

Rooms 7 (4 with terrace), with telephone, satellite TV, safe. **Price** Double 350-400,000L, suite 450,000L. **Meals** Breakfast included, served 8:30-10:30. **Restaurant** Service 8:30PM - mealtime specials 60,000L. **Credit cards** Amex, Visa, Eurocard, MasterCard. **Pets** Dogs not allowed. **Facilities** Swimming pool, parking. **Nearby** Siena - Vineyards Chianti Classico (S222) from Impruneta to Siena - Impruneta (grape harvets festival, Fair of Saint Luke with is an important horse market, center of porcelain manufacture) - San Gimignano - Firenze – Dell'Ugolino golf course (18-hole) in Grassina. **Closed** Jan 10 - Mar 10.

The drastic regulations governing building and even restoration in Tuscany, while they are a burden to locals, have allowed the preservation of unique sites like the one where La Locanda is situated. A few kilometers from the ilittle village of Volpaia, you go through the woods before finally arriving on a hill that overlooks the whole of the surrounding plain. Guido and Martina left Milan to open this marvellous inn. The restoration is exemplary: one building houses the drawing room and the dining room which is extended by a terrace. The welcome is what you would expect in a friends' house. There is not really a restaurant, but if you ask, they will always make you a plate of regional products or pasta. In the other building, all the rooms are exquisite: pretty furniture, pretty fabrics, and comfortable bathrooms; numbers 5 and 6, with their loggia overlooking the little village of Volpaia, are even better. You absolutely must visit.

How to get there *(Map 13): 30km north of Siena by SS222 towards Firenze. Castellina, Radda in Chianti. Onleaving Radd, towards Firenze. After 4km turn right for Volpaia. On the little town square at Volpaia, take the street to the right which becomes a road for 3km. On the left, take the road for Montanino as far as La Locanda.*

Podere Terreno 🌲

Volpaia - 53017 Radda in Chianti (Siena)
Tel. 0577-73 83 12 - Fax 0577-73 84 00
Sig.ra Marie-Sylvie Haniez
E-mail: podereterreno@chiantinet.it

Rooms 7 with shower, WC. **Price** With half board 170-180,000L (per pers., 2 nights min. in high season). **Meals** Breakfast included, served 8:30-10:30. **Restaurant** Service 8:00PM - mealtime specials - Tuscan and Mediterannean cuisine. **Credit cards** Amex, Visa, Eurocard, MasterCard. **Pets** Dogs allowed. **Facilities** Mountain bike, parking. **Nearby** Lake - Siena - Vineyard Chianti Classico (S222) - Impruneta - San Gimignano - Firenze – Dell'Ugolino golf course (18-hole) in Grassina. **Closed** Christmas.

Volpaia is one of those pretty villages in the region of Chianti Classico, in an estate with oak and chestnut trees, olive orchards and a vineyard, which produces quality wine and excellent olive oil. The old traditional Tuscan kitchen has been converted into a salon. The large couch in front of the fireplace, the rustic antique furniture and Marie-Sylvie's and Roberto's collections, all add to the decor. The very charming rooms are comfortable and decorated with taste and simplicity. Marie-Sylvie makes the jellies she serves for breakfast and Roberto supervises the kitchen. Meals are served around a large common table, accompanied by wine from the estate vineyards. The billiards room and library in the cellar are good places to spend a quiet moment alone, as is the arbor in the garden.

How to get there *(Map 13): 30km north of Siena by SS222 towards Firenze. Castellina, Radda in Chianti. At the Radda exit, towards Firenze. After 4km turn right for Volpaia and Podere Terreno.*

Vescine - Il Relais del Chianti

Vescine - 53017 Radda in Chianti (Siena)
Tel. 0577-74 11 44 - Fax 0577-74 02 63
Sig.ra Flora Ferri
E-mail: vescine@chiantinet.it

Rooms 24 with air-conditioning, telephone, bath or shower, WC, TV, minibar. **Price** Double 260-350,000L, suite 350-500,000L. **Meals** Breakfast included, served 8:00-10:30. **Restaurant** 700m from the hotel, closed Thurs. **Credit cards** Amex, Visa, Eurocard, MasterCard. Pets Dogs allowed (10,000L). **Facilities** Swimming pool, tennis, parking. **Nearby** Siena - Vineyard Chianti Classico (S222) - Impruneta - San Gimignano - Firenze – Dell'Ugolino golf course (18-hole) in Grassina. **Open** Mar – mid Nov.

If it's calm and solitude you're seeking, don't hesitate — Vescine is the place for you. In the heart of Chianti, this little hamlet surrounded by 75 hectares of land has been reconverted into a country inn and offers a unique setting for a stay in Tuscany. Completely restored and renovated, the various buildings are connected by pretty cobbled paths lined with masses of flowers. The woman who runs the place has managed to combine a gentle Tuscan atmosphere with very functional facilities. The rooms are sober and functional as well. You can make your stay more pleasant by enjoying the fine swimming-pool. The welcome is rather impersonal.

How to get there *(Map 13): 54km south of Firenze. A1 Firenze-Certosa exit, then take superstrada for Siena, San Donato exit in Poggio to Catellina in Chianti. The hotel is on the road no. 429 between Castellina and Radda in Chianti.*

Torre Canvalle

La Villa - 53017 Radda in Chianti (Siena)
Tel. 0577-73 83 21 - Fax 0577-73 83 21
Enrico and Lele Vitali
E-mail: canvalle@chiantinet.it - Web: www.chiantiline.com

Apartment 1 with kitchen, lounge, 2 bedrooms, telephone, bath or shower. **Price** Apart./week 1 300,000L. **Credit cards** Not accepted. **Pets** Dogs allowed. **Facilities** Swimming pool, parking. **Nearby** Siena - Vineyard Chianti Classico (S222) - Impruneta (grape harvest festival, Fair of Saint Luke with is an important horse market, center of porcelain manufacture) - San Giminiano - Firenze – Dell'Ugolino golf course (18-hole) in Grassina. **Open** Mar 1 – Jan 31.

Many people will love the idea of renting a Tuscan tower in the Chianti region. The idea is unexpected and quite delightful. Sanding alone in the estate, the tower, built in the early 19th Century, overlooks a small lake and all the surrounding countryside. The owners do not live far away and have done it up to house four people. On the ground floor is a sitting room with kitchen attached, then each bedroom has its own floor, with a bathroom on the first. The décor is simple and rustic, but elegant. If you think that holidays mean not doing the cooking, then you can arrange through Lele to have half-board at the family restaurant, Le Vigne, at the podere Le Vigne. The welcome is warm and the family, which has lived around here for a long time, is always ready with advice if you need it.

How to get there *(Map 13): 54km south of Florence. On A1 exit firenze-Certosa than take the superstrada for Siena, exit San Donato in Poggio. Go as far as Castellina in Chianti. In the village, by the Restaurant Miranda, take the road for Canvalle as far as the tower.*

Hotel Borgo Pretale

Borgo Pretale
53018 Sovicille (Siena)
Tel. 0577-34 54 01 - Fax 0577-34 56 25 - Sig. Rizzardini
E-mail: info@borgopretale.it - Web: www.emmeti.it/borgopretale

Category ★★★★ **Rooms** 35 with telephone, bath, WC, TV, minibar. **Price** Double 185,000L (per pers.), junior suite 200,000L, suite 225,000L (per pers.). **Meals** Breakfast included, served 7:30-10:00; half board 70,000L (per pers., 3 days min.). **Restaurant** Service 7:30PM-9:30PM - mealtime specials 80,000L, also à la carte - Tuscan and Italian cuisine. **Credit cards** All major. **Pets** Dogs not allowed. **Facilities** Swimming pool, tennis, archery, fitness center with sauna, mountain bikes, golf practice, parking. **Nearby** Villa Cetinale in Sovicille - Abbey of Torri in Rosia - Abbey of Torri in Rosia - Abbey of San Galgano - Siena. **Open** Apr – end Oct.

Eighteen kilometers from Siena, in a village that has kept its Tuscan colors and all its authenticity, the Torre Borgo Pretale has been transformed into a hotel. There are eight marvelous rooms in the tower itself; the others are located in cottages at garden level. The interior amenities are very comfortable and in excellent taste. The service is most attentive. From June to September, a buffet lunch is served at the swimming pool. The availability of swimming, archery, tennis and other recreations are a plus, even for those who have come primarily on a pilgrimage of the Quattrocento, as Borgo Pretale is located in the heart of historic Tuscany.

How to get there *(Map 13): 18km southeast of Siena via S73 towards Rosia. Follow signs.*

Azienda Agricola Montestigliano 🌳

53010 Rosia (Siena)
Tel. 0577-34 21 89 - Fax 0577-34 21 00
Sig. Donati
E-mail: montes@ftbcc.it

Apartments 10 (3-8 pers.) and 1 villa (12 pers.) with kitchen, shower, WC, telephone. **Price** Per day 130-255,000L (3-4 pers.), 170-350,000L (6-8 pers.), 300-675,000L (villa Donati 12 pers.). **Meals** Breakfast 12,000L, served 8:30-10:00. **Evening meals** (For residents, on request, 2 times a week). Service 8:00PM - mealtime specials 450,000L - Tuscan cuisine. **Credit cards** Not accepted. **Pets** Small dogs allowed. **Facilities** 2 swimming pools, parking. **Nearby** La Montagnala: Church of S. Giovanni in Rosia, Abbey of Torri, Abbey of San Galgano - Monteriggioni - Abbadia Isola - Siena. **Open** All year.

Only 16 kilometers from Siena, discover the property of Montestigliano, which has been in the Donati family for over 50 years. The various farm buildings form a veritable village overlooking fields of olive trees that cover the broad plain of the Merse River. The farmhouses and noble estates have all been restored in traditional style and furnished in a pleasant country manner. They are all comfortable: The kitchens are well-equipped (they all have washing machines and the villa also has a dishwasher) and each one has a terrace or a private garden. If you wish, you can have your breakfast and dinner in a wing of the main house, which also contains the offices of the cereal farm, or better still, on the well-shaded terrace of the owners' stately home. For the greater comfort of the guests, there are two swimming pools. The warm welcome is both Italian and English - Susan Pennington will advise you on all the possible walks to be done in the Montagnola area.

How to get there *(Map 13): 15km south of Siena via SS73 to Rosia. L'Azienda is 5km after Torri, Stigliano and Montestigliano on right.*

Casa Bolsinina

Montauto 53041 Monteroni d'Arbia (Siena)
Tel. and fax 0577-71 84 77 - Marcello Mazzotta
E-mail: bolsinina@bolsinina.com - Web: www.bolsinina.com

Rooms 5 and 1 suite (2-4 pers.) and 4 apartments with telephone, bath, WC, satellite TV, minibar. **Price** Double 150-200,000L (3 days min.), suite 190-310,000L, apart./week 750-1 750,000L. **Meals** Breakfast included, served 8:00-10:30. **Restaurant** By reservation, service 7:30PM-8:30PM - mealtime specials 50,000L. **Credit cards** All major. **Pets** Small dogs allowed on request. **Facilities** Swimming pool, parking. **Nearby** Abbey of Sant'Antimo at Montalcino - Abbey of Monte Oliveto Maggiore - Asciano-Siena crete road - Siena - Pienza - Montepulciano. **Open** Mar 15 – Jan 15.

Casa Bolsinina is close to the oddest location in Tuscany, the region of the Crete, southeast of Siena. The origin of this discrepency lies in a geological phenomenon. On the S438 between Siena and Asciano, one discovers with astonishment a lunar landscape of bare hills which change in color from grey to red according to season. A dirt road of two kilometers winds its way towards this elegant old brick house, burnt sienna in color. The same bricks are to be found inside, enhancing a vault, an arcade or a pillar. The interior has been entirely restored, respecting the original forms. On the ground floor are all the shared areas which are comfortably furnished, with taste and without affectation. The same applies to the rooms, each of which has the name of a dog, an animal which is well-liked here, though not over-obtrusive. There is a very clear view from the house. The loggia and terraces allow you to enjoy the panorama, and you can also laze or cook a barbecue on the banks of the pond. There are fine walks around and some of the most interesting abbeys in the region.

How to get there *(Map 13): 20km southeast of Siena by S2 as far as Buonconvento-Montalcino. 1km of Bivio via Casale Caggiolo.*

Hotel Vecchia Oliviera

53024 Montalcino (Siena)
Porta Cerbaia/angolo Via Landi, 1
Tel. 0577-84 60 28 - Fax 0577-84 60 29 - Marisa Stefanelli

Rooms 11 with air-conditioning, telephone, bath, satellite TV, minibar. **Price** Single 110-160,000L, double 220-320,000L, triple 260-380,000L, suite (per 4 pers.) 300-450,000L. **Meals** Breakfast included, served 7:30-10:00. **Restaurant** See p. 555. **Credit cards** All major. **Pets** Dogs not allowed. **Facilities** Swimming pool, parking. **Nearby** Montalcino - Abbey of Sant'Antimo at Montalcino - Abbey of Monte Oliveto Maggiore - Asciano-Siena crete road - Siena - Pienza - Montepulciano **Closed** 2 weeks in Nov.

The history of Montalcino is closely tied in with the wine-growing traditions of the region which produces Brunello, one of the best wines in Italy. The hotel is near the Porta Cerbaia which leads into this fortified village overlooking the valleys of the Ombrone and the Asso. It occupies an old oil press surrounded by olive groves; hence its name. No trace of this former function remains inside and the décor tends rather towards the cozy and comfortable with 17th- and 18th-century style furniture in the shared areas. All the bedrooms are named after flowers; they are on the ground floor with direct access to the large terrace (not attached to any one of them), or else on the second floor with views over the countryside (our preference goes to Viola and Veronica). The suite, Ortensia, is meant to house four people, but overlooks the street. All the rooms are comfortable with well-designed bathrooms, pretty white walls trimmed with light bucolic friezes and painted iron bedsteads. The sitting rooms are pleasant: the reading room opens directly on to the lawn and the dining room on to the swimming pool. There is no restaurant, but plenty of good ones in town, with a Michelin star for Poggio Antico.

How to get there *(Map 13): 40km southeast of Siena.*

375

Castello di Modanella

Modanella 53040 Serre di Rapolano (Siena)
Tel. 0577-70 46 04 - Fax 0577-70 47 40
Sig.ra Cerretti
E-mail: modanell@tin.it

Apartments 47 with bath, WC, TV. **Price** For 1 week 805-1 300,000L (with 2 rooms), 1 010-1 655,000L (3 rooms), 1 640-2 405,000L (4 rooms), 1 695-2 515,000L (5 rooms). **Restaurant** In Aciano and in Montalcino, see p. 555. **Credit cards** All major. **Pets** Dogs allowed. **Facilities** 3 swimming pools, tennis, ping-pong, parking. **Nearby** Rapalano Terme - Bagno Vignoni - Petriolo - the crestroad from Asciano to Siena - Abbey of Monte Oliveto Maggiore - Abbey of Sant'Antimo - Montalcino - Pienza - Lucignano - Arezz. **Open** All year.

Leave behind the marble and travertine quarries of the industrial zone of Serre di Rapolano and make your way confidently, for as soon as you cross the railroad tracks you will catch sight of the castle of Modanella and its farm buildings scattered over a large wine-growing estate. To provide such a large number of apartments, they have transformed all the stables, barns, granges, silos and even the old schoolhouse. All designed with taste and simplicity, they charmingly combine rusticity and comfort: white walls, blond wood furniture, comfortable bedding, a well-equipped kitchen and handsome bathrooms (all done in tavertine stone, of course). There are no rooms in the castle itself, as it is still being restored. All in all, a beautiful place, but the new extensions make it seem slightly like a holiday club.

How to get there *(Map 13): 35km from Siena; 30km from Arezzo; in Siena take road E78 326 to km 28, then turn left, and you will see the sign for Modanella after 3.5km.*

TUSCANY

Azienda Piccolomini Bandini

Lucignano d'Asso 53020 San Giovanni d'Asso (Siena)
Tel. 0577-80 30 68 - Fax 0577-80 30 82
Angelica Piccolomini Naldi Bandini
E-mail: piccolomini@comune.siena.it - Web: www.nautilus-mp.com/piccolomininaldi

Houses 6 with kitchen, sitting room, 2-4 rooms, bath, TV. **Price** For 1 week "Casa Maria" (2 pers.) 2 500,000L - "Casa Severino" (2-4 pers.) 2 000,000L - "Casa Amedeo" (4-6 pers.), "Casa Clementina" (2-4 pers.), "Casa Remo" (2-4 pers.) 3 000,000L - "Casale Sarageto" (7 pers. and privat swimming pool) 7 000,000L. **Credit cards** Not accepted. **Pets** Dogs allowed. **Facilities** Panoramique swimming pool. **Nearby** Val d'Orcia: Pienza, Montepulciano, Monticchiello, Montalcino (Brunello's cellars) and Abbey of Sant'Antimo, Terme di Bagno Vignoni, Collegiata San Quirico d'Orcia, Castiglione d'Orcia, Rocca d'Orcia, Campiglia d'Orcia, Abbey of Sant'Anna Camprena, Abbey of Monte Oliveto Maggiore (N48). **Open** All year.

If you dream of houses in Tuscany, of the light and the landscape of the Sienese masters, treat yourself to a stay in the hamlet of Lucignano d'Asso where six houses have been done up with exquisite taste and a real flair for decoration. They are all equally equipped with household and sanitary facilities of the highest quality. Each one has its own charm. The largest, the "Casa Sarageto" is quite spectacular with its grand salon and its trophy-cases, its superb bedrooms, a garden and a private swimming pool. The others can make use of a superb panoramic swimming pool. Nearby, you will find a typical little grocer's shop, well-stocked with products from the estate (wine and olive oil), where you can even go to have lunch. In such marvelous surroundings, you can give free range to the emotions produced by art and nature in the heart of Tuscany.

How to get there *(Map 13): 35km south of Siena, towards Montalcino-S. Quirico d'orcia. In Torrenieri, towards S. Giovanni d'Asso. Halfway take the road on the right for Lucignano d'Asso and Lucignanello Bandini.*

Locanda dell'Amorosa

L'Amorosa
53048 Sinalunga (Siena)
Tel. 0577-67 94 97 - Fax 0577-63 20 01 - Sig. Citterio - Sig.ra Chervatin
E-mail: locanda@amorosa.it - Web: www.amorosa.it

Category ★★★★ **Rooms** 15 and 6 suites with air-conditioning, telephone, bath, WC, TV, minibar. **Price** Standard 410,000L, superior 480,000L, deluxe 560,000L, suite 620,000L, luxury suite 1 200,000L. **Meals** Breakfast included, served 7:30-10:30. **Restaurant** Service 12:30PM-2:30PM, 8:00PM-9:30PM - closed Mon and Tues at noon, except for residents - à la carte - New regional cooking, very good Italian wines. **Credit cards** All major. **Pets** Dogs not allowed. **Facilities** Swimming pool, parking. **Nearby** Collegiata di San Martino and Church of S. Croce de Sinalunga - Museo Civico - Palazzo Comunale - Church of Madonna delle Averce in Lucignano - Monte San Savino (loggia) - Pienza - Montepulciano - Perugia - Savino (loggia) - Arezzo - Siena. **Closed** Jan 7 – Mar 5.

After crossing the plain where Piero della Francesca was born, a long cypress-lined path will lead you to the entrance of the Locanda. Once you have gone through the vaulted archway, you will find enchanting old buildings built out of a mixture of stone, brick and the pink terra cotta of Siena. Quiet comfort and good taste are the great luxuries of this inn, one of the most beautiful in Italy. The cuisine, made from numerous products from the farm, is excellent. The selection of wines from the region is also nice. Don't miss this place if you can afford it.

How to get there *(Map 13): 50km southeast of Siena via S326; via A1, Val di Chiana exit; 2km south of Sinalunga to L'Amorosa.*

La Chiusa

53040 Montefollonico (Siena)
Via della Madonnina, 88
Tel. 0577-66 96 68 - Fax 0577-66 95 93
Sig.ra Masotti and Sig. Lucherini

Rooms 6 and 6 apartments with telephone, bath, WC, TV, minibar. **Price** Double 350,000L, suite 590,000L, luxe 690-850,000L. **Meals** Breakfast included, served 8:30-10:30. **Restaurant** Service 12:30PM-3:00PM, 8:00PM-10:00PM - closed Tues - mealtime specials 160,000L, also à la carte - Specialties: Collo d'oca ripieno - Pappardelle Dania - Coniglio marinato al romarino - Piccione al vinsanto. **Credit cards** All major. **Pets** Dogs allowed. **Nearby** Montepulciano - Monticchiello - Montalcino - Terme in Bagno Vignoli - Val d'Orcia villages (Castiglione d'Orcia, Rocca d'Orcia, Ripa d'Orcia, Campiglia d'Orcia) - Pienza - Collegiale San Quirico d'Orcia - Museo Nazionale Etrusco in Siusi - Chianciano Terme - Siena. **Open** Mar 15 — Dec 15, Dec 26 — Jan 9.

L a Chiusa is more than just a famous restaurant and inn–it's the lovely and welcoming house of Dania who passionately loves her work and takes pleasure in receiving her guests as if they were good friends. The delicious meals are always prepared with fresh products from the farm. The rooms and the apartments are very comfortable and very well kept. The breakfasts, of homemade jellies and brioches and fresh fruit juices are generous. When you watch the sun set over the Val di Chiana and the Val d'Orcia, you will start planning your next trip back.

How to get there *(Map 13): 60km south of Siena via A1, Valdichiana exit - Bettole, Torrita di Siena Montefollonico.*

La Dionora

53040 Montepulciano (Siena)
Tel. 0578-71 74 96 - Fax 0578-71 74 98 - Dr Mario Angelini
Web: www.dionora.it

Rooms 6 with air-conditioning, telephone, bath with jacuzzi, WC, satellite TV, minibar. **Price** Single 350,000L, double 400-430,000L, suite 500,000L. **Meals** Breakfast included, served 8:00-10:30. **Restaurant** See p. 556. **Credit cards** All major. **Pets** Dogs not allowed. **Facilities** Swimming pool, mountain bike, sauna, parking. **Nearby** Pienza - Monticchiello - Montalcino - hot baths of Bagno Vignoni - villages of the Val d'Orcia (Collegiale San Quirico d'Orcia, Castiglione d'Orcia, Rocca d'Orcia, Ripa d'Orcia, Campiglia d'Orcia) - Abbey of Sant'Anna Camprena - Spedaletto - Chiusi - Cetona - Chianciano. **Closed** Jan 10 – Feb 10.

In the plain of the Chiana which extends below Montepulciano, the Dianora is more a luxury hotel in the countryside than a comfortable stopping place for agriturismo. The rooms are shared between the two adjacent buildings. In the main house is the sitting room with large sofas covered in fine Ferragamo fabrics. The rooms are reached by a stone staircase. They are very attractive and luxurious with elegant decoration in natural colors. The bathrooms are very comfortable. The rooms in the second building are done in the colors of the name they have been given: sunflower, olive... Opening directly on to the garden or the little courtyard, they are sophisticated and all welcome you, if you wish, with an open fire in the appropriate season. Breakfast is served in the Orangery beside the swimming pool and, at your feet, you will see that Renaissance jewel which is the little town of Pienza. A wonderful place to stay.

How to get there *(Map 13): On A1, exit Chiusi-Chianciano towards Montepulciano. Do not go up intot he village. Take a left towards Pienza, then towards Poggiano. The entrance is 1.5km on the left.*

La Sovana 🌲

Sovana 53047 Sarteano (Siena)
Tel. 0578-27 40 86 - Fax 0578-27 40 86 - Tel. and Fax 075-600 197
Sig. Giuseppe Olivi
E-mail: info@lasovana.com - Web: www.lasovana.com

Suite-apatments 15 (4-5 pers.) with bath or shower, kitchen. **Price** (3 days min., 1 week for Christmas and in summer) suite 105-155,000L (per pers.). **Meals** Breakfast (buffet) included, served 8:30-9:30 - half board +45,000L (per pers.). **Restaurant** Service 8:00PM - mealtime specials. **Credit cards** Not accepted. **Pets** Dogs not allowed. **Facilities** Swimming pool, tennis. **Nearby** Pienza - Monticchiello - Montalcino - hot baths of Bagno Vignoni - villages of the Val d'Orcia (Collegiale San Quirico d'Orcia, Castiglione d'Orcia, Rocca d'Orcia, Ripa d'Orcia, Campiglia d'Orcia) - Abbey of Sant'Anna Camprena - Spedaletto - Chiusi - Cetona - Cianciano. **Closed** Jan 8 – Feb 10, Nov 10 – Dec 22.

L a Sovana is a pleasant, very well-organized holiday residence. The two old buildings face one another and house a series of well-designed apartments which are entirely self-contained. Further back in the property, another house also has apartments, which lead out on to private terraces. These are quieter. The interior design is outstanding. Pretty old rustic furniture is combined with modern décor composed of fabrics and flooring in coordinated pretty colors. No aspect of comfort has been neglected. A new dining room extends into a very large covered terrace opening on the garden. On the estate there is still a large swimming pool and a pond with perch, tench and wild duck. A very interesting place to stay, given its position between Tuscany and Umbria.

How to get there *(Map 13): On A1 exit Chiusi Chianciano, towards Sarteano, 1km from the motorway on the left.*

381

La Saracina

53026 Pienza (Siena)
Strada Statale, 146 (km 29,7)
Tel. 0578-74 80 22 - Fax 0578-74 80 18 - Simonetta Vessichelli
E-mail: info@lasaracina.it - Web: www.lasaracina.it

Rooms 2, 3 suites and 1 apartment with telephone, bath, WC, TV. **Price** Double 300-380,000L, apartment 400,000L, suite 420,000L. **Meals** Breakfast included. **Restaurant** See p. 556. **Credit cards** All major. **Pets** Dogs not allowed. **Facilities** Swimming pool, tennis, mountain bike rentals, parking. **Nearby** Pienza (Duomo, Palazzo Piccolomini) - Montepulciano - Monticchiello - Montalcino - Terme in Bagno Vignoni - villages in Val d'Orcia (Collegiale San Quirico d'Orcia, Castiglione d'Orcia, Rocca d'Orcia, Ripa d'Orcia, Campiglia d'Orcia) - Abbey of Sant'Anna Camprena (frescoes of Sodoma) - Spedaletto - Chiusi - Cetona - Chianciano. **Open** All year.

The Saracina is in an old farmhouse on a small hill, which has a view of Pienza, Monticchiello and Montefollonico. The rooms are very beautiful; they are decorated with antique furniture and have large bathrooms and very comfortable salons. Everything has been done with exquisite taste. A delicious breakfast is served in the shade of the pretty garden or on the terrace. Be sure to spend some time visiting the enchanting town of Pienza, which has remained intact since the Renaissance and is not a tourist trap. It was the work of Pope Pius II of Piccolomini, who wanted, with the help of architect B. Rossellino, to create the ideal town. Several palaces and the cathedral were built before the work was interrupted by the sudden death of the two sponsors. Fortunately, no one has disturbed the harmony of this small town which served as the set of Zefferelli's Romeo and Juliet.

How to get there *(Map 13): 52km southeast of Siena. Motoway A1 exit Valdichiana or Chiusi-Chianciano.*

Relais Il Chiostro di Pienza

53026 Pienza (Siena)
Corso Rossellino, 26
Tel. 0578-74 84 00/42 - Fax 0578-74 84 40 - Sig.ra Loriana Codogno
E-mail: ilchiostro@jumpy.it

Category ★★★ **Rooms** 37 with telephone, bath or shower, WC, TV, minibar – 2 rooms for disabled persons. **Price** Single 200,000L, double 300,000L, suite 400,000L. **Meals** Breakfast included **Restaurant** Service 12:30PM-2:30PM, 8:00PM-9:30PM - closed Mon - mealtime specials, also à la carte - Regional cooking. **Credit cards** All major. **Pets** Dogs not allowed. **Facilities** Swimming pool. **Nearby** Pienza (Duomo, Palazzo Piccolomini) -, Montepulciano - Monticchiello - Montalcino - Terme in Bagno Vignoni - villages in Val d'Orcia (Collegiale San Quirico d'Orcia, Castiglione d'Orcia, Rocca d'Orcia, Ripa d'Orcia, Campiglia d'Orcia) - Abbey of Sant'Anna Camprena (frescoes of Sodoma) - Spedaletto - Chiusi - Cetona - Chianciano. **Closed** Jan 4 – Mar 21.

Pienza, which long deserved to have a hotel of charm, has now found one in the Relais Il Chiostro di Pienza, set in a former 15th-century monastery in the center of the historic old town. The building has been beautifully restored: We see arches, beams and frescoes and, of course, the old cloister of the convent. The rooms are large, soberly furnished and decorated. The whole place has a great calm and serenity. An excellent spot from which to discover the wonderful little Renaissance town of Pienza, as well as the medieval and Roman/Etruscan sites nearby.

How to get there *(Map 13): 52km southeast of Siena. Motorway A1, Valdichiana or Chiusi-Chianciano exit.*

L'Olmo 🌳

53020 Monticchiello di Pienza (Siena)
Tel. 0578-755 133 - Fax 0578-755 124
Sig.ra Lindo
E-mail: olmopienza@iol.it - Web: www.nautilus.mp.com/olmo

Suites 5 and 1 apartment, 1 double room with telephone, bath, WC, TV, minibar, safe. **Price** Single 270,0000L, suite 375-395,000L, apart. 470,000L. **Meals** Breakfast included, served 8:30-10:30. **Restaurant** For residents - mealtime specials 65,000L. **Credit cards** Visa, Eurocard, MasterCard. **Pets** Dogs not allowed. **Facilities** Heated swimming pool, parking. **Nearby** Pienza - Montepulciano - Montalcino - Terme de Bagno Vignoni - Villages of Val d'Orcia (Collegiale San Quirico d'Orcia, Castiglione d'Orcia, Rocca d'Orcia, Ripa d'Orcia, Campiglia d'Orcia) - Abbey of Sant'Anna Camprena (fresco of Sodoma) - Spedaletto - Chiusi - Cetona - Chianciano. **Open** Mar – Oct.

The Olmo is an elegant country inn where the service is attentive without being effusive. Thanks to a respectful restoration, the house has regained its noble appearance in keeping with its old stones. Inside, there are exposed beams in the ceilings, but for the rest, the spaces have been treated in a more contemporary way. The entire installation has a refined look, mingling antique furniture, hand-crafted objects, fine fabrics and traditional floors. Each lodging is different in size and style. Two suites open directly onto the garden and a private terrace. Of those upstairs, the largest has two rooms and can sleep three, others have a fireplace, and one offers a panoramic view of the Val d'Orcia. The public areas have the same tasteful luxury. With notice in advance, you can dine by candlelight. The same careful attention has been given to the garden and swimming pool, which blend beautifully with the surroundings.

How to get there *(Map 13): 52km southeast of Siena. On highway A1 Valdichiana exit, towards Torina di Siena, Pienza e monticchiello 110.*

Castello di Ripa d'Orcia

Ripa d'Orcia 53023 Castiglione d'Orcia (Siena)
Tel. 0577-89 73 76 - Fax 0577-89 80 38
Famiglia Aluffi Rossi
E-mail: info@castelloripadorcia.com - Web:www.castelloripadorcia.com

Category ★★★ **Rooms** 6 with shower or bath and 7 apartments fully equipped. **Price** Double 190-230,000L, breakfast included; apart. 800-950,000L (2 pers., 1 week), 1 250-1 400,000L (4 pers., 1 week). **Restaurant** Service 7:30PM-8:30PM - closed Mon, also à la carte 35-50,000L - Tuscan cuisine. **Credit cards** All major. **Pets** Dogs not allowed. **Facilities** Parking. **Nearby** Val d'Orcia: Peinza, Montepulciano, Monticchiello, Montalcino and Abbey of Sant' Antimo, Terme de Bagno Vignoni - villages of the Val d'Orcia (Collegiale San Quirico d'Orcia, Castiglione d'Orcia, Rocca d'Orcia, Ripa d'Orcia, Campiglia d'Orcia) - Abbey of Sant'Anna Camprena - Spedaletto - Chuisi - Cetona - Chianciano. **Open** Mar – Nov.

Ripa d'Orcia is one of those wonderful little medieval hamlets that have remained just as they were in the Middle Ages. To get there, you must leave the road at San Quirico and drive into the countryside for about 5 kilometers. Don't be impatient — the road may not be very well-kept, but the castello makes it all worth it when you see it rising up from behind a wall of cypresses. An intelligent restoration has given new life to some old houses in a village deserted by its inhabitants. There are a variety of rooms and apartments with facilities to enable independent living: a reading or television room, a restaurant and a marvelous meeting room. The bedrooms are attractive and comfortable; the apartments are more rustic in style, but some recent renovations should make them just as inviting as the rest. In the heart of a protected natural setting, Ripa d'Orcia is well worth a tour. You can always buy olive oil there, and wine or *grappa*.

How to get there *(Map 13): 45km south of Siena (towards lago di Bolsena and Viterbo) via S2 to San Quirico and Ripa d'Orcia. A1, Val di Chiana or Chiusi-Chanciano exit and towards Pienza.*

Cantina Il Borgo

Rocca d'Orcia 53023 Castiglione d'Orcia (Siena)
Tel. and Fax 0577-88 72 80
Sig. Tanganelli

Rooms 3 with air-conditioning, shower, WC, TV – WC for disabled persons. **Price** 110-130,000L.
Meals Breakfast included, served 8:30-10:00. **Restaurant** Service 12:00PM-2:30PM, 7:00PM-9:30PM -
closed Mon, à la carte 40,000L. **Credit cards** Amex, Visa, Eurocard, MasterCard. **Pets** Dogs allowed.
Nearby Val d'Orcia - Peinza - Montepulciano - Monticchiello - Montalcino and Abbey of Sant' Antimo
- Terme de Bagno Vignoni - villages of the Val d'Orcia (Collegiale San Quirico d'Orcia, Castiglione
d'Orcia, Rocca d'Orcia, Ripa d'Orcia, Campiglia d'Orcia) - Abbey of Sant'Anna Camprena - Spedaletto
- Chiusi - Cetona - Chianciano. **Closed** Jan 16 – Feb 14.

You can see the Rocca di Tentennano, the imposing military fortress,
towering above the Val d'Orcia from a distance. The old Medieval town is
discreetly set back, down below, as if to protect itself from a few curious
tourists. The village looks like it has been asleep for centuries. The telephone
booth (from which you can easily call long distance) is the only reminder of the
present. The restaurant, the Cantina Il Borgo, is in one of the austere houses on
the site–a refurbished coach house–across from a superb octagonal, cited in
texts since the 12th century. The owner will welcome you simply, but he's more
than willing to share what he loves in this region with you: its wine, cuisine, and
the numerous trails which criss-cross the Val d'Orcia. The three carefully
prepared rooms have whitewashed walls, wrought iron beds, antique furniture,
and an array of fabrics combining stripes and gingham, for a modern touch. The
shower rooms are comfortably equipped. This place is surprisingly nice.

How to get there *(Map 13): 50km south of Siena (towards lago di Bolsena and
Viterbo) via S2, towards Castiglione d'Orcia and Rocca. A1, Val di Chiana or
Chiusi-Chanciano exit towards Pienza.*

La Frateria

53040 Cetona (Siena)
Convento San Francesco
Tel. 0578-23 80 15 / 23 82 61 - Fax 0578-23 92 20
E-mail: frateria@ftbcc.it - Web: www.mondox.it

Category ★★★★ **Rooms** 7 withair-conditiong bath, WC. **Price** Single 250,000L, double 380,000L,
suite 500-000L. **Meals** Breakfast included, served 7:30-10:00. **Restaurant** Service 1:00PM, 8:00PM -
closed Tues except on request - mealtime specials 120,000L - New traditional cuisine. **Credit cards**
Amex in the restaurant only, Visa, Eurocard, MasterCard. **Pets** Dogs not allowed. **Facilities** Parking.
Nearby Montepulciano - Monticchiello - Montalcino - Terme de Bagno Vignoli - Val d'Orcia villages
(Castiglione d'Orcia, Rocca d'Orcia, Ripa d'Orcia, Campiglia d'Orcia) - Pienza - Collegiale San Quirico
d'Orcia - Museo Nazionale Etrusco in Siusi - Chianciano Terme - Siena. **Closed** Jan 7 – Feb 10.

A young Franciscan priest decided to restore an abandoned convent with the
help of a community of troubled youth called "Mondo X." The result is
nothing short of extraordinary. After a considerable amount of restoration, the
convent once again has its chapels, cloisters with laurel flowers, meditation
room, and very recently, dining hall. The garden is overloaded with clematis,
camellias and azalies. In summer, the rose bushes and kiwi trees take over. The
feeling here is harmony with nature. The cuisine in the restaurant consists of
Tuscan specialties made exclusively with products from La Frateria's farm.
The rooms are very nicely decorated and have a slightly monastic feel to them.
If you didn't know that the founder of the order, Saint Francis of Assisi, had
a taste for nice things, you might be surprised by so much elegance.

How to get there *(Map 13): 89km of Siena, via A1, Chiusi exit; Chianciano*
Terme and S428 to Sarteano, towards Cetona.

Albergo Sette Querce

53040 San Casciano dei Bagni (Siena)
Via Manciati, 2-5
Tel. 0578-58 174 - Fax 0578-58 172 - Daniela Boni
Web: www.settequerce.it

Category ★★★ **Rooms** 9 with air-conditioning, telephone, bath, WC, satellite TV, minibar. **Price** 250-400,000L per pers. **Meals** Breakfast included, served 7:30-10:30 - half board and full board 170-220,000L, 210-260,000L (per pers., 3 days min.). **Restaurant** "Daniela", service 1:00PM-2:30PM, 8:00PM-11:00PM - mealtime specials 50,000L, also à la carte - Italian cuisine. **Credit cards** Amex, Visa, Eurocard, MasterCard. **Pets** Small dogs allowed. **Facilities** Arrangement with the Fonteverde thermal center. **Nearby** Chiusi - Chianciano Terme - Montepulciano - Siena - Montalcino - Bagno Vignoni - Orvieto. **Closed** Jan.

It is hard not to be well-situated in Tuscany, given the richness of the cultural and ecological heritage - and Etruscan Tuscany, adjoining Etruscan Umbria, also holds many treasures. A stop at Sette Querce will allow you to discover the region. The hotel is in a village house. The decoration was carried out by the Cabinet Designer Guild of London, under the personal supervision of Patricia Guild: those who know her work will recognize her color palette here. The nine suites are themed in yellow on the first floor and sky blue on the second, with sponge painting on the walls and fabrics in which stripes, squares and diamonds explore the chromatic scale. All of them are delightful and spacious with a sitting room corner and a jacuzzi. The one we prefer is number 309 on the top floor because of its large terrace with panoramic view. In summer breakfast is served in the garden in the shade of the hundred-year old oaks which give their name to the hotel. The restaurant, on the village square, with its "acid drop" décor, serves genuine Italian cooking. A very lovely place to know.

How to get there *(Map 13): 80km south of Siena, via A1 exit Chiusi and S321 towards Cetona, Piazze and S. Casciano dei Bagni.*

La Palazzina

Le Vigne 53040 Radicofani (Siena)
Tel. 0578-55 585 - Fax 0577-8999 85
Sig.ra Nicoletta Innocenti
E-mail: collection@verdidea.net

Rooms 10 with bath, WC. **Price** With half board 125-140,000L, full board 130-150,000L (per pers., 3 days min.). **Meals** Breakfast included, served 8:00-10:00. **Restaurant** Service 12:45PM-1:30PM, 8:00PM-8:30PM - mealtime specials 38-48,000L - Specialties: Zuppe e vellutate di stagioni - Pici - Gnochetti agli aromi - Tagliolini d'ortica arrosto alla cannella o alla mentta - Mousse al limone - Bianco mangiare alle mandorle. **Credit cards** Amex, Visa, Eurocard, MasterCard. **Pets** Dogs allowed (15,000L). **Facilities** Swimming pool, parking. **Nearby** Montepulciano - Monticchiello - Montalcino - Terme de Bagno Vignoli, Val d'Orcia villages (Castiglione d'Orcia, Rocca d'Orcia, Ripa d'Orcia, Campiglia d'Orcia) - Pienza - Collegiale San Quirico d'Orcia - Museo Nazionale Etrusco in Siusi - Chianciano Terme - Siena. **Closed** 2nd week in Nov and third week in Mar.

Here in this little corner of Tuscany we have found what may well be a paradise on earth: a verdant landscape of gently rolling hills, bathed in a soft light. On the hilltops, signs of man-made beauty, old farmhouses, or villas like the Palazzina, surrounded by walls of tall dark cypress trees. Life in this handsome *fattoria* is essentially run by two women, Bianca and Nicoletta, mother and daughter, and each of the rooms (all prettily arranged) bears a woman's name. In an atmosphere of great refinement, you will nevertheless be close to nature. With baroque music in the background, you can taste dishes that are simple but delicious, all with home-made products, including the excellent wine that the owner can tell you so much about. All this in surroundings that resemble a Lorenzetti or Simone Martini or some such landscape of the Sienese school.

How to get there *(Map 13): 80km south of Siena via A1, Chiusi-Chianciano Terme exit, to Sarteano. Turn on the left for Radicofani. Before 14th kilometer turn on left towards Celle sul Rigo. 1.5km, on right.*

Locanda d'Elisa

Massa Pisana 55050 Lucca
Via nuova per Pisa, 1952
Tel. 0583-37 97 37 - Fax 0583-37 90 19
Sig. Ruggiero Giorgi

Category ★★★★ **Rooms** 2 and 8 junior suites with air-conditioning, telephone, bath, WC, satellite TV, minibar, safe. **Price** Single 330-360,000L, double 450-520,000L, junior suite 490-790,000L. **Meals** Breakfast 32,000L, served 8:00-10:00. **Restaurant** Service 12:30PM-2:30PM, 7:30PM-10:30PM - closed Sun - mealtime specials à la carte 80-130,000L. **Credit cards** All major. **Pets** Dogs not allowed. **Facilities** Parking. **Nearby** Lucca: Duomo, S. Michele in Foro, S. Frediano, via Fillungo and Via Guinigi, Villa Guinigi museum, house of Puccini (Corte S. Lorenzo); events: sagra musicale lucchese, estate musicale lucchese, second-hand market 3rd Sunda of the month - Villa Mansi near Segromigno Monte - Villa Torrigiani near Camigliano - Villa royale at Marlia - Pistoia - Pisa - Viareggion - Versilioa Golf Club (18-hole). **Open** All year.

L a Locanda l'Elisa is an old 18th-century villa, entirely restored early in the 19th Century by a Napoleonic civil servant who had followed Elisa Baciocchi, Duchess of Lucca, to her home town. The décor preserves the spirit of this, with suites and drawing rooms having walnut furniture in Empire style, old portraits, fabrics and carpets inpired by prints and illustrations of the period and woodwork restored on the basis of pieces discovered in an outbuilding in the garden. The rooms are chiefly very warm suites in variations on themes of pink and orange. The dining room of the Gazebo restaurant is in a Victorian style veranda opening on the garden. The garden, too, has been entirely replanted with an abundance of flowers and bushes mingling with the aquatic plants growing beside the stream. Refinement and comfort are everywhere throughout the house.

How to get there (Map 9): 3.5km south of Lucca by S12bis.

Villa La Principessa

Lucca Massa Pisana 55050
Via nuova per Pisa, 1616
Tel. 0583-37 00 37 - Fax 0583-37 91 36 - Famiglia Mugnani
E-mail: info@hotelprincipessa.com - Web: www.hotelprincipessa.com

Category ★★★★ **Rooms** 37 and 8 junior suites with air-conditioning, telephone, bath, hairdryer, plug for modem, sattelite TV – Elevator. **Price** Single 300,000L, double 350-450,000L, junior suite 600-700,000L. **Meals** Breakfast (buffet) 30,000L, served 7:30-10:00. **Restaurant** Service 7:30PM-10:00PM - à la carte 85-95,000L. **Credit cards** All major. **Pets** Small dogs allowed. **Facilities** Swimming pool, parking. **Nearby** Lucca: Duomo, S. Michele in Foro, S. Frediano, via Fillungo and Via Guinigi, Villa Guinigi museum, house of Puccini (Corte S. Lorenzo) - Events: sagra musicale lucchese, estate musicale lucchese, second-hand market 3rd Sunda of the month - Villa Mansi near Segromigno Monte - Villa Torrigiani near Camigliano - Villa royale at Marlia - Pistoia - Pisa - Viareggion - Versilioa Golf Club (18-hole). **Closed** Nov 6 – Mar 16.

La Principessa still evokes the memory of Elisa Baciocchi to whom her famous brother, Napoleon, gave the Duchy of Lucca. It was the Bourbon-Parmas who later adapted the house to receive distinguished guests. The building is impressive with its great loggia painted siena pink and covered by an untamed vine. The great drawing room on the ground floor with its large, deep sofas and its soft lighting is very British. As for the rooms, they have a Sixties décor which is not always in the best taste, especially in the case of those situated in the annex (which are available all year round). Yet all are spacious and comfortable. In this town where the historic center has not a single hotel of real charm, the Principessa is a house of character and atmosphere with, in particular, a magnificently Romantic garden, lined with shade alleyways, hundred-year old trees, lawns and terraces where breakfasts and light meals are served.

How to get there *(Map 9): 3.5km south of Lucca by S12bis (towards Pisa), exit Massa Pisana.*

California Park Hotel

55042 Forte dei Marmi (Lucca)
Via Colombo, 32
Tel. 0584-78 71 21 - Fax 0584-78 72 68 - Sig. Mario Viacava
E-mail: info@californiaparkhotel.com - Web: www.californiaparkhotel.com

Category ★★★★ **Rooms** 44 with air-conditioning, telephone, bath or shower, WC, satellite TV, safe – Elevator. **Price** Double 280-620,000L, suite 500-1 200,000L. **Meals** Breakfast included, served 8:00-10:00 - half board 190-380,000L, full board 200-400,000L (per pers., 3 day min.). **Restaurant** (For residents) Served 12:30PM-2:00PM, 8:00PM-9:30PM - mealtime specials, also à la carte. **Credit cards** All major. **Pets** Dogs not allowed. **Facilities** Swimming pool, parking. **Nearby** Duomo de Carrara - Cave di marmo di Colonnata, cava dei Fantiscritti - Lucca - Pisa - Viareggio – Versilia Golf club (18-hole). **Closed** Oct.

In the residential quarter of this seaside resort and only 300 meters from the beaches, a park full of luxuriant trees and flowers protects the three villas that make up the California Park Hotel. They are large modern buildings in Mediterranean style, built around a swimming pool. The bedrooms are bright, the furnishings functional but pleasant. Many of them have a balcony or terrace, or are directly on the garden. Well-prepared traditional cooking, served in a dining room that opens onto the park. The park, with tables and beach chairs, is indeed a wonderful and quiet place to sit if the swimming pool gets too hectic for you. The service and welcome are professional.

How to get there *(Map 9): 35km from Pisa via A12 (Genova-Livorno), Versilia exit - Forte dei Marmi.*

Hotel Byron

55042 Forte dei Marmi (Lucca)
Viale Morin, 46
Tel. 0584-78 70 52 - Fax 0584-78 71 52 - Sig. Franco Nardini
E-mail: byron@versilia.net - Web: www.versilia.toscana.it/byron

Category ★★★★★ **Rooms** 24 and 6 suites with air-conditioning, telephone, bath or shower, WC, satellite TV, minibar – Elevator. **Price** Single 340-475,000L, double 450-600,000L, suite 650-1 030,000L. **Meals** Breakfast 45,000L, served 7:30AM-12:00PM - half board 355-490,000L, full board 385-520,000L (per pers., 3 day min.). **Restaurant** Service 1:00PM-2:30PM, 8:00PM-9:30PM - mealtime specials 90,000L, also à la carte - Specialties: Scampi in passatina di cannellini - Crêpes alla crema di asparagi - Risotto con zafferno - Scampi e zucchine - Pesce misto all'acqua pazza - Torta al limone. **Credit cards** All major. **Pets** Dogs not allowed. **Facilities** Swimming pool, billards, parking. **Nearby** Duomo de Carrara - Caves di marmo di Colonnata, cava dei Fantiscritt - Lucca - Pisa - Viareggio – Versilia Golf club (18-hole). **Open** All year.

A few meters from the sea, which you can contemplate from the terraces, the Hotel Byron is composed of two villas dating from the turn of the century. In the most residential area of Forte dei Marmi, protected from the outside world by a verdant rampart of foliage, it is a haven of peace and comfort on this rather frenetic coast. The whole place has the calm and serene feeling of a colonial mansion. Salons and bedrooms have kept their elegance despite a few modern notes introduced during recent renovations. The balconies face either the sea or a vast garden that contains a large swimming pool. A pleasant luxury vacation.

How to get there *(Map 9): 35km from Pisa via A12 (Genova-Livorno), Versilia exit - Forte dei Marmi.*

Hotel Tirreno

55042 Forte dei Marmi (Lucca)
Viale Morin, 7
Tel. 0584-78 74 44 - Fax 0584-787 137
Sig.ra Daddi Baralla

Category ★★★ **Rooms** 59 with telephone, bath or shower, WC. **Price** Single 150,000L, double 260,000L. **Meals** Breakfast (buffet) included, served 7:00-11:00 - half board 190-220,000L, full board 200-240,000L (per pers., 2 days min.). **Restaurant** Service 1:00PM-2:00PM, 8:00PM-9:00PM - mealtime specials 50-80,000L, also à la carte - Tuscan cuisine. **Credit cards** All major. **Pets** Dogs not allowed. **Nearby** Duomo de Carrara - Cave di marmo di Colonnata, cava dei Fantiscritti - Lucca - Pisa – Versilia golf course (18-hole). **Closed** Oct – Mar.

The part of the hotel which is visible from the street is a little disconcerting–it is 70s' style–but there is a surprise deep in the garden: the outbuilding, an old 19th-century summer house. Don't plan to stay anywhere in Tirreno but here, in one of the rooms on the pretty garden (57, 58, and 60) or on the sea. The hotel is both centrally located in Tirreno and close to the beach. The service is meticulous and the Tuscan cuisine is great.

How to get there *(Map 9): 35km north of Pisa via A12 (Genova-Livorno); Versilia exit, Forte dei Marmi.*

Albergo Pietrasanta

55045 Pietrasanta (Lucca)
Via Garibaldi, 35
Tel. 0584-79 37 26 - Fax 0584-79 37 28 - Marisa Giuliano
E-mail: a.pietrasanta@versilia.toscana.it - Web: albergopietrasanta.com

Categoria ★★★★ **Rooms** 14 and 8 suites with air-conditioning, telephone, bath, WC, satellite TV, minibar, safe. **Price** Single 200-300,000L, double 300-500,000L, junior suite 500-650,000L, suite 550-850,000L. **Meals** Breakfast included, served 7:30-3:00. **Restaurant** See p. 558. **Credit cards** All major. **Pets** Dogs allowed on request. **Facilities** Fitness, garage (30,000L). **Nearby** Marina di Pietrasanta - Duomo de Carrara - Marble quarries: cave di mrmo di Colonnata, cava dei Fratiscritti - Lucca - Pisa - Viareggio (beaches) - Forte dei Marmi (beaches) – Versilia Gold Club (18-hole). **Closed** Jan 6 – Feb 28.

Pietrasanta is close to Carrara and still an active center of the marble industry. Many sculpture schools and workshops still keep up the tradition - and if you have illusions of grandeur, you may like to know that you can have your bust done as a Roman emperor. Though it lies at the foothills of the Apuan Alps, it is still only a few kilometers from the Riviera della Versilia. The hotel, modestly describing itself as albergo, is situated in the Palazzo Barsanti-Bonetti which dates from the 17th Century. With its two caryatids on either side of the entrance and its elegant red and gray façade, it is easy to find in the historic center of town. The reception rooms are spacious with fine flooring in marble mosaic. Paintings by contemporary artists and a splendid collection of carafes decorate the drawing room which extends by a veranda into the garden. The rooms are large and luxurious with frescoes and canopies in some and marble bathrooms for all. A bottle of liqueur and some crisps welcome you, a kind though by the director, Marisa Giuliano.

How to get there *(Map 9): 30km from Pisa by A12, exit Versilia-Forte dei Marmi.*

Hotel Viila Rinascimento

55038 Santa Maria del Giudice (Lucca)
Tel. 0583-37 82 92 - Fax 0583-37 02 38
Carla Tersteeg - Emilio and Fabio Zaffora
E-mail: hotelvr@mbox.lognet.it

Category ★★★ **Rooms** 17 (some with air-conditioning), with telephone, shower, WC, satellite TV. **Price** Double in the villa 215-245,000L (+10,000L whith air-conditioning), double in the annex 150-175,000L. **Meals** Breakfast included, served 7:30-10:30. **Restaurant** Service 12:30PM-1:30PM, 7:30PM-9:30PM - closed Sun - mealtime specials 45,000L, also à la carte. **Credit cards** Amex, Diners. **Pets** Dogs allowed. **Facilities** Swimming pool, tennis, parking, garage. **Nearby** Romanesque churches of Santa Maria del Giudice - Lucca - Pisa – Versilia Golf Club (18-hole). **Closed** Nov – Feb.

The delightful village of Santa Maria del Giudice is situated halfway between Lucca and Pisa in the fertile valley of the Serchio which borders the Garfagnana and separates the Appenines from the Apuan Alps. The Villa Rinascimento itself, as its name suggests, is a superb example of the holiday houses of a rich 19th-century family. Indeed, this fine house has everything that one could expect of it: aristocratic pink stonework, vaulted ceilings, magnificent loggia with harmonious arcades and a terrace from which one enjoys a superb view over vineyards and olive groves. The interior has the rustic atmosphere of a country house. There are traditonal iron bedsteads and large regional wardrobes furnishing the rooms, which still have their ceiling beams and terracotta flooring. The annex is more recent and less charming, but benefits from the same setting, as well as the swimming pool and tennis court. This hotel has the addiitonal advantage of being only ten kilometers away from two historic towns which themselves have few hotels of charm.

How to get there *(Map 9): 9km south of Lucca on S12r, or 11km north of Pisa.*

Hotel Plaza e de Russie

55049 Viareggio (Lucca)
Piazza d'Azeglio, 1
Tel. 0584-44 449 - Fax 0584-44 031
Sig. Claudio Catani

Category ★★★★ **Rooms** 52 with air-conditioning, telelephone, bath or shower, WC, satellite TV, minibar– Elevator. **Price** Single 170-285,000L, double 250-430,000L, suite 375-520,000L. **Meals** Breakfast (buffet) included, served 7:00-11:00 - half board 180-350,000L, full board 230-410,000L (per pers., 3 day min.). **Restaurant** Service 12:30PM-2:30PM, 7:00PM-10:30PM - mealtime specials 80-120,000L, also à la carte - Specialties: Sparnocchi in pllata di finochio - Stracci neri ai frutti di mare, - Filetto di branzino al limone candito. **Credit cards** All major. **Pets** Dogs not allowed. **Facilities** Parking. **Nearby** Duomo de Carrara - Cave di marmo di Colonnata, cava dei Fantiscritti - Lucca - Pisa - Viareggio –Versilia Golf club (18-hole). **Open** All year.

Built in 1871, this was the first hotel in Viareggio, a little resort town that has still managed, despite a flourishing tourism industry, to preserve some of the charm it had at the turn of the century. Located just a few steps from the sea and the beaches, it has been completely renovated and at the same time enhanced by the addition of marble and chandeliers. Still, the bedrooms are sober and elegant, and have kept their original parquet floors. If possible, avoid the bedrooms on the first floor, as they face a promenade that remains rather noisy till late into the night. The restaurant, featuring all the products of the sea, has a terrace with an outstanding view of the sea and the town. This can serve as an excellent base for anyone who wants to visit Pisa, Lucca and the region, without giving up the pleasures of a holiday by the sea.

How to get there *(Map 9): 25km from Pisa via A12 (Genova-Livorno), Viareggio exit*

Il Frassinello

56040 Montecatini Val di Cecina (Pisa)
Tel. and Fax 0588-300 80 - Handy: 0348-650 80 17
Sig.ra Elga Schlubach Giudici
E-mail: frassinello@sirt.pisa.it

Rooms 3 and 4 apartments (2-6 pers.) with bath or shower. **Price** Double 150,000L (3 days min.), apart. 4 nights min. 160,000L (2 pers.), 260,000L (4 pers.). **Meals** Breakfast 12,000L, served about 8:00-10:00. **Evening meals** By reservation; 32,000L. **Credit cards** Not accepted. **Pets** Dogs allowed. **Facilities** Parking. **Nearby** Volterra - San Gimignano - Siena - Lucignano - Marina di Cecina (beach) - Pisa. **Open** Easter – end Oct.

This is an old farmhouse turned into an appealing little guest house, located in a region where few tourists venture. You will discover a more genuine Tuscany (even though your hostess is of German origin) only 50 kilometers from the world-famous sites. Il Frassinello is rather isolated and not so easy to reach — the last 4 kilometers are on a dirt road. But you will have the added surprise of seeing the Elga deer farm, the largest in Europe. You will be in the heart of a grandiose and unspoiled natural site, better suited to a longer stay than just a stopover. The ambiance in the rooms and small apartments is pleasantly rustic but not lacking in comfort. Civilization is not so far away, and your hostess is happy to suggest restaurants for a dinner out: the Locanda del Sole at Querceto, the Trattoria San Lorenzo at Saline di Volterra, the Scaccipensieri in Cecina or the Don Beta da Nicola in Volterra.

How to get there *(Map 12): 60km northwest of Siena (towards Firenze); Colle di Val d'Elsa-South exit, towards Volterra and Monticatini Val di Cecina. On the A12 (Genova-Grosseto), take exit S. P. Palazzi, no. 68, towards Volterra.*

Casetta delle Selve

56010 Pugnano
San Giuliano Terme (Pisa)
Tel. and Fax 050-85 03 59
Sig.ra Nicla Menchi

Rooms 6 with bath or shower, WC. **Price** Double 125,000L. **Meals** Breakfast 15,000L, served about 9:00. **Restaurant** See p. 557. **Credit cards** Not accepted. **Pets** Dogs allowed. **Facilities** Parking. **Nearby** Certosa di Calci - Pisa - Lucca - beach and sea. **Open** Apr – Oct.

The enchantment will start as soon as you leave the road to take the scented path that leads up to the casetta. Flooded with light, surrounded by chestnut and olive trees, the house offers a stunning view of the Tuscan hills with, in the background, the sea and the islands of Corsica and Gorgona. It is a simple, pleasant place and Nicla provides a warm and friendly welcome. She has artistically seen to the comfort and decoration of each room, to the point of adding her own handmade rugs and pillow cases, not to mention her paintings that adorn the walls. At breakfast, you can appreciate her homemade jams as you enjoy the view from the delightful terrace. A good base for visiting Pisa and Lucca, both close by.

How to get there *(Map 9): 10km south of Lucca, via A11 Lucca exit; then SS12 and SS12bis towards San Giuliano Terme; in Pugnano (13km) follow the small partly unpaved road.*

Grand Hotel Villa di Corliano

Rigoli 56010 San Giuliano Terme (Pisa)
Via Statale, 50
Tel. 050-81 81 93 - Fax 050-81 88 97 - Sig. Agostini della Seta
E-mail: villadicorliano@viladicorliano.com - Web: www.villadicornalio.com

Category ★★★ **Rooms** 18 with telephone (8 with bath, WC). **Price** Double 120-200,000L, suite for 3 pers. 300-350,000L. **Meals** Breakfast 18,000L, served 8:00-10:00. **Restaurant** On the property. Specialties: Seafood. **Credit cards** Visa, Eurocard and MasterCard. **Pets** Dogs allowed. **Nearby** Santa Maria del Giudice - Pisa - Lucca. **Open** All year.

The Villa di Corliano is, like a jewel, its own lovely jewel box. A jewel of measured and elegant architecture amid extensive grounds that have been allowed to remain natural. In front of the house, a large prairie stretches toward a background of wooded hills. The interior has kept its original appearance with chandeliers, gilded wood and antique furniture. Unfortunately, all this splendor is just a decor and not accessible to guests. The bedrooms are more modest and the owner not always very affable. Still, the spot is unique and the prices reasonable for the facilities offered. So perhaps it's worth taking advantage of before it is restored and redecorated, with who knows what result. A good restaurant on the property is also worth mentioning.

How to get there *(Map 9): 8km north of Pisa via SS12bis to San Giuliano Terme, then northwest S12 towards Rigoli.*

Albergo Villa Nencini

56048 Volterra (Pisa)
Borgo San Stefano, 55
Tel. 0588-86 386 - Fax 0588-80 601
Sig. Nencini

Rooms 34 and 1 suite with telephone: 31 with shower, WC, satellite TV; 21 with telephone, bath, WC, satellite TV – Wheelchair access. **Price** Single 100,000L, double 130,000. **Meals** Breakfast 15,000L, served 7:00-10:00. **Restaurant** In the new part of the hotel - Service 12:30PM-1:30PM, 7:30PM-9:00PM - Regional cooking. **Credit cards** Visa, Eurocard, MasterCard. **Pets** Dogs allowed. **Facilities** Swimming pool. **Nearby** Volterra: piazza dei Priori, Duomo, Museo Etrusco Guarnacci, Les Balze - San Gimignano - Lucignano - Siena - Firenze - Piza. **Open** All year.

The Villa Nencini is just outside the walls of Volterra, an ancient Etruscan, Roman and medieval town, with "one of the most beautiful medieval squares in Italy," the Piazza dei Priori. On the edge of town, it has a great view of the valley. The house is very old; the interior is unpretentious and friendly. A wing has been added onto the house; the rooms there are more modern and more comfortable ; and there is a restaurant. The rooms in the villa are more traditional and authentic. The very pretty garden and swimming pool overhanging the valley are good places to take in the marvelous panorama.

How to get there *(Map 12): 60km northwest of Siena, via SS or A1; Colle di Val d'Elsa exit.*

Hotel Grotta Giusti

51015 Monsummano Terme (Pistoia)
Via Grotta Giusti, 17
Tel. 0572-51 165/6 - Fax 0572-51 269 - Sig. Alessandro d'Onofrio
E-mail: info@grottagiustispa.com - Web: www.grottagiutispa.com

Category ★★★★ **Rooms** 70 with air-conditioning, telephone, bath, WC, satellite TV, safe, minibar – Elevator. **Price** Whith half board single 230-330,000L, double 150-250,000L (per pers.) - with full board single 250-350,000L, double 170-270,000L (per pers.). **Meals** Breakfast included, served 7:30-10:00. **Restaurant** Service 12:30PM-2:00PM, 7:30PM-9:00PM - mealtime specials 55,000L, also à la carte - Tuscan and international cuisine. **Credit cards** All major. **Pets** Small dogs allowed. **Facilities** Swimming pool, tennis, sauna, health center (thermal swimming pool). **Nearby** Montecatini - Serra Pistoiese - Pistoia - Villa Mansi near Segromigno Monte - Lucca – Golf course (18-hole) in Pievaccia and in Monsummano. **Open** Mar – Jan.

This former residence of the rich poet Giusti is built around an amazing grotto with a stream of hot blue water. Giuseppe Verdi was often a guest at this house. You can still see some of the splendor of the original decor in the reception area. The rooms are functional, but the ones in the old building, which look out over the park, are by far the nicest. They all have hot running spring water, so ask for one with a bathtub. In addition, beautiful grounds with a spring water swimming pool, a tennis court and running trail make this hotel an ideal place for a relaxing stay.

How to get there *(Map 9): 37km northwest of Firenze; 13km west of Pistoia via A11, Montecatini exit; then S435 to Monsummano Terme.*

Grand Hotel e La Pace

51016 Montecatini Terme (Pistoia)
Viale della Toretta, 1
Tel. 0572-9240 - Fax 0572-784 51 - Sig. Claudio Tongiorgi
E-mail: htlapace@tin.it - Web: www.grandhotellapace.it

Category ★★★★★ **Rooms** 136 and 14 apartments with telephone, bath, WC, TV, minibar – Elevator. **Price** Single 320-350,000L, double 490-550,000L. **Meals** Breakfast 30,000L, served 7:30-10:30. **Restaurant** Service 12:30PM-2:00PM, 8:00PM-9:30PM - à la carte - Tuscan cuisine. **Credit cards** All major. **Pets** Dogs allowed (with extra charge). **Facilities** Heated swimming pool, sauna, tennis, health center, parking. **Nearby** Pescia - church in Castelvecchio - Collodi - Lucca - Pistoia - Firenze - Pisa – Golf course (18-hole) in Pievaccia and in Monsummano Terme. **Open** Apr – end Oct.

All of the traditional splendor of this 1870 palace is completely intact. The hotel's sumptuous, thick carpeted salons, first-class dining room with a bay window and very comfortable rooms, decorated in harmonious pastel colors, make the atmosphere warm. On the superb five-acre grounds there is a large heated swimming pool, a tennis court and a spa for medically supervised mud baths, saunas, massages, ozone baths and algae beauty treatments.

How to get there *(Map 9): 49km northwest of Firenze; 15km west Pistoia via A11, Montecatini exit.*

Villa Lucia

51015 Montevettolini (Pistoia)
Via Bronzoli, 1443
Tel. 0572-61 77 90 - Fax 0572-62 88 17
Sig.ra Vallera

Rooms 10 with air-conditioning, telephone, 9 with shower, WC, 4 with satellite TV. **Price** (2 days min.) double 300-400,000L, apart. 1 500-3 000,000L (1 week min.). **Meals** Breakfast included **Restaurant** For residents only, by reservation. Service 8:30PM - mealtime specials 30-50,000L. **Credit cards** Not accepted. **Pets** Dogs allowed. **Facilities** Small swimming pool. **Nearby** Firenze - Montecatini - Serra Pistoiese - Pistoia - Villa Mansi near Segromigno Monte - Lucca — Golf course (18-hole) in Pievaccia and in Monsumanno. **Open** Apr 15 – Nov 15.

The Villa Lucia is part bed and breakfast and part Tuscan inn. Everything is pretty and authentically Tuscan, though there is a hint of California as well. This is no accident: it is run by a charming lady who caters to the many Americans who come here for the warm convivial atmosphere, the pretty copper beds, the regional furniture and a nice glass of *vinsanto* (fortified dessert wine) and *cantuccini* (almond biscuits). Her savory cuisine is based on house recipes. On summer evenings there are parties on the lawn. You may not make much progress with your Italian while you are here, but you are sure to have a great time.

How to get there *(Map 9): 40km of Firenze; 13km west Pistoia via A11, Montecatini exit; then S435 to Monsummano Terme and little road for Montevettolini.*

Il Convento

51030 Pontenuovo (Pistoia)
Via San Quirico, 33
Tel. 0573-45 26 51 / 2 - Fax 0573-45 35 78
Sig. Petrini

Rooms 24 with telephone, bath, WC, TV. **Price** Single 150,000L, double 170,000L. **Meals** Breakfast 13,000L, served 7:30-9:30 - half board 140,000L; full board 180,000L (per pers., 3 days min.). **Restaurant** Service 12:30PM-2:30PM, 7:30PM-10:00PM - closed Mon from Jan – Easter - mealtime specials 55-60,000L, also à la carte - Tuscan cuisine. **Credit cards** Visa, Eurocard, MasterCard. **Pets** Dogs not allowed. **Facilities** Swimming pool, parking. **Nearby** Pistoia - De Maresca - Lake of Scaffaiolo - Corno alle Scale (1 945 m) - Firenze - Lucca – Dell'Ugolino golf course (18-hole) in Grassina. **Open** All year.

This old Franciscan monastery, in keeping with its name, still has a small chapel and a tranquil atmosphere. Surrounded by a vast flower garden overlooking the plain, this charming hotel is a little old and could use some modernizing. But it is a pleasant place from which to visit Pistoia and the northern part of Tuscany. A pool above the garden is at your disposal. The restaurant serves very good, traditional Tuscan cuisine.

How to get there (Map 9): 40km of Firenze; 5km east of Pistoia towards Montale then to Pontenuovo.

Le Pisanelle

58014 Manciano (Grosseto)
Strada Provinciale Nr. 32,km 3,9
Tel. 0564-62 82 86 - Fax 0564-62 58 40 - Roberto and Milly Maurelli
E-mail: lepisanelle@laltramaremma.it - Web: www.laltramaremma.it/le-pisanelle

Rooms 5 with air-conditioning, telephone, bath or shower, WC, TV, minibar. **Price** Single 180-190,000L, double 200-210,000L. **Meals** Breakfast included, served 8:00-9:45 - half board 145-155,000L (per pers., 3 days min.). **Restaurant** Service 8:00PM-8:30PM - closed Sun and Mon - mealtime specials 50-55,000L, also à la carte - Regional cooking. **Credit cards** All major. **Pets** Small dogs allowed. **Facilities** Sauna, riding, moutain bike, exterior pool with hydromassage, parking. **Nearby** Etruscan country: Viterbo, Tarquinia, Le Argentare, Pitigliano - Cerveteri, Veio - Isola Bisentina - Lago di Bolsena – Golf Le querce (18-hole) at Viterbo **Closed** Jan 10 – 25, Jul 5 – 20.

$\mathbf{B}$etween Ortebello and Pitigliano there is a string of Etruscan sites along the often fortified medieval villages that cling to the rocky spurs overhanging the plain. Manciano is a former Siennese fortress, but you will find Le Pisanelle in the open marshy countryside. It is a delightful guest house set up by Roberto and Milly in a casolare converted with affection and talent. The rooms are very well decorated in the cozy style of an English cottage and offer the standards of comfort of a very good hotel, while the restaurant aims to be still more convivial, inviting you to join in the set menu. The cooking is of very high quality, with a preference for the good products of the region, and the service is elegant. Sanding on the border between Tuscany and Latium, the area and the inn are worth a detour if you are going down towards Rome, but still more a longer stay which will allow you to discover a new aspect of a Tuscany that tends to be limited to the monuments of the Quattrocento.

How to get there *(Map 13): 60km south of Grosetto. At Maciano, strada provinciale no. 32 twoards Farnese as far as km 3,9.*

Rifugio Prategiano

58026 Montieri (Grosseto)
Via Prategiano, 45
Tel. 0566-99 77 00 - Fax 0566-99 78 91 - Sig. Paradisi
E-mail: prategiano@bigfoot.com - Web: www.prategiano.heimatseite.com

Category ★★★ **Rooms** 24 with telephone, bath, WC, TV. **Price** Single 90-152,000L, double 142-216,000L. **Meals** Breakfast included - half board 95-140,000L (per pers.,3 days min.). **Restaurant** Service 1:00PM, 8:00PM - mealtime specials - Specialties: Tortelloni - Cinghiale - Acqua Cotta. **Credit cards** All major. **Pets** Dogs allowed. **Facilities** Swimming pool, tennis, riding, parking. **Nearby** Roman and Etruscan ruins of Roselle - Vetulonia - Montepescali - National Park of Maremma - Volterra. **Open** All year.

The Prategiano is on Montieri Hill, an old Medieval citadel deep in the High Maremma part of the little-known Métallifère Forest in Tuscany. The ambiance is that of a mountain inn. The decor is very simple and rustic, as most of the hotel guests are horseback riders. There are riding lessons and daytime excursions for children and beginners, while more experienced riders can gallop through the Tuscan hills, crossing woods and forests to the deserted beaches of Punta Ala to get to Volterra. The setting is perfect and the owner is friendly and very careful about the security of his guests. This is the perfect address for those (including some guests who come back year after year) seeking a small adventure.

How to get there (*Map 13*): *50km southwest of Siena via S73 to Bivio del Madonnino, then S441 (15km); on the right towards Montieri.*

Hotel Il Pellicano

Lo Sbarcatello 58018 Porto Ercole (Grosseto)
Tel. 0564-858 111 - Fax 0564-83 34 18
Sig. Fanciulli
E-mail: info@pellicanohotel.com - Web: www.pellicanohotel.com

Category ★★★★ **Rooms** 50 with air-conditiong, telephone, bath, WC, TV, minibar. **Price** Double 380-1 060,000L, suite 785-2 090,000L. **Meals** Breakfast included, served 7:30-10:30. **Restaurant** Service 1:00PM-2:30PM, 8:00PM-10:00PM - mealtime specials 125,000L, also à la carte - Specialties: Risotto mantecato con astice e champagne - Ravioli di verdura con pesto di rucola e pomodoro pachino - Spaghetti saltati con calamari origano e olive nere. **Credit cards** All major. **Pets** Dogs not allowed. **Facilities** Sea-water swimming pool, health center, tennis, private beach, parking. **Nearby** Giannutri and Giglio islands - Tombolo di Feniglia - Sovona - Sorano - Pitigliano. **Closed** Oct 29 – Apr 7.

The guest book of the Pelicano is full of prestigious names. Inaugurated in 1975 in the presence of Charlie Chaplin, it has been visited by celebrities ever since. Nestled in a little valley of cypress trees overlooking the gulf of Argentaro, the hotel consists of a number of villas, contiguous but independent. It is a luxury establishment with the atmosphere of a private home. The sitting rooms are arranged around the fireplace or the library. In the summer the restaurant serves on the terrace, from which you have a view of the sea through the branches of pine trees. A large swimming pool has been cut directly into the rock face of the cliff. It is reached by an elevator. The quality service comes up to the standards of its demanding clientele.

How to get there *(Map 13): 55km south of Grosseto via SS51, then along the coast to Porto Ercole; then strada panoramica to Lo Sbarcatello.*

Hotel Cala del Porto

58040 Punta Ala (Grosseto)
Via Cala del Pozzo
Tel. 0564-92 24 55 - Fax 0564-92 07 16
E-mail: cala.puntaala@baglionihotels.com

Category ★★★★ **Rooms** 36 and 5 apartments with air-conditioning, telephone, bath, WC, TV, minibar. **Price** Single 300-580,000L, double 420-850,000L, apartment 650-1 000,000L. **Meals** Breakfast included, served 7:30-10:30 - half board 350-550,000L, 360-550,000L (per pers.,3 days min.). **Restaurant** Service 1:00PM-3:00PM, 7:30PM-9:30PM - mealtime specials 70-90,000L, also à la carte - Mediterranean cuisine, seafood. **Credit cards** All major. **Pets** Small dogs allowed. **Facilities** Swimming pool, tennis (35,000L), private beach, parking. **Nearby** Tombolo - Massa Maritima - Volterra - National Park of Maremma –Punta Ala golf course (18-hole). **Closed** Oct – Apr.

Punta Ala is the chic beach resort of Grossetto, which is at the tip of the Gulf of Follonica across from the Island of Elba. The Cala del Porto is a comfortable modern hotel with a beautiful flower garden. The rooms are elegantly furnished and have balconies with views of the historical island. Pleasant Tuscan-inspired cuisine is served on the beautiful terrace.

How to get there *(Map 12): 41km west of Grosseto via S327, along the coast to Punta Ala.*

Piccolo Hotel Alleluja

58040 Punta Ala (Grosseto)
Via del Porto
Tel. 0564-92 20 50 - Fax 0564-92 07 34
E-mail: alleluja.puntaala@baglionihotels.com

Category ★★★★ **Rooms** 38 with air-conditioning, telephone, bath, WC, safe, minibar– Elevator. **Price** Single 270-630,000L, double 410-900,000L. **Meals** Breakfast 30,000L, served 7:30-10:30 - half board 310-940,000L, full board 370-1 060,000L (per pers.,3 days min., oblig. in Jul – Aug). **Restaurant** Service 1:00PM-2:30PM, 7:30PM-9:30PM - mealtime specials 75-90,000L, also à la carte - Regional and international cooking and seafood. **Credit cards** All major. **Pets** Dogs not allowed. **Facilities** Swimming pool, private beach, tennis, parking. **Nearby** Tombolo - Massa Maritima - Volterra - National Park of Maremma – Punta Ala golf course (18-hole). **Open** Mar – Nov.

The pink roughcast walls, tile roofs and exposed beams of this recently built hotel reflect the architect's respect for the region. An airy space opens onto the impeccably maintained lawns. The hotel is decorated with simple unpretentious furniture. The rooms open onto either an Italian-style terrace or a small garden on the lake. The numerous advantages of this hotel include a private beach, tennis courts and a nearby golf course.

How to get there *(Map 12): 41km west of Grosseto via S327, along the coast to Punta Ala.*

Fattoria di Peruzzo

Peruzzo 58028 Roccatederighi (Grosseto)
Tel. 0564-56 98 73 oder 56 98 08 - Fax 0564-56 87 70
Sig. Giuseppe Marruchi
E-mail: peruzzo.fattoria@tiscalinet.it - Web: web.tiscalinet.it/peruzzo

Apartments 7 (2-8 pers.) with kitchen, lounge, bath (1 or 2 bedrooms, garden corner). **Price** Apart. 900-2 100,000L (weekly). **Meals** Breakfast not included. **Credit cards** All major. **Pets** Dogs not allowed. **Facilities** Swimming pool. **Nearby** Massa Marittima - Pitigliano - Sovana - Capalbio - Castiglione della Pescaia - Siena - Montalcino - Pienza - Abbeys of S. Galgano, Sant'Antimo, S. Raban, S. Salvatore - Etrucan grottoes. **Open** All year.

La Fattoria di Peruzzo is part of the huge agricultural estate of the Marruchi family, set up in 1873. The original 1 500 hectares have since been divided between the members of the family who have continued to cultivate them. The Fattoria is the property of Giuseppe Marrichi who still produces a renowned brand of olive oil. With his daughter, Giuseppe has also created a splendid stopping place for tourists on his land. The three best apartments are in the 18th-century casa padronale, on a little hill 300 m up, giving a fine view over the valley, the castles and medieval villages. Our own preference is for La Torre, in the oldest part of the house, the top level being occupied by a terrace with a view extending as far as the isle of Giglio. The décor is high-standard countryhouse with additional modern comfort. As for Il Giardino, it opens directly on to the garden, while La Logetta has a fine uninterrupted view from its terrace. There is a house offering four other apartments on the heights of La Serratina; they are comfortable, but with less charm, although they still enjoy the magnificent setting which, apart from its vineyards, also has an orchard, three little lakes, and a farm where they rear deeer and moufflons.

How to get there *(Map 13): 30km north of Grosetto. On A1 exit Braccagni, towards Montemassi, Roccatederighi-Sassofortino, Peruzzo.*

Auberge Azienda Pereti

Pereti 58028 Roccatederighi (Grosseto)
Tel. 0564-56 96 71 - Fax 0564-56 96 71
Frances Gruter-Napier

Rooms 4 with shower. **Price** With half board 145,000L (per pers.). **Meals** Breakfast included, served 8:30-10:00. **Evening meals** Service 8:00PM - mealtime specials - Tuscan and La Maremma cuisine. **Credit cards** Visa, Eurocard, MasterCard. **Pets** Dogs not allowed. **Facilities** Swimming pool, parking. **Nearby** Massa Marittima - Pitigliano - Sovana - Capalbio - Castiglione della Pescaia - Siena - Montalcino - Pienza - Abbeys of S. Galgano, Sant'Antimo, S. Raban, S. Salvatore - Etrucan grottoes. **Closed** End Nov - end Jan.

The south of Tuscany is less visited, yet it has natural beauty, abundant vegetation and many tourist itineraries. This little inn with only a small number of rooms has been opened by a Swiss-Scottish couple who are very keen that their guests should enjoy a quiet stay and a feeling of well-being. The inn is built on the heights and the panoramic view extends as far as the blue of the sea, which is some thirty kilometers away. The garden is full of greenery: arbors of vines or wisteria, a pond with water plants and a botanical garden where the displays of flowers change according to season. The interior is equally well-designed, with comfortable, well-kept rooms opening on a private pergola. Since half-board is recommended, one should be careful not to disappoint, because the owner has become a veritable cordon bleu, even making the bread and jam for breakfast himself. Discipline and conviviality can thus sometimes happily live together. A multilingual welcome.

How to get there *(Map 13): 30km north of Grosetto. On A1, exit Braccagni, towards Montemassi. Before reaching Montemassi, take the right towards Preti (signposted).*

Pieve di Caminino

Via Provinciale di Peruzzo 58028 Roccatederighi (Grosseto)
Tel. 0564-56 97 37/055-21 48 98 - Fax 055-26 75 819
D. Marrucchi
E-mail: caminino@caminino.com - Web: www.caminino.com

Apartments 8 (2-5 pers.), with kitchenette, lounge, 1-2 bedrooms, shower. **Price** Apart./week 750-1 900,000L. **Credit cards** Visa, Eurocard, MasterCard. **Pets** Dogs not allowed. **Facilities** Parking. **Nearby** Massa Marittima - Pitigliano - Sovana - Capalbio - Castiglione della Pescaia - Siena - Montalcino - Pienza - Abbeys of S. Galgano, Sant'Antimo, S. Rabano, S. Salvatore - Etruscan grottoes. **Open** All year.

It was in 1873 that the Marrucchi family acquired these religious buildings, the origins of which go back to 1075. The apartments are named after the most important figures in the long history of the monastery. The whole place has been excellently restored by the owner, who is an architect. The six suites in the buildings beside the church, like La Segrestia, have preserved elements of Romanesque architecture: ceiling arches in S. Feriolo, wooden framework and ached windows in La Bifora. All of them have a superb view over the countryside immortalized in the famous fresco by Simone Martini, Guidoriccio da Fogliano. The interior, rustic but comfortable, harmonizes with the noble austerity of the site. All the apartments have either a terrace, or else a private spot in the garden and a fireplace where guests can make grills or barbecues. If you do not get the opportunity to hear one of the concerts given in the nave of the church, ask to visit it. Now transformed into a private drawing room, it has many remains as well as a fine collection of pictures painted by artists in the family.

How to get there *(Map 13): 30km north of Grosetto. On A1 exit Braccagni, towards Sassofortino, for 2km, and Caminino is on the right.*

Hotel Terme di Saturnia

58050 Saturnia (Grosseto)
Provinciale della Follonata
Tel. 0564-60 10 61 - Fax 0564-60 12 66 - Sig. San Giovanni
E-mail: info@termedisaturnia.it - Web: www.termedisaturnia.com

Category ★★★★ **Rooms** 80 and 10 suites with air-conditioning, telephone, bath or shower, WC, satellite TV, safe, minibar – Elevator. **Price** Double 600-700,000L, suite 1 030,000L. **Meals** Breakfast included, served 7:15-10:30. **Restaurant** Service 12:45PM-2:00PM, 8:00PM-9:15PM - closed Mon - mealtime specials 75,000L, also à la carte - Regional cooking. **Credit cards** All major. **Pets** Dogs allowed. **Facilities** Swimming pool, tennis, thermal baths, parking. **Nearby** Tombolo - Massa Maritima - Volterra - National Park of Maremma – Punta Ala golf course (18-hole). **Open** All year.

The Hotel Terme di Saturnia is located in the historical Saturnia woods, where legend has it that you can still hear the Etruscans, whose brilliant and mysterious civilization and language we know so little about. Tuscany is named after the "Tusci", as the Etruscans were called, its first known inhabitants. Saturnia is also famous for its Renaissance heritage, and is surrounded by interesting vestiges such as Pitigliano, Sovana, and Sorano. The hotel is profoundly attached to this historical context, as well as the spring water which has flowed here from deep in the ground for thousands of years at 37.5°, beneficial for both body and mind. This is why the entire hotel is laid out around an immense pool, the centerpiece of a modern health and beauty complex. If you prefer, you can enjoy all of the comfort of the hotel, the garden, and the fine cuisine without doing a treatment. The staff, most of whom have worked there for more than 10 years, are very friendly and attentive.

How to get there *(Map 13): 57km southeast of Grosseto via A1 (towards Roma) Manciano exit, then Montemerano, towards Saturnia.*

Villa Clodia

58050 Saturnia (Grosseto)
Via Italia, 43
Tel. 0564-60 12 12 - Fax 0564-60 13 05 - Sig. Giancarlo Ghezzi
E-mail: villaclodi@laltramaremma.it - Web: www.laltramaremma.it

Category ★★★ **Rooms** 8 and 2 suites with air-conditiong, telephone, shower, WC, TV, minibar. **Price** Single 95,000L, double 150,000L, suite 180,000L. **Meals** Breakfast included, served 8:00-10:30. **Restaurant** See p. 559. **Credit cards** Visa, Eurocard, MasterCard. **Pets** Dogs not allowed. **Facilites** Swimming pool. **Nearby** Tombolo - Massa Marittima - Voltera - National Park of Maremma –Punta Ala golf course (18-hole). **Closed** Dec.

S aturnia is a spa town where many people come to take the cure. It can also be a stop on the way to Rome and the south or a base for those who want to visit the Etruscan sites of Tuscany and Latium. The Villa Clodia is a jewel of a small hotel, lovingly looked after by its owners. The house is built right up against the mountain and after extensive remodeling of the interior, the rooms are laid out on different levels all the way down to the garden. The decor is simple and in the finest taste. The color scheme is blue and white, in harmony with the thermal waters and the well-being they have produced for centuries. All the rooms but one have a panoramic view of the valley. Both suites are really spacious and have a terrace as well. In the little garden lawn that seems to be suspended in its natural setting, the blue waters of the star-shaped swimming pool add a final decorative touch to this adorable house.

How to get there *(Map 13): 57km southeast of Grosseto via A1 (via Roma) Manciano exit, then Montemerano, towards Saturnia.*

Park Hotel Napoleone

Isola d'Elba
57037 San Martino di Portoferraio (Livorno)
Tel. 0565-91 85 02/91 11 11 - Fax 0565-91 78 36 - Sig. Marcello Costantini
E-mail: phnapoleone@elbalink.it - Web: www.elbalink.it/hotel/phnapoleone

Category ★★★★ **Rooms** 64 with air-conditioning, telephone, bath, WC, TV, minibar. **Price** Single 120-205,000L, double 170-410,000L. **Meals** Breakfast included, served 8:00-10:00 - half board 155-252,000L (per pers., 3 days min.). **Restaurant** Service 12:30PM-2:00PM, 7:00PM-9:00PM - open Apr – Oct - mealtime specials 60,000L - Italian and international cuisine. **Credit cards** All major. **Pets** Small dogs allowed (except in restaurant and on the beach (40,000L). **Facilities** Swimming pool, private beach (30,000L), 2 tennis (27,000L), riding, parking. **Nearby** Portoferraio (Napoleon House) - Villa Napoleone in San Martino - Madonna del Monte in Marciana – Dell'Acquabona golf course (9-hole). **Open** Apr 23 – Oct 3.

The Park Hotel Napoleone is close to the Emperor's villa, which you can see from certain windows. The hotel itself has historical significance: it was built at the end of the last century by a famous aristocratic Roman family. It is surrounded by a lush garden dotted with white canvas chairs. The rooms are tastefully furnished. The hotel has a beautiful swimming pool and a private beach a few miles away. Being near the Imperial Villa has several drawbacks, however. The path is lined with small souvenir shops, but they disappear at nightfall.

How to get there *(Map 12): Ferry services from Livorno (2hrs.50mn.) or Piombino (1hr.); the hotel is 6km southwest of Portoferraio.*

Hotel Hermitage

Isola d'Elba
La Biodola 57037 Portoferraio (Livorno)
Tel. 0565-93 69 11 - Fax 0565-96 99 84 - Sig. De Ferrari
E-mail: info@elba4star.it - Web: www.elba4star.it

Category ★★★ **Rooms** 130 with air-conditioning, telephone, bath, WC, satellite TV, minibar, safe.
Price Single and double 120-750,000L. **Meals** Breakfast 25,000L, served 7:30-10:00 - half board
160-500,000L, full board +40,000L (per pers., 3 days min.). **Restaurant** Service 12:30PM-2:00PM,
7:30PM-9:00PM - mealtime specials 60-70,000L - Italian and regional cooking. **Credit cards** All major.
Pets Dogs allowed.(+35-45,000L). **Facilities** Swimming pool, tennis (25,000L), private beach,
parking. **Nearby** Portoferraio (Napoleon House) - Villa Napoleone in San Martino - Madonna del Monte
in Marciana - Dell'Acquabona golf course (9-hole). **Open** May - end Sept.

The lovely isle of Elba often seems to have much in common with its
neighbor Corsica, which is visible in clear weather. Both are linked to the
name of Napoleon who, after his abdication in 1814, became its governor until
1815 and left numerous traces of his passage. Sheltered in a charming bay, the
Hermitage is hidden, like all the houses here, in a forest of pines. Discreet and
luxurious, it is in the wealthiest part of the island. A beautiful private beach,
three sea water swimming pools, tennis and miniature golf - a host of
advantages to win favor with the guests. The bedrooms are simply decorated
but all have a balcony with view of the sea. A large staff and attentive service.
Need it be mentioned, however, that in August the whole town of Biodola is
taken by storm.

How to get there *(Map 12): Ferry services from Livorno (2hrs.50mn) or
Piombino (1hr.); the hotel is 7km east of Portoferraio.*

Hotel da Giacomino

Isola d'Elba
Capo Sant'Andrea 57030 Marciana (Livorno)
Tel. 0565-90 80 10 - Fax 0565-90 82 94 - Sig. Giacomino Costa
E-mail: hgiacomino@tiscalinet.it - Web: www.hoteldagiacomino.it

Category ★★★ **Rooms** 33 with telephone, shower, WC. **Price** Single 50-80,000L, double 80-130,000L. **Meals** Breakfast 20,000L, served 8:00-9:30 - half board 75-145,000L, full board 85-165,000L (per pers.). **Restaurant** Service 1:00PM-2:00PM, 8:00PM-9:00PM - mealtime specials 45,000L - Familial and regional cooking. **Credit cards** All major. **Pets** Dogs allowed. **Facilities** Swimming pool, beach, parking at hotel. **Nearby** Portoferraio (Napoleon House) - Villa Napoleone in San Martino - Madonna del Monte in Marciana – Dell'Acquabona golf course (9-hole). **Open** Apr - Oct.

On a little promontory that separates it from the very touristy Bay of Sant'Andrea, the Hotel da Giacomino is perfectly suited to anyone who wants a quiet spot by the sea. Its shaded gardens go right down to the water. There is no beach but a jagged rocky shoreline with lots of private little nooks for swimming. However, you may prefer the swimming pool with a panoramic view of the little bay. The nice family-style service, run by the owner, Signor Giacomino, will help you forget (as much as possible) the rather unfortunate decor. The comfort of the bedrooms is adequate, but the decoration is minimal and the pastel colors a bit strident. Some of the bungalows have kitchen facilities, so you can isolate yourself even more from the seasonal hyperactivity. This is an unpretentious hotel offering unbeatable value for price in an island known to be very expensive.

How to get there *(Map 12): Ferry services from Livorno (2hrs.50mn) or Piombino (1hr.); the hotel is 33km from Portoferraio.*

Parkhotel Laurin

39100 Bolzano
Via Laurin, 4
Tel. 0471-31 10 00 - Fax 0471-31 11 48 - Sig. Havlik
E-mail: info@laurin.it - Web: www.laurin.it

Category ★★★★ **Rooms** 96 with air-conditioning, telephone, bath, WC, cable TV, minibar, safe – Elevator. **Price** Single 205-305,000L, double 305-415,000L. **Meals** Breakfast included, served 7:30-10:30. **Restaurant** Service 12:00PM-2:00PM, 7:00PM-10:00PM - mealtime specials 41-56,000L, also à la carte - Regional and Italian cuisine. **Credit cards** Amex, Visa, Eurocard, MasterCard. **Pets** Dogs allowed (20,000L). **Facilities** Heated swimming pool, parking. **Nearby** Wine road (N 42) from Appiano to Caldaro Lake - Bolzano - Castel Roncolo and Sarentina valley to Vitipeno. **Open** All year.

This old palace in the center of Bolzano, six hundred and fifty feet (200 meters) from the train station, remains an important address for a clientele of businessmen and upper-class families. The dining room, salons and guest rooms are large and "international palace" style. The hotel has every modern convenience and a very attentive personnel. *Le Laurin* is one of the best known restaurants in the region. The rooms look out onto the grounds and are all decorated with contemporary paintings from the hotel's own collection. The swimming pool, hidden in a box of greenery and coolness, is very pleasant. This establishment confirms the advantages of tradition.

How to get there *(Map 4): 140km north of Verona via A22, Bolzano-South or North exit toward the stazione (railway station).*

Hotel Castel Labers

39012 Merano (Bolzano)
Via Labers, 25
Tel. 0473-23 44 84 - Fax 0473-234 146
Sig. G. Stapf-Neubert

Category ★★★ **Rooms** 32 with telephone, bath or shower, WC (TV and minibar on request). **Price** 125-200,000L (per pers.). **Meals** Breakfast included, served 7:30-10:00 - half board 145-200,000L (per pers., 3 days min.). **Restaurant** Service 12:00PM-2:30PM, 7:30PM-9:00PM - mealtime specials 45-65,000L, also à la carte - Italian and Tyrolese cuisine. **Credit cards** Amex, Visa, Eurocard, Master-Card. **Pets** Dogs allowed (20,000L). **Facilities** Heated swimming pool, tennis (20,000L), parking, garage. **Nearby** Castel Tirolo - Castel Scena - Castel Coira in Sluderno - Glorenza - Abbey of Monte Maria near Malles Venosta – Golf in Lana; Petersberg golf course in Karersee. **Closed** Nov 4 – Apr 6.

On a perfectly quiet site surrounded by vineyards, is Castel Labers, a pretty Dolomite castle. An intimate atmosphere and an unusually warm welcome await the traveler here. Antique furniture and paintings decorate the salons and the foyer. You can get to the rooms either by a charming stairway or a pretty elevator. The rooms are comfortable and have old fashioned charm–and they open onto a dazzling panorama. The service is attentive and efficient. The owners are true art and music lovers and they sometimes organize concerts for hotel guests.

How to get there *(Map 3): 28km northwest of Bolzano via A22, Bolzano-South exit; then S38 to Merano-South - Sinigo, towards Scena, then via Labers (5km).*

Hotel Castel Frasburg

Labers 39012 Merano (Bolzano)
Via Fragsburgerstrasse, 4
Tel. 0473-24 40 71 - Fax 0473-24 44 93 - Famiglia Ortner
E-mail: info@fragsburg.com - Web: www.fragsburg.com

Category ★★★★ **Rooms** 12 and 4 suites with telephone, bath or shower, WC, satellite TV, safe – Elevator. **Price** With half board 140-200,000L (per pers.). **Meals** Breakfast included, served 8:00-10:00. **Restaurant** Service 12:00PM-2:00PM, 6:45PM-8:30PM - mealtime specials 50-60,000L, also à la carte. **Credit cards** Not accepted. **Pets** Dogs allowed (+10,000L). **Facilities** Swimming pool, sauna, fitness, parking. **Nearby** Casel Tirolo - Casel Scena - Castel Coira at Sluderno - Glorenza - Benedictine abbey of Monte Maria near Malles Venosta – Petersberg Golf course at Karersee. **Open** Easter – Nov.

The road leading to the hotel is quite charming. After leaving Merano you drive through green fields, gradually entering a forest of larch trees with streams and torrents. After seven kilometers the landscape becomes quite grandiose. The house, half-chalet, half-castello, is typical of the architecture hereabouts with its great wooden balconies, sculpted wood, white façade and red shutters. The drawing rooms are spacious and elegant with lighting that creates an atmosphere of intimacy and well-being. The dining room opens on a long terrace with a panoramic view, shaded by a trellis, beautifully communing with nature. The view is magnificent: the ring of mountains, with Merano in the valley. The rooms are spacious and all different. The overall feel combines the mountain ambiance with deep comfort and lots of embroidered fabrics showing birds and animals of the forest. Nature and tradition have lived together in these mountains since time immemorial. A rare niche.

How to get there *(Map 3): 28km northwest of Bolzano via A22, exit Merano-South - Sinigo, towards Schenna, via Labers and Fragsburg.*

Hotel Oberwirt

Marlengo 39020 Merano (Bolzano)
Via San Felice, 2
Tel. 0473-447 111 - Fax 0473-447 130 - Sig. Josef Waldner
E-mail: oberwirt@dnet.it

Category ★★★★ **Rooms** 40 with telephone, bath or shower, WC, TV, minibar. **Price** Double 105-152,000L, suite 140-198,000L. **Meals** Breakfast included, served 7:30-10:30. **Restaurant** Mealtime specials 54-85,000L, also à la carte. **Credit cards** All major. **Pets** Small dogs allowed (15,000L). **Facilities** Indoor and outdoor swimming pool, sauna, tennis, riding, parking, garage (12,000L). **Nearby** Castel Tirolo - Castel Scena - Castel Coira in Sluderno - Glorenza - Abbey of Monte Maria near Malles Venosta – Petersberg golf course in Karersee. **Open** Mar 15 – Nov 11.

The Hotel Oberwirt is in Marling, a village on the outskirts of Merano, near the racetrack in the hills of the town. It has been run by the same family for two centuries, so there is no lack of professionalism. The hotel only has about forty rooms, all comfortably furnished in traditional and more modern styles. Our favorite is the one in the tower. The traditional *Stube* and the salons have the warmth of Tyrolean style. The Franz Liszt salon was the workplace of the famous musician during the summer of 1874. The hotel has two covered, heated swimming pools and a farm where you can go horseback riding; you can also do a week-long tennis clinic on the grounds (around $675 for half board per person per week). The region offers wonderful possibilities for hikes in the woods.

How to get there *(Map 3): 28km northwest of Bolzano via A22, Bolzano-South exit; then Superstrada to Merano-South. After leaving the superstrada, towards Lana-Marlengo.*

Hotel Schloss Korb

39050 Missiano (Bolzano)
Hocchepan, 5
Tel. 0471-63 60 00 - Fax 0471-63 60 33 - Famiglia Dellago
E-mail: hotel-schloss-korb@dnet.it - Web: www.highlight-hotels.com/korb

Category ★★★★ **Rooms** 56 with telephone, bath, WC, TV – Elevator. **Price** Double 110-200,000L.
Meals Breakfast included, served 7:30-10:00. **Restaurant** Service 12:00PM-2:00PM, 7:00PM-9:30PM -
mealtime specials 65,000L, also à la carte - Regional and Italian cuisine. **Credit cards** All major.
Pets Dogs allowed. **Facilities** 2 Swimming pool, sauna, tennis, parking and garage (15,000L).
Nearby Wine road (N 42) from Appiano to the Caldaro Lake - Bolzano. **Open** Apr 1 – Nov 2.

On top of a hill, the Schloss Korb is an old castle transformed into a hotel-restaurant by its present owners. Surrounded by vineyards, which make it absolutely quiet, it has a superb view over Bolzano and Monte Catinaccio. It is decorated in a Baroque style reminiscent of the Tyrol. Colors, hand crafted objects, a profusion of gilded wood and bouquets of flowers give the place a look of comfortable luxury. You can go for a pleasant walk to the ruins of a neighboring castle where a picnic is served with wine from the property, in a small shelter set up for hotel guests. A Grand Hotel in a delightful setting.

How to get there *(Map 4): 13km west via S42 to San Paolo, then towards Missiano.*

Pensione Leuchtenburg

39052 Caldaro sulla Strada del Vino (Bolzano)
Klughammer, 100
Tel. 0471-96 00 93 - Fax 0471-96 01 55 - Sig. Sparer
E-mail: pensionleuchtenburg@iol.it - Web: www.kalterersee.com/pensionleuchtenburg

Category ★★ **Rooms** 17 and 1 suite with shower, WC. **Price** Double 160,000L, suite 220,000L. **Meals** Breakfast included - half board +20,000L (per pers.). **Restaurant** Service 12:00PM-1:30PM, 7:00PM-8:30PM. **Credit cards** Visa, Eurocard, MasterCard. **Pets** Dogs allowed. **Facilities** Private beach, windsurfing, mountain biking, sauna, whirlpool, bikes rental, parking. **Nearby** Wine road (N42) from Appiano to the Caldaro Lake - Appiano - Merano — Petersberg golf course. **Open** Mar — Nov (closed Wed).

The region of Caldaro is very attractive and deserves to be discovered. After leaving the Bolzano autostrada and making your way through the maze of little roads bordered by dwarf apple trees which perfume the air, you drive above Lake Caldaro. Here the mountain is gentle and welcoming, covered in meadows and vineyards. The pensione is in the outbuildings of the Leuchtenberg castle. It is a very pleasant house with pretty arbor-covered courtyards and a large terrace, filled with flowers, on the lake. The interior is simple but charming. The tavern is typical of the region and the rooms are decorated with pretty painted wood furniture. A private beach, sailboards and mountain bikes are at the disposal of hotel guests at no charge. This is a good place for a nice vacation at a low price.

How to get there *(Map 4): 25km south of Merano, via A22, Ora-Lago Caldaro exit (Kaltern); on the left bank of the lake.*

Berghotel Zirmerhof

39040 Redagno (Bolzano)
Oberradein, 59
Tel. 0471-88 72 15 - Fax 0471-88 72 25 - Sig. Perwanger
E-mail: info@zirmerhof.com - Web: www.zirmerhof.com

Rooms 32 with bath or shower, WC. **Price** With half board (per pers., 3 days min.) 101-165,000L, 140-180,000L (suite). **Meals** Breakfast 17,000L, served 8:00-10:00. **Restaurant** Service 12:00PM and 7:30PM (for residents only) - closed Mon, mealtime specials 40-60,000L - Specialties: Minestra di vino - Zirmertorte - Sella di vitello. **Credit cards** Not accepted. **Pets** Dogs allowed. **Facilities** Sauna, parking. **Nearby** Wine road (N 42) from Appiano to the Caldaro Lake - Appiano - Merano – Petersberg golf course. **Closed** Nov 8 – Dec 25, Mar 30 – May 15.

Away from the hordes of tourists, the Redagno region and the Monte Corno Reserve have not lost any of their natural beauty. This inn, which opened in 1890, was a popular vacation spot for the aristocracy and upper classes of Vienna and Berlin and a place where intellectuals came for inspiration. The rooms are cozy and comfortable, the stube and the family library still have that "Magic Mountain" atmosphere, and the great "Sala Grimm" the work of Ignaz Sthol, has kept its beautiful frescos. The fine cuisine of the house restaurant is still influenced by the recipes of the nonna Hanna Perwanger, of German origin, who loved the Upper Adige very much. Friendly service is a priority here, as is the happiness of the guests. The swimming poll may be ready for this year, and the wine cellar is open now for tastings.

How to get there *(Map 4): 40km south of Bolzano via A22, Egna Ora exit towards Cavalese to Kaltenbruno; after on your left towerds Redagno.*

Albergo Monte San Vigilio

Monte San Vigilio
39011 Lana (Bolzano)
Tel. 0473-561 236 - Fax 0473-561 731
Sig. Burger

Category ★★★ **Rooms** 40 with telephone, bath or shower, WC. **Price** With half board 85-120,000L (per pers., 3 days min.). **Meals** Breakfast included, served 8:00-10:00. **Restaurant** Service 12:00PM-2:00PM, 7:00PM-8:30PM - mealtime specials 30-40,000L. **Credit cards** All major. **Pets** Dogs allowed. **Facilities** Swimming pool, garage (5,000L). **Nearby** Skiing - Castel Tirolo - Castel Scena - Castel Coira in Sluderno - Glorenza - Abbey of Monte Maria near Malles Venosta — Petersberg golf course in Karersee. **Closed** Nov 8 – Dec 19.

This chalet is the perfect place for mountain lovers. The obligatory access by cable car will satisfy even the most demanding aficionados of rest and fresh air. Decorated with naive paintings, this chalet is undoubtedly one of the most charming places in this guide. There is a nice family atmosphere, warmly fostered by the manager, who willingly acts as a guide for guests who want to explore one of the many hiking trails in the area. The lifts work during the summer too, so you can get to beautiful natural sites and shelters where it is pleasant to stop and rest for awhile. The rooms all have a superb panoramic view. The cuisine is simple and good. This place is ideal for a family vacation.

How to get there *(Map 3): 30km northwest of Bolzano via S38, towards Merano to Portal, then Lana; in Lana take the funicular (summer 8:00AM-7:00PM, winter 8:00AM-6:00PM).*

Hotel Turm

39050 Fié allo Sciliar (Bolzano)
Piazza della Chiesa, 9
Tel. 0471-72 50 14 - Fax 0471-72 54 74
Sig. Pramstrahler

Category ★★★★ **Rooms** 26 with telephone, bath, WC, TV. **Price** Single 102-164,000L, double 204-328,000L, suite 264-368,000L. **Meals** Breakfast included, served 8:00-10:00 - half board 127-422,000L (per pers.). **Restaurant** Service 12:00PM-2:00PM, 7:00PM-9:00PM - closed Thurs - mealtime specials 38-65,000L, also à la carte. **Credit cards** Visa, Eurocard, MasterCard. **Pets** Dogs allowed (12,000L). **Facilities** Swimming pool, sauna, garage (7,000L). **Nearby** Alpe di Siusi (16km) - Bolzano. **Closed** Nov 5 – Dec 18.

This hotel is in Fié, a small village in Val Gardena, a superb region just below the spectacular and impressive Mount Sciliar. It is in the old town hall, right in the middle of Fié and has been run by the same family for three generations. Very comfortable and nicely decorated interior, it has antique furniture and a large collection of paintings. Most of the rooms are cozy and tastefully furnished and have a superb view of the mountains. Stefano, the owner's son and manager of the restaurant, is also an excellent cook: his fine inventive cuisine skillfully blends the particularities of regional cuisine with the sophistication of recipes of the great French chefs. In the summer, this is a marvelous place for hiking around the lake and in the winter, you can go cross-country skiing, skating and downhill skiing at Alpe di Suisi, only twenty minutes away.

***How to get there** (Map 4): 16km east of Bolzano (via A22 Bolzano-North exit) via S49 to Prato all'Isarco, then Fié.*

Hotel Cavallino d'Oro

39040 Castelrotto (Bolzano)
Piazza Kraus
Tel. 0471-706 337 - Fax 0471-707 172 - Sig. and Sig.ra Urthaler
E-mail: cavallino@cavallino.it - Web:www.cavallino.it

Category ★★★★ **Rooms** 20 with telephone, bath or shower, WC, TV, safe. **Price** Single 70-100,000L, double 125-180,000L. **Meals** Breakfast included, served 7:30-10:00 - half board 80-150,000L, full board 102-174,000L. **Restaurant** Service 11:30AM-2:00PM, 6:00PM-9:00PM - closed Sun dinner - mealtime specials 25-50,000L, also à la carte - Italian and regional cooking. **Credit cards** All major **Pets** Dogs allowed (with extra charge). **Facilities** Sauna. **Nearby** Skiing - Alpe de Siusi - Val Gardena - Ortisei. **Open** All year (closed Tues).

The Cavallino d'Oro is a traditional inn typical of Southern Tyrol. It is in Castelrotto, a village in the Val Gardena where Ladin is still spoken and where the inhabitants still dress in traditional costume and live in houses with painted façades. The stube (locale) is friendly and the restaurant features local specialties. The rooms are very well kept. In the summer, a small terrace is set up on the square, the prettiest spot in the village. The hotel is constantly being improved and you can now enjoy sauna or steam baths in what were once the 600-year old wine cellars. This still relatively unvisited region is worth exploring, especially at these prices.

How to get there *(Map 4): 26km northeast of Bolzano via S12 to Ponte Gardena, then towards Castelrotto.*

Albergo Tschötscherhof

39040 Siusi allo Sciliar (Bolzano)
San Osvaldo, 19
Tel. 0471-70 60 13 - Fax 0471-70 48 01
Famiglia Jaider
E-mail: info@tschoetscherhof.com - Web: www.tschoetscherhof.com

Rooms 8 with bath or shower, WC. **Price** Double 80-90,000L. **Meals** Breakfast included, served 7:30-10:00 - half board 50-59,000L (per pers.). **Restaurant** Service 11:30AM-2:00PM, 6:00PM-9:00PM - mealtime specials 25-50,000L, also à la carte - Regional cooking. **Credit cards** Not accepted. **Pets** Dogs not allowed. **Nearby** Val Gardena - Ortisei - Alpe di Siusi - Skiing. **Open** Feb –Dec.

You dream of finding a mountain protected from mountain bikes and a village where there are more farms than hotels; you will discover all this at San Osvaldo along the little road that winds through the meadows where lovely fat cows are grazing. The hamlet that extends below is dominated by the traditional bulbous tower of its church. The house is a postcard vision, a delightful chalet with green shutters where the balconies are bending beneath the weight of the vines and the geraniums. You cross the great terrace to get to the reception, on the first floor. The interior is simple and rustic: low ceilings, walls covered with wood or whitewashed. The living rooms are furnished with regional furniture and popular objets d'art. The rooms are more modest, but very well kept and not lacking in comfort. This is a place that will attract lovers of walking (the Siusi park is quite near) and all those who enjoy the revitalizing air and pure light that can only be found in the mountains. Convivial atmosphere.

How to get there (Map 4): 26km northeast of Bolzano by A22, exit Bolzano-North, then S12 (towards Brennero) as far as Prato Isarco, then towards Castelrotto, Seis and San Osvaldo.

Hotel Adler

39046 Ortisei/Val Gardena (Bolzano)
Via Rezia, 7
Tel. 0471-77 5000 - Fax 0471-77 5555 - Famiglia Sanoner
E-mail: info@hotel-adler.com - Web: www.hotel-adler.com

Category ★★★★ S **Rooms** 123 with telephone, bath, hairdryer, WC, TV, minibar, safe – Elevator. **Price** With half board and full board 171-353,000L (single), 145-330,000L (per pers. in double room); full board +25,000L. **Meals** Breakfast included, served 7:00-10:00. **Restaurant** Service 12:00PM-2:00PM, 7:00PM-9:30PM - mealtime specials 30-49,000L, also à la carte - Tyrolese cuisine. **Credit cards** Visa, Eurocard, MasterCard **Pets** Dogs not allowed. **Facilities** Heated indoor swimming pool, tennis, sauna, health center, garage, parking. **Nearby** Alpe di Siusi (1996 m) and Seceda (2500 m) by cabble car - Castelrotto - Val Gardena - Bolzano. **Open** May 17 – Oct 20, Dec 16 – Apr 20.

In the center of Ortisei, this hotel, born from the fusion of two buildings with very different architectural styles, is an island of greenery and quiet. It is also the meeting place for German tourists staying in the region. In summer and winter it is frequented by a clientele of regulars for whom solitude and proximity to the slopes are not priorities; they enjoy the animated ambiance of the little village of Ortisei. All of the rooms have been redone.

How to get there *(Map 4): 35km east of Bolzano via A22; Chiusa exit (or S12 to Ponte Gardena), then S242 to Ortisei.*

Piccolo Hotel Uhrerhof Deur

Bulla 39046 Ortisei
Tel. 0471-79 73 35 - Fax 0471-79 74 57
Famiglia Zemmer
E-mail: uhrerhof@val-gardena.com - Web: val-gardena.com/hotel/uhrerhof

Rooms 10 suites (no smoking) with telephone, bath or shower, WC, TV. **Price** With half board 120-170,000L (per pers. 3 days min.). **Restaurant** (By reservation). Service 7:00PM - closed Wed - mealtime specials 40-60,000L. **Credit cards** Visa, Eurocard, MasterCard. **Pets** Dogs not allowed. **Facilities** Sauna, steam bath, solarium (20,000L), whirlpool, parking, **Nearby** Alpe di Siusi (1 996 m) and Seceda (2 500 m) by cable car - Castelrotto - Val Gardena - Bolzano. **Closed** Apr 20– 28, Nov 1 – Dec 4.

Ortisei is a large resort in Val Gardena where all those who love the mountains can enjoy skiing or hiking in the forests of Rasciesca or on the slopes of Alpe di Siusi. Its charm lies also in its people's attachment to local tradition, which lends a picturesque quality to village life. The Uhrerhof Deur is faithful to this spirit. Located just a few kilometers from the village, it has the feel of a guest house and you are welcomed like a friend. The house, whether in the bedrooms, the drawing rooms or the reading room, is welcoming, the site grandiose and the cooking excellent, but we would emphasize (in case you missed it above) that the house is completely non-smoking - a good way for smokers to test the degree of their dependence.

How to get there *(Map 4): 35km east of Bolzano via A22, Chiusa or Bolzano-North exit (or S12 to Ponte Gardena), then S242 to Ortisei. Bulla is 5km from Ortisei.*

Hotel Elephant

39042 Bressanone (Bolzano)
Via Rio Bianco, 4
Tel. 0472-83 27 50 - Fax 0472-83 65 79 - Famiglia Heiss-Falk
E-mail: elephant.brixen@acs.it - Web: www.acs.it/elephant

Category ★★★★ S **Rooms** 44 with telephone, bath, WC, TV. **Price** Single 136-193,000L, double 272-386,000L. **Meals** Breakfast 26,000L - half board 213-277,000L (per pers., 3 days min.). **Restaurant** Service 12:00PM-2:15PM, 7:00PM-9:30PM - closed Mon - mealtime specials 65-75,000L, also à la carte. **Credit cards** All major. **Pets** Dogs allowed except in restaurant (15,000L). **Facilities** Heated swimming pool, tennis, parking (12-15,000L). **Nearby** Plose (2504 m) - Convent of Novacella - Val Gardena (castle of Velturno, Chiusa, Ortisei). **Open** Mar 10 – Nov 6, Dec 1 – Jan 7.

The many Episcopal monasteries and castles around Bressanone testify to the artistic, cultural and spiritual influence this town had on the region during the 18th-century. The Hotel Elephant is the ideal base for exploring the area. The paneled reception rooms are decorated with antique furniture, tapestries and rugs. The rooms are all very comfortable and most of them look out onto the swimming pool or the mountains (only certain rooms face north). The cuisine is remarkable and the personnel is excellent. The hotel has consistently lived up to its reputation since 1550 when a convoy with an elephant, given to the Emperor Ferdinand of Habsbourgby the King of Portugal, stayed here.

How to get there *(Map 4): 40km northeast of Bolzano via A22; Bressanone exit. The hotel is northwest of town center: from via Roma, via Fichini, then via Rio Bianco.*

La Perla

39033 Corvara in Badia (Bolzano)
Str. Col Alt 105
Tel. 0471-83 61 32 - Fax 0471-83 65 68
Famiglia Costa
E-mail: perla@altabadia.it - Web: www.altabadia.it/perla

Category ★★★★ **Rooms** 52 with telephone, bath, WC, TV. **Prices** Single 190-380,000L, double 340-720,000L, suite 460-840,000L. **Meals** Breakfast included, served 7:30-10:30; half board 188-378,000L (per pers., 3 days min.). **Restaurant** "La Stüa de Michil" (Dec 15 – Apr 1), service 7:00PM-9:00PM - closed Mon - mealtime specials 98-118,000L - Specialties: Tarte di fresco - Risotto con castagne e tartufo nero - Ravioli ripieni con polenta nera - Crema di zucca con finferli e speck rosolato - Sella di maialino con funghi di bosco - Tortino al papavero con salsa al cioccolato e frutti di bosco. **Credit cards** Amex, Visa, Eurocard, MasterCard. **Pets** Dogs not allowed. **Facilities** Heated swimming pool, massage, sauna, fitness, garage, parking. **Nearby** Skiing - Val Badia - Great road of Dolomites (N48) - Ortisei. **Closed** Sept 23 – Dec 6, Apr 1 – Jun 22.

The Hotel La Perla is a real gem. A beautiful chalet in a quiet part of the center of Corvara, it is perfect in every way. It is more elegant than rustic, and it manages to maintain a certain intimacy despite the numerous services worthy of a grand hotel (sauna, wine cellar, heated pool and a baths with the latest equipment). In the restaurant the chef, Markus Wolfsgruber, cooks specialties that incorporate some of the special features of southern Tyrolese cuisine. Just twenty seven miles (45km) from Cortina d'Ampezzo, this place is great all year round.

How to get there *(Map 4): 65km east of Bolzano via A22; Chiusa exit (or S12 to Ponte Gardena), then S242 to Corvara via Ortisei.*

Hotel Armentarola

39030 San Cassiano (Bolzano)
Via Prè de Vì, 12
Tel. 0471-84 95 22 - Fax 0471-84 93 89 - Famiglia Wieser
E-mail: info@armentarola.com - Web: www.armentarola.com

Category ★★★★ **Rooms** 50 with telephone, bath or shower, WC, safe, TV, minibar. **Price** With half board: single 175-260,000L, double 175-280,000L (per pers.), suite 210-300,000L (per pers.). **Meals** Breakfast included, served 7:30-11:00. **Restaurant** Service 11:00PM-6:00PM, 7:00PM-9:00PM - mealtime specials 45-70,000L, also à la carte - Regional cooking. **Credit cards** Not accepted **Pets** Dogs allowed (25,000L). **Facilities** Indoor swimming pool, fitness center, tennis, riding, sauna, solarium, garage (10,000L). **Nearby** Skiing - Cortina d'Ampezzo - Great road of Dolomites (N48) - Ortisei. **Open** Dec 1 – mid Apr, mid Jul – mid Oct.

The story of the Armentarola began with the Wieser family in 1938, when Paolo and Emma transformed the family chalet into an inn. It is isolated at an altitude of 5,200 feet (1,600 meters), in an enchanting landscape of pastures and woods with the Dolomites in the background, but the Armentarola has continually adapted to the changing standards of modern comfort, while keeping all of its original charm intact. There are plenty of well-organized leisure activites here all year round. In summer, you can play tennis and go horseback riding, and in winter, you can swim in the covered swimming pool or take the ski lift from the hotel, which is linked to the large ski *carrousel* of the upper Badia Valley. Enjoy the grandeur of nature at this hotel, only a few kilometers from Cortina d'Ampezzo.

How to get there *(Map 4): 75km east of Bolzano via S12, S242d and S242 towards Selva di Valgardena; then S243 to Corvara and S244.*

Parkhotel Sole Paradiso

39038 San Candido - Innichen (Bolzano)
Via Sesto, 13
Tel. 0474-91 31 20 - Fax 0474-91 31 93 - Famiglia Ortner
E-mail: parkhotel@sole-paradiso.com - Web: www.sole-paradiso.com

Category ★★★★ **Rooms** 39 and 4 suites with telephone, bath or shower, WC, TV. **Price** Single 130-200,000L, double 250-400,000L. **Meals** Breakfast included (buffet), served 8:00-10:30 - half board 125-250,000L, full board 155-280,000L (per pers., 3 days min.). **Restaurant** Service 12:30PM-1:30PM, 7:00PM-8:30PM - mealtime specials 45-70,000L - Specialties: Schlutzkrapfen - Maccheroni alla boscaiola - Trota del vivaio Kaiserschmarrn. **Credit cards** All major. **Pets** Dogs not allowed. **Facilities** Indoor swimming pool, tennis, sauna, garage (15,000L). **Nearby** Lago di Braies - Lago di Misurina - Croda Rossa - Tre cime di Lavaredo - Cortina d'Ampezzo. **Closed** Oct 8 – Dec 17, Mar 31 – May 31.

The architecture and the red and yellow colors of this large chalet will remind you, if you need to be reminded, that you are only a few miles from the Austrian border. The warm cozy atmosphere of a mountain home pervades the hotel. The walls are covered with blond wood and the ceiling and table lamps are made of very beautiful sculpted wood. The rooms have large canopy beds, heavy drapes and pretty flower-covered balconies with nice views of the Val Pusteria. The hotel is very well equipped for leisure activities: There is a tennis court, a heated swimming pool open year round, cross-country ski trails and a ski shuttle bus which stops just in front of the hotel.

How to get there *(Map 4): 100km northeast of Bolzano via A22, Bressanone exit; then S49 to San Candido. 200m north of Venice via A27.*

Hotel Uridl

39038 S. Cristina Val Gardena (Bolzano)
Tel. 0471-79 32 15 - Fax 0471-79 35 54
Sig. Helmar Delmetz
E-mail: uridl@val-gardena.com - Web: www.val-gardena.com/hotel/uridl

Category ★★★ **Rooms** 15 with telephone, bath, WC, satellite TV —Elevator. **Price** With half board 93-144,000L (per pers.); full board +10-22,000L. **Meals** Breakfast included, served 8:00-10:00. **Restaurant** Service 12:00PM-1:30PM, 6:30PM-8:30PM - mealtime specials 40,000L, also à la carte - Regional cooking. **Credit cards** All major. **Pets** Dogs not allowed. **Facilities** Access tennis, squash in the Ortisei sports center, 4km away, parking and garage (5,000L). **Nearby** Alpe di Siusi (1 996m) and Seceda (2 500m) by cable car - Castelrotto - Val Gardena - Bolzano **Closed** Oct – Christmas and May.

Val Gardena provides a marvellous setting for the winter sports resorts such as Santa Cristina, a crossroads for various excursions in every season. This little village, 1 500 meters above sea level, in th heart of the Dolomites, has kept its prestige of former times thanks particularly to initiatives such as the Hotel Uridl, where the chalet has been restored with taste and intelligence. On the first level are the panelled reception and drawing room, as you would expect. The restaurant occupies three small rooms, but our preference, here too, is for the most traditional which still has its old wooden decors, including its shutters. The large porcelain stove, the cuckoo clocks and the stube tirolese are still there to remind one of the old traditional customs of the region. The bedrooms are less charming, but do provide you with all the comforts of modernity. The extraordinary view that some have over the mountains will easily compensate for a lack of interest in the internal decoration. Note that in the basement there is a large games room with ping-pong, billiards and table football...

How to get there *(Map 4): 40km east of Bolzano by A22, exit Chiusa (or S12 to Ponte Gardena), then S242 as far as S. Cristina.*

436

Albergo Accademia

38100 Trento
Vicolo Colico, 4-6
Tel. 0461-23 36 00 - Fax 0461-23 01 74 - Sig.ra Fambri
E-mail: info@accademiahotel.it - Web: www.accademiahotel.it

Category ★★★★ **Rooms** 43 with air-conditioning, telephone, bath or shower, WC, satellite TV, mini-bar – Elevator. **Price** Single 180,000L, double 260,000L. **Meals** Breakfast included, served 7:00-10:30. **Restaurant** Service 12:30PM-2:30PM, 7:30PM-10:30PM - closed Sun - mealtime specials 45-55,000L, also à la carte - Specialties: Langostine grigliate al profumo di menta - Tagliolini freschi in guazzetto - coda di rospo con funghi porcini - Babà al rum. **Credit cards** All major. **Pets** Dogs allowed. **Nearby** Trento - Lake Garda - Brenta Dolomites - Lake Toblino - La Paganella - the "Ormeri" di Segonzaro. **Closed** Dec 24 – Jan 6.

The Albergo Accademia is in an old house from the Middle Ages on a small square in this pretty neighborhood of this medieval town. The decor is resolutely modern, but highlights what remains of the original architecture and a few antique pieces. The rooms are large, light, quiet and very comfortable. The hotel restaurant, La cucina del sole, is renowned for its traditional Neapolitan cuisine, with an emphasis on fish. The old inner courtyard is now a garden where breakfast is served and the terrace is a nice place from which to enjoy the view of the rooftops, the towers and the bell-towers of Trento. This is a charming address in a town that is really worth the trip.

How to get there *(Maps 3 and 4): 101km north of Verona via A22, Trento exit; the hotel is located in the town center.*

Castello Pergine

38057 Pergine Valsugana (Trento)
Tel. 0461-53 11 58 - Fax 0461-53 13 29
Sig. and Sig.ra Schneider-Neff
E-mail: verena@castelpergine.it - Web: www.castelpergine.it

Rooms 21 with telephone, bath or shower, WC, TV. **Price** With half board: 115,000L (per pers.). **Meals** Breakfast included, served 8:00-9:30. **Restaurant** Service 12:30PM-2:00PM, 7:30PM-9:30PM - closed Mon lunchtime; carte 50,000L - Specialties: Strangola con su salsa formaggiconiglio disossaso farciso con la verza - Carpaccio di carne salada. **Credit cards** Amex, Visa, Eurocard, MasterCard. **Pets** Dogs allowed in rooms. **Facilities** Parking. **Nearby** Caldonazzo Lake (San Cristoforo al Lago) - Canal of the Brentaby (N47) after Primolano - Trento. **Open** Easter - Oct.

On the border between Latin and German civilization, Trento is an interesting town, its Duomo and Castello del Buonconsiglio well worth a visit. The mountainous back country is also pleasant, with small rural villages like Pergine Valsugana. The hotel is in a medieval castle. Known primarily for its good restaurant, serving regional specialties, the building has undergone alterations that have made the rooms more comfortable. The location and the green surroundings create an atmosphere of serenity. An appealing place.

How to get there *(Map 4): 11km east of Trento via S47; 2.5km from the town.*

Lido Palace Hotel

Lago di Garda
38066 Riva del Garda (Trento)
Viale Carducci, 10
Tel. 0464-55 26 64 - Fax 0464-55 19 57 - Sig. Genetin
E-mail: lidopalace@anthesi.com - Web: www.garda.com/hotels/riva/lido

Category ★★★★ **Rooms** 63 with telephone, bath or shower, WC, minibar, TV – Elevator. **Price** Double 220-300,000L. **Meals** Breakfast included, served 7:30-10:00; half board 135-175,000L (per pers., 3 days min.). **Restaurant** With air-conditioning. Service 12:30PM-2:00PM, 7:30PM-9:00PM - mealtime specials 40,000L - International and Italian cuisine. **Credit cards** All major. **Pets** Dogs allowed (15,000L). **Facilities** Swimming pool, tennis, parking. **Nearby** Cascade of Varone - Lake of Tenno - Trento. **Open** Apr – Oct 31.

The main attraction of the Lido is its proximity to the small port of Riva del Garda. The grounds are next to the public garden and the lakeside docks where you will find a quaint 19th-century spa atmosphere. The building is from the same period and has been very tastefully renovated. The rooms are bright and simple; from them you can see the lake through the foliage of cedar trees. A family atmosphere pervades the hotel despite its conventional, classic appearance.

How to get there *(Map 3): 50km southwest of Trento; 87km north of Verona via A22; Rovereto-South exit, then S240.*

Palace Hotel

38050 Roncegno (Trento)
Casa di Salute Raphael
Tel. 0461-772 000 - 0461-76 40 12 - Fax 0461-76 45 00
E-mail: mail.info@casaraphael.com - Web: www.casaraphael.com

Category ★★★★ **Rooms** 85 with telephone, bath or shower, WC, TV — Elevator. **Price** Single 185,000L, double 330,000L. **Meals** Breakfast included, served 8:00-9:30 - half board 215,000L, full board 235,000L (per pers., 3 days min.). **Restaurant** Service 12:30PM-2:00PM, 7:00PM-9:30PM - meal-time specials 55-60,000L, also à la carte - Vegetarian cooking. **Credit cards** Amex, Visa, Eurocard, MasterCard. **Pets** Dogs not allowed. **Facilities** Indoor swimming pool, tennis, squash, health center, parking. **Nearby** Ruins of the castles of Borgo Valsugana - Canal of the Brenta (N47) after Primolano - Trento. **Open** Apr — Oct.

B uilt at the beginning of the century on twelve and a half acres, the Palace Hotel still has all of the elegance and the picturesque quality of that time. It has long been the summer meeting place for the Italian aristocracy. The salons and the dining room testify to its past. It has been completely renovated and has all the requisite amenities of a four-star hotel, including a squash court, a health center with an indoor pool and a sauna. This blend of old-fashioned elegance and modern efficiency is the main appeal of this hotel.

How to get there *(Map 4): 33km east of Trento via S47.*

Hotel Cipriani e Palazzo Vendramin

30133 Venezia
Isola della Giudecca, 10
Tel. 041-520 77 44 - Fax 041-520 39 30/77 45 - Sig. N. Rusconi
E-mail: info@hotelcipriani.it - Web: www.hotelcipriani.it

Category ★★★★ **Rooms** 106 with air-conditioning, telephone, bath, WC, TV, minibar – Elevator. **Price** Single 825-1 200,000L, double 1 300-2 040,000L. **Meals** Breakfast included, served 7:00-10:30. **Restaurant** Service 12:30PM-3:00PM, 8:00PM-10:30PM - à la carte - Regional cooking. **Credit cards** All major. **Pets** Small dogs allowed. **Facilities** Swimming pool, tennis (45,000L), sauna (50,000L), turkish bath, private port. **Nearby** Events: Carnival of Venice, the Regata Storica (Sept), the Mostra of Venice (Aug – Sept), Venice Biennale - Murano - Torcello (S. M. Assunta, S. Fosca) - Villa Foscari in Fusina - Venetian villas (cruise along the Brenta Canal with the boat "Il Burchiello") – Al Lido Alberoni golf course (18-hole). **Open** All year.

On the floating docks that border the Piazza San Marco, the Cipriani is the only hotel that has a spot for its own private craft — luxurious small boats of varnished wood, which assure the hotel's own shuttle service. Everything here is exceptional, for the name Cipriani has come to mean high quality and luxury. Giuseppe Cipriani also founded Harry's Bar, world famous for its cuisine as well as for its famous cocktail, the Bellini. Located at one end of the island of Giudecca, the hotel offers its guests many other luxuries: an Olympic swimming pool, a private yacht club, salons and bedrooms with great refinement and superb views of the lagoon with San Giorgio Maggiore and the Palladian domes of the Redentore and Zitelle. As for the Palazzo Vendramin, the luxurious annex of the Cipriani, what can we say except that we prefer the original? As for the new Palazzetto, it houses a few apartments and a bar-restaurant opposite La Salute.

How to get there *(Map 4): On Isola della Giudecca.*

441

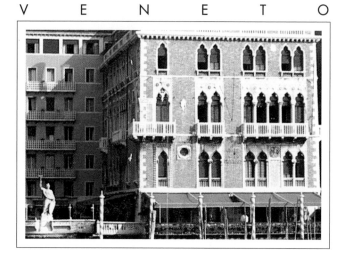

Bauer Grünwald and Grand Hotel

30124 Venezia
Campo San Moise, 1459
Tel. 041-520 70 22 - Fax 041-520 75 57
Sig. D'Este

Category ★★★★★ **Rooms** 214 with air-conditioning, telephone, bath or shower, WC, TV, minibar, some rooms with lounge —Elevator. **Price** Rooms in the Palazzo: Palatial Room 570-1 180,000L, Deluxe suite 800-2 500,000L, excecutive suite 1 600-3 600,000L. Rooms in the Hotel: Superior Room 410-950,000L, suite 650-1 500,000L. **Meals** Breakfast 50,000L, served 7:00-10:30. **Restaurant** Service 12:30PM-2:30PM, 7:00PM-10:30PM - mealtime specials 90,000L, also à la carte - Specialties: Risotto alla torcellana - Fegato alla veneziana. **Credit cards** All major. **Pets** Dogs allowed (60,000L). **Nearby** Events: Carnival of Venice, the Regata Storica (Sept), the Mostra of Venice (Aug – Sept), Venice Biennale - Murano - Torcello (S. M. Assunta, S. Fosca) - Villa Foscari in Fusina - Venetian villas (cruise along the Brenta Canal with the boat "Il Burchiello") —Al Lido Alberoni golf course (18-hole). **Open** All year.

The Bauer Grünwald was born out of Italian unity: a young Venetian man, Jules Grünwald, married Miss Bauer. First they opened a tavern, which was a great success, and then they built the Grand Hotel. The difference between the Bauer and other palaces in Venice is its "class": An atmosphere of quiet luxury reigns here. Only a few steps from Piazza San Marco, it also has the advantage of having a terrace on the Grand Canal, where you can dine by candlelight facing the Salute and the island of San Giorgio.

How to get there *(Map 4): Near Piazza San Marco, along the Grand Canal, between Chuch of Salute and San Giorgio island.*

Gritti Palace Hotel

30124 Venezia
Campo Santa Maria del Giglio, 2467
Tel. 041-79 46 11 - Fax 041-520 09 42 - Sig. Feriani
E-mail: laura.fanecco@luxurycollection.com

Category ★★★★★ **Rooms** 82 and 9 suites with air-conditioning, telephone, bath or shower, WC, safe, TV, minibar —Elevator. **Price** Single 850-880,000L, double 1 250-1 720,000L, suite 2 900-5 800,000L. **Meals** Breakfast 50-85,000L, served 7:00-11:00 or at any time in room. **Restaurant** Service 12:30PM-3:00PM, 7:30PM-10:30PM - mealtime specials 170-220,000L, also à la carte - Specialties: Bresaola Gritti Palace - I risotti del Gritti - Scampi fritti in erbaria. **Credit cards** All major. **Pets** Small dogs allowed (except in restaurent). **Nearby** Events: Carnival of Venice, the Regata Storica (Sept), the Mostra of Venice (Aug — Sept), Venice Biennale - Murano - Torcello (S. M. Assunta, S. Fosca) - Villa Foscari in Fusina - Venetian villas (cruise along the Brenta Canal with the boat "Il Burchiello") — Al Lido Alberoni golf course (18-hole). **Open** All year.

Ernest Hemingway wrote of this 15th-century palace built by Andrea Gritti, "The best hotel in Venice, which is a town made of grand hotels." Its splendid and famous terrace on the Grand Canal is a magic place. Everything here, from the rooms and suites to the salons and dining rooms, emanates luxury and refinement. The restaurant is also one of the best in Venice. If you are planning to stay at the Gritti, try to get a room on the Grand Canal so you can enjoy the show for longer.

How to get there *(Map 4): Near San Marco, on the Grand Canal.*

Hotel Monaco e Grand Canal

30124 Venezia
San Marco - Calle Vallaresso, 1325
Tel. 041-520 02 11 - Fax 041-520 05 01 - Sig. Ciaceri
E-mail: mailbox@hotelmonaco.it

Category ★★★★ **Rooms** 72 with air-conditioning, telephone, bath or shower, WC, TV, minibar –
Elevator. **Price** Single 440-520,000L, double 730-950,000L, suite 1 150-1 250,000L. **Meals** Breakfast
included, served 7:00-11:00 in room, 8:00-10:30 in restaurant. **Restaurant** Service 12:30PM-3:00PM,
7:30PM-10:00PM - à la carte. **Credit cards** All major. **Pets** Small dogs allowed. **Nearby** Events:
Carnival of Venice, the Regata Storica (Sept), the Mostra of Venice (Aug – Sept), Venice Biennale -
Murano - Torcello (S. M. Assunta, S. Fosca) - Villa Foscari in Fusina - Venetian villas (cruise along the
Brenta Canal with the boat "Il Burchiello") –Al Lido Alberoni golf course (18-hole). **Open** All year.

The elegant atmosphere, plush salons, flowering patio and small but very
well-decorated rooms make this one of the great hotels of Venice. It also
has a superb terrace on the Grand Canal, where you can have lunch and dinner.
The restaurant is excellent, but very expensive. In the summer, it is nicer to
have a room on the interior patio. If you really want to have a view of the
Grand Canal, try to get room farthest from the *vaporetto* station at the foot of
the hotel. Our favorite is Room 308. Prices are reasonable, especially off-
season.

How to get there *(Map 4): Near Piazza San Marco.*

Hotel Londra Palace

30122 Venezia
Riva degli Schiavoni, 4171
Tel. 041-520 05 33 - Fax 041-522 50 32 - Sig. Lorenzo Righi
E-mail: info@hotelondra.it - Web: www.hotelondra.it

Category ★★★★ **Rooms** 53 with air-conditioning, telephone, bath, WC, safe, satellite TV, whirl pool, hairdryer, minibar – Elevator. **Price** Double 600-1 000,000L, suite 700-1 500,000L. **Meals** Breakfast included, served 7:00-10:30. **Restaurant** Service 12:30PM-3:30PM, 7:30PM-11:30PM - mealtime specials 90-110,000L, also à la carte - Venitian and Italian cuisine. **Credit cards** All major. **Pets** Dogs not allowed. **Nearby** Events: Carnival of Venice, the Regata Storica (Sept), the Mostra of Venice (Aug – Sept), Venice Biennale - Murano - Torcello (S. M. Assunta, S. Fosca) - Villa Foscari in Fusina - Venetian villas (cruise along the Brenta Canal with the boat "Il Burchiello") – Al Lido Alberoni golf course (18-hole). **Open** All year.

Situated on the edge of the San Marco basin, the two palazzi which make up the Londra Palace have just been entirely done up for the new millennium. Rocco Magnoli, famous for his work on Versace boutiques, supervised the work. The combination of Venetian style and modernity is a complete success. The cleaned façades open still more on the lagoon, the drwing rooms have become more intimate and the bedrooms more full of light. The palette of colors is subtle: pale green silk, shimmering whites, Aubusson carpets in faded tints making a fine foil to the deep red velvet of the seats. Finally, the mirrors and glass recall the fragile beauty of the city and, as a souvenir of Tchaikovsky who composed his fourth symphony here, a few fragments of a letter from the composer have been reproduced on the walls at the entrance. This restoration is a fine attempt to project timeless Venice into the third millennium.

How to get there *(Map 4): Near Piazza San Marco.*

Hotel Gabrielli Sandwirth

30122 Venezia
San Marco-Riva degli Schiavoni, 4110
Tel. 041-523 15 80 - Fax 041-520 94 55 - Famiglia Perkhofer
E-mail: hotelgabrielli@libero.it

Category ★★★★ **Rooms** 110 with telephone, bath or shower, WC, TV. **Price** Single 450,000L, double 750,000L. **Meals** Breakfast included, served 7:15-10:00 - half board 850,000L, full board 920,000L (2 Pers.). **Restaurant** "Trattoria al Buffet", service 12:00PM-2:30PM, 7:00PM-9:30PM - 65,000L - Buffet of Italian and Venetian cuisine. **Credit cards** All major. **Pets** Dogs allowed. **Nearby** Events: Carnival of Venice, the Regata Storica (Sept), the Mostra of Venice (Aug – Sept), Venice Biennale - Murano - Torcello (S. M. Assunta, S. Fosca) - Villa Foscari in Fusina - Venetian villas (cruise along the Brenta Canal with the boat "Il Burchiello") – Al Lido Alberoni golf course (18-hole). **Closed** Nov 26 – Feb 15.

This old 13th-century Veneto-Gothic palace is on the Riva degli Schiavoni, among some of the most luxurious hotels in Venice. It has been expanded to incorporate two other medieval houses and the interior is now a real maze. The rooms are decorated in a classical style and are very comfortable. The ideal is to get one with a loggia on the San Marco Basin, facing the San Giorgio Church. There is no trace of the old palace left in the modern decor of the bar, but this hotel is the only one on the Riva degli Schiavoni with an inner courtyard and a palm tree-shaded rose garden where you can dine by candlelight and Venetian lanterns. There is also a terrace on the roof with a view of the Grand Canal and the lagoon.

How to get there (Map 4): *Near Piazza San Marco.*

Hotel Metropole

30122 Venezia
San Marco - Riva degli Schiavoni, 4149
Tel. 041-520 50 44 - Fax 041-522 36 79 - Sig. Beggiato
E-mail: hotel.metropole@venere.it - Web: www.venere.it/venezia/metropole

Category ★★★★ **Rooms** 73 with air-conditioning, telephone, bath or shower, WC, safe, TV, minibar. **Price** Single 250-500,000L, double 350-770,000L, suite 600-850,000L. **Meals** Breakfast included, served 7:00-10:30 - half board 62,000L, full board 124,000L. **Restaurant** "Al Buffet", service 12:30PM-3:00PM, 7:00PM-10:00PM - buffet: 62-65,000L - Italian and Venetian cuisine. **Credit cards** All major. **Pets** Small dogs allowed. **Nearby** Events: Carnival of Venice, the Regata Storica (Sept), the Mostra of Venice (Aug – Sept), Venice Biennale - Murano - Torcello (S. M. Assunta, S. Fosca) - Villa Foscari in Fusina - Venetian villas (cruise along the Brenta Canal with the boat "Il Burchiello") –Al Lido Alberoni golf course (18-hole). **Open** All year.

We will say this up front: this hotel, in one of the most busy parts of Venice, is more pleasant off-season. Behind its slightly banal façade you will find it deliciously quaint. The salon is vast and pleasant and the breakfast room on the canal is exquisite. In the hallways you will find pretty collections of objects, mirrors and Venetian paintings. The rooms are fairly spacious and look like the rest of the hotel. The ones on the top floor have small terraces with a phenomenal view of the rooftops of Venice.

How to get there *(Map 4): On the laguna, near Piazza San Marco, entrance by the Riva degli Schiavoni and by the Canale di San Marco.*

Pensione Accademia - Villa Maravegie

30123 Venezia
Dorsoduro - Fondamenta Bollani 1058
Tel. 041-521 01 88 / 523 78 46 - Fax 041-523 91 52 - Sig. Dinato
E-mail: info@pensioneaccademia.it - Web: www.pensioneaccademia.it

Rooms 27 with telephone, bath or shower, TV. **Price** Single 150-220,000L, double 240-420,000L.
Meals Breakfast included, served 7:15-10:30. **Restaurant** See pp. 563-568. **Credit cards** All major.
Pets Dogs not allowed. **Nearby** Events: Carnival of Venice, the Regata Storica (Sept), the Mostra of
Venice (Aug – Sept), Venice Biennale - Murano - Torcello (S. M. Assunta, S. Fosca) - Villa Foscari in
Fusina - Venetian villas (cruise along the Brenta Canal with the boat "Il Burchiello") – Al Lido
Alberoni golf course (18-hole). **Open** All year.

This charming *pensione* whose popularity never wavers is located just near
the Accademia and the Guggenheim Foundation, at the end of a small
canal and surrounded by a romantic garden. The interior is just as beguiling,
with poetic little sitting rooms offering antique furniture and nicely-decorated
bedrooms, no two alike. Some are in the villa, others in an adjacent house
which has been cleverly joined together to form one ensemble. Family
furniture and souvenirs collected over the years create the climate of a real
private home. You can choose a view on the canal or on the garden — both are
attractive. It's the sort of place where you feel like a privileged guest — and
many return again and again. This also means that if you are interested, you'd
best make your arrangements well in advance.

How to get there *(Map 4): Vaporetto no. 1 to Accademia stop, no. 2 to Zattere
stop.*

Hotel Flora

30124 Venezia
Via XXII Marco, 2283 A
Tel. 041-520 58 44 - Fax 041-522 82 17 - Sig. Romanelli
E-mail: info@hotelflora.it - Web: www.hotelflora.it

Category ★★★ **Rooms** 44 with air-conditioning, telephone, bath or shower, satellite TV, safe, WC – Elevator. **Price** Single 300,000L, double 400,000L. **Meals** Breakfast included. **Restaurant** See pp. 563-568. **Credit cards** All major. **Pets** Dogs allowed. **Nearby** Events: Carnival of Venice, the Regata Storica (Sept), the Mostra of Venice (Aug – Sept), Venice Biennale - Murano - Torcello (S. M. Assunta, S. Fosca) - Villa Foscari in Fusina - Venetian villas (cruise along the Brenta Canal with the boat "Il Burchiello") – Al Lido Alberoni golf course (18-hole). **Open** All year.

A t the end of a small hidden street not far from the Piazza San Marco you will find the Hotel Flora, a true oasis of cool, quiet greenery. The decor is of mostly English inspiration, a vestige of the time when the clientele was primarily British. If you make your reservation early enough, you might be able to have a room on the garden. All the bathrooms are tiny. The salon and the dining room are delightful but there is nothing like breakfast in the verdant garden around the fountain. The Saint Moses Church near the hotel has many 17th- and 18th-century paintings, including a Tintoretto and a "Cène" by Palma the Younger.

How to get there *(Map 4): Vaporetto, San Marco stop, behind the Museo Correr.*

Hotel Torino

30124 Venezia
Calle delle Ostreghe, 2356
Tel. 041-520 52 22 - Fax 041-522 82 27 - Sig. Luigi Moro
E-mail: info@hoteltorino.it - Web: www.hoteltorino.it

Category ★★★ **Rooms** 20 with air-conditioning, telephone, shower, WC, satellite TV, minibar, safe.
Price Single 150-250,000L, double 200-360,000L. **Meals** Breakfast included, served 7:30-10:00.
Restaurant See pp. 563-568. **Credit cards** All major. **Pets** Dogs allowed. **Nearby** Events: Carnival of
Venice, the Regata Storica (Sept), Mostra of Venice (Aug – Sept), Venice Biennale - Torcello (S. M.
Assunta, S. Fosca) - Burano - Villa Foscari in Fusina - Venetian Villas - cruise along the Brenta Canal
the "Il Burchiello" – Al Lido Alberoni golf course (18-hole). **Open** All year.

Behind the Piazza San Marco, near the Correr Museum, is a street called Larga XXII Marzo, one of the main shopping streets in Venice. This street has an extension toward Santa Maria del Giglio and this is where the Hotel Torino is located. The entrance is quiet and intimate. A staircase leads to the upper floors, where you will find a small salon and a breakfast room filled with lovely bouquets of fresh flowers. The rooms are well-kept and decorated in antique style. The shower rooms are small, as is this whole miniature palace. Better ask for a room facing the rear if you're sensitive to noise and choose a higher floor if you want more light. But you won't have much choice unless you book well in advance, for an address of this quality is very sought after and the place fills up early.

How to get there *(Map 4): Vaporetto no. 1 stazione Santa Maria del Giglio then towards piazza San Marco or no. 82 stazione San Marco then via XXII Marzo and calle delle Ostreghe.*

Hotel Bel Sito & Berlino

30124 Venezia
San Marco - Campo Santa Maria del Giglio, 2517
Tel. 041-522 33 65 - Fax 041-520 40 83 - Sig. Serafini
E-mail: belsito@iol.it

Category ★★★ **Rooms** 38 with air-conditioning, telephone, bath or shower, WC (19 with minibar).
Price Single 195-227,000L, double 216-345,000L, triple 280-443,000L. **Meals** Breakfast included,
served 8:00-10:00. **Restaurant** See pp. 563-568. **Credit cards** Amex, Visa, Eurocard, MasterCard.
Pets Dogs allowed. **Nearby** Piazza San Marco, Grand Canal, Gallery of the Academy, Ca' d'Oro,
Guggenheim collection, scuola di San Rocco, scuola di San Giorgio degli schiavoni, the Ghetto, the
Lido and lagoon, Murano (Venetian glass), Burano (center of lacemaking), Torcello (S. M. Assunta,
S. Fosca), Venetian villas (cruise along the Brenta Canal the "Il Burchiello" or by rented car: Amex) -
Events: Carnival of Venice, the Regata Storica (Sept), the Mostra of Venice (Aug – Sept), Venice
Biennale – Al Lido Alberoni golf course (18-hole). **Open** All year.

The Hotel Bel Sito is in San Marco near Gritti. The rooms are furnished in
Venetian style and are comfortable, air-conditioned and quiet, especially
the ones on the canal. Our favorite ones are in the front, however: notably,
Rooms 30 and 40, which are sunny and have flowering balconies and a view
of the Baroque sculptures of the church of Santa Maria del Giglio. Breakfast
and bar service on the terrace will allow you to enjoy the magic atmosphere
unique to Venice. The vaporetto is not very far off, but if you want to play the
Venice game as soon as you arrive, put your suitcases in a taxi-boat and get it
to take you to the entrance on the canal. On the whole, however, the hotel
needs a little more care and attention.

How to get there *(Map 4): Vaporetto no. 1, Santa Maria del Giglio stop.*

Hotel La Fenice e des Artistes

30124 Venezia
San Marco - Campiello de la Fenice, 1936
Tel. 041-523 23 33 - Fax 041-520 37 21 - Sig. Facchini
E-mail: fenice@fenicehotels.it

Category ★★★ **Rooms** 68 with air-conditioning, telephone, bath or shower, WC, satellite TV –
Elevator. **Price** Single 150-420,000L, double 300-450,000L, junior suite 320-470,000L, suite 360-
550,000L, triple 340-480,000L. **Meals** Breakfast included, served 7:30-10:30. **Restaurant** See 563-
568. **Credit cards** All major. **Pets** Dogs allowed. **Nearby** Events: Carnival of Venice, the Regata
Storica (Sept), the Mostra of Venice (Aug – Sept), Venice Biennale - Murano - Torcello (S. M. Assunta,
S. Fosca) - Villa Foscari in Fusina - Venetian villas (cruise along the Brenta Canal with the boat "Il
Burchiello") – Al Lido Alberoni golf course (18-hole). **Open** All year.

The hotel is on a quiet little square, behind the Fenice Theatre. It consists of
two pretty houses connected by a patio where you can have a nice
breakfast or unwind after hours of running around Venice. The rooms are all
comfortable, but ask for one of the three rooms with terraces, which are also
the most pleasant ones: Rooms 354, 355, and 406. The hotel has no restaurant,
but it is next door to the famous *Taverna La Fenice*, a Venice classic.

How to get there *(Map 4): Near La Fenice.*

Hotel Do Pozzi

30124 Venezia
Via XXII Marzo, 2373
Tel. 041-520 78 55 - Fax 041-522 94 13 - Sig.ra Salmaso
E-mail: hotel.dopozzi@flashnet.it - Web: www.hoteldopozzi.it

Category ★★★ **Rooms** 35 with air-conditiong, telephone, bath or shower, satellite TV, minibar – Elevator. **Price** Single 140-230,000L, double 230-350,000L. **Meals** Breakfast included, served 7:00-10:30 - half board 50,000L, full board 100,000L (per pers.). **Restaurant** "Da Raffaele", service 12:00PM-3:00PM, 6:45PM-10:30PM - closed in Dec, Jan and Thurs - mealtime specials 50,000L, also à la carte - Venetian and Italian cuisine. **Credit cards** All major. **Pets** Dogs allowed. **Nearby** Piazza San Marco, Grand Canal, Gallery of the Academy, Ca' d'Oro, Guggenheim collection, scuola di San Rocco, scuola di San Giorgio degli schiavoni, the Ghetto, the Lido and lagoon, Murano (venetian glass), Burano (center of lacemaking), Torcello (S. M. Assunta, S. Fosca), Venetian villas (cruise along the Brenta Canal the "Il Burchiello" or by rented car: Amex) - Events: Carnival of Venice, the Regata Storica (Sept), the Mostra di Venice (Aug – Sept), Venice Biennale – Al Lido Alberoni golf course (18-hole). **Closed** Jan.

After plowing your way through the crowds on the small commercial streets of the San Marco quarter, it is easy to miss the little cul de sac which leads to the Hotel Do Pozzi. Hidden in one of those tiny squares so typical of Venice, the hotel is sheltered from the crowds. The rooms and bathrooms are small, modern and well equipped. The *campullo* full of flowers makes the hotel feel like an inn, there is also a restaurant, *Da Raffaele*. In summer, you can dine next to the canal and in winter, in a large picturesque room with a fireplace, decorated with old weapons and copper.

How to get there *(Map 4): Vaporetto, San Marco stop. In the via XXII Marzo, behind the Museo Correr, on a very small street.*

Hotel Panada

30124 Venezia
Calle dei Specchieri, 646
Tel. 041-520 90 88 - Fax 041-520 96 19
E-mail: info@hotelpanada.com - Web: www.hotelpanada.com

Category ★★★ **Rooms** 48 with air-conditioning, telephone, bath, WC – Elevator. **Price** Single 180-400,000L, double 220-500,000L, triple 270-570,000L, 320-640,00L (4 pers.). **Meals** Breakfast included, served 7:00-10:30. **Restaurant** See pp. 563-568. **Credit cards** All major. **Pets** Dogs allowed. **Nearby** Events: Carnival of Venice, the Regata Storica (Sept), the Mostra of Venice (Aug – Sept), Venice Biennale - Murano - Torcello (S. M. Assunta, S. Fosca) - Villa Foscari in Fusina - Venetian villas (cruise along the Brenta Canal with the boat "Il Burchiello") – Al Lido Alberoni golf course (18-hole). **Open** All year.

The hotel is on the hard to find calle dei Specchieri, just a few yards from the Basilica of San Marco (northeast of the Torre dell'Orologio). It is worth the effort, though, because it would be hard to find anything better (at this price) right in the heart of Venice. As soon as you walk in, the noise and the crowds fade in the distance. The hotel is quiet and comfortable. The rooms are cozy and have Venetian-style furniture in different pastel shades. All have comfortable bathrooms. There is no restaurant, but there is a bar, "Ai Speci," which is very popular with locals. This is a good place to relax, to meet friends for a drink or to have a light meal.

How to get there *(Map 4): Vaporetto nos. 1 and 82, 52, San Marco stop. Behind Basilica of San Marco.*

Hotel Ai Due Fanali

30120 Venezia
S. Croce, 946
Tel. 041-71 84 90 - Fax 041-71 83 44 - Sig.ra Ferron
E-mail: ai2fanali@venicehotel.com - Web: www.venicehotel.com/ai2fanali

Category ★★★ **Rooms** 16 with air-conditiong, telephone, bath or shower, WC, TV, safe, minibar.
Price Single 160-275,000L, double 200-360,000L, triple 260-390,000L, apart. 350-600,000L. **Meals**
Breakfast included, served 7:30-10:00. **Restaurant** See pp. 563-568. **Credit cards** Amex, Visa,
Eurocard, MasterCard. **Pets** Dogs not allowed. **Nearby** Events: Carnival of Venice, the Regata Storica
(Sept), the   Mostra of Venice (Aug – Sept), Venice Biennale - Murano - Torcello (S. M. Assunta,
S. Fosca) - Villa Foscari in Fusina - Venetian villas (cruise along the Brenta Canal with the boat "Il
Burchiello") –Al Lido Alberoni golf course (18-hole). **Closed** Jan 10 – 30.

In the sestiere of Santa Croce, just near the Santa Lucia railroad station and
the car park of piazzale Roma, one comes across this pretty hotel in what
was once the school of the church San Simeon Grando. The dimensions of the
building have made it possible to create a reception area furnished in antique
style, extending into a salon. Breakfast is served in the dining room on the
third floor or if the weather is fine, on the terrace. The bedrooms, done in
Venetian style, are sober and elegant, not very large but with good amenities.
There are also two apartments on the Riva degli Schiavoni with a view on the
San Marco basin and the isle of San Giorgio.

How to get there (Map 4): Vaporetto no. 1 Riva di Biario stop.

Hotel La Residenza

30122 Venezia
Castello 3608 Campo Bandiera e Moro
Tel. 041-52 85 315 - Fax 041-52 38 859 - Sig. Giovanni Ballestra
E-mail: info@venicelaresidenza.com - Web: www.venicelaresidenza.com

Category ★★ **Rooms** 15 with air-conditioning, telephone, bath or shower, WC, TV, minibar. **Price** Single 100-180,000L, double 160-280,000L; extra bed 50-60,000L. **Meals** Breakfast included, served 7:45-9:30. **Restaurant** See pp. 563-568. **Credit cards** Amex, Visa, Eurocard, MasterCard. **Pets** Dogs not allowed. **Nearby** Events: Carnival of Venice, the Regata Storica (Sept), Mostra of Venice (Aug – Sept), Venice Biennale - Burano - Torcello (S. M. Assunta, S. Fosca) - Villa Foscari in Fusina - Venetian Villas (cruise along the Brenta Canal the "Il Burchiello") – Al Lido Alberoni golf course (18-hole). **Open** All year.

L a Residenza is on the Campo Bandiera e Moro, a quiet square near the quays of the Arsenal and the church of San Giovanni in Bragora (where you can see a fine painting by Cima da Conegliano). The building, which once belonged to the Gritti family, has preserved the charm of an old palazzo, with a gothic façade, 18th-century frescoes, stuccos and dazzling chandeliers of Murano glass - like something you dream about when you think of the city of the Doges. The salon is particularly regal, but be forewarned that the bedrooms are not quite the same - much smaller and simpler, in Venetian laccato style, with bathrooms dating from the 1950s. Aside from this, you can appreciate this hotel for its quiet and its "invitation to the palace" ambiance.

How to get there *(Map 4): Vaporetto Arsenale stop. On the quay, turn on left, after the bridge 1st alley on right, the place is at the end of the alley on left.*

V E N E T O

Locanda Ai Santi Apostoli

30131 Venezia
Strada Nova, 4391
Tel. 041-521 26 12 - Fax 041-521 26 11 - Sig. Stefano Bianchi Michiel
E-mail: aisantia@tin.it

Category ★★★ **Rooms** 11 with air-conditioning, telephone, bath or shower, WC, TV, minibar –
Elevator. **Price** Single 250-400,000L, double 320-520,000L, 560-720,000L (4 pers.with 1 bath).
Meals Breakfast included, served 7:20-10:50. **Restaurant** See pp. 563-568. **Credit cards** All major.
Pets Dogs allowed. **Nearby** Events: Carnival of Venice, the Regata Storica (Sept), the Mostra of Venice
(Aug – Sept), Venice Biennale - Murano - Torcello (S.M. Assunta, S.Fosca) - Burano - Villa Foscari in
Fusina - Venetian villas (cruise along the Brenta Canal the"Il Burchiello") –Al Lido Alberoni golf
course (18-hole). **Closed** Dec 15 – Feb 28.

On the Grand Canal, just near the Rialto, the Locanda Ai Santi Apostoli, on
the third floor of an old palazzo, offers the atmosphere and hospitality of
a patrician home of bygone times. The owners have the knack of receiving
guests with warmth, attention and discretion, and the ambiance, glamourous
and cozy at the same time, make this a very good place to know. The
bedrooms, all recently restored, are elegantly decorated with pieces of family
furniture. Two of them face the Grand Canal, a spectacle you shouldn't miss:
You can see the famous Rialto Bridge and the fish market and hear the
serenades of the gondoliers. These rooms are much in demand, of course, and
if they are not available, don't hesitate to accept another room, for you can
always enjoy the same view from the very pleasant living room. Also in the
neighborhood (Rialto and San Polo) are some of the nicest restaurants, both
large and small, in Venice.

How to get there (Map 4): Vaporetto no. 1, Ca'd'Oro stop.

Hotel Santo Stefano

30124 Venezia
San Marco - Campo San Stefano, 2957
Tel. 041-520 01 66 - Fax 041-522 44 60 - Sig. Roberto Quatrini
E-mail: info@hotelsstefano.com - Web: www.hotelscelio.sstefano.com

Category ★★ **Rooms** 11 with telephone, bath, WC, satellite TV, safe, minibar (air-conditioning on request) – Elevator. **Price** Single 180-350,000L, double 250-450,000L, triple 300-490,000L, suite 350-570,000L. **Meals** Breakfast included, served 8:30-10:00. **Restaurant** See pp. 563-568. **Credit cards** Amex, Visa, Eurocard, MasterCard. **Pets** Small dogs allowed. **Nearby** Events: Carnival of Venice, the Regata Storica (Sept), the Mostra of Venice (Aug – Sept), Venice Biennale - Murano - Torcello (S. M. Assunta, S. Fosca) - Villa Foscari in Fusina - Venetian villas (cruise along the Brenta Canal with the boat "Il Burchiello") – Al Lido Alberoni golf course (18-hole). **Open** All year .

The Santo Stefano stands on the large *Campo* that is the main point of passage between the Piazza San Marco and the Accademia. The hotel occupies a small *palazzo*, six stories high but with only two rooms per floor. The rooms have all the amenities, including air-conditioning and well-equipped bathrooms. The modern Venetian decor sometimes borders on *kitsch*, but it is never in poor taste. Everything is miniature here — the reception area, the breakfast room, the patio and the terrace facing the open square, where you look out on the church of San Stefano. Its campanile, lovely but distinctly out of plumb, makes you realize that it's not only in Pisa that old towers tend to lean.

How to get there (Map 4): Vaporetto no. 82 San Samuele stop - no. 1, Accademia stop.

V E N E T O

Pensione Seguso

30123 Venezia
Dorsoduro-Zattere, 779
Tel. 041-528 68 54 - Fax. 041-522 23 40
Sig. Seguso

Category ★★ Rooms 36 with telephone (16 with bath or shower, 10 with WC) — Elevator, wheelchair access. **Price** With half board (with or without bath): for 1 pers. 235-260,000L; for 2 pers. 360-390,000L; for 3 pers. 500-530,000L. **Meals** Breakfast included, served 8:00-10:00. **Restaurant** Service 1:00PM-2:00PM, 7:30PM-8:30PM - closed Wed - mealtime specials 40,000L - Home Venetian cuisine. **Credit cards** Amex, Visa, Eurocard, MasterCard. **Pets** Dogs allowed. **Nearby** Events: Carnival of Venice, the Regata Storica (Sept), the Mostra of Venice (Aug — Sept), Venice Biennale - Murano - Torcello (S. M. Assunta, S. Fosca) - Villa Foscari in Fusina - Venetian villas (cruise along the Brenta Canal with the boat "Il Burchiello") — Al Lido Alberoni golf course (18-hole). **Open** Mar — end Nov.

The Zattere quarter is a rather quiet area, a residential part of Venice. It is bordered by the Giudecca Canal, where you can watch the ceaseless ballet of the large ships sailing back and forth to the Lido and the vaporetti crossing the canal. From the terrace of the Pensione Seguso you can sit and watch the sun set over the island and church of San Giorgio — an unforgettable spectacle. This little building, slightly set back off the street, has been run for years by the same family, carrying on the tradition of the family pension, with dinner at the hotel (except March, July, August and September) served in the cozy dining room by a Venetian mamma. The rooms are old-fashioned but very well kept, and most have a good view. It is another one of those places that it's a good idea to get to before it is "updated" to conform with European standards.

How to get there *(Map 4): Vaporetti nos. 51, 61 and 82, stop Zattere.*

Pensione La Calcina

30123 Venezia
Dorsoduro Zattere, 780
Tel. 041-520 64 66 - Fax 041-522 70 45 - Sig. and Sig.ra Szemere
E-mail: la.calcina@libero.it

Category ★★ **Rooms** 29 with air-conditiong, telephone, bath or shower. **Price** Single 150-170,000L, double 200-300,000L. **Meals** Breakfast included, served 7:30-10:00. **Restaurant** Small meals until 11:00PM. Or see pp. 563-568. **Credit cards** All major. **Pets** Dogs not allowed. **Nearby** Events: Carnival of Venice, the Regata Storica (Sept), the Mostra of Venice (Aug – Sept), Venice Biennale - Murano - Torcello (S.M. Assunta, S.Fosca) - Burano - Villa Foscari in Fusina - Venetian villas (cruise along the Brenta Canal on the "Il Burchiello") – Al Lido Alberoni golf course (18-hole). **Open** All year.

This pensione is situated on the Zattere (meaning "the rafts"), one of the favorite spots of real Venetians who appreciate its calm and the long promenade along the waterfront, with the floating docks, where people come to sun themselves. From here the view of the canal, at any hour of the day or night, is one of the finest you can have in Venice. La Calcina is a good address for its location, comfort, service and moderate prices. The entrance hall, living and dining rooms, all facing the quay are pleasant and inviting, as is the large, flowered waterside terrace, reserved for residents. The bedrooms are nicely decorated with family furniture ; all of them are pleasant, but of course the ones we recommend are those that face the Giudecca Canal. Our favorites are numbers 2, 4, 22 and 32. Be careful, only 11 rooms have a view and their prices vary depending on whether they are on the front, side or corner. Numbers 37, 38 and 39 have a balcony.

How to get there *(Map 4): Vaporeti nos. 51, 61 and 82, stop Zattere.*

Pensione Alla Salute Da Cici

30123 Venezia
Fondamenta Cà Balla, 222
Tel. 041-523 54 04 - Fax. 041-522 22 71
Sig. Cici

Rooms 48 with telephone, shower (35 with bath and WC). **Price** Single 140-190,000L, double 180-250,000L, triple 250-350,000L. **Meals** Breakfast included, served 8:00-9:30. **Restaurant** See pp. 563-568. **Credit cards** Not accepted. **Pets** Dogs not allowed. **Nearby** Events: Carnival of Venice, the Regata Storica (Sept), the Mostra of Venice (Aug – Sept), Venice Biennale - Murano - Torcello (S. M. Assunta, S. Fosca) - Villa Foscari in Fusina - Venetian villas (cruise along the Brenta Canal with the boat "Il Burchiello") –Al Lido Alberoni golf course (18-hole). **Open** Mar 8 –Nov 14, Dec 26 – Feb 25.

Alla Salute "da Cici" is one of the old pensiones of Venice, in one of the most poetic places in the town–on a canal behind the Salute. Though the house has lost some of its traditional appearance, the old family furniture is still in the large rooms. All of them are spacious and very well kept, some even being able to house as many as four people. Ask for the ones on the canal; even though the toilets are outside the rooms, the view is attractive and the neighborhood is quiet. The bar service in the small adjoining garden is very pleasant and the welcome friendly. Note that in March, July and August, the hotel has a reduction in prices.

How to get there *(Map 4): Vaporetto no. 1, La Salute stop (at the exit take the bridge in wood, walk to the next bridge; take on left the Fondamenta Cà Balla); take no. 52, Zattere stop. Take no. 82 Accademia stop.*

Hotel Pausania

30123 Venezia
Dorsoduro, 2824
Tel. 041-522 20 83 - Fax 041-52 22 989
Sig. Gatto

Category ★★★ **Rooms** 26 with air-conditioning, telephone, bath or shower, WC, TV, minibar. **Price** Single 100-265,000L, double 160-399,000L. **Meals** Breakfast included, served 7:30-10:30. **Restaurant** See pp. 563-568. **Credit cards** Amex, Visa, Eurocard, MasterCard. **Pets** Small dogs allowed. **Nearby** Piazza San Marco, Grand Canal, Gallery of the Academy, Ca' d'Oro, Guggenheim collection, scuola di San Rocco, scuola di San Giorgio degli schiavoni, the Ghetto, the Lido and lagoon, Murano (venetian glass), Burano (center of lacemaking), Torcello (S. M. Assunta, S. Fosca), Venetian villas (cruise along the Brenta Canal the "Il Burchiello" or by rented car: Amex) - Events: Carnival of Venice, the Regata Storica (Sept), the Mostra of Venice (Aug – Sept), Venice Biennale – Al Lido Alberoni golf course (18-hole). **Open** All year.

The Hotel Pausania is in the quarter of Dorsoduro, just near the *sestiere* of San Polo, a real working class district where you will at last be able to see the people of Venice at work, the children going to school and even the yapping little Venetian dogs, a species of lap dog that you can see depicted in the old paintings. It's also just near the Ca' Rezzonico palace and the two marvels — the Scuola Grande del Carmine, with its superb Tiepolo ceilings, and the Gothic church of Santa Maria del Carmelo. All this has decidedly more charm than the hotel itself, but it is a good address nonetheless — quiet, comfortable and friendly.

How to get there *(Map 4): Vaporetto no. 1, Ca' Rezzonico stop.*

Hotel Agli Alboretti

30123 Venezia
Dorsoduro - Rio Terrà Foscatini, 884
Tel. 041-523 00 58 - Fax 041-521 01 58 - Sig.ra Linguerri
E-mail: alboretti@cash.it - Web: www.cash.it/alboretti

Category ★★ **Rooms** 19 with air-conditioning, telephone, bath or shower, WC, satellite TV. **Price** Single 175,000L, double 270,000L. **Meals** Breakfast included, served 7:30-9:30. **Restaurant** Closed Wed, 3 weeks between Jul and Aug, Jan - mealtime specials 60-80,000L, also à la carte - Venetian cuisine, very good Italian wines. **Credit cards** Amex, Visa, Eurocard, MasterCard. **Pets** Dogs allowed. **Nearby** Events: Carnival of Venice, the Regata Storica (Sept), the Mostra of Venice (Aug – Sept), Venice Biennale - Murano - Torcello (S. M. Assunta, S. Fosca) - Villa Foscari in Fusina - Venetian villas (cruise along the Brenta Canal with the boat "Il Burchiello") – Al Lido Alberoni golf course (18-hole). **Open** All year.

The entrance to the Hotel Agli Alboretti has a blond wood parquet floor and an atmosphere, which is as warm as the welcome Isabella and Federica Linguerri will give you. The rooms are all pleasant, though some are larger than others. The most charming ones are on the interior gardens, such as Room 18, and especially Room 15, which has a balcony big enough to have breakfast on. The owner's, daughter Anna, is a certified wine-waitress and runs the restaurant with a talented chef. She will help you select the right wine, which you can order by the glass, to accompany dishes. The dining room is pleasant, but the interior terraces and the *pergola* are really charming. This hotel is the best value in Venice.

How to get there *(Map 4): Vaporetto nos. 1 and 82, Accademia stop.*

Hotel Belle-Arti

30123 Venezia
Rio Terrà Foscarini, 912/A - Dorsoduro
Tel. 041-522 62 30 - Fax 041-528 00 43
E-mail: info@hotelbellearti.com - Web: www.hotelbellearti.com

Category ★★★ **Rooms** 66 with air-conditioning, telephone, bath, TV, minibar. **Price** Single 220,000L, double 340,000L. **Meals** Breakfast included, served 7:30-10:30. **Restaurant** See pp. 563-568. **Credit cards** Amex, Visa, Eurocard, MasterCard. **Pets** Dogs not allowed. **Nearby** Events: Carnival of Venice, the Regata Storica (Sept), the Mostra of Venice (Aug – Sept), Venice Biennale - Murano - Torcello (S. M. Assunta, S. Fosca) - Villa Foscari in Fusina - Venetian villas (cruise along the Brenta Canal with the boat "Il Burchiello") – Al Lido Alberoni golf course (18-hole). **Open** All year.

This recently-established hotel in the district of Dorsoduro (the one we most like for staying in), between the Accademia and the zattere, is comfortable; it has a further advantage in the form of a fine terrace leading to a garden which has obviously been installed on a former tennis court, the surfacing of which has not been removed. The décor lacks refinement and the Venetian style is not used to best advantage. However the rooms are very pleasant, being large, well-designed and airconditioned in summer. The bathrooms are also impeccable and the service is good. All in all, then, a good address for this city where it is hard to find somewhere to stay, whatever the season.

How to get there *(Map 4): Vaporetti nos. 1 and 82, stop Accademia or Zattere.*

Hotel La Galleria

30123 Venezia
Rio Terrá Antonio Foscarini/Dorsoduro, 878 A
Tel. 041-523 24 89 - Fax 041-523 24 89
E-mail: galleria@tin.it - Web: www.hotelgalleria.it

Category ★★ **Rooms** 10 with telephone, shower. **Price** Double with private bath outside the room 160,000L, double with bath 190-240,000L. **Meals** Breakfast included, served 7:30-10:00. **Restaurant** See pp. 563-568. **Credit cards** Visa, Eurocard, MasterCard. **Pets** Dogs not allowed. **Nearby** Events: Carnival of Venice, the Regata Storica (Sept), the Mostra of Venice (Aug – Sept), Venice Biennale - Murano - Torcello (S. M. Assunta, S. Fosca) - Villa Foscari in Fusina - Venetian villas (cruise along the Brenta Canal with the boat "Il Burchiello") – Al Lido Alberoni golf course (18-hole). **Closed** Jan.

L a Galleria will suit those for whom charm can exist without a certain degree of comfort. Situated at one end of the Academia bridge, the hotel occupies the first floor of a house on the corner of the little square and the canal. There is no drawing room and no breakfast room (breakfast is served in the bedrooms) and only ten attractively arranged rooms .Not all of these are to be recommended, since only the four overlooking the canal have their own bathroom - and the view is, moreover, the major asset of the place. You should also know that the rooms are very small (like no. 7, which is our favourite, and no. 9); only no. 8 has an acceptable flooring. But having said all that, if you are even slightly responsive to the spectacle and life of the canal, you will have a private box here, and take away marvellous memories of drinking your coffee by the windowsill and sleeping with your window open and your feet almost in the water - but remember to turn your bed round in the right direction and try not to grumble too much about the comings and goings on the lagoon. In any case, we have warned you that charm here does not mean tranquillity.

How to get there *(Map 4): Vaporetti nos. 1 and 82, stop Accademia or Zattere.*

Palazzetto da Schio

30123 Venezia
Dorsoduro 316/B - Fondamenta Soranzo
Tel. and Fax 041-523 79 37 - Comtesse da Schio
E-mail: avenezia@tin.it - Web: web.tin.it/sangregorio

Apartments 3 with air-conditiong, 1 or 2 rooms, lounge, kitchen, bath, telephone, TV. **Price** 1 740,000L (1 week), 3 180,000L (2 weeks); water, electricity, gaz and telephone not included. **Restaurant** See pp. 563-568. **Credit cards** Not accepted. **Pets** Dogs not allowed. **Nearby** Events: Carnival of Venice, the Regata Storica (Sept), the Mostra of Venice (Aug – Sept), Venice Biennale - Murano - Torcello (S. M. Assunta, S. Fosca) - Villa Foscari in Fusina - Venetian villas (cruise along the Brenta Canal with the boat "Il Burchiello") – Al Lido Alberoni golf course (18-hole). **Open** All year.

If you are traveling with your family and plan to spend more than two nights in Venice, a pleasant apartment in the center of town is undoubtedly the most economical option. The small but charming Palazzetto da Schio is in a palace, close to the Academy. It is a good place to relax after a day of sightseeing. There are two light, spacious apartments. The antique family furniture creates an atmosphere which is both Romanesque and intimate. The owners are very nice and live downstairs on the "noble floor" of the house. Staying here will allow you to live like a Venetian for a while (without having to go to the Rialto market as a tourist). You will also enjoy both the intimacy of a home and the comfort of a hotel (maid service is available for all of your household needs). A deposit and references are required.

How to get there (Map 4): Vaporetto no. 1 La Salute stop, (at the exit take the bridge in wood, go to the first bridge after the canal; take immediately on your left la Fondamenta (the river Cà Balla); take no. 52, Zattere stop. Take no. 82 Accademia stop.

Palazzetto S. Lio 🌳

30125 Venezia
Castello, 5715 - Calle del Frutariol
Tel. 041-720 620 - Fax 041-721 677

Apartments 8 (possibility air-conditioning with extra charge) with 1 or 2 bedrooms, kitchen, bath (possibility telephone and TV with extra charge). **Price** Apart./week 870-1 800,000L (+ cleaning 85-120,000L, + charge 37,000/pers.) **Restaurant** See pp. 563-568. **Credit cards** Not accepted. **Pets** Dogs not allowed. **Nearby** Events: Carnival of Venice, the Regata Storica (Sept), the Mostra of Venice (Aug – Sept), Venice Biennale - Murano - Torcello (S. M. Assunta, S. Fosca) - Villa Foscari in Fusina - Venetian villas (cruise along the Brenta Canal with the boat "Il Burchiello") – Al Lido Alberoni golf course (18-hole). **Open** All year.

The Palazzetto S. Lio is an old family house which the owners have converted into several apartments which can be rented by the week (Saturday to Saturday). Situated in a central, popular and lively area of Venice, the building is at the end of a street and enjoys some peace and quiet. The renovation/ conversion has been very well carried out. The entrance is very elegant; the only thing that still awaits restoration is the house's little private chapel. The apartments are comfortable, the smallest, which are rather dark, being on the ground floor. The largest, on the upper floors, enjoy more light and space. The old furniture creates a good atmosphere and some rooms even have a little terrace overlooking the inner courtyards and the roofs of Venice. Since some facilities are extra to the prices indicated, let the management know what you require when you reserve. Also ask for someone to accompany you, since the address is hard to find for a non-Venetian.

How to get there (Map 4): Vaporetti nos. 1 and 82, stop Rialto.

Hotel des Bains

30126 Venezia
Lido - Lungomare Marconi, 17
Tel. 041-526 59 21 - Fax 041-526 01 13

Category ★★★★ **Rooms** 191 with air-conditioning, telephone, bath, TV, minibar – Elevator. **Price** Single 400-650,000L, double 600-1 000,000L, suite 860-2 000,000L. **Meals** Breakfast included., served 7:00-10:30 - half board +132,000L, full board +231,000L (per pers.). **Restaurant** Service 12:30PM-2:30PM, 7:30PM-10:30PM - mealtime specials 130-165,000L; also à la carte - Specialties: Pesce. **Credit cards** All major. **Pets** Small dogs allowed. **Facilities** Swimming pool (open: May – Sept), tennis, private beach (open: Jun – Sept 15), sauna, parking. **Nearby** Events: Carnival of Venice, the Regata Storica (Sept), the Mostra of Venice (Aug – Sept), Venice Biennale - Murano - Torcello (S.M. Assunta, S.Fosca) - Burano - Villa Foscari in Fusina - Venetian villas (cruise along the Brenta Canal in the "Il Burchiello") – Al Lido Alberoni golf course (18-hole). **Open** Mar 16 – Nov 10.

The Hotel des Bains has been forever immortalized by Visconti's film "Death in Venice." Though not quite as sumptuous as the film version, it still preserves much of the charm the Lido beaches must have had at the turn of the century when they were frequented by Thomas Mann and other illustrious visitors of that elegant era. Grand salons filled with nostalgia for the past, comfortable bedrooms (we prefer those facing the famous cabins of the Lido), large dining rooms for the two restaurants, La Pagoda and Le Liberty, terraces, gardens and, above all, that "Grand Hotel" atmosphere that only such former palaces have retained.

How to get there *(Map 4): Vaporetto via the Lido from piazza San Marco.*

Albergo Quattro Fontane

30126 Venezia
Lido - Via delle Quattro Fontane, 16
Tel. 041-526 02 27 - Fax 041-526 07 26 - Famiglia Friborg-Bevilacqua
E-mail: quafonve@tin.it - Web: www.quattrofontane.com

Category ★★★★ **Rooms** 61 with air-conditioning, telephone, bath, TV. **Price** (except during the Cinema's Festival): single 315-375,000L, double 450-500,000L. **Meals** Breakfast included, served 7:00-10:30 - half board 280-355,000L, full board 380-450,000L (per pers. 3 days min.). **Restaurant** Service 12:45PM-2:30PM, 7:45PM-10:30PM - mealtime specials 90-100,000L, also à la carte - Specialties: Seafood. **Credit cards** All major. **Pets** Dogs allowed. **Nearby** Events: Carnival of Venice, the Regata Storica (Sept), the Mostra of Venice (Aug – Sept), Venice Biennale - Murano - Torcello (S.M. Assunta, S. Fosca) - Villa Foscari in Fusina - Venetian villas (cruise along the Brenta Canal with the boat "Il Burchiello") – Al Lido Alberoni golf course (18-hole). **Open** Apr 20 – Oct 20.

For those who would like to see a different Venice, the Albergo Quattro Fontane is a fabulous villa in the Lido run by two very friendly sisters, heiresses of great Venetian voyagers, one with a passion for Africa and the other for South America. A fabulous collection of memorabilia from their travels decorates the salons of the villa. Everything is perfectly elegant and comfortable here: the well-kept gardens, the shaded flagstone terraces with wicker furniture, the personalized rooms on the garden and the impeccably served Venetian cuisine. The annex built in the style typical of the islands of the lagoon, has newer and even more comfortable rooms.

How to get there (Map 4): *Vaporetto via the Lido from Piazza San Marco.*

V   E   N   E   T   O

Hotel Villa Mabapa

30126 Venezia
Lido - Riviera San Nicolo, 16
Tel. 041-526 05 90 - Fax 041-526 94 41 - Sig. Vianello
E-mail: info@villamabapa.com - Web: www.villamabapa.com

Category ★★★★ **Rooms** 70 with air-conditioning, telephone, bath, WC, hairdryer, safe, minibar, TV – Elevator. **Price** Single 170-310,000L, double 270-500,000L. **Meals** Breakfast included (buffet), served 7:30-10:00 - half board +45-60,000L, full board +80-110,000L (per pers., 3 days min.). **Restaurant** Service 12:30PM-2:00PM, 7:30PM-9:30PM - mealtime specials 60-75,000L, also à la carte - Venetian cuisine and seafood. **Credit cards** All major. **Pets** Small dogs allowed except in restaurant. **Facilities** Parking, private landing stage. **Nearby** Events: Carnival of Venice, the Regata Storica (Sept), the Mostra of Venice (Aug – Sept), Venice Biennale - Murano - Torcello (S. M. Assunta, S. Fosca) - Villa Foscari in Fusina - Venetian villas (cruise along the Brenta Canal with the boat "Il Burchiello") – Al Lido Alberoni golf course (18-hole). **Open** All year.

It is possible to find a bit of quiet country in Venice, even in the middle of August. These are the two major attractions of this property, built in the Lido in 1930 and subsequently transformed into a hotel. It is still run by the same family; the name Mabapa comes from the first syllables of "mama, bambini, papa." The interior of the villa still looks like a private house. The most charming rooms are the ones on the second floor of the main house. In the summer you can have your meals in the garden on the lagoon. A bit far from the center of town, but close to the Lido beach and convenient *vaporetto* (ferry) service, the Mabapa is a nice refuge for those who fear the tourist frenzy of Venice in the summer.

How to get there *(Map 4): From the rail station, Vaporetto nos. 1, 52, 82 (in summer). By car, from Tronchetto ferry-boat ligne no. 17 (30mn). From the airport, boat "Cooperativa S. Marco" (40mn).*

Locanda Cipriani

30012 Venezia
Isola Torcello - Piazza S.Fosca, 29
Tel. 041-73 01 50 - Fax 041-73 54 33 - Sig. Brass
E-mail: info@locandacipriani.com - Web: www.locandacipriani.com

Category ★★★ **Rooms** 6 with air-conditioning, telephone, bath, WC. **Price** With half board 260,000L, full board 350,000L (per pers.). **Meals** Breakfast included, served 7:00AM-12:00PM. **Restaurant** Service 12:00PM-3:00PM, 7:00PM-10:00PM - mealtime specials 90-100,000L, also à la carte - Specialties: Risotto alla torcellana - Zuppa di pesce. **Credit cards** Amex, Visa, Eurocard, MasterCard. **Pets** Dogs not allowed. **Nearby** Events: Carnival of Venice, the Regata Storica (Sept), the Mostra of Venice (Aug – Sept), Venice Biennale - Murano - Torcello (S. M. Assunta, S. Fosca) - Villa Foscari in Fusina - Venetian villas (cruise along the Brenta Canal with the boat "Il Burchiello") – Al Lido Alberoni golf course (18-hole). **Closed** Jan 6 – Feb 12, and Tues.

Giuseppe Cipriani discovered this old inn on the island of Torcello while driving a visiting couple around the lagoon. It was love at first sight and he ended up buying it. The Locanda has four rooms and is known for its fine cuisine, notably the fish specialties. The exterior has kept its rustic flavor, but the salons and rooms are elegantly decorated. Meals are served in the garden or in the gallery with arcades. It is hard to stay very long in Torcello, where there's only the Santa Fosca Church and the superb Veneto-Byzantine Santa Maria Assunta Cathedral, but this old inn's isolation and charm make it well worth spending at least one evening here. Reservations are a must.

How to get there *(Map 4): From San Marco, boat via Torcello (30-45mn.).*

Villa Ducale

30031 Dolo (Venezia)
Riviera Martiri della Libertà, 75
Tel. 041-56 080 20 - Fax 041-56 080 04

Category ★★★ **Rooms** 11 with air-conditioning and soundproofing, telephone, bath or shower, WC, satellite TV, safe, minibar. **Price** Single 180,000L, double 240-300,000L; extra bed 60,000L. **Meals** Breakfast included (buffet), served 7:00-10:00 - half board 60,000L (per pers.). **Restaurant** Closed Tues - mealtime specials, also à la carte - Specialties: Seafood. **Credit cards** Amex, Visa, Eurocard, MasterCard. **Pets** Small dogs allowed. **Facilities** Parking. **Nearby** Riviera del Brenta and Palladian Villas (S11) between Padua and Venice (Villas Ferretti-Angeli in Dolo, Villa Venier-Contarini-Zen in Mira Vecchia - Palais Foscarini in Mira - Villa Widmann - Villa Piscani in Srada - Villa Malcontenta in Malcontenta) – Ca' della Nave golf course (18-hole) in Martellago. **Open** All year.

The Villa Ducale is, alas, next to a rather noisy road. But the building is majestic. The lobby has marvelous decorated ceilings and is very elegant. The rooms have beautiful period furnitureare very comfortable and they are air-conditioned and soundproofed, so traffic noise from the road is not a problem. The hotel provides quality round-the-clock service and has a fine restaurant. In this sublime setting you will feel like you are in a waking dream, especially if you are lucky and have a room with a terrace facing the grounds.

How to get there *(Map 4): 22km west of Venezia via A4, Dolo-Mirano exit then towards Dolo; 2km east of town center via S11, towards Venezia.*

Hotel Villa Margherita

30030 Mira Porte (Venezia)
Via Nazionale, 416/417
Tel. 041-426 58 00 - Fax 041-426 58 38 - Familly Dal Corso
E-mail: hvillam@tin.it - Web: www.villa-margherita.com

Category ★★★★ **Rooms** 19 with air-conditioning, telephone, bath or shower, WC, satellite TV, safe, minibar. **Price** Single 195-230,000L, double 345-390,000L, triple 420,000L, junior suite 440,000L. **Meals** Breakfast included, served 7:30-10:30 - half board +70,000L (per pers.) **Restaurant** Service 12:00PM-2:30PM, 7:00PM-10:00PM - closed Tues dinner, Wed - à la carte - Venetian cuisine and seafood. **Credit cards** All major. **Pets** Small dogs allowed. **Facilities** Parking. **Nearby** Riviera del Brenta and Palladian Villas - Asolo - Treviso - Conegliano - Venezia - Padova – Cà della Neva and Lido Albertoni golf course. **Open** All year.

This old 17th-century patrician villa is ideally on the tourist circuit of villas which rich Venetians built on the banks of the Brenta. It is luxuriously decorated; and particular attention has been paid to architectural details such as the quality of materials used, the studied mixture of antique and contemporary furniture, the richness of the decor with frescos, the trompe l'œil, the drapes and the fabrics. The rooms are less well-decorated than the public areas. The quietest are those overlooking the fields ; avoid the ones on the road. The restaurant is in another building, 50m away. The personnel is charming and discreet and the price is justified.

How to get there *(Map 4): 15km west of Venezia via A4, Dolo-Mirano exit; then S11 towards Dolo/Venezia.*

Villa Soranzo Conestabile

30037 Scorzé (Venezia)
Via Roma, 1
Tel. 041-44 50 27 - Fax 041-584 00 88 - Sig.ra Martinelli
E-mail: vsoranzo@tin.it - Web: www.villasoranzo.it

Category ★★★ **Rooms** 20 (5 with air-conditioning) with telephone, bath or shower, WC, TV. **Price** Single 140-200,000L, double 200-300,000L, suite 300-500,000L. **Meals** Breakfast included, served 7:30-10:30 - half board +42,000L (per pers.). **Restaurant** Service 7:30PM-10:00PM - open Mon to Fri from Mar to Oct - mealtime specials 42,000L, also à la carte - Venetian cuisine. **Credit cards** Amex, Visa, Eurocard, MasterCard. **Pets** Dogs allowed (25,000L). **Facilities** Parking. **Nearby** Riviera del Brenta and Palladian Villas (N11) between Padua and Venice – Ca' della Nave golf course (18-hole) in Martellago. **Open** All year.

A holiday home for a noble Venetian family since the 16th Century, this villa, badly damaged in the last war, was restored in 1960 and turned into a hotel. The façade is a fine example of neo-Classical style and the interior, too, is also typical of the architecture of Venetian villas, with its double staircase, columns and balusters. The rooms and the suites, which have recently been renovated, are large and calm; special mention should be given to the Contessa Soranzo suite which was once the room of the mistress of the house. The hotel is twenty kilometers from Venice and thirty kilometers from Padua and, even though the proximity of the two cities has somewhat spoiled the countryside, one may also enjoy the charm of a Romantic park designed by Giuseppe Jappelli, who is more famous for making the Café Pedrocchi in Padua.

How to get there *(Map 4): 28km northeast of Padua by A4, exit Padova-East, towards Treviso.*

Hotel Bellevue

32043 Cortina d'Ampezzo (Belluno)
Corso Italia, 197
Tel. 0436-88 34 00 - Fax 0436-86 75 10 - Sig.ra Fabiani
E-mail: h.bellevue@cortinanet.it - Web: www.cortinanet.it/bellevue

Category ★★★★ **Rooms** 20 and suites 45 with telephone, bath or shower, WC, satellite TV, safe, minibar – Elevator. **Price** Double 310-570,000L. **Meals** Breakfast included - half board 200-330,000L (per pers.). **Restaurant** "L'Incontro al Bellevue", service 12:30PM-2:00PM, 8:00PM-11:00PM - mealtime specials 45-70,000L, also à la carte - Italian cuisine. **Credit cards** All major. **Pets** Dogs allowed. **Facilities** Garage. **Nearby** Skiing - excursions by cable car to the Tofana (10,543 feet) and to the Cristallo - Ghedina lake - Misurina lake - Tiziano's house in Pieve di Cadore. **Open** Dec – Apr and Jul – Sept.

The historical Hotel Bellevue has been one of the most popular inns in Cortina with celebrities since the beginning of the century. It is the jewel of this famous resort. Wood–used as the main decorative element in the hotel–is paneled, painted, parqueted and sculpted, and the result is magnificent. Most of the work has been done by hand using traditional techniques, which gives the entire hotel an atmosphere of elegant warmth. Beautiful fabrics by Pierre Frey and Rubelli complement the regional antique furniture. You will find the same atmosphere in the restaurant, which has excellent cuisine. This hotel is a model of simplicity and good taste–the essential ingredients of what we call "class."

How to get there *(Map 4): 168km north of Venezia via A27 to Alemagna, then S51 to Cortina d'Ampezzo.*

Hotel de la Poste

32043 Cortina d'Ampezzo (Belluno)
Piazza Roma, 14
Tel. 0436-42 71 - Fax 0436-86 84 35 - Sig. Manaigo
E-mail: posta@hotels.cortina.it - Web: www.hotels.cortina.it/delaposte

Category ★★★★ **Rooms** 81 with telephone, bath, WC, satellite TV, safe, minibar – Elevator. **Price** Single 150-300,000L, double 250-480,000L. **Meals** Breakfast 27,000L - half board 190-400,000L, full board 210-430,000L (per pers.). **Restaurant** Service 12:30PM-2:30PM, 7:30PM-9:30PM - mealtime specials and also à la carte 95,000L - Italian cuisine. **Credit cards** All major. **Pets** Dogs not allowed. **Facilities** Garage (+25,000L). **Nearby** Skiing - excursions by cable car to the Tofana - Ghedina lake - Misurina lake - Tiziano's house in Pieve di Cadore. **Closed** Apr, May, Oct, Nov.

The pearl of the Dolomites has its historic hotel - the Hotel de la Poste, around which the life of sophisticated Cortina revolves. You will find here, of course, all the usual assets of a mountain inn. Situated in the center, in a sunny spot, peaceful, with its popular bar (don't forget that the local cocktail is called the Dolomite), beautifully-prepared cuisine and attentive service. Despite the drawbacks caused by its fame, it is still one of the nicest places in the region. The bedrooms are inviting, comfortable and quiet. This is recommended to all those who like the mountains but who don't want to give up the pleasures of shopping and meeting people.

How to get there *(Map 4): 168km north of Venezia via A27 to Alemagna, then S51 to Cortina d'Ampezzo.*

Hotel Ancora

32043 Cortina d'Ampezzo (Belluno)
Corso Italia, 62
Tel. 0436-32 61 - Fax 0436-32 65 - Sig.ra Flavia Sartor
E-mail: info@hotelancoracortina.com - Web: www.hotelancoracortina.com

Category ★★★★ **Rooms** 31, 9 junior suites and 11 suites with telephone, bath or shower, WC, satellite TV, safe, minibar – Elevator. **Price** Whith half board per pers. single 250-350,000L, double 220-320,000L, junior suite 280-420,000L, suite 320-520,000L. **Meals** Breakfast included, served 8:00-10:00 - half board +40,000L; for Christmas and New year's day (per pers, 10-14 days min.) 4 200-5 040,000L. **Restaurant** Service 12:30PM-2:00PM, 7:00PM-9:00PM - mealtime specials 60-70,000L, also à la carte - Italian cuisine. **Credit cards** All major. **Pets** Dogs allowed (+30,000L). **Facilities** Garage. **Nearby** Skiing - excursions by cable car to the Tofana - Ghedina lake - Misurina lake - Tiziano's house in Pieve di Cadore. **Open** Jan – Mar and Jul – Dec.

This wonderful place owes a lot to its owner, Flavia, an expert in antiques and decoration, who has given this pretty hotel a lot of personality. Behind the traditional façade of a simple chalet lies a hidden elegance and refinement, quiet comfort in the salons and bedrooms, and a restaurant, La Petite Fleur, which serves a creative cuisine of Italian inspiration. The Terrazza Viennese is the meeting place for all those who flock here after the day's skiing to enjoy a sachertorte or a drink at the piano bar. In a perfect location - this is the "in" to be in Cortina.

How to get there *(Map 4):168km north of Venezia via A27 to Alemagna, then S51 to Cortina d'Ampezzo.*

Hotel Pensione Menardi

32043 Cortina d'Ampezzo (Belluno)
Via Majon, 110
Tel. 0436-24 00 - Fax 0436-86 21 83 - Famiglia Menardi
E-mail: hmenardi@sunrise.it - Web: www.sunrise.it/cortina/alberghi/menardi

Category ★★★ **Rooms** 49 with telephone, bath or shower, WC, satellite TV. **Price** Single 90-180,000L, double 160-350,000L. **Meals** Breakfast 15,000L, served 7:30-10:00 - half board 130-240,000L, full board 145-260,000L (per pers.). **Restaurant** Service 12:30PM-2:00PM, 7:30PM-9:00PM - mealtime specials 35,000L - Italian cuisine. **Credit cards** All major. **Pets** Dogs not allowed. **Facilities** Garage. **Nearby** Skiing - excursions by the cable car to the Tofana (10,543 feet) and to the Cristallo - Ghedina lake - Misurina lake - Tiziano's house in Pieve di Cadore. **Open** Dec 22 – end Apr, Jun 17 – Sept 18.

The Hotel Menardi is an old postal inn. It is charming: as soon as you enter the village you can't help noticing this pretty building with light green wood balconies covered with flowers in the summer. You will find the same charm and warmth inside the house which is wood with regional decor. Don't get the wrong idea from its location next to the road; the hotel has large grounds in the back. The quietest rooms are on the garden and have a nice view of the Dolomites. The kindness of the Menardi family and their dedication to running their hotel well has earned them a clientele of regulars. The prices are also particularly good, considering the quality of the service.

How to get there *(Map 4): 168km north of Venezia via A27 to Alemagna, then S51 to Cortina d'Ampezzo.*

Franceschi Park Hotel

32043 Cortina d'Ampezzo (Belluno)
Via Cesare Battisti, 86
Tel. 0436-86 70 41 - Fax 0436-2909 - Famiglia Franceschi
E-mail: h.franceschi@cortinanet.it - Web: www.cortinanet.it/franceschi

Category ★★★ **Rooms** 49 with telephone, bath, WC, TV – Elevator. **Price** (rooms and suites): 65-470,000L, apart. 200-580,000L. **Meals** Breakfast included, served 7:40-10:15. **Restaurant** Service 12:30PM-1:45PM, 7:30PM-8:45PM - mealtime specials 43-75,000L - Italian cuisine. **Credit cards** All major. **Pets** Dogs not allowed. **Facilities** Tennis, sauna, turkish bath, whirl pool, play room, beauty, solarium, parking. **Nearby** Skiing - excursions by the cable car to the Tofana (10,543 feet) and to the Cristallo - Ghedina lake - Misurina lake - Tiziano's house in Pieve di Cadore. **Open** Jun 22 – Sept 16, Dec 18 – Mar 26.

This pretty turn-of-the-century building has housed the Franceschi family hotel for three generations. It is on large grounds with a pretty garden, near the center of town. The hotel has kept its old-time flavor. Woodwork, parquet floors and blond wood exposed beams make the atmosphere very warm, as does the furniture and the large Austrian stove. The cozy, comfortable rooms have the same decor. This hotel is ideal for a family vacation.

How to get there *(Map 4): 168km north of Venezia via A27 to Alemagna, then S51 to Cortina d'Ampezzo.*

Baita Fraina

Fraina 32043 Cortina d'Ampezzo (Belluno)
Tel. 0436-36 34 - Fax 0436-86 37 61
Familly Menardi

Category ★★ **Rooms** 6 with telephone, bath or shower, WC, TV. **Price** Double 140-220,000L. **Meals** Breakfast included, served 7:00-9:00 - half board 115-155,000L (per pers.). **Restaurant** Service 12:30PM-2:30PM, 7:30PM-9:30PM - closed Mon in low season - mealtime specials 50-60,000L - Specialties: Filetto di cervo al rirtillo rosso. **Credit cards** All major. **Pets** Dogs not allowed. **Facilities** Sauna. **Nearby** Skiing - excursions by cable car to the Tofana - Ghedina lake - Misurina lake - Tiziano's house in Pieve di Cadore. **Closed** Apr 20 – June 25, Oct 1 – Dec 15.

A little away from the chic effervescence of Cortina, here you will appreciate the beauty of the site without getting caught up in the whirlwind of tourism. In winter as in summer, it is completely immersed in nature, only one kilometer from the center. The hotel has only six rooms, modest but comfortable. The place is run in family style, which only enhances the intimacy and simplicity, two aspects to be appreciated. A good address to know at reasonable prices in Italy's most upscale ski resort.

How to get there *(Map 4): 168km north of Venezia via A27 to Alemagna, then S51 to Cortina d'Ampezzo.*

Villa Marinotti

32040 Tai di Cadore (Belluno)
Via Manzago, 21
Tel. 0435-322 31 - Fax 0435-333 35 - Sig. and Sig.ra Giacobbi de Martin
E-mail: villa.marinotti@libero.it

Suites 5 and 2 bungalows, with telephone, bath, WC. **Price** Suite 120-140,000L (single.), 200-220,000L (double), bungalow 110-120,000L (single), 160-180,000L (double). **Meals** Breakfast included, served until 10:00. **Restaurant** "Le Ristorantino", service 12:00PM-2:00PM, 7:30PM-9:00PM - closed Wed. **Credit card** Amex, Visa, Eurocard, MasterCard. **Pets** Small dogs allowed. **Facilities** Tennis (15,000L), sauna (20,000L), parking. **Nearby** Skiing in Pieve di Cadore (2km) and in Cortina d'Ampezzo (25km) - Tiziano's house in Pieve di Cadore - Great Dolomite Road. **Open** All year.

The owners of this house had the fortunate idea of transforming the family chalet into a small hotel, which is still a precious secret. The house has only five rooms, or rather five suites, as each one has a small, private salon. Simplicity and good taste pervade the decor (the "Rosa" suite is the nicest one). The house is surrounded by large grounds, which have a tennis court. Breakfasts are excellent. In the villa, a restaurant, independently managed, means that you get meals on the spot, an additional advantage. You can expect a charming, warm welcome here.

How to get there (Map 4): 34km north of Belluno via S51.

Golf Hotel

34070 San Floriano del Collio (Gorizia)
Via Oslavia, 2
Tel. 0481-88 40 51 - Fax 0481-88 40 52 - Comtesse Formentini
Web: www.isabellaformentini.com

Category ★★★★ **Rooms** 14 and 1 apartment (some with air-conditioning) with telephone, bath or shower, WC, TV. **Price** Single 200,000L, double 350,000L, apart. 540,000L. **Meals** Breakfast included. **Restaurant** Service 12:00PM-2:00PM, 8:00PM-9:30PM - closed Mon and Tues lunch - mealtime specials 70-90,000L, also à la carte - Regional cooking. **Credit cards** All major. **Pets** Dogs allowed. **Facilities** Swimming pool, tennis, golf (9-hole), parking. **Nearby** Fortress of Gradisca d'Isonzo - Gorizia castle - Trieste - Monastery of Kostanjevica - Cividale (medieval city) - Cathedral of Grado and of Aquileja. **Open** Mar – Nov 15.

Two houses of the San Floriano castle make up this hotel. Each of the rooms bears the name of one of the famous regional wines. They are all furnished in a blend of styles, from 17th-century to Biedermeier, like in old family houses where each generation has left its mark. The hotel has a nine-hole golf course with a practice and putting green. The restaurant Castello Formentini is next to the castle and is one of the region's finest.

How to get there *(Map 5): 47km northwest of Trieste via A4, Villesse-Gorizia and San Floriano exit.*

Haus Michaela

32047 Sappada (Belluno)
Borgata Fonta, 40
Tel. 0435-46 93 77 - Fax 0435-66 131 - Sig. Piller Roner
E-mail: hmichaela@sunrise.it - Web: www.dolomiti.com/sappada/michaela

Category ★★★ **Rooms** 20 with telephone, shower and 1 with bath, WC, satellite TV. **Price** Double 100-160,000L, suite 170-210,000L. **Meals** Breakfast 15,000L, served 8:00-10:00 - half board 75-145,000L, full board 85-160,000L (per pers., 3 days min.). **Restaurant** Service 12:30PM-1:30PM, 7:30PM-8:30PM - mealtime specials 35-45,000L - Regional cooking and sappadina. **Credit cards** Visa, Eurocard, MasterCard. **Pets** Dogs not allowed. **Facilities** Swimming pool, sauna, parking. **Nearby** Skiing - Cortina d'Ampezzo - Titien house in Pieve di Cadore. **Open** Dec 5 – end Mar, May 20 – end Sept.

Haus Michaela is located in Sappada, a beautiful town on the outskirts of Venetia, where you can already feel the charms of Austria (just 5km away). It extends down to the floor of a valley dominated by the majestic furrowed summits and sharp peaks of the Dolomites. You can enjoy the mountains to the fullest here year round: it is a fine ski resort in the winter and a marvelous vacation spot in summer. Among the many hiking trails don't miss the one going up to the sources of the Piave, the legendary river which is the main supplier of the lagoon of Venice and flows through all of Venetia.The hotel offers simply decorated but highly comfortable rooms, and three large studios ideal for family vacations. Hotel facilities include a heated pool, a complete health care complex with Turkish baths, and a restaurant featuring local and Tyrolian specialties, notably a wide variety of deer dishes.

How to get there *(Map 5): 169km north of Venezia. A27, Vittorio Veneto exit, then towards Cortina, then towards Sappada.*

Albergo Leon Bianco

35122 Padova
Piazzeta Pedrocchi, 12
Tel. 049-65 72 25 - Fax 049-875 61 84 - Sig. Morosi
E-mail: leonbianco@toscanelli.com - Web: www.toscanelli.com

Category ★★★ **Rooms** 22 with air-conditioning, telephone, bath or shower, WC, TV, minibar – Elevator. **Price** Single 106-131,000L, double 155-167,000L. **Meals** Breakfast 15,000L, served 7:30-10:30. **Restaurant** See p. 570. **Credit cards** All major. **Pets** Dogs allowed (+12,000L). **Facilities** Garage (25,000L). **Nearby** Padova: Piazza delle Erbe and Palazzo della Ragione, Basilica di San Antonio, Chiesa degli Eremitani, Cappella degli Scrovegni (frescoes of Giotto) - Pallandian villas: tour in car from Padua to Venice via the Brenta Riviera-N11 (Villa Pisani, Villa "La Barbariga," villa Foscari) by boat *Il Burchiello* - Villa Simes in Piazzola sul Brenta - Villa Barbarigo in Valsanzibio - Abbey of Praglia - Pétrarque's house in Arqua Petrarca – Valsanzibio and Frassanelle golf course (18-hole). **Open** All year.

When Théophile Gautier visited Padua, he was struck by two sights (described in his *"Italia"*): the café Pedrocchi, which is still there, "monumentally classic, with pillars and columns... all very large and all very marble...," and the Scrovegni chapel, with its frescoes by Giotto. Aside from these, though, the lively university city of Padua has many more attractions worth visiting. The Albergo Leon Bianco is right in the center of town. It is a small hotel that constantly endeavors to improve its comfort, service and hospitality. Though the decoration in the bedrooms is standardized, it is nevertheless a nice place for a stopover in Padua.

How to get there *(Map 4): 37km east of Venezia via A4, Padova-East exit; then towards town center, Palazzo della Ragione.*

Hotel Villa Regina Margherita

45100 Rovigo
Viale Regina Margherita, 6
Tel. 0425-36 15 40 - Fax 0425-313 01

Category ★★★★ **Rooms** 22 with air-conditiong, telephone, bath or shower, WC, TV, minibar – Elevator. **Price** Single 150,000L, double 190,000L, triple 210,000L suite 250,000L. **Meals** Breakfast included (buffet), served 7:30-9:30. **Restaurant** Service 12:30PM-2:00PM, 7:30PM-10:00PM - mealtime specials 35-50,000L, also à la carte - Seasonal cooking. **Credit cards** All major. **Pets** Dogs not allowed. **Facilities** Parking. **Nearby** Villa Badoer (Palladio) - Villa Bragadin - Villa Molin in Fratta Polesine - Abbey of the Vangadizza in Badia Polesino - Padua - Ferrara. **Open** All year.

This charming hotel and its excellent restaurant are in a very pretty Art Deco villa. In the center of the little town of Rovigo, on a beautiful and slightly old-fashioned residential avenue, the Hotel Regina Margherita has recently been tastefully renovated. The stained glass, in vogue in the 1930s, has been preserved, along with some beautiful pieces of furniture which, combined with pretty, warm colors, make the salons and the lobby particular charming. The rooms, some of which are on the garden, are pleasant, comfortable and particularly well kept. The hotel restaurant deserves special mention for its remarkable setting, service and cuisine.

How to get there *(Map 10): 45km south of Padova via A13, Boara exit.*

Hotel Villa Cipriani

31011 Asolo (Treviso)
Via Canova, 298
Tel. 0423-52 34 11 - Fax 0423-95 20 95 - Sig. Burattin
E-mail: giampaolo.burattin@sheraton.com - Web: www.sheraton.com

Category ★★★★ **Rooms** 31 with air-conditioning, telephone, bath, WC, TV, minibar – Elevator.
Price Single 374-484,000L, double 484-792,000L. **Meals** Breakfast (buffet) 58,300L, served 7:00-
10:30 - half board 150,000L (per pers.). **Restaurant** Service 12:30PM-2:30PM, 8:00PM-10:00PM -
mealtime specials 130,000L, also à la carte - Specialties: Risotto Asolo - Pasta - Seafood. **Credit
cards** All major. **Pets** Dogs allowed (except in restaurant). **Facilities** Garage (26,000L). **Nearby**
Possagno (casa and tempio del Canova d'Antonio Canova) - Villa Barbaro in Maser - Villa Rinaldi-
Barbini - Villa Emo in Panzolo – Golf (7km). **Open** All year.

A solo is a must during any visit to Venetia. Don't worry if you have to drive
through some industrial zones to get there — it will seem all the more
beautiful once you reach it, perched on its hill in the middle of the countryside,
a little medieval village with the castle as its crown. The lovely Villa Cipriani
is a must in itself. It offers you elegant rooms, a lovely garden scented with
rose trellises, a beautiful vista of the distant landscape and in the evening
before dinner, a singer of charm murmuring those irresistible Italian melodies.
An unforgettable spot.

How to get there (*Map 4*): *65km northwest of Venezia; 35km northwest of
Treviso via S348 to Montebelluna, then S248 to Asolo; towards Bassano,
D/Grappa.*

Albergo al Sole

31011 Asolo (Treviso)
Via Collegio, 33
Tel. 0423-52 81 11 - Fax 0423-52 83 99 - Silvia de Checchi
E-mail: albergoalsole@sevenonline.it - Web: www.sevenonline.it/albergoalsole

Category ★★★★ **Rooms** 23 and 5 suites no smoking, with air-conditioning, telephone, bath, WC, satellite TV, minibar, safe – Wheelchair access. **Price** Single 180-250,000L, double 280-350,000L junior suite and suite 350-450,000L. **Meals** Breakfast included, served 7:30-10:00. **Restaurant** See p. 571. **Credit cards** All major. **Pets** Dogs allowed. **Facilities** "Technogym", fitness center, parking. **Nearby** Possagno (casa and tempio del Canova d'Antonio Canova) - Villa Barbaro in Maser - Villa Rinaldi-Barbini - Villa Emo in Fanzolo – Golf (7km).**Open** All year.

The finest of the Venetian villas open to visitors are to be found between Treviso and Bassano. Asolo is an ideal stopping-place not only because of its superb geographical setting, but also because the village itself is very pleasant to visit, since it remains more or less unspoilt. The orange façade of the hotel, recently cleaned, overlooks the main square. The reception area and the salon-bar which are furnished with several armchairs and sofas, display the comfortable décor of a grand hotel. The rooms are more personalized, all spacious and comfortably fitted out. Prefer the ones on the left side, which have views over the village. The finest of all are the suites, which are still large and have lovely old furniture. The terrace on the first floor which overlooks the square and the gardens, is the ideal place to take breakfast or an aperitif at sundown. Another asset of the place: it allows you to stay relatively cheaply in this charming village.

How to get there *(Map 4): 65km northwest of Venice - At 35km northwest of Treviso by S348 as far as Montebelluna, then S248 to Asolo, towards Bassano, D/Grappa.*

Villa Abbazia

31051 Follina (Treviso)
Via Martiri della Libertà
Tel. 0438-97 12 77 - Fax 0438-97 00 01 - Sig.ra Zanon De Marchi
E-mail: info@hotelabbazia.it - Web: www.hotelabbazia.it

Category ★★★★★ **Rooms** 14 and 4 suites with air-conditioning, telephone, bath or shower, WC, satellite TV, minibar. **Price** Single 180-240,000L, double 280-350,000L, suite 440-600,000L. **Meals** Breakfast included, served 7:30-10:00. **Restaurant** In Miane see p. 572 or Lino in Solighetto see p. 491. **Credit cards** All major. **Pets** Dogs allowed on request. **Facilities** Parking. **Nearby** Abbey of Follina, from Conegliano (white wine road to Valdobbiadene (Spumante) - Palladian villas tour - Treviso - Venice - Asolo – Asolo golf course (27-hole) in Cavaso del Tomba (16km). **Open** All year.

The Hotel Abbazia is a pretty, 17th-century house in the soft green Venetian Pre-Alps, facing a splendid Cistercien abbey. It is a small, luxurious hotel that offers everything you can imagine in terms of comfort, service and elegance. The rooms, some of which have pretty flower-filled terraces, are vast and each one is differently with antique furniture, pretty engravings decorated and soft, quiet colors. This dream house does not have a garden, but Follina is in the heart of the marvelous province of Treviso, which is filled with often undiscovered villas and Palladian farms. If you stay four nights in July and August you'll get one night free.

How to get there *(Map 4): 40km north of Treviso. Via A4, A27 Vittorio Veneto exit towards Lago Revine; Follina is located at 15km.*

Villa Stucky

31021 Mogliano Veneto (Treviso)
Via Don Bosco, 47
Tel. 041-590 45 28 - Fax 041-590 45 66 - Sig. Zanon
E-mail: info@villastucky.it - Web: www.villastucky.it

Category ★★★★ **Rooms** 20 with air-conditioning, telephone, bath, fax, bath or shower (7 with whirlpool), WC, TV, video, safe, minibar – Elevator. **Price** Single 195,000L, double 320,000L, suite 375,000L. **Meals** Breakfast included, served 7:30-10:30. **Restaurant** Service 7:30PM-10:30PM - à la carte. **Credit cards** All major. **Pets** Dog not allowed. **Facilities** Parking. **Nearby** Venice - Treviso – Villa Condulmer golf course (18-hole). **Open** All year.

Villa Stucky is an 18th-century Venetian villa built by the Countess Seymour. It had become pretty run down until major renovations were undertaken to transform it into the luxury hotel it is today. It has twenty rooms, which all look out onto the grounds, but are all different. Each one has decor that corresponds to the name it bears. "Princess Sissi" is precious with pastel colors; others are simpler and more elegant. In the ones on the top floor you can sleep in the moonlight, thanks to a skylight which you can open.

How to get there *(Map 4): 12km south of Treviso via S13.*

Villa Giustinian

31019 Portobuffolé (Treviso)
Via Giustiniani, 11
Tel. 0422-85 02 44 - Fax 0422-85 02 60

Category ★★★★ **Rooms** 35 and 8 suites with air-conditioning, telephone, bath or shower , WC, TV, radio, minibar. **Price** Single 120-140,000L, double 220-250,000L, suite 450-600,000L. **Meals** Breakfast 15,000L, served 7:30-10:00. **Restaurant** Service 12:30PM-2:30PM, 7:30PM-10:30PM - closed Sun evening and Mon - à la carte. **Credit cards** All major. **Pets** Dogs not allowed. **Facilities** Parking. **Nearby** Venice, from Conegliano (White Wine Road to Valdobbiadene (Spumante), Red Wine Road to Roncade) - Treviso. **Closed** Aug 6 – 24.

The Villa Giustinian is in Portobuffolé, a beautiful medieval village on the border between Venetia and Frioul. Around 1700, a noble Venetian family built this magnificent villa in a classical architectural style on a large piece of land. The interior is sumptuously Baroque, with stucco, frescos of the Veronese school and trompe l'œil. In this grandiose decor you will nonetheless find an intimate atmosphere. A superb stairway leads up to the suites, which are as big as ballrooms and have Venetian furniture. The presidential suite, which has a bed in a sculpted alcove, is amazing. Though the breakfast room also enjoys this same décor, the bedrooms are in the barchessa, an annex found with every Venetian building. They are of different sizes, much more ordinary, but comfortable. This where you will also find the restaurant with its good cooking and excellent wine list. A discovery, too, because of its prices, which are reasonable by Italian standards.

How to get there *(Map 5): 40km northeast of Treviso, towards Oderzo, Portobuffolé-Pordenone.*

Locanda Da Lino

31050 Solighetto (Treviso)
Via Brandolini, 31
Tel. 0438-84 23 77 - 0438-82 150 - Fax 0438-98 05 77 - Sig. Marco Toffolin
E-mail: dalino@tmn.it - Web: www.seven.it/locanda-da-lino

Category ★★★ **Rooms** 17 with telephone, bath, WC, TV, minibar. **Price** Single 110,000L, double 150,000L, suite 170,000L. **Meals** Breakfast included, served 8:00-11:00. **Restaurant** Service 12:00PM-3:00PM, 7:00PM-10:00PM - closed Mon, Christmas and in Jul - à la carte 60-70,000L - Specialties: Tagliolini alla Lino - Spiedo - Faraona con salsa peverada - Dolci della casa. **Credit cards** All major. **Pets** Dogs allowed. **Facilities** Parking. **Nearby** Venice - Villa Lattes in Istrana - Villa Barbaro Maser - Villa Emo Fanzolo di Vedelago - Conegliano (White Wine Road to Valdobbiadene (Spumante) - Red Wine Road to Roncade) - Treviso – Villa Condulmer golf course (18-hole). **Closed** Jul and Mon.

Da Lino is a character who regularly makes news in his village of Solighetto. He started by opening a restaurant, which quickly put the town, in the beautiful countryside of Montello and at the foothills of the Pre-Alps, between Venice and Cortina, famous for its Prosecco and its Marzemino sung by Don Juan, on the map. His painter, novelist and poet friends, among whom Zanzotto is the most faithful, have an open table and it is here that the great singer Toti del Monte came to spend her last days. In her memory, Lino has created the Premio Simpatia, a cultural event. Marcello Mastroianni used to enjoy the atmosphere of well-being in the house. Nowadays his son Marco continues the tradition and the spirit remains. The rooms bear the names of regulars and friends: "Marcello" (Mastroianni) and "Marta Marzotto" are comfortable and decorated with originality. In the restaurant, there are two rooms frequented by regulars; one is bigger and more touristy.

How to get there *(Map 4): 33km northwest of Treviso.*

Hotel Villa Condulmer

31020 Zerman Mogliano Veneto (Treviso)
Via Zermanese
Tel. 041-45 71 00 - Fax 041-45 71 34 - Sig. M. Zuin
E-mail: condulmer@tin.it

Category ★★★★★ **Rooms** 51 with air-conditioning, telephone, bath, WC, TV. **Price** Single 280,000L, double 390,000L, junior suite 460,000L, suite 550,000L. **Meals** Breakfast included, served 7:00-10:30. **Restaurant** Service 12:30PM-2:30PM, 7:30PM-10:00PM - mealtime specials 80-100,000L, also à la carte - Regional cooking. **Credit cards** All major. **Pets** Dogs not allowed. **Facilities** Swimming pool, tennis, golf (27-hole), riding, parking. **Nearby** Venice - Treviso. **Open** All year.

The Venetian villas flourished in the 18th century, when the wealthy merchants who traded with the Orient decided to convert their fortunes into real estate. This was the birth of a new architectural style consisting of a central, often sumptuous, building, where the family lived, flanked by two wings called *barchesse*, that were used as storage space. At the Villa Condulmer the reception rooms are still very well preserved and one can still admire the ceiling with ornate stuccos and large Venetian chandeliers, painted medallions that adorn the walls and a floor of terra cotta tile. The nicest rooms are those in the villa, though the others have more modern amenities. To be able to live in the country, with a large swimming pool and just near a golf course, is really a blessing during the summer months — and it's only 20 kilometers from Venice.

How to get there *(Map 4): 18km north of Venezia via A4, Mogliano Veneto exit; then towards Zerman.*

Locanda Al Castello

33043 Cividale del Friuli (Udine)
Via del Castello, 20
Tel. 0432-73 32 42 / 73 40 15 - Fax 0432-70 09 01 - Sig. Balloch
E-mail: castello@ud.nettuno.it - Web: www.infotech.it/castello

Category ★★★ **Rooms** 17 with telephone, bath or shower, WC, hairdryer, satellite TV, minibar, safe – Elevator, wheelchair access and rooms for disabled persons. **Price** Single 110,000L, double 145,000L; extra bed 30,000L. **Meals** Breakfast 15,000L - half board 130,000L, full board 150,000L (per pers, 3 days min.) **Restaurant** Service 12:00PM-2:30PM, 7:00PM-10:00PM - closed Wed - mealtime specials 45,000L, also à la carte - Specialties: Antipasti misti di pesce e di selvagigina - Pesce e carne ai ferri - Maltagliata alla longoborda. **Credit cards** All major. **Pets** Dogs allowed. **Facilities** Parking. **Nearby** Tempietto - Duomo and Archeological Museum - Udine - Villa Manin in Passariano – Golf course (9-hole) in Lignano, golf course (9-hole) in Tarvisio. **Closed** Nov 1 – 15.

For the curious traveler who wants to venture deeper into Italy, Friuli offers its smiling countryside and some interesting towns. Cividale del Friuli has a museum of architecture with some fine pieces from the early Middle Ages, and the Duomo (16th century) contains paintings by Palma the Younger and a wonderful altarpiece of pure silver. The Locanda Al Castello is in an unpretentious but pleasant stopping place. It is a typical provincial small town inn, with rooms that exude a prosperous comfort, a restaurant that serves generous meals and a hospitality that is simple and natural.

How to get there *(Map 5): 17km east of Udine via A23, Udine exit; then towards Cividale (1.5km from Cividale).*

Hotel Gabbia d'Oro

37121 Verona
Corso Porta Borsari, 4a
Tel. 045-800 30 60 - Fax 045-59 02 93 - Sig.ra Balzarro
E-mail: gabbiadoro@easynet.it

Category ★★★★★ **Rooms** 5 and 22 suites with air-conditioning, telephone, bath, WC, TV, minibar – Elevator. **Price** Double 310-680,000L (per 1 pers.), double 400-600,000L, suite 550-1 000,000L. **Meals** Breakfast 45,000L, served 7:00-11:00. **Restaurant** See pp. 569. **Credit cards** All major. **Pets** Small dogs allowed. **Facilities** Parking (50,000L). **Nearby** In Verona: Piazza delle Erbe, Piazza dei Signori, the Arena, Juliet's House, Arche Scaligere, Church of San Zeno, Castelvecchio - Events: Festival of Verona in the Arena (end Jun – beg Sept) - Villa Boccoli-Serego in Pedemonte - Villa della Torre in Fumane - Soave - Castle Villafranca di Verona – golf course (18-hole) in Sommacampagna. **Open** All year.

The luxurious Hotel Gabbia d'Oro is a discreet 18th-century palace, recently transformed into a no less discreet luxury hotel. At first glance it seems like a secret place. The entrance is barely distinguishable from the street. There are two small salons with superb exposed beams, very beautiful period furniture and nice armchairs around an old fireplace. The rooms, not very large but very luxurious, are arranged around the orangery, with its pretty flowers.There is a profusion of luxury here. Alas, nothing is perfect–the prices are high, but justifiably so. The hotel is in a historical pedestrian area. If you come by car, a taxi (at the hotel's expense) will accompany you to the nearest garage–one less thing to worry about.

How to get there *(Maps 3 and 4): Via A4, Verona-South exit. Via A22, Verona-West exit. The hotel is near the Piazza delle Erbe.*

V E N E T O

Hotel Due Torri

37121 Verona
Piazza Sant' Anastasia, 4
Tel 045-59-50-44 - Fax 045-800 41 30 - Sig. Mariotti
E-mail: duetorri.verona@baglioni-palacehotels.it - Web: www.baglionihotels.com

Category ★★★★ **Rooms** 81 and 8 suites with air-conditioning, telephone, bath, WC, TV, minibar – Elevator, rooms for no smoking. **Price** Single 300-540,000L, double 450-750,000L, suite 720-1,300,000L, extra bed 150,000L. **Meals** Breakfast included, served 7:30-10:30. **Restaurant** "Aquila", service 12:30PM-2:30PM, 7:30PM-10:00PM - mealtime specials 65,000L, also à la carte - Regional cooking. **Credit cards** All major. **Pets** Dogs not allowed. **Facilities** Parking. **Nearby** In Verona: Piazza delle Erbe, Piazza dei Signori, the Arena, Juliet's House, Arche Scaligere, Church of San Zeno, Castelvecchio - Events: Festival of Verona in the Arena (end Jun – beg Sept) - Villa Boccoli-Serego in Pedemonte - Villa della Torre in Fumane - Soave - Castle Villafranca di Verona – golf course (18-hole) in Sommacampagna. **Open** All year.

Former residence of the Scaglieri, lords of Verona, this palace was already receiving the private guests of the Della Scala family in the 13th Century. Successive restorations have not detracted from the ceremonial feel of the place. Adjacent to the church of Santa Anastasia, the two buildings enclose the little town square, unfortunately invaded by the car park. After passing the entrance door, with its two caryatids, you go into the monumental hall, which seems even larger because of its checkerboard flooring. The ceiling still has some fine pieces of fresco and the arcades suggest the architecture of a cloister. The furniture and the choice of colors give the whole a theatrical atmosphere which seems to appeal to the artists and festival goers who meet in the evening in the famous arena of Bel Canto. The best rooms overlook the square or the ones on the top floor with their views over the red and ochre roofs of the town. Proud of having once housed Mozart, Goethe and Garibaldi, the hotel maintains its reputation as the grand hotel of Verona.

***How to get there** (Maps 3 and 4): In the historic center.*

Hotel Aurora

37121 Verona
Piazza Erbe, 2
Tel. 045-59 47 17 - Fax 045-801 08 60
Sig.ra Rossi

Rooms 19 with air-conditioning, telephone, bath or shower, WC, satellite TV – Elevator. **Price** Single 130-190,000L, double 160-210,000L, apartment with 2 double rooms and 1 bath 250-350,000L. **Meals** Breakfast (buffet) included, served 7:30-10:00. **Restaurant** See p. 569. **Credit cards** All major. **Pets** Dogs allowed. **Nearby** In Verona: Piazza delle Erbe, Piazza dei Signori, the Arena, Juliet's House, Arche Scaligere, Church of San Zeno, Castelvecchio - Events: Festival of Verona in the Arena (end Jun – beg Sept) - Villa Boccoli-Serego in Pedemonte - Villa della Torre in Fumane - Soave - Castle Villafranca di Verona – Golf course (18-hole) in Sommacampagna. **Open** All year.

The Albergo Aurora is on the Piazza dell'Erbe in the heart of the town (a pedestrian area). It is very well kept and very comfortable (air-conditioning and well-equipped shower room). The service is discreet and charming and the prices are very competitive. There is one sour note, however, the decor and the lighting are reminiscent of a train station. So, should you decide to come here, choose the front rooms with a view of the piazza (they are the smallest but there are plans to enlarge them). The terrace, which looks out on those famous sun umbrellas, is a wonderful place to sit back and relax.

How to get there *(Maps 3 and 4): A4, Verona-South exit; A22, Verona-North exit. (Parking, Cittadella, piazza Arsenale, here you can phone a taxi for the center).*

Hotel Villa del Quar

37020 Pedemonte (Verona)
Via Quar, 12
Tel. 045-680 06 81 - Fax 045-680 06 04 - Sig.ra Acampora Montresor
E-mail: villadelquar@e-point.it

Category ★★★★ **Rooms** 22 with air-conditiong, telephone, bath or shower, WC, TV, minibar – Elevator. **Price** Double 430-480,000L, suite 595-670,000L. **Meals** Breakfast included, served 7:30-10:00. **Restaurant** Service 12:30PM-2:00PM, 7:30PM-10:00PM - closed Mon in low deason - mealtime specials 120,000L - Specialties: Capesante marinate alla vaniglia bourbon - Filetti di rombo in crosta di pistacchi - Meringa al polline, gelato di frutti di bosco. **Credit cards** All major. **Pets** Dogs allowed. **Facilities** Swimming pool, parking **Nearby** Villa Boccoli-Serègo in Pedemonte - Verona - Villa della Torre in Fumane - Soave - Castle Villafranca di Verona - Lago di Garda - Mantova - Venise - Events: Festival of Verona in the Arena (end Jun – beg Sept) – Golf course (18-hole) in Sommacampagna and in Garde. **Open** All year.

The younger generation of owners of the Villa del Quar have transformed the family estate into a luxury hotel, continuing to cultivate the hectares of vineyards that surround the villa (which means that you can take part in a tasting). The building is typical of the region, with three wings around a central garden. There are beautiful salons and bedrooms, each differently furnished, that combine a refined setting and good amenities. Elegance is the key word here, even if you're way out in the country. And what a joy it is to stroll through the vineyard in the morning, knowing you're only a few kilometers from Verona.

How to get there *(Map 3): 5km northeast of Verona, via Trento; before Parona take the Valpolicella road towards Pedemonte. Via A4, Verona-North exit, highway towards S. Pietro in Cariano, right (towards Verona) to Pedemonte.*

Foresteria Serego Alighieri

37020 Gargagnago di Valpolicella (Verona)
Tel. 045-770 36 22 - Fax 045-770 35 23
Sig. Pieralvise Serego Alighieri
E-mail: serego@easynet.it - Web: www.seregoalighieri.it

Apartments 8 with air-conditioning, telephone, bath, WC, TV, minibar. **Price** 2-4 pers. 230-550,000L (1 night), 190-450,000L (1 night during 5 days). **Meals** Breakfast included, served 8:00-10:00. **Restaurant** In Verona, see p. 569. **Credit cards** All major. **Pets** Dogs not allowed. **Facilities** Parking. **Nearby** Verona - Events: Festival of Verona in the Arena (end Jun – beg Sept) - Vineyards of Valpolicella (Villa Boccoli-Serego, Villa della Torre, Fumane, S. Floriano, San Giorgio, Volargne and the Villa del Bene) - Soave – Golf course (18-hole) in Sommacampagna. **Closed** Jan.

Go up the long path lined with majestic cypress trees and you will soon see a massive residence with a large enclosed courtyard of flagstones in the middle of the Valplolicella vineyards. Dante used to come here on vacation when he lived in Verona. The Casal dei Ronchi was bought in 1353 by his eldest son, Pietro, and has been the home of the poet's descendants ever since. Today it is a prosperous estate with a working farm with wine and oil you can taste during your stay here. Eight elegantly decorated apartments are available (for 2 to 4 people). Between Lake Garda and Verona, and Venice less than 60 miles away, this villa is a magical, rare delight.

How to get there *(Map 3): 20km of Verona via A22, Verona-North exit; then towards S. Ambrogio di Valpolicella.*

Relais Villabella

37047 San Bonifacio (Verona)
Via Villabella, 72
Tel. 045-61 01 777 - Fax 045-61 01 799
Famiglia Cherubin

Category ★★★ **Rooms** 10 with air-conditiong, telephone, bath or shower, WC, TV, minibar. **Price** Double 300,000L, romantic room 350,000L. **Meals** Breakfast included. **Restaurant** Service 12:00PM-2:00PM, 8:00PM-10:00PM - closed Sun and Mon, Jan 22 – Feb 4 and in Nov - à la carte 80-120,000L. **Credit cards** All major. **Pets** Dogs allowed. **Facilities** Swimming pool with hydrommassage, parking. **Nearby** In San Bonifacio: Churche of S. Abbondio, Abbey of S. Pietro Apostole - Verona - Soave - Vicenza - Events: Wein Feast in Soave, Festival of Verona in the Arena (end Jun – beg Sept) – Golf course (18-hole) in Sommacampagna. **Open** All year.

The most famous town in the Alpone Valley, Soave is known for its extraordinary medieval fortifications and its wine. Just a few kilometers away from this pleasant fortified village is Villabella, with the hotel of the same name, a traditional villa of the region now converted into a comfortable country inn. The excellent decoration of the bedrooms and the great attention paid to the cooking attract both a regional clientele, who want to spend a weekend in the country, and tourists who are looking for a quiet country hideaway after their day's touring. And quiet though it is, the Villabella is easy to reach, located just off the autostrada.

How to get there *(Map 4): 20km west of Vierona, via A4, Soave exit; Villabella is located near the highway.*

Coop. 8 Marzo - Ca' Verde

Ca'Verde 37010 Sant' Ambrogio di Valpolicella (Verona)
Tel. 045-686 22 72 - Fax 045-686 79 52
Sig.ra Vilma Zamboni

Rooms 10 (4 with bath, WC). **Price** Single 60-105,000L, double 75-120,000L; extra bed 25-50,000L.
Meals Breakfast (buffet) included, served 8:30-10:00. **Restaurant** Service 12:30PM-2:00PM, 7:30PM-
9:30PM - closed Mon - à la carte 35,000L - Specialties: Pasta fatta in casa - Gnocchi di ricotta - Garni
alla griglia - Piatti vegetariani. **Credit cards** Visa, Eurocard, MasterCard. **Pets** Dogs not allowed.
Facilities Parking. **Nearby** Verona - Villa Boccoli-Serègo in Pedemonte - Villa della Torre in Fumane -
Soave - Castel of Villafranca di Verona - Lake Garda. **Closed** Jan and Feb.

Arustic site, it officially became an agricultural cooperative some ten years
ago after its owners had occupied unused land. Today it functions as a
cooperative, with a team that have divided up the tasks, both the farming and the
commercial work, with the aim of distributing their products directly. They have
opened a latteria where dairy products (milk, yogurt and cheese) and honey, all
organically produced on the farm, are sold to the public, and have also created
facilities to enable them to receive guests. There are two kinds of lodgings. In one
wing are the recently-built, more comfortable rooms. In the other there are
dormitories, as well as several large rooms suitable for families, but with showers
outside. There are several large picnic tables on the property, but the restaurant
prices are low enough to tempt anyone to sample the cooking, which is family-
style and based on home-made products. Ca`Verde is not easy to get to. Once you
have left the road you have to drive 2 kilometers further on a dirt track before you
catch a glimpse of it, standing there completely surrounded by farmland.

How to get there *(Map 3): 20km from Verona, Verona-North exit to S. Ambrogio.*
In the village, towards Monte; 3nd turning point, take road on the left after 2km.

Hotel Gardesana

Lago di Garda - 37010 Torri del Benaco (Verona)
Piazza Calderini, 20
Tel. 045-722 54 11 - Fax 045-722 57 71 - Sig. Lorenzini
E-mail: gardesana@easynet.it - Web: www.hotel-gardesana.com

Category ★★★ **Rooms** 34 with air-conditioning (in Jul and Aug), telephone, bath or shower, WC, TV – Elevator. **Price** Single 75-100,000L, double 100-200,000L. **Meals** Breakfast 25,000L, served 7:00-11:00. **Restaurant** Service 7:00PM-11:00PM - mealtime specials 50-90,000L, also à la carte - Specialties: Zuppetta di pesci del Garda - Carpaccio di trota - Filetti di pesce persico. **Credit cards** All major. **Pets** Dogs not allowed. **Facilities** Parking. **Nearby** Cap San Vigilio (Villa Guarienti) - Verona – Golf course (18-hole) in Marciaga. **Open** Mar – Oct 25, Dec 26 – Jan 15.

This 15th-century harbormaster's office faces the ruins of the Scalinger castle built on the other side of the port. From the terrace, where breakfast and dinner are served, you can look down onto the small port on Garde Lake. The rooms all have identical decor; ask for those on the third floor overlooking the lake, with balconies ; they are quieter. The famous restaurant attracts clientele from outside of the hotel and on certain evenings celebrities from the world of art, literature, show business and sports host the dinner. Torri del Benaco is one of the most charming places on the lake. André Gide enjoyed his stay here and Room 23 bears his name. The owner and his family will make you feel at home too.

How to get there *(Map 3): 39km northwest of Verona via A4, Peschiera exit; Via A22, Affi-Lago di Garda exit.*

Hotel Villa Michelangelo

31011 Arcugnagno (Vicenza)
Via Sacco, 19
Tel. 0444-550 300 - Fax 0444-550 490 - Sig. Sebastiano Leder
E-mail: reception@hotelvillamichelangelo.com - Web: www.hotelmichelangelo.com

Category ★★★★ **Rooms** 52 and 6 suites with air-conditioning, telephone, bath, WC, satellite TV, minibar, safe – Elevator, wheelchair access. **Price** Single 210-235,000L, double 300-365,000L, suite 480-550,000L. **Meals** Breakfast included, served 7:00-10:30 - half board +65,000L (per pers.). **Restaurant** Service 12:30PM-2:30PM, 8:00PM-10:30PM - à la carte 85-110,000L. **Credit cards** All major. **Pets** Dogs allowed except in restaurant. **Facilities** Swimming pool (covered in winter), parking. **Nearby** Possagno - Villa Barbaro in Maser - Villa Rinaldi-Barbini - Villa Emo in Panzolo – Golf course (7km). **Open** All year.

L ess than seven kilometers from the town of the famous Palladio, the Villa Michelangelo has a succession of façades looking out on a great lawn that overhangs the Venetian countryside offering a panoramic view of the Berici mountains. The restaurant is on a level with the garden and extends into a terrace through a loggia where meals are served in summer. The dining room is elegant with impeccably laid tables, prettily decorated with flowers. The bar, which is more intimate, also offers pleasant moments. The rooms are less individualized but luxurious and comfortable. Two suites are more remarkable for their gigantic glazed bays, open for fifteen meters which allow you to commune with the landscape. No. 301 is also worth choosing. In the basement, the large covered swimming pool can also fold back its glazed façade which looks out at the hills. As the hotel is well enough organized to serve as a conference center, enquire about what is due to happen when you make your booking.

How to get there *(Map 4): 7km from Vicenza. On A4, exit Vicenza-West, then southwest towards Arcugnagno via the Berici ridge.*

502

Il Castello 🌳

36021 Barbarano Vicentino (Vicenza)
Via Castello, 6
Tel. 0444-88 60 55 - Fax 0444-88 60 55 - Sig.ra Elda Marinoni
E-mail: castellomarinoni@tin.it - Web: www.castellomarinoni.it

Apartment 4 with kitchen, bath, WC. **Price** 35-40,000L (per pers., 7 days min.) +10,000L for heating in low season. **Restaurant** In Vicenza, see p. 571. **Credit cards** Not accepted. **Pets** Dogs not allowed. **Facilities** Parking. **Nearby** Vicenza - Venetian villas road: villas Guiccioli, Valmarana, La Rotonda - In Arcugnano: Villa Franceschini or Canera di Salasco - In Costoza di Longare: Villa Trento-Carli and Villa Garzadori-Da Schio - In Montegalda: La Deliziosa - In Barbano di Grisignano: Villa Ferramosca-Beggiato - In Vancimuglio: Villa Trissino-Muttoni - In Bretisina da Vicenza: Villa Ghislanzoni-Curti and Villa Marcello-Curti. **Open** All year.

When people mention Venetian villas, we think immediately of those that line the Brenta Canal. In fact, over a period of three centuries, more than 2,000 villas were built on all the hills near Venice.To explore those of the Berici mountains,take up residence in the Castello, a fine wine-growing estate which also produces olive oil, honey and grappa. The entrance way leads through the building directly into the garden which serves the castello in which lives Elda Marinoni, a farmhouse and an outbuilding which have been made over into apartments for rent. A pleasant entrance is hung with old photos that depict life in Barbarano at the turn of the century. The apartments are functional and comfortable. One can enjoy the large meadow that overlooks the little valley. There is also a romantic Italian-style garden at a lower level, planted with orange trees. The welcome is not effusive but very kind.

How to get there *(Map 4): 25km southeast of Vicenza. On highway A4 Vicenza-East exit towards Noventa as far as Ponte di Barbarano and Barbarano.*

Azienda A & G da Schio

36023 Costozza di Longare (Vicenza)
Piazza da Schio, 4
Tel. 0444-55 50 73 - Fax 0444-55 50 99 - Conte Giulio da Schio

Apartment 1 (10 pers.) with telephone, 3 bath, kitchen, 3 bedrooms, sitting room, TV. **Price** 2 800,000L/week. **Restaurant** In Vicenza, see p. 571. **Credit cards** Not accepted. **Pets** Dogs allowed. **Facilities** Garage. **Nearby** Venetian villas of the Berici mountains: Guiccioli Vlamarana, La Rotonda villas - At Arcugnagno: Villa Franceschini or Canera di Salasco (visit on request) - At Cosoza di Longare: Villa Trento-Carli and Villa Grzadori-Da Schio - At Montegalda: La Deliziosa - At Barban di Grisignano: Villa Ferramosca-Beggiato - At Vancimuglio: Villa Trissino-Muttoni - At Bretisina da Vicenza: Villa Ghislanzoni-Curti and Villa Marcello-Curti - Vicenza - Verona - Padua. **Open** All year.

If you dream of the villas of Vicenza, you will want to know that the village of Costozza alone has the Villa Trento-Carli, which is decorated with frescoes, some of which are attributed to Nicholas Poussin, and the Villa da Schio, famous for its age-old grotto, used as a wine cellar, as well as for its marvellous garden with its espaliers and for having housed the studio of the sculptor Marinali (1643-1720), whose statues decorate the finest of the villas. Recently, the Count da Schio has converted some former stables to make an apartment which can receive up to ten guests in great comfort. Much care has been given to fitting out the premises, while the family furniture and old prints lend charm to he house. The gardens and orchards are open and no one will complain if you want to have a barbecue. The surroundings are rich in historic sites, the nearest being the Eolia tavern in the village, the vaulted ceiling of which is decorated with 17th-century frescoes and which enjoys a constant temperature ensured by the nearby grottoes. A holiday adddress to share with friends.

How to get there *(Map 4): 11km southeast of Vicenza. On A4, exit Vicenza-East towards SS247 Riviera Berica. Costozza is 5km further on.*

Relais Ca' Masieri

Masieri 36070 Trissino (Vicenza)
Tel. 0445-490 122 - Fax 0445-490 455
Sig. Vassena
E-mail: camasieri@primopiano.it - Web: www.camasieri.com

Rooms 7 and 5 junior suites (9 with air-conditioning), telephone, bath, WC, TV, minibar. **Price** Single 120,000L, double 180,000L, junior suite 240,000L; extra bed 40,000L. **Meals** Breakfast 16,000L, served 7:30-11:00. **Restaurant** (Tel. 0445-96 21 00) Service 12:30PM-2:00PM, 7:30PM-10:00PM - mealtime specials 70-90,000L - Specialties: Insalata di capresante - Bigoli al torchio - Filetto bollito. **Credit cards** All major. **Pets** Dogs allowed. **Facilities** Swimming pool, parking. **Nearby** In Trissino: Park of the villa Marzotto, from Montecchio Maggiore, Castellodi (panorama), Bellaguardia and Castello della Villa, Romeo and Juliet's castle, Villa Cordellina-Lombard - Vicenza. **Closed** End Jan – beg Feb.

A little inn in countryside near Vicenza, known and appreciated primarily for its cooking and its wines. It will also make a pleasant stopover in your explorations of this region of Palladian art. The surroundings are calm, with soft rolling hills. Inside, it is very comfortable. The rooms, which are vast with with decor to suit every taste, have been intalled in the outbuildings; these were inspired by the style of the great Venetian architect Carlo Scarpa. The apartments, four quite recently added, are even larger and most have a terrace. Adjoining the hotel is an attractive restaurant where you can have delicious meals. The hospitality is courteous and pleasant; professionalism rules throughout.

How to get there *(Map 4): 20km northwest of Vicenza. On highway A4 Montecchio Maggiore exit, 15km towards Valdagno.*

Grand Hotel Duchi d'Aosta

34121 Trieste
Piazza Unità d'Italia, 2
Tel. 040-760 00 11 - Fax 040-36 60 92 - Sig.ra Hedy Benvenuti
E-mail: info@magesta.com - Web: www.magesta.com

Category ★★★★ **Rooms** 48 with air-conditioning and 2 suites with telephone, bath or shower, WC, TV, minibar – Elevator. **Price** Single 340,000, double 456,000L, suite 920,000L. **Meals** Breakfast included, served 7:00-10:30. **Restaurant** Service 12:30PM-2:30PM, 7:30PM-10:30PM - mealtime specials, also à la carte - Specialties: Seafood. **Credit cards** All major. **Pets** Dogs allowed. **Facilities** Garage (37,000L), parking. **Nearby** Trieste (Piazza dell'Unita, Roman theater, Cathedral of S. Giusto, the port) - Castello di Miramare - Grotta Gigante - Church of Monrupino - Extending the trip to include Yugoslavia: Lipizza stud, Basilica at Porec, caves of Postojna. **Open** All year.

Like the rest of the town of Trieste, the Hotel Duchi d'Aosta has the nostalgic charm of one of those places with a fabulous history, which is now overlooked. It is a palace from another century, where you might expect to see some rich Austro-Hungarian family with its entourage, stopping off for an evening on the way to Venice, enter one of the plush salons. It is an excellent hotel with vast, pleasant rooms, equipped with every modern convenience. The service is in the fine and all too rare tradition of the international hotels of yesteryear. The trilingual personnel is omnipresent, attentive, friendly, discreet and efficient. The restaurant is also excellent. The hotel is right in the center of the old part of Trieste, only a few minutes away from the fort.

How to get there *(Map 5): Via A4, Trieste-Costiera exit.*

RESTAURANTS

Maratea

- **Taverna Rovita**, via Rovita 13 - tel. (0973) 876 588 - Closed Nov. 1 – Mar. 15 - 35-50,000L. A pretty restau-

rant on a narrow street in the historical center of Maratea. It serves regional cuisine, has a good wine cellar.

Fiumicello

5km from Maratea
- **La Quercia** - tel. (0973) 876 907 - Closed October 1 – Easter - 30-40,000L. It Serves seafood and traditional regional Italian cuisine in a romantic atmosphere. Meals are served in a rustic but elegant dining room, or in the garden in the shade of the big oak tree. - **Za' Mariuccia**, on the port - tel. (0973) 876 163 - Closed Thursday except in the summer and from December to February - 50-80,000L. Wide variety of fish specialties.

Matera

- **Il Terrazzino**, Bocconcino II, vico San Giuseppe 7 - tel. (0835) 332 503

- Closed Tuesday - 40,000L. The town's amazing vestiges of the Troglodyte period are worth seeing. Terrazzino is a great place to stop in for a family meal. Matera has some of the best bread in Italy. - **Trattoria Lucana**, via Lucana 48 - tel. (0835) 336 117 - Closed Sunday from September 1 to 15 - 35,000L. Two brothers carry on the regional culinary tradition with passionate enthusiasm.

LOCAL SPECIALTIES
- **Il Buongustaio**, piazza Vittorio Veneto 1 - It features smoked ham from Lauria, Picerno, and Palazzo San Gervasio, and the *Aglianico* wine.

Potenza

- **Taverna Oraziana**, via Orazio Flacco 2 - tel. (0971) 21 851 - Closed Sunday, August - 40-50,000L. This classic restaurant has long been the haunt of town notables who come for rich hearty regional cuisine. *Aglianico dei Vulture* is a good local wine.

Altomonte

- **Barbieri**, via San Nicolas 32 - tel. (0981) 948 072 - A famous restaurant, regional cooking.

LOCAL SPECIALTIES
- **Bottega di Casa Barbieri**, has a very good selection of regional prod-

ucts such as the *Ciro classico*, one of the best wines of Calabria.

Cosenza

- **Da Giocondo**, via Piave 53 - tel. (0984) 29 810 - Closed Sunday, August - 30-50,000L. It is very small, so reservations are a must.

Castrovillari

- **La Locanda di Alia**, via Jetticelle 69 - tel. (0981) 46 370 - Closed Sunday - 50-70,000L. It is located a few miles from the ancient Greek town of Sibari, and serves traditional Calabrian cuisine in a very lovely decor.

Reggio di Calabria

- **Bonaccorso**, via Nino Bixio 5 - tel. (0965) 896 048 - Closed Monday, August - 45-60,000L. Italian and French cuisine with some Calabrian specialties, *fettucine, cinzia, semifreddi*. - **Conti**, via Giulia 2 - tel. (0965) 29 043 - Closed Monday - 45-60,000L. It has 2 rooms, one is elegant, the other more casual with a piano bar. - **Caffé Arti e Mestieri**, via Emilia S. Pietro 16 - tel. (0522) 432

202 - Closed Sunday, Monday, Christmas Day and New Year's Day - 40-60,000L. Both a bar and a restaurant, with service on the terace in summer. - **La Cupola**, via Santi 13 - tel. (0522) 337 010 - Closed Monday and in January and August - 60-100,000L. Fish and seafood restaurant. Reservation essential.

Gallina

2km from Reggio di Calabria
- **La Collina dello Scoiattolo**, via Provinciale 34 - tel. (0965) 682 255 - Closed Wednesday, November - 35-40,000L. There is an avalanche of *antipasti, penne all'imbriacata* and very good desserts, in pleasant surroundings, but it is always overcrowded.

Soverato

- **Il Palazzo**, Corso Umberto I 40 - tel. (0967) 25 336 - Closed Monday, November - 40,000L. Old very well restored and tastefully decorated palace and features regional cuisine. In the summer, meals are served in the garden.

Catanzaro Lido

- **La Brace**, 102 via Melito di Porto Salvo, tel. (0961) 31 340 - Closed Monday, July - 40-60,000L. A pretty restaurant with a panoramic view on the Gulf of Squillace, fine cuisine (spaghetti with zucchini flowers, octopus ravioli, homemade pie) and a good selection of Calabrian wine.

Napoli / Naples

- **La Sacrestia**, via Orazio 116 - tel. (081) 7611051 - Closed Monday, August - 70-100,000L. People come here religiously for its elegant simplicity, very good cuisine, and great Campanian wines. - **Ciro a Mergellina**, via Mergellina, 21 - tel. (081) 68 17 80 - Closed Monday, Friday from July 15 to August 25. Find the push-cart vender wandering on the boardwalk, and try his *Ostrecaro Ficico* and other seafood specialties. - **Amici Miei**, via Monte di Dio 78 - tel. (081)

764 60 63 - Closed Sunday, Monday, August - 40,000L. Has good traditional family-style cuisine and a friendly atmosphere. - **Ciro a Santa Brigida**, via Santa Brigida 71 - tel.

(081) 552 40 72 - Closed Sunday, Christmas, August 15-31 - 60,000L. People come here to enjoy simple authentic Neopolitan cuisine. - **I Primi**, via Margellina 1 - tel. (081) 761 61 08 - Closed Sunday, May - 45,000L. Mediteranean cooking. - **Don Salvatore**, via Mergellina 5 - tel. (081) 681 817 - Closed Wednesday, June - 50,000L. Unmissable for pizza - which does not mean excluding other

Neapolitan specialties and fish. - **Bellini**, via Santa Maria di Costantinopoli 80 - tel. (081) 459 774 - Closed Wednesday, August - 45,000L. Has good pizza and other Neopolitan specialties. - **Giuseppone a Mare**, via F. Russo 13 - tel. (081) 575 60 02 - Closed Monday, Christmas and New Year - 25-40,000L. Typically Neopolitan restaurant in an inlet in Posilippe which serves seafood specialties. - **Dante et Beatrice**, piazza Dante 44 - tel. (081) 549 94 38. Typical Neopolitan trattoria. - **Al Poeta**, piazza Giacomo, 134, is the in restaurant for young Neopolitans. - **A'Fenestrella**, Calata Ponticello a Marcechiaro - tel.

(081) 769 00 20 - Closed Sunday, for middaymeals in August and in the second fortnight in August - 40-60,000L. Balcony overlooking the sea.

Santa Lucia and Borgo Marinari

- **Bersagliera**, Borgo Marino - tel. (081) 764 60 16, faces the Castel dell'Ovo, on the small port of Santa Lucia. It is is famous, so you must reserve. - **La Cantinella**, via Cuma 42 - tel. (081) 764 86 84 - Closed Sun., Aug. 13-31, Christmas and New Year - 45-90,000L. It has a nice view on Vesuvius and serves elegant cuisine in the great Neopolitan tradition.

CAFFE'-BARS

- **Scaturchio**, piazza San Domenico Maggiore - Closed Thursday. The best place to try real traditional rum cake and *brevettata* (chocolate cake) Bar Marino, via dei Mille, 57. - **Gambrinus**, via Chiaia 1, is an old Neopolitan cafe, once closed down by the fascist regime and transformed into a bank,

now restored in the finest tradition. - **Caffe' Latino**, Gradini di Chiesa, 57, the best *espresso*. - **Bilancione**, via Posillipo, 238 - Closed Wednesday, the best ice creams in Naples.

LOCAL SPECIALTIES, CRAFTS

- **Pintauro**, via S. M. di Constanti-

nopoli and vico d'Affuto, has made *sfogliatelle*, a specialty of the house since 1848. - **Light**, via Chiaia, 275, is a coral boutique. - **Marinella**, via Chiaia, 287 is where you can find the same silk ties as Don Corleone!

Pompeii

- **Il Principe**, piazza B. Longo 8 - tel. (081) 850 55 66 - Closed Mon., Aug. 1-15 - 50-70,000L. You will find only the best, the most elegant, and the most expensive here. - **Zi Caterina**, via Roma - Closed Tues., June 28 – July 8 - 30-50,000L, more traditional and less expensive.

Caserta

- **Antica Locanda-Massa 1848**, via Mazzini, 55 - tel. (0823) 321 268 - Serves regional specialties, with service in the garden in the summer. It is only about thirty kilometers from Naples. Don't miss the Palazzo Reale and the Parco-Giardino in Caserta.

CASERTA VECCHIA (10 KM AWAY)
- **La Castellana**, Closed Thursday - 20-50,000L - It is rustic, regional, and has a cool terrace in the summer.

Capri

CAPRI:
- **La Capannina**, via Le Botteghe 12b - tel. (081) 8370 732 - Closed Wed., Nov. 7 – Mar. 15 except for Chrismast Holidays - 50-75,000L. It is elegant and serves very good fish from Capri. - **La Pigna**, via Roma 30 - tel. (081) 837 0280 - Closed Tues. in low season, Oct. 15 – Easter - 50-60,000L. It has been a wine bar since 1876, and is today one of the most popular restaurants on the

island. It has an elegant room, a beautiful garden with lemon trees, and a view on the Bay of Naples. - **Luigi**, ai Faraglioni - tel. (081) 837 0591 - Closed Oct. – Easter - 60-80,000L. It has good cuisine, a flower-covered terrace, and a great view. Take a walk to the Faraglioni, the famous rocks across from Capri, a half an hour away on foot, or go there by boat from Marina Piccola. - **Pizzeria Aurora**, via Fuorlovado 18 - tel. (081) 837 0181 - Closed Tues., Dec. 10 – Mar. 10 - 40-50,000L. Excellent cuisine by Peppino.

Anacapri

- **Da Gelsomina**, at Migliara 72 (30 min on foot) - tel. (081) 837 14 99 - Closed Tues. in low season, Feb. 1-15. You can see the sea and the gulf from the terrace through the vineyards and the olive trees.

CRAFTS

- **Capri Flor**, via Tragara, is a nursery. Capri will make you start dreaming about gardens, and **Carthusia**, via Matteotti 2, will about perfumes. - **Massimo Godericci** offers a large selection of pottery and fine Italian china.

Ischia

ISCHIA PONTE
- **Giardini Eden**, via Nuova Portaromana - tel. (081) 993 9091 - Closed the evening, Oct.-Apr. - 40-50,000L. Away from the hordes of tourists, come have a quiet lunch and enjoy good southern Italian cuisine in this garden full of exotic flowers. - **Gennaro**, via Porto - tel. 992 917, has a convivial, typical atmosphere.

Ischia-forio

- **Umberto a Mare**, via Soccorso 2 - tel. 081 99 7171 - Sea foods eaten on a wide terrace overlooking the sea. Pleasant atmosphere. - **La Bussols**, via Marina 40 - tel. 081 997645 - Wide choice of fresh grilled fish, friendly welcome and good value for money.
BAGNO-LIDO PORTO-D'ISCHIA
- **Alberto**, tel. 981 259 - Closed Mon. evening, Nov. – Mar. - 40,000L. This friendly trattoria has a veranda on the beach, regional cuisine, and good house wine by the pitcher.

Ravello

- **Palazzo della Marra**, via della Marra 7 - tel. 089 858302 - Closed Tues. except from Apr. to Oct. - 30-50,000L. Very popular in the evening. - **Garden**, via Boccaccio 4 - tel. (089) 857 226 - Closed Tues. in the winter - 30-45,000L. In the summer, you can dine on the picturesque terrace with a view on the gulf.

Sorrento

- **O Parrucchiano**, Corso Italia 71 - tel. (081) 878 13 21 - Closed Wed. in the winter - 35-50,000L. It has been the "must-see" of Sorrento for more than a century now. Be sure to end your meal with a *limoncello*, the liquor of the house. - **Il Glicine**, via Sant'Antonio 2 - tel. (081) 877 2519 - Closed Wed. off season, Jan. 15 – Mar. 1 - 30-50,000L. Elegant, friendly, reservations necessary - **La Pentolaccia**, via Fuorimura 25 - tel. (081) 878 5077 - Closed Thurs. - 35,000L. A classic restaurant in the heart of town serving traditional cuisine.

CRAFTS

- **Handkerchiefs**, via Luigi di Maio 28. Sells beautiful handkerchiefs, one of the specialties of Sorrento, monogrammed to your specifications.

Sant'Agata Sui Due Golfi

9 km from Sorrento

- **Don Alfonso 1890**, piazza Sant'Agata - tel. (081) 878 0026 - Closed Mon. in high season, Tues. in low season - 70-95,000L. It is the best restaurant in Campania, and in Italy, superbly located on a little hill between Sorrento and Amalfi, featuring traditional cuisine made with produce fresh from the market.

Vico Equense

- **Pizza A Metro Da Gigino**, via Nicotera 10 - tel. (081) 879 8426 - 35,000L, has a wide selection of delicious pizzas and local specialties.

Salerno

- **Vicolo della Neve**, Vicolo dell

Neve 24 - tel. (089) 225 705 - Closed Wed., Christmas - 30,000L. Despite its name, it is not a pizzaria, and serves fine local traditional cuisine made with fresh produce from the grounds. - **Al Fusto d'Oro**, via Fieravecchia 29, unpretentious pizzeria and seafood dishes - **La Brace**, lungomare Trieste 11 - tel. 225 159 - Closed Sun. and from Dec. 20 to 31 - 40-60,000L. - **Il Caminetto**, via Roma 232 - tel. 089 22 96 14 - Closed Wed. - 40,000L. Real pizza and an excellent menu of good local products, well-prepared.

Paestum

- **Nettuno**, closed in the evening, and Mon. except July, Aug., Christmas - 30-50,000L. It is on the archaeological site and has a lovely dining room and terrace with a view on the temples.

Palinoro

- **Da Carmelo**, in Iscia - tel. (0974) 931 138 - Closed Wed. out of season, and mid-Oct. to mid-Nov. - 45,000L. On the coast towards Matera, a halt not to be missed. It has a rustic dining room, a pretty verdant garden, and traditional cuisine with seafood specialties.

Positano

- **Chez Black**, via Brigantino 19 - tel. (089) 875 036 - Closed Januar 7-Februar 7 - 35-45,000L. Is a charming place near the beach, serving pizzas, grilled fish, and spaghetti - **Da Constantino**, via Corvo 95 - tel. (089) 875 738 - Closed November 1- December 31 - 20,000L. Is 5 km from Positano, and has a marvelous view on the sea. A minibus will take you to the restaurant. Reservations are a must in the summer. - **San Pietro**, via Laurito 2, 2km from Positano - tel. (089) 875 455 - Dinner on the terrace perched on a rocky crag is magic. The view is sublime and the cuisine delicious

Praiano

9km from Positano
- **La Brace**, via G. Capriglione - tel. (089) 874226 - Open March 15-October 15 - Closed Wednesday in low season. You can enjoy a superb view of Posiatno and the *faraglioni* of Capri from the terrace.

Amalfi

- **Da Gemma**, via Cavalieri di Malta - tel. (089) 871 345 - Closed Tuesday, Jan. 15-Feb. 15 - 35-45,000L. The

best old restaurant where you can have delicious Neopolitan specialties such as *genovese*, along with good regional wines - **Il Tari'**, via Capuano - tel. (089) 871 832 - Closed Tuesday, Nov. - 40-70,000L. Good seafood specialties. - **La Caravella**, via M. Camera - tel. (089) 871 029 - Closed Tuesday and Nov. 40-70,000L. Here is another classic Amalfi address. Reservations are required.

Bologna

- **I Carracci**, via Manzoni 2 - tel. (051) 270 815 - Closed Sun., Aug. - 60-80,000L. It features fine cuisine for elegant suppers. - **Il Battibecco**, via Battibecco 4 - tel. (051) 223 298 - Closed Sun. between Christmas and New Year's Day, Aug. 10-20 - 60-90,000L. It has delicious risottos, spaghetti with clams, and roast beef pie. - **Il Bitone**, via Emilia Levante 111 - tel. (051) 546 110 - Closed Mon., Tues., Aug. - 50-80,000L. The favorite restaurant of the Bolognese. There is a large garden where you can have tea in the summer - **Torre de'**

Galluzzi', corte de' Galluzzi 5-A - tel. (051) 267 638. Located inside the old tower, fine meat and fish dishes - **Diana**, via Indipendenza 24 - tel. (051) 231 302 - Closed Mon., Aug. - 50,000 L. A traditional restaurant with classic cuisine - **Rodrigo**, via della Zecca 2-h - tel. 220 445 - Closed Sun., Aug. 4-24. Excelent. - **Rosteria Da Luciano**, via Nazario Sauro 19 - tel. (051) 231 249 - Closed Wed., Aug., Christmas and New Year - 35-60,000L. One of the best restaurants in Bologna, reservation. - **Anna Maria**, via delle Belle Arti 17 - tel. (051) 266 894 - Closed Mon., Aug. 1-20 - 45,000L. Here they celebrate la *cucina povera*, quality not calories.

Only one menu, but you won't be disappointed by the choice imposed on you. - **Rostaria Antico Brunetti**, via Caduti di Cefalonia 5 - tel. (051) 234 441 - 40,000L. A very old restaurant with delicious pasta, and good *lambrusco*. - **Antica Trattoria del Cacciatore**, Casteldebole - tel. (051) 564 203 Closed Sun. evening, Mon., Aug., Jan. - 50,000 L. Located west of Bologna, it is a rustic but very chic trattoria, with fine cuisine.

LOCAL SPECIALTIES

- **Bottega del vino Olindo Faccioli**, via Altabella 15/B, large selection of wines. Among Emilian wines, try the young and bubbly *Lambrusco*, and the *Sangiovese*. - **Salsamenteria**

Tamburini, via Caprarie 1, features ham from Parma, *mortadelle* and *culatello*, reputed to be the best Italian salami. - **Casa della Sfoglia**, via Rialto 4. Here they make traditional Bolognese pasta and tagliatelles, invented, legend has it, for the wedding of Lucrecia Borgia and the Duke of Ferrara in 1487.

Imola
30km from Bologna
- **San Domenico**, via Sacchi 1 - tel. (0542) 29 000 - Closed Monday, January 1-13, end-July to end-August - 90-130,000L. Gourmets from all over the world come here for the San Domenico pilgrimage as well as for this restaurant's ingenious interpretation of regional Italian cuisine.

Brisighella
- **La Grotta**, via Metelli 1 - tel. (0546) 81 829 - Closed Tuesday, January - 30-70,000L. La Grotta shares the gastrionomic honors of this very pretty little town with **Gigiolé**, piazza Carducci 5 - tel. (0546) 81 209 - Closed Monday -

Trust in Tarcisio Raccagni who will advise you in your choice of one of the menus that have made the name of his restaurant.

Ferrara
- **Grotta Azzurra**, piazza Sacrati 43 - tel. (0532) 209 152 - Closed Wednesday, Sunday evenings, January 2-10, August 1-15 - 45,000L. The decor is Mediterranean, but the cuisine is traditional northern Italian, with some Emilian specialties. - **La Provvidenza**, corso Ercole I d'Este 92 - tel. (0532) 205 187 - Closed Monday, August 11-17 - 40-60,000L. The interior resembles a farmhouse with a little garden full of regular customers. You will need a reservation.
- **Quel Fantastico Giovedi**, via Castelnuovo 9 - tel. (0532) 76 05 70 - Closed Wednesday and July 10 to the last 10 days in January - Menu: 25,000L (lunch), 45,000L (diner).

Unsure what to call his restaurant, Marco gave it the name of the Steinbeck novel he was reading at the time. Since that day in 1985, his set menu has always been a great success, so reserve in advance. - **Enoteca Al Brindisi**, via degli Adelardi II. The Guinness Book of World Records says this is the oldest tavern in the world. Benvenuto Cellini, the Titien was said to have frequented this "Hostaria del Chinchiolino". There are wine tastings and wine is also sold here. - **Centrale**, via Boccaleone 8 - tel. 0532-306 735 - Closed Sunday and Wednesday evening, July 20 to August 20 - 20-50,000 L - Terrace

Argenta

34km from Ferrara

- **Il Trigabolo**, piazza Garibaldi 4 - tel. (0532) 804 121 - Closed Sunday evening, Monday - 100-130,000L. A good place to enjoy fine cuisine in Emilia-Romagna.

Modena

- **Bianca**, via Spaccini 24 - tel. (059) 311 524 - Closed Saturday at noon, Sunday, August, Christmas, New Year - 45-65,000L. You will like this tratto-

ria and the authentic cuisine served here. - **Fini**, rua Frati Minori 54 - tel. (059) 223 314 - Closed Monday, Tuesday, August, Christmas - 80-100,000L. Fini's *tortellini* and *zamponi* are almost as famous as the Ferraris of Modena. - **Hostaria Giusti**, vivolo Squallore 46 - tel.

(059) 222 553 - Open only at noon, diner only on request - Closed Sunday, Monday, November, December, August - 50,000L. A few tables at the back of the famous salumeria Giusti, for you to taste the shop's Emilian cuisine.

Ravenna

- **Al Gallo**, via Maggiore 87 - tel. 0544-213 775 - Closed Sunday evening, Monday, Tuesday. Christmas,

Easter - 50,000L. The trattoria had been in this fine building with its cortiletto and pergola, for almost a hundred years, so its reputation is well-established. Reserve. - **Tre Spade**, via Faentina 136 - tel. (0544) 500 5222 - Closed Sunday nights, Monday, August - 50-70,000L. It features Italian cuisine from different provinces in a pretty decor. - **La Gardèla**, via Ponte Marino 3 - tel. (0544) 217 147 - Closed Thursday,

August 10-25. It serves savory cuisine. - **Enoteca Ca' de Ven**, via Ricci 24 - Closed Monday. This wine bar in an old palace offers wine tasting and sales, and light meals.

Parma

- **La Greppia**, via Garibaldi 39 - tel.

(0521) 233 686 - Closed Monday, Tuesday, July - 50-70,000L. Near the Opera, and has very good Italian cuisine and a cheery decor. Reservations

are recommended - **L'Angiol d'Or**, vicolo Scutellari 1 - tel. (0521) 282 632 - Closed Sunday, Christmas, August 14-15, January 10-20. At the corner of the piazza del Duomo - You can enjoy savory cuisine and the illuminated baptistry at night in this elegant restaurant - 65,000L - **Gallo d'Oro**, Borgo della Salina 3 - tel. (0521) 208 846 - Closed Sunday. A tavern. Try their famous *culatello de Parme, maltaglioti,* and *tortellini.* -

Croce di Malta, Borgo Palmia - tel. 0521-235 643. A small restaurant with innovative cuisine and a terrace

in the summer. - **La Filoma**, via XX Marzo 15 - tel. (0521) 234 269 - Closed Sunday, August - 50-70,000L.

One of our favorites with an intimate atmosphere and personalized regional cuisine. - **Il Cortile**, borgo Paglia 3 - tel. 0521-285 779 - Closed Sunday, Monday noon, August 1-22 - 30-50,000L. Reservations are recommended. - **Vecchio Molinetto**, viale Milazzo 39 - tel. 0521-526 72. Traditional trattoria.

AROUND PARMA

Sacca di Colorno, 15km from Parma
- **Le Stendhal** - tel. (0521) 815 493 - Closed Tuesday, January 1-15, July 20-August 10. If you are following the footsteps of Fabrice del Dongo, try the Stendhal.

NOCETO, 14km from Parma
- **Aquila Romana**, via Gramsci 6 - tel. (0521) 62 398 - Closed Monday, Tuesday, 15 July 15-August 15, 30-50,000L. An old postal inn, famous for its regional specialties inspired by old recipes.

BUSSETO, 35km from Parma
- **Ugo**, via Mozart 3. Country atmosphere.

POLESINE PARMENSE, Santa Franca 6km from Busseto
- **Da Colombo** - tel. (0524) 98 114 - Closed Monday evening, Tuesday, January, July 20- August 10 - 40,000L. It is famous, so you'd better reserve.

ZIBELLO, 10km from Busseto
- **Trattoria La Buca** - tel. (0524) 99 214 - Closed Monday evening, Tuesday, July 1-15 - 45,000L. It is very popular, so you will need a reservation.

BERCETO, 50km from Parma
- **Da Rino**, piazza Micheli 11 - tel. (525) 64 306 - Closed Monday, December 20-February 15 - 45,000L. The masters of the mushroom in season, and of ravioli of all sorts year round.

Reggio nell'Emilia
- **5 Pini-da-Pelati**, viale Martiri di Cervarolo 46 - tel. (0522) 5536 63 - Closed Tuesday evening, Wednesday, August 1-20 - 45-70,000L - **La Zucca**, piazza Fontanesi 1/L - tel. 0522-437 222 - Closed Sunday, January 5-12, August. - **Enoteca Il Pozzo**, viale Allegri 6/A. It has wine tasting and sales, and a restaurant with garden.

Santarcangelo di Romagna
- **Osteria La Sangiovese**, via Saffi 27 - tel. 0541 620 710 - Closed at midday and on Modnays, Christmas and New Year - 45,000L. Cooking and atmosphere of Romagna. - **Osteria della Violina**, vicolo Denzi 3/5 - tel. 0541 6720 416 - Closed on Wednesday and from August 6 to 22 - 35,000L. Choose the ground-floor dining room where local food is served in a more rustic atmosphere.

Roma / Rome

Near Villa Borghèse

- **Il Caminetto**, viale Parioli 89 - tel. (06) 808 3946 - Closed Thurs., Aug. - 50,000L. Success has not spoiled the quality of this restaurant.

Near Pantheon

- **La Campana**, vicolo della Campana 18 - tel. (06) 686 7820 - Closed Mon., Aug. - 45-55,000L. One of the oldest, if not the oldest trattoria of the capital, with good Roman cuisine and good house wine. - **Il Bacaro**, via degli Spagnoli 27 - tel. (06) 686 4110 - Closed Sun. - 60,000L. Has an elegant bistro decor. - **L'Eau Vive**, via Monterone 85 - tel. (06) 688 01 095 - Closed Sun., Aug. - 50-70,000L. Missionary sisters serve their specialties every day. - **La Rosetta**, via della Rosetta 9 - tel. (06) 686 1002 - Closed Sat. noon, Sun., Aug. - 80-100,000L - Is well known for its fish specialties. - **Papà Giovanni ai Sediari**, via dei Sediari 4/5 - tel. 06 68 80 48 07 - Closed Sun. and in Aug. - 80 000 L. Between Palazzo Madama and the Pantheon, a very old Hostaria. Tradition and Roman nouvelle cuisine in the fine dining room with its display of the many wines on offer. The same building hosues a *tavola calda* which, "Mare e Vino", which sells high-class snacks at any time. - **Trattoria al Panthéon**, vial del Panthéon 55 - tel. (06)

679 27 88.

Near Piazza di Spagna

- **Nino**, via Borgognona 11 - tel. (06) 679 5676 - Closed Sun. - 50,000L. Near the stairs of the Piazza di Spagna, it is frequented by local artists and writers who come here for Tuscan specialties and the "Mont Blanc", a house dessert. - **Osteria Margutta**, via Margutta 82 - tel. (06) 679 8190 - Closed Sun. - 40,000L. Friendly trattoria with a nice atmosphere, very close to the Piazza di Spagnanice, closed Sundays. There are many galleries and antique shops on this street where Fellini used to live. - **Da Mario**, via delle Vite - tel. (06) 678 38 18 - Closed Sun. and Aug. - 50,000L - Tuscany cooking. - **Alfredo l'Originale**, piazza Augusto Imperatore 30 - tel. (06) 678 10 72. Typical, reservation.

Near piazza del Popolo

- **Gusto**, piazza Augusto Imperatore 10 - tel. 06 322 62 73 - In a very lovely New York penthouse decor, plus all the refinement of Italian design, you will find under the same roof a pizzeria, a wine merchant, a bookshop and a wine bar. Well placed near to the Mausoleum of Augustus, it can be reached from Piazza di Spagna and the via dei Condotti and from Piazza del Popolo by via del Corso. - **Dal Bolognese**, piazza del Popolo 1/2 - tel. 06 361 14 26 - A good restaurant, chic and stylish, where the food is served on the terrace as soon as the weather allows.

Near Piazza Navona

- **Pino e Dino**, piazza di Montevecchio 22 - tel. (06) 686 1319 Closed Mon., Aug. - 70,000L. Is an intimate place near the Piazza Navona, hidden behind heavy curtains on this Renaissance square so dear to Raphael and Bramante, where Lucrecia Borgia formented numerous intrigues. Reservations are necessary. - **Majella**, 45 piazza Sant' Appolinare 45 - tel. (06) 65 64 174 - Closed Sun. The restaurant is in a beautiful old house, and features. - **Trattoria della Pace**, via della Pace 1 - tel. 06-686 48 02 - For a typical trattoria.

Near Piazza di Trevi

- **Al Moro**, vic. delle Bollette 13 - tel. (06) 67 83 495 - Typically Italian trattoria. Reservation.

Near Terme di Caracalla

- **Checcino dal 1887**, Via Monte Tes-

taccio 30 - tel. (06) 574 38 16 - Closed Sunday evening, Monday, August, Christmas - 60-80,000L. A old vaulted dining room where they serve typical Roman cooking; specialty: *coda alla vaccinara*; very good cellar.

Near Piazza del Campidoglio and Teatro di Marcello

- **Vecchia Roma**, Via della tribuna di Campitelli - tel. (06) 686 46 04 - Closed Wednesday, August 10-25 - 50-60,000L. Roman specialties and fish. - **Da Giggetto**, via del Portico d'Ottavia 21/a - tel. (06) 686 11 05. Typical - Patio.

Near Janicule

- **Antica Pesa,** via Garibaldi 8 - tel. (06) 58 09 236 - Closed Sunday - You can dine in the room decorated with frescoes painted by artist-customers, or else by candlelight on the patio. Specialty of the house: *rittico di pastasciutta.*

Near Piazza Barberini

- **Il Giardino**, 29 via Zucchelli - Closed Monday. Is one of the best trattorias in town, with low prices. - **La Carbonara**, piazza Campo dei Fiori - tel. (06) 68 64 783 - Closed Tuesday. One of the most beautiful market places in Rome, featuring fish specialties. - **El Tartufo**, vicolo Sciarra - tel. (06) 678 02 26 - Closed Sunday. An authentic place. The *Navone* meal is a true delight.

Dinners in the Trastevere

- **Romolo**, via di Porta Settimania - tel. (06) 581 8284 - Closed Monday, August. Dine by candlelight in the garden Raphael used to visit. The interior is also has charm and atmosphere. - **Sabatini I**, piazza Santa Maria in Trastevere 10 - tel. (06) 581 2026 - Closed Wednesday and twoweeks in August - 60,000L. It is the most famous and popular restaurant in the Trastevere. If it is full, you can always try the **Sabatini II**, vicolo di Santa Maria in Trastevere 18 - tel. (06) 581 8307 - **Checco er Carettiere**, via Benedetta 10 - tel. (06) 581 70 18 - Closed Sunday evening, Monday, August, New Year - 50-75,000L - An osteria typical of the Trastevere with a decor reminiscent of the time when the *carettieri* came here, and very good Roman cuisine with old recipes. - **La Tana de Noiantri**, via della Paglia 13 - Closed Tuesday. Friendly and inexpensive, with simple cuisine and tables on the sidewalk in the summer. - **Alberto Ciarla**, piazza San Cosimato - tel. (06) 581 86 68 - Closed at noon, Sunday, 1-15 August, 1-13 January - 70-90,000L. Intimate, on the terrace in summer. Reservation.

PIZZERIAS

- **Pizzeria Berninetta**, via Pietro Cavallini 14 - tel. (06) 360 3895 - Closed Monday, August, open only in the evening - 25,000L is also very popular, a good place for pizza, *crostini*, and pasta. - **Pizzeria Da Fieramosca ar Fosso**, piazza de Mercanti 3 - tel. (06) 589 0289 - Closed Sunday - Open only in the evening - 20-30,000L. The best pizzeria in the Trastevere. - **Pizzeria San Marco**, via Taano 29 - tel. (06) 687 8494 - Closed Wednesday, August - 20,000L. It has fine, crisp Roman pizza and a clientele of Roman yuppies who won't think twice about having champagne with their pizza. There is a good selection of wines

too. - **Ivo a Trastevere**, via di San Francesco a Ripa 150. Delicious pizzas in a tiny room.

CAFFE' - BARS
near the piazza Navona

- **Tre Scalini**, piazza Navona, is across from the Bernin fountain, and has the

best *granita di caffe, tartufo* and *triumfo*. - **Cul de Sac**, piazza di Pasquino73, behind the piazza Navona - a delightful wine bar, with good Roman and French cooking and a very wide choice of wines - **Antico Caffe' della Pace**, via della Pace 6, has a turn of the century artistic atmosphere, and is frequented in the evening by a hip intellectual crowd. - **Enoteca Navona**, piazza Navona offers wine tasting and *crostini*.

near the via Veneto
- **Gran Caffe' Doney**, via Veneto 39, was born in Florence in 1822, moved to Rome in 1884 and to the Via Veneto in 1946. Coctails, salads, and pastries are served here. - **Harry's Bar**, via Veneto 148. Like its brothers, it is chic and elegant.

near the piazza del Popolo
- **Casina Valadier**, Pincio, Villa Borghese. The chic terrace restaurant is a great

good cocktails and fine ice cream when the weather gets warm. - **Caffe' Rosati**, piazza del Popolo, serves sandwiches and pastries. The large terrace has been completely overrun.

near the piazza di Spagna

- **Caffe' Greco**, via Conditi 86. Casanova mentioned this place in his memoirs, and Stendhal, Goethe, D'Annunzio, and De Chirico... have all been here. You can have small sandwhiches in a nice Napoleon III-style decor. Try the *paradiso*, a house specialty - **Babington's english tea room**, on the Piazza di Spagna - The other institution of this square since it was opened by two English sisters in 1893. For tea all'inglese. - **Dolci e Doni**, via delle carrozze 85, for its cioccolatini, made on the day you eat them... - **Grand Caffé le Caffetiera**, via Margutta 61a - Decor in the grand manner, with refined service for a light lunch. - **Le Cornacchie**, piazza Rondanini. This place has style, an upbeat friendly atmosphere, and family-style cuisine.

THE BEST CAPPUCCINO: **Caffe' San Eustachio**, piazza San Eustachio La Tazza d'Oro, via degli Orfani, near the piazza del Pantheon.

THE BEST GELATI: **Giolitti**, Offici del Vicario 40.

THE OLDEST BAKERY IN ROME: **Valzani**, via del Moro 37.

SHOPPING

- **Gamarelli**, via Santa Chiara 34 - Closed Saturday - Sells religious accessories. Lay people come here to buy their famous socks, violet for bishops, and red for cardinals - **La Stelletta**, via delle Stelletta 4 - Is great for costme jewelry. - **Aldo Fefe**, via delle Stelleta 20b - Closed Sat. - Sells beautiful cardboard boxes. - **Papirus**, via Capo le case - Has a large selection of elegant stationery. - **Libreria antiquaria Cascianelli**, largo Febo 14 - Is specialized in old and modern works on Rome, across from the **Hotel Raphaël Limentani**, via Portico d'Ottavia 25 is in the old ghetto, in a basement, and offers a wide selection of household linens. - **Ai Monasteri**, corso Rinascimento 72 - Sells liquors, elixirs, and other products produced by monastic orders, in a beautiful Neo-Gothic decor. - **Trimani Wine Bar**, via Cernaia 37-B - Is a good place for tasting and buying fine Italian food products. - **Antique Shops** via del Babbuino, via dei Coronari, in the Corso Emanuele distric.

NEARBY ROMA

Tivoli

- **Le Cinque Statue**, via Quintilio Varo 1 - tel. (0774) 20 366 - Stop in while visiting the Villa d'Este gardens in Tivoli. - **Sibella**, via della Sibella 50 - tel. (0774) 20281 - 45,000L. Has the same beautiful interior and garden which Chateaubriand admired in 1803.

Villa Adriana

- **Albergo Ristorante Adriano** - tel. (0774) 382 235 - Closed Sun. evening - Has terra cotta walls, Corinthian columns decorating the interior, and a beautiful shady garden in the summer, a nice place to relax after visiting Hadrian's villa.

Frascati, 22km from Roma
- **Cacciani**, via Armando Diaz 13 - tel. (06) 9420 378 - Closed Mon., Jan. 7-17, August 17-27- 50,000L. Thirty years of great Roman cooking, delicious house wine and a beautiful terrace in the summer make this place well worth the trip. - **Cantina Comandini**, via E. Filiberto - Closed Sun. A good place to buy wine and has a nice wine bar. - **Pasticceria Renato Purificato**, piazza del Mercato or Bar degli Specchi , via Battisti 3 - Try the lady-shaped *biscottini*. - **Villa Simone**, via Toricella 2 at Monteporzio Catone. You will find the best *Frascati* of the region and very good olive oil here.

Castel Gandolfo, 22km from Roma
- **Sor Campana**, corso della Repubblica - Closed Mon. -Is one of the oldest restaurants of the region.

Anagni
- **Del Gallo**, Via V. Emanuele 164 - tel. (0775) 727 309 - Has a long family tradition of fine regional cuisine.

Alatri
- **La Rosetta**, via Duomo 35 - tel. 0775-43 45 68 - Closed Tues. and Nov. 5 to 30.

L'Aquila
- **Ernesto**, (Ai benefattori del Grillo), piazza palazzo 22 - tel. (0862) 2 10 94 - Closed Sun. and Mon., Aug. - After having *Sagnarelle alla pastora, pastasciutta*, or *bigolo al torchio*, be sure to visit the two "botti a camera", superb rooms whe re wine is stored. - **Tre Marie**, via Tre Marie - tel. (0862)

413 191 - Closed Sun. evening, Mon. This historical monument has a superb decor, very good cuisine, and

a delicious dessert "Tre Marie".

Isola di Ponza
- **Gennarino al mare**, via Dante - tel. 0771 805 93 - Closed Thu. and from Oct. to May - 50-70,000L. Good cooking with sea views and views of the port, plus an attractive terrace on the water for fine weather. - **Acqua Pazza** - tel. 0771 806 43 - Closed Dec. and Jan. Traditional cuisine in a charming décor.

Viterbo
- **Il Grottino**, via della Cava 7 - tel. (0761) 308 188 - Closed Tues., June 20-July 10 - 50,000L. Limited number of places, reservation preferable. - **Aquilanti**, La Quercia, 3km - tel. (0761) 341 701 - Closed Sun. evening, Tues., Aug. 1-20 - 50,000L. You will need a reservation for this classic regional restaurant with a beautiful "Etruscan room" among the other more modern ones.

Bolsena
- **Angela e Piero**, via della Rena, 98d - Closed Tues. and in Oct. View over the lake.

L I G U R I A

San Remo

- **Da Giannino**, lungomare Trento e Trieste 23 - tel. (0184) 504 014 - Closed Sunday evening, Monday, May 15-31 - 80-90,000L. This is the chic gourmet restaurant of the town. - **Paolo e Barbara**, via Roma, 47 - tel. (0184) 53 16 53 - Closed Wednesday, December-15-January-6, 10 days in June and in July - 80-100,000L. Excellent interpretation of regional recipes. Reserve. - **Pesce d'oro**, corso Cavalotti 300 - tel. (0184) 576 332 - Closed February 15-March 15, Monday - 65,000L. It has some of the best food on the Italian Riviera. - **Osteria del Marinaio da Carluccio**, via Gaudio 28 - tel. (0184) 501 919 - Closed Monday, October, December - 70-90,000L. This very small osteria serves excellent seafood cuisine to a distinguished clientele. Reservations are a must.

Cervo

35km from San Remo
- **San Giorgio**, in the historic center, via Volta 19 - tel. (0183) 400 175 - Closed Tuesday, Christmas vacation - 50-60,000L. This adorable little restaurant serves seafood *antipasti*, excellent cuts of meat, and *zabaione*.

Savona

- **Vino e Farinata**, Via Pia 15 R - 20,000L - Popular, typical, friendly.

Genova / Genoa

- **Gran Gotto**, viale Brigate Bisagno 69r - tel. (010) 564 344 - Closed Sat. noon, Sun., Aug. - 60-80,000L. This is the chic restaurant of the town with an elegant decor and very good classic Ligurian cuisine. - **Giacomo**, Corso Italia - tel. (010) 369 67 - Closed Sun., Aug. - 65-80,000L. It is an elegant place with a beautiful view on the sea. - **Il Cucciolo**, viale Sauli 33 - tel. (010) 546 470 - Closed Mon., Aug. - 40-50,000L, has great Tucsan cuisine. If you don't know your way around town, you'd better come by taxi. - **Da Walter**, vico Colasanto 2 rosso - tel. (010) 290 524 - Open at noon every day and all the Sat. night - Closed Sun., Christmas, Aug. - 40,000L. In

the port district, so go byu taxi, because it is very hard to find. Your perseverence will be rewarded. - **Antica Osteria el Bai**, via Quarto 12, Quarto dei Mille - tel. (010) 387 478 - Closed Mon., Jan. 1-20, Aug. 1-20 - 55-90,000L. After leaving the port, follow the coastal road twoards Nervi. Magnificent menu of fish and seafood.

- **L'Angolo della Luciana**, via della Libertà - tel. (010) 54 00 63 - Closed Mon. and 3 weeks in July. 50,000L. Very few tables, so you must reserve. Good ingredients, well-cooked. - **Edilio**, corso Dre Stefanis 104 r - tel. (010) 81 12 60 - Closed Mon. and from Aug. 1 to Aug. 20 - 80,000L. A small menu with a preference for seafoods and seasonal ingredients. A good addition to the Genoese scene.

Porto Antico

- **Bruxaboschi**, at San Desiderio, via Mignone 8 - Closed Sunday evening, Monday, Christmas, August - 50,000L. Go up the valley of the Sturla on the hills. Cuisine of the Ligurian hinterland: *picaggia al pesto antico, frito misto, cuculli*. - **Da Rina**, via Mura delle Grazie 3r - tel. (010) 246 6475 - 80-100,000L. To try *burrida di seppie*, its specialty. - **Vittorio**, via Sottoripa 59r - tel. (010) 247 29 27 - 30-40,000L - Grilled fish. - **Trattoria Bedin**, via Dante 54r - tel. (010) 58 09 96. To discover *farinata genovese*. - **Ferrando**, in San Cipriano, in on the hill - tel. (010) 75 19 25 - Closed Sunday, Monday and Wednesday evening. Specialties: mushroom dishes.

CAFFE' IN GENOVA
- **Caffe' Mangina**, via Roma 91 - Closed Monday. You can admire the equestrian statue of Victor Emmanuel II on Corvetto Square from this elegant cafe. - **Caffe' Klainguti**, piazza Soziglia 98. This is one of Italy's historical cafés.

Finale Ligure
- **Osteria della Briga**, altipiano delle Marie - tel. (019) 698 579 - Closed Tuesday, Wednesday - 25,000L. It has a rustic family atmosphere, and memorable *lasagne alle ortiche* and *grappe "al latte"*.

Rapallo
- **Da Monique**, lungomare Vittorio Veneto 6 - tel. (0185) 50 541 - Closed Tues., Feb. - 45-50,000L. It is the most famous seafood restaurant of the port. - **U Giancu**, in San Massimo 3km - tel. (0185) 260 505 - Closed Wed., Thurs. noon, Oct. 4-13, Nov. 13- Dec. 6 - 30,000L. Nice country atmosphere, and service on the terrace in the summer.

Santa Margherita Ligure
- **Trattoria Cesarina**, via Mameli 2 - tel. (0185) 286 059 - Closed Wed., Dec. - 85,000L - Is one of the better restaurants on the Ligurian coast, with excellent service. - **Trattoria l'Ancora**, via Maragliano 7 - tel. (0185) 280 559 - Closed Mon., Jan., Feb. - Serves a mostly local clientele. Marinated spaghetti is a house specialty.

Portofino
- **Delfino**, piazza M. dell' Olivetta 40

come here for sandwiches, cocktails, to see and be seen. - **Caffe' Excelsior**, piazza M. Olivetta. A good place to drink expresso and read the morning paper.

- tel. (0185) 269 081 - Closed Thursday, November, December - 75,000L. One of the most stylish restaurants of this port town. - **Puny**, piazza M. Olivetta 7 - tel. (0185) 269 037 - Closed Thursday - 45-70,000L. It is a classic Portofino restaurant, with a nautical decor and a beautiful view of the port. - **Il Pistoforo**, Molo Umberto 1 - tel. (0185) 269 020 - Closed Tuesday, Wednesday noon, January, February - 70-100,000L. It serves fish soup, fish stew, and grilled fish in the shade of the centuries-old *pistoforum*. - **Da Ü Batti**, vico Nuovo 17 - tel. (0185) 269 379 - Is a small fish trattoria. Reservations are a must. - **Chuflay Bar**, on the port - The new bar-restaurant of the Splendido Mare, the hotel annexe of the Splendido. Serves all meals from breakfast to supper. The new fashionable terrace of Portofino. - **Tripoli**, piazza M Olivetta 1 - On the port, simple but good traditional cuisine.

CAFFE' - BARS
- **Bar Sole**, piazza Olivetta. People

Sestri Levante
- **El Pescador**, via Pilade Queirolo 1 - tel. (0185) 41 491 - Closed Tuesday, frm December 15 to March 1st- Specialties: fish. - **San Marco**, port - tel. (0185) 41 459 - Closed Wednesday except August, February 1st-15, November 15-30 - 40-60,000L. Fish. - **Santi's**, viale Rimembranza 46 - tel. (0185) 48 50 19 - Closed Monday, and November 5 to December 13 - 60,000L. - **Polpo Mario**, 136 via XXV aprile - An address all the more precious for being well-hidden. - **Fiammenghilla Fieschi**, at Erigox, Riva Trigoso 2 km via Pestella 6 - tel. (0185) 481 041 - Closed Monday at noon off season - 50-85,000L. It has very good traditional cuisine and a pretty garden.

Portovenere
- **La Taverna del Corsaro**, lungomare Doria 102 - tel. (0187) 790 622 - Closed Tuesday, Mid-November, June 1-22 - 60,000L. There is a very nice view of the island of Palmaria from the dining room. The cusisne is based on fish fresh and produce from the market as well as local specialties.

L O M B A R D Y

Milano / Milan
Historical center

- **Trattoria Bagutta**, via Bagutta 14 - tel. (02) 7600 27 67 - Closed Sunday, Christmas holidays. 60-100,000L. The sequential rooms are decorated with characatures. This is undoubtedly the most famous trattoria in town (a litterary award is given here every year). Although the cuisine is nothing to write home about, the decor is nonetheless attractive. - **Papper Moon**, via Bagutta 1, (near Via Spiga et Montenapo-leone) - tel. (02) 76 02 22 97. One of the best and most friendly trattorias in Milan - Right next door, it is also worth looking into **Moon fish**, opposite No 2, above the garage - tel. (02) 76 00 57 80 - Closed on Sundays. - **Tavola calda Snack Bar Peck**, via Victor Hugo 4 - tel. (02) 86 10 40 - Closed Sun. and from Jan. 1 to 10 and July 1 to 20 - 50,000L. Traditional gourmet cuisine in the snack bar (street level) and good Milanese specialties; there is also a restaurant in the basement. Work on restructuring should improve standards of comfort and service in the restaurant. - **Il Salumaio**, via Monte-napoleone 12 - An elegant restaurant in a pretty courtyard where meals are served in summer. Ideal for lunch in this luxury shopping area. - **Caffete-ria Milano**, alla Scala, Piazza Scala - An elegant restaurant for lunch which shares the first floor of Trussardi's. -

Trattoria Milanese, via Santa Marta 11 - tel. (02) 864 519 91 - Closed Tues., it is true to tradition. - **Don Lisander**, via Manzoni 12 - tel. (02) 7602 0130 - 68-105,000L - Closed Sat. evening and Sun. The restaurant is especially nice in the summer, as it serves fine cuisine to its upscale clientele on a very pleasant canvas-covered terrace with an Italian-style decor and flowering plants. You will need a reservation. - **Franco il Contadino**, via Fiori Chiari 20 - tel. (02) 8646 3446 - Closed Tues., Wed. at noon, July - 45-60,000L. It has a nice atmosphere and is frequented by artists. It is open Sundays. - **Boeucc**, piazza Belgioioso 2 - tel. (02) 760 20224 - Closed Sat., Sun. at noon, Dec. 23-Jan. 5, Aug.

- 60-80,000L. Reservations are necessary for this chic restaurant, where you can dine on the terrace as soon as the weather permits. - **Stendhal**, Via Ancona - tel. (02) 659 25 89 - The Milanese crowd in here, but it is not possible to reserve. In summer, meals are served on the terrace with view of the Gothic chuch of San Marco.

DOPO SCALA
- **Le Santa Lucia**, via San Pietro

all'orto 3, (near via Montenapoleone) - tel. (02) 760 23155 - The Milanese equivalent of the Brasserie Lipp, where it is preferable to dine quite late if you don't want to be driven mad by a maître d'hôtel whose only thought is to see you leave and make way for the next customer. - **Biffi Scala**, piazza della Scala - tel. (02) 86 66 51 -Closed Sun. and Chrismas, August 10.-20. Traditionnel - **Don Carlos**, via Manzoni 99. Don Carlos is the restaurant at the superb Grand Hotel et de Milan where Verdi spent

his last days. The atmosphere is appropriately theatrical.

Navigli
- **Osteria del Binari**, via Tortona 1 - tel. (02) 8940 9428 - Closed at noon, Sun., Aug. 10-20 - 50,000L. This is an atmosphere restaurant, with a very convivial dining room, a very shady garden, and somewhat traditional cuisine. - **Le Braque**, via Bugatti 13 - tel. (02) 581 862 47 - Near the Genova station. Atmosphere and clientele from the fashion world, décor to match. - **La Bella Aurora**, via Abamonti 1 - Friendly half-bistro, half-trattoria.

Porta Romana, Corso Vittoria
- **Giannino**, via Amatore Sciesa 8 - tel. (02) 551 955 82 - Closed Sun., Aug. - 60-100,000L. You will enjoy some of the finest gourmet cuisine in Lombardy here in this classic chic Milanese restaurant - **Masuelli San Marco**, viale Umbria - tel. (02) 551 841 38 - Closed Sun., Mon. noon, Dec. 25-Jan. 6, Aug. 15-Sept. 15 - 50,000L. - **Da Giacomo**, via B. Cellini angle via Sottocorno 6 - tel. (02) 760 23 313 - Closed Mon. and from Dec. 24 to Jan. 2, and in Aug. - 50-80,000L. Attractive decor of classic trattoria type, with embroidered curtains, 1930s lighting and goo seafood. Reserve.

Porta and Corso Venezia
- **Rosy e Gabrielle**, via Sirtori 26 - tel. 02-295 259 30 - Pizzeria, a classic of the district. - **Transatlantico**, via Malpigi 3 - tel. (02) 295 260 98 - On the ground floor of a fine apartment block decoarted with 1900 frescoes.

Near centro direzionale

- **La Tana del Lupo**, viale Vittorio Veneto, 30 - tel. (02) 6 59 90 06 - Open only for the dinner, closed Sunday, end-July, August - 40-65,000L. Specialties from Trentino and Veneto

country. - **Rigolo**, largo Treves angle via Solferino - tel. (02) 8646 3220 - Closed Monday, August. 30-50,000L. It is in the Brera quarter, and is frequented by a stylish crowd of regulars. Another plus, it is open Sundays. - **Alla Cucina delle Langhe**, corso Como, 6 - tel. (02) 6 55 42 79 - Closed Sunday, three weeks in July, Christmas - 60,000L. Typical

Piemontian cuisine. - **Corso Como Café**, corso Como 10 - tel. (02) 290 135 81 - The most 'in' place at the moment. Near Porta Garibaldi. Italian cuisine with exotic flavors. - **Trattoria della Pesa**, Via Pasubio - tel. (02) 65 55 74 - Closed Sunday and in August - 70,000L. One of the best

restaurants in Milan. Its reputation is such that you must book a table as soon as you arrive if you want to have a chance of eating here.

Fiera -Sempione

- **Alfredo Gran San Bernardo**, via Borghese 14 - tel. (02) 331 90 00 - Closed Christmas, August, Sunday, Saturday in June and July - 65-99,000L. An excellent place to eat *risotto all'osso buco*. - **Pizzeria il Mozzo**, via Marghera (corner of via Ravizza) - tel. (02) 498 47 46 - Closed Wednesdays and in August - open until 2:00 am. Rustic décor, good cooking, elegant. - **Torre di Pisa**, via Fiori Chiari 21 - tel. (02) 874 877 - Closed Sunday - 40-50,000L. It is a Tuscan restaurant frequented by designers and people from the fashion industry.

CAFFE'- BARS

- **Bar Zucca**, galleria Vittorio

Emanuele 21 - One of the oldest bistros in town, situated in the lovely covered arcade near the Duomo and the Scala. Salon de thé on the first floor. - **Caffè del Sole**, via della Spiga 42 - A café of charm and atmosphere. - **Cova**, via Montenapoleone 8 - Is the most elegant café in Milan, and serves teas, coffee, pastries, champagne, and cocktails. - **Pozzi**, piazza Cantore 4, glacier. Features a wide assortment of ice cream and sherbert. - **Pasticceria Marchesi**, via santa Maria alla Porta, 1. This is a good place for a coffee and an Italian croissant with jelly. They have made the best holiday pastries, (Panattone at Chrismas and Colombe at Easter) since 1824. - **Bar del Comparino**, the original Frescos and Liberty-style mosaics have recently been restored in this historical landmark, the former haunt of Toscanini, Verdi, and Carrà - **Sant Ambrœus**, corso Matteoti 7 - Specialties of Ambrogitto, is the most elegant tearoom in Milan, but there is also **Biffi**, corso Magenta 87, Taveggia, via Visconti di Modrone 2 - **Galli**, corso di Porta Romana 2 which has delicious candied chestnuts.

SHOPPING

- **Casa del formaggio**, via Speronari 3 - Has a wide asssortment of cheeses from all over Italy. - **Peck**, via Spadari 9 - Is still the finest gourmet food store in Milano. - **La Fungheria di Bernardi**, viale Abruzzi 93 - Has a wonderful variety of fresh and canned mushrooms. - **Enoteca Cotti**, via Solferino 32. - **Principessa Hortensia**, via Bigli 24 - Luxury boutique for food presents. You can also have lunch. - **Memphis Design** for Ettore Sottsass' creations. - **De Padova**, corso Venezia 14, modern furniture by Vico Magistretti and Gae Aulenti - **Magazzini Cappellini**, via Santa Cecilia 4 a new showroom for his contemporary furniture. - **Fontana Arte**, via Santa Margherita 4 - A showroom on four floors for furniture and lighting. - **Flos**, Corso Monforte 9 - A major supplier of contemporary lightings. - **Vivere**, via Ugo Foscolo 4 - The architect Antonio Citterio designed this huge space offering an excellent choice of household wares. - **Alessi**, Corso Matteotti 9 - A classic of design for the arts of the home: great masters and new talents. - **Marino alla Scala** - A vast space opened by the house of Trussardi with a shop for accessories, an art gallery and a restaurant. - **Fornasetti**, via Manzoni 45 - Reeditions of the artist's famous works. - **DaDriade**, via Manzoni 30 - Has created a style with its choice of household waresmade by the finest designers. - **2 Link**, via Milano 58b, Cantú - Anyone who is mad about design will travel the 20 km to Cantú to see the very latest in international design, in a contemporary decor by Christophe Pillet, extending over three floors. - **Frette**, via Manzoni 11 - Famous for its elegant decorations for beds and tables. - **Pratesi**, via Montenapoleone 27, supplies the finest house linen. - **Venini**, via Montenapoleone 9 - Still displaying wonderful Murano glass. - **Barovier & Toso**, via Manzoni 40 - Supplies Murano glass. - **Libreria Rizzoli**, galleria Vittorio Emanuele 79, has rare French publications and art books. - **Libreria Hoepli**, via Hoepli 5, has modern works, manuscripts, and authentic signatured drawings. - **Feltrinelli**, via Manzoni 12, - a good bookshop where you can also find the international press.

Bergamo

- **Lio Pellegrini**, via San Tomaso 47 - tel. (035) 247 813 - Closed Monday, Tuesday at noon, January 4-11, August 2-24 - 50-90,000L. Resevation advised. - **Taverna del Colleoni**, piazza Vecchia 7 - tel. (035) 232 596 - Closed Monday, August 15-31 - 50-70,000L. It serves regional cuisine in a Renaissance decor. The *tagliatelle* and the *filetto alla Colleoni* are house specialties. There is also **Il Gourmet**, via San Vigilio, 1 tel. (035) 437 30 04 - Closed Tuesday, January 1-6 - 40-60,000L - Service on the terrace with panoramic view in summer. - **La Marianna**, largo Colle Aperto 2/4 - tel. (035) 237 027 - Closed Monday, from January 1 to 14. You can dine on a beautiful flower-covered terrace when the weather is nice.

Brescia

- **La Sosta**, via San Martino della Battaglia 20 - tel. (030) 295 603 - Closed Monday, August - 50-80,000L. The handsome 17th century building and fine cuisine make it worth stopping off here for a meal.

Cremona

- **Ceresole**, via Ceresole 4 - tel. (0372) 23 322 - Closed Sunday

evening, Monday, January, August - 60-80,000L. It is considered to be something of an institution in this town famous for its violins. If you are interested, you can visit the Antonio Strativari Museum. - **Antica Trattoria del Cigno**, via del Cigno 7 - tel. (0372) 21 361 - Closed Sunday, January, July 20 - October 4 - 30,000L. In the shadow of the Torrazzo, this old trattoria is the favorite of the inhabitants of Cremona.

Mantova / Mantua

- **San Gervasio**, via San Gervasio 13 - tel. (0376) 323 873 - Closed Wednesday, August 12-31 - 40-70,000L. Grilled pike and *polenta*, cepes or tortellini and wonderful home-made grissini. Meals served insummer on two charming patios. - **L'Aquila Nigra**, vicolo Bonacolsi 4 - tel. (0376) 327 180 - Closed Sunday, Monday, Christmas, August - 45,000L. It is famous for its cuisine, which you will enjoy in a beautiful decor of frescos in a former monastery. - **Cento Rampini**, piazza delle Erbe 11 - tel. (0376) 366 349 - Closed Sunday evening, Monday at noon, Christmas, August 1-15. - It is nicely located under the portico of the Palazzo Comunale, and has service on the terrace.

- **Caravatti**, from 1865 in the piazza delle Erbe. Specialties: la *Sbrizolona*.

Villastrada-Dosolo

-**Nizzoli** - tel. (0375) 89 150 - Cclosed Wednesday and from December 24 to 29 - 25-50,000L. While you are touring the villages of the Po Valley, do try to stop at Nizzoli, 40km from Mantua, for its beautiful dining room and its specialties: pork, and dishes based on *zucca, lumaca, rana* and *melone*.

Pavia

- **Antica Trattoria Ferrari da Tino**, via del Mille 111 - tel. (0382) 310 33 - Closed Sunday evening, Monday, August - 35-70,000L. This traditional country trattoria serves savory cuisine.

Certosa di Pavia

- **Vecchio Mulino**, via al Monumento 5 - tel. (0382) 925 894 - Closed Sunday evening, Monday, January 1-10, August 1-20 - 60-80,000L. This is a good place to dine when visiting the famous monastery. Be sure to make a reservation. - **Chalet della Certosa**, opposite the Certosa - Closed Monday, January 11-24.

Iseo

– **Il Volto**, via Mirolte 2 - tel. (030) 98 14 62 - Closed Wednesday, Friday at noon, July 1-15 - 60,000L. Simple and elegant dining room, cuisine from the Brescia region.

Sirmione

- **La Rucola**, vicolo Strendelle - tel. (030) 91 63 26 - Only thirty places, excellent cooking. 75-110,000L.
AT LUGANA, 5 km from Sirmione
- **Vecchia Lugana**, piazzale vecchia Lugana 1 - tel. (030) 91 90 12 - Closed Monday evening, Tuesday and from January 9 to February 22 - Only 30 places, excellent cuisine. 60-100,000L - The place to go if you want to try the finest cuisine of the region. Meals served on the terrace overlooking the lake on fine days.

Ancona

- **Passetto**, piazza IV Novembre - tel. (071) 33 214 - Closed Sun. night, Mon., Aug. 1-25 - 55-70,000L. There is a nice view of the Adriatic from the terrace which is open in the summer. - **Osteria Teatro Strabacco**, via Oberdan 2 - tel. (071) 542 13 - Closed Mon., May -

Viviani Palace. - **Self-Service Franco**, via de Poggio - tel. (0722) 24 92 - Closed Sun. - 15,000L. Located near the museum, it has reasonable prices - **Vanda**, Castelcavallino - tel. (0722) 34 91 17 - Closed Wed., Christmas and from July 8 to 20 - 40,000L. Another fine classic restaurant in the town.

40,000L. A very convivial atmosphere created by a mixed clientele of all ages, open until 3 am with a menu that will end the war between generations.

Urbino

- **Vecchia Urbino**, via dei Vasari 3 - tel. (0722) 4447 - Closed Tues. off season - 40-60,000L. It serves regional cuisine, (the *formaggio di fossa* is remarkable) in a pleasant room in the

Ascoli Piceno

- **Gallo d'Oro**, corso V Emanuele 13 - tel. 0736 535 20 - Closed Mon. and in Aug. - People come here for the famous *pollo alla diavola*, but also for the Adriatic fish and for the truffles. - **Tornassaco**, piazza del Popolo 36 - Closed Fri. and in July - **Caffè Meleni**, piazza del Popolo - Satre aznd Hemingway came here.

Perugia

- **Osteria del Bartolo**, via Bartolo 30 - tel. (075) 573 15 61 - Closed Sunday, January 7-15, July 25-August 7 - 60,000L. Very good home-style cuisine and old Umbrian dishes. - **La Taverna**, via delle Streghe 8 - tel. (075) 572 41 28 - Closed Monday - 40,000L. Country cuisine in a large room with a vaulted ceiling. - **Del Sole**, via delle Rupe 1 - tel. (075) 65 031 - Closed Monday, December 23-January 10 - 35,000L.

CAFFE'- BARS

- **Pasticceria Sandri**, corso Vannucci 32 - For pastry buffs. - **Caffe' del Cambio**, corso Vannucci 29. It can get

pretty crowded in this student cafe.

Assisi

- **Buca di San Francesco**, via Brizi 1 - tel. (075) 812 204 - Closed Monday, January, July - 30-60,000L. It serves traditional Umbrian cuisine in a Medieval palace with a pretty garden in the summer. - **Medio Evo**, via Arco del Priori 4 - tel. (075) 81 3068 - Closed Wednesday, January, July - 45,000L. It has beautiful architecture and meticulously fine cuisine. - **La Fortezza**, Vic. Fortezza 2-B - tel. (075) 812 418 - Closed Thursday - 30,000L. Some vestiges of the ruins of the typical Roman house it was built on remain. The cuisine is Umbrian-style. - **Taverna del Arco da Bino**, via S Gregorio 8 - tel. (075) 81 24 18 - Closed Sunday evening and Turesday, and from January 7 to February 13, and June 30 to July 15 - 40-70,000L.

Spello

- **Il Cacciatore**, via Giulia 42 - tel. (0742) 65 11 41 - Closed Monday, July 6-20 - 30-50,000L. Pleasant trattoria with a beautiful terrace. - **Il Molino**, piazza Matteotti - tel. (0742) 65 79 05 - Closed Tuesday - 40-50,000L.

Spoleto

- **Il Tartufo**, piazza Garibaldi 24 - tel. (0743) 40 236 - Closed Wednesday, August 15-10 - 35-70,000L. This is an excellent tavern serving regional cuisine. The house specialty is *fettucine al tartufo*. - **Sabatini**, corso Mazzini 52/54 - tel. 22 18 31 - Closed Monday, August 1st-10. - **Tric Trac da Giustino**, p. del Duomo - tel. (0743) 44 592 - 20-50,000L. Very busy during the "Two World Festival".

CAMPELLO SUL CLITUNNO, 9km from Spoleto.

- **Casaline** - tel. (0743) 62 213 - Closed

Monday - 45,000L. After your visite of Tempietto sul Clitunno. Have lunch in this country inn after visiting the Tempietto sul Clitunno. The cuisine is made with local products, and the *crostini* with truffles are marvelous.

Todi

- **Umbria**, via San Bonaventura, 13 - tel. (075) 89 42 737 - Closed Tuesday, December 19-January 8 - 40-60,000L.
- **Jacopone-da Peppino**, piazza jacopone, 5 - tel. (075) 89 48 366 - Closed Monday, July 10-30 - 40-60,000L.

Trevi

- **L'Ulivo**, 3 km - tel. (0742) 78 969 - Closed Saturday, Monday and

Tuesday. The owner offers a daily menu with an emphasis on traditional Umbrian cuisine.

Gubbio

- **Alle Fornace di Mastro Giogio**, via Mastro Giogio 3 - tel. (927) 5740 -

Closed Sunday evening, Monday, February, 60,000L. - **Taverna del Lupo**, via G. Ansidei 21 - tel. (075) 927 43 68 - Closed Monday, January. 30-50,000L. It serves delicious local specialties in a beautiful Medieval tavern decor.

Orvieto

- **Giglio d'Oro**, piazza Duomo 8 - tel. (0763) 341 903 - Closed Wednesday - 40-70,000L. Classical and good. - **Grotte del Funaro**, v. Ripa Serancia 41 - tel. (0763) 343 276 - Closed Monday in low season. In an old grotto; typical cusine. - **Dell'Ancora**, via di Piazza del Popolo 7 - tel. (0763) 342 766 - Closed Thursday, January - 35,000L. Local home-style cuisine.

LOCAL SPECIALTIES

- **Dai Fratelli**, via del Duomo 11, it has all kinds of cheese and the famous Umbrian sausages and ham.

Torino / Turin

- **Vecchia Lanterna**, corso Re Umberto 21 - tel. (011) 537 047 - Closed Saturday noon, Sunday, August 10-20 - 30-100,000L. This is one of the best restaurants in Italy. The owner, Armando Zanetti with new flavors, but also does an admirable job with traditional recipes. The wine cellar is superbly well stocked with Italian wines. - **Del Cambio**, piazza Carignano - tel. (011) 546 690 - Closed Sunday and August - 60-95,000L - Located in the historical center of Turin, birthplace of the unification of Italy, this restaurant has kept all of the luster of the old days when Cavour came to eat here every day. The atmosphere, cuisine, and service are straight out of the 19th century. - **Mina**, via Ellero 36 - tel. (011) 696 3608 - Closed Sunday evening in June and July, Monday, August - 70,000L. It serves genuine Piemontian home-style cuisine *(antipasti, sformati, finanzeria)*. - **Al Gatto Nero**, corso Turati 14 - tel.

(011) 590 414 - Closed Sunday and August - 70,000L. Delicious Tuscan cuisine. For your first meal, we recommend *assassini*, an assortment of the finest specialties of the house. - **Trattoria della Posta**, strada Mongreno 16 - tel. (011) 8980 193 - Closed Sunday evening, Monday, July. It is famous for its cheeses and its excellent wine cellar. - **Tre Galline**, via Bellezia 37 - tel. (011) 436 65 53 - Closed Sunday, Monday noon - 50,000L. Typical Piemontian cuisine. - **Salsamentario**, via Santorre di Santarosa 7-B - tel. (011) 819 50 75 - Closed Sunday evening, Monday, August 15-22. There is a large buffet for 35,000L, just next door to a caterer. - **Il Ciacalon**, viale 25 Aprile - tel. (011) 661 09 11 - Closed Sunday, August 11-24. Located near the fairgrounds, beautiful restaurant with a simple friendly atmosphere. - **Ostu Bacu**, corso Vercelli 226 - tel. (011) 265 79. Closed Sunday. Typical Piemontian cuisine served in a rustic family atmosphere.

CAFFE' - BARS

- **Caffe' al Bicerin**, piazza della Consolata 5. Has had famous customers such as Alexander Dumas who perhaps came to try the famous *bicerin*, a house specialty made from chocolate, coffee, milk, and sugar cane syrup. - **Caffe Il Florio**, via Po, called "caffe dei condini" because it used to be a meeting place for the most conservative people of the time. Try the *Sabaione, gelato al gianduia*. - **Caffe' San Carlo**, piazza San Carlo 156. Opened in 1822, and used to be

the meeting point of the European intellegensia. Historical café frequented by d'Azeglio, Cavour, Cesare Pavese and James Stewart. - **Caffe' Mulassano**, piazza Castello 15. His large cafe has a lot of atmosphere,

and delicious *tramezzini* (32 varieties of small sandwiches).

LOCAL SPECIALTIES
- **Stratta**, piazza San Carlo 191 specialties: *caramelle alla gioca di gelatinases*, "marrons glacés", *amaretti, meringhe con panna montata*. - **Peyrano**, corso Moncalieri 47

- Is a laboratory for the famous Turinese chocolates, *givu, diablottini*, and the most famous *giandujotti*, also sold at the pastry shop **Peyrano-Pfatisch**, corso V. Emanuele II, 76 - **Cantine Marchesi di Barolo**, via Maria Vittoria sells Piedmont wines *Barolo Barbera, Barbaresco, Gattinara, l'Asti Spumante* of course, and the *grappe*.

Carmagnola
29 km from Turin
- **La Carmagnole**, via Sottotenente Chiffi 31 - tel. (011) 971 26 73 - 120,000L. Dine in an old palace, reservations a must.

Lozanzé
46 km from Turin
- **Panoramica**, Lungo Tanaro, 4 tel. (0125) 66 99 69 - Closed Sat. noon, Sun. evening, Christmas. -50-95,000L. This is still one of the best restaurants in Piedmont.

Alba
- **Il Vicoletto**, via Bertero, 6 - tel. (0173) 36 31 96 - Closed Mon., July20-Aug. 15 - 50-80,000L. Gastronomic cooking, specialtie: *langarola*. - **Osteria dell'Arco**, piazza Savona 5 - tel. (0173) 36 39 74 - Closed Sun., Mon. at noon except from Sept. 25 to Nov. 25 - 30-45,000L. In the historic center. - **Daniel's**, corso canale, 28 - tel. (0173) 44 19 77 - Closed Christmas and New year. Aug. 1-15, Sun. except from Oct. to Dec. - 45-60,000L. 1km of town center. Typical cooking in a typical house - **Porta san Martino**,

via Enaudi 5 - tel. (0173) 36 23 35 - Closed Mon., Aug. 20-Sept. 20 - 45-60,000L. Particularly tasty recipes, especially in the truffle season.

Asti

- **Gener Neuv**, Lungo Tanaro 4 - tel. (0141) 557 270 - Numerous brief periods of closure, so the best is to phone - 85,000L. This is one of the best places for traditional Piedmont cuisine. - **L'Angolo del Beato**, via Guttuari 12 - tel. (0141) 531 668, Closed Sun., July 1st-10, Aug. 1st-20 - 50,000L. A beautiful old house, reservation advised. - **Il Cenacolo**, viale al Pilone 59 - tel. (0141) 531 110 - Closed Mon. and Tuesday at noon, January 10-20 and Aug. 5-20 - 40,000L. Savory regional cuisine is served in this intimate reasturant. Reservations required.

Castigliole d'asti
15km from Asti

- **Guido**, Piazza Umberto I 27 - tel. (0141) 966 012 - Closed at noon, Sun., Aug. 1-24, Dec. 22- Jan. 10 - 100,000L. Elegantly reinvented specialties of Langhe are served here. By reservation only.

Canelli
29 km from Asti

- **San Marco**, via Alba 136 - tel. (0141) 82 35 44 - Closed Tuesday evening, Wednesday, from July 20 to august 13. A la carte: 40-65,000L. Great cuisine, you will need a reservation.

Cannobio

- **Del Lago**, in Carmine Inferiore

3km away - tel. (0323) 705 95 - Closed November, February - 60-100,000L. Reservation. This restaurant on a lake offers very good classical cuisine.

Aosta

- **Le Foyer**, Corso Ivrea 146 - tel. (0165) 32136 - Closed Monday evening, Tuesday, July 5-20, January 15-31 - 50,000L. Local specialties are served in this friendly comfortable restaurant. - **Vecchia Aosta**, piazza Porta Pretoria, 4 - tel. (0165) 3611 86 - Closed Tuesday night, Wednesday, June 5-20 and October 15-30- 30-40,000L. Much appreciated local cuisine, so book. - **Vecchio Ristoro**, via Tourneuve 4 - tel. (0165) 3 32 38 - closed in June, onSundays and a midday on Mondays out of season - 40-70,000L - Authentic Alpine and Val d'Aostan haute cuisine served in an old water mill. Not many places, so it is essential to book.

Saint-Christophe
4 km from Aosta

- **Casale** - tel. (0165) 54 12 03 - Closed from January 5 to 20 and June 5 to 20 - 50,000L. Val d'Aostan specialties, a few kilometers from Aosta,

in a warm, rustic setting in winter and on the terrace in summer. A restaurant not to be missed.

Breuil-Cervinia

- **Cime Bianche** - tel. (0166) 949 046 - 30-50,000L - Is on the ski slopes in the winter, and serves regional cuisine in a pretty mountain decor, with a superb view on the Cervin. - **Le Mattherhorn** - tel. (0166) 948 518 - Is in the center of town, and serves pizzas, steaks, and fish. - **Maison de Saussure**, via Carrel 4, - tel. (0166) 948 259 - It is essential to book, given the popularity of authentic local cooking- Hostellerie des guides, is open from 7 am to midnight, and is famous for its Irish coffee.

Courmayeur

- **Pierre Alexis 1877**, via Marconi 54 - tel. (0155) 84 35 17 - Closed October, November, Monday (except August), Tuesday at noon from December to March. - **Leone Rosso**, via Roma 73 - tel. (0165) 845 726 - Closed Monday in low season, May 15-June 15, October - 50,000L. Seasonal regional cuisine in an elegant rustic setting.

- **Al Camin**, via dei Bagni - tel. (0165) 844 687 - Closed Tuesday off season, November, Mountain atmosphere and home-style cuisine.

- **Caffe' Della Posta**, via Roma 41. It is a hundred-year-old bar where you can drink traditional Alpine alcohols and cocktails, comfortably installed in plush sofas. *(Grappas, Genepi, grolla dell'amicizia).*

Entrèves

4km from Courmayeur
- **La Maison de Filippo** - tel. (0165) 89 668 - Closed Tuesday, June-July 15, November - 50,000L. You must make a reservation for this famous

tavern.

Planpincieux Val Ferret

7km from Courmayeur
- **La Clotze** - tel. (0165) 869 720 - Closed Wednesday, June, November - 45,000L. Good regional cuisine.

La Palud Val Ferret

5km from Courmayeur
- **La Palud-da-Pasquale** - tel. (0165) 89 169 - Closed Wednesday, November - 30-40,000L. Regional and mountain specialties.

Plan-de-Lognan Val Veny

12km from Courmayeur
- **Le Chalet del Miage**, Closed July, September. Mountain-style cuisine.

Cogne

- **Lou Ressignon**, rue des Mines 22 - tel. (0165) 74 034 - Closed Monday evening, Tuesday. It has excellent cuts of meat, *fonduta, carbonara* (meat cooked in beer) and also delicious cheeses and desserts.

Verres

- **Chez Pierre**, via Martorey 43 - tel. (0125) 929 376 - Closed Monday and Tuesday except August - 50-80,000L. This adorable litttle restaurant, 22 miles (37km) from Aoste, has a friendly atmosphere and regional cuisine.

P U G L I A

Alberobello

- **Trullo d'Oro**, via Cavallotti 31 - tel. (080) 721 820 - Closed Monday, January 7- February 8 - 40-60,000L. It is picturesque, with a country-style decor and regional cuisine. - **Cucina dei Trulli**, piazza San Fernandino 31 - tel. (080) 721 179 - Closed Thursday except in summer - 20,000L. Varied local cuisine. - **Il Poeta Contadino**, via Indipendenza 21 - tel. (080) 721 917 - Closed Sunday evening, Monday, January, June - 65,000L. Excellent cuisine.

Castel del Monte

- **Ostello di Federico**, Castel del Monte - tel. (0883) 56 98 77 - Closed Monday, 2 weeks in January and two in November - 40,000L. The ideal place to go after a visit to the monumental castle, the Crown of Puglia:

tortieri di riso e patate, cannelloni di baccalà e ricotta.

Bari

- **Nuova Vecchia Bari**, via Dante Alighieri 47 - tel. (080) 521 64 96 - Closed Friday, Sunday evening - 50,000L. Pugilian cuisine is served in this rustic former oil press house. - **La Pignata**, corso Vittorio Emanuele 173 - tel. (523) 24 81 - **Deco'**, largo Adua 10 - tel. (524) 60 70. Elegant.

Polignano al Mare

- **Grotta Polazzese**, via Narcisso 59 - tel. (080) 740 0677 - 65-90,000L. It serves lobster and fish dishes inside a natural grotto in the summer.

Martina Franca

- **Da Antonietta**, via Virgilio 30 - tel. (080) 706 511 - Closed Wednesday off season - 25,000L. Flavorful cuisine. - **Rosticceria Ricci**, via Cavour 19. Behind a butcher's shop, so the meat is good. - **Trattoria delle**

Ruote, via Ceglie 4,5km - tel. (080) 883 74 73 - Closed Monday - 30-45,000L. A nice place with limited seating so be sure to make a reservation. - **Ristorante In**, piazza Magli 6 - tel. (080) 705 021 - Closed Tuesday night, Wednesday, two weeks in November - 50,000L. Set in the heart of this magnificent town, this restaurant is an elegant version of the regional architectural style and the food is of high quality (for example,

the *galantina d'anatra al pistacchio*). - **Caffe' Tripoli**, piazza Garibaldi, is a wonderful old cafe serving pastries and almond paste. - **Bar Derna**, piazza Settembre 4 - Delicious pastries.

Taranto

- **Il Caffé**, via San Tomaso d'Aquino 8 - tel. (099) 452 5097 - Closed on Sunday evenings, Monday lunchtime and for two weeks inAugust - 50,000L. A very good place for fresh fish, as well as the *papardelle al pesce affumicato* and the desserts of

the owner's daughter, Francescaromana, who makes as much a success of these as of her law studies.

Lecce

- **Villa della Monica**, via SS Giacomo e Filippo 40 - tel. (0832) 458 432 - Closed Tuesday and from November 1 to 20 - 20-40,000L. In the fine setting of a 16th-century palazzo. - **Gino e Gianni**, via Adriatica, 2 km away - tel. (0832) 399 210 - Closed Wednesday - 45,000L. Traditional cuisine in this theatrical-looking town. - **Il Satirello** - tel. (0832) 3768 672 - Closed Tuesday. It is in an old farmhouse with a beautiful garden when the weather is warm, 9km from the road to Torre Chianca. - **Barbablù**, via Umberto I - tel. (0832) 24 11 83 - Closed Sunday evening, Monday and the first week in June. 50,000L. On the first floor of a fine restored palazzo, Tonio Pireci and his daughter Paola display the regional recipes that the restauranteur published in *Oltre le orecchiette*.

Alghero

- **Le Lepanto**, via Carlo Alberto 135 - tel. (079) 979 116 - Closed Monday off season - 50,000L. After your visit to the Grottos of Neptune, you will undoubtedly be delighted to have a lobster Lepanto or to try other regional specialties here. - **Al Tuguri**, via Majorca 113 or **Dieci Metri**, vicolo Adami 37.

Santa Teresa Gallura

- **Canne al Vento**, via nazionale 23 - tel. (0789) 754 219 - Closed October, November, Saturday off season - *Zuppa galurese, antipasti del mare*, seafood delicacies cooked with love.

Nuoro

- **Canne al Vento**, viale Repubblica 66 - tel. (0784) 201 762. It has a nice selection of meat and fish.

Monte Ortobene

7 km from nuoro

- **Dai Fratelli Sacchi** - tel. (0784) 31200. The Sacchi brothers warmly welcome their guests with savory cuisine.

Dorgali

- **Il Colibri**, via Gramsci 44 - tel. (0784) 960 54 - Closed December-February, Sunday from October to May - 50,000L. This is a good place to stop off for a Sardinian meal on your way to visit the Dolmen Mottore and the Grottos di Ispinigoli.

Olbia

- **Ristorante dell' hotel Gallura**, corso Umberto 145 - tel. (0789) 246

48. It has served fish and seafood dishes cooked with delicious simplicity for more than fifty years. - **Leone et Anna**, via Barcelona 90 - tel. (0789) 263 33 - Closed January, Wednesday off season - Sardinian cuisine, fish, and some Venetian specialties.

Cagliari

- **Dal Corsaro**, viale Regina Margherita 28 - tel. (070) 664 318 - Closed Sunday, Christmas, August - 60,000L. If you spend a night in Cagliari before moving on down the coast, you can come here for high quality authentic Sardinian cuisine. - **Antica Hostaria**, via Cavour 60 - tel. (070) 665 870 - Closed Sunday, August. It is one of the nicest restaurants in Cagliari. Antonello Floris has skillfully adapted traditional recipes, and his wife Lilly makes great desserts.

Isola san Pietro-carloforte
- **Al Tonno di Cosa**, via Marconi 47 - tel. (0781) 855 106 - Closed Monday, October-November 10 - It serves delicious local cuisine (*tonno alla carlofortina*, "casca" regional couscous) on a terrace overlooking the sea - **Miramare**, piazza Carlo Emanuele 12 - tel. (0781) 85 653, Carlofortan, Sardinian, and Arab specialties.

Porto Cervo
- **Il Pescatore**, sul molo Vecchio - tel. (0789) 92 296 - Closed October-May, open in the evening only - 65,000L. You can have dinner by candlelight on a flower-covered terrace. - **Bar degli archi**, piazzetta degli Archi. People come here for breakfast, a sandwhich at noon, and a drink in the evening. - **Pevero Golf Club**, Pevero - tel. (0789) 96 210 - Closed November-April - 80,000L. This is one of the nicest golf courses. The cuisine served in the clubhouse

restaurant is elegant and light, just like the clientele.

Isola la Maddalena
- **La Grotta**, via Principe di Napoli 3 - tel. (0789) 737 228 - Closed November - 30-50,000L. Typical trattoria for fish and seafood. - **Mangana**, via Mazzini - tel. (0789) 738 477 - Closed Wednesday, December 20-January 20 - 35-60,000L. There are all-fish meals here, too.

Oristano
- **Il Faro**, via Bellini 25 - tel. (0783) 700 02 - Closed Sunday, July 11-25 -

60,000L. Inventive cuisine based on regional recipes.

Palermo

- **Renato l'Approdo**, via Messina Marina 28 - tel. (091) 630 2881 - Closed Wed., Aug. 10-25 - 50-70,000L. One of the best restaurants on the island, featuring dishes made from old Silicioan recipes. - **La Scuderia**, viale del Fante 9 - tel. (091) 520 323 - Closed Sun. - 55-80,000L. It has one of the prettiest terraces in town. Dinners here are exquisite. - **Al Ficondindia**, via Emerico Amari 64 - tel. (091) 324 214 - Closed Thu. - 25,000L. A country tavern serving local regional cuisine. - **Gourmand's**, via Libertà 37-E - tel. (091) 323 431 - Closed Sun., Aug. 2-25. Elegant, and fine cuisine. Smoked fish is a house specialty. - **Trattoria del Buongustaio**, via Venezia 79 - tel. (091) 33 47 14 - Closed Mon. and in Aug. - 40,000L. Family-run restaurant with home cooking combining delight with simplicity: *calamaretti alla palermitana* and *parfait di mandorla al cioccolato* are among the specialties.

IN MONREALE, 8km from Palermo

- **La Botte**, contrada Lenzitti 416 - tel. (091) 414 051 - Closed Mon., July, Aug. - 45,000L. Delicious cuisine. Don't miss the superb cathedral.

IN MONDELLO, 11 km from Palermo

- **Charleston le Terrazze**, viale Regina Elena - tel. (091) 450 171 - Opened from June to Sept. On the most elegant beach of Palermo. It is the summer quarters of the *Charleston* of Palermo, with an superbly elegant terrace on the sea. - **Gambero Rosso**, via Piano Gallo 30 - tel. (091) 454 685 - Closed Mon., Nov. - 45,000L. This trattoria serves good seafood dishes.

CAFFE' - BARS

- **Caffe' Mazzara**, via Generale Magliocco 15. Tomaso di Lampedusa wrote many chapters of "the Cheetah" here. - **Bar du Grand Hotel des Palmes** - The hotel has been dropped from our selection because the rooms are overpriced, but the superb salons are still worth a visit.

Cefalù

- **La Brace**, via XXV Novembre 10 - tel. (921) 23 570 - Closed Mon., Dec. 15-Jan. 15. This small restaurant offers traditional Italian cuisine.

Messina

- **Alberto**, via Ghibellina 95 - tel. (090) 710 711. Alberto Sardella has served marvelous cuisine here since his return from the U.S. 30 years ago. One of his specialties is *spiedini di pesce spada* - Simple, but welcoming. - **Pippo Nunnari**, via Ugo bassi 157 - Closed Mon., June - 50,000L.

Taormina

- **La Griglia**, corso Umberto 54 - tel. (0942) 239 80 - Closed Tues., Nov. 20-Dec. 20 - 40-60,000L , serves carefully prepared country-style regional cuisine. - **A' Zammàrra**, via Fratelli Bandieri 15 - tel. (0942) 24 408 - Closed Wed., Jan. - 45,000L. Finely interpreted regional cuisine. - **Rosticepi**, via S. Pancrazio, 10 - tel. (0942) 24149, is the trattoria of Toarmina. - **Giova Rosy Senior**, corso Umberto 38 - tel. (0942) 24 411 - Closed Thur., Jan., Feb. - 50,000L. There is a large cart of antipasti and fish on a lovely jasmin-covered terrace. - **Maffei's** - A pretty terrace among the banana trees. Chic and refined. - **Ciclope**, corso Umberto - tel. (0942) 625 910 - Closed Wed. - 25-35,000L. One of the best Sicilian-style trattorias, terrace in summer. - **La Chiocca d'Oro**, via Leonardo da Vinci - tel. (942) 28 066 - Closed Thur. and Nov. - 30-45,000L.

Catania

- **La Siciliana**, via Marco Polo 52-A - tel. (095) 376 400 - Closed Mon., Aug. 15-31 - 50-60,000L. One of their specialties, the *Rippiddu nivicatu*, is a miniature. - **Etna Costa Azzura**, via de Cristofaro at Ognina (4km) - tel. 494 920 - Closed Mon. A beautiful terrace for the summer; seafood.

ACIREALE, 16km
- **Panoramico**, Sta Maria Ammalati - Closed Mon. View of Etna and wonderful *pastaciutta al raguttiino di mare*, the "castellane di Leonardo".

Siracusa

- **Archimede**, via Gemellaro 8 - tel. (0931) 69 701 - Closed Sunday, May - 40,000L. Its name is a homage to the

most illustrious of Syracusans and its cooking a homage to the fruits of the sea, for example its *zuppa di pesce* and its *riso al nero di seppia e ricotta fresca*. - **Darsena**, riva Garibaldi 6 - tel. (0931) 66 104 - Closed Wednesday - 25-50,000 L. Seafood, views over the sea. - **Don Camillo**, via Maestranza 92-100 - tel. (0931) 67 133 - Closed Sunday - 40-60,000L - **La Follia** - Another good restaurant.

Agrigente

- **Taverna Mosé**, contrada San Biagio 6 - Has a terrace with a view on the

Junon temple. They serve spaghetti that Pirandello is said to have liked! - **Le Caprice**, strada panoramica dei Tempi 51 - tel. (0922) 264 69 - 30-60,000L - Closed Friday, July 1-15 - It overlooks the Valley of the Temples.

SAN LEONE, 7 km from Agrigento.
- **Il Pescatore** - Recommended by a reader.

Eolie-Lipari

- **Filippino**, piazza Municipo - tel. (090) 981 1002 - Closed Monday in low season, November 15- December 15 - 45,000L. Traditional cuisine, and the best fish on the island. - **E Pulera**, via Stradale Diana 51 - tel. (090) 981 1158 - Open June-October, closed at noon - 35-65,000L. You can dine under a charming pergola. Reservations are a must. - **Pescecane**, Corso V. Emanuele - Very good pizzas.

Eolie-Vulcano

- **Lanterna Bleu**, Porto Ponente, via Lentia - tel. (090) 985 2287 - 40,000L. The best one on this small untamed island, good fish.

Eolie-Panarea

- **Da Pina**, via S Pietro and Trattoria da Adelina, on the port, are the two best restaurants on the island.

Eolie-Salina

- **Da Franco**, in Santa Marina. Typical cooking.

Firenze / Florence

- **Enoteca Pinchiorri**, via Ghibellina
87 - tel. (055) 24 27 57 - Closed Sun.,
Mon. at noon, Aug., Feb., Christmas,
New Year's - 125-150,000L. One of
the most refined kitchens and cellars in
Italy, where the food is served in
porcelain with silver tableware and the
wine in crystal. The keynote is elegance. - **Trattoria Coco Lezzone**, via
del Parioncino 26r - tel. (055) 287 178

- Closed Sun., Tues. evening, Aug.,
Christmas - 45-80,000L. You will find
simple perfection here is a row of
small rooms where regulars and locals
rub elbows with international celebrities. The manager announces the delicious specialties of the day one after
another as they are prepared. You don't
have to try them all, but you will be
tempted to. - **Da Gannino**, piazza del
Cimatori - tel. (055) 214 125 - Closed
Sun., Aug. This typical little osteria
near the Signoria has service on the
small square in the summer. - **Il
Latini**, via Palchetti - tel. (055) 210
916 - Closed Sun., Aug. - 30,000L.
Hidden on a back street, people stand

on line a glass of wine in hand while
waiting to be seated in this noisy convivial restaurant. There is a common
table, *prosciutto* and *vitello arosto*, a
house specialty. - **Il Cibreo**, via dei
Macci 118r - tel. (055) 234 1100 -
Closed Sun., Mon., Aug., Christmas -
60,000L. Near Santa Croce, the surroundings of a trattoria, but serving
delicious Italian nouvelle cuisine.
Reservation essential. - **Trattoria
Cammillo**, borgo San Iacopo 57 - tel.
(055) 212 427 - Closed Wed., Thu., 1st
week of Aug., Christmas - This is one
of most popular trattorias in town,
serving traditional Florentine-style
cuisine with a few innovations, such as
the curried *tortellini*. Reservation. -
Mamma Gina, borgo S. Iacopo 37 -
tel. (055) 2396 009 - Closed Sun.,

Aug. - 30-40,000L. Traditional cuisine. - **Cantinone del Gallo Nero**, via San Spirito 6 - tel. (055) 218 898 - 25,000L. It has great *Crostini*, *Chianti*, and *Tiramisu*. It is in a cellar a few yards away from and opposite Cammillo, and the entrance can be a little hard to find. - **Sostanza**, via della Porcellàna - tel. (055) 212 691 - Closed

Sat., Sun., Aug. - 40,000L. A little restaurant and grocer's near Santa Maria Novella which has become popular for its authentic atmosphere rather than its plain family cooking. To avoid ordering roast chicken or pasta al burro, note that the house specialty is cabbage soup and bistecca alla fiorentina. Friendly.
- **13 Gobbi**, Via del Porcellana 9 r - tel. (055) 2398 769. Enjoy local cuisine around tables with benches in this softly lit restaurant. - **Sabatini**, via de Panzani 9/A - tel. (055) 210 293 - Closed Mon. - 70,000L. The house

antipasti will give you a taste of good classic Tuscan cuisine. Chic. - **Da Noi**, via Fiesolana, 46r - tel. (055) 242 917 - Closed Sun., Mon., Aug., Christmas - 50,000L. This small elegant restaurant serves creative cuisine and seafood.
- **Dino**, via Ghibellina 51r - tel. (055) 241 452 - Closed Sun. evening, Mon., Aug. - 35-50,000L. One of the oldest restaurants in Florence, where each day Tuscan tradition is renewed with products fresh from the market. - **Cantinetta Antinori**, piazza Antinori 3 - tel. (055) 292 234. Hidden in the courtyard of the Antinori palace near the town hall. People come here for simple meals and good Tuscan wine. - **Buca Lipi**, via del Trebbio 1r - tel. (055) 213 768 - Closed Wed., Aug. - 30-50,000L. This picturesque cellar serves local cuisine. - **Buca Mario**, piazza Ottaviani, 16 l - tel. (055) 214 179 - Closed Wed. and Aug. - 30-50,000L. Typical regional cuisine and wine. - **Le Fonticine**, via Nazionale 79 r - tel. (055) 282 106. Is a large country-style restaurant with walls covered with paintings, Tuscan cuisine, and a few Emilian delicacies. The only drawback is that the tables are a little too close.
- **Campannina di Sante**, piazza Ravenne - tel. (055) 68 8343. It has a nice view of the Ponte Vecchio and the Signoria tower. It serves only fish dishes. There is a very pretty walk you can take in the evening along the Arno to the da Verrazzano bridge.
- **Antico Fattore**, via Lambertesca 1 - tel. (055) 238 12 15 - Closed Sun., Mon., Aug. - 35,000L. Family tratto-

ria near the Uffizi Museum serving traditional Tuscan specialties.

- **Fagioli**, Corso Tintori 47r - tel. (55) 244 285 - Closed Sat., Sun., Aug., Christmas - 30-40,000L. Typical regional specialties prepared by a real Tuscan. One of the few places where you meet more Florentines than tourists.

CAFFE' - BARS

- **Rivoire**, piazza della Signoria. It has a large terrace on the most beautiful square in the world, a nice place to have sandwhiches and pastries and relax after visiting the Offices. It is

famous for its *gianduiotti* and the *Cantucci di Prato* which is great with a glass of *Vino Santo*.

- **Gilli**, piazza della Repubblica. It has a Belle Epoch interior, and a large terrace on the busiest square in Florence, sheltered by palm trees Giacosa, via

Tornabuoni 83. Nice place to have cappuccino and pastries. It is always crowded.

- **Vivoli**, via Isola delle Strinche - Closed Mon. Very good ice cream and pastries.

- **Dolce Vita**, piazza del Carmine. The meeting place for hip young Florentines.

- **Paszkowski**, piazza della Repubblica 6, concert cafe and restaurant.

SHOPPING

- **Pineider**, piazza della Signoria 13r - Used to supply Napolean and Verdi with paper, and has continued to make stationery and desk sets for the rich and famous, and esthetes who come here to buy ink or to have their stationery monogrammed.

- **Taddei**, via Sta Margherita 11, pretty hand-crafted leather goods store.

- **Boutique de la Leather School**, also sells items made in the neighbor-

ing schools.

- **Officina Profumo Farmaceutica di Santa Maria Novella**, piazza Santa Maria Novella. Is in a 14th century chapel, and sells perfumes, cologne, elixirs, and soap. You can visit the superb back rooms by appointment.

- **Florentine jewelry**, old and new, in the shops on Ponte Vecchio.
- **Gusceli Brandi-marte**, via Bar-

tolini 18, Gold and silversmith.
- **Bottega Orafa di Cassigoli e Costanza**, via degli Ramaglienti 12 Craft jeweler.
- **The Via de' Tornabuoni**, is where you can find boutiques. For silk and traditional Florentine Renaissance brocade, try, **Antico Sattificio Fiorentini**, via Bartolini. For embroidered handkerchiefs, or house linens, go to Loretta Caponi, borgo Ognissanti 10-12r.
- **Procacci**, via de' Tornabuoni, sells quality groceries, **Gastronomia Palmieri**, via Manni 48 r and **Gastrononomia Vera**, piazza Frescobaldi 3r, has sausages and ham, wine, cheeses and other Tuscan products.
- **Mandarina Duck**, 25 Corso S Floriano - You will find several Mandarina Duck shops, selling bags and lug-

gage, in this large street leading to the Ponte Vecchio.
- **Fornasetti**, borgo degli Albizi, 70 R
- If you like this contemporary artist,

you will find his furniture, tableware and other decorative objects here.

Prato

- **Enoteca Barni**, via Ferrucci 22 - tel. (0574) 60 78 45. Everyone has been coming here since Clinton and Blair dropped in to try the cooking and the wine cellar. - **Il Piraña**, via Valentini 110 - tel. (0574) 25746 - Closed Sat. noon, Sun. and Aug. - 60-80,000L. Fine cuisine in a modern elegant decor - **Tonio**, piazza Mercatale 161 - tel. (0574) 21 266 - Closed Sun., Mon., Aug. Seafood specialties.

Siena

- **Cane e Gatto**, via Pagliaresi 6 - tel. (0577) 28 75 45 - Reserve for lunch. Good trattorias in the small street just opposite the pinacoteca. - **Guido**, Vic. Pettinaio, 7 - tel. (0577) 28 00 42 - Closed Wed., Jan. 10-25, July 15-30 - The most genuine cuisine. - **Al Mangia**, or **Il Campo**, piazza del Campo 43 - 45-50,000L. Its location on the famous Place del Campo makes it worth the visit, but it is not a tourist trap. - **Osteria Le Logge**, via del Porrione 33 - tel. (0577) 480 13 - Closed Sun. - 40-50,000L In a former grocer's, quite stylish, book if you want to be in the more pleasant of the downstairs rooms. - **Grotta Santa Caterina da Bogoga**, via della Galluzza 26 - tel. (0577) 282 208 - Closed Sun. evening, Mon., July - 30,000L. Country-style cuisine and atmosphere. - **Antica Trattoria Botteganova**, strada Chiantigiana 29 - tel. (0577) 284 230 - Closed Sun., Mon. at noon, 10 days in Aug. - 40-70,000L. This very pleasant restaurant is worth the trip: the cuisine and service are meticulously well done.

- **Nello La Taverna**, via del Porrione 28 - tel. (0577) 289 003 - Closed Mon., Feb. - 25-50,000L. Taverne frequented by Siene families, with fine cuisine and a selection of Tuscan wine.

CHIANTI COUNTRY

Fiesole
5km from Firenze

- **Trattoria Cave di Maiano**, in Maiano 3 km away, via delle cave 16 - tel. (055) 591 33 - Closed Thur., Sun. evening, Aug. - 35,000L. In the summer you can dine on large wooden tables on a shady terrace, and in the winter, in a picturesque tavern setting.

Sesto Fiorentino
8km from Florence

- **L'Ulivo Rosso**, via Le Catese 2 - tel. (055) 448 18 90. Verdi supplies the theme, with rooms named after the characters from Falstaff and a background of opera. Country specialties and wines.

Bagno a Ripoli
9km from Firenze

- **Cent'Anni**, via Centanni 7 - tel. (055) 630 122 - Closed Sat. noon, Sun., Aug. - 50,000L. This pretty restaurant has a lovely garden. The traditional Tuscan dishes served here are a family affair. Mamma Luciani does the cooking, her son Luciano makes the pastries, and Silvano takes care of the wine.

Settignano
7km from Firenze
- **Caffe' Desiderio**, is an old cafe dating from the end of the 19th-century, where you can have coffee, chocolate, pastries, and cocktails while enjoying a superb view of the Fiesole hills.

Serpiolle
8km from Firenze
- **Lo Strettoio**, via di Serpiolle 7 - tel. (055) 4250 044 - Closed at noon and Sun., Mon., Aug. Is in a beautiful room in an old villa which still has an olive oil press (which is why it has this name). The atmosphere is elegant, and the seasonal cuisine is served by *cameriere* dressed in black with white collars.

Carmignano
22km from Firenze
- **Da Delfina**, Artimino 6km, via della Chiesa - tel. (055) 871 8074 - Closed Mon. evening, Tues., Aug., Jan. 1-15. Mamma Delfina oversees the entire operation, and everything comes from the family estate (vegetables, eggs, and poultry) and is homemade, notably the *pappardelle*. An address to note.

San Casciano in Val di Pesa
18km from Firenze
IN MERCATALE
- **La Biscondola** - tel. (055) 821 381 - Closed Mon., Tues. at noon, Nov. - 40-50,000L.

CERBAIA, 6 km
- **La Tenda Rossa**, piazza del Monumento - tel. (055) 826 132 - Closed Wed., Thur. at noon, Aug. 5-28 - 75,000L. This small family-run restaurant, with a very high reputation, serves savory cuisine prepared with the freshest ingredients. Reservation.

Monterriggioni
15km from Siena
- **Il Pozzo**, piazza Roma 2 - tel. (0577)

304 127 - Closed Sun. evening, Mon., Jan., end-July-Aug. 15 - 40-50,000L. This excellent restaurant has a wide selection of wines and regional gourmet cuisine.

Castelnuovo Berardenga
20km from Siena
- **La Bottega del 30**, in Villa a Sesta, 5km from Castelnuovo - tel. (0577) 35 92 26 - Closed at noon except Sun. and National Days, Thu. and Wed. - 40-80,000L. A very popular restaurant in the region (with one Michelin star to reward Hélène Camelia), so it is best to reserve.

San Piero a Sieve
21km of Siena
- **Villa Ebe**, borgo San Lorenzo - tel. (0551) 845 7507 - Closed Mon. -

40,000L. The village and the countryside alone are worth the trip, but it's Signora Ebe's fresh pasta that makes this place truly irrestable.

Castellina in Chianti
26km from Siena
- **Antica Trattoria La Torre** - tel. (0577) 740 236 - Closed Friday, Sept. 1-15 - 30-45,000L. The longstanding family tradition of serving fine cuisine made with local products is contiuned here

Gaiole in Chianti
28km from Siena
- **Badia**, in Coltibuono, 5km - tel. (0577) 749 424 - Closed Mon., Nov. 1-Dec. 15 - 45,000L. The Benedictine tradition of humanism and fine gourmet cuisine continues here in this very pleasant place.

Brolio
25km from Siena.
- **Castello di Brolio** - Recently opened, but the reputation of the chef, Seamus de Pentheny O'Kelly, is well-established in the area. The setting, in the gardens of the Castello di Brolio, is an additional asset. Essential to reserve.

Colle Val d'Elsa
25km from Siena
- **Arnolfo**, piazza Santa Caterina 2 - tel. (0577) 920 549 - Closed Tues., Aug. 1-10, Jan. 10-Feb. 10 - 60-100,000L. On the trail of San Gimignano and Volterra, Arnofolo is a good place to stop off for a meal. The young chef in charge of the kitchen serves traditional and innovative cuisine. Reservation. - **Antica Trattoria**,

piazza Arnolfo 23 - tel. (0577) 92 37 47 - Closed Tues., and from Dec. 22 to Jan. 8. - 50-60,000 L. An institution. Small menu and few tables, but outstanding Tuscan cuisine. Reserve.

Abbey of Monteoliveto Asciano
32km from Siena
- **Osteria della Pievina**, stratale 438, Lauretana - A great place to stop after visiting the abbey of Monteoliveto on the way back to Siena via the peak route from Asciano. Atmospheric restaurant

with good cooking and cellar. - **La Torre**, in the gardens of the abbey - Closed Tues. - 50,000L. Very pleasant taverna while waiting for the opening of the monastery which closes at lunchtime. In fine weather the tables are set out under the trellis. Sandwiches.

San Antimo Abbey Montalcino
41km from Siena
- **La Cucina di Edgardo**, via Saloni, 33 - tel. (0577) 84 82 32 - Closed Wed. and in Jan. Good regional cuisine, rustic setting. - **Poggio Antico**, in Poggio Antico, 4km tel. (0577) 849 200 - Closed Mon. - 60-80,000L. Famous, Reservation. - **Taverna della Fattoria dei Barbi**, in Podernovi, 5 km from Montalcino - tel. (0577) 849 357 -

Closed Thus. evening and Wed., July 1-15, second week of Jan. - 50,000L. After visiting the abbey of San Antimo (unmissable), try all the farm produce of the fattoria here.

Montefollonico
60km from Siena
- **La Chiusa**, via Madonnina - tel. (0577) 669 668 - Closed Tues., except

from Aug. to Sept., 5 Jan. 5-Mar. 19, Nov. 5- Dec. 5 - 80-120,000L. Here you will enjoy delicious cuisine prepared by a pretty woman, and a good wine cellar, in a charming setting.

Pienza
52km from Siena
- **Dal Falco**, piazza Dante Alighieri 7 - tel. (0578) 748 551 - Closed Fri., July 10-20 and Nov. 10-30 - 30-40,000L. It serves house delicacies in a family atmosphere. - **Il Prato**, piazza Dante Alghieri 25 - tel. (0578) 748 601 -

Closed Wed., July 1-20. Friendly atmosphere and regional cuisine.

San Gimignano
38km from Siena
- **Le Terrazze**, piazza della Cisterna - tel. (0577) 575 152 - Closed Tues., Wed. noon, Jan. 1st-Feb. 10 - 40,000L. Tuscan specialties and a nice view of the Elsa Valley. - **Dorando'**, vicolo dell' oro, 2 - Closed Mon. Elegant atmosphere and very good cuisine, right near the Duomo - 50,000L. - **La Griglia** - tel. 0577-940 005 - Closed Thur., Dec. 15-Mar. 1st. A nice view on the valley.

Arezzo
- **Buca di San Francesco**, via San Francesco - tel. (0575) 23 271 - Closed Mon. evening, Tues., July - 55,000L. Delicious cuisine in a Renaissance decor thick with atmosphere. - **Al Principe**, 7km from Giovi - tel. (0575) 362 046 - Closed Mon., July 20-Aug. 20 - 50,000L. An old trattoria in the tradition.

Cortona
28km from Arezzo
- **Il Falconiere**, in S. M. a Bolena 3km away - Closed Wed. - 60,000L. Very good. - **La Grotta**, Piazzetta Baldini, 3 - Good traditional trattoria. - **Preludio**, via Guelfa, 11 - **Dardano**, via Dardano, 24. Two sympatical addresses.

Sogna - Bucine
30km from Arezzo
- **Le Antiche Sere**, 3km from ambra - tel. 055 -998 149 - Closed at midday except on Sat., Sun. and Tues. - The

restaurant is in one of the houses of this little medieval village. Superb setting and excellent cuisine. Do not miss. Reservation ssential.

Lucignano

27km from Arezzo

- **Osteria da Toto**, piazza Tribunale 6 - tel. (0575) 836 988 - Closed Tues., Nov., Feb. This is a nice place in a beautiful village.

Lucca

- **Buca di Sant' Antonio**, via della Cervia 1 - tel. (0583) 55 881 - Closed Sun. evening, Mon., July - 75,000L. Opened 1782, warm, intimate interior, one of the best restaurants in the region which has welcomed several well-known personalities. - **Puccini**, corte S Lorenzo 1 - tel. (0583) 31 61 16 - Closed Tues., and Wed. midday. 45,000L - Specialty: fish. Reserve. - **Antico Caffe' delle Mura**, piazzale Vittorio Emanuele 2 - tel. (0583) 47 962 - Closed Tues., 20 days in Jan., 10 days in Aug. - 40,000L. This old cafe serves hearty regional cuisine. - **Da Giulio in Pelleria**, via delle Conce 45 - tel. (0583) 55 948 - Closed Sun., Mon. - 40,000L. Flavorful genuine local family-style cuisine.

ROUND ABOUT.

- **Solferino**, San Macario in Piano, 6km - tel. (0583) 59 118 - Closed Wed.y, Tues. noon, two weeks in August and one for Christmas. - **Vipore**, in Pieve Santo Stefano 9km away - tel. (0583) 39 4107 - 60,000L. Closed Mon., Tues. evening. This 18th-century farmhouse has been transformed into an adorable restaurant with a nice view of the Lucca plain.

Pugnano San Giulano Terme

- **Le Arcate** - tel. (050) 850 105 - Closed Mon., Aug. - Traditional cooking. - Sergio the famous Pisan restaurant, has opened up at the Villa di Corliano, in Rigoli San Giuliano Terme.

Pisa

- **Al Ristoro dei Vecchi Macelli**, via Volturno 49 - tel. (050) 20 424 - Closed Wed., Sun. at noon, Aug. 10-20 - 60,000L - Individualized regional cooking. We liked the colorita (red bean soup), the fish and to round off

the meal, the zabaione gratinato. - **Sergio**, lungarno Pacinotti 1 - tel. (050) 58 0580 - Closed Sun., Mon. noon, Jan. - 75,000 L. The best place in Pisa, with market-fresh inventive cuisine and delicious desserts. - **Emilio**, via Roma 26 - tel. (050) 562 131 - Closed Fri. - 35,000L. Between the Arno and the Tower, this is a nice place to have lunch, with a large buffet of *antipasti*. - **Da Bruno**, via Bianchi 12 - tel. (050) 560 818 - Closed Mon. evening, Tues., Aug. 5-18 - 40,000L. It serves traditional cuisine in a friendly setting - Close to the station. - **Lo Schiaccianoci**, via Vespucci 104 - tel. (050) 21024. Closed Sun. and holidays - 50,000L. Authentic cuisine, despite the menu translated for tourists. Good Tuscan specialties, and also from Liguria, where the owner was born: bucatini all'amatriciana, ribollita, gamberi all'erba cittolina. Just by the station.

Volterra

60km from Pisa

- **Da Beppino**, via delle Prigioni 15 - tel. (0588) 86 051 - Closed Wed., Jan. 10-20. Traditional trattoria in a histor-

ical center - 30,000L. - **Etruria**, piazza dei Priori 8 - tel. (0588) 86 064 - Closed Thur., Nov. - 45,000L. The restaurant is in a former palazzo on the magnificent town square of Volterra. Delicious, highly flavored cooking, such as the recipes with wild boar in season.

Pietrasanta

- **Lo Sprocco**, via Barsanti 22 - tel. 0584 707 93 - Closed at midday from June to Sept. and on Wed. in other months - 35-55,000L. Terrace in good

weather. - **Martinatica** - tel. 0584 79 25 34 - Closed Tues. - 50-70,000L. At Baccatoio, 1km - A good place to know. - **Il Baffardello**, at Fiumetto-Marina di Pietrasanta - tel. (0584) 21 034 - Closed on Tues. at midday in summer - Pizzeria.

Livorno

- **La Barcarola**, viale Carducci 63 - tel. (0586) 402 367 - Closed Sun., Aug. - 40-60,000L. The best Livornan specialties: caciucco, fish soup, and *loup a la livournaise* in a 1900 palace. - **Gennarrino**, via Santa Fortunata 11 - tel. (0586) 888 093 - Closed Wed., Feb. - 45,000L. This is a good classic restaurant. - **Il Fanale**, Scali Novi Lena 15 - tel. (0586) 881 346 - Closed Tues. - 50,000L. Reservation advised.

Viarregio

- **Grand Caffé Margherita**, lungomare Margherita 30 - tel. (0584) 962 553 - Closed Sun. and Aug. - 50,000L. Oriental style architecture

for the façade, art nouveau for the interior, a café which has regained all its former splendor and a restaurant serving high-quality classical cuisine. - **L'Oca Bianca**, via Coppino 409 - tel. (0584) 38 84 77 - Closed at midday in July and Aug., and Tues. and

Wed. from Setp. to June. 90,000L. The place to go in Viareggion for fish, and also for cooking that combines mare e monti.

Saturnia
- **I Due Cippi da Michele**, piazza Veneto 26 - tel. (0564) 60 10 74 - Closed from Dec. 20 to 24 and on Tues. except in summer - 50,000L. Good Tuscan and French fare, served on the terrace in summer.

Grosseto
- **La Locanda**, via Vinzaglio 11 - tel. (056) 42 22 39 - Closed Sun. - 35,000L. Typical, authentic and well-prepared.

Castiglione della Pescaia
23km from Grosseto
- **Romolo**, corso della Libertà 10 - tel. (0564) 93 35 33 - Closed Tues. and in Nov. - 40-70,000L. The menu offers regional and seafood specialties. Good selection of wines (for example, Bianco de Pitigliano).

Isola d' Elba
- **Publius**, Poggio (Marciana) - tel. (0565) 99 208 - Closed from the second fortnight in Oct. until Easter. - 35-70,000L. Reputed to be the best restaurant on the island, with a beautiful view of the sea - **Rendez-vous da Marcello**, in Marciana Marina, piazza della Vittoria 1 - tel. (0565) 99 251 - Closed Wed., Jan. 10 to Feb. 10 - 40-60,000L.

T R E N T I N O
D O L O M I T E S

Trento

- **Chiesa**, via San Marco 64 - tel. (0461) 238 766 - Closed Sun., Aug. 10-25 - 60-80,000L. The specialties vary according to the seasons. During the apple season, all the dishes are made with them. In the spring, there are many early vegetables, and in the summer, fine fresh water fish from the lake. - **Antica Trattoria Due Mori**, via San Marco, 11 - tel. (0461) 98 42 51 - Closed on Mon. - 50,000L. A very good restaurant which combines Italian cuisine (specialty: *risotto*, prepared in dozens of ways) and local specialties with numerous dishes accompanied by fruit or red fruits, such as the excellet *tagliatelli* with blueberries; game in season. - **Hostaria del Buon consiglio**, via Suffragio 23 - tel. (0461) 986 619 - Open in the evening only except on Sun. - 30,000L. Rustic and friendly. - **Birreria Forst**, via Oss Mazzurana 38 - tel. (0461) 235 590 - Closed Mon. - 30,000L. Good place for lunch, either at the bar, or in the back room. - **Le Bollicine**, via dei Ventuno 1 - tel. (0461) 983 161 - Closed Sun., Aug. - 35,000L. Restaurant and tavern on the road to Buon Consiglio Castle.

IN CIVEZZANO, 6 km from Trento
- **Maso Cantanghel**, via Madonnina 33 - tel. (0461) 858 714 - Closed Sun., Easter, Aug. - 35,000L. This beautiful old farmhouse located just outside of town, has been nicely restored, and offers carefully prepared cuisine and attentive service.

CAFFE' - BARS
- **Caffe' Campregher**, via Mazzini. Delicious cocktails made with *Spumante*, a sparkling regional wine.

Calavino
19km from Trento

- **Castel Toblino** - tel. (0461) 44 036. Located in a marvelous landscape of mountains and lakes, this beautiful castle on Lake Garde now has a restaurant in one of its most charming rooms.

Riva del Garda
28km from Trento

- **Vecchia Riva**, via Bastione 3 - tel. (0464) 555 061 - Closed Tues. and Wed. evening in low season - 50,000L. Elegant, with meticulous service and cuisine. - **Bastione**, via Bastione 19-A - tel. (0464) 552 652 - Closed Wed., Nov. 4-Dec. 11 - 30,000L. Typically Trentinan cuisine in a warm friendly atmosphere. You will need a reservation.

Madonna di Campiglio

- **Prima o Poi**, Pozze 8 - tel. (0465) 57 175 - Closed Wednesday, June. A few kilometers from the center of town on the road to Pinzolo, do stop at this little wooden house where the Recagni family is waiting to offer you some generous portions of mountain fare.
- **Rifugio Malghette**, Pradalago - tel. (0465) 41 144 - Closed September 20-Christmas, May-June 10 - 30,000L. This warm friendly castle is located in the Andamello-Brenta Reserve. The best time of year to visit the forest is at the beginning of July when the rhododendrons are in bloom. The mushroom and blueberry risotto and homemade pasta are always a delight.

Bolzano

- **Da Abramo**, piazza Gries 16 - tel. (0471) 280 141 - Closed Sunday and August - 45-65,000L. Elegant restaurant.
- **Chez Frederic**, via Armando Diaz 12 - tel. (0471) 271 011 - 35,000L. It serves French-inspired cuisine. Dining in the shaded courtyard in the summer is especially pleasant.
- **Castel Mareccio**, via Claudia de' Medici 12 - tel. (0471) 979 439. An elegantly rustic castle surrounded by vineyards.

LOCAL SPECIALTIES
- **Antica Salumeria Salsamenteria Guiliano Masé**, via Goethe 15 has homemade *spek tirolese, salami di selvagina*, and other delicacies.

Bressanone

- **Fink**, Portici Minoni 4 - tel. (0472) 83 48 83 - Closed Wednesday, July 1-15. Typical mountain cuisine in an old palace located under the Medieval arcades of the center of Bressanone -
Oste Scuro, vicolo Duomo 3 - tel. (0472) 83 53 43 - Closed Sunday evening, Monday, January 10-February 5 - 40,000L. Tyrolean cuisine in a Baroque dining room, and on

a beautiful terrace in the summer.

Fie allo Scilliar

- **Tschafon**, Fié di Sopra 57 - tel. (0471) 72 5024 - Open in the evening only, closed Monday, January 9-22, November 1-14. If you are a fan of French cuisine, you can expect a warm welcome from Therese Bidart. If you come between October and April, try her extraordinary fish buffet.

Merano

- **Sisi**, via Galilei 44, - tel. 0473 123 10 62 - Closed Monday and the first three weeks in July - 60,000L. 'Promises to be a good replacement for Andrea' (the highly regarded restaurant that was for a long time at this address), according to a well-informed reader. - **Flora**, via Portici 75 - tel. (0473) 231 484 - Closed Sunday, Monday at noon, January 15-February 28 - 55-85,000L. Sophisticated Tyrolean and Italian cuisine.

LOCAL SPECIALTIES

- **Casa del Miele Schenk**, via casa di Risparmio 25. Honey, royal jelly, and an assortment of hand-crafted candles.

Santa Gertrude - Val D'ultimo

28 km from Merano
- **Genziana**, via Fontana Bianca 116 - tel. (0473) 79 133 - Closed Friday, November 1st-December 26 - 50,000L. One of the best, and certainly one of the highest (2000 meters) restaurants in Italy. Cooking of the Tyrol and Trentino: polenta, porcini and also linzer, strudel and sacher torte.

Villabassa

- **Friedlerhof**, via Dante 40 - tel. (0474) 75 003 - Closed Tuesday, June - 40,000L. 23km from Brunico, Lovely restaurant with Tyrolean meals and decor, 23km from Brunico.

Ortisei

- **Ramoser**, via Purger 8 - tel. (0471) 796 460 - Closed Thursday - 40,000L. This warm friendly restaurant, one of the best in Val Gardena, serves authentic regional cuisine. - **Janon**, via Rezia 6 - tel. (0471) 796 412 - Closed Tuesday, November - 30,000L. Typically Tyrolean cuisine and good desserts.

Venezia / Venice
near San Marco

RESTAURANTS:

- **Harry's Bar**, calle Vallaresco 1323 - tel. (041) 528 5777 - Closed Monday, January 4-February 15 - 110,000L. The *Bellini, carpaccio*, and *risotto* are house specialties famous all over the world. The best table is the one near the bar. Reservations are a must. - **Trattoria alla Colomba**, Piscina-Frezzeria 1665, San Marco - tel. (041) 522 11 75 - Closed Wednesday in low season - 70-100,000L. One of the most popular trattorias in Venice. It has excellent cuisine and works by contemporary artisits on the walls. - **Antico Martini**, across from the opera - tel. (041) 522 41 21 - Closed Tuesday, Wednesday noon - 70-120,000L - Delicious. - **Al Teatro**, Campo San Fantin 1917 - tel. (041) 523 72 14 -

Closed Monday - 40,000L. The walls of this pizzeria-tobacco shop are covered with dedications from actors and performers who come after their shows. Pleasant for its terrace with view over the Fenice (even when the theatre is shrouded in scaffolding). - **La Caravella**, via XXII Marzo - tel (041) 520 89 01 - Closed Wednesday in winter - 75-132,000L. - **Vini da Arturo**, calle degli Assassini 3656 - tel. (041) 528 69 74. Only seven tables which you must reserve if you want to stand a chance of having the excellent meat served here. Snobbish. - **Da Raffaele**, San Marco 2347 - tel. (041) 523 23 17 - Closed Thursday, Christmas. You can dine near a large fireplace in the winter. In the summer the tables are set up along a picturesque little canal on a gondola route. - **Do Forni**, calle dei Specchieri 457 - tel. (041) 523 77 29 - Closed Thursday in winter and end of November-beginning of December- 60-90000L.

CAFFE' ET BACARI

- **Quadri**, piazza San Marco. is across the square on the sunny side, and is also very elegant. - **Caffe' Lavena**, piazza San Marco 134. Despite the fact that it is 200 years old, the Lavena holds its own with its two illustrious neighbors. - **Florian**, piazza San Marco 56 - Closed Wednesday. Travelers and Venetians have appreciated its sumptuous interior and large terrace on the shady side of Saint Mark Square since 1720. At five o'clock, people

come here to take chocolate; before dinner, they come for a *Bellini* (spumante and fresh peach juice in summer) or *Tintoretto* (spumante and fresh apple juice in winter). After dinner, it's time for grappa. - **Caffe' Paolin**, campo San Stefano, 2692 San Marco. Has a large sunny terrace on the campo where you can enjoy the best ice cream in town or a spritz (*Prosecco* and *bitter*). - **Vino Vino**, Ponte delle Veste 2007A, is a small bar popular with gondoliers who come here to take a break, just a few steps away from the Fenice Theatre. There is a good selection of Italian wine, which you can enjoy along with a dish of *pasta e fagioli*. - **Enoteco Volto**, calle Cavalli, 4081 San Marco 4081 - tel. (041) 522 89 45. Is the ideal place for lunch. You can have delicious little sandwiches on rye bread along with an *ombre* (white venetian wine), or other equally good wines such as *Brunello, Barello,* or *Barbaresco*. There is also a

wide assortment of beers - **Al Bacareto**, San Samuele 3447, crowed.

near Rialto

RESTAURANTS:
- **Trattoria Madonna**, calle de la Madonna 594 - tel. (041) 522 38 24. Closed Wednesday, Christmas, August 1st-15 - 40,000L. One of the most typically Venetian trattorias, but it can be difficult to find a table here. - **Poste Vecie**, Pescheria Rialto - tel. (041) 721

822. Near the Rialto fisch market. Right next to the fish market. Fine décor in the dining rooms, and large, very romantic terrace beside the canal (covered in winter), plus excellent fish menus - but a very touristy place. - **Al Graspo de Ua**, calle de Bombaseri 5094 - tel. (041) 522 36 47 - Closed Mon., Tues., Dec. 20-Jan. 10, August 1st-15 - 70,000L. It has a picturesque decor and lives up to its reputation as the best seafood restaurant in town.

BACARI
- **Vini da Pinto**, campo della Pescaria - The favorite bar with the market fish vendors who come to warm up at the counter with a little glass of white wine and crostini, a plate of fish and prawns. Pleasant terrace at lunchtime

in summer. - **Alla Botte**, near the Rialto bridge and the Campo san Bartolomeo - a real Italian-style bar where they serve mortadella sliced to order and wine by the glass. Ideal for lunch.

San Polo

- **Osteria da Fiore**, calle del Scaleter

- tel. (041) 72 13 08 - Closed Sunday, Monday, Christmas, August - Seafood - Reservation advised.
- **Ai Mercanti**, Pescheria Rialto, tel. (041) 524 02 82 - Closed Sunday - 60,000L.

- **Da Ignazio**, calle del Saoneri - tel. (041) 523 48 52 - Closed Saturday - 60,000L. The vaporetto stop is San Tomé, then near the Casa Goldoni. A welcoming restaurant with a terrace in summer, famous for its *baccalà mantecado* and its fish.

near Cannaregio

- **Fiaschetteria Toscana**, S Giovanni

Crisostomo - tel. (041) 528 52 81 - Seafood specialities, salted bass, risotto. - **Vini da Gigio**, near Ca' d'Oro - tel. (041) 528 51 40 - Closed Sunday evening and Monday, August, January - 45,000L. - **Osteria Al Million S. Giovanni Crisostomo**, 5841 - Closed Wednesday. One of the oldest baccari in Venise. Try *Soave* or *Prosecco* if you like while wine, or *Valpolicella* or *Bardolino* if you prefer red, to go with you *molecche* (soft crab) or *cichetti*. - **Ca d'Oro** or **alla Vedova** (the widow's), calle del Pistor. Typical bar where you can eat good fish and the house specialty, polpete d'Alda (meat balls).

BACARI

- **Do Mori**, calle dei Do Mori, near the Rialto brige. The one place you must not miss in this quarter. Careful, it closes at 13:00 for lunch.
- **Do Spade**, calle Le do Spade, an extension of des do Mori street. Counter service.
- **Alla Pergola**, fondamenta della Sensa Cannaregio 3318 - Close to

Tintoretto's house, a typical bacaro serving authentic family cuisine. **Antica Mola**, fondamenta Ormesini - in the ghetto, the old Jewish quarter of Venice which tourists tend to ignore. Very nostalgic atmosphere, where movie fans will recognise the square that was used by visconti for a scene in Senso... Terrace overlooking the canal.

with a view of the mills of Stuky,fish specialties.

near Dorsoduro Accademia

RESTAURANTS

- **Ai Cugnai**, Dorsoduro San Vio. Typical trattoria, loca customers. - **Ai Gondolieri**, Dorsoduro San Vio 366 - San Vio - tel. (041) 528 63 96 - Closed Tuesday - 90,000L - Specialty: meat. Snobbish, expensive atmosphere. Reservation.
- **Locanda Montin**, fondamenta di

Borgo 1147 - tel. (041) 522 71 51 - Closed Tuesday evening, Wednesday - 30,000L. It is located very close to the Guggenheim Foundation, and serves traditional cuisine. In the summer, the tables are set up under an arbor in the large courtyard.
- **Le Riviera**, Zattere 1473 - tel (41) 522 76 21 - Closed in August - A hard-to-findentrance on the zattere, with a terrace in summer by the canal

- **Cantinone Storica**, San Vio 661 - tel. (041) 52 39 577 - A delightful fish restaurant with service beside the canal in summer and a boos, Alessandro, who will give you a very Italian welcome.

- **L'incontro**, campo Santa Margherita - tel. (041) 522 24 04 - Closed Modnays - Very friendly atmosphere on a square where young Venetians gather in summer on the café terraces, off the tourist track. - **Tattoria da Silvio**, San Pantalon 3818 3748 - tel. (041) 520 58n 33 - Near Campo San Margherita. Ideal in summer when the food is served in the pretty inner courtyard. Always crowded. Reservation essential.

BAR AND BACARI
- **Cantinone Già Schiavi**, San

Trovaso 992 - A favorite haunt of students who come here for panini and spritz al bitter, because of its closeness to the university and the academy.

Between riva degli Schiavonni, Giardini and Arsenale.

RESTAURANTS
- **Corte Sconta**, calle del Pestrin 3886 - tel. (041) 522 70 24 - Closed Sunday, Monday - 60,000L. This subtly elegant restaurant serves truly excellent cuisine. It is the best place in Venice, frequented by a clientele of intellectuals and artists, who have had no trouble keeping it relatively secret, as it is not very easy to find (Vaporetto: stazione Arsenale. On left to 4th bridge and street on right) - **Al Cavo**, campiello della Pescaria 3968 - tel. (041) 522 38 12 - Closed Wednes-

day, Thursday, August 10-20 - 60,000L. A favorite haunt of Venetians. - **Hostaria da Franz**, fondamenta San Isepo 754 - tel. (041) 522 75 05 - Closed Tuesday off season, January - 50-60,000L. Specialties: seafood. In the summer the tables are set up along the canal. By reservation. (Vaporetto: n° 18, stazione Giardini). Chic.

La Giudecca

RESTAURANTS
- **Cip's at the Palazzetto** - The new restaurant-pizzeria-grill of the new

annexe to th Cipriani. A floating terrace with a view of San Marco and the Salute. - **Harry's Dolci**, fondamenta San Biagio - tel. (041) 522 48 44 - Closed Monday, November 10-March 10 - 70,000L - Less touristy than Harry's Bar - Excellent cuisine. This is the summer headquarters of ultra-chic Venetians. - **L'Altanella**. As you walk along the canal on the Giudecca, you will notice the small Virginia creeper-covered terrace of the Altanella, where you can have Venetian family-style cuisine.

SHOPPING
- **Stefano Zanin** has sculpted gold-leaf picture frames.
- **Renato Andreatta** has frames for mirrors or pictures, and masks.
- **Mondonovo**, ponte dei Pugni, 3063 - Dorsoduro. - **Giano Lavato** makes superb masks, and also does work for the theater.
- **Legatoria,** Piazzesi S. Maria del Giglio 2511 -You will find marbled and traditional "carta varese" hand

printed stationery, and other Venitian handicrafts, old-fashioned book bindings, and beautiful collectors' items.

- **Antichita` V. Troïs**, Campo S. Maurizio - For splendid fabrics by Fortuny made at la Giudecca.
- **Rubelli**, palais Cornerspinelli, Campo S. Gallo. Superb damask, silks, and brocades.
- **Delphos**, and **Venetia Studium**, campo S. Fantin, 1997, have dresses, handbags, and Fortuny scarves in a wide assortment of colors, as well as lamps created by Fortuny.
- **Chez Mazzaron**, sells handmade lace including the famous "Venitian stitch".
- **Jesurum**, Ponte della Canonica S. Marco, offers house linens and old lace.
- **Pauly**, piazza S. Marco, beautiful glass art objects.
- **Venini**, Piazzetta Leoncini 314, San Marco.
- **L'Isola**, campo S.-Moise, glass art objects of Carlo Moretti.
- **Rigattieri**, calle de la Mandola, glass art objects of Seguso, Barovier and Toso, Venini...
- **Archimede Seguso**, piazza San Marco. The doyen of craftsmen in glass.
- **Industie Veneziane** near the San Marco station or Battiston, calle Vallaresco 1320 have the famous "Harry's Bar" pitchers here.
- **Codognato**, calle del Ascension, sells antique Art-Deco, Cartier, Fabergé, and Tiffany jewelry.
- **Nardi**, piazza S. Marco, is one of the best jewelers and has a superb series of Othellos, each one of a kind.

- **M. Antiquités**, sells jewels by Monica Zecchi, silk velvet dresses and capes by Mirella Spinella.
- **Enoteca Al Volto**, calle Cavalli 4081, has good selection of Veneto wines.
- **Pasticceria Dal Col**, San Marco 1035 has all kinds of traditional Venitian candies.

Murano

- **Venini**, Fondamenta Veltrai 50 - If you only visit one, come here to see the work of the grand-daughter of Mario Venini.
- **Carlo Moretti**, Fondamenta Manin 3 - To see the work of this other great artist.
- **Ai Frati** - tel (041) 736 694 - Closed Thursday, February. This is the oldest osteria in Murano serving typically Venetian meals.The terrace on the

grand canal is particularly pleasant in the summer.

Torcello

- **Locanda Cipriani** - tel (041) 735433. Closed Tuesday, January, February 1st-18 - 80-100,000L. Adjoining the cathedral of Santa Maria Assunta, where the mosaics make it an essential

stop. Quality in the Cipriani tradition. - **Ponte del Diavolo** - tel. (041) 730 401. Closed Thursday, January, February, every evening except Saturday - 40-70,000L. A pleasant inn serving seafood specialties. In the summer you can dine in a pretty garden.

Burano

- **Osteria ai Pescatori** - tel. (041) 730 650 - Closed Monday, January - 50,000L. Boasts two centuries of activity and fidelity to authentic *buranella* cuisine, a pretty dining room, and a small garden for warm sunny days. - **Al Gato Nero-da Ruggero** - tel. (041) 730 120 - Closed Monday, January 30-February 10, October 30-November 15 - 50,000L. Regional cuisine atmosphere.

Verona

- **Arche**, via delle Arche Scaligere 6 - tel. (045) 800 7415 - Closed Sun., Mon. noon, Jan. - 80,000L. Across from the famous Della Scala mau-

soleum this old tavern is also a marvelous elegant restaurant. - **Il Desco**, via Dietro San Sebastiano 7 - tel. (045) 595 358 - Closed Sun., Christmas, Eastern, June - 70-100,000L. In the historical center of Verona, you can enjoy Italain-style nouvelle cuisine and a very nice wine cellar. - **Nuovo Marconi**, via Fogge 4 - tel. (045) 591 910 - Closed Sun., July - 70,000L. An elegant restaurant with fine Italian cuisine and friendly service. - **Re Teodorico**, piazzale Castel San Pietro - tel. (045) 8349 990 - Closed Wed., Jan. - 55,000L. It has a nice view of Verona and the Adige. - **12 Apostoli**, vicolo Corticella San Marco 3 - tel. (049) 596 999 - Closed Sun. evening,

Mon., Jan. 2-8, end-June - 85,000L. This is the "must-see" of Verona. - **Bottega del Vino**, via scudo di Francia 3 - tel. (045) 80 04 535 - A pleasant wine bar right by the piazza dell'Erbe, which serves traditional cooking in a jolly, informal atmosphere. When you reserve, ask for a table in the first room with the bar. - **Rubiani**, piazetta Scalette Rubiani 3 - tel. (045) 800 68 30 - Closed Fri., Jan. - 60,000L. One of the best restaurants in this district close to the arena and full of tourist restau-

rants. Try risotto ai bruscandoli and, for the adventurous, *coniglio al caffè*. - **Osteria dal Duca**, via Arche Scaligere 2 - tel. (045) 59 44 74. The clientele is made up of regulars who come for the *pastisada de caval* (horse stew), the specialty of Verona. - **Trattoria Al Camiere**, piazza San Zeno 10 - tel. (045) 803 0765 - Closed Wed. evening, Thur., July. Meticulous cuisine, with an emphasis on local produce. - **Osteria all' Oste Scuro**, vicolo San Silvestro 10 - tel. (045) 59 26 50 - Closed Sat. at noon and Sun., Christmas, Aug. 20-31 - 80-100,000L. Two small, warm rooms in a palazzo in the historic center of town. A small menu offers excellent fish specialties. A restaurant much liked by the locals, so you are advised

to book. - **Osteria le Vecete**, via Pelliciai 32 - Closed on Sun. - Wine bar, pork products, convivial. - **Trattoria Sant'Anastasia**, corso Sant'Anastasia 27 - tel. (045) 800 91 77 - Closed Wed. and ten days in Sept. - 20-55,000L. Tasty fare: *torteli di zucca, spedini misti di mare caramelle di mascaprone e basilico al sugo di ciliegino fresco*, and for dessert *zabaione al caffè*.

CAFFE' - BARS

- **Caffe' Dante**, piazza dei Signori. Has a warm friendly atmosphere and opens onto the superb square surrounded by palaces and the Loggia del Consiglio. Restaurant on the terrace in fine weather, a gem. - **Campidoglio**, piazzetta Tirabosco 4. A yuppie bar in a former convent with its original frescos. - **Enotheque Dal Zovo**, Vicolo San Marco in Foro, 7 - has a large selection of wines to taste, *amarone* and *reciota*.

Padova / Padua
- **Antico Brolo**, Corso Milano 22 - tel. (049) 656 088 - Closed Sun., Aug. 8-28 - 50-90,000L. It serves cuisine made from fresh products from the market. In the summer you can dine by candlelight in the garden. - **El Toula'**, via Belle Parti 11,tel. (049) 8751822 - Closed

Sun., Mon. evening, Aug. - 65-80,000L. People always love the elegant but conventional Toula'. - **l Michelangelo**, corso Milano 22 - tel. (049) 65 60 88 - Closed Sat. noon, Mon., end-Aug. - 45,000L. Reservation. - **Mario e Mercedes**, via San Giovanni da Verdara 13 - tel. (049) 871 97

31 - Closed Wed., Christhmas and New Year, Aug. 15-31. 45,000L. All the specialties of Venezia in a nice place.

CAFÉS, BARS.

- **Caffè Pedrocchi** - Opened in 1831 by A. Pedrocchi, this was the most elegant cultural café in Europe. The octagonal room has now been restored to its original size and the three historic salons have been renovated; they are in the 3 colors, white, red and green, of the Italian flag. The adjacent neogothic Pedrocchino has become a patisserie.

Dolo
19km from Padoue
- **Locanda alla Posta** - tel. (041) 410 740 - Closed Mon. - 55,000L. Seafood restaurant.

Vicenza
- **Scudo di Francia**, Contrà Piancoli 4 - tel. (0444) 323322 - Closed Sun. evening, Mon., Aug. - 50,000L. Enjoy Venetian delicacies in a Venetian-style palace, near the piazza Signori, specialites seafood - **Cinzia e Valerio**, piazzetta Porto Padova 65 - tel. (0444) 505 213 - Closed Mon., Jan. 1st-7, Aug. - 70,000L. Seafood restaurant - **Gran Caffe' Garibaldi**, piazza dei Signori 5 - tel. (0444) 544 147 - Closed Tues. evening, Wed., Nov. - 35,000L. You can either have a drink and a small sandwich on one of the marble tables in a beautiful spacious room on the ground floor, or enjoy classic Italian cuisine in the restaurant upstairs. - **Osteria Cursore**, stradella Cursore 10 - tel. (0444) 32 35 04. Friendly and popular.

Treviso
- **Le Beccherie**, piazza Ancillotto 10 - tel. (0422) 56 601 - Closed Sun. evening, Mon., end-july. One of the oldest and most prestigious restaurants in town, and is doing its part to revive

the great culinary tradition of the region. - **Al Bersagliere**, via Barberia 21 - tel. (0422) 541 988 - Closed Sun., Sat. noon, beg-Jan. and beg-Aug. Good Trevisan cuisine. Reservation.

Asolo

- **Aio Due Archi**, via Roma 55 - tel. 0423 95 22 01 - Closed Wed. evening, Thrus. and from Jan. 15 to 30 - 45,000L. - **La Tavernetta**, via Schiavonesca 45, 2km away - tel. 0423 95 22 73 - Closed Tues. - 30-50,000L. Limited number of places, so reserve.

Miane

- **Da Gigetto**, via A. de Gasperi 4 - tel. (0438) 960020 - 50,000L. Closed Mon. evening, Tues., Jan. 7-22, Aug. 1st-22. An excellent restaurant in a luxurious country-style setting, serving fine innovative Italian cuisine inspired by nouvelle cusisne, but without the drawbacks of its French counterpart. The wine cellar is excellent, as is the service.

Belluno

- **Al Borgo**, via Anconetta 8 - tel. (0437) 926 755 - Closed Mon. evening, Tues., Jan. 15-30 - 35,000L. It combines fine cuisine and culture in a beautiful Venetian villa on the border between Veneto and Alto Adigea.

Mel, 14km from Belluno

- **Antica Locanda al Cappello**, piazza Papa Luciani - tel. (0437) 753 651 - Closed Tues. evening, Wed., 2 weeks in July - 30,000L. The old sign still outside this17th century palace testifies to its past as a postal inn. Cuisine based on old recipes is served here.

Cortina d' Ampezzo

- **Bellavista-Meloncino**, in Gillardon

- tel. (0436) 861 043 - Closed Tues., June, Nov. - 50,000L. A small restaurant, very popular among the regulars at the resort. From the center of Cortina, follow the signs to Falzarego. - **El Toulà**, Ronco 123 - tel. (0435) 3339 - Closed Mon., open Dec. 20-April 12, July 20-end-August - 90,000L. The elegant restaurant of Cortina. - **Da Beppe Sello**, via Ronco 67 - tel. (0436) 3236 - 40-50,000L. We like the hearty cuisine served in this small three star chalet-hotel, in the pretty Tyrolean-style dining room or on a terrace in the summer. - **Da Leone e Anna**, via Alverà 112 - tel. (0436) 2768 - 50-60,000L. Sardinian specialties. - **El Zoco**, via Cademi 18 - tel. 860 041 - 50-70,000L. Reservation preferable.- **Baita Fraina**, Fraina - tel. (0436) 3634 - Closed Mon., Oct., Nov., May, June - 40,000L. This chalet deep in the mountains has a warm convivial atmosphere and family-style cuisine. - **Il Meloncino al Lago**, lago Ghedina - tel. (0436) 860 376, Closed Tues., July, Nov. It serves good authentic cuisine in a rustic but elegant chalet in a very beautiful natural setting.

CAFFE' - BARS

- **Bar del Posta**, Hotel de la Poste, piazza Roma. Quiet atmosphere and a small bar which Hemingway loved. The *Dolomite* is the house cocktail.

Udine

- **Alla Vedova**, via Tavagnacco 8 - tel. (0432) 470 291 - Closed Sun. evening, Mon., Aug. - 45,000L. Savory cuisine in a friendly atmosphere.

Trieste

- **Harry's Grill**, Hotel Duchi d'Aosta, piazza dell' Unita d'Italia - tel. (040) 62 081 - 90,000L. The hotel bar is the meeting point for the town businessmen, and the restaurant is also very popular for its seafood specialties. - **Ai Fiori**, piazza Hortis 7 - tel. (040) 300 633 - Closed Sun., Mon., June 15-July 15 - 40,000L. Elegant seafood restaurant. - **Suban**, via Comici 2 - tel. (040) 54 368 - Closed Mon., Tues., 20 days in Aug. - 60,000L. When it opened in 1865, it was a country inn. The town has now surrounded it, but the interior remains unchanged. Try the delicious herb risotto. In the summer, meals are served under a lovely pergola. - **Elefante Bianco**, riva Tre Novembre 3 - tel. (040) 365 784 - Closed Sat. noon, Sun. - 35-75,000L. You must reserve if you want to stand a chance of getting a table. - **Al Granzo**, piazza Venezia 7 - tel. (040) 306 788 - Closed Wed. - 50,000L. One of the star restaurants for fish and seafood in Trieste. Try to get a table facing the very picturesque fish market. - **Al Bragozzo**, riva Nazario Sauro 22 - tel. (040) 303 001 - Closed Sun., Mon., June 25-July 10. One of the most popular restaurants of the port.

CAFFE' - BARS

- **Caffe' San Marco**, opened in 1904 under the Austro-Hungarian Empire. It has been recently restored to recreate the atmosphere of days gone by when it was a literary cafe where Umberto Saba, Italo Svevo, and more

recently contemporary writers such as Claudio Magris and Giorgio Voghera would gather. The San Marco is twinned with the Hungaria in Budapest and the Florian in Venice, two other cafes which have played an important role in the cultural life of the center of Europe. - **Caffe' degli Specchi**, piazza dell'Unita de' Italia, is on the largest square in Trieste, a good starting point for your visit to the town. Have a drink in the evening and watch the sun go down over the sea. - **Para Uno**, via Cesare Battisti 13, has marvelous cappuccino.

INDEX

INDEX

A

Agrigento
    Villa Athena 239
    Foresteria BaglioBaia di Luna.....................................240
Alba (Cuneo) : Villa La Meridiana - Cascina Reine 192
Alberobello (Bari) : Hotel dei Trulli 216
Alghero (Sassari) : Hotel Villa Las Tronas 231
Altomonte (Cosenza) : Hotel Barbieri..1
Amalfi (Salerno)
    Hotel Luna Convento..28
    Hotel Santa Caterina 29
    La Conchiglia 30
Amalfi - Conca dei Marini (Napoli) : Hotel Belvedere 31
Amelia (Terni) : El Piccolo Hotel del Carleni 188
Arcugnano (Vicenza) : Hotel Villa Michelangelo 502
Artimino - Carmignano (Firenze)
    Hotel Paggeria Medicea 329
    Fattoria di Bacchereto *(220/260 000 L)* 330
Arzachena-Cannigione (Sassari) : Hotel Li Capanni 232
Asolo (Treviso)
    Hotel Villa Cipriani 486
    Hotel del Sole 487
Assisi (Perugia)
    Hotel Fontebella...162
    Hotel Umbra...163
    Le Silve di Armenzano *(Armenzano)* 164
    Podere La Fornace *(Tordibetto)*..................................165

B

Baia Domizia (Caserta) : Hotel Della Baia 5
Barbarano Vicentino (Vicenza) : Il Castello 503
Barberino Val d'Elsa (Firenze)
    La Callaiola 320
    Il Paretaio *(San Filippo)* 321
    La Spinosa *(Scheto)* 322
    Fattoria Casa Sola *(Cortine)* 323
    La Chiara di Prumiano *(Prumiano)*............................324
Bergamo : Agnello d'Oro 111
Bevagna (Perugia) : L'Orto degli Angeli 166
Bologna
    Hotel Corona d'Oro 45
    Hotel Commercianti..46
    Hotel Orologio...47
Bolsena (Viterbo) : Hotel Royal 90
Bolzano
    Park Hotel Laurin...419

Bovara di Trevi (Perugia) : Casa Giulia 167
Bressanone (Bolzano) : Hotel Elephant................................432
Breuil Cervinia (Aosta)
   L'Hermitage..205
   Les Neiges d'Antan 206
Brisighella (Ravenna)
   Il Palazzo 58
   Relais Torre Pratesi (*Cavina*) 59
Bussetto (Parma)
   I Due Foscari 56

C

Caldaro (Bolzano) : Pensione Leuchtenburg 424
Camogli (Genova) : Hotel Cenobio dei Dogi 96
Canalicchio (Perugia)
   – Relais Il Canalicchio 168
Canelli (Asti) : La Luna e i Falo' 193
Canizzaro-Catania : Grand Hotel Baia Verde 242
Cantello (Varese)
   – Albergo Madonnina 145
Capri Isola di (Napoli)
   Villa Brunella...10
   Europa Palace Hotel 11
   Hotel Luna 12
   Hotel Punta Tragara 13
   Hotel Villa Sarah 14
   Pensione Quattro Stagioni......................................15
Castel del Piano Umbro (Perugia) : Villa Aureli 158
Castel di Tusa (Messina) : Museo Albergo L'Atelier sul Mare 253
Castelfranco Emilia (Modena) : Villa Gaidello Club 52
Castellina in Chianti (Siena)
   Palazzo Squarcialupi 358
   Hotel Salivolpi 359
   Tenuta di Ricavo (*Ricavo*) 360
   Hotel Villa Casalecchi 361
   Locanda Le Piazze 362
   Albergo Fattoria Casafrassi (*Casafrassi* 363
   Hotel Belvedere di San Leonino (*San Leonino*) 364
Castelnuovo Berardenga (Siena)
   Castello di Montalto 339
   Hotel Villa Arceno *San Gusmè* 340
   Hotel Relais Borgo San Felice *San Felice* 341
Castelrotto-Siusi (Bolzano)
   Hotel Cavallino d'Oro 428
   Albergo Tschötscherhof 429
Castiglion Fiorentino (Arezzo) : Relais San Pietro in Polvano 274
Castiglione di Ravello (Salerno) : Hotel Villa San Michelle 32
Castelvecchio di Rocca Barbena(Savona) -: Casa Cambi 107
Castiglioni di Rufina (Firenze) : La Sosta A' Busini 317
Castiglione d'Orcia-Rocca d'Orcia (Siena) : Cantina Il Borgo 386

Cenito (Salerno) : Giacaranda 23
Certaldo Alto (Firenze) : Osteria del Vicario 327
Cesaro (Messina) : Villa Miraglia 255
Cetona (Siena) : La Frateria 387
Champoluc (Aosta) : Villa Anna Maria 207
Cioccaro di Penango (Asti) : Locanda del Sant'Uffizio 197
Cisternino (Brindisi) : Villa Cenci...218
Citta di Castello (Perugia) : Hotel Tiferno 169
Cividale del Friuli (Udine) : Locanda al Castello 493
Cogne (Aosta) : Hotel Bellevue...208
Colle di San Paolo di Tavernelle (Perugia) : Villa di Monte Solare .170
Colline di Iseo - Iseo (Brescia) : I Due Roccoli 112
Cologne Franciacorta (Brescia) : Cappuccini 113
Cortina d'Ampezzo (Belluno)
    Hotel Bellevue 475
    Hôtel de la Poste 476
    Hôtel d'Ancora 477
    Hotel Pensione Menardi 478
    Hotel Franceschi 479
    Baita Fraina *(Fraina)*...480
Corvara in Badia (Bolzano) : Hotel La Perla 433
Cortona (Arezzo)
    Albergo San Michele 275
    Hotel Il Falconiere *(San Martino)*..276
Costozza di Longare (Vicenza) : Azienda A & G da Schio 504
Courmayeur-Arnouva (Aosta) : Chalet Val Ferret 211
Courmayeur-Entrèves (Aosta)
    La Grange 212
    Hotel La Brenva 213

D
Dolo (Venezia) : Villa Ducale 472

E
Erbusco (Brescia) : L'Albereta 114
Erice (Trapani) : Hotel Elimo Erice 262

F
Farnese (Viterbo) : Il Voltone 92
Fasano (Brindisi) : Masseria Marzalossa 219
Ferrara
    Hotel Duchessa Isabella 48
    Locanda della Duchessina 49
    Locanda Borgonuovo 50
Fié Allo Sciliar (Bolzano) : Hotel Turm......................................427
Finale Ligure (Savona) : Hotel Punta Est 108
Firenze
    Hotel Helvetia & Bristol 281
    Hotel Regency 282
    Hotel Brunelleschi 283

Hotel J & J 284
Hotel Monna Lisa 285
Grand Hotel Minerva 286
Hotel Montebello Splendid...................287
Hotel Lungarno 288
Hotel de la Ville 289
Torre di Bellosguardo 290
Villa Belvedere 291
Villa Carlotta (...................................292
Hotel Hermitage 293
Hotel Loggiato dei Serviti....................294
Hotel Splendor....................................295
Hotel Morandi alla Crocetta 296
Hotel Pensione Pendini 297
Pensione Annalena 298
Hotel Tornabuoni Beacci 299
Hotel David 300
Hotel Boticelli 301
Residenza Johanna I 302
Residenza Johanna II...........................303
Villa La Massa *(Candeli)*....................304
Villa San Michele *(Fiesole)* 305
Pensione Bencistà *(Fiesole)*...............306
Hotel Villa Le Rondini *(Trespiano)* 307
FattoriaI Milione *(Giogoli)* 308
Tenuta Le Viste *(Scandici)*.................309
Follina (Treviso) : Hotel Abbazia 488
Formia (Latina) : Hotel Castello Miramare 63
Forte dei Marmi (Lucca)
California Park Hotel 392
Hotel Byron 393
Hotel Tirreno.......................................394

G

Gaeta (Latina) : Gran Hotel Le Rocce 64
Gaiole in Chianti (Siena) :
Castello di Spaltenna............................364
Borgo Argenina *(Argenina)* 365
L'Ultimo Molino *(Ripresa di Vistarenni)* ...366
Gangi (Palermo) : Tenuta Gangivecchio 248
Gargagnano di Valpolicella (Verona) : Foresteria Serègo Alghieri ...498
Garlenda (Savona) : La Meridiana......................109
Gubbio (Perugia) : Villa Montegranelli Hotel *(Monteluiano)*.........172
Gressoney-la-Trinité (Aosta) : Hotel Lo Scoiattolo 214
Gressoney-Saint-Jean (Aosta) : Hotel Lo Scoiattolo 215
Grimaldi Inferiore (Imperia) : Baia Benjamin 105
Grottaferratta (Roma)-: Park Hotel Villa Grazioli 85

I

Impruneta (Firenze) : Castello di Caffagio 311
Isola d'Elba (Livorno)
Park Hotel Napoleone................................416

Hotel Hermitage 417
Hotel da Giacomino 418
Isole Eolie ou Lipari (Messina)
  Lipari
  Hotel Carasco 265
  Villa Augustus Hotel..266
  Villa Meligunis...267
  Panarea : Hotel Raya..268
  Salina
  Hotel Signum..269
  Stromboli
  Hotel La Sciara Residence 270
  La Locanda del Barbablu...271
  La Sirenetta Park Hotel...272
  Vulcano : Les Sables Noirs 273
Isola d'Ischia (Napoli)
  Park Hotel Miramare 16
  Pensione Casa Garibaldi 17
  Pensione Casa Sofia 18
  Hotel Villarosa...19
  Hotel Bagattella...20
  Albergo Terme San Montano...21
  Hotel Residence Punta Chiarito 22
Isola di Lampedusa (Agrigento) : Club Il Gattopardo...........264
Isola di Ponza (Latina) : Hotel Cernia................................65
Isola di San Pietro - Carloforte (Cagliari)
  Hotel Hieracon 227
  Pensione Paola e primo Maggio 228

L

Lago di Como
  Como
  Albergo Terminus 122
  Hotel Villa Flori 123
  Bellagio
  Grand Hotel Villa Serbelloni...124
  Hotel Florence..125
  Cernobbio : Grand Hotel Villa D'Este 126
  Moltrasio : Grand Hotel Imperiale 127
  Lenno : San Giorgio Hotel..128
  Menaggio : Grand Hotel Victoria...................................129
  San Mamete : Hotel Stella d'Italia 130
  Tremezzo : Grand Hotel Tremezzo 131
  Varenna
  Hotel Royal Vittoria 132
  Hotel Olivedo 133
Lago di Garda
  Fasano di Gardone Riviera (Brescia)
  Villa del Sogno...115
  Grand Hotel Fasano 116
  Gardone Riviera : Villa Fiordaliso..................................117

Gargnano
Baia d'Oro...118
Villa Giulia..119
Salo : Hotel Laurin 120
Sirmione : Villa Cortine Palace Hotel 121
Riva del Garda (Trento) : Lido Palace Hotel 439
Lago Maggiore (Varese)
Ranco (Varese) : Albergo Ristorante Il Sole di Ranco 148
Cannobio (Novara) : Hotel Pironi 199
Ghiffa (Novara) : Hotel Ghiffa 200
Stresa (Novara) : Hotel Verbano 201
Lago d'Orta
Orta San Giulio
Villa Crespi 202
Hotel San Rocco 203
Lago Trasimeno (Perugia)
Passignano sul Trasimena : Poggio del Belvedere 173
Isola Maggiore : Hotel da Sauro..............................175
Lecce (Salento) : Hotel Patria 225
Lecchi - SanSano (Siena) : Residence San Sano 343
Lecchi - Tornano (Siena) : Castello di Tornano 342
Le Valli-Incisa Val d'Arno : Residenza San Nicolo d'Olmeto 312
Le Vigne (Siena) : La Palazzina 389
Lucca-
Locanda L'Elisa 390
La Principessa 391
Lucignano d'Asso (Siena) : Azienda Picolomini Bandini.....377

M

Maleo (Milano) : Albergo del Sole 146
Manciano (Grosseto) : Le Pisanelle 406
Mantova : Albergo San Lorenzo 135
Maratea (Potenza)
Locanda delle Donne Monache.................................2
Martina Franca (Taranto) : Hotel Villa Ducale 226
Matera : Hotel Sassi 3
Menfi (Agrigento) : Casa Ravidà...............................241
Merano (Bolzano)
Hotel Castel Labers...420
Castel Fragsburg...421
Hotel Oberwirt *(Marling)* 422
Mercatale (Firenze) : Salvadonica.............................313
Milano
Hotel Four Seasons 137
Excelsior Hotel Gallia 138
Grand Hotel del Duomo 139
Hotel Pierre Milano 140
Hotel Diana Majestic 141
Hotel Spadari al Duomo 142
Hotel de la Ville..143

Antica Locanda dei Mercanti 144
Mira Porte (Venezia) : Hotel Villa Margherita............................473
Missiano - Appiano (Bolzano) : Hotel Schloss Korb....................423
Modanella-Serre di Rapolano (Siena) : Castello di Modanella 376
Modena : Canalgrande Hotel...51
Mogliano Veneto (Treviso) : Villa Stucky..................................489
Monopoli (Bari) : Il Melograno...217
Monsummano Terme (Pistoia) : Hotel Grotta Giusti.....................402
Montagnane (Firenze) : Castello di Montegufoni 314
Montalcino : Hotel Vechia Oliviera 375
Montali - Tavernelle di Panicale : Azienda Agrituristica Montali 171
Montauto - Monteroni (Siena) : Casa Bolsinina 374
Monte San Savino (Arezzo) : Castello di Gargonza......................278
Montebenichi - Bucine (Arezzo) Castelletto di Montebenichi 277
Montecatini Terme (Pistoia) : Grand Hotel e la Pace 403
Montecatini Val di Cecina (Pisa) : Il Frassinello 398
Montefalco (Perugia) : Villa Pambuffeti....................................175
Montefiridolfi (Firenze) : Fattoria La Loggia 315
Montefollonico (Siena) : La Chiusa...379
Montepulciano (Siene) : La Dionora 380
Monteriggioni (Siena) : Hotel Monteriggioni 344
Monterosso al Mare (La Spezia) : Hotel Porto Roca 110
Montevetollini (Pistoia) : Villa Lucia..404
Monticchiello di Pienza (Siena) : L'Olmo 384
Montieri (Grosseto) : Rifugio Prategiano 407

N
Napoli
   Hotel Santa Lucia 6
   Hotel Elxelsior 7
   Grand Hotel Parker's 8
   Hotel Paradiso 9

O
Ortisei (Bolzano)
   Hotel Adler...430
   Pension Uhrerhof Deur *(Bulla)* 431
Orvieto (Terni) :
   Villa Ciconia 189
   Hotel Ristorante La Badia..190
   Hotel Virgilio 191
Ostuni (Brindisi)
   Grand Hotel Masseria Santa Lucia 223
   Il Frantoio 224

P
Paciano (Perugia) : Locanda della Rocca 176
Padova : Albergo Leon Bianco...484

Palermo
   Grand Hotel Villa Igiea 243
   Centrale Palace Hotel...244
   Grand Hotel et des Palmes 245
   Hotel Principe di Villafranca 246
   Massimo Plaza Hotel 247
Panzano in Chianti (Firenze) : Villa Le Barone 316
Parma : Hotel Verdi...55
Pedemonte : – Hotel Villa del Quar..497
Pergine Valsugana : Castello Pergine..438
Perugia
   Locanda della Posta...155
Perugia-Cenerente - carte 14
   Castello dell' Oscano...156
   Villa Ada 157
Pesaro (Varese) :
   Hotel Vittoria 152
   Villa Serena 153
Pettineo (Messina) : Casa Migliaca 254
Pezze di Greco (Brindisi) : Masseria Salamina...............................220
Pienza (Siena)
   La Saracina...382
   Il Chiostro di Pienza 383
Pietrasanta (Lucca) : Albergo Pietrasanta 395
Pieve a Elsa - Colle di Val d'Elsa (Siena) La Piccola Pieve 345
Pissignano-Campello (Perugia) : Albergo Vecchio Molino..............177
Poggibonsi (Siena) : Hotel Villa San Lucchese 346
Poggio (Rieti) : Hotel Borgo Paraelios..68
Poggio d'Ancona (Arezzo) Il Trebbio 280
Palo Laziale (Roma)-: Posta Vecchia 87
Pomino-Rufina (Firenze) : Fattoria di Petrognano 318
Pomponesco (Mantova) : Il Leone 136
Pontenuovo (Pistoia) : Il Convento 405
Pontessieve (Firenze) : Tenuta di Bossi 325
Portico di Romagna (Forli) : Hotel Al Vecchio Convento 53
Porto Cervo (Sassari)
   Hotel Cala di Volpe...234
   Hotel Ginestre...235
   Hotel Romazzino 236
Porto Conte (Sassari) : El Faro..238
Porto Ercole (Grosseto) : Il Pellicano 408
Porto San Paolo (Sassari) : Hotel Don Diego.............................233
Portobuffolé (Treviso) : Villa Giustinian....................................490
Portofino (Genova)
   Albergo Splendido 98
   Albergo Splendido Mare 99
   Piccolo Hotel 100
   Hotel Nazionale 101
Portonovo (Ancona)
   Hotel Fortino Napoleonico 149
   Hotel Emilia..150

Positano (Salerno)
Hotel San Pietro 33
Le Sirenuse 34
Hotel Poseidon 35
Hotel Palazzo Murat 36
Albergo Casa Albertina 37
La Fenice 38
Casa Cosenza 39
Prato (Firenze)
Villa Rucellai - Fattoria di Canneto.................................328
Pretale-Sovicille (Siena) : Albergo Borgo Pretale 372
Pugnano (Pisa) : Casetta delle Selve 399
Puinello (Reggio Nell'Emilia) : Casa Matilda 62
Punta Ala (Grosseto)
Hotel Cala del Porto 409
Piccolo Hotel Alleluja 410

R

Radda in Chianti (Siena)
Relais Fattoria Vignale 367
La Locanda (*Volpaia*) 368
Podere Terreno (*Volpaia*)..369
Vescine - Il Relais del Chianti (*Vescine*) 370
Torre Canvalle (*La Villa*) 371
Ragusa-Giubiliana : Eremo della Giubiliana.......................250
Ravello (Salerno)
Hotel Palumbo-Palazzo Gonfalone 40
Palazzo Sasso 41
Hotel Caruso Belvedere 42
Villa Cimbrone 43
Villa Maria..44
Redagno (Bolzano) : Berghotel Zum Zirmerhof 425
Regello - Vaggio (Firenze) : Villa Rigacci 319
Reggio Nell'Emilia
Hotel Posta...60
Albergo delle Notarie...61
Rigoli - San Giuliano Terme (Pisa) : Hotel Villa di Corliano 400
Roccatederighi (Grosseto)
Fattoria di Peruzzo 411
Auberge Azienda Peretti 412
Pieve di Caminino..413
Roma
Hotel Lord Byron 69
Hotel Giulio Cesare 70
Hotel d'Inghilterra..71
Hotel Raphaël 72
Hotel Sole Al Pantheon 73
Hotel dei Mellini 74
Hotel Carriage 75
Mecenate Palace Hotel..76
Hotel Villa Grazioli 77

Hotel Gregoriana 78
Hotel Locarno 79
Hotel Teatro di Pompeo 80
Hotel Sant'Anselmo 81
Hotel Villa del Parco 82
Pensione Scalinata di Spagna 83
Pensione Parlamento 84
Roncegno (Trento) : Palace Hotel 440
Rosia (Siena) : Azienda Montestigliano 373
Rovigo : Hotel Regina Margherita 485

S

Salvetrini di Fasano (Brindisi) : Masseria San Domenico 221
Santarcangelo di Romagna (Forli) : Hotel della Porta 54
San Candido (Bolzano) : Parkhotel Sole Paradiso 435
San Casciano dei Bagni (Siena) : Sette Querce 388
San Cassiano - Armentarola (Bolzano) : Hotel Armentarola 434
San Fedele d'Intelvi (Como) : Villa Simplicitas e Solferino 134
San Felice Circeo (Latina) : Hotel Punta Rossa 66
San Floriano del Collio (Gorizia) Golf Hotel 482
San Fruttuoso (Genova) : Albergo Da Giovanni 97
San Gimignano (Siena) - carte 13
Hotel L'Antico Pozzo *(190 000 L)* 347
Hotel La Cisterna *(146 000/186 000 L)* 348
Hotel Bel Soggiorno *(150 000 L)* 349
La Collegiata *(550/650 000 L)* 350
Villa San Paolo *(180/320 000 L)* 351
Hotel Le Renaie *(135/180 000 L)* 352
Villa Remignoli *(Casaglia)* 353
Il Casale del Cotone *(Il Cotone)* 354
Il Casolare di Libbiano *(Libbiano)* 355
Hotel Pescille *(Pescille)* 356
Casanova di Pescille *(Pescille)* 357
San Giorgio Monferrato (Alessandria) : Castello di San Giorgio 204
San Pantaleo-Sasima (Sassari) : La Sasima 237
San Pietro a Dame (Arezzo) : Stoppiacce 279
San Quirico d'Orcia-Ripa d'Orcia : Castello di Ripa d'Orcia 385
San Remo (Imperia) : Hotel Royal 106
San Vigilio - Lana (Bolzano) : Albergo Monte San Vigilio 426
Sant'Ambrogio di Valpolicella (Verona) : Coop 8 Marzo-Ca`Verde 500
Santa Cristina (Bolzano) : Albergo Uridl 436
Santa Maria del Guidice (Lucca) : Hotel Villa Rinascimento 396
Santa Maria di Castellabate (Napoli) Palazzo Belmonte 24
Santa Margherita de Pula (Cagliari) : Is Morus Hotel 229
Sappada : Haus Michaela 483
Saturnia (Grosseto)
Hotel Terme di Saturnia 414
Hotel Villa Claudia 415
Sauze d'Oulx (Torino) : Il Capricorno 196
Scopello (Trapani)-: Pensione Tranchina 263
Scorze (Venezia) : Villa Conestabile 474

Selva di Fasano (Brindisi) : Sierra Silvana.................................222
Seripola-Orte (Viterbo) : La Chiocciola 93
Sesto Fiorentino (Firenze) : Villa Villoresi 310
Sestri Levante (Genova)
    Grand Hotel Villa Balbi 102
    Hotel Helvetia 103
    Hotel Miramare 104
Siena
    Park Hotel...331
    Hotel Certosa di Maggiano 332
    Grand Hotel Villa Patrizia...333
    Hotel Villa Scacciapensieri 334
    Palazzo Ravizza 335
    Hotel Antica Torre 336
    Hotel Santa Caterina...337
    Villa dei Lecci..338
Sinalunga (Siena) : Locanda dell'Amorosa 378
Siracusa
    Villa Lucia 251
    Grand Hotel di Siracusa 252
Sirolo (Ancona) : Hotel Monte Conero...............................151
Solighetto (Treviso) : Locanda Da Lino.............................491
Soragna (Parma) : Locanda del Lupo 57
Sorrento (Napoli)
    Grand Hotel Excelsior Vittoria 25
    Hotel Bellevue Syrene...26
Sperlonga (Latina) : Park Hotel Fiorelle..............................67
Spello (Perugia)
    Hotel Palazzo Bocci 182
    Hotel La Bastiglia 183
Spoleto (Perugia)
    Hotel Gattapone 178
    Palazzo Dragoni 179
    Hotel San Luca 180
    Hotel Eremo delle Grazie *(Monteluco)* 181
Su Gologone-Oliena (Nuoro) : Hotel Su Gologone 230

T

Tai de Cadore (Belluno) : Villa Marinotti 481
Taormina (Messina)
    San Domenico Palace Hotel 256
    Hotel Villa Belvedere 257
    Hotel Villa Ducale 258
    Villa Paradiso 259
    Hotel Riis 260
    Hotel Villa Schuler..261
    Hotel Villa Sant'Andrea *(à Mazzarro)*........................262
Telese Terme (Benevento) : Grand Hotel Telese 4
Titignano-Orvieto (Terni) : Fattoria di Titignano 187
Tivoli (Roma) : Hotel Ristorente Adriano 86

Todi (Perugia)
Hotel Fonte Cesia 184
Poggio d'Asproli *(Asproli)*...185
Tenuta di Canonica *(Canonica)* 186
Torgiano (Perugia)
Relais Le Tre Vaselle 159
La Bondanzina 160
Torino
Villa Sassi-Toula..194
Hotel Victoria 195
Torri del Benaco (Verona) : Hotel Gardesana.............................501
Tuscania (Viterbo) : Hotel Al Gallo 94
Trabia (Palermo) : Hotel Tonnara Trabia 249
Trento : Albergo Accademia...437
Trieste : Hotel Duchi d'Aosta...506
Trissino (Vicenza) : Relais Ca' Masieri.......................................505

U
Urbino : Hotel Bonconte 154

V
Valnontey (Aosta)
Hotel Herbetet 209
Hotel Petit Dahu 210
Varese : Hotel Colonne 147
Venafro (Isernia) : Dimora DelPrete di Belmonte 95
Venezia
Hotel Cipriani et Palazzo Vendramin 441
Bauer Gründwald et Grand Hotel 442
Gritti Palace Hotel 443
Hotel Monaco e Grand Canal 444
Hotel Londra Palace 445
Hotel Gabrielli Sandwirth 446
Hotel Metropole 447
Pensione Accademia-Villa Maravegie 448
Hotel Flora 449
Hotel Torino 450
Hotel Bel Sito & Berlino)...451
Hotel La Fenice et des Artistes 452
Hotel Do Pozzi 453
Hotel Panada 454
Hotel Ai due Fanali 455
Hotel Residenza 456
Locanda Ai Santi Apostoli 457
Hotel Agli Alboretti 458
Hotel Santo Stefano 459
Pensione Seguso 460
Pensione La Calcina 461
Pensione Alla Salute da Cici 462
Hotel Pausania 463
Hotel Belli Arte 464

Hotel La Galleria 465
Palazzetto da Schio 466
Palazzetto San Lio..467
Hotel des Bains *(Lido)* 468
Albergo Quattro Fontane *(Lido)*...469
Hotel Villa Mabapa *(Lido)* 470
Locanda Cipriani *(Torcello)* 471
Verduno : Albergo del Castello...198
Verona
   Hotel Gabbia d'Oro 494
   Hotel Due Torri..495
   Albergo Aurora..496
Viareggio (Lucca) : Hotel Plaza e de Russie 397
Vicchio (Firenze) : Villa Campestri 326
Vico Equense (Napoli) : Hotel Capo La Gala.............................27
Vignola (Chieti) : Villa Vignola..88
Villabella-S. Bonifacio (Verona) : Relais Villabella 499
Viterbo: Country Hotel Il Rinaldone 89
Volterra (Pisa) : Albergo Villa Nencini....................................401

Z

Zerman-Mogliano Veneto (Treviso) : Hotel Villa Condulmer 492

HUNTER RIVAGES

3RD EDITION

H O T E L S
of Character and Charm
I N   P A R I S

• WITH COLOR MAPS AND PHOTOS •

HUNTER RIVAGES

4TH EDITION

HOTELS AND COUNTRY INNS

of Character and Charm

IN FRANCE

• WITH COLOR MAPS AND PHOTOS •